THE KARMAPA'S MIDDLE WAY

The Nitartha Institute Series
published by Snow Lion Publications

Nitartha Institute was founded in 1996 by The Dzogchen Ponlop Rinpoche, under the guidance of Khenchen Thrangu Rinpoche and Khenpo Tsültrim Gyamtso Rinpoche, the leading contemporary teachers of the Karma Kagyü tradition of Tibetan Buddhism. The Institute, under the aegis of Nitartha *international*, aims to fully transmit the Buddhist tradition of contemplative inquiry and learning; it offers Western students training in advanced Buddhist view and practice, as taught by the Karma Kagyü and Nyingma lineages of Tibet.

The Institute is pleased to ally with Snow Lion Publications in presenting this series of important works offering a wide range of graded educational materials that include authoritative translations of key texts from the Buddhist tradition, both those unique to the Kagyü and Nyingma lineages and those common to the wider scope of Indo-Tibetan Buddhism; modern commentaries by notable lineage scholar-practitioners; manuals for contemplative practice; and broader studies that deepen understanding of particular aspects of the Buddhist view. The initial releases are from the Kagyü tradition and will be followed by publications from the Nyingma tradition.

This publication is an Advanced Level Nitartha book.

The Karmapa's Middle Way

Feast for the Fortunate

THE NINTH KARMAPA, WANGCHUK DORJE

Translated under the guidance of
Dzogchen Ponlop Rinpoche

and according to the explanations of
Acharya Lama Tenpa Gyaltsen
& Acharya Tashi Wangchuk
by Tyler Dewar
With editing by Andy Karr

SNOW LION PUBLICATIONS
ITHACA, NEW YORK

Snow Lion Publications
P. O. Box 6483, Ithaca, NY 14851 USA
(607) 273-8519 • www.snowlionpub.com

ISBN-10: 1-55939-289-4
ISBN-13: 978-1-55939-289-1

Library of Congress Cataloging-in-Publication Data

Dbaṅ-phyug-rdo-rje, Karma-pa IX, 1556-1603.
 ['Jug ṭīk dwags brgyud grub pa'i śiṅ rta bde bar 'dren byed skal bzaṅ dga'
ston. English]
The Karmapa's middle way : feast for the fortunate / the Ninth Karmapa,
Wangchuk Dorje ; translated under the guidance of Dzogchen Ponlop
Rinpoche and according to the explanations of Acharya Lama Tenpa
Gyaltsen & Acharya Tashi Wangchuk by Tyler Dewar ; with editing by
Andy Karr.
    p. cm. — (The Nitartha Institute series)
    Includes bibliographical references and index.
    ISBN-13: 978-1-55939-289-1 (alk. paper)
    ISBN-10: 1-55939-289-4 (alk. paper)
    1. Kar-ma-pa (Sect)—Doctrines—Early works to 1800. 2. Candrakīrti.
Madhyamakāvatāra. 3. Atīśa, 982-1054. Madhyamakopadeśa. I. Karr,
Andy. II. Candrakīrti. Madhyamakāvatāra. English III. Atīśa, 982-1054.
Madhyamakopadeśa. English IV. Title.
BQ7682.4.D313 2008
294.3'923—dc22   2008005238

: Contents

⦂ An Aspiration by His Holiness the Seventeenth Karmapa, Ogyen Trinley Dorje

You realize that whatever appears dawns within the play
    of the mind
And that mind itself is the dharmakāya free of clinging.
Through the power of that, you, the supreme siddhas, master
    apparent existence.
Precious ones of the Kagyü lineage, please bestow excellent virtue.

Through the heart of a perfect Buddha awakening in you,
You possess the blossoming glorious qualities of supreme insight.
You genuine holder of the teachings by the name Dzogchen Ponlop,
Through your merit, the activity of virtue,

You publish the hundreds of flawless dharma paintings
That come from the protectors of beings, the Takpo Kagyü,
As a display of books that always appears
As a feast for the eye of intelligence of those without bias.

While the stream of the Narmadā* river of virtue
Washes away the stains of the mind,
With the waves of the virtues of the two accumulations rolling high,
May it merge with the ocean of the qualities of the victorious ones.

---

* The image here alludes to this river being considered as very holy by Hindus—even its mere sight is said to wash away all one's negative deeds (it rises on the summit of Mount Amarakaṇṭaka in Madhya Pradesh in Central India, and after a westerly course of about eight hundred miles ends in the Gulf of Cambay below the city of Bharuch).

This was composed by Karmapa Ogyen Trinley Dorje as an auspicious aspiration for the publication of the precious teachings called The Eight Great Texts of Sūtra and Tantra *by the supreme Dzogchen Ponlop Karma Sungrap Ngedön Tenpe Gyaltsen on April 18, 2004 (Buddhist Era 2548). May it be auspicious.*

⋮ A Statement by His Holiness the Seventeenth Karmapa, Ogyen Trinley Dorje

In Tibet, all the ravishing and beautiful features of a self-arisen realm—being encircled by ranges of snow mountains adorned by superb white snowflakes and being filled with Sal trees, abundant herbs, and cool clear rivers—are wonderfully assembled in a single place. These wonders make our land endowed with the dharma the sole pure realm of human beings in this world. In it, all aspects of the teachings of the mighty sage, the greatly compassionate teacher skilled in means, are perfectly complete—they include the greater and lesser yānas as well as the mantrayāna. They are as pure and unblemished as the most refined pure gold; they accord with reasoning through the power of things; they dispel the darkness of the minds of all beings; and they are a great treasury bestowing all benefit and happiness one could wish for, just as desired. Not having vanished, these teachings still exist as the great treasure of the *Kangyur*, the *Tengyur*, and the sciences as well as the excellent teachings of the Tibetan scholars and siddhas who have appeared over time. Their sum equals the size of the mighty king of mountains, and their words and meanings are like a sip of the nectar of immortality. Headed by Dzogchen Ponlop Rinpoche with his utterly virtuous pure intention to solely cherish the welfare of the teachings and beings, many dedicated workers of Nitartha *international*, striving with devotion, diligence, and prajñā, undertook hardships and made efforts over many years to preserve these teachings and further their transmission, and restore them. In particular, they worked toward the special purpose of propagating the excellent stream of teachings and practices of the unequaled Marpa Kagyü lineage, the great family of siddhas, in all directions and times, like the flow of a river in summertime. Through these efforts, the *Eight Great Texts of Sūtra and Tantra* publication series, inclusive of all the essential meanings of the perfectly complete teachings of the Victor, is magically manifesting in such a way that many appear from one. Bearing this in mind, while being in the process of making efforts myself in the preparatory stages of accomplishing the protection of the teachings and beings, from the bottom of my heart, I rejoice in this activity and toss flowers of praise upon it. I pray that, through this excellent activity, the intentions of our noble forefathers may be fulfilled in the expanse of peace.

Karmapa Ogyen Trinley Dorje
Gyütö Ramoche Temple
July 19, 2002 (Buddhist Era 2547)

⦂ A Verse on the Essence of the Middle Way by Khenpo Tsültrim Gyamtso Rinpoche

༄༅། ཆོས་ཀུན་གནས་ལུགས་སྐྱེ་བ་མེད་པ་དང་།།
རང་བཞིན་འོད་གསལ་འགག་པ་མེད་པ་གཉིས།།
སེམས་ཉིད་འོད་གསལ་སྐྱེ་འགག་མེད་པར་འདུས།།

ཞེས་མཁན་པོ་ཚུལ་ཁྲིམས་རྒྱ་མཚོ་རིན་པོ་ཆེས་གསུངས་སོ།།

The unborn true nature of all phenomena
And the unceasing true nature of luminous clarity
Are encompassed by mind itself, luminous clarity, unborn and
   unceasing.

—Khenpo Tsültrim Gyamtso Rinpoche,
Dechen Ling, Seattle, U.S.A., March 30, 2008

This verse was spoken in response to the request of Dzogchen Ponlop Rinpoche and Tyler Dewar for an introductory and blessing verse from one of the most highly accomplished scholar-yogis of the Karma Kagyü lineage.

Translated by Ari Goldfield.

⋮ Foreword by Dzogchen Ponlop Rinpoche

THE PRECIOUS TEACHINGS on emptiness from Nāgārjuna's tradition are an invaluable support for breaking through the veils of fabrications about the natural state of phenomena. As the greatest abbot of the historic Nālandā University, the epicenter of Buddhist philosophy in the golden age of Indian Buddhadharma, Nāgārjuna founded the tradition that came to be known as the Middle Way by clarifying the Buddha Shākyamuni's discourses on the lack of inherent nature of all phenomena.

All Buddhist philosophical systems explain how they adhere to a "middle way" or middle path, whether that middle way is one of view, meditation, or conduct. However, it is only the system of Nāgārjuna outlined in his six treatises on reasoning, along with the tradition of exposition that stemmed from that system, that are universally renowned as the Middle Way.

In Tibet, the works of Chandrakīrti, who lived some three hundred years after the time of Nāgārjuna, became renowned amongst the masters of all four of Tibet's Buddhist schools—Kagyü, Geluk, Sakya, and Nyingma—as representing the authoritative interpretation of Nāgārjuna's thought. Chandrakīrti composed two works on the meaning of Nāgārjuna's main text, the *Treatise on the Middle Way*, also known as the *Fundamental Wisdom of the Middle Way*. The first of these was *Lucid Words*, a "word commentary" on the original text's line-by-line meaning; the second was the *Entrance to the Middle Way*, a "meaning commentary" designed both to prepare students to study *Fundamental Wisdom* in depth and to supplement Nāgārjuna's work by examining topics not treated directly by Nāgārjuna.

Of these two key texts by Chandrakīrti, the *Entrance to the Middle Way* holds a special place in the curricula of Tibetan Buddhist colleges. It is mandatory reading for all students who wish to engage in the discipline of

Middle Way studies. Commensurate with its title, it is the first major text of the Middle Way tradition which is studied.

In the Karma Kagyü lineage, the most important text on Nāgārjuna's Middle Way approach is the Eighth Karmapa, Mikyö Dorje's *Chariot of the Takpo Kagyü Siddhas*, which in turn is an extensive commentary on Chandrakīrti's *Entrance*. The *Chariot*, since it was composed in the twilight of the Eighth Karmapa's lifetime, is thought by many to be the repository of his definitive positions on the most profound topics of the view. Because of its special qualities, such as his pith instructions that join the view of the Middle Way with the meditation practice of Mahāmudrā, the *Chariot* is one of the greatest literary treasures of not only the Karma Kagyü tradition, but of Tibetan Buddhadharma as a whole.

Despite the uniqueness and profundity of the Eighth Karmapa's text, the extensiveness of the *Chariot* presents some difficulties to Western students challenged by time constraints. To our great fortune, the Ninth Karmapa, Wangchuk Dorje, abridged the *Chariot* into a more accessible edition, which he named *Feast for the Fortunate*, the text translated in this publication. In this text, the Ninth Karmapa distills the essence of the Eighth Karmapa's unique and powerful approach to determining the Middle Way view and integrating it with direct experience; yet, at the same time, he preserves many of the extended dialogues and debates that make the Eighth Karmapa's text so rich.

With the publication of this text, for the first time Western students of Buddhadharma can enjoy an opportunity to study and reflect upon a complete Kagyü lineage commentary to the *Entrance to the Middle Way*. I am therefore confident that this book will provide a great contribution to the field of Middle Way studies and enlighten English language readers as to a unique and relatively unexplored presentation of the vital concept of emptiness.

I am delighted by the work of my student Tyler Dewar, who has translated this text under my guidance and with assistance from my two wonderful colleagues, Acharya Lama Tenpa Gyaltsen and Acharya Tashi Wangchuk. The text was translated under the auspices of Nitartha Institute and would not have been possible without the generous support of David Lunsford and the Bodhi Foundation and Eric Colombel and the Tsadra Foundation. To these two patrons I am wholeheartedly grateful.

Finally, I feel that it is auspicious that this book, which contains the enlightened words of two of the most prolific authors in the lineage of successive Karmapa manifestations, is being published in the same year as the historic first visit to the West of the current holder of this lineage, His Holiness the Seventeenth Gyalwang Karmapa, Ogyen Drodul Trinley Dorje. I dedicate the merit of this publication to His Holiness's long life and to the unhindered flourishing of his profound activity for the benefit of all beings in the world.

May all sentient beings realize and manifest the incredibly profound Middle Way, free from clinging to the extremes of eternalism and nihilism. Through this, may the world be filled with great love, harmony, and prosperity.

Dzogchen Ponlop Rinpoche
Nalanda West
April 26, 2008

: Translator's Acknowledgments

IT HAS BEEN a great honor to translate a key work of the Karmapa at the direction, under the guidance, and with the constant inspiration and encouragement of my guru, Dzogchen Ponlop Rinpoche. Rinpoche began teaching Chandrakīrti's *Entrance to the Middle Way* at Nitartha Institute's annual, month-long summer sessions in 1997. He taught the entire text from start to finish between then and 2000, basing himself on the Eighth Karmapa Mikyö Dorje's commentary, *Chariot of the Takpo Kagyü Siddhas*.

Returning to the *Entrance to the Middle Way* once more in 2004, he emphasized the difficult points of the text's general meaning and, in particular, the approach to the Consequentialist Middle Way of the early Tibetan masters and the Karmapas. During this cycle he taught from *Feast for the Fortunate*, the Ninth Karmapa Wangchuk Dorje's abridgement of the Eighth Karmapa's text, for which I had prepared a draft translation. These teachings, which drew on the vast wealth of Rinpoche's years of studies of the Middle Way and the literature of the Karmapas, provided insight into the uniqueness of the Karmapa's work and much information to correct and improve my translation. Over the course of this translation project, Rinpoche patiently and kindly advised me in a way that greatly shaped the tone and content of the present work. I offer my profound gratitude and appreciation to him, along with heartfelt aspirations for his long life and for the abundant treasury of his instructions to be enjoyed by an ever-increasing number of those interested in wisdom and compassion.

I also received invaluable guidance from Acharya Lama Tenpa Gyaltsen, who selflessly granted me most of his waking hours during an intense week of discussions and reading in Boulder, Colorado in February, 2005. These sessions with Lama Tenpa brought my contemplations of the Middle Way to a deeper level and enabled me to translate some of the most difficult sections of the text with newfound confidence. My main reading mentor for this project was Acharya Tashi Wangchuk, resident teacher at Nalanda West in Seattle, Washington. Acharya Tashi gave freely of his time over the course of several months in 2003 and 2004 and once again toward the end of the project, painstakingly explaining line after line of text. He also helped research the sources of quotations and compared different editions of *Entrance to the Middle Way* commentaries. For the extraordinary opportunity to learn from these two great Acharyas, I am ever thankful.

Several translators influenced and informed this work. Ari Goldfield has been generous to me in sharing his translations, published (in *The Moon of Wisdom*, Snow Lion Publications, 2005) and unpublished, of the root verses of the *Entrance to the Middle Way* and portions of the Eighth Karmapa's commentary. These were a primary reference for my work, as were Elizabeth Callahan's draft translations of sections of Mikyö Dorje's text, which she produced for Ponlop Rinpoche's teachings at Nitartha Institute.

I would be in a sorry state without the encyclopedic knowledge of Karl Brunnhölzl, who corrected several errors in my draft translation, righted my reading of the Karmapa's chapter on the Consequentialist-Autonomist distinction, and answered all of my many questions with acuity. Cyrus Stearns kindly checked my translation of the longest section on Dolpopa Sherab Gyaltsen and gave helpful suggestions on approaching Buddhist polemics. Mark Seibold shared his intimacy with the Eighth Karmapa's *Chariot of the Takpo Kagyü Siddhas* in many helpful and stimulating conversations and gave detailed counsel on tricky passages. Scott Wellenbach, Co-Director of Nitartha Institute, and Jules Levinson offered seasoned advice at key junctures in the project. I rejoice in the opportunity to both walk in the footsteps of and learn directly from these and other senior translators.

I and readers of this book alike are indebted to Andy Karr, my editor, whose Strunk and White-like deftness, insight, and hard work led to a markedly more pleasant read. Thanks also to Jirka Hladiš, who kindly researched and provided several Sanskrit terms, and to Cindy Shelton, a valued colleague whose experience in publishing and editing is continually beneficial. The Nitartha International Document Input Center (NIDIC) provided me with an edited electronic input of the Ninth Karmapa's text, and also produced the edition of the Eighth Karmapa's text that I consulted throughout the project. To the NIDIC's editors and input staff I am truly grateful. I thank David Karma Choephel, who provided important information on Wangchuk Dorje's bibliography, and the many others who have provided feedback, encouragement, and support during this book's journey into English. A special note of appreciation goes to Jeff Cox and Sidney Piburn of Snow Lion Publications for their interest and willingness to publish this text and to Steve Rhodes for his exacting work in readying the text for printing.

Even with the help of these great masters, translators, teachers, and friends, it would be difficult for any translator to produce a faultless translation of a work of this nature. All errors in the translation, or other aspects of the text, are solely my responsibility.

I am extremely grateful for the financial support of David Lunsford and the Bodhi Foundation and Eric Colombel and the Tsadra Foundation. The completion of this project would have been impossible without the vision and kindness of these two great organizations. Their generosity, patience, and encouragement throughout the course of the project were remarkable.

For organizational and community support, I would like to thank Steve Seely, Phil Stanley, and Tashi Wangmo, Co-Directors of Nitartha Institute, along with all of the Institute's administrators, faculty, and students. It is wonderful to participate in Snow Lion's Nitartha Institute Series and have the opportunity, year after year, to attempt to deepen my study and contemplation of the dharma, along with my understanding of translation, at Nitartha Institute.

I would like to thank Martin Marvet, Lynne Conrad Marvet, and the staff of Nitartha *international* and Mark Power, Kim McMeans, and the teachers, administrators, and members of Nalandabodhi. These organizations, under the guidance of Dzogchen Ponlop Rinpoche, have not only created the conditions for my own education and work as a translator to be possible, they have helped the Buddha's genuine dharma, free of compromise, to continue its transplantation in the West and remain a vital pillar of wisdom in the East.

Finally, I would like to thank my wife, Shirley, and my daughter, Saeran, for their inspiration and support and for their patience with me throughout this project's trials and joys.

By whatever positive contribution this translation has offered, may all sentient beings realize the Middle Way, free from extremes, and may peace, harmony, and prosperity flourish in all corners of the world.

Tyler Dewar
Nalanda West
Seattle, Washington
March 31, 2007

⠶ Technical Notes

THE TRANSLITERATION OF SANSKRIT names and terms follows the
IAST method, with the exception of *ṛ*, *c*, *ch*, *ś*, and *ṣ*, which are rendered
as *ri*, *ch*, *chh*, *sh*, and *ṣh*, respectively. Sanskrit and Tibetan equivalents for
important names and terms, along with birth and death dates when available, are provided on the first occurrence of the name or term in parentheses in italics. Both phonetic renderings and Wylie transliterations are
provided for the Tibetan terms in the following format: *(phonetic render-
ing/Wylie transliteration)*. In the main body of the text, root verses from
the *Entrance to the Middle Way* are indented and bolded. When available,
the name of a text quoted by the Karmapa is given in parentheses in italics, directly before the quotation, if it is not mentioned in the body of the
text. Brackets enclose material inserted by the translator; text in parentheses in roman type is the original author's material.

I have chosen not to crowd the text with references to Tibetan page
numbers in addition to the already plentiful extraneous material in the
body of the text. Also with the nonspecialist reader in mind, I have used
brackets sparingly, opting not to use them in instances where the implied
content of the Tibetan phrases could be reliably ascertained, and where
there was no substantive scholarly concern to alert the reader to an insertion by the translator.

⋮ Introduction

AROUND 2,550 YEARS AGO, our Teacher, the Buddha Shākyamuni, fully awakened to perfect enlightenment by actualizing the deepest potential of human nature. Unleashing the boundless love, wisdom, and abilities of the true nature of mind, he presented a plentiful banquet of instructions for sentient beings of all dispositions and inclinations to attain perfect happiness.

In the *Perfection of Supreme Knowledge (Prajñāpāramitā, Sherab kyi Parol tu Chinpa/shes rab kyi pha rol tu phyin pa)* sūtras of the second turning of the wheel of dharma, he presented the Middle Way by which sentient beings may become ultimately free from suffering. The Middle Way undermines suffering's deepest root: mistaken beliefs about the nature of reality and experience. In instructions given to his disciple Kāshyapa, the Buddha described the Middle Way succinctly:

> Kāshyapa, saying "it exists" is one extreme. Saying "it does not exist" is a second extreme. The center of these two is the middle way, inexpressible and inconceivable.

The Middle Way lies between the two extremes of existence and nonexistence, eternalism and nihilism. Furthermore, when we use our discriminating intelligence to analyze the nature of any phenomenon, we discover that, once we transcend the two conceptual extremes, there is no "middle" or "center" left over. There is no final resting place for the conceptual mind to dwell. The end result of our analysis is to allow reifying thoughts to dissolve into the peace that is free of all contrivance. Nāgārjuna, the founder of the Middle Way tradition based on the Buddha's teachings on the perfection of supreme knowledge, praised the Buddha's instructions for transcending the limitations of concept:

You taught that whatever arises dependently
Is free of ceasing, free of arising;
Free of extinction, free of permanence;
Free of coming, free of going;
Free of being one, free of being many—
You taught perfect peace, the easing of all elaborations.
Perfect Buddha, supreme among speakers,
I pay homage to you.

If the true or ultimate nature cannot be identified with any quality of arising, ceasing, coming, or going, how are we to relate to all the things we see and feel in our day-to-day lives that seem to arise and cease? Is it all just nothing, to be ignored? No. Since the confused appearances and projections of sentient beings *exist* from the perspective of the confusion that perceives them, we need to know what to adopt and what to reject for as long as we have not realized the true nature of these appearances.

To help sentient beings form a path to ultimate realization while still living and taking part in the everyday world, the Buddha taught the two truths: the relative truth and the ultimate truth. The relative truth, the appearances and experiences all ordinary people believe to be real, can become a stepping stone to realizing the ultimate truth, the true nature of phenomena that is beyond the labels and contrivances of thoughts. In fact, there is no other stepping stone for realizing the ultimate than the relative.

THE MIDDLE WAY IN INDIA

NĀGĀRJUNA AND THE *FUNDAMENTAL WISDOM* OF THE *MIDDLE WAY*

Somewhere between the first and third centuries, C.E.,[1] during the period of the Mahāyāna's emergence in India, the noble Nāgārjuna founded the system of philosophical inquiry known as the Middle Way. The preeminent abbot of Nālandā, the greatest Buddhist educational institution of Indian Buddhism's golden era, he is renowned as the author of three collections of treatises: the collection of texts on reasoning *(rik tsok/rigs tshogs)*, the collection of praises *(tö tsok/bstod tshogs)*, and the collection of counsels *(tam tsok/gtam tshogs)*. His most famous work is *Verses on the Fundamental Wisdom of the Middle Way (Prajñā-nāma-mūla-madhyamaka-kārikā, Uma Tsawe Tsik le-ur Jepa Sherab/dbu ma rtsa ba'i tshig le'ur byas pa shes rab)*, which comes from the collection on reasoning. In the *Fundamental Wisdom's* twenty-seven crisp and pithy chapters, Nāgārjuna, in metered verse, dismantled all attempts to freeze reality into definable entities.

In *Fundamental Wisdom*, Nāgārjuna mainly addressed the views of the lower-vehicle Buddhist schools, since other Buddhist schools had effectively refuted the prevalent non-Buddhist views of the day, such as the Enumerator *(Sāṃkhya, Drangchenpa/grangs can pa)* school of Hinduism. Because of their universally accepted status as the unerring sources of the Middle Way system, Nāgārjuna and his heart disciple, Āryadeva (ca. third century), became known as the Middle Way Progenitors, or Authors of the Model Texts *(Shung Chimö Umapa/gzhung phyi mo'i dbu ma pa)*.

ONE PURPOSE, TWO TRUTHS, AND THREE LEVELS OF ANALYSIS

Since the Middle Way tradition is an expression of the Mahayana, its sole purpose is to liberate all sentient beings from suffering by means of wisdom and compassion working together. This is an essential Buddhist objective. Followers of the Middle Way do not pursue philosophical investigation for the purpose of knowledge itself, but only seek wisdom that will undermine the root of suffering. No matter how alluring a philosophical system may seem, it will merely be a conceptual elaboration, and thus part of the problem, if it does not cut through this root. Even though freedom from conceptual elaboration is the final objective, we must rely on nothing other than our current projections, perceptions, and confusion in order to open our eyes of supreme knowledge to the true state of things. There is a baby of intelligence in the washwater of our discursiveness. As Nāgārjuna said in *Fundamental Wisdom*:

> Without relying on conventions,
> One cannot realize the ultimate.
> Without realizing the ultimate,
> One cannot attain nirvāṇa. (24.10)

By working with what we know ordinarily, the relative truth, we can connect with the extraordinary knowledge of ultimate truth. The approach of the progenitors of the Middle Way is that the mundane and the sublime can, and must, complement each other. This approach is explained as "three stages of analysis"—no analysis, slight analysis, and thorough analysis—which were described by Āryadeva in his preeminent work, the *Four Hundred Verses (Chatuḥshataka, Shibgyapa/bzhi brgya pa)*:

> In the beginning one reverses nonvirtue.
> In the middle one reverses the view of a self.
> In the end one reverses all views.
> Those who know this way are wise. (8.15)

And by Nāgārjuna in *Fundamental Wisdom*:

> The buddhas impute a "self,"
> Teach "selflessness,"
> And teach that there is neither
> Self nor selflessness. (18.6)

The first stage, no analysis, does not delve into the subtle issues of examining one's perceptions of what truly exists. Operating on the basis of what is commonly accepted in the world, one simply tries to lead a virtuous life and avoid the coarser forms of suffering, such as involuntary rebirth in the lower realms, that would prevent one from continuing to practice effectively on the path to liberation. To help beings at this level, the Buddha spoke of the person and phenomena as existing things. He did not challenge beings' preconceptions about existence, for such a challenge would overwhelm most people with a truth they were not prepared to assimilate, or turn them away in aversion from the Buddha's teachings altogether. To avoid this, the Buddha taught about the mundane level of causality: virtuous actions, beneficial to self and other, produce happiness; nonvirtuous actions, harmful to self and other, produce suffering. With these and other teachings, the Buddha's students could habituate themselves to progressively deeper understandings of causality, enabling them gradually to consider causality's more profound implications.

The second stage, slight analysis,[2] introduces the natural, yet radical, outcome of a thorough contemplation of cause and effect. Since all phenomena, including the person, arise interdependently, no phenomenon has any independent, solid, singular, permanent, ultimate, or genuine existence of its own. When we analyze things carefully and look for an enduring quality of objectivity, we cannot find it. The *Heart Sūtra* proclaims:

> There is no eye, no ear, no nose, no tongue, no body, no mind.

It is at this stage that the ever-vital concept of emptiness *(shūnyatā, tongpa nyi/stong pa nyid)* is introduced. When analyzed with precise reasonings, such as the "five great reasonings of the Middle Way,"[3] it is found that phenomena are empty precisely of themselves. All phenomena are without an inherent nature. At this stage, emphasizing things' lack of inherent existence is important, because, for the vast majority of sentient beings, the source of suffering is clinging to solid existence. (Not many beings cling to the utter *non*existence of everything.)

Even though familiarizing ourselves with phenomena's lack of true existence when analyzed goes a long way in exhausting our tendencies to superimpose labels onto our experience (whether we make these labels consciously or unconsciously), the thought of nonexistence cannot be our final destination. This is so because emptiness has no stopping point. There is no thing—including emptiness—that is not empty of its own nature.

The stage of thorough analysis, therefore, involves transcending completely all levels of coarse and subtle concepts—labels of existence, nonexistence, emptiness, nonemptiness, and so on. When we arrive at the stage of thorough analysis, therefore, we experience the genuine Middle Way directly. "Thorough" analysis means "beyond" the analysis of conceptuality.

Nāgārjuna and *Fundamental Wisdom* inspired a vibrant flow of exposition, debate, and composition on how to realize and guide others toward the Middle Way. Most of the Indian commentaries that followed, either explicitly or essentially, aimed to explicate and complement his root texts, especially *Fundamental Wisdom*. Let us now take a brief tour of some key subsequent moments of Indian, and then Tibetan, Middle Way history that set the stage for our present study, the Ninth Karmapa's *Feast for the Fortunate*.

BUDDHAPĀLITA, BHĀVAVIVEKA, AND CHANDRAKĪRTI

Around the early sixth century, a scholar named Buddhapālita composed a famous commentary on *Fundamental Wisdom*, aptly entitled *Buddhapālita (Sangye Kyang/sangs rgyas bskyangs)*. In unpacking Nāgārjuna's verses refuting the views of realist philosophical schools, Buddhapālita strictly adhered to Nāgārjuna's main logical tool, the absurd consequence: rather than offering a position of his own in response to his counterparts' positions (which would then be subject to further conceptual speculation), Buddhapālita simply exposed the logical flaws inherent in his counterparts' systems by stating their absurd consequences.

Some years later, another scholar named Bhāvaviveka composed his own *Fundamental Wisdom* commentary, the *Lamp of Wisdom (Prajñāpradīpa, Sherab Drönma/shes rab sgron ma)*. Although he did not differ with Buddhapālita on the nature of the experience of ultimate reality, he criticized Buddhapālita's approach of relying solely on absurd consequences to refute the wrong views of opponents. In order to instill certainty about the correct view in others, he said, one must affirmatively prove that view using structured logic statements, or "autonomous probative arguments," that rely not on the opponents' mistakes, but on one's own unmistaken perceptions. In advocating this approach, Bhāvaviveka had a strong wind behind him, as the sophisticated logic system of Dignāga, the famed Valid Cognition scholar, was becoming prominent in Indian Buddhist thought.[4] Though Buddhapālita's and Bhāvaviveka's distinct approaches each had strong followings, Bhāvaviveka's would eventually become dominant, at least for a while.

Enter Chandrakīrti, around one hundred years later. In his commentary on *Fundamental Wisdom* called *Lucid Words (Prasannapadā, Tsiksal/tshig gsal)*, Chandrakīrti, with great vigor and precision, defended the consequential approach of Buddhapālita and assailed Bhāvaviveka's adherence to affirmative statements from one's own perspective as "a wellspring of many serious faults." For Chandrakīrti, it was antithetical to the Middle Way to adopt a philosophical stance of one's own, since the true Middle Way is beyond any conceptions whatsoever. Arguing in this way, he founded what Tibetan scholars would later refer to as the Consequentialist *(Prāsaṅgika, Talgyurwa/thal 'gyur ba)* branch of the Middle Way. Bhāvaviveka's followers would later become known as proponents of the Autonomist *(Svātantrika, Rang-gyüpa/rang rgyud pa)* branch.[5]

THE *ENTRANCE TO THE MIDDLE WAY*

Chandrakīrti's fiery polemic in *Lucid Words* on how to correctly uphold Nāgārjuna's intention was supplemented by his *Entrance to the Middle Way (Madhyamakāvatāra, Uma la Jukpa/dbu ma la 'jug pa)*, a verse-form composition accompanied by his own prose commentary. Since this autocommentary explicitly describes the text as an *entrance* into the topics of *Fundamental Wisdom*, *Lucid Words* and *Entrance to the Middle Way* are generally considered a pair in which *Lucid Words* is a word commentary to *Fundamental Wisdom* and *Entrance* is the meaning commentary.

The *Entrance to the Middle Way* is composed of ten main chapters, each corresponding to one of the ten *bhūmis*, or bodhisattva grounds, the progressive steps to buddhahood on the Mahāyāna path. Additional chapters cover the special qualities the bodhisattvas attain on each ground and the distinct features of the final result, buddhahood. The ten bodhisattva grounds correspond with ten transcendent virtues, or *pāramitās*, which are described in each chapter. As *Entrance* is a Middle Way treatise, it is natural that the majority of its text is contained in the sixth chapter, which focuses on the perfection of supreme knowledge *(prajñā, sherab/shes rab)*. However, in addition to a thorough exploration of wisdom—the Mahāyāna's *profound* dimension—it also explains compassion, the pāramitas, and the stages of a bodhisattva's progression through the bhūmis, the *vast* aspects of the Mahāyāna.[6] A section by section overview of the *Entrance's* contents is provided below.

As an aside, it is worth noting that Chandrakīrti was no ordinary scholar. In addition to a formidable intellect, he evidently had attained some degree of meditative accomplishment. As the colophon to *Entrance* relates, he once helped his colleagues at Nālandā transform their clinging to true existence by drawing milk from a painting of a cow!

The *Entrance to the Middle Way* is taught throughout all four lineages of Tibetan Buddhism as the main introduction to Middle Way studies. Virtually all of the most famous Tibetan masters of the Middle Way have authored commentaries to it, and many, such as the Eighth and Ninth

Karmapas, have used their commentaries on it as the main vehicle for presenting their heart teachings on the Middle Way.

THE MIDDLE WAY IN TIBET

AUTONOMIST BEGINNINGS AND THE EARLY CONSEQUENTIALISTS

In the eighth century, Buddhadharma was established in Tibet, in large part due to the combined efforts of three great personages: Padmasambhava, an Indian tantric adept, Trisong Detsen, the benevolent "dharma king" of Tibet, and Shāntarakṣhita, an exceptionally gifted Indian scholar and monk. Since Shāntarakṣhita's approach to logic borrowed partially from Bhāvaviveka's use of autonomous probative arguments, he is considered to have been an Autonomist. His brand of the Middle Way, which also incorporated some elements of the Indian Yogāchāra school's views, was predominant in Tibet for around four hundred years.

During this time, little was known of Chandrakīrti's Middle Way approach in Tibet. However, of notable interest is the legendary Atisha (982-1054), who, though he did not specifically advocate for the Consequentialist approach over and above that of the Autonomists, praised Chandrakīrti and identified his writings as a primary source for the correct understanding of emptiness.[7] Atisha's student Naktso Lotsawa (1011-1064)[8] made an early translation of *Entrance to the Middle Way*.

One of the last great Tibetan Autonomist stalwarts was Chapa Chökyi Senge (*phywa pa chos kyi seng ge,* 1109-1169), a follower of Dignāga and Dharmakīrti who is said to have cleverly refuted Consequentialism, even defeating Jayānanda (ca. twelfth century), the author of the only known Indian commentary on the *Entrance to the Middle Way,* in debate.[9] Nevertheless, Jayānanda explained the texts and system of Chandrakīrti to an especially brilliant translator and teacher, Patsap Nyima Drak (*pa tshab nyi ma grags,* 1055-?), and Patsap made what would become the authoritative Tibetan translation of the *Entrance.*

Patsap Lotsawa went on to teach extensively in Tibet on the *Entrance* and other texts that explained Chandrakīrti's Consequentialist approach. Through his efforts and those of his disciples, such as the "four sons of Patsap"[10] and others, the Consequentialist system came to be almost universally regarded in Tibet as the pinnacle of Middle Way thought.[11]

In addition to Patsap Lotsawa, some of the most important Tibetan Consequentialist masters from whom our present study draws inspiration and derives authority are Majawa Chanchub Tsöndrü (*rma bya ba byang chub brtson 'grus*, ca. twelfth century), Rendawa Shönu Lodrö (*red mda' ba gzhon nu blo gros*, 1349-1412), and Lochen Kyapchok Palzang (*lo chen skyabs mchog dpal bzang*, ca. fifteenth century). In Tibetan doxography, the Middle Way masters who preceded Tsongkapa (introduced below) are considered to be Early Followers of the Middle Way *(Uma Ngarabpa/dbu ma snga rabs pa)*, and Tsongkapa and his followers are considered Later Followers of the Middle Way *(Uma Chirabpa/dbu ma phyi rabs pa)*.

THE MIDDLE WAY LINEAGES OF THE KARMA KAGYÜ TRADITION

Feast for the Fortunate details five distinct Middle Way lineages that came to be assimilated into the dharma transmissions of the Karmapas *(karma pa)*, the chief holders of the Kagyü lineage. The lineages that came through Nāropa (1016-1100), Maitripa (1012-1097), Atisha, and Patsap Lotsawa were all received by the First Karmapa, Düsum Khyenpa (*dus gsum mkhyen pa*, 1110-1193), and passed down through his lineage to the present day. The fifth lineage, a special dialectic lineage of reading transmissions and debate, was received by the Eighth Karmapa, Mikyö Dorje (*mi bskyod rdo rje*, 1507-1554), and passed down through the Karmapa lineage. The detailed steps of each lineage are described in *Feast for the Fortunate*, starting on page 83.

The First Karmapa, Düsum Khyenpa, marked the beginning of the special transmission of the Middle Way within the Karma Kagyü lineage. He studied directly with Patsap Lotsawa,[12] perhaps the greatest of the first generation of Tibetan Consequentialists. Furthermore, his importance to the Kagyü Middle Way is reflected in the subtitle of the Eighth Karmapa's seminal *Entrance to the Middle Way* commentary: *The Oral Transmission of the Glorious Düsum Khyenpa*.

THE EIGHTH KARMAPA AND THE *CHARIOT OF THE TAKPO KAGYÜ SIDDHAS*

The Eighth Karmapa Mikyö Dorje was a great practitioner-scholar and the most prolific author of all the Karmapas. In addition to voluminous writings on the view and practice of both sūtra and tantra, he also authored works on such fields as astrology and medicine and founded the Karma Gadri *(karma dga' bris)* style of thangka painting.[13] His significance to the intellectual tradition of the Karma Kagyü lineage can hardly be overestimated, as he composed the main commentaries for four of the five major sūtra topics studied in the Karma Kagyü monastic universities: the Vinaya or Ethics *(dulwa/'dul ba)*, the Abhidharma or Clear Categorization of Phenomena *(chö ngönpa/chos mngon pa)*, the Perfection of Supreme Knowledge *(sher chin/sher phyin)*, and the Middle Way.[14] He also completed the Seventh Karmapa, Chödrak Gyamtso's commentary to the fifth topic, Valid Cognition *(pramāṇa, tsema/tshad ma)*, through his editing and compilation.[15]

Born in eastern Tibet, his birth and early signs of prodigy mirrored the typical pattern of the life examples of all the Karmapas. He was formally enthroned as the Karmapa at age seven at the monastery of Tshurpu *(tshur phu)*, the historic Tibetan seat of the Karmapas and the Karma Kagyü lineage. Though he studied diligently with many exalted teachers on a wide range of topics, he held his root guru to be Sangye Nyenpa Tashi Paljor *(sangs rgyas mnyan pa bkra shis dpal 'byor,* 1505-1569), whom he identified as his main source of transmission for the highest and most difficult aspects of the Middle Way view.

At the age of thirty-eight (ca. 1545),[16] Mikyö Dorje embarked on the composition[17] of the *Chariot of the Takpo Kagyü Siddhas,*[18] a commentary on Chandrakīrti's *Entrance to the Middle Way.* Dzogchen Ponlop Rinpoche, in an introduction to a recent publication of the Tibetan text of the *Chariot,*[19] remarked on the significance of the composition's timing: because the Karmapa wrote the *Chariot* in the latter part of his life (he passed away at forty-seven), at a time when all of his major studies of the view were complete, it is reasonable to infer that the *Chariot* contains his true heart intention regarding many essential topics of the view.[20]

The Karmapa did not relate to this composition merely as a vehicle for providing a word commentary to illuminate the *Entrance to the Middle Way's* root verses. He used it as an opportunity to thoroughly examine many difficult, profound, and much-debated Middle Way issues that hovered just on the peripheries of the topics taught directly in the *Entrance* itself. The *Chariot,* or, as the Ninth Karmapa would later call it, the "*Ṭīkā,*"[21] is filled with several sections that run page after page in which the Karmapa explores an issue related, if sometimes indirectly, to a particular root verse. Other sections, conversely, move briskly through the text of the *Entrance*, offering illuminating glosses of the root verses but returning the reader to Chandrakīrti's poetry in steady, short intervals.

In the "general meaning" *(chi dön/spyi don)* sections, as these exploratory sections are traditionally called, the Karmapa often draws upon the views of other Middle Way scholars, mostly Tibetan masters who preceded him, as reference points in the journey toward a correct understanding of the topic at hand. Fittingly for a follower of Nāgārjuna's tradition, these references to others mostly involve the Karmapa refuting their views. Although occasionally bereft of diplomacy, his refutations serve an elevated purpose. Their purpose is not to show that another master is inferior, or to place the Karmapa and his view on a high pedestal. Rather, by maneuvering students around certain aspects of others' philosophies, the Karmapa leads them to a subtle and refined understanding that, if processed correctly, entails no aversion toward others' views as inferior, or arrogance toward one's own view as supreme.[22] More remarks on the purpose and spirit of Buddhist debates will follow below.

In this vein, the most refuted master in the *Tīkā* is the great Tsongkapa *(tsong kha pa,* 1357-1419), perhaps the most famed Middle Way scholar in Tibetan history and founder of the Geluk *(dge lugs)* lineage of Tibetan Buddhism.[23] In refuting Tsongkapa's unique views, which were widely criticized by those outside of Tsongkapa's tradition as innovations with no basis in the Indian source texts, Mikyö Dorje corroborates his own counterpoints with references to the Indian Consequentialist masters and to Early Tibetan Consequentialists such as the ones identified above as his predecessors.

Others whose views find a place under the Karmapa's microscope in the *Tīkā* are Dolpopa Sherab Gyaltsen *(dol po pa shes rab rgyal mtshan,* 1292-1361), Bodong Chokle Namgyal *(bo dong phyogs las rnam rgyal,* 1376-1451), and Shākya Chokden *(sh'akya mchog ldan,* 1428-1507)—all of whom propounded varying interpretations of the "other-emptiness" *(shentong/gzhan stong)* doctrine[24]—as well as Gorampa Sonam Senge *(go rams pa bsod nams seng ge,* 1429-1489), another of Tsongkapa's most vocal critics. The diversity of the scholars refuted by the Karmapa show us something of the uniqueness of his approach in a key period of Middle Way exposition in Tibet.

Finally, one more special feature of the *Ṭīkā* that bears mention here is its occasional forays into Mahāmudrā pointing-out instructions, along with lengthy quotations from the spontaneous realization songs of the great siddhas of India and Tibet. The Karmapa, elegantly and seamlessly, weaves together the intellectual inquiries of his debates with powerful intuitive instructions on the true nature of mind, occasionally calling out to his guru with invocations that show a heart heavy with gratitude and devotion. This provides not only a rare glimpse of how Buddhism's meditative and scholarly streams of teaching can intimately work together, but also a wonderful refreshment in the midst of what, for some, can often seem an overly cerebral endeavor.

Pawo Tsuklak Trengwa

The Eighth Karmapa's two main students were the fifth Shamar *(zhva dmar)* incarnation, Könchok Yenlak *(dkon mchog yan lag, 1525-1583)*, who would go on to tutor the Ninth Karmapa, and Pawo Tsuklak Trengwa *(dpa' bo gtsug lag phreng ba, 1504-1566)*, the second Pawo incarnation. While Könchok Yenlak was considered the "sunlike" disciple, Pawo Rinpoche was considered the "moonlike" disciple, and as such he reflected the rays of the Karmapa's Middle Way view brightly in his long commentary on Shāntideva's *Entrance to the Conduct of a Bodhisattva (Bodhicharyāvatāra, Changchub Sempe Chöpa la Jukpa/byang chub sems dpa'i spyod pa la 'jug pa)*. In this text, especially in the commentary to the ninth chapter on wisdom,[25] he preserves many of the Eighth Karmapa's Middle Way teachings. It is traditionally held that Karmapa Mikyö Dorje's *Ṭīkā* and Pawo Rinpoche's commentary on Shāntideva are the two main texts that reveal the Karma Kagyü lineage's approach to the Middle Way.[26]

To round out this rough sketch of the history of the Karma Kagyü Middle Way lineage, before introducing the author of the present text, it is fitting to briefly mention the work of Jamgön Kongtrul Lodrö Thaye *('jam mgon kong sprul blo gros mtha' yas, 1813-1899)*, the Kagyü lineage's most prolific author. Jamgön Kongtrul authored over ninety volumes of texts, and, from among these, his *Treasury of Knowledge (Sheja Dzö/shes bya mdzod)*, along with its autocommentary, offers penetrating and concise treatments of the Middle Way and its historical background. While he approaches some topics differently than the Eighth Karmapa, his succinctness and clarity have proven extremely useful to contemporary students.[27]

THE NINTH KARMAPA AND *FEAST FOR THE FORTUNATE*

The Ninth Karmapa, Wangchuk Dorje (*dbang phyug rdo rje,* 1556-1603), also a prolific author on a wide range of sūtra and tantra topics, is most renowned in the Kagyü tradition for his instructions on Mahāmudrā. These are presented in his short, medium length, and extensive Mahāmudrā works: *Pointing Out the Dharmakāya (Chöku Dzup Tsuk/chos sku mdzub tshugs), Dispelling the Darkness of Ignorance (Marik Münsel/ma rig mun sel),* and the *Ocean of Definitive Meaning (Ngedön Gyamtso/nges don rgya mtsho).*

Born in the lower Trewö region of eastern Tibet, he was enthroned at the age of six by Könchok Yenlak. After receiving the complete lineage transmissions from the Shamarpa, he taught widely throughout Tibet, moving from place to place with a traveling camp at which the practice of meditation was emphasized. He also made important visits to Mongolia and Bhutan.[28]

Perhaps the Ninth Karmapa's greatest contributions to Kagyü scholarship in the sūtra category are his offerings of shorter, more accessible commentaries on the great sūtra texts as complements to the longer works by the Eighth Karmapa. He composed a commentary on the *Treasury of Abhidharma* called *Play of the Youthful (Shönu Namrol/gzhon nu rnam rol)* and, basing himself on the *Chariot of the Takpo Kagyü Siddhas,* he compiled the present volume, *Feast for the Fortunate.*[29]

He also wrote a text on Valid Cognition called *The Essence of the Texts on Reasoning (Tsema Rikshung Nyingpo/tshad ma rigs gzhung snying po).* Two other short, prose-form Middle Way texts, *A Short Summary of the Middle Way (Ume Döndu Düpa/dbu ma'i don bsdu bsdus pa* and *An Abridgement Called "The Lion's Roar" (Sur Kol Senge Ngaro/zur bkol seng ge nga ro)* have also been attributed to him.[30]

According to his colophon, Wangchuk Dorje began his work on *Feast for the Fortunate* at the age of twenty-three (ca. 1578) and finished at age twenty-five (ca. 1560). Aside from the opening verses, some intermediary verses, and the concluding verses, the text does not contain lengthy portions of commentary newly composed by Wangchuk Dorje. However, he did make edits and paraphrases of many of the Eighth Karmapa's phrasings, clarifying key sections of the text. He also adduced several quotations not found in the *Ṭīkā*. He frequently directs readers to the Eighth Karmapa's text for a more extensive exploration of salient points.

Though, compared to the *Ṭīkā*, *Feast* may be called an "abbreviated" work,[31] Wangchuk Dorje was certainly liberal in selecting material from the original text: he preserves all of the Eighth Karmapa's word commentary sections and includes healthy portions of some of the most important general meaning sections. The general meaning sections, especially, reveal the unique profundity of the Karmapa's Middle Way outlook. Since time is an increasingly rare commodity, and since it is rare for the editor of a new edition of a book to be the original author's reincarnation, those interested in the Karmapa's literary legacy are indeed fortunate to avail themselves of this feast of contemplation.

CONSIDERATIONS ON THE DEBATES IN THIS BOOK

As mentioned above, one of the Eighth Karmapa's preferred methods of guiding students to an understanding of his Middle Way view was refuting the views of others. Many of his refutations in the *Ṭīkā* are preserved by the Ninth Karmapa in this book. Though intellectually stimulating, the study of Buddhist polemics can involve major pitfalls for the reader who does not understand the purpose and spirit of Buddhist debate. In the sūtras, the Buddha gave this advice:[32]

> Those who study a teaching and become attached to it
> Will become angry when they hear something that is not that
>   teaching.
> Their pride and conceit will defeat them
> And lead them only to suffering.

Therefore, when reading debates between great masters of the Middle Way, if we worry too much about who is right and who is wrong, who has the best view and who has the worst view, we will miss the opportunity to engage in a penetrating analysis of the topic at hand. The purpose of debate is to offer two or more different approaches to an issue as sticks to be rubbed together until the flame of our intelligence burns brightly on its own. Our approach to debate should be free from partisanship, as Chandrakīrti says in the present text:

> Attachment to one's own view and
> Aversion to the views of others are nothing more than conception.
> Therefore, if you first overcome attachment and aggression
> And *then* analyze, you will be liberated. (6.119)

Liberation from mundane, confused thoughts is the hallmark of a successful debate or of an analysis of competing views. Moreover, since Chandrakīrti and the Karmapa were masters of the Mahāyāna, compassion was always foremost for them.

Another key point to keep in mind when reading the debates in this book is that, as mentioned above, the Karmapa uses the views of others to help students understand *his own* approach. His job, as it were, is not to thoroughly present the view of the master he is refuting. Rather, he need only refer to the aspects of his counterparts' views that are relevant to the point he is making. Therefore, one should not read the Karmapa's refutations of Tsongkapa, for example, and hope to walk away thinking, "Now I know what Tsongkapa's view was, so I don't need to read his books." In fact, if you are interested in thoroughly understanding Tsongkapa's views, you *must* read Tsongkapa's books, as there certainly is not enough space to explain the details of all of his positions in the footnotes of this book. This principle applies to all of the other masters whose views are analyzed in *Feast for the Fortunate*.

Finally, sometimes the Karmapa's longer refutations and exchanges use language and logic drawn from the techniques of Indian and Tibetan debate. Those readers who have not put in long hours in the debate courtyards may find some of these sections daunting, or even impenetrable. Don't worry. If you don't understand an argument after several readings, move on. You will be able to pick up the thread. Keep in mind that even when writing for beginners, authors of texts such as this inevitably address some sections at peers. Try not to let these difficulties diminish your enjoyment of this amazing treatise.

AN OVERVIEW OF *ENTRANCE TO THE MIDDLE WAY* AND *FEAST FOR THE FORTUNATE*

The following is a brief summary of some key topics explored by our root text and commentary, offered with the hope to enhance the reader's appreciation of the full treatment they are given in *Feast*.

THE FIRST BODHISATTVA GROUND AND THE PERFECTION OF GENEROSITY

After a brief preamble in which he introduces the scriptural context for the present study, the importance of realizing emptiness, and the source text, the *Entrance to the Middle Way*, the Karmapa describes the five lineages, mentioned above, whose wisdom informs his commentary. In addition to listing the names of all of the main holders of each lineage, the Karmapa also provides insightful comments about the emphasis the lineages placed on Middle Way studies, and on what differences and similarities there are in their approaches to the view, concluding with a very interesting, if cryptic, discussion of the Middle Way in the context of secret mantra, or Vajrayāna.

Following the Indo-Tibetan philosophical custom, the Karmapa next explains the title of the treatise on which he will comment. In connection with this, he then provides pithy descriptions of ground, path, and fruition Middle Way, and of the "Middle Way of statements," where he affirms that the *Entrance to the Middle Way* is intended to be an entrance, or introduction, to Nāgārjuna's *Fundamental Wisdom*. Here he makes a statement of what is probably the most repeated declaration of his entire commentary:

> . . . in following the Middle Way, one dismantles the views of others while at the same time not positing a position of one's own view.

Concluding this subchapter, he outlines the layers of purpose in undertaking this composition, the most essential purpose being to help all sentient beings attain buddhahood.

The Karmapa embarks on his commentary on the opening root verses by explaining why Chandrakīrti chose to begin his text with an homage to a quality of mind, compassion, rather than to a buddha, bodhisattva, or meditation deity. Chandrakīrti's logic is to praise the cause before the result, for it is through establishing the correct cause that all beneficial results will come about. Thus compassion (along with the wisdom of nonduality and bodhichitta, the altruistic desire to awaken) is the cause for an ordinary being to become a noble bodhisattva; through traversing the stages of bodhisattvahood one arrives at the citadel of perfect enlightenment, the supreme of all results. Compassion, he explains, has three categories: the compassion that arises in observation of sentient beings' suffering, the compassion born of knowing suffering's root causes, and the compassion that is beyond any conceptual reference point whatsoever.

After this, the text enters in earnest the presentation of the ten "grounds," or stages of a bodhisattva's spiritual growth, the first of which being named *Supreme Joy*. On this first ground, the aspirant on the path experiences his or her first direct perception of the reality of emptiness. As opposed to being frightening, this experience entails great delight, because one's experience of reality is for the first time completely freed of all confused, conceptual overlays.[33] It is at this stage that, in the tradition of Chandrakīrti, one attains the name of a "bodhisattva."[34]

Because of the strength of their pure intention and compassion, the bodhisattvas' merit surpasses that of the hearers and solitary realizers, but at this stage their wisdom does not. They are likened to the chicks of an unrivaled species of bird: though they are at present dwarfed by others vying in the same disciplines, that they have taken birth into their special family (for the bodhisattvas, the family of those who have engendered bodhichitta) guarantees that they will outshine their counterparts in all respects before long.

From Chandrakīrti's perspective, the bare realization of the true nature of reality at the level of the first bodhisattva ground is the same realization that buddhas have. The only difference between buddhas and bodhisattvas in terms of wisdom is that buddhas have perfected familiarization with this realization, whereas bodhisattvas have just been introduced to it. In terms of wisdom, therefore, the progression through the bodhisattva grounds involves increasing familiarity with what one had already cognized, rather than the cognition of anything new.

A vital distinction to bear in mind regarding the progression of the bodhisattvas' wisdom, leading to the stage of buddhahood, is that between meditative equipoise *(nyamshak/mnyam bzhag)* and postmeditation or "subsequent attainment" *(jetop/rjes thob)*. The direct realization of emptiness as possessed by first-ground bodhisattvas only occurs during meditative equipoise. Thus a large part of the bodhisattvas' progress through the grounds pertains to the degree to which their postmeditation experience is informed by the wisdom of their meditative moments. Not until full buddhahood is attained does the distinction between equipoise and postmeditation fall away completely—buddhas are the only ones capable of sustaining the realization of the true nature of reality uninterruptedly in all times and situations.

The most important philosophical moment in this chapter takes place in the commentary to verse 1.8, in which Chandarkīrti makes a passing reference to the seventh bodhisattva ground, where, he says, the bodhisattvas' wisdom, as well as their merit, surpasses the wisdom of the hearers and solitary realizers.

One may wonder how it could be possible for bodhisattvas, who are generally considered of a higher rank, to have wisdom inferior to that of the hearers and solitary realizers at any point. However, the wisdom of the hearers and solitary realizers consists of a deep and long-cultivated familiarity with the emptiness of the aggregates *(skandha, pungpo/phung po)*, constituents *(dhātu, kam/khams)*, and sense sources *(āyatana, kyemche/skye mched)* of their own respective continua. Bodhisattvas train in realizing the selflessness of all phenomena—not only those of their own continua—but their realization of emptiness on the first ground is new; it is not a realization with which they have been cultivating familiarity for a long time.

Wisdom, or cognitive maturity, therefore, contains two main components: realization, or bare cognition, and familiarity with what one has realized.[35] The hearers and solitary realizers are more deeply familiar with the emptinesses they have cognized than are the first-ground bodhisattvas with their emptinesses, even though the bodhisattvas have a broader appreciation of emptiness' implications and applications.

The Hearers and Solitary Realizers Realize Phenomenal Selflessness

In the Tibetan exegetical tradition, particular attention has been paid to the question of whether the hearer and solitary realizer arhats of the foundational vehicles realize the selflessness of phenomena in addition to realizing the selflessness of persons. (It is widely agreed that they realize the selflessness of persons.) Some scholars have held that the arhats only realize personal selflessness—the fact that the aggregates, constituents, and sources of their own continua are empty of the personal self. Others hold that the arhats realize both forms of selflessness: that they realize not only that there is no self in the aggregates, constituents, and sources, but that the aggregates, constituents, and sources themselves also do not inherently exist.

The Karmapa, along with most other *Entrance* commentators, yet with the notable exception of Jamgön Mipham,[36] takes the latter position. He uses Chandrakīrti's comparison of the arhats' and bodhisattvas' wisdom as an opportunity to prove, using "three reasonings and seven scriptural quotations," that the arhats do indeed realize phenomenal selflessness. The central logic of the Karmapa's position is revealed perhaps most clearly in the third reasoning, where he uses the example of a chariot and its parts to illustrate his contention that, if the arhats viewed their aggregates, constituents, and sources as real, it would be impossible for them not to view the self as being real as the possessor of those elements, or as the whole of which the aggregates, constituents, and sources are considered parts. Therefore, the arhats realize personal selflessness *precisely because* they see the emptiness of the aggregates, constituents, and sources—phenomena—that constitute their own personal continua.

The Karmapa relates that, according to Nāgārjuna's explanation of emptiness, when one realizes the emptiness of one phenomenon, one will have realized the emptiness of all phenomena. As Āryadeva, Nāgārjuna's heart disciple, famously stated in his *Four Hundred Verses*:

> Whatever is the viewer of one,
> That is the viewer of all.
> Whatever is the emptiness of one,
> That is the emptiness of all.

Furthermore, if the arhats did not realize phenomenal selflessness, it would follow that their wisdom would be surpassed by even the first ground bodhisattvas, because they would not have understood that all phenomena lack an inherent nature, whereas the bodhisattvas on the first ground have. This would contradict Chandrakīrti's position that the arhats are not outshone by the bodhisattvas until the latter's attainment of the seventh ground. The Karmapa continues with further consequences and proofs.

If both the arhats and the bodhisattvas equally realize phenomenal self-lessness, what, in the end, makes the wisdom of the Mahāyāna superior? In his *Ṭīkā*, the Eighth Karmapa clarifies that the difference lies in the bodhisattvas' ability to apply emptiness as a true nature of phenomena to a greater number of appearing subjects than can the arhats. The arhats' realization of phenomenal selflessness is complete, but they only apply it to the phenomena of their own continua and to "the uncontaminated truth of the path."[37]

The *Entrance* next describes the perfection of generosity, which achieves its summit on the first ground. Because of their newfound insight into the true nature, bodhisattvas on the first ground can not only give generously of their time, resources, and energy; they are also capable, should the need arise, of giving their own flesh away. Yet generosity is a practice for ordinary beings as well, as all mundane happiness is connected to material enjoyments, which in turn arise as the karmic result of having given. Furthermore, generosity can produce positive results for the giver even if he or she gives with an improper motivation or an irritated mind. Giving can lead one into situations where more profound instructions for attaining lasting happiness are available. Since generosity can be practiced by anyone, regardless of whether one's mind is refined in the trainings of loving-kindness and compassion, the Buddha taught it first from among the ten perfections.

Chandrakīrti next draws a clear line between two types of perfections, transcendent and mundane, regarding the practice of any of the ten perfections. In the case of generosity, any act of giving that involves clinging to the existential solidity of the gift, giver, or recipient is a mundane perfection. Conversely, when one is free of observing those "three spheres" in a reifying manner, one's perfection has reached the transcendent level. In order to make any act of virtue transcendent, therefore, supreme knowledge, or *prajñā*, is required.

THE SECOND BODHISATTVA GROUND AND THE PERFECTION OF DISCIPLINE

The chapter on the second bodhisattva ground focuses mostly on the qualities of that ground's associated perfection, ethical discipline. Though much of the teachings on discipline focus on actions to avoid in body and speech, working with discipline involves nothing other than working with one's own mind and cultivating the ability to not mentally engage the disturbing emotions of anger, lust, jealousy, pride, and so on in a way that will lead one down the path of performing actions harmful to oneself or others.

Specifically, the second-ground bodhisattvas perfect their ability to refrain from the ten nonvirtuous actions: the three nonvirtuous actions of body (killing, stealing, and sexual misconduct), the four nonvirtuous actions of speech (lying, harsh speech, inciting discord, and idle chatter), and the three nonvirtuous actions of mind (malicious intent, covetousness, and wrong view).

The functional benefit of practicing discipline is that discipline produces the karmic result of rebirth in the higher realms, or pleasant existences, and of leading one ever closer to the ultimate goals of liberation from saṃsāra and complete enlightenment. Again, the quality essential to making any form of virtue "perfect" is transcendent wisdom. Therefore, the second-ground bodhisattvas, as opposed to allowing their stainless ethics to become grounds for arrogance, always maintain the awareness that the agent, action, and object of their ethical discipline are empty of inherent nature.

THE THIRD BODHISATTVA GROUND AND THE PERFECTION OF PATIENCE

The bodhisattvas' realization of emptiness continues to influence their behavior on deeper and deeper levels on the third ground, on which the quality of patience is highlighted and reaches its peak. Chandrakīrti masterfully interweaves descriptions of the profundity of bodhisattva patience with extremely practical encouragements for ordinary beings to practice patience. Why, he asks rhetorically, would one insist on resentment as a response to harm done to oneself? Would that resentment remove the destruction the aggressor has already inflicted? Better than resentment or desire for revenge, therefore, is to remember that the cause of all harm inflicted upon oneself, in a deeper analysis, is one's own negative actions of the past. Furthermore, contemplating the downfalls of anger in comparison to the benefits of patience will lead one to become more capable of choosing intelligent patience over impulsive aggression in all situations.

Along with the attainment of the third ground comes the acquisition of such powers as the four concentrations, the four formless meditative states, and the five higher cognitions. Patience is the last of the perfections the Buddha taught primarily to laypeople and is also the last of the perfections whose engagement leads primarily to the accumulation of merit from among merit and wisdom.

THE FOURTH BODHISATTVA GROUND AND THE PERFECTION OF DILIGENCE

Diligence, the perfection highlighted on the fourth ground, produces all good qualities; Shāntideva famously defined it as "delight in virtue." By applying diligence to virtuous actions such as generosity, discipline, and patience, we ensure that the flow of beneficial results from those actions will never cease but continue to flourish ever further. The practice of diligence accumulates both merit and wisdom, and, on the wisdom side of the coin, Chandrakīrti explains, bodhisattvas on the fourth ground exhaust their clinging to concepts of the self and entities connected to the self, the usually incessant thoughts of "me" and "mine."

THE FIFTH BODHISATTVA GROUND AND THE PERFECTION OF MEDITATION

On the fifth ground, *Difficult to Overcome*, the bodhisattvas' perfection of meditation reaches its culmination. Meditation in the context of the fifth perfection relates to the ability not only to calm and concentrate the mind, but to be able to do so willingly at any time one desires and in any situation one finds oneself in. The ability to calm and relax the mind is in most cases taught as a necessary prerequisite to developing prajñā, or supreme knowledge, the penetrating and discriminating insight into the true nature of appearing phenomena.

Even though the perfection of concentration becomes preeminent on this ground, the bodhisattvas here are of course also continuously refining their prajñā. They now gain the ability to analyze and comprehend the four noble truths in a way that was inaccessible to them before. In presenting this development, the Karmapa briefly explores the correlation of the four noble truths to the two truths, the latter being the set of truths or realities employed more frequently in Middle Way analyses of what is and what is not a truth or reality, and on what levels. Essentially, from a conventional perspective the truths of suffering, origin, and path are relative realities, while the truth of cessation is ultimate because of being unconditioned by karmic formations. However, in the final analysis all four truths, including cessation, are relative truths because of depending on each other for their designation as truths. All presentations of truths, the Karmapa concludes, should be understood in this way. In fact, even the ultimate truth, when presented as a dichotomous opposite to the relative truth, is a relative truth, because it exists merely as a conventional counterpoint to the relative; it does not exist as an entity known as "ultimate truth" in its own right.

THE SIXTH BODHISATTVA GROUND AND THE PERFECTION OF SUPREME KNOWLEDGE

Supreme knowledge is the central focus of our present inquiry, and as such it is given by far the most attention from among the ten perfections explained in *Entrance to the Middle Way*. The general definition of prajña is "the intelligence that thoroughly differentiates phenomena." When we can clearly see the characteristics of any given phenomenon, without overlaying the characteristics of other phenomena onto the one we are investigating, that is prajña. However, in the Mahāyāna, and especially in the Middle Way, prajña is taken to a much deeper level. Rather than clarifying our awareness of the appearing characteristics of phenomena, we are trained to probe with the most subtle faculties of intelligence we can access to try and find the core of the existence of phenomena themselves. The sixth chapter presents logical reasonings to help us deconstruct our assumptions about the way things are and to encourage our mind of analysis toward greater and greater levels of subtlety.

Introduction to the Teachings on Emptiness

Chandrakīrti and the Karmapa begin their exploration of supreme knowledge by situating the sixth-ground bodhisattvas in prime position for ultimate insight to develop: the bodhisattvas have perfected concentration, the ability to both relax the mind in a stable and malleable way and to focus the mind on any desired object or topic of contemplation, without the slightest distraction toward outer objects of the five senses or inner discursive thoughts.

The structure of Chandrakīrti's treatise is unique. Usually, the authors of Indian treatises begin, with the first verse of their text, with an opening homage followed by the pledge of composition. We have already discussed how Chandrakīrti's opening homage is unique; the other quality that sets this treatise aside from others is that its pledge of composition does not appear until we are already six chapters into the text, at verse 6.3. Its appearance here in the chapter on prajñā only underscores that the central focus of the text is supreme wisdom and the reality that wisdom sees, emptiness.

The Karmapa reveals the essential sectional outline for the sixth chapter: the two main sections explain emptiness in terms of the two types of selflessness and in terms of the sixteen types of emptiness, respectively. The two types of selflessness are explained individually: phenomenal selflessness and personal selflessness.

In introducing the scriptural basis for his explanation of the selflessness of phenomena, Chandrakīrti calls upon the *Sūtra on the Ten Grounds* (*Dashabhūmikasūtra, Sa Chupey Do/sa bcu pa'i mdo*). According to this sūtra, all phenomena are of the nature of equality, and their equality can be demonstrated in reference to ten main criteria. When analyzed, phenomena are equal with each other 1) in their absence of signs; 2) in their absence of characteristics; 3) in being free from arising; 4) in being unarisen; 5) in their voidness; 6) in their primordial purity; 7) in their absence of elaborations; 8) in being free from adoption and rejection; 9) in being like illusions, dreams, hallucinations, echoes, water-moons, reflections, and emanations; and 10) in not being things or nonthings.

According to Chandrakīrti, if one realizes how phenomena are free from arising (the third type of equality), one will easily realize the other nine equalities. Therefore the *Entrance* concentrates on revealing the logic by which any assertion of phenomena's inherent arising is refuted.

The main logical framework around which the explanation of the selflessness of phenomena is based is the refutation of "arising from the four extremes." If phenomena were to truly or inherently arise in a way that could be verified by analysis, they would have to arise either from themselves, from others, from both self and other, or from no causes at all. Chandrakīrti teaches that all of the Buddhist and non-Buddhist schools that cling to the notion of objective, truly existent phenomena do so by asserting one or more of these four extremes of arising. By refuting these attempts of the philosophical schools to cling to true existence, Chandrakīrti provides readers with the opportunity to identify and transform their own confusion that grasps onto phenomena as independently real and onto the person as a solid self.

A key distinction to bear in mind here is that between two types of ignorance: innate *(lhen kye/lhan skyes)* ignorance and imputed *(kuntak/kun btags)* ignorance. Innate ignorance is the basic fixation on the thought of "I" shared by all sentient beings, from dung beetles and dogs on up through scholars and scientists. All ordinary sentient beings have a strong tendency to think of themselves as real persons separate from others and of their environments as objectively existing. Imputed ignorance, however, is more specialized. In addition to our basic ignorance of ego-fixation and duality, we develop all kinds of sophisticated labels and concepts to enhance our sense of being a distinct entity in our world. In particular, we may develop elaborate theories to justify the existence of ourselves and our environment by relying on religious, scientific, or sociological philosophies (e.g., "I think, therefore I am."). These more elaborate forms of conception are expressions of imputed ignorance.

In refuting arising from the four extremes in the *Entrance*, Chandrakīrti, on the explicit level, is dealing with imputed ignorance. The four extreme notions of arising that he invalidates with reasoning are assertions of specific philosophical schools of ancient Indian thought. Lest one were to think that ordinary sentient beings, not only philosophers, conceive of "arising from other," thus making arising from other an expression of innate ignorance, Chandrakīrti states very clearly that the refutation of arising from other applies to philosophical assertions (namely to the Buddhist schools of the foundational vehicles and the Mind Only proponents of the Mahāyāna), not to ordinary beings' conceptions of the way things arise:

> Because worldly people will merely plant a seed
> And say, "I produced this boy"
> Or think, "I planted this tree,"
> Arising from other does not even exist for the world. (6.32)

Therefore, on the explicit level, the refutation of arising from the four extremes remedies the imputed ignorance of philosophical systems. The four extreme types of arising are all asserted by their proponents *after* engaging in philosophical analysis.

However, this does not mean that the refutation of arising from the four extremes and other refutations in the *Entrance to the Middle Way* are of no value in overcoming the innate ignorance due to which all ordinary beings suffer. By familiarizing our intellects with the illogic of the attempts of philosophical schools to reify arising, we gain more tools to examine and dismantle our own similar internal rationales for believing that things truly arise. Reading the *Entrance to the Middle Way* and the Karmapa's commentary is therefore not just a study regimen. When engaged fully, these texts form a comprehensive manual of analytical meditation that can help us cut through our doubts about the existence of phenomena, see our patterns of reification more clearly, and independently engender the insights of selflessness and emptiness.

The "four theses," posited by Chandrakīrti in verse 6.8ab to begin his refutation of inherent arising, are a reiteration of Nāgārjuna's famed first verse (after the opening homage) in *Fundamental Wisdom*:

Not from themselves and not from others,
Not from both nor causelessly—
In things, of whatever type they may be,
Arising never exists. (1.1)

However, we must read the word "theses" here with a grain of salt. As the Karmapa states again and again throughout the commentary, the genuine Followers of the Middle Way, from their own side and in terms of their own take on things, have no thesis about anything whatsoever. Therefore any appearance of their adopting a "thesis" is an instance of their using the language of others in order to skillfully communicate. In voicing such theses, they temporarily adopt the perspective of others in order to lead others to the result of seeing genuine reality, which is beyond theses, for themselves. For someone who has penetrated the illusions and gone to the other shore of language, concepts, and perception, all talk of "emptiness," "nonemptiness," "seeing," "nonseeing," "arising," "nonarising," "positing a thesis," and "not positing a thesis" has no bearing on direct experience. The genuine Followers of the Middle Way abide in the wisdom of the noble ones' enlightenment. Nevertheless, they may take on the appearance of adopting positions in order to skillfully lead beings along the path. As Nāgārjuna's *Fundamental Wisdom* relays:

> We do not assert "emptiness."
> We do not assert "nonemptiness."
> We do not assert "both" or "neither."
> We use these only as labels. (22.11)

The Consequentialist approach is to help others overcome their wrong views while not holding a view of one's own. For in the end, any and all *views*—concepts of what reality might be—are limiting to direct experience and to be relinquished. Therefore, the designation of the lack of arising from the four extremes as a "thesis" or set of theses is merely a temporary label used for convenience in the context of refuting the four positions of arising.

The lack of arising from the four extremes is not a thesis that the Consequentialists hold from their own side in general. For example, in order to communicate in debate with a follower of the Enumerator *(Sāṃkhya, Drangchenpa/grangs can pa)* school of Indian philosophy, a school that asserts arising from self, the Consequentialists may say, "Things do not arise from themselves." However, their philosophical commitment does not go beyond simply making that utterance. They do not hold a position of "the lack of arising from self" from their own side.

The principle of making statements for the perspective of others while holding onto no conceptual construct whatsoever of one's own is explained many times, in many different ways, and in many different contexts throughout this book. Justifying the redundancy involved in these explanations, the Karmapa, in a later section, remarks,

> Since this is an important point, I have made it not once but several times, and will continue to make it!

Concluding his general introduction to the sixth chapter, the Karmapa shares that his explanation has been based on that of the "early Consequentialist" masters such as Atisha, Naktso Lotsawa, and Dromtönpa.

He specifically mentions Rendawa Shönu Lodrö and Lochen Kyapchok Palzang as being among the few masters of the later period of Tibetan Middle Way exposition who accurately explain the Middle Way approach of Nāgārjuna and Chandrakīrti as it was passed down through the early Tibetan masters.

The Consequentialist-Autonomist Distinction

Also prefacing the actual refutation of arising from the four extremes is the Karmapa's synopsis of the distinction between two trends of logical practice and thought in the Middle Way tradition that Tibetan scholars came to call Consequentialist *(Prāsaṅgika, Talgyurwa/thal 'gyur ba)* and Autonomist *(Svātantrika, Rang-gyüpa/rang rgyud pa).*[38] This is the only major section in the Ninth Karmapa's entire commentary that is purely an "independent" composition of the Karmapa, written without being based on any of the *Entrance's* root verses.

The outline of the Karmapa's section headings highlights an important point related to his explanation of the Consequentialist-Autonomist distinction. The section on this distinction is placed as the first heading under the refutation of arising from the four extremes. Thus, for the Karmapa, the distinction between the Consequentialists and Autonomists primarily lies in the *methods* the two groups use to refute arising from the four extremes, not in differences of beliefs regarding what constitutes reality on the ultimate or relative levels.

It seems that throughout his explanation of this topic the Karmapa is often more interested in debunking myths (which, for him, mostly are derived from the explanations of Tsongkapa and his followers) about the Consequentialist-Autonomist distinction than he is in presenting a clearly defined boundary between the Consequentialists and Autonomists in an affirmative manner. His most pointed remarks seem to be aimed at elevating the esteem of the Autonomists as genuine Followers of the Middle Way, thus rescuing their reputation from the status of inauthentic Followers of the Middle Way that had been assigned to them by Tsongkapa and his followers.

He begins by identifying two misunderstandings: first, that the Autonomists accept the perceptions of ordinary beings as valid cognition, and, second, that the Autonomists approach logic in the exact same manner as Dignāga and Dharmakīrti, the masters of the Valid Cognition tradition. In general, however, the most important myth of which readers are to be disabused is the belief that the Autonomists either mistakenly apprehend or are incapable of fully understanding emptiness.

For the Karmapa, the basic view of the Autonomists is the same as that of the Consequentialists: all phenomena are, from the beginning, free from all conceptual elaborations of existence, nonexistence, and so on. However, the Autonomists make presentations of the relative truth, from the perspective of others, "to encourage the discovery of suchness." The Consequentialists found that in doing so the Autonomists wound up committing themselves to problematic logical implications, and thus the split between the two approaches remained intact.

The Karmapa claims that, contrary to popular belief, the Autonomists do not believe that the phenomena of the relative truth are real on the level of the relative. Rather, they speak of such phenomena from the perspective of their performing functions. On the relative level, phenomena have the power to perform functions, and thus the cognition of function-performing things is valid in the relative. However, the Karmapa insists that the Autonomists make this presentation of valid cognition at the level of no analysis only with the intention of "clearing away all poisonous clinging to outer and inner things." Nevertheless, even the most sympathetic Consequentialist finds problems in this presentation. For the Consequentialists, calling anything "valid cognition" necessarily ascribes the quality of being undeceiving. Undeceiving in turn necessitates being, on some level, real. Therefore, for the Consequentialists the Autonomist approach to communicating with others about emptiness—and communication is really what this distinction is about—entails a certain level of clinging to conventional terms and objects.

Does this mean that one could not achieve the realization of emptiness using the Autonomist approach? No. By using the Autonomist approach to reasoning—the logic of "beyond one or many" and so on—one will gain progressive familiarity with the actual Middle Way, through which any residual clinging to conventions will naturally dissolve.

Even though the Karmapa certainly identified more with the Consequentialist approach, his respect for the Autonomist tradition is clear:

> The Consequentialists and Autonomists differ in regard to the words they use to communicate, but their intentions are the same. The slight differences in their approaches are similar to a doctor treating different kinds of illnesses by administering

sweet medicine to some and sour medicine to others: Consequentialists and Autonomists teach differently in order to eradicate sentient beings' different propensities to cling to the true
existence of things.

Another key issue in the distinction that the Karmapa investigates—
and in relation to which, as preserved in an appendix to this book,
Chandrakīrti takes Bhāvaviveka to task—is that of "commonly appearing subjects." Bhāvaviveka, the progenitor of the Autonomist system, held
that in order for a Follower of the Middle Way to communicate effectively with a counterpart in debate, there must be a subject of debate that
appears commonly to both of the debate's participants. For Chandrakīrti
and the Consequentialists, however, this type of common appearance is
impossible: Followers of the Middle Way who abide in the genuine insight
of suchness have no clinging to the existence of any objects of the relative
truth. To participate in a discussion in which the two participants were
not talking about the same thing would not be a helpful way to communicate. Therefore, the Consequentialists primarily highlight the internal
contradictions of their counterparts' philosophies, without holding any
philosophies of their own.

Next the Karmapa draws on an important section of Chandrakīrti's
Lucid Words to explain the key differences between the approaches of
Chandrakīrti and Bhāvaviveka and, by extension, between the Consequentialists and Autonomists. Since an annotated translation of the full
excerpt from *Lucid Words* is presented as an appendix in this book, this
section of the Karmapa's commentary will not be summarized here.

In concluding this introductory glance at the Consequentialist-Autonomist distinction, it may be helpful to note that the Karmapa comments
on the distinction (and, more precisely, on others' misunderstandings of
the distinction) not only in this section explicitly dedicated to it alone,
but in many general meaning sections interspersed throughout *Feast for
the Fortunate*. It seems that the Karmapa holds the Consequentialist-
Autonomist distinction to be a powerful key to unlocking the secrets of
Middle Way view.

The Refutation of Arising from Self
The main refutation of the self of phenomena is carried out using the argument sometimes known as the "Vajra Slivers" but is in this book simply

called the refutation of arising from the four extremes. Phenomena do not arise from themselves, others, both self and other, or causelessly. Therefore, they lack an inherent nature. This is proven first by refuting the notion of arising from self as it was advanced by the Enumerator *(Sāṃkhya, Drangchenpa/grangs can pa)* school of the Hindu tradition of India.

The Enumerators propose that phenomena are indeed produced in dependence upon a process of causality, but that the results of phenomena are present as the essential nature of their causes. A sprout, they would say (according to the reading they are given by Tibetan philosophers), is present as the essential nature of its seed at the time of the seed's existence. Therefore, sprouts arise "from themselves." For the Enumerators, the only difference between the stage of cause and the stage of result is the difference between the result's being "clearly manifest" or not: at the time of the cause, the result is hidden; when the essential nature of the cause becomes clearly manifest, it is called a result.

The Followers of the Middle Way respond with straightforward logic: if something already existed, it wouldn't need to "arise" or be produced again. If already existing things produced already existing things, it would in fact be impossible for a seed to produce a sprout, because seeds would simply produce themselves in infinity. There would be no chronological process of earlier and later stages, because those stages must be different from each other. Moreover, if things produced themselves, the result would never cancel its cause (just as a sprout, in order to be a sprout, must cause the disintegration of its own seed; the seed cannot keep existing as a seed through the stage of being a sprout), because the result and cause are of the same entity. Since both of these consequences are logically inevitable and also undesirable to the Enumerators, the Followers of the Middle Way conclude that arising from self does not exist.

In conclusion, since not even normal worldly people observe or speak about things arising from themselves, the notion that they do should be rejected on both the ultimate and relative levels.

The Refutation of Arising from Other

Having made short work of arising from self, the *Entrance* next turns its attention for a much longer stretch to refuting arising from other. The main refutation of arising from other refutes the lower vehicles of Buddhism, and a supplementary section refutes the system of the Proponents of Consciousness of the Mahāyāna. This latter section provides a significant supplement to the texts of Nāgārjuna because, due to the historical evolution of the schools, the system of the Proponents of Consciousness was not refuted by Nāgārjuna himself.

Staying close to the wording of Chandrakīrti's autocommentary, the Karmapa begins the first section, which refutes the arising asserted by Buddhism's abhidharma schools, not by commenting on a root verse but by briefly describing the assertions by the hearers that relate to causes and results. The abhidharmikas believed that the inherent nature of things lies in the process of causality: because specific things arise in an undeceiving way due to specific, observable causes, things therefore have an inherent nature and are not free from arising.

Chandrakīrti begins his refutation of the lower vehicle rendition of arising from other by stating an unavoidable absurd consequence to his counterparts' view: if things really did arise from things that were inherently different from themselves, arising would be random and nonsensical; flames could arise from sheer darkness, precisely because flames and darkness are also inherently "different" from each other. In other words, in order for two phenomena to be truly different from each other, they would have to be unconnected to each other. To assert arising from other, therefore, is to assert that any cause could produce any result.

The hearers may respond that Chandrakīrti's refutation does not apply to their view because they assert arising in specific, observable instances within the same continuum of cause-result relationships. For example, they say, it can be seen that only barley seeds produce barley sprouts; therefore there would be no absurd consequence that arising would be nonsensical. Chandrakīrti rejects that defense. Precisely because the hearers assert the cause to be "different" from the result, they lose their ability to posit the cause as sharing the result's continuum. Something that is inherently different from another thing cannot belong to that other thing's continuum.

It may be helpful to recall here that the Followers of the Middle Way are not suggesting that seeds do not arise from sprouts. On the level of worldly reality, seeds arise from sprouts, fire is hot and burning, and actions lead to consequences. What the Followers of the Middle Way see as problematic is the attempt by philosophers to ascribe true existence or other philosophical concepts to the process of arising *after* analysis. Therefore, the problem is not that the hearers say that causes produce results. Rather, what the Followers of the Middle Way wish to refute is the notion, presented as being backed by logical reasoning, that causes and results truly exist and that "arising from other" is a verifiable phenomenon.

To further clarify the illogic of arising from other, the *Entrance* next demonstrates the impossibility of inherently different causes and results being earlier and later moments or being simultaneous occurrences. Inherently existing causes and results as earlier and later moments is impossible, because in the context of earlier and later moments otherness or difference itself is impossible. One can speak of two different people, for example, as being different from each other on the basis of observing them simultaneously. However, in the production of phenomena, when the cause is present the result is absent, and when the result is present the cause is absent. Otherness cannot exist when one member of the pair of mutual others does not exist.

Nor can causes and results exist simultaneously as mutually different from each other. If a result, such as an eye consciousness, existed simulaneously with its cause, such as an eye faculty, what need would there be to call it a result? It would already exist, so why would it need to be produced "again" by a cause? Since there would be no such need, arising from other cannot be asserted in that permutation either.

The Two Truths

Chandrakīrti's discussion of the two truths is introduced by way of an objection made by a hypothetical opponent to his refutation of arising from other. The interlocutor suggests that perhaps logical reasonings are not needed to prove arising from other, since every ordinary person directly sees that other things arise from other things. The Karmapa's heading above Chandrakīrti's next verse offers the first response: even if arising from other were established for the worldly perspective, it would not invalidate the refutations of arising from other set forth by the Followers of the Middle Way. For, as Chandrakīrti then states in one of the more famous moments of the *Entrance*, everything can be seen in two ways, from either a relative *(saṃvṛti, kundzob/kun rdzob)* or an ultimate *(paramārtha, döndam/don dam)* perspective.

A key point in understanding Chandrakīrti's distinction between the two truths is that, for Chandrakīrti, the distinction is not drawn from the side of the object. As verse 6.23 clearly teaches, the distinction is drawn from the side of the perceiving subject: ultimate truth is what is seen by the wisdom of realized, enlightened beings, beings who have removed the cataracts of their ignorance; relative truth is what is seen by ordinary, confused sentient beings.

The Two Truths Are Neither the Same Nor Different

The Indo-Tibetan study tradition is rich in profound and vast critical investigations related to the two truths. While the Eighth Karmapa delves into great detail in his exploration of topics related to verse 6.23, the Ninth Karmapa, quoting or closely paraphrasing the Eighth Karmapa's words, centers his discussion around one key question, which he treats succinctly: are the two truths of one entity (or essence), or are they different? For the Karmapa, the two truths are of neither the same or different entities. Using scriptural quotations and tenable logic, he explains the undesirable consequences entailed in asserting either that the two truths are of the same entity or that they are of different entities.

If they were of the same entity, all sentient beings would see ultimate reality, because observing the characteristics of the relative truth would necessarily be equal to observing the characteristics of the ultimate truth. Since countless sentient beings still have not attained liberation from suffering, obviously that is not the case. If the two truths were of inherently different entities, it would be impossible for beings to attain liberation, because the ultimate truth would not be the true nature of the relative truth. In order to see ultimate truth, one would have to view a completely different set of phenomena rather than realize the nature of phenomena themselves.

The Karmapa concludes on this point by stating that the two truths are beyond all conceptual elaborations of being the same or different. This is the case regarding any phenomena that depend on each other for their respective designations. In the case of the two truths, truth (the ultimate truth) is posited in dependence upon falsity (the relative truth), and vice versa. The Karmapa neatly joins his explanation with a verse from Nāgārjuna's *Fundamental Wisdom*:

> When something originates in dependence upon something else,
> The [depender] is not the same as [the depended-on],
> Nor is it different from it.
> In this way, nihilism and permanence are transcended. (18.10)

Relative Truth and the Mere Relative
In the next lines of the *Entrance's* root text, Chandrakīrti elucidates his clear and straightforward Middle Way description of the relative truth: relative truth is whatever ordinary, worldly beings consider to be real. The world accepts whatever appears to unimpaired sense faculties as real; what appears to impaired faculties, along with entities imagined to exist by non-Buddhist philosophical systems (such as the "primal matter" of the Enumerators) and apparitions such as mirages, does not exist for the worldly perspective and is therefore not even relative *truth*.

Relative *truth*, therefore, is simply what appears to be real to ordinary beings. Yet the appearance of phenomena does not necessarily entail clinging to true existence from the side of the perceiving subject. Bodhisattvas, for example, in their postmeditation experience, perceive various appearances but understand them to be like illusions and dreams. They do not ascribe any true existence to them. Therefore, in postmeditation, that which appears to the bodhisattvas is called the *mere relative*. Relative appearances manifest, but they are not considered to be *truths* or *realities* in themselves. When bodhisattvas and the other noble beings (the realized hearers and solitary realizers) dwell in meditative equipoise, however, not even the appearances of the mere relative manifest, for at that time all movement of consciousness and conceptual elaborations is completely pacified.[39]

Clinging to True Existence Is an Afflictive Obscuration
Because of the distinction between relative truth and the mere relative, the Karmapa, in notable agreement with Tsongkapa and in open contrast with Gorampa and Shākya Chokden, holds that all instances of clinging to true existence *(den-dzin/bden 'dzin)* are afflictive obscurations *(nyön-drip/nyon sgrib)* and that there are no instances of clinging to true existence that are only cognitive obscurations *(she-drip/shes sgrib)*. Ordinary beings cling to true existence because of not having relinquished the afflictive ignorance *(nyönmong chen gyi marikpa/nyon mongs can gyi ma rig pa)* that is the cause of that clinging. Due to clinging to things as being real, all other afflictive mental states, such as desire and anger, arise.

The postmeditation of noble beings, on the other hand, involves relative appearances, but it does not involve clinging to true existence, because noble beings have reversed afflictive ignorance. Due to still having nonafflictive ignorance *(nyönmong chen mayinpe marikpa/nyon mongs can ma yin pa'i ma rig pa)*, the bodhisattvas have the mere apprehension of subtle characteristics *(tsen-dzin/mtshan 'dzin)* in their postmeditation states. The final vestiges of apprehending subtle characteristics vanish only at the stage of buddhahood.

The section on the two truths concludes with a pithy explanation of the ultimate truth: ultimate truth is what is seen when ignorance is removed. It is not an autonomous entity unto itself. One can speak of ultimate reality, the experience of noble beings, in comparison with relative reality, what is experienced by ordinary beings, but there is no "ultimate reality" established as a real thing apart from that comparison. When one breaks through the veils of ignorance and finds that the vases, trees, and rocks of the relative truth do not truly exist, that "nonseeing" is the seeing of the ultimate. Even though "appearance" is usually equated with relative truth and "emptiness" with the ultimate, both appearance and emptiness, the relative and the ultimate, are designated merely in mutual dependence. Neither of them possesses true existence. For this reason, one of the sixteen modes of emptiness taught by the Buddha in the Mahāyāna sūtras was *the emptiness of emptiness.*

Therefore, it seems that in the final analysis of the Karmapa, emptiness itself is merely a pedagogical tool. One must rely heavily on emptiness during the second of the three stages of analysis, but when one arrives at the third stage, thorough analysis, the view of the genuine Followers of the Middle Way themselves, one understands that there is no emptiness or nonemptiness. One is free, furthermore, of having or not having opinions of one's own about the existence or nonexistence, emptiness or nonemptiness, of phenomena. Nevertheless, to arrive at such a subtle and incredibly profound understanding, the reasonings that demonstrate emptiness, the lack of inherent nature of all phenomena, are crucial. The Karmapa underscores this key point—along with the status of emptiness as a pedagogical tool—in the section on personal selflessness:

> What, then, *is* emptiness? All phenomena from form through omniscience are, from the outset, not established whatsoever as any extreme elaboration such as existent, nonexistent, arisen, ceased, permanent, impermanent, empty, not empty, true, or false. To that lack of establishment, mere conventional terms

such as "emptiness" and "suchness" are given. It is nothing more than that.

This emptiness—that conventionally all phenomena are empty of their own entities—is the natural being *(rang bab/ rang babs)*, the abiding mode, of all knowable objects. Resting in equipoise within it is the antidote to all obscurations. It is the sun that conquers the darkness of wrong views, the supreme medicine that clears away the snake poison of reification, the essential nectar of the Buddha's teachings. Everyone who sincerely desires liberation and omniscience should engage it through applying great effort in hearing, contemplating, and meditating.

In the above quotation, the Karmapa's use of the word "conventionally" is key. From the perspective of thorough analysis—the meditative equipoise of the noble ones—both appearing phenomena *and* emptiness are merely conventions, conceptual elaborations. However, at the second stage of analysis it is crucial to determine that appearing phenomena are of the nature of emptiness. When not engaged in any analysis, the Followers of the Middle Way simply repeat whatever worldly people say about existence and nonexistence. Out of compassion, they do whatever they can to help beings transcend their wrong assumptions.

Freedom from Elaborations
By arriving at the stage of thorough analysis, one experiences "freedom from elaborations" *(niṣhprapañcha, trödral/spros bral)*,[40] a very important term in the Karmapa's writing and in the entirety of the Kagyü lineage in general. The genuine experience of the genuine reality is beyond any correlation to concepts: emptiness or nonemptiness, existence or nonexistence, refutation[41] or affirmation. When understood correctly, "emptiness" can also indicate the same freedom (as in the emptiness of emptiness), but *niṣhprapañcha* is helpful in that it explicitly indicates that emptiness too is not to be reified. In the Mahāmudrā tradition and in the explanations of the Kagyü lineage's creation and completion stage practices of the Vajrayāna, *niṣhprapañcha* is used to succinctly remind the practitioner of the correct understanding of emptiness, which at those stages is presupposed.

Though the formal section of the root text and commentary indicated

by the Karmapa to be the "presentation of the two truths" is fairly brief, we
will see issues that directly relate to the two truths raised again and again
throughout the text. The analysis of the two truths lies at the very core of
Middle Way debate, explanation, and composition.

Continuation of the Refutation of Arising from Other

The next series of root verses describes how the two truths fit with each
other, the proper context for emphasizing each of the truths, and the reasons why the worldly perspective on arising and existence does not invalidate the refutations of the Followers of the Middle Way. Chandrakīrti
offers his first direct response to the question posed by the interlocutor at
verse 6.22 (the one who suggested that arising from other could be proven
simply by relying on the ordinary perceptions of worldly people) by stating that the worldly perspective cannot be regarded as an authoritative
source for any definite statement about the way things are. For if worldly
beings saw things accurately, what need would there be for a "path to
enlightenment" or any notion of enlightenment to strive for? We would
all already be seeing true reality. However, that is obviously not the case.
We experience suffering, time and again, because of the discord between
our thoughts and perceptions and the way things really are. Therefore, in
no instance whatsoever can worldly perceptions be relied on as valid cognition.

Though Chandrakīrti mentions no names in his root verses or autocommentary, it may be inferred that in verse 6.30 he is criticizing the explanations of conventional reality of the Indian epistemology and logic masters
Dignāga and Dharmakīrti, whose tradition includes the direct sense perceptions of ordinary beings in the category of valid cognition. Verses 6.34
through 6.36, which pursue similar themes, have also been interpreted
as refutations of the Autonomist approach to the relative truth. Dzogchen Ponlop Rinpoche has noted[42] that, although Wangchuk Dorje does
not identify a particular master or school at which these verses are aimed,
the refutations seem to be directed at the followers of the lower Buddhist
vehicles, the Proponents of Consciousness, and some, but not necessarily
all, Autonomist masters.[43]

In any case, verses 6.34 through 6.36 express three absurd or undesirable consequences for those who hold the view that the perceptions of
worldly people are valid. Firstly, if what worldly people see were authori-

tative, emptiness, and the realization of emptiness, would be a denigration of appearing phenomena. Things' characteristics would be existent from the outset, and when the bodhisattvas rested in the equipoise in which things' characteristics were not observed, they would be committing a denial of the actual state of things. Emptiness would become like a hammer of the ultimate destroying a vase of the relative. But as the Buddha taught in the *Heaps of Jewels Sūtra* and other places, emptiness does not empty phenomena of their characteristics; phenomena are empty of their own characteristics from the outset.

Secondly, if worldly perceptions were valid cognition, conventional reality, because of being verified by logic and analysis, would become ultimately reality. There would be no further or more profound reality to discover apart from the mundane appearances of form, sound, smell, taste, touch, and mental objects, because these would have already been established by analysis as valid. Yet this is not the case, because when we analyze phenomena we discover that they are empty of their own natures. It is for this reason that Chandrakīrti points out that, if one wants to maintain an observation of conventional reality, it should not be analyzed in terms of whether it exists unto itself or not. Once one has begun such an analysis, one has already crossed over into the analysis of seeking the ultimate.

Thirdly, if the perceptions of worldly people were verifiably existent, the reasonings that investigate ultimate reality would be incapable of refuting arising. But that is not the case: reasonings demonstrate that, not only is arising from self, other, both, and neither impossible ultimately, such arising does not even exist conventionally.

Tsongkapa's Object of Refutation by Reasons

In this section the Karmapa takes Tsongkapa to task for the first of many occasions in the commentary on the latter's description of "what is to be refuted by reasonings" or "the object of refutation by reasons" *(rikpe gakja/ rigs pas dgag bya* or *tak kyi gakja/rtags kyis dgag bya)*. Tsongkapa, we are told, insists that in order for a refutation of any phenomenon's inherent existence to be meaningful, one must precisely identify "true existence," the quality being refuted, and then direct the refutation at that target. For example, when refuting the inherent existence of a vase, one does not demonstrate that the vase itself is empty of its own entity; rather, one isolates "the true existence of the vase" as the target of refutation. This is how

Tsongkapa is said to explain the principle of self-emptiness or intrinsic emptiness *(rangtong/rang stong)*. The formula "the vase is not empty of the vase; the vase is empty of true existence" is often associated with Tsongkapa's approach to the logic of emptiness.

The Karmapa states that, by explaining intrinsic emptiness in this way, Tsongkapa takes as his own position precisely what was refuted by Chandrakīrti as a view of the *opponents* of the Followers of the Middle Way. For the Karmapa, what makes the Middle Way profound is its ability to refute the existence, after analysis, of all phenomena. Middle Way reasonings demonstrate that all phenomena, from form through omniscience, are empty of their own entities—they are empty precisely of themselves. The Karmapa contends that Tsongkapa advocates not for a profound emptiness, but for a partial emptiness *(nyitsewey tongpanyi/nyi tshe ba'i stong pa nyid)*, for Tsongkapa's explanation does not target the real source of sentient beings' confusion: reification of things themselves. Sentient beings do not cling to "the true existence of the vase," they cling to "the vase." Tsongkapa's critics have difficulty with his isolating something other than appearing phenomena themselves and then calling the emptiness of that "the emptiness of phenomena." Arguing for an approach more closely aligned with the Karmapa, the great twentieth-century Tibetan scholar Gendün Chöpel *(dge 'dun chos 'phel,* 1903-1951), in his *Ornament to Nāgārjuna's Thought (Ludrup Gong-gyen/klu sgrub dgongs rgyan),* wrote:

> No matter how much one verbally distinguishes the objects that are to be negated by reasoning, the truth is that, as far as refutation is concerned, you need to refute the vase; you need to refute the pillar; you need to refute existence; you need to refute nonexistence. What use is there in positing the vase and then refuting a "truly existent vase" off to the side?
>
> In regard to this approach, not only the early scholars of Tibet, but also those of the Gendenpa faction[44] who possess experience are clearly of similar thought. For example, Changkya [Rolpe Dorje] *(lcang skya rol pa'i rdo rje,* 1717-1786) offered these displeased words:

> Leaving alone all vivid appearances,
> They look for something with horns to refute.

Gungthang Tenpey Drönme (*gung thang bstan pa'i sgron me,* 1762-1823) and Panchen Lobsang Chögyen (1570-1662) also taught in the exact same manner.

There are those who fear that if vases, pillars and so on were refuted through reasoning, everyone would come to espouse nihilistic views of nonexistence. Their worries are pointless. For in the case of ordinary, everyday beings who are looking at a vase presently in front of them, how is it possible that a nihilistic view regarding the vase to be utterly nonexistent could arise? Even if such an outlook did happen to arise in someone, he or she would directly cognize that the vase can still be seen and touched. Therefore, if a mind naturally arose that thinks, "The vase is appearing to me, but while appearing, it is utterly nonexistent," that is the Middle Way view known as "the twofold collection of appearance and emptiness that cognizes how appearing phenomena do not exist in the way they appear." How is that nihilism?[45]

Gendün Chöpel's text continues with an extensive refutation of the traditional Geluk interpretation of the "object of refutation by reasons," and Ju Mipham's commentary to the *Entrance,* along with the Eighth and Ninth Karmapas' texts, is also rich in similar criticisms.

Returning to the *Entrance's* root verses, the next focus is reconciling karma and ultimate truth. If nothing, including actions and results, is established by way of its nature, is the relationship between actions and results therefore meaningless? Are actions therefore inconsequential? No. Even though a reflection of an object is considered not to be a real object in the world, it can still be seen. In the same way, even though actions and results are empty of their own natures, from the confused perspective of apparent reality results perfectly arise as precise reflections of the actions that were their causes. For as long as relative appearances manifest, one must therefore be heedful of the relationship between actions and results.

Even though some actions ripen into resultant experiences many lifetimes after they were committed, there does not need to be a special or truly established phenomenon devoted to the function of keeping the dormant potential of the actions alive. For Followers of the Middle Way, neither actions nor their results inherently arise, nor do they inherently cease. Because the nature of actions and results is emptiness, it is entirely possible for a result to ripen long after the action that was its cause was performed.

Refuting Postdisintegration as a Thing

Another controversial theory of Tsongkapa's tradition that receives first mention in this section of the text is his explanation of the connection between causes and their results. Tsongkapa asserts "postdisintegration as a thing" *(shikpa ngöpo/zhig pa dngos po)*,[46] the state (or states) following an action or other cause's disintegration. According to Tsongkapa, postdisintegration is a function-performing thing that makes it possible for results to ripen, even if the actions or other causes had ceased long ago. The Karmapa does not describe Tsongkapa's position on postdisintegration to the same extent that he describes the latter's position on the object of refutation by reasons. This is likely because the Karmapa assumes the reader's familiarity with the position he is refuting, since the unique assertions of Tsongkapa had been widely disseminated in Tibetan philosophical circles by the time the Eighth and Ninth Karmapas composed their *Entrance* commentaries.

Postdisintegration as a function-performing thing is renowned as one of the "eight great difficult points" of the Consequentialist system as asserted by Tsongkapa.[47] In his own commentary to *Entrance* entitled *Illuminating the Intention (Gongpa Rapsal/dgongs pa rab gsal)*, Tsongkapa directs readers to his commentary on Nāgārjuna's *Fundamental Wisdom* called the *Ocean of Reasoning (Rikpe Gyamtso/rigs pa'i rgya mtsho)*[48] for his full explanation of this phenomenon.[49] To be brief, it seems that Tsongkapa ascribes creative power to the passive state of absence that immediately follows the disintegration of any given cause and that begins a stream of similar moments of disintegratedness until the cause's result arises. For Tsongkapa, this postdisintegration, or disintegratedness, must be acknowledged as performing a vital function of ensuring that a cause's potential carries through to the result, since an action that is a cause in many cases ceases long before its result becomes manifest. In some cases many lifetimes, it is said, can transpire during this interim. Even when results ripen immediately, there are no instances of causes directly contacting results.

For the Karmapa, however, any attempt at analyzing conventional

reality on so subtle a level will become an analysis of the ultimate. Moreover, he says, the master Chandrakīrti clearly explained that even though
actions do not inherently cease, they are able to produce results. Actions,
results, and the connection between them are simply posited from the
worldly perspective. According to the Karmapa, this, and simply this, is
the way that Followers of the Middle Way should speak about karma. If
one posits a relationship between causes and results *after* analysis, one is
following the system of the Proponents of Things. When analyzing, one
sees that results do not arise from either disintegrated causes or nondisin-
tegrated causes.

The Ninth Karmapa devotes less space to refuting postdisintegration
than does the Eighth Karmapa in the *Chariot of the Takpo Kagyü Siddhas*.
In *Feast for the Fortunate*, the main refutations of postdisintegration are
found in this section and in the section on personal selflessness. Throughout *Feast*, far more of the Ninth Karmapa's emphasis is placed on refuting
the "object of refutation by reasons" of Tsongkapa and his followers.

The next root verses of the *Entrance* describe the essential relationship
between karma and emptiness: virtuous actions produce happiness and
nonvirtuous actions produce suffering. Moreover, once an action ripens
into a result, it does not ripen again. Nevertheless, both actions and results
lack an inherent nature from the outset. Knowing the ways of karma, and
especially the way in which karma is empty, leads to liberation.

In verse 6.43 Chandrakīrti, for the first time in the text, refers to the
distinction between definitive meaning *(nītārtha, ngedön/nges don)* and
provisional meaning *(neyārtha, drangdön/drang don)*. A more thorough
exploration of this distinction is offered during the refutation of the system of the Proponents of Consciousness; here, Chandrakīrti makes use
of the distinction briefly, for two verses (6.43 and 6.44), in order to dispel the misconception that the basis or support for actions and results is
truly existent.

In various sūtras, the Buddha did teach about "the person," "the all-
base consciousness," and "the aggregates" in order to help sentient beings
understand the infallibility of actions and results and so that students
could gradually approach the notion of emptiness without becoming
frightened away from the Buddha's teachings. Chandrakīrti declares that
these statements were made with only emptiness in mind; they are not to
be understood literally or definitively. Rather, they serve the temporary

purpose of taking care of students at a certain level of ability and guiding them to the actual meaning when they are ready. The Buddha, after all, had to communicate with ordinary beings who had solid conceptions of the self. He used words such as "I" and "mine," even though he knew that these words referred to no true entities. In the same way, every time the Buddha described something as "existent," he was making a statement of only the provisional, and not the definitive, meaning.

The Refutation of the Proponents of Consciousness

Although the Karmapa's section heading calls Chandrakīrti's discussion of the Proponents of Consciousness *(Vijñāptivādin, Namrik Mawa/rnam rig smra ba)*[50] an "ancillary refutation," in terms of the major topics covered in the sixth chapter its length is second only to that of personal selflessness. In composing an introduction or supplement to Nāgārjuna's *Fundamental Wisdom*, Chandrakīrti no doubt sensed a responsibility on his part to examine the system of the Proponents of Consciousness in the context of Nāgārjuna's Middle Way, given that the Proponents of Consciousness did not emerge as a powerful philosophical school in the Mahāyāna of India until after the time of Nāgārjuna.

As an expression of what is perhaps a unique respect for his refutation's target, a school born of the same Mahāyāna ethic in which he was trained, Chandrakīrti devotes three full root verses simply to stating the position of his counterparts. On Chandrakīrti's reading of their system, the Proponents of Consciousness assert that the true nature of reality is mere consciousness, free from the duality of perceiver and perceived. The source for the arising of all appearances of duality is the all-base consciousness *(ālayavijñāna, kunshi namshe/kun gzhi'i rnam shes)*, which is likened to an ocean from which the waves of appearances manifest due to the winds of ignorance.

The bulk of Chandrakīrti's refutation focuses not on the "all-base consciousness" per se (although in other sections he indeed clearly proclaims it does not exist), but on the "consciousness of the dependent nature *(paratantra, shenwang/gzhan dbang)*,"[51] which the Proponents of Consciousness assert to possess three main qualities: 1) it is free from outer apprehended objects yet entails dualistic appearances due to habitual tendencies, 2) it substantially exists as the basis for dualistic appearances and the conceptions of the self of phenomena and the self of persons, and 3) its own nature is free from conceptual elaborations of thoughts and terms.

Chandrakīrti first takes apart at great length the notion of a consciousness without outer apprehended objects. His refutation involves disproving the validity of three main examples given by the Proponents of Consciousness to prove that consciousness can exist without outer objects. The three are the dream example (dream objects do not exist but the dreaming mind does), the diseased vision example (the minds of people with diseased vision who see nonexistent strands of hair exist without objects), and the example of skeletons (meditators who contemplate repulsiveness can come to see the world filled with skeletons—this is an example of a mind without objects). Chandrakīrti's refutations are quite straightforwardly understood by reading the root text and the Karmapa's commentary.

Refuting a Common Object of Perception
The issues raised by verse 6.71ab created a great controversy amongst commentators on the *Entrance*. In the verse, Chandrakīrti refers to hungry ghosts perceiving a river as pus and says that their perception is equivalent to that of someone with diseased vision who sees the false appearance of falling hairs: from the perspective of the confused perceiver, both the object and subject appear to exist. But from the perspective of someone free from the confusion with which the perceiver is afflicted, neither the subject nor the object exists. The central question that Tibetan commentators drew from this verse was: is there a basis of appearance that is shared in common between the six classes of beings in saṃsāra? Hungry ghosts see the Ganges as pus; humans see it is as water. But is there some entity or entities "out there" that serve as the ground for these different perceptions? Is there any common object behind our differing perceptions *(taja tunmongwa/blta bya thun mong ba)*?

The Karmapa's short answer is no. For the Karmapa, the pus example of the hungry ghosts applies to all relative phenomena. It is not the case that there is actually water in the river that is being mistaken as pus by the hungry ghosts. Rather, due to ignorance, mental afflictions, and karma, hungry ghosts have the relative—i.e., false—perceived object of pus and its corresponding perceiving subject. Human beings as well, due to ignorance, mental afflictions, and karma, have the relative—and equally false—

perceived object of a water-river, along with its corresponding perceiving subject. This becomes a key point of logic in refuting the Proponents of Consciousness: the ground of appearances does not exist; therefore consciousness is established as not truly existing.

For the Followers of the Middle Way, there is no difference between apprehended objects and mind in terms of the degree to which they exist. On the nonanalytical, worldly level, these phenomena of course perform different functions, but that does not make one more existent than the other. The very defining characteristic of mind is that it is aware of objects. Therefore, if consciousnesses exist, objects must exist as well. When objects do not exist, consciousnesses must also be declared nonexistent.

Refuting Self-Awareness, Even Conventionally

In refuting the second claim about the dependent nature consciousness, the claim that it substantially exists, Chandrakīrti moves quickly toward the Proponents of Consciousness's assertion of self-awareness. Self-awareness constitutes another major key topic on which Tsongkapa and the Karmapa are in agreement in their *Entrance* commentaries: for them, self-awareness does not even exist conventionally. Therefore, it is negated as a proof for the Proponents of Consciousness of the existence of the dependent nature consciousness.

The Proponents of Consciousness say that the dependent nature's substantial existence is verified by self-awareness: the dependent nature consciousness cognizes itself. However, according to Chandrakīrti and the Karmapa, it is contradictory for a thing to perform its function on itself. Even well trained acrobats cannot ride on their own shoulders, a sword cannot cut itself, and an eye cannot turn to look at itself. A consciousness apprehending itself is the same.

The Proponents of Consciousness employ memory as a proof that self-awareness exists. They describe mind as being similar to fire, which illuminates both itself and objects external to itself. Mind, they say, cognizes both itself and external objects. They say that if this were not the case, memory or recollection of experience would be impossible: in order to have the recollection, "I saw that thing," one must have been aware not only of the content of the experience but of the experience of seeing itself. Furthermore, if consciousness did not experience itself, it would have to be apprehended by a consciousness other than itself, but that view would entail the logical fault of endlessness, for an endless stream of consciousnesses would need to arise in order cognize themselves. Therefore, they conclude, since memory is established as existing for everyone, and since without self-awareness there would be the fault of endlessness, self-awareness must be accepted.

Chandrakīrti's reply is that memory cannot be used a proof for selfawareness because memory is only spoken of in the confused, worldly perspective—it does not exist, and therefore the Proponents of Consciousness have done nothing but rely on a nonexistent in an attempt to prove another nonexistent. The Proponents of Consciousness may rejoin that memory may not be established when analyzed, but it is established conventionally. But since self-awareness does not exist conventionally, it cannot be spoken of conventionally as memory's cause. (We will recall that the Proponents of Consciousness spoke of memory as the *result* of self-awareness.)

For Chandrakīrti, there is nothing special about the phenomenon of memory. Worldly people merely have the recollection, "I experienced such-and-such previously." This is simply how conventions function in the confused, worldly perspective, and this confusion cannot be relied on in an attempt to prove a sophisticated philosophical concept such as self-awareness.

In brief, performers of actions, objects of action, and actions themselves are not identical with each other. Therefore it is impossible to posit the phenomenon of self-awareness, either conventionally or ultimately. The following response by the Karmapa to other commentators' views on self awareness makes his own position very clear:

> There are some, such as Gorampa and Shākya Chokden, who say that this verse [verse 6.75 of the *Entrance*] proves that Chandrakīrti holds, from his own perspective, that self-awareness exists conventionally. They also say that in Chandrakīrti's tradition the all-base, self-awareness, outer objects, and the person all exist conventionally, but they do not exist as "conventional phenomena that can withstand analysis."
>
> These positions are untenable. The master Chandrakīrti does not, as his own position, accept any phenomenon as existent or nonexistent in either ultimate or conventional truth. What

need is there to mention his position on the "existence" of self-awareness? Since the earlier and later consciousnesses are not [inherently] different substances, it is possible to say, [repeating after worldly people], that what is experienced initially is also experienced by memory and that what is unique to that experience is also unique to its memory.

Thus a later consciousness can remember something by thinking, "I saw it before." Yet this relation between experience and memory is simply the way conventions work in the world. It is not to be thoroughly analyzed: worldly conventions are by nature false.

Chandrakīrti moves on to refute the third main claim about the dependent nature consciousness—that it exists free from conceptual elaborations—by using a combination of logic and ridicule. The dependent nature consciousness is not apprehended by any other consciousness, and it has already been proven that it does not apprehend itself. If this is the case, and if, as the Proponents of Consciousness say, it is beyond all conceptual elaborations, its status of existence would be equivalent to the childless woman's son, or the horns of a rabbit, or flowers growing in the sky. By what bias, Chandrakīrti chidingly probes, do the Proponents of Consciousness not declare the childless woman's son to be something that exists beyond conceptual elaborations?

Since the dependent nature does not even slightly exist, it cannot be the cause or basis of relative appearances as the Proponents of Consciousness claim. By positing an utterly false basis of the relative truth, the Proponents of Consciousness lose the relative truth of the world completely. In the view of Chandrakīrti, the worldly perspective alone is all that is needed for positing relative truth. Chandrakīrti identifies the relative truth of the world of no analysis as the method, and the ultimate truth, the realization of the way things are, as what arises from relating to that method skillfully. As Nāgārjuna's *Fundamental Wisdom* proclaims:

Without relying on conventions,
One cannot realize the ultimate.
Without realizing the ultimate,
One cannot attain nirvāṇa. (24.10)

The correct way to engage in and speak of the relative is summarized by the Karmapa:

> When using conventions in conventional reality, rather than fitting their descriptions to the views of philosophical systems, [the Followers of the Middle Way] describe the relative in precisely the way it is renowned in the world for all beings, high and low, of the six realms.

What the Buddha Really Meant by "Mind Only"

In the verses under the heading "Reconciling apparent contradictions in the refutation [of the Proponents of Consciousness]," and in particular in the section on "Reconciling apparent contradictions with scripture," Chandrakīrti reveals his interpretation of what the Buddha *really* meant when he taught about "mind only" *(sem tsam/sems tsam)*. In particular, the Tibetan tradition generally regards this section of the *Entrance* as Chandrakīrti's explanation of the significance of the term "only" *(tsam dra/tsam sgra).*[52]

Referring mainly to the *Sūtra on the Ten Grounds (Dashabhūmikasūtra, Sa Chupe Do/sa bcu pa'i mdo)* and the *Descent into Laṅka Sūtra (Laṅk-āvatāra, Langkar Shegpa/langkar gshegs pa)*, two of the most cited scriptures of the Proponents of Consciousness, Chandrakīrti explains that when the Buddha spoke of how the three realms are "mind only," he was refuting the notion of external creators of phenomena such as Īshvara. All phenomena appear due to karma, and karma in turn would not occur were it not for the mind.

There is therefore no other creator in this world other than mind. Because of mind's power as the root of all the bodies, worlds, and environments we experience, mind is considered foremost among all phenomena in terms of its function. The distinction between mind and form, therefore, is one of *function*; it is not a distinction of different levels of *existence*. It may be said that mind is more important than form, but it may not be said that mind alone exists and form does not. *That*, says Chandrakīrti, is what the Buddha had in mind when he said "mind *only*." For in the *Perfection of Supreme Knowledge* sūtras, the Buddha refuted the existence of mind and form equally. And, in the sūtras on abhidharma, the Buddha spoke equally of the existence of both form and mind.

Provisional Meaning and Definitive Meaning

This discussion of what the Buddha really meant when making certain statements leads Chandrakīrti to outline the distinction between provisional meaning and definitive meaning, mentioned above briefly. When the Buddha said that form does not truly exist and that mind appears as all varieties of appearances, he was making a provisional meaning statement in order to counter the clinging of those who are extremely attached to form. The Buddha emphasized the teachings on "mind only" to beings with certain styles of clinging to true existence, in the same way that a doctor will administer even poison to cure certain types of illnesses. That both form and mind are equally nonexistent is demonstrated extensively throughout the *Entrance*; here, Chandrakīrti mentions that many beings have excessive clinging to form, and, for that reason, the Buddha placed more emphasis on refuting the existence of form in the beginning.

For Chandrakīrti, the distinction between definitive meaning and provisional meaning is simple: sūtras that teach about emptiness, the suchness that is the true nature of reality, are definitive meaning. Sūtras that teach about anything else are provisional meaning. The Karmapa adds "buddha nature" and "emptiness of other" *(shentong/gzhan stong)* to Chandrakīrti's list of topics that the Buddha taught as provisional meaning, a list that had already included such phenomena as the person, the aggregates, and the all-base consciousness. This discussion is accompanied by an interesting general meaning commentary by the Karmapa on the topic of the provisional and definitive meanings. One of the key points the Karmapa makes is that *all* of the Buddha's teachings, be they provisional or definitive, are supreme causes of liberation for beings of various dispositions and abilities.

The Refutation of Arising from Both

The historical reference to the view of arising from both self and other is drawn from the Jain school of India. On Chandrakīrti's reading of their system, the Jains say that a clay vase, for example, arises from elements that are "itself" (such as clay) and elements that are "other" (such as the craftsmen's efforts). Chandrakīrti's logic in refuting this assertion is simple: arising from self and other is impossible, because the lack of arising from both self and other individually has already been established. Therefore, since bringing self and other together will not yield any additional truly existent production, "arising from both" does not exist for the world or for those who analyze suchness.

The Refutation of Causeless Arising

Chandrakīrti's refutation of arising due to no causes is aimed at India's Chārvāka *(Gyangpenpa/rgyang 'phen pa)* school. The Chārvākas say that things arise from their own essences or entities, but this view is slightly different from the view of the Enumerators, who propound arising from self. For the Chārvākas, there is no distinction between causal phases and resultant phases whatsoever: there are no causes or results—things simply arise due to what they are. Chandrakīrti attributes to them the somewhat laughable probative example of the colors of a peacock's feathers: "No causes could have possibly created such intricacy."

Chandrakīrti states that if things could arise without any causes whatsoever, the causes and noncauses of any given result would be equivalent. As in arising from other, anything could arise from anything, because everything would be equivalent in not being a cause. Worldly people would not have to go through hardships to accomplish the results they desire, such as tilling fields for abundant harvests. Yet this contradicts what is directly perceived by everyone. Furthermore, if there were no causes to anything at all, everything would be like the scent and color of flowers that grow in the sky, which also have no causes: nothing at all would be perceptible. But, in fact, the phenomenal world in all its brilliance is perceptible to everyone. Therefore, if one wishes to speak of arising, one must acknowledge causes.

Other assertions of the Chārvākas that Chandrakīrti deals with are the assertion that the elements truly exist, the assertion that primary minds and mental events arise from the elements, and the assertion that a world or life beyond that of the present utterly does not exist. Chandrakīrti does not refute the Chārvākas' assertions about the elements extensively, because the existence of the elements has already been implicitly refuted during the refutations of arising from self, from other, from both, and causelessly. With regard to the assertion of the utter nonexistence of past or future lifetimes, Chandrakīrti, somewhat cryptically from the perspective of this translator, instructs the Chārvākas that they are viewing knowable objects incorrectly, and that their incorrect view is based on the body. It seems that Chandrakīrti is saying that, if one carefully examines the ultimate and relative natures of the body, one will come to understand the correct view of knowable objects, which, on the mere level of no analysis, entails the existence of past and future lifetimes.

The Conclusion to the Refutation of the Self of Phenomena

Chandrakīrti concludes that, due to the logic explained thus far, phenomena have no inherent nature, because they do not arise from any of the four extremes. Having thus neatly sewn up his refutation of the self of phenomena, and before proceeding to explain the selflessness of persons, he takes the opportunity of the gap between the two main sections of the sixth chapter to address a series of hypothetical objections to what some Proponents of Things of the lower Buddhist vehicles may perceive as self-contradictions on the part of the Followers of the Middle Way. He also uses this opportunity to impart profound heart instructions on why the Middle Way is taught and how it should be followed.

Why, one may wonder, do things appear even though they do not inherently arise or exist? Appearances manifest due to ignorance. Things exist from the perspective of worldly people, whose vision is obscured by ignorance. This is just like the example of someone with diseased vision seeing strands of hair. For as long as the disease persists, the strands of hair will exist for that person. For as long as sentient beings have ignorance, they will perceive phenomena to exist. The noble beings, on the other hand, overcome ignorance with supreme knowledge. Knowing that all phenomena lack inherent existence, they abandon ignorance and, due to that, gain liberation from saṃsāra.

The Proponents of Things may object that it is incorrect to say that phenomena do not exist in the true nature of reality, because if that were the case, no phenomena could exist conventionally, and everything would be like the horns of a rabbit or the childless woman's son—utterly nonexistent and inconsequential. This objection is shown to be unfounded. The phenomena that Middle Way reasonings demonstrate as lacking an inherent nature in suchness are the phenomena that appear to worldly people. These phenomena exist for the world, yet are found to be primordially unarisen when analyzed. Therefore, the consequence that everything would be like the childless woman's son does not apply.

The arising that does occur in the relative truth is dependent arising. Dependent arising is distinct from arising from the four extremes, because the principle of dependent arising itself demonstrates the lack of inherent existence. In fact, the dependent arising of the relative is the only thing that can serve as a stepping stone to realizing ultimate reality. The deep profundity of the Middle Way tradition is that it presents the relative truth in exactly the way it is renowned in the world, and this itself is all that is required for the realization of the ultimate. As the Karmapa explains:

> How, then, do [the Followers of the Middle Way] use the presentation of interdependent, relative phenomena to guide students to realize that, in the ultimate truth, causes and results are empty of their own entities? They do so by explaining how all dualistic opposites depend on each other for their existence. "Dualistic opposites" refers to such phenomena as performers and actions, the self and the aggregates *(nyerlen/nyer len)*, causes and results, viewers and the viewed, expressers and the expressed, parts and wholes *(yenlak chen/yan lag can)*, features and bases of features, characteristics and things that illustrate characteristics *(tsenshi/mtshan gzhi)*, truth and falsity, saṃsāra and nirvāna, and the permanent and the impermanent. Since every one of these phenomena depends on its counterpart, there is no phenomenon that is established in and of itself, independent of anything else. By realizing this, students will gain liberation from the extremes of eternalism and nihilism.

Chandrakīrti and the Karmapa continue by praising dependent arising as the supreme method for transcending all wrong views.

The Analyses of the Middle Way Are an Expression of Compassion
Why is the Middle Way taught and studied? The Middle Way is a blueprint for analysis and analytical meditation on the true nature of things. As ordinary beings, we are fettered by nothing other than our reifying concepts. The reversal, or unraveling, of these very concepts is the true result of engaging with Middle Way reasonings. Therefore Nāgārjuna did not set forth this stream of intense philosophical inquiry known as the Middle Way so that scholars could have heated exchanges with each other and see who could pronounce the sharpest refutations. Rather, the debates and analyses associated with the Middle Way are a profound expression

of compassion, the compassion that wishes for all beings to overcome the deepest roots of suffering: mistaken conceptions.

Students are to be heedful, therefore, that, in order for their analysis of competing views to bear meaningful fruit, they must clear away their emotional allegiances to their own preconceived notions of what the best view is and their fears and aversions toward what they believe to be inferior views. Cultivating the ability to analyze objectively in this way will swiftly lead one to liberation. Nāgārjuna's *Sixty Stanzas on Reasoning* sums up this principle beautifully:

> Genuine beings who are free from debate
> Have no position of their own.
> For those who have no own-position,
> How could a position of others exist? (50)

The Selflessness of Persons

Chandrakīrti's refutation of the self of persons and discussion of personal selflessness is outlined by the Karmapa in three main headings: the reasons why it is necessary to refute the self of persons, the logic of the refutation itself, and the conclusion following the refutation that the person is a mere dependent imputation. The Karmapa uses the first verse of the first section as a springboard for a long discussion on the different ways beings conceive of a self, the divisions of selflessness, his own approach to refuting and speaking about the self, and the problems he sees in the way Tsongkapa and his followers describe the self and selflessness.

All mental afflictions, such as desire, anger, and bewilderment, and all suffering, such as birth, old age, sickness, and death, arise due to the view of the transitory collection *(jiktsok la tawa/'jig tshogs la lta ba)*. For this reason, students on the path to liberation who practice the Buddha's teachings as personal instructions endeavor to uproot this view. In the system of Nāgārjuna and his followers, this view—self-fixation *(dak-dzin/ bdag 'dzin)*—is uprooted by engaging in thorough analysis and analytical meditation of the view of transitory collection's object, the self. The Karmapa declares that the analysis of the selflessness of persons is the supreme method for accomplishing liberation.

The explanations and meditations of personal selflessness are considered by the Buddhist tradition to be unique to Buddhism. Other spiritual traditions may speak in their own ways about how certain phenomena do not truly exist in the way they appear, but it is only the Buddha's tradition that establishes without question that the self, ego, or soul of the person does not exist. It is with personal selflessness that the path of analytical meditation most often begins. In the context of explanation, phenomenal selflessness is customarily taught first, but in the context of practice, it is more common to begin with personal selflessness.[53]

As to the above-mentioned "view of the transitory collection," the "collection" refers to the five aggregates or skandhas *(pungpo/phung po)*—the five groups of physical and mental phenomena (forms, feelings, discriminations, mental formations, and consciousnesses) that become the basis for sentient beings' conception of a self. "Transitory," or, more literally, "disintegrating," means that each of these groups of phenomena is disintegrating, changing, in every passing moment. "View" refers to the mistaken conception of a true "me" or "I" that all beings generate and regenerate when observing the five aggregates of their own continua of experience.

Through solidifying the view of the transitory collection, sentient beings become attached to thoughts of "me" and "mine," the self *(dak/bdag)* and entities connected to the self *(dakgiwa/bdag gi ba).* There are two different types of the view of the self:[54] the connate *(lhen kye/lhan skyes)* view of the self and the imputed[55] *(kuntak/kun btags)* view of the self. The connate view of the self is something all sentient beings possess: every ordinary, confused being conceives of "I" or "me" in one way or another, whether the being uses language or not. The imputed view of the self, on the other hand, consists of the sophisticated labels we attribute to ourselves once we have reified the basic notion of "I." The latter category of self-fixation is traditionally spoken of as originating with incorrect philosophical systems and misguided teachers.

How the Entrance to the Middle Way Works with the Imputed and Connate Views of Self

In the *Entrance,* Chandrakīrti's logic that refutes the self of persons is aimed primarily at the imputed view of a self as it was expressed by non-Buddhists and by the Saṃmitīyas *(Mangkurwa/mang bkur ba)* and Vātsīputrīyas *(Ne Mabupa/gnas ma bu pa)* of the Buddhist tradition.[56] This is the quality of his refutations' focus on the explicit level. However, it is not the case that by studying these refutations one will not develop tools with which one may transcend the connate view of the self, saṃsāra's deepest and most powerful root. As the Karmapa explains, the connate self is not to be refuted on the conventional level of no analysis. It would be impossible, moreover, to do so. However, in the context of analysis, the logic used to refute the selves asserted by the non-Buddhists, the Saṃmitīyas, and the Vātsīputrīyas will also become logic that undermines the view of the connate self.

The Karmapa considers the self that is the object of the connate view to be an imputed existent, in the same manner that a vase is an imputed existent. Both of these phenomena are imputed and accepted to exist in the everyday, conventional world. The self that is an object of the imputed view, however, is, at all times, nonexistent in both the world and in the realm of analysis.

One of the main events of this general meaning section of the commentary is a continuation of the debate about Tsongkapa's "object of refutation by reasons," this time in the context of personal selflessness. The Karmapa also questions a claim attributed to Tsongkapa that only the Consequentialist system, and not any other Buddhist philosophical system, presents unerring methods for realizing selflessness. Probing Tsongkapa's assertions in a long, debate-style dialogue, the Karmapa sets forth absurd consequences of Tsongkapa's views and also presents his own positions. Because of its length and its back-and-forth structure that would be difficult to condense, this dialogue will not be summarized here.

Returning to the *Entrance*, Chandrakīrti's refutation of the self of persons is outlined in section headings by the Karmapa in a way that highlights the thoroughness of the investigation at hand. First, Chandrakīrti searches for anything findable as a "self" in any of four different relationships with the aggregates: a self that is different from the aggregates (asserted by the non-Buddhist tīrthikas), a self that is the same as the aggregates (asserted by the Saṃmitīyas), a self in a relationship of support-supporter with the aggregates, and a self that possesses the aggregates. Next, he searches for a self that could not be expressed as being the same as or different from the aggregates (asserted by the Vātsīputrīyas). Finally, he concludes that there is simply no truly findable entity whatsoever behind the label "me."

Refuting a Permanent Self

For the investigation of the self asserted by the non-Buddhist tīrthikas,[57] Chandrakīrti and the Karmapa provide a detailed presentation of the Enumerators' assertions, with which, we are told, the other tīrthikas' assertions of the self harmonize but for slight differences here and there. In short, the Enumerators assert a deep separation between what they call "primal matter" and the person, the enjoyer of the primal matter's manifestations. They say that the person neither arises from causes nor produces results. However, the state of bondage consists of the person's being caught up in enjoying the primal matter's manifestations. Liberation is attained when, due to meditation, the primal matter's manifestations retreat back into primal matter, whereupon the person is isolated and thus set free. The Enumerators assert that the self is an enjoyer, is a permanent thing, is not a creator, has no qualities, and is inactive.

Chandrakīrti begins his refutation by stating that, firstly, since this self is asserted to not arise it is therefore equivalent to the childless woman's son: it is utterly nonexistent. Since this self itself is unarisen, a fact that the Enumerators themselves accept, it cannot possibly possess any of the features the Enumerators ascribe to it. The Enumerators are far off the mark in claiming a self outside the five aggregates, for it is only in observation of the aggregates that the conception of "I" *(ngar-dzin/ngar 'dzin)* arises. A self that is permanent and so forth is not observed by ordinary beings, such as animals, but nonetheless all ordinary beings still engage the conception of "I." It is impossible for a permanent self to be the support for the conception of "I."

Refuting the Five Aggregates or the Mind Alone as the Self

The next assertion of self to be examined is that of the Saṃmitīyas, who claim variously that the self is all five aggregates or that the self is only the mind. Chandrakīrti first refutes these assertions in three phases of refutation: logic, scripture, and the perceptions of yogins. As for logic, if the aggregates were the self, there would be several selves, because the aggregates are multiple. This consequence would also apply if the self were strictly mind, because there are many classifications of mind. Furthermore, the self would be severed at the time that an arhat attained nirvāṇa, since when one attains nirvāṇa the aggregates cease to exist. Even before nirvāṇa the self would arise and disintegrate in each moment, just as the aggregates do.

As for scripture, the Buddha left fourteen questions unspoken, questions such as whether the Tathāgata exists or not after passing into parinirvāṇa. These questions are accepted by the Saṃmitīyas as being indicative of entities that do not exist, and the person in relationship to the aggregates is congruent with the principles implicit in the fourteen unspoken topics.

Furthermore, if the self were the aggregates, the yogins' perception of selflessness, also accepted by the Saṃmitīyas, would eradicate the aggregates. When yogins had the insight, "all things are selfless," the five aggregates would disappear, because, according to the Saṃmitīyas, the five aggregates are the self. Many other logical faults, as the *Entrance* describes, would accrue from asserting the self as the aggregates in this way.

The Saṃmitīyas may be tempted to defend themselves by pointing out to Chandrakīrti that the Buddha himself declared the aggregates to be the self. Chandrakīrti responds by clarifying that the Buddha made such statements provisionally in order to refute concepts of a self external to the aggregates, and in order to show that it is only in observation of the aggregates that the thought of "I" arises. However, in other sūtras the Buddha made it very clear that forms, feelings, discriminations, formations, and consciousnesses are definitely not the self.

Chandrakīrti forces the Saṃmitīyas to accept that they are asserting the *collection* of aggregates to be the self, not the aggregates themselves, since otherwise it would be necessary for each aggregate to be a self. A collection, moreover, does not exist as a real entity. It is only a concept.

The hypothetical Saṃmitīyas' rebuttal to the refutation of the collection prompts Chandrakīrti to wheel out for the first time the example of the chariot, an example which he also uses powerfully and famously in a lengthy section later in this chapter to demonstrate how the self is unfindable in relation to the aggregates. The Saṃmitīyas say that the collection is valid, because the collection is inseparable from its components and therefore produces meaningful effects. However, it is illogical to say that a collection is equivalent to its components. The component parts of a chariot, such as the axle and so on, cannot be posited as the chariot, and vice versa. The Buddha taught that the self, the sentient being, the person, and so on are mere imputations made on the basis of the aggregates. Therefore the mere collection of the aggregates is not the self.

Though they assert a self in the manner described above, the Saṃmitīyas nevertheless attempt their own explanation of selflessness and the way the view of a self is relinquished by yogins who practice the path: they say that it is the view of a *permanent* self that is relinquished when yogins engender the realization of selflessness. Chandrakīrti responds by pointing out that the permanent self is not even the support for ordinary beings' conception of "I."

Refuting the Imputed Self Does Not Equal Eradicating Connate Clinging

The refutation of the Saṃmitīya approach to cognizing selflessness makes a very important point. The view of a permanent self falls into the category of imputed self-fixation, whereas clinging to the thought of "I" in observation of the aggregates is the connate form of self-fixation. It would be extremely mistaken to think that, by eradicating concepts about the former type of self, clinging to the latter type of self will also be transcended. Even though we may use the logic that refutes the imputed selves to assist us in seeing through our tendencies toward the connate view of a self, putting a stop to the coarse views of the imputed self is by no means equivalent to cutting through the connate clinging to the "I," the root of saṃsāra. Accordingly, Chandrakīrti ridicules the Saṃmitīyas, comparing them to someone who pacifies the fear of snakes by assuring the fearful that there are no elephants present.

Chandrakīrti next refutes the self as existing in a support-supported relationship with the aggregates. The self is not supported by the aggregates, nor are the aggregates supported by the self, because, as has already been demonstrated, the self is not different from the aggregates. The same logic applies to the assertion of the self possessing the aggregates: since the self does not exist, no meaning of "possession" would apply.

The Twenty Views of the Transitory Collection

All of the above examinations of the self in relation to the aggregates are summarized by Chandrakīrti's refutation of the twenty views of the transitory collection:

> Form is not the self; the self does not possess form;
> The self does not exist in form; form does not exist in the self.
> These four statements should be understood to apply to all
> the aggregates.

The reversals of these statements represent the twenty views of
the self. (6.144)

When yogis and yoginīs realize selflessness, all twenty of these views
dissolve, together with any other conceptions about the self.

Refuting an Inexpressible Self

The Vātsīputrīyas' assertion of a self that cannot be expressed as being the
same as or different from the aggregates is refuted by the *Entrance* next.
The Vātsīputrīyas say that the self, a substantially existent entity that is the
basis for the conception of "I," is not different from the aggregates, because
worldly people know the self through no other means. However, the self is
not equivalent with the aggregates, for if it were, it would arise and disintegrate. Therefore, they say the self is inexpressible in these terms and also
in terms of being permanent or impermanent.

If the self were substantially existent, says Chandrakīrti, it would not be
inexpressible. Mind, for example, is not inexpressible in relation to form.
It is *different* from form. In the same way, the self would have to be expressible in relation to the aggregates. If the self were inexpressible, it would
necessarily be a mere imputation, and not a substantial thing.

The Self Is a Mere Imputation:
The Sevenfold Analysis of the Chariot

As a result of all of the above analyses, Chandrakīrti concludes that the
object to which the thought of "I" refers does not exist. It is not different
from the aggregates, it is not the aggregates themselves, it does not support the aggregates, and does not possess the aggregates. What is the self?
It is a mere *imputation* made in *dependence* upon the aggregates.

To explain further how the self is a mere dependent imputation, Chandrakīrti employs the sevenfold analysis of the chariot:

A chariot is not asserted to be different from its parts.
It is not the same as its parts, nor does it possess them.
It does not depend on its parts, nor do its parts depend on it.
It is not its parts' mere assembly, nor is it their shape. (6.151)

In an approach similar to the above analyses of all possible permutations in the relationship between the self and the aggregates, Chandrakīrti

demonstrates that all relative phenomena, including the person, are mere imputations made on the basis of their components. Even though no objective referent of "chariot" or "person" can be found either conventionally or ultimately when analyzed, the chariot and the person are nonetheless renowned and referred to in the world of no analysis. Therefore, Chandrakīrti cautions readers not to make the analysis of the chariot a nihilistic denial of worldly beings' experience:

> "How can the chariot exist, since when it is analyzed in these
>   seven ways it is seen not to exist at all?"
> Thus the yogis and yoginīs do not find the existence of the
>   chariot.
> Through this they also easily engage in suchness,
> But, in the relative, the existence of the chariot should be accepted
>   in accordance with the world. (6.160)

How the Label of the Person Is Used Conventionally on the Path
After further illumination of the chariot example to cut through conceptual elaborations of true existence, Chandrakīrti returns to the worldly perspective of how the self, the aggregates, the sense sources, and other relative phenomena are spoken of conventionally. This leads the Karmapa to a fascinating discussion of how the different schools employ the concept of the person on the conventional level. After briefly discussing the presentation of the person in the Particularist, Sūtra Follower, and Proponent of Consciousness systems, the Karmapa elucidates the approach of the Vajrayāna, which uses the special conventional assertion of buddha nature as the basis of imputation for the person. Even though he clearly treats buddha nature as provisional meaning and conventional as opposed to ultimate, the Karmapa does not equate this status with a lack of power. He remarks:

> Many noble yogis and yoginīs, during the impure stages of
> ground and path, have skillfully used these conventions. They
> cannot be defeated by debates from dharma lectures.

The Karmapa goes on to discuss the mistakes involved if one were to posit buddha nature as the person *after* analysis. He also states that the true nature of reality may become a basis for positing the person, in the sense that when one realizes that all phenomena are free from signs and characteristics, one is posited as a buddha, and for as long as one does not realize this, one is posited as a sentient being.

However, in the context of analysis, even in the Vajrayāna the person does not exist. After stating this, and supporting his position with quotations from the tantras, the Karmapa briefly examines some views about the self of Shākya Chokden, the Jonangpas, and Tsongkapa.

Chandrakīrti next clearly reconciles the two truths with regard to the self. The self is not a thing; it is not stable or unstable; it does not arise or disintegrate; it is not permanent, impermanent, both, or neither; and so on. Therefore when analyzed it is seen not to exist in any manner whatsoever. Nevertheless, in dependence upon the aggregates, worldly beings use the convention of a self, just as they use the conventions of vases and sweaters. These conventions are not to be refuted in the world, as disputing with the mundane world was not the intention of the Buddha.

The Analysis of Contact versus No Contact

Perhaps disconcertingly to the Western reader, before concluding this section Chandrakīrti drops his reconciliation of the contexts of analysis and no analysis and returns to another analysis of true production, this time a refutation of the Proponents of Things' understanding of cause and effect. If causes were to truly produce results, they must do so either by contacting their results or by having no contact with their results. If they contacted their results, there would be no separation between cause and result. It would be impossible to say, "This, the cause, produces this, the result." If there were no contact between causes and results, either no results would be produced at all (as in a barley sprout not being produced by a rice seed due to lack of contact) or anything could arise from anything. Due to these faulty consequences, Chandrakīrti concludes that causes and results do not inherently exist.

However, since Followers of the Middle Way regard causes and results as merely illusions, those faulty consequences do not apply to their explanations. Moreover, if the Proponents of Things attempt to question the refutations of the Followers of the Middle Way by claiming that those refutations are equally susceptible to the analysis of contact versus no contact (the means of refutation and the object of the refutation cannot logically contact or avoid contacting each other), the Followers of the Middle Way would clarify that their absurd consequences only apply to those who assert inherent production.

In fact, it is absolutely correct that Middle Way refutations do not inherently refute their objects of refutation. This, for the Followers of the Middle Way, is not problematic, for there were never any inherently existent "wrong views" to refute in the first place. The approach of the Followers of the Middle Way is similar to using logic in a dream in order to refute something illogical in a dream. Even though Middle Way refutations lack true existence, and therefore ultimately there is no "logic" at all, they are still capable of accomplishing their intended purpose: to reverse the misconceptions of sentient beings regarding the way things are. The Followers of the Middle Way are free from holding any position of their own.

Therefore, the Karmapa maintains that the self exists only for the confused sentient beings who are afflicted by self-fixation. Noble beings, who are free from ignorance, hold no position of self or selflessness.

Summary of the Two Selflessnesses

Before introducing the sixteen emptinesses, Chandrakīrti summarizes his presentation of emptiness by way of the two forms of selflessness. So that beings of various dispositions may gain liberation, the Buddha taught emptiness in two ways: the selflessness of phenomena and the selflessness of persons. For the liberation of the hearers and solitary realizers the selflessness of persons was taught; for the liberation of those with the Mahāyāna aptitude the Buddha taught the selflessness of phenomena.

One may wonder why personal selflessness was taught separately for the hearers and solitary realizers, since it is the Karmapa's position that they equally realize the selflessness of phenomena. It is true that the hearers and solitary realizers possess equal realization of the selflessness of phenomena, but their cultivation of familiarity with selflessness is limited mostly to the aggregates, sense sources, and constituents of their own personal continua. Bodhisattvas, on the other hand, cultivate familiarity with selflessness in relation to the limitless excellent phenomena of the two types of bodhichitta, relative and ultimate. Due to the differences regarding familiarity, the hearers and solitary realizers enter the absorption of one-sided peace, whereas the bodhisattvas attain the vast and profound dharmakāya of buddhahood.

The Sixteen Emptinesses

Chandrakīrti begins his presentation of the Mahāyāna's sixteen emptinesses by clarifying that this sixteenfold categorization is simply a further
elaboration of the two types of selflessness taught above. Actually, there
are limitless numbers of types of emptiness, corresponding to the limitless numbers of concepts and appearing phenomena there are. However,
the sixteen emptinesses touch on the most important and beneficial phenomena for us to join with the understanding, experience, and realization
of emptiness.[58] In expanding the presentation of twofold selflessness, the
Buddha made the elaborate presentation of the sixteen emptinesses. Con-
densing the sixteen, he also made a presentation of four emptinesses.

The sixteen emptinesses are the emptiness of 1) the inner, 2) the outer,
3) the outer and inner, 4) emptiness, 5) the great, 6) the ultimate, 7) the
conditioned, 8) the unconditioned, 9) what is beyond extremes, 10) the
beginningless and endless, 11) what is not to be discarded, 12) nature, 13)
all phenomena, 14) defining characteristics, 15) nonobservation, and 16)
the nonexistence of things. Aside from the emptiness of defining characteristics, to which he devotes fourteen and a half root verses, Chandrakīrti
explains the emptinesses succinctly, devoting no more than two root verses
to each.

However, it is the first emptiness, the emptiness of the inner, that receives the most attention from the Karmapa. The Karmapa's general
meaning commentary following the root verses on inner emptiness comprises the majority of text for the entire section on the sixteen emptinesses. For emptinesses two through sixteen, aside from the occasional
brief foray into debate mode, the Karmapa comments straightforwardly
on Chandrakīrti's root verses.

In his lengthy general meaning commentary, the Karmapa discusses
emptiness in an even more subtle way than in the previous sections of
the text. The first issue he explores outside his word commentary on the
root verses is emptiness as a *nature* of phenomena. Since phenomena are
free from arising and beyond conceptual identification, they lack a nature.
To this very lack of nature, the conventional label "nature" is given. It is
tenable to speak of the lack of a nature as a nature in this way, because
this description harmonizes with the conventional world. Phenomena's
lack of nature does not change; therefore, in comparison to the appearing
phenomena to which beings cling, emptiness is uncontrived. Therefore,

speaking of emptiness as the nature of phenomenon does not constitute reification or the creation of an "assertion" for Followers of the Middle Way. Calling emptiness the "nature of phenomena" is simply another way in which the Followers of the Middle Way skillfully relate with worldly people in the worldly perspective of no analysis. In the context of analysis, there is no inherently established nature in either of the two truths.

Dolpopa's Emptiness of Other

The Karmapa proceeds to analyze, in the context of several topics, the views of Tsongkapa, some masters of the Shangpa Kagyü tradition, and Dolpopa Sherab Gyaltsen (dol po pa shes rab rgyal mtshen, 1292-1361), the important Kālachakra Tantra scholar of the Jonang tradition who founded in earnest the empty of other (shentong/gzhan stong) school of Tibetan philosophy. The following few paragraphs will selectively and briefly discuss the Karmapa's section on Dolpopa.

On the Karmapa's reading of his system, Dolpopa questions the authoritativeness of Chandrakīrti's explanation of emptiness. The reader is referred to a quotation from the Kālachakra Tantra, adduced by Dolpopa, that forms the basis of Dolpopa's apparent critique of Chandrakīrti·

> The emptiness of analyzing the aggregates
> Is, like a banana tree, without pith.[59]

Dolpopa says that in his own Middle Way system, the ultimate truth, known as the "supreme other," is beyond interdependence. It is completely isolated from the relative because it is empty of what is other than itself (shentong/gzhan stong) and does not depend on relative phenomena, which are empty of themselves (rangtong/rang stong). He says that phenomena that are empty of other are real in the way they appear to the mind, whereas phenomena that are empty of themselves are not. Thus Dolpopa, we are told, suggests that Chandrakīrti's system, due to teaching only how phenomena are empty of themselves and not teaching how ultimate reality is empty of other, is inferior.

The Karmapa replies by stating that it is illogical for Followers of the Middle Way to posit a true nature of reality that has no relationship to appearing phenomena. Both the true nature of reality and appearing phenomena are beyond elaborations of existence, nonexistence, and so on.

Therefore it is impossible for only one of them to be "existent" or "real" on its own.

Furthermore, the quotation about the emptiness of analyzing the aggregates does not indicate that tantra is superior to sūtra regarding the view of emptiness. To the contrary, the tantric and sūtric views of emptiness are the same. Whether one is practicing in a context of sūtra or tantra, engaging emptiness through hearing and contemplating alone will only result in a general understanding of emptiness, not a direct realization. In both the sūtra and tantra paths, the supreme knowledge born of meditation directly produces the realization of emptiness.

There is a difference between sūtra and tantra, however, with regard to the skillful methods the practitioner may use to accelerate the process of engendering the supreme knowledge born of meditation. In this regard, the sūtra methods do not possess the efficacy of the tantra methods. *That*, says the Karmapa, is the meaning of Dolpopa's quotation. Aside from that, there is no difference between sūtric and tantric emptiness in terms of profundity. The Karmapa continues by expressing many other refutations of Dolpopa's presentation of emptiness of other.

In addition to the debates on the views of other Tibetan masters, the Karmapa's general meaning commentary in this section also offers a wonderful and eloquent synopsis of the four Buddhist philosophical systems' approach to emptiness. For each school, and also for Tsongkapa's system, the Karmapa describes the unique assertions of the bases of emptiness, of what those bases are empty, and how the schools present their emptiness as tenable. As quoted earlier in this introduction, he concludes that "emptiness" is a mere conventional label given to phenomena's lack of establishment in any way that could correspond with conceptual elaborations.

Returning to the *Entrance*, in explaining the sixteen emptinesses Chandrakīrti not only explains how each of the sixteen types of appearing phenomena are empty, he also teaches, sometimes in great detail, about the qualities, functions, and significance in the relative truth of the appearing phenomena themselves. In particular, when reading his explanation of the emptiness of defining characteristics, during which Chandrakīrti describes many of the key phenomena of ground, path, and fruition, one has the sense that Chandrakīrti is "powering down" the *profound* aspect of his treatise to turn his attention back to the *vast* aspect of the journey of the bodhisattvas through the grounds and, eventually, to the perfect enlightenment of buddhahood. After the sixteen emptinesses, the *Entrance* focuses mostly on the relative truth perspective of bodhisattvahood and buddhahood.

In this chapter Chandrakīrti also presents the four emptinesses that are condensed from the sixteenfold presentation: 1) the emptiness of things, 2) the emptiness of nonthings, 3) the emptiness of phenomena's own entities, and 4) the emptiness of other entities.

Since no new logic for determining phenomena as lacking an inherent nature is introduced in this section, making for straightforward reading, the sixteen emptinesses and the four emptinesses will not be summarized individually here.

The Seventh through Tenth Bodhisattva Grounds and Their Respective Perfections

On the seventh ground, the bodhisattvas attain the perfection of methods and gain the ability to enter into and arise from the meditative absorption of cessation in every moment. Through this, they surpass the hearers and solitary realizers even in terms of wisdom. Though they can enter into and arise from cessation in every moment, they do not fully actualize cessation, because they have no affection for personal peace and have great interest in continuing the bodhisattva journey for the benefit of beings. After referring to the hearers' and the Mahāyāna abhidharma's definitions for cessation, the Karmapa relates the definition of Nāgārjuna's tradition, drawn from Chandrakīrti's autocommentary to the *Entrance*, which states that cessation is equivalent with freedom from elaborations.

On the eighth ground, the bodhisattvas attain the perfection of aspirations and, with their forbearance toward freedom from arising increasing ever further, gain irreversible momentum toward the wisdom of buddhahood. There is a great distinction between the eighth ground and those previous with regard to effort. Relying on a quotation from the Buddha, the commentary explains that the ease with which the bodhisattvas engage the wisdom of enlightenment and accumulate merit is similar to the ease of a mighty ship sailing smoothly in a strong wind, following a long period of intense efforts to initiate the ship's movement.

Since on the eighth ground, the first of the "three pure bodhisattva grounds," all mental afflictions without exception are relinquished, the bodhisattvas can effortlessly engage the dharmadhātu. For this reason, it is taught that they must occasionally be roused from their absorptions by the buddhas, who urge them to finish the path to full buddhahood and not be deceived that their current state is the final result. Though the absorption from which the bodhisattvas are roused is not nirvāṇa, it is sometimes called nirvāṇa. This is explained in a wonderful quotation from a text called *Brilliance of the Sun,* which enumerates eight types of nirvāṇa.

Although the bodhisattvas of the eighth ground are unsurpassable and completely pure, their qualities do not rival those of buddhas, whose qualities are as limitless as space. Though saṃsāra has ceased for them, these bodhisattvas continue to relate to sentient beings through their attainment of the ten masteries, which are enumerated in the commentary.

On the ninth ground, the bodhisattvas attain the perfection of powers. They gain the four correct and discerning awarenesses: those of phenomena, meanings, contextual etymologies, and confidence. On the tenth, the bodhisattvas attain the perfection of wisdom and receive empowerments from the buddhas in all ten directions. They become regents of the buddhas, and their positive qualities are utterly inconceivable.

QUALITIES OF THE BODHISATTVA GROUNDS AND THE RESULTANT STAGE OF BUDDHAHOOD

Having presented the nature of all ten bodhisattva grounds, Chandrakīrti next will explain the various qualities that the bodhisattvas on those grounds attain. The bodhisattvas on the grounds attain twelve sets of qualities that increase in magnitude with the attainment of each subsequent ground. For example, bodhisattvas on the first ground can see one hundred buddhas, while bodhisattvas on the second ground can see one thousand buddhas. The next few verses give details, and many high numbers, of the miraculous qualities and abilities through which bodhisattvas benefit beings.

Does the Buddhas' Wisdom Exist, and What Do Buddhas See?
The next topic addressed in the *Entrance* is the resultant ground of buddhahood itself. After identifying the place of the buddhas' enlightenment as Akaniṣhṭha, Chandrakīrti describes how buddhas realize the equality of everything and gain the full knowledge of everything to be known.

Following this root verse, the Karmapa launches into a discussion of an important topic of debate about the *Entrance* in the monastic colleges, the topic of whether or not the wisdom of the buddhas really exists, and whether or not the buddhas perceive appearances of any sort.

In harmony with the worldly relative, the Followers of the Middle Way may say, from the perspective of others, that the wisdom of the buddhas exists and the objects of this wisdom are all knowable objects. The Karmapa states that the wisdom of the buddhas, when described at the level of no analysis, must be explained in harmony with the worldly perspective. The presentations of the non-Buddhists and of the Buddhists from the Particularists through the Autonomists are not even correct on the conventional level. As emphasized in other contexts before, the Followers of the Middle Way are utterly free from positions of their own about the existence, nonexistence, and so on of the wisdom of the buddhas and its appearances. The Karmapa remarks:

> When thoroughly analyzing, it is like this: regarding the state-
> ment, "In our own system we do not speak of the buddhas' wis-
> dom as being existent or nonexistent," we do not say even that!
> Therefore when the Proponents of Things criticize us, saying,
> "Refraining from asserting either existence or nonexistence is
> itself your own system," their criticisms do not apply.

Chandrakīrti's root verses pick up the discussion where the Karmapa left off by raising a hypothetical objection: if all phenomena are free from arising and elaborations, how could they possibly be known? Wouldn't it be illogical to speak of a "mind" of a buddha "perceiving objects"?

There is no contradiction, because in the context of nonarising, the mind of the buddhas as well is free from elaborations. In dependence upon conventions, the wisdom of the buddhas is posited merely in reference to the aspect of knowing the objects' freedom from arising. Therefore it is entirely possible for buddhas to teach beings in the world. Through the blessings of the dharmakāya (the actual buddha), the sambhogakāya, the nirmāṇakāya, and even inanimate phenomena such as space can teach beings about suchness, the true nature of reality. Beings can receive these teachings and realize suchness as a result.

For this teaching to occur, no effort is required from the side of the

buddhas. Just as a craftsman's wheel spins effortlessly after initial application of effort, the buddhas' activity for the benefit of beings occurs
effortlessly due to previously accumulated merit and aspiration prayers.
The teachings of the buddhas arise due to the merit of the sentient beings
receiving them and the aspirations made by the buddhas when they were
bodhisattvas. In the final analysis, however, these special causes and results
related to buddhahood are inconceivable.

Chandrakīrti next presents the buddhas' kāyas, the dimensions of
enlightenment. The dharmakāya represents the perfect benefit for oneself, while the form kāyas represent the perfect benefit for others.

All phenomena are primordially free from elaborations. When the realization of just this is attained in a stable and final way, the dharmakāya of
buddhahood becomes manifest. It is not the case, however, that something that did not exist previously arises anew. Moreover, when the fixation of primary minds and mental events dissolves, it is said that "mind
ceases," but it is not the case that something previously existent becomes
nonexistent.

The Karmapa returns briefly to the issue of whether or not wisdom
exists for buddhas. Underscoring his previous points that 1) on the level
of no analysis and from the perspective of others wisdom exists and 2)
the Followers of the Middle Way are free from any position of their own
regarding existence or nonexistence, he adds:

What *is* wisdom? It is as explained in the perfection of supreme
knowledge teachings: all phenomena are free from elaborations, and when the perceiving subject as well becomes equally
free from elaborations, that is wisdom. In particular, the wisdom of the buddha consists in the pacification of the elaborations and their habitual tendencies in relation to suchness.
It is the inseparability of the expanse and wisdom. It is free
from singularity and multiplicity, quality and qualified. It realizes the nonduality of subjects and objects. In it all phenomena—saṃsāra and nirvāṇa, faults and qualities, and so on—are
always undifferentiable and equal. Outside of that, there is no
way to posit wisdom.

And:

In a nonanalytical context of repeating what others accept, we Followers of the Middle Way describe knowable objects as existing. The wisdom of the buddhas is the same. Since we speak of all phenomena as existing from the perspective of others (even though from our own perspective they are free of the elaborations of existence and nonexistence), it is unreasonable to debate solely about the existence or nonexistence of the wisdom of buddhas.

Chandrakīrti's explanation of the form kāyas adds a less renowned category, the "kāyas of natural outflow" (gyu tünpe ku/rgyu mthun pa'i sku) to the more famous pairing of the sambhogakāya and the nirmāṇakāya. After Chandrakīrti lays out the main characteristics of the sambhogakāya (it is luminous and free of concept, it remains until all beings are liberated, it possesses the "five certainties," and appears only to those whose minds are free from elaborations), the Karmapa takes on some assertions of Shākya Chokden regarding the relationship of the dharmakāya and the form kāyas.

On the Karmapa's reading of Shākya Chokden's system, the latter claims that 1) the form kāyas are not the buddha and that 2) the form kāyas are of the nature of consciousness. The Karmapa refutes these assertions by explaining that the dharmakāya and the form kāyas exist in a relationship of supported and support. The dharmakāya is the supported quality; it is freedom from elaborations itself. Even when buddhas see it, they see it in a manner of not seeing anything. The form kāyas are the support. They can appear in the pure mirrors of the minds of sentient beings, and sentient beings can relate with them and extract the essence of their intention through hearing, contemplating, and meditating.

However, it is not the case that the form kāyas are not the buddha. For if they were not, the speech that emanates from those kāyas would not be the teachings of the buddha, and those who practice and uphold those teachings would not be the saṅgha. It is also untenable to say that the form kāyas are of the nature of consciousness, because the form kāyas appear to the visual consciousnesses of sentient beings. If they were consciousness, it would absurdly follow that consciousness possesses shape and color.

Furthermore, if there were scriptures stating that the form kāyas are not the buddha, those scriptures are teaching on the same level as the scriptures that teach that emptiness is the nature of fire: they are indicating that the form kāyas cannot be posited as actual buddhahood following analysis. The scriptures that do teach the form kāyas to be the buddha are similar to the scriptures that teach hotness as the nature of fire: they are describing the appearing qualities of relative truth phenomena on the level of no analysis.

One should not be attached to only one way of explaining the dharmakāya and the form kāyas. Sometimes their roles as support and supported are reversed, and the explanations of which are relative and which are ultimate can also vary, depending on the context and purpose of the teaching being imparted.

Chandrakīrti's teachings on the kāyas of natural outflow present many of the buddhas' supreme qualities, foremost among which are the ten powers. The nirmāṇakāya is the emanation of the buddhas that appears due to compassion to help the beings of the world. The descriptions in these sections of the text are straightforward.

The Teaching That There Are Three Vehicles Is Provisional Meaning
The next verses in the root text clarify that in the definitive meaning there is only one vehicle of the Buddha's teachings, and that vehicle is the realization of the suchness of phenomena. Any presentation of multiple vehicles, such as the three vehicles, is provisional meaning. Because of the buddhas' great compassion, they provide an array of avenues for beings of all capacities to enter the path to liberation, just like a tour guide from a story in a sūtra emanated an illusory city (analogous to the provisional meaning teachings) in which his clients could take their rest on the way to the genuine destination (analogous to emptiness).

The section on the resultant stage of buddhahood concludes with Chandrakīrti's teachings on the time of attaining buddhahood (buddhas actualize enlightenment continually, over the course of eons equal in number to the atoms in all the pure realms) and the time for which buddhas remain in the world. In relation to the latter topic, Chandrakīrti beautifully praises the buddhas' great compassion, by which they forsake their own peace in order to ceaselessly take care of all beings in all worlds, who, due to being tormented by the various sufferings born of clinging to existence and nonexistence, are without exception the worthy objects of compassion.

THE CONCLUSION OF THE *ENTRANCE TO THE*
MIDDLE WAY AND *FEAST FOR THE FORTUNATE*

Having imparted all of his central messages, Chandrakīrti now prepares
to sign off. As for his commentary, the Karmapa, saving some of his most
challenging prose for the end, chooses this location of the text to reveal
some of the key explanations of his own Middle Way system *(rangluk/
rang lugs)*.

First, Chandrakīrti states that his *Entrance* has been based on Nāgārjuna's
Fundamental Wisdom and other scriptures and key instructions. He
instructs readers to ascertain that, just as no treatise author teaches emptiness as authoritatively as Nāgārjuna in *Fundamental Wisdom*, in the same
way there is no follower of Nāgārjuna whose instructions surpass his in the
Entrance to the Middle Way.

According to the Karmapa, verses 13.1 and 13.2 indicate that the Proponents of Things do not realize emptiness, that the Followers of the Middle
Way do, that the Autonomists are Followers of the Middle Way, and that
the system of Chandrakīrti is superior to that of the Autonomists. The
Karmapa also presents some key differences between the Consequentialists and Autonomists and refutes some assertions of the Jonangpa School
about the status of the Consequentialists and Autonomists as Followers
of the Middle Way.

There are some who have been frightened by the profundity of Nāgārjuna's mind, which Chandrakīrti likens to a deep, dark ocean. The Karmapa, following Chandrakīrti's autocommentary, comments that Indian
authors who came after Nāgārjuna, including Vasubandhu, Dignāga,
Dharmakīrti, and Dharmapāla, became frightened by Nāgārjuna's teachings upon merely reading the words and abandoned the Middle Way.

Asaṅga as a Follower of the Middle Way
Although Bhāvaviveka derided Asaṅga for "pull[ing] students away"
from the Middle Way teachings, the Karmapa clarifies that Asaṅga should
be respected as a Follower of the Middle Way who, in order to take care of
certain types of beings, wrote some texts on Mind Only, as did the bud-
dha-regent Maitreya. Therefore, Asaṅga should not be exempt from being
regarded as a Follower of the Middle Way simply because he composed
Mind Only texts.

For Chandrakīrti and the Karmapa, the reason why some people come to abandon the Middle Way is because suchness will only be comprehended by cultivating familiarity with it over time. If one does not possess the karmic seeds of previous habituation and the accumulation of merit, the view of emptiness may frighten one away, as it cannot be fathomed simply through extensive study alone. Therefore, so that students may approach the unerring explanations of suchness, Chandrakīrti encourages his readers to abandon all affection for the teachings outside of Nāgārjuna's way and devote themselves to the genuine Middle Way completely.

After Chandrakīrti dedicates the merit of his composition so that all beings may realize suchness and swiftly proceed to the blissful state of buddhahood, the Karmapa begins a lengthy "essential explanation of dependent arising" based on the thought of the Eighth Karmapa, Mikyö Dorje. In this general meaning section, the Karmapa further underscores key differences between the Consequentialists and the Autonomists, provides clear classifications of the different types of "Followers of the Middle Way," discusses how the Consequentialists relate to the relative and how they perform refutations, and, to no surprise, analyzes the system of Tsongkapa in the context of some of these topics.

What Is a Follower of the Middle Way?
Though the general meaning section will not be summarized in detail here, one of its most interesting moments is the Karmapa's presentation of the different levels of being a "Follower of the Middle Way." He confirms in explicit terms what he had been implying throughout the entire commentary: genuine Followers of the Middle Way are buddhas and the other three types of noble beings dwelling, not in postmeditation, but in meditative equipoise within the true nature of reality.

However, it is also admissible to call others "worldly Followers of the Middle Way." This latter category consists of noble beings in postmeditation and ordinary sentient beings who are capable of describing at least some knowable objects in harmony with interdependence, i.e., as lacking true existence.

The Karmapa seals the conclusion of *Feast for the Fortunate* by thanking those who helped him compose the text, making positive aspirations for the future study and practice of the genuine Buddhadharma, and dedicating the merit of his efforts to the enlightenment of all sentient beings.

: Feast for the Fortunate

A Commentary on the *Entrance to the Middle Way*
That Easily Pulls Along the *Chariot of the Takpo Kagyü Siddhas*

: Preamble

You taught your students well exactly what you yourself had realized:
The suchness of profound interdependence free from the eight
    extremes,
Ultimate peace—the complete pacification of all elaborations.
To you, highest of the Shākyas, supreme among speakers, I respectfully
    bow.

You are the embodiment of the wisdom that knows everything
    without obstruction.
Wielding the sword that cuts through ignorance
And a volume of scripture of the profound meaning,
You hold the secret of the speech of all victorious ones.
Eldest of the victors' heirs, protector Mañjushrī, I place the crown
    of my head at your feet.

You attained the ground *Supreme Joy* and were prophesied
By the victorious Transcendent Conqueror in many sūtras and tantras:
The *Great Drum*,[60] *Great Clouds*,[61] the *Descent into Laṅka*,[62]
The *Root Tantra of Mañjushrī*,[63] and others.
Great charioteer, venerable Nāgārjuna, I respectfully bow to you.

With the light of the moon,[64] the excellent tradition of the
    Consequentialists,
You clearly illuminated the intention of Nāgārjuna on the high peak
    of the mountain of freedom from extremes—
Fearless scholars whose renown fills the world,
Buddhapālita and Chandrakīrti, I bow at your feet.

All the rivers of practice and study descending from those masters
Flow into the great ocean of the Buddha's teachings
That combines them into one: the glorious Takpo Kagyü.
Extractor of that ocean's jewels of definitive meaning, Könchok Yenlak,
   I bow to you.

Eternally you build your abode on the snow mountain of discipline.
You clothe your body with the garments of the three baskets
And, with your sharp fangs and claws of scripture and reasoning,
You defeat the elephants, your dialectic opponents' pride.
Lord of lions, my spiritual tutor Namgyal Drakpa, may you be
   victorious.

Karmapa of great compassion with lotus in hand,[65]
The eighth lord, adorned with the crown of the victor Akṣhobhya,[66]
Assimilated in his mind the ultimate intention of all sugatas.[67]
Then, relying on the supreme text[68] of the glorious Chandrakīrti,

He explained this intention with the great *Chariot of the Takpo Kagyü
   Siddhas,*
A chariot that blissfully leads one down the vast and profound path of
   excellent nonabiding—
The Middle Way, the peak of all vehicles.
Here, in an honest fashion, I will teach in a way that pulls that *Chariot*
   along.

You who desire liberation, take this deathless nectar
And pour it into the vase of your discriminating intelligence.
Completely purifying all illnesses of reification *(ngö-dzin/dngos 'dzin)*,
Touch the genuine states of purity, self, bliss, and permanence!

Our Teacher, Shākyamuni, buddha of the fortunate eon and supreme light
of the world, possesses not even the slightest fault and is fully endowed
with all excellent qualities. In this world he set into motion all of the limitless dharma wheels *(chökyi korlo/chos kyi 'khor lo)*, dharma discourses
(chökyi tam/chos kyi gtam), and dharma gates *(chökyi go/chos kyi sgo)*[69]—
both the topics expressed and the means of expression. If classified into

succinct categories, there are those that are known as the three wheels of the teachings *(ka korlo sum/bka' 'khor lo gsum),*[70] the three discourses *(tam sum/gtam gsum),* the eighty-four thousand gates of dharma, and, the category that subsumes all of those, the twelve branches of scripture.[71] Thus it is said in Nāgārjuna's *Verses on the Fundamental Wisdom of the Middle Way (Mulamādhyamakakārikā, Uma Tsawa Tsikle-ur Jepa Sherab/dbu ma rtsa ba tshig le'ur byas pa shes rab):*

> The buddhas impute a "self,"
> Teach "selflessness,"
> And teach that there is neither
> Self nor selflessness.[72] (18.6)

Also, the victorious Ajita *(Mapampa/ma pham pa)*[73] said *(Highest Continuum, Uttaratantra, Gyü Lama/rgyud bla ma):*

> Knowing the methods of the terms
> Of impermanence, suffering, selflessness, and peace,
> The Buddha enabled sentient beings
> To engender sadness toward the three realms and excellently enter
>   the path of nirvāṇa.

> To those who had already entered this path of peace in a complete
>   way
> And had an outlook *(du-she/'du shes)* focused on attaining nirvāṇa,
> The Buddha, in the *White Lotus of Genuine Dharma*
>   *(Saddharmapuṇḍārika, Damchö Pema Karpo/dam chos padma
>   dkar po)* and other sūtras,
> Taught the suchness of phenomena.

> Through this, he reversed beings' previous forms of fixation.[74]
> Uniting skillful means and knowledge,
> He ripened them into the supreme vehicle
> And prophesied their attainment of supreme enlightenment.

The master Āryadeva said *(The Four Hundred Verses, Chatuḥshataka, Shibgyapa/bzhi brgya pa):*

In the beginning one reverses nonvirtue.
In the middle one reverses the view of a self.
In the end one reverses all views.
Those who know this way are wise.[75] (8.15)

All of the approaches to the dharma mentioned above join students with the two paths of the higher realms *(ngönto/mngon mtho)*[76] and definite excellence *(ngeleg/nges legs)*.[77] From among those approaches, it is not necessary for an individual who has a disposition toward only the paths of the higher realms to receive teachings on personal and phenomenal selflessness, emptiness, the supreme knowledge *(prajñā, sherab/shes rab)* that realizes emptiness, and the yoga of special seeing *(vipashyanā, lhaktong/ lhag mthong)* that gives rise to such supreme knowledge in one's mindstream. However, for an individual to traverse the path of definite excelence, if their path does not rely on the teachings on selflessness, it will certainly be incapable of bringing about definite excellence. The sūtras say:

> Not knowing the way of emptiness, peace, and nonarising,
> One wanders in saṃsāra.

And from Nāgārjuna's *Praise of the Transcendent (Lokātītastava, Jikten Detö/'jig rten 'das bstod)*:

> You taught that there is no liberation
> Without realizing the absence of characteristics.
> Therefore, in the Mahāyāna,
> You taught it in a comprehensive way.

The extensive teachings on emptiness are thus presented in the precious scriptures of the Mahāyāna —those of the Middle Way and of the Mind Only school—and in the limitless scriptures of tantra. From among all of these, emptiness is presented in an extremely clear fashion in all of the sūtras *(ka/bka')* and treatises of the Middle Way. This is so because this tradition teaches all conceptual fabrications *(trötsen/spros mtshan)* as emptiness without leaving behind even the slightest remainder. It presents the full body of emptiness.

One may wonder, "Who founded this tradition that is known as the 'Middle Way?'" This tradition was well founded by the great master, the venerable Nāgārjuna, who was prophesied by the Victorious One himself. After Nāgārjuna came his students Āryadeva (*Phagpa Lha/'phags pa lha,* ca. third century), Āchāryashūra (*Lobpön Pawo/slob dpon dpa' bo,* second century),[78] Shāntideva (*Shiwa Lha/zhi ba lha,* ca. eighth century) and others.[79] Since there is no disagreement about these early masters being Followers of the Middle Way, they are known as the Middle Way Progenitors *(Shung Chimö Umapa/gzhung phyi mo'i dbu ma pa).*[80]

Later on, the master Bhāvaviveka opposed the explanation of the meaning of the Middle Way that was set forth by the master Buddhapālita. Since that opposition in turn also contained elements that required analysis, the master Chandrakīrti arrived in this world and, in order to investigate those points further, extensively taught on the meaning of the freedom from extremes. Since that time, there have been limitless other masters of the Middle Way who explained the view slightly differently from Chandrakīrti, in such texts as the *Ornament to the Middle Way,*[81] the *Light of the Middle Way,*[82] and *Distinguishing the Two Truths.*[83] However, there is not even the slightest difference between them with respect to their final view being the intention of the Middle Way. They all speak of nothing other than the Middle Way itself. As it is said:

> The teachings of the eighty-four thousand
> Classes of dharma
> All lead to emptiness.

Limitless such statements have been made. Yet some talkative scholars here in Tibet assert that, regarding the tenets by which the view is realized, there is a difference between such masters as Chandrakīrti and Bhāvaviveka, that one's view is good and the other's bad, one's high and the other's low. Their assertions are untenable.

If such differences existed, whoever held the lower view would not even be a Follower of the Middle Way. They and their views would merely bear the name of "Follower of the Middle Way" and "the Middle Way," but they would not fulfill the objectives of the Middle Way at all. Their scenario would be just like that of the False Aspectarian Followers of the Middle Way.[84]

One may wonder, then, "Who among these great masters is endowed with the greatest power of intelligence by which they may quickly vanquish the pride of the Buddhist and non-Buddhist tīrthikas[85] through explaining the intended meaning of the Middle Way?"

Addressing this question, the glorious Dipaṃkara[86] said, "The venerable master Chandrakīrti is without peer," and what he said is certainly true. The master Chandrakīrti composed several texts on the Middle Way, compositions that were entirely his own as well as commentaries on the works of others. Here, I wish to offer a summary of one of his independent compositions, *The Entrance to the Middle Way*.

⦂ Lineages

THE TEXT HAS two main sections:

1. The lineage through which this teaching has been passed down
2. The actual explanation of the teaching

1. THE LINEAGE THROUGH WHICH THIS
TEACHING HAS BEEN PASSED DOWN
1.1. The lineage due to the kindness of which certainty in this teaching system can arise in students who rely on the three types of supreme knowledge
1.2. The lineage through which were passed down the reading transmissions *(laglung/klag lung)* and logic structures *(drujor/'bru sbyor)* that are renowned in contemporary Tibet

1.1. THE LINEAGE DUE TO THE KINDNESS OF WHICH CERTAINTY IN THIS TEACHING SYSTEM CAN ARISE IN STUDENTS WHO RELY ON THE THREE TYPES OF SUPREME KNOWLEDGE[87]
1.1.1. The lineage of the precious Kagyü itself
1.1.2. The command lineage of the lord Dipaṃkara
1.1.3. The lineage of Patsap Lotsawa

1.1.1. THE LINEAGE OF THE PRECIOUS KAGYÜ ITSELF
1.1.1.1. The lineage of lord Nāropa
1.1.1.2. The lineage of lord Maitripa

1.1.1.1. THE LINEAGE OF LORD NĀROPA
The Kadampas[88] assert that Chandrakīrti was a direct student of Nāgārjuna, but that is not the case. After the protector Nāgārjuna had passed away,

the [teachers and students] of Nālandā cried out, "The sun of the world has set!" In response to this, many ḍākinīs in unison voiced this prophecy from the sky:

> Five hundred years from now,
> In a large city named Sani,
> Though the sun will have set, the moon[89] will rise to dispel darkness.
> A paṇḍita born of pure reasoning,
> The wise Chandrakīrti will appear.

It has been said that Chandrakīrti, the master prophesied by that quotation, was a student of Āryadeva.[90] Therefore, this lineage of lord Nāropa was passed down by the following individuals: the perfect Buddha; the lords of the three families;[91] Nāgārjuna; Āryadeva; Chandrakīrti; Mātaṅgi; Tilopa (988-1069 C.E.); Nāropa (1016-1100); Marpa (*mar pa*, 1012-1097); Milarepa (*mi la ras pa*, 1040-1123); Gampopa (*sgam po pa*, 1079-1153); Düsum Khyenpa (*dus gsum mkhyen pa*, 1110-1193); Drogön Rechen (*'gro mgon ras chen*, 1088-1158); Pomdrakpa (*spom brag pa*); Karma Pakshi (*karma pakshi*, 1206-1283); Ogyenpa (*o rgyan pa*, 1230-1309); Rangjung Dorje (*rang byung rdo rje*, 1284-1339); Yungtönpa (*g.yung ston pa*, 1284-1365); Rölpay Dorje (*rol pa'i rdo rje*, 1340-1383); Khachö Wangpo (*mkha' spyod dbang po*, 1350-1405);[92] Deshin Shekpa (*de bzhin gshegs pa*, 1384-1415); Ratnabhadra (ca. fifteenth century); Tongwa Dönden (*mthong ba don ldan*, 1416-1453); Jampal Sangpo (*'jam dpal bzang po*, ca. late fifteenth/early sixteenth century); Paljor Döndrup (*dpal 'byor don grub*, 1427-1489);[93] the lord of victorious ones Chödrak Gyatso (*chos grags rgya mtsho*, 1454-1506); the one who served the latter, Nyewo Goshri (*snye bo go shri*); Jetsun Repa Chenpo (*rje btsun ras pa chen po*, 1505-1569);[94] the omniscient Mikyö Dorje (*mi bskyod rdo rje*, 1507-1554); the sole protector of all beings, the glorious Könchok Yenlak (*dkon mchog yan lag*, 1526-1583),[95] chief subject of the supreme Shākya and excellently ripened master; and the great master Vijāyakīrti (*Namgyal Drakpa/rnam rgyal grags pa*, 1469-1530). From those two latter masters in person, the lineage was then passed down to me, Palden Mipham Chökyi Wangchuk (*dpal ldan mi pham chos kyi dbang phyug*).

1.1.1.2. THE LINEAGE OF LORD MAITRIPA

The victorious master Maitripa fully understood and also taught others that the meaning intended by the Middle Way systems of the older and younger Sarahas[96] and of the masters Nāgārjuna and Chandrakīrti is the same. The teaching cycle of his tradition of the Middle Way is known as "freedom from mental engagement" *(yi la mijepe chökor/yid la mi byed pa'i chos 'khor)*. Master Maitripa is also known as "victorious" because of his gaining victory in debate over the master Shantipa, who held the view of the False Aspectarian Mind Only school *(Semtsam Namdzunpa/sems tsam rnam rdzun pa)*.

Here in Tibet, there have been three different styles of fulfilling the intention of the master Maitripa's Middle Way of freedom from mental engagement: 1) the practice emphasizing the profound and luminous Middle Way of secret mantra, 2) the practice emphasizing the profound Middle Way of the sūtras, and 3) the practice emphasizing the Middle Way of the False Aspectarian Mind Only school.

The view of the third of these consists in teaching the ultimate establishment of self-aware, self-luminous consciousness, empty of perceiver and perceived, as the meaning of the dohas. There have been a great many masters who propound this view in both India and Tibet: the Indian master Chakna *(phyag na)*; Palpo Asu *(bal po a su)*; Kornirūpa; and others.

As for the teaching traditions of the first two of the three above systems, both of these were fully held and practiced by masters such as the lords Marpa and Milarepa. Lord Gampopa, moreover, placed special emphasis on the second by creating terminology for and vastly propagating the teaching of what he himself had realized. Gampopa was highly praised by the Sugata himself in the *King of Samādhi (Samādhirāja, Tingdzin Gyalpo/ting 'dzin rgyal po)* sūtra as the one who would propagate the sūtra meaning of the Middle Way as explained in the *King of Samādhi*.

This teaching tradition of Maitripa's Middle Way lineage was given the name "Mahāmudrā," the same name that is renowned in the anuttara class of secret mantra as the wisdom of bliss and emptiness. Various terms have been created to give a name to the state in which the view of this form of the Middle Way has taken birth in one's mindstream. They include "making manifest the ordinary mind" and "making manifest the dharmakāya." Also, when apparent phenomena *(chöchen/chos can)*—sprouts, thoughts, and so on—are realized not to exist apart from their own true nature *(chönyi/chos nyid)*, this realization has been called "thoughts dawning as the dharmakāya."

The lineage for this teaching system is the same as the lineage described above from Gampopa onward, starting with lord Düsum Khyenpa.

1.1.2. The command[97] lineage of the lord Dipaṃkara

This lineage was held by the master Nāgārjuna, Āryadeva, Chandrakīrti, the older and younger Rigpe Kujugs *(rig pa'i khu byug)* and so on, the lord Atisha (982-1054), and Gewe Shenyen Tönpa Chenpo *(dge ba'i bshes gnyen ston pa chen po)*.[98] Gampopa studied with many Kadampa masters, including Dromtönpa's heart student Chen Ngawa Tsultrim Bar *(spyan snga ba tshul khrims 'bar,* ca. 1033-1103), Jayulwa *(bya yul ba,* 1075-1138), and others. Alternatively, a lineage was passed down via Potowa *(po to ba,* ca. 1031-1105), the great sage Sharawa *(sha ra ba,* 1070-1141), and the glorious Düsum Khyenpa.[99] The lineage after Düsum Khyenpa is the same as the lineage that was fully explained above.

One may wonder, "Are the two teaching systems discussed above, the Middle Way teaching of Maitripa's lineage, which bears the name of Mahāmudrā, and the Middle Way teaching of Atisha's lineage, the same or different?" Though there is no difference between them in the final sense, one could speak of a difference as follows: In the latter one determines the view by way of analysis and rests in equipoise through the supreme knowledge that arises due to obtaining a slight experience of clarity about the nonimplicative negation.[100] In the former, the very supreme knowledge performing the analysis itself is also determined as baseless and rootless. Just as a fire is extinguished when its firewood has exhausted, one rests in equipoise in a reality that is free of both affirmations and refutations.

1.1.3. The lineage of Patsap Lotsawa

This lineage was held by Chandrakīrti, his direct student Mañjushrīkīrti, Devachandra (ca. tenth century), the Brahmin Ratnavajra (ca. late tenth/early eleventh century), Parahita (ca. eleventh century), Hasumati (ca. late eleventh/early twelfth century), Patsap Lotsawa,[101] and Düsum Khyenpa. The rest of the lineage is the same as in the full lineage presented above.

One may wonder, "Is this teaching system the same as the Middle Way teaching system of the lineage of Atisha?" Not only are they the same, their use of terminology is also very similar. However, a difference can be spoken of in the following sense. In the latter, the view of the Middle Way is determined by the inferences arising from hearing. After that, one rests in equipoise by means of supreme knowledge in the meaning arrived at through hearing. In the former, the view is determined by all forms of reasoning—those connected with hearing, contemplation, *and* meditation. After that, one rests in equipoise by means of supreme knowledge without even focusing on the object of evaluation that was arrived at earlier.

1.2. THE LINEAGE THROUGH WHICH WERE PASSED DOWN THE READING TRANSMISSIONS (LAGLUNG/KLAG LUNG) AND LOGIC STRUCTURES (DRUJOR/'BRU SBYOR) THAT ARE RENOWNED IN CONTEMPORARY TIBET

This lineage is the same as the above up to Patsap Lotsawa. From Patsap it was passed down to Shangtang Sagpa *(zhang thang sag pa)*, Drom Wangchuk Dragpa *('brom dbang phyug grags pa)*, Sherab Dorje *(shes rab rdo rje)*, the brothers Tentsul *(bstan tshul)* and Drakden *(grags ldan)*, Dewe Lha *(bde ba'i lha)*, Jetsun Urawa *(rje btsun dbu ra ba)*, Sherab Pal *(shes rab dpal)*, Darma Sherab *(darma shes rab)*, Bangtön Sherin *(bang ston shes rin)*, Sonam Senge *(bsod nams seng ge)*, Bangtön Samzang *(bang ston bsam bzang)*, Bangtön Shönsam *(bang ston gzhon bsam)*, Tangnagpa *(thang nag pa)*, Treseng *(bkras seng)*, Shönu Zangpo *(gzhon nu bzang po)*, Sekangpa Chödrak *(gsas khang pa chos grags)*, Tangsagpa Shöngyal *(thang sag pa gzhon rgyal)*, Gyal Morongpa Chenpo *(rgyal mo rong pa chen po)*, Jamchen Rabjampa Sangye Pel *(byams chen rab 'byams pa sangs rgyas 'phel)*, Bumtrak Sumpa *('bum phrag gsum pa)*, the lord of speech Karma Trinleypa *(karma phrin las pa)*, the omniscient Mikyö Dorje, and then, from my two spiritual tutors[102] to me, Palden Mipham Chökyi Wangchuk.

One may wonder, "Is there a way of teaching the Middle Way in the mantrayāna that is superior to the Middle Way teachings of the master Nāgārjuna, his students, and their followers?"

There is no difference[103] between sūtra and mantra regarding the freedom from elaborations *(trödral/spros bral)* that does not affirm anything after all fixation on the extremes and on the elaborations has been refuted. Nevertheless, there are differences with respect to certain methods of the Middle Way used for determining the view. In particular, the mantrayāna possesses the special view of naturally present emptiness—

free of elaborations and endowed with all supreme aspects—along with the wisdom that realizes such a view, whereas the sūtrayāna does not. In the mantrayāna, this view is realized not by means of intellectual effort, but by employing the secret, key principles of binding.

There is also a difference between the Middle Ways of sūtra and mantra in the sense that in the mantrayāna the basis upon which the conceptual elaborations are cut through is different. This basis becomes a special subject in the mantrayāna. Further, in the mantrayāna the ultimate truth, the nature of phenomena, is isolated from the relative truth, the appearing subject, and is then designated itself as an appearing subject. On the basis of that, one strives to attain the fruition that consists in transforming [relative appearances] into the unified bodies *(ku/sku)* and wisdoms *(yeshe/ye shes)*. This type of result is not sought after in the sūtrayāna.

Regarding all of the differences that have been posited, the venerable Karmapa Mikyö Dorje, in the *Ṭīkā*, relates how he had understood all of these points from the outset but did not have full permission from his master, the lord Repa,[104] to explain them. Later, he said, he was granted permission and explained them fully.

Also in this section of the *Ṭīkā* the Karmapa presents the individual assertions of the Jonangpas, Zilungpa,[105] Podongwa,[106] and Tsongkapa,[107] which are different from what was mentioned above, on the differences between the Middle Way views of sūtra and mantra. Refutations and affirmations connected with these are presented extensively in the *Ṭīkā*.

⋮ The Title and Translator's Homage

2. THE ACTUAL EXPLANATION OF THE TEACHING
2.1. The connections of the treatise
2.2. The actual treatise
2.3. The statement of the author's colophon and the translator's colophon to the treatise

2.1. THE CONNECTIONS OF THE TREATISE
2.1.1. The meaning of the title
2.1.2. The homage to the chosen deity
2.1.3. The explanation of the purpose and connections of the treatise

2.1.1. THE MEANING OF THE TITLE
2.1.1.1. The translation of the title
2.1.1.2. The explanation of the title
2.1.1.3. To what the name was given
2.1.1.4. The purpose of naming the text

2.1.1.1. THE TRANSLATION OF THE TITLE

> In the language of India, *Madhyamakāvatāra-kārikā-nāma*[108]
> In the language of Tibet, *Uma la Jukpe Tsikle-ur Jepa She Jawa/ dbu ma la 'jug pa'i tshig le'ur byas pa zhes bya ba*[109]
> In the English language, the *"Entrance to the Middle Way," Set in Verse*

This treatise, written in Sanskrit, one of the four language families of India, is called *Madhyamakāvatāra-kārikā-nāma*. Translated into [English], it is called the *"Entrance to the Middle Way," Set in Verse.*[110]

2.1.1.2. THE EXPLANATION OF THE TITLE
2.1.1.2.1. The actual Middle Way: what is to be expressed
2.1.1.2.2. The Middle Way of statements: the means of expression

2.1.1.2.1. THE ACTUAL MIDDLE WAY: WHAT IS TO
BE EXPRESSED
All phenomena, on the relative, conventional level, are mere collections of causes and conditions. Their arising is imputed merely dependently, therefore their existence is also posited merely dependently. They are superimpositions of mere names and mere conventional terms. In the ultimate truth, phenomena do not abide within any of the extreme elaborations *(trö ta/spros mtha')* of existence or nonexistence, arising or ceasing, and so on. They do not even abide within any state that could be called "the middle." This is called "the Middle Way of the ground: the union of the two truths."

Through understanding this ground, one comprehends that the relative truth consists of phenomena that are nothing more than names. Since all phenomena are free of arising and so on, one realizes the freedom from confused superimpositions and denials. At the same time, one trains in dependently arisen, illusionlike great compassion for the limitless dependently arisen, illusionlike sentient beings, all of whom have been one's mother. One also trains in the dependently arisen, illusionlike and spacelike two accumulations, which consist of the six perfections that are in turn an outflow of compassion. This stage of training is called "the Middle Way of the path: the union of relative and ultimate bodhichitta."

By training in the path, one achieves the result. Through arriving at the pinnacle of clear experience of ultimate bodhichitta, one completely eradicates the three obscurations[111] along with their seeds and latent tendencies. By becoming free from all elaborations, one attains the benefit for oneself, the state of dharmakāya. Additionally, by arriving at the pinnacle of clear experience of relative bodhichitta, one manifests activity that is spontaneously present until saṃsāra is emptied for the benefit of those to be tamed in accordance with their capabilities and dispositions. Mastering the elaborations[112] of enlightened activity (turning the wheel of dharma and so on), one attains the benefit for others, the state of the form kāyas. This is known as "the Middle Way of the result: the union of the two kāyas."

2.1.1.2.2. THE MIDDLE WAY OF STATEMENTS: THE MEANS
OF EXPRESSION
The Middle Way of statements consists of the Buddha's short, middling,
and extensive teachings [on the perfection of supreme knowledge], as well
as the treatises of Nāgārjuna and his heart disciples such as the *Fundamental Wisdom of the Middle Way (Mūlamadhyamakakārikā, Uma Tsawa
Sherab/dbu ma rtsa ba shes rab)*. These texts are universally renowned as
the treatises of *the Middle Way that is the means of expression*. The *Entrance
to the Middle Way* is called an "entrance" because it is an entrance into the
Middle Way treatise *Fundamental Wisdom*.

In relation to the persons who follow the Middle Way, there are two
categories: someone who accepts the view and someone who has developed realization. The four permutations of these two categories, along
with illustrating examples, are presented in the *Ṭīkā*.[113]

Accepting the view of the Middle Way is done only for the sake of
reversing the misconceptions of students. It is not done as a position of
one's own. This is because in following the Middle Way, one dismantles
the views of others while at the same time not positing a position of one's
own view.

2.1.1.3. TO WHAT THE NAME WAS GIVEN
The title or name is given to the scripture that consists of what is to be
expressed and the means of expression.

2.1.1.4. THE PURPOSE OF NAMING THE TEXT
There is a purpose in naming the text, because, in dependence upon the
name, one realizes the meaning. As was said *(Descent into Laṅka Sūtra,
Laṅkāvatārasūtra, Langkar Shekpe Do/langkar gshegs pa'i mdo)*:

> If he did not assign names,
> The whole world would be confused.
> Therefore, to dispel confusion,
> The Protector assigned names.

2.1.2. THE HOMAGE TO THE CHOSEN DEITY

Homage to the noble Mañjushrī, the youthful one.

With great loving-kindness that is *noble* or exalted in that it is superior to the qualities of naïve beings, he makes *gentle*[114] the mindstreams of oneself and others. Since he has accomplished the two benefits, he is the *glory* of all beings, and since he has crossed over the impure grounds and possesses the qualities of the pure grounds, as well as youth and vitality, he is *youthful*. Thus the translators and scholars [who translated this text into Tibetan], in order to accomplish the two benefits,[115] pay respectful homage to him with their three gates.

2.1.3. THE EXPLANATION OF THE PURPOSE AND CONNECTIONS OF THE TREATISE[116]

The object of expression of this treatise is all of the types of the Middle Way that were just explained: the Middle Way of ground, of path, and of result. Since the means of expression are also discussed, they are themselves also objects of expression.

As to the purposes for which this text was written, first there is the purpose of exclusion *(namche/rnam bcad)*, which is to remove all mistakenness. Mistakenness here refers to doubts some people may have about whether or not the intention of Nāgārjuna is the ultimate intention of the Tathāgata. Mistakenness also refers to the Autonomists' positing the intention of Nāgārjuna as consisting of two types of positions: positions from one's own standpoint and positions from the standpoint of others.[117] In order to prove that these two exist, the Autonomists use logic in an attempt to rationalize conventional reality.

The second type of purpose is the purpose of inclusion *(yongchö/yongs gcod)*: to establish students who are worthy of the teachings of this tradition in the state of omniscience. In order to do this, one must dispel all objections to the teachings of the Transcendent Conqueror, as elucidated by the venerable Nāgārjuna, that clarify the natural state.

The essential purpose is to enable students to attain in stages the five paths[118] and the eleven grounds[119] through hearing, contemplating, and meditating on this treatise, which expresses the topics explained above.

As for the connections, the above three elements are connected in the following way. The essential purpose depends on the purposes, and the purposes depend on the object of expression of the treatise.

⠶ The Three Causes of Bodhisattvas

2.2. THE EXPLANATION OF THE ACTUAL TREATISE
2.2.1. The branches of entering into the composition of the treatise
2.2.2. The extensive explanation of the nature of the treatise to be composed
2.2.3. Bringing the composition to completion

2.2.1. THE BRANCHES OF ENTERING INTO THE COMPOSITION OF THE TREATISE
2.2.1.1. The praiseworthiness of great compassion, the root of all virtue and excellence
2.2.1.2. The praise describing its focal objects

2.2.1.1. THE PRAISEWORTHINESS OF GREAT COMPASSION, THE ROOT OF ALL VIRTUE AND EXCELLENCE
2.2.1.1.1. The teaching on how all noble beings are born from the three qualities of compassion and so on
2.2.1.1.2. The teaching on how compassion is foremost even from among these three qualities

2.2.1.1.1. THE TEACHING ON HOW ALL NOBLE BEINGS ARE BORN FROM THE THREE QUALITIES OF COMPASSION AND SO ON

> Hearers and middling buddhas arise from the lords of sages,
> Buddhas are born from bodhisattvas,
> And compassionate mind, nondual intelligence,
> And bodhichitta are the causes of the victors' heirs. (1.1)

At the outset of this supreme being's activity of composing this treatise, which enters the Middle Way in a vast and profound way, it is appropriate for him to first praise and pay homage to an exalted object and then embark upon the main composition. This verse lists, from the lowest to highest in praiseworthiness and worthiness for homage, the hearers *(shrāvaka, nyentö/nyan thos)*, the solitary realizers *(pratyekabuddha, rang sangye/rang sangs rgyas)*, perfect buddhas, bodhisattvas, and the great compassion of the heirs of the victorious ones *(gyalwe se/rgyal ba'i sras)*, or bodhisattvas.

Hearers and middling buddhas[120] arise from the lords of sages,[121] because the liberations of the hearers and solitary realizers are produced through the tathāgatas'[122] teaching the dharma. One may wonder, "If the solitary realizers manifest their own realization without depending upon others, how is it that they arise from the lords of sages?" In the beginning, those bearing the disposition of a solitary realizer hear the profound dharma of interdependence from a tathāgata. After that, they do not pass into nirvāṇa during that lifetime, but through the cause [of their previous training] they actualize nirvāṇa in their final lifetime, a lifetime during which no buddha appears in the world. Therefore the birth of the solitary realizers from the lords of sages is logical.

As to the meaning of the term "hearer," certain individuals are called hearers because when they attain the results of the authentic instructions, they proclaim those instructions to others.[123] Alternatively, they are called hearers because they proclaim instructions to those who are dedicated to the path of perfect buddhahood after they hear teachings on that path from a buddha in person. From that perspective, the term "hearer" can also be applied to bodhisattvas. The *White Lotus of Genuine Dharma* says:

> Protector, today we have become hearers.
> We will correctly proclaim genuine enlightenment
> And fully express the terms of enlightenment.
> Therefore, we are like inexhaustible[124] hearers.

Moreover, since the bodhisattvas not only hear the dharma but also teach it to others, the term "hearer" applies to the qualities of bodhisattvas that are shared with the hearers proper.

Perfect buddhas are born from bodhisattvas, because they arise due to the causes of persistence on the path and exertion in gathering and purifying. One may wonder, "Are the bodhisattvas not called 'heirs of the victorious ones?'" This is true from the point of view that the victorious ones act as the dominant condition that produces bodhisattvas through teaching them the dharma. Nevertheless, it is not contradictory to say that the heirs of the victorious ones themselves are the cause of the victorious ones. For, the victorious transcendent conquerors (bhagavan, chomden de/bcom ldan 'das) transform into buddhas from the state of bodhisattvas. Furthermore, all victorious ones take a bodhisattva as their master in the beginning. They are able to attain the resultant state of the victorious through relying on bodhisattvas, who in turn serve as the dominant conditions for their attainment of buddhahood.

One may wonder, "What are the causes for becoming such a bodhisattva?" The causes of the victors' heirs are compassionate mind (the focal objects and aspects of which will be explained later); nondual intelligence, supreme knowledge free of all extremes such as conceptions of the existence or nonexistence of things; and bodhichitta, the desire to attain enlightenment for the benefit of others (a desire congruent with supreme knowledge). Bodhichitta is the cause that enables someone to be called a bodhisattva.

2.2.1.1.2. THE TEACHING ON HOW COMPASSION IS FOREMOST EVEN FROM AMONG THESE THREE QUALITIES

> Since it is asserted that love is the seed of the victorious ones'
>   abundant harvest,
> Is like the water that causes it to grow,
> And is the ripening that allows it to be enjoyed for a long time,
> I therefore praise compassion first. (1.2)

Since compassion itself is the cause of the other two causes of becoming a bodhisattva, it is praised first. To have an abundant harvest, the seed, water, and ripening are essential in the beginning, middle, and end, respectively. Compassion is praised here in correlation to the harvest example. Why is it praised? Because love—great compassion—is essential to the victorious ones' abundant harvest in all of its three phases.

In the beginning, compassion is like a seed that produces all the qualities of the buddhas, since it gives rise to the sprouts of the two types of bodhichitta that have not yet arisen. It is essential in the middle because it is like water that causes the bodhichitta that has already arisen, and the virtue of the two accumulations, to grow and flourish. Without the nour-ishment of the water of compassion, some types of students would pro-ceed to attain an inferior nirvāṇa, even if they have generated bodhichitta previously.

It is essential in the end because it is asserted to be like the ripening of the harvest that is the enjoyment upon which the hosts of ordinary and noble students depend for a long time. Even if one attains the dharmakāya for one's own benefit, if one lacks the form kāyas, which are ripened by the compassion that benefits others, the disciples will not enjoy any harvests for a long time. Conversely, if the form kāyas that are fully ripened by com-passion are available to the hosts of ordinary and noble disciples as objects of reliance, the continuity of enlightened activity will flourish for a long time, until saṃsāra is emptied.

For these reasons, the master Chandrakīrti praises great compassion first, at the outset of composing this treatise.

2.2.1.2. THE PRAISE DESCRIBING ITS FOCAL OBJECTS
2.2.1.2.1. The praise to compassion that focuses on sentient beings
2.2.1.2.2. The praise to compassion that focuses on phenomena and nonreferential compassion

2.2.1.2.1. THE PRAISE TO COMPASSION THAT FOCUSES ON
SENTIENT BEINGS

> First, thinking "I," they cling to a self.
> Then, thinking "This is mine," attachment to things develops.
> Beings are powerless, like a rambling water mill.
> I bow to compassion for these wanderers. (1.3)

Compassion is of three types: the compassion that focuses on sentient beings, the compassion that focuses on phenomena, and nonreferential compassion. Those three types of compassion all possess the aspect of desire for sentient beings to be free from suffering.

The first compassion focuses on sentient beings whose substantial exis-tence as persons and so on has been superimposed. The second compas-sion focuses on sentient beings as being mere imputations in reference to the aggregates and so on. This compassion entails the realization that sentient beings are devoid of substantial existence. The third compassion observes the absence of inherent nature, in relation to which the existence of sentient beings is a mere label. This compassion entails the realization that both sentient beings and phenomena are devoid of inherent nature.

One may wonder, "In whose mindstream do these types of compassion arise?" In the system that holds that hearers and solitary realizers do not realize the selflessness of phenomena, the three arise in ordinary beings, hearers and solitary realizers, and heirs of the victorious ones, respectively. When correlated to the philosophical systems, they arise in tīrthikas, Proponents of Things *(Ngö Mawa/dngos smra ba)*,[125] and followers of the Middle Way, respectively. In terms of the stages of Mahāyāna, they arise in those who have attained the Mahāyāna paths of accumulation and juncture, those dwelling on the seven impure grounds,[126] and those dwelling on the three pure grounds[127] and upwards,[128] respectively.

From the standpoint of this tradition, [that of Chandrakīrti], in which the hearers and solitary realizers do realize the selflessness of phenomena, the latter two types of compassion are taught to be the same basic mental state, but with different modes of perceptual focus. Thus it is taught that all noble beings possess the latter two types of compassion.

Before beings begin to cling to the world as something that could be possessed by a self, they think "I," reifying the self even though the self does not exist. Consequently, attachment to things develops: all things not fixated on as "I" are thought of as "mine." This includes sentient beings and nonsentient objects.

These beings, who cling to "me" and "mine," or self and entities connected to the self, are like the flow of a rambling water mill: due to karma and mental afflictions they are powerless. They wander without pause from beginningless time in the great well of saṃsāra, from the Avīchi hell to the peak of existence.[129] Thus the praise is made by Chandrakīrti: "I bow to the compassion that delights in saving these beings from such suffering."

2.2.1.2.2. THE PRAISE TO COMPASSION THAT FOCUSES ON PHENOMENA AND NONREFERENTIAL COMPASSION

Beings are like a moon on rippling water:
They move and are empty of inherent nature. (1.4ab)

Again an example is used: when the image of a moon appears on the surface of a very clear pool of water that has been blown gently by the wind, the actual moon seems to appear simultaneously with the water, the basis for the reflection. Genuine beings[130] understand that the reflection of the moon, along with the water that is its support, is impermanent, changing from moment to moment. They also understand that the moon is empty of an inherent nature. The example illustrates its meaning in the following way.

In the ocean of the views of the transitory collection, which is moved by the winds of incorrect conception, beings appear in the eyes of bodhisattvas like the reflection of a moon. They are born from the interdependence of their previous actions, which in turn depend on the vast blue waters of ignorance. The bodhisattvas, overcome with compassion, see that these beings, who exist in dependence upon karma and mental afflictions, are moved—they suffer the changes of impermanence from moment to moment.

Bodhisattvas also see that all of these phenomena are empty of an inherent nature. Seeing in this way, they form a desire to attain the state of the only true friend of beings, buddhahood itself, which vanquishes the suffering of movement and possesses the nectar of genuine dharma, free from all mistaken conceptions.

Thus, "I bow to the compassion for beings that is a transcendent conqueror."

⋮ Ground One: Supreme Joy

2.2.2. The extensive explanation of the nature
of the treatise to be composed
2.2.2.1. The explanation of the cause, the bodhisattva grounds
2.2.2.2. The explanation of the result, the ground of buddhahood

2.2.2.1. The explanation of the cause, the bodhisattva
grounds
2.2.2.1.1. The explanation of the actual ten grounds
2.2.2.1.2. The explanation of the grounds' qualities

2.2.2.1.1. The explanation of the actual ten grounds
2.2.2.1.1.1. Supreme Joy *(Pramuditā, Rabtu Gawa/rab tu dga' ba)*
2.2.2.1.1.2. The Stainless *(Nirmala, Drima Mepa/dri ma med pa)*
2.2.2.1.1.3. The Luminous *(Prabhākari, Ö Jepa/'od byed pa)*
2.2.2.1.1.4. The Radiant *(Archiṣhmati, Ö Trowa/'od 'phro ba)*
2.2.2.1.1.5. Difficult to Overcome *(Sudurjayā, Jang Kawa/sbyang dka' ba)*
2.2.2.1.1.6. The Manifest *(Abhimukhī, Ngöndu Gyurpa/mngon du gyur pa)*
2.2.2.1.1.7. Gone Far Beyond *(Dūraṃgamā, Ringdu Songwa/ring du song ba)*
2.2.2.1.1.8. The Immovable *(Achala, Miyowa/mi gyo ba)*
2.2.2.1.1.9. Excellent Intelligence *(Sādhumatī, Lekpe Lodrö/legs pa'i blo gros)*
2.2.2.1.1.10. Cloud of Dharma *(Dharmameghā, Chökyi Trin/chos kyi sprin)*

2.2.2.1.1.1. The explanation of Supreme Joy *(Pramuditā, Rabtu Gawa/rab tu dga' ba)*
2.2.2.1.1.1.1. The brief teaching on this ground's nature, the basis of distinct features

2.2.2.1.1.1.2. The extensive explanation of the distinct features or qualities of the ground

2.2.2.1.1.1.3. A concluding summary describing the ground's qualities

2.2.2.1.1.1.1. THE BRIEF TEACHING ON THIS GROUND'S NATURE, THE BASIS OF DISTINCT FEATURES

> **The victors' heirs see this and, so that these beings may be freed completely,**
> **Their minds are overcome by compassion. (1.4cd)**
> **Fully dedicating their virtue with the *Aspiration of Samantabhadra*,**
> **They abide in supreme joy—this is called "the first." (1.5ab)**

"The bodhisattva grounds" *(bhūmi, sa/sa)* is a phrase that refers to the divisions of the uncontaminated wisdom of bodhisattvas. These categories are made in dependence upon the methods, such as compassion, that embrace their wisdom. The grounds are the supports or bases for excellent qualities, just as the "ground" is known as a support in the world. However, the grounds themselves are indivisible from their own side, because the uncontaminated knowledge that realizes emptiness has no divisions. As it is said *(Avataṃsaka Sūtra, Do Palpo Che/mdo phal po che)*:

> Just as the trace of a bird in the sky
> Is extremely hard to describe and indemonstrable,
> The grounds of the sugatas' heirs
> Are not objects of the rational mind.

The grounds are differentiated on the basis of the following four factors: distinctions regarding the number of qualities the bodhisattvas possess (which increase as the bodhisattva progresses to higher grounds);[131] distinctions regarding powers such as miracles;[132] distinctions regarding which perfections, such as generosity, become preeminent; and distinctions regarding how bodhisattvas reincarnate due to the increase of karmic maturation.[133] Therefore, the *Supreme Joy* of the bodhisattvas is the first level of generating bodhichitta, and *Cloud of Dharma* is the tenth.

So that beings may be completely freed, these bodhisattvas, heirs of the victorious ones who have given rise to the first level of bodhichitta, are overcome by nonreferential compassion. They excellently abide in the supreme joy that comes from fully dedicating their virtue with the aspiration of the bodhisattva Samantabhadra. This stage is called the first generation of bodhichitta. It is an illustration of the result that is caused by nondual intelligence.

As to the aspirations of the bodhisattvas, there is the one that is excerpted as follows *(Aspiration for Excellent Conduct, Bhadrachāryapranidhana, Zangchö Mönlam/bzang spyod smon lam):*

> All the victorious ones who appear in the three times
> Awaken into enlightenment through the excellent conduct
> Of various aspiration prayers for awakened conduct—
> May I perfect all of these.[134]

This aspiration is one of the "ten great aspirations," which themselves belong to the "one hundred vigintillion[135] aspirations," all of which are made on this first bodhisattva ground.

Bodhisattvas on the paths of the conduct of devoted interest[136] have not given rise to the first generation of bodhichitta. Their bodhichitta is similar to the hearers who have yet to enter into the result of definite separation *(nge-je/nges 'byed).*[137]

2.2.2.1.1.1.2. THE EXTENSIVE EXPLANATION OF THE DISTINCT FEATURES OR QUALITIES OF THE GROUND
2.2.2.1.1.1.2.1. The special accompanying qualities
2.2.2.1.1.1.2.2. The primary quality, the perfection of generosity

2.2.2.1.1.1.2.1. THE SPECIAL ACCOMPANYING QUALITIES
2.2.2.1.1.1.2.1.1. The qualities of attaining a special name
2.2.2.1.1.1.2.1.2. The qualities of attaining the special significance of that name

2.2.2.1.1.1.2.1.1. THE QUALITIES OF ATTAINING A SPECIAL NAME

From that time onward, the one who attains that state
Is called by the term "bodhisattva." (1.5cd)

From the time of entering into the ground of *Supreme Joy* onward, the heirs of the victorious ones are noble ones. They attain the primary quality that allows them to be called by that name—the supreme knowledge that directly realizes the true nature of reality. They are not to be called by names such as "ordinary being"; they are called only by the term "bodhisattva." The *Lady Transcendent Conqueror*[138] sūtras say:

> The term "bodhisattva" is an epithet *(ladak/bla dvags)* for beings who possess realization and who realize and understand all inner phenomena. What do they understand? They understand what does not arise, what genuinely does not arise, and what is incorrect. They understand phenomena in a way that is unlike the way phenomena are labeled by naïve, ordinary beings and is unlike the way phenomena are discovered by naïve, ordinary beings. Therefore, they are called "bodhisattvas."

This and other statements were made in the sūtras, and their basic meaning is as follows: beings who conceptualize the three spheres,[139] strongly cling to things, and have pride that thinks "me" are not bodhisattvas.

However, we are not completely excluding the use of the term "ordinary being bodhisattvas." Ordinary beings can possess the relative bodhichittas of aspiration and application, as well as the bodhichitta of mental engagement in and devoted interest toward ultimate reality or suchness. Still, the only bodhisattvas who completely fit the explanations and applications of the term "bodhisattva" are the ones who have attained the grounds. In a similar vein, the *Highest Continuum (Uttaratantra, Gyü Lama/rgyud bla ma)* says:

> Impure, both impure and pure,
> And completely pure:
> These three descriptions apply respectively to the stages
> Of sentient beings, bodhisattvas, and buddhas.

2.2.2.1.1.1.2.1.2. THE QUALITIES OF ATTAINING THE SPECIAL SIGNIFICANCE OF THAT NAME
2.2.2.1.1.1.2.1.2.1. The qualities of being born into the family of tathāgatas and so forth
2.2.2.1.1.1.2.1.2.2. The qualities of advancing from ground to ground and so forth
2.2.2.1.1.1.2.1.2.3. The qualities of outshining other noble ones

2.2.2.1.1.1.2.1.2.1. THE QUALITIES OF BEING BORN INTO THE FAMILY OF TATHĀGATAS AND SO FORTH

> They are born into the family of the tathāgatas
> And relinquish the three entanglements.
> These bodhisattvas possess extraordinary joy
> And can cause a hundred worlds to quake. (1.6)

Not only are the bodhisattvas given a new name when they engender the first level of bodhichitta, they are also born into the family of tathāgatas, because they have gone beyond the grounds of ordinary beings, hearers, and solitary realizers, and because the grounds and paths that lead to buddhahood have taken birth in them.

It should be understood that the "family of tathāgatas" refers to "family" from the perspective of the immediate causes of enlightenment. From the perspective of the long-term causes of enlightenment, one is said to be born into this family after first giving rise to the bodhichitta arising from signs.[140] For example, Shāntideva said *(Entrance to the Conduct of Bodhisattvas, Bodhicharyāvatāra, Changchub Sempe Chöpa La Jugpa/byang chub sems dpa'i spyod pa la 'jug pa)*:

> Today I am born into the family of the buddhas.
> Now I am a child of the buddhas. (3.26cd)

On the first ground, the bodhisattvas entirely relinquish the three entanglements *(kuntu jorwa sum/kun tu sbyor ba gsum)*: the view of the transitory collection *(jigtsog la tawa/'jig tshogs la lta ba)*, doubt *(tetsom/ the tshom)*, and holding their ethical discipline and yogic conduct to be supreme *(tsultrim tulshuk chogdzin/tshul khrims brtul zhugs mchog 'dzin)*. Once those three have been relinquished they do not arise again, because the bodhisattvas have directly realized the selflessness of the person. It is due only to not seeing selflessness that one superimposes the existence of a self, takes on the view of the transitory collection, and is led down wrong paths by doubt.

These bodhisattvas possess and sustain a most excellent joy that transcends the world. Through attaining the qualities born of certainty, and through relinquishing the faults that are overcome by this bodhisattva ground, a great multitude of unique joys arises. This ground is called

Supreme Joy because it possesses joy that is especially exalted. At this stage the bodhisattvas also gain the ability to cause a hundred worlds to quake. These qualities are among the twelve sets of hundredfold qualities they attain at this stage.[141]

2.2.2.1.1.1.2.1.2.2. THE QUALITIES OF ADVANCING FROM GROUND TO GROUND AND SO FORTH

> **Advancing from ground to ground, they excellently move ever higher.**
> **At that time, all paths to the lower realms are sealed off.**
> **At that time, all grounds of ordinary beings are exhausted.**
> **They are taught to be like the eighth of the noble ones. (1.7)**

These bodhisattvas advance from the lower grounds to the higher grounds and excellently progress ever upward. For, through further familiarizing themselves with the realities that they have already comprehended, they experience great delight in advancing to the second ground and onward.

At that time, all paths in the continua of these bodhisattvas that cause one to fall to the lower realms due to karmic actions are sealed off, because they successfully restrain themselves from performing nonvirtuous actions. Their actions no longer cause them to take birth in any other unfavorable existence, such as the states of no-leisure.

Also at that time, all grounds of ordinary beings who have clinging—nondiscrimination *(dushe mepa/'du shes med pa)*, Uttarakuru *(Dra Minyenpa/sgra mi snyan pa)*, the level of Mahābrāhma *(Tsangchen/tshangs chen)*, and so on—are exhausted, because they directly see true reality.

In sum, for the stream-enterers—the eighth of the noble ones—faults disappear and qualities arise in a measure corresponding to their realization of the dharmas of noble ones.[142] In the same way, for these bodhisattvas qualities arise and faults are exhausted in harmony with their realization of the first ground. Therefore the eighth of the noble ones is the example used to illustrate the first bodhisattva ground.

One may object, "It is not tenable to posit the stream-enterers as the eighth of the noble ones, because the eighth of the noble ones are the pre-stream-enterers" *(gyün shug shugpa/rgyun zhugs zhugs pa)*. However, that fault does not apply here, because if one takes the "eighth" (the stream-enterer) that is mentioned here and applies the categorization scheme of the four pairs,[143] both the pre-stream-enterer and the stream-enterer who has attained the result will be included under the name "stream enterer." The eighth noble one referred to in this verse is used as an example of someone who has attained the qualities of the hearers' path of seeing, so it makes no difference which of the two terms (stream-enterer or pre-stream-enterer) is used.[144]

2.2.2.1.1.1.2.1.2.3. THE QUALITIES OF OUTSHINING OTHER NOBLE ONES

2.2.2.1.1.1.2.1.2.3.1. On the first ground, they outshine the hearers and solitary realizers through their generation of bodhichitta, their compassion, and their pure intention

2.2.2.1.1.1.2.1.2.3.2 On the seventh ground, they outshine the hearers and solitary realizers through the power of their knowledge

2.2.2.1.1.1.2.1.2.3.1. ON THE FIRST GROUND, THEY OUTSHINE THE HEARERS AND SOLITARY REALIZERS THROUGH THEIR GENERATION OF BODHICHITTA, THEIR COMPASSION, AND THEIR PURE INTENTION

> **Even those who abide on the first level of the view of perfect bodhichitta**
> **Surpass those born of the sages' speech and the solitary realizers**
> **Through their merit, which continues to perfectly increase.**
> **(1.8abc)**

Even bodhisattvas who abide on the first ground of the dharmadhātu, due to the view of perfect bodhichitta that realizes ultimate reality, outshine and surpass those born of the lord of sages' speech—the hearers—and the solitary realizers through the merit of their pure intention that wishes to attain the qualities of buddhahood so that they may accomplish the short- and long-term welfare of sentient beings. The bodhisattvas' merit increases even further. As the Transcendent Conqueror said *(Sūtra on the Ten Grounds, Dashabhūmikasūtra, Sa Chupe Do/sa bcu pa'i mdo)*:

> O child of noble family, not long after the son of a king is born, that son will take the name of the king. Through his greater ancestry he will come to outshine the entire upper echelon

of elder ministers. In the same way, not long after a beginner bodhisattva gives rise to bodhichitta, through being born into the family of the tathāgatas, the kings of dharma, they will outshine the hearers and solitary realizers, long-practiced in the conduct of purity *(tsangpar chepa/tshangs par spyad pa)*, through the power of their bodhichitta and compassion.

O child of noble family, not long after a chick has been born to the king of garudas, the chick will grow until the force of its wings, its sharp eyes, and all of its other qualities will be unrivalled by all the other flocks of elder birds. In the same way, once bodhisattvas give rise to the first level of bodhichitta, they genuinely enter into the family of the great king-of-garuda tathāgatas. The children of the great king of garudas, through the power of their wings, the wish to attain the state of omniscience, will inherit qualities—the ability to surpass others, pure intention, pure vision, and so on—unrivalled by any hearers or solitary realizers, who have trained in renunciation for hundreds or even thousands of eons.

The masters Abhayakāra[145] and Jayānanda[146] interpret the above quotation as corresponding to the first level of the generation of bodhichitta arising from signs. [Even though that interpretation differs from that of Chandrakīrti, who interprets the quotation as corresponding to the first bodhisattva ground], their interpretation is nonetheless valid. The quotation can be correctly interpreted in either way, because no form of merit can compare with the merit of bodhichitta, be it worldly merit or the transcendent merit of hearers and solitary realizers.

2.2.2.1.1.1.2.1.2.3.2 ON THE SEVENTH GROUND, THEY OUTSHINE THE HEARERS AND SOLITARY REALIZERS THROUGH THE POWER OF THEIR KNOWLEDGE

On the ground *Gone Far Beyond,* their knowledge also becomes superior. (1.8d)

When these bodhisattvas who have given rise to the first level of bodhichitta arrive at the seventh bodhichitta generation, called *Gone Far Beyond,* not only do they surpass the hearers and solitary realizers in terms of their mind of relative bodhichitta, they also surpass them with their knowledge of ultimate bodhichitta. Their supreme knowledge that realizes the two truths becomes extraordinarily superior, because on the seventh ground they attain the perfection of skillful means, and their minds enter into and arise from cessation in every moment.

Also, at that time they abide in the greatness that consists in knowing fully, and just as it is, the object that is the dharmadhātu without characteristics. This knowledge differs from understandings of the dharmadhātu based on conceptual reference points such as the contents of the sūtras. This quality is not present in hearers, solitary realizers, or on grounds below the seventh. For, it was said in the sūtras *(Sūtra on the Ten Grounds)*:

> O children of the victorious ones, when the son of a king is born into his royal family, he will take the name of the king, and his birth alone will cause him to outshine the entire assembly of ministers. This is not because of his discriminating intelligence, but because of the splendor of his royal ancestry. Later, when the son comes of age and his intelligence matures, he completely passes beyond all the activities of ministers. O children of the victorious ones, in the same way bodhisattvas as well, as soon as they generate bodhichitta, outshine the hearers and solitary realizers. This is not because of the power of their discriminating intelligence, but because of the greatness of their pure intention. The bodhisattvas abiding on the seventh bodhisattva ground abide in the greatness of knowing the object [of dharmadhātu]. They pass completely beyond all the activities of the hearers and solitary realizers.

The above quotation demonstrates that hearers and solitary realizers possess the realization of phenomenal selflessness. That they do realize phenomenal selflessness will be proven here by three reasonings and seven scriptural quotations.

THE FIRST REASONING[147]
Given hearers and solitary realizers, the subject: it follows that the power of their knowledge is outshone even by the bodhisattvas who have generated the first level of bodhichitta,[148] because they are persons who have not

fully understood that things lack an inherent nature,[149] just as in worldly freedom from attachment.[150]

THE SECOND REASONING
Given hearers and solitary realizers, the subject: it follows that they have not relinquished all of the mental afflictions *(tra-gye/phra rgyas)* of the three realms,[151] because they mistakenly observe phenomena such as form to have an entity *(ngowo/ngo bo)* that is truly existent, just as in the freedom from attachment of non-Buddhists.[152]

THE THIRD REASONING
Given hearers and solitary realizers, who apprehend the aggregates as being impermanent and selfless, the subject:[153] it follows that they actually do not even realize the selflessness of the person, because they hold a view that reifies the aggregates, which are the cause for the imputation and positing of a self. This is just as in the case where if one does not stop clinging to the parts of a chariot (the wheels, etc.) as being real, one will not stop clinging to the chariot, the bearer of those parts, as being real.

THE FIRST SCRIPTURAL QUOTATION
From Nāgārjuna's *Precious Garland (Ratnāvalī, Rinchen Trengwa/rin chen phreng ba)*:[154]

> For as long as there is clinging to the aggregates,
> There will be clinging to an "I."
> Where there is clinging to an "I" there is karma,
> Which is followed by birth. (1.35)

> These three paths[155] are without beginning, middle, or end.
> In saṃsāra, like a firebrand's wheel,
> They are each the result of the other,
> Cycling round and round. (1.36)

> When saṃsāra is seen not to exist in itself, in something different,
> In both, or in the three times,
> Clinging to an "I" is exhausted.
> Due to that, action and birth are exhausted as well. (1.37)

This quotation demonstrates how the presence or absence of clinging to things, such as the aggregates, causes saṃsāra to continue or be reversed, respectively.

THE SECOND SCRIPTURAL QUOTATION[156]

Just as the eye, due to delusion,
Perceives a firebrand to be a circle,
In a similar way the faculties
Apprehend the objects of the present. (4.57)

The faculties and their objects
Are asserted to be of the nature of the five elements.
Yet since each of the five elements has no essence
    individually,
All of them in actuality are devoid of essence. (4.58)

If the elements were distinct from each other,
It would follow that there could be fire without fuel.
If they merge, they would lose their defining characteristics—
This logic applies to all the other elements. (4.59)

Since the elements do not exist in these two ways,[157]
An "assembly" is meaningless.
Since assemblies are meaningless,
"Form" is also, in actuality, meaningless. (4.60)

Consciousnesses, feelings, discriminations,
And mental formations as well
Are without an essence of their own identity.
Therefore, in ultimate truth, [the sense pleasures] are
    essenceless. (4.61)

Just as we fancy the decrease of suffering
To be real happiness,
We also fancy the removal of happiness
To be real suffering. (4.62)

Since suffering and happiness are devoid of an essence,
If you relinquish craving to meet with happiness
And craving to be free of suffering,
You will be liberated by seeing. (4.63)

What is it that sees?
Conventionally, we call it mind.
Yet without mental events there is no mind.
Since both are essenceless, we do not assert their existence. (4.64)

In this way, through precisely and genuinely
Understanding that beings do not exist ultimately,
One becomes just like a fire devoid of its cause:
One passes into nirvāṇa, not being susceptible to further births
    and not taking further births. (4.65)

This quotation teaches that unless one understands the lack of inherent
nature of things such as the aggregates, one will not attain nirvāṇa. However, if you think that the quotation [in the final verse] is referring to nonabiding nirvāṇa, that is incorrect: hearers and solitary realizers attain a
nihilistic nirvāṇa through their realization that things lack an essence.
Noble bodhisattvas, who attain the same realization, do not. This is verified by the verse following the above quotation:

Bodhisattvas see [this possibility]
And come to desire the enlightenment [that is emancipation from
    birth and death].
Yet, due to their compassion,
They remain in existence until the [complete] enlightenment [of
    nonabiding nirvāṇa is attained]. (4.66)

THE THIRD SCRIPTURAL QUOTATION

Forms are like foam on water,
Feelings are like water bubbles,
Discriminations are like mirages,
Formations are like banana trees,

And consciousnesses are like illusions:
Thus taught the Friend of the Sun.[158]

THE FOURTH SCRIPTURAL QUOTATION[159]

In the Mahāyāna, the Buddha taught nonarising.
[In the lower vehicles, he taught] emptiness as the exhaustion of
    all extraneous things.[160]
Since exhaustion and nonarising are in actuality
The same, accept [the Mahāyāna teachings]. (4.86)

THE FIFTH SCRIPTURAL QUOTATION[161]

The Transcendent Conqueror, through his knowledge
Of things and nonthings,
In the *Instructions to Kātyāyana* sūtra,
Refuted both existence and nonexistence. (15.7)

The above three quotations demonstrate that the five aggregates are without an inherent nature through comparing them to five things such as illusions. In particular, in the sūtras of the hearer and solitary realizer vehicles,
the Buddha taught that all formations are devoid of an inherent nature
in order for the hearers and solitary realizers to relinquish the afflictive
obscurations.

THE SIXTH SCRIPTURAL QUOTATION
From the *Precious Garland*:

In the vehicle of the hearers,
There are no teachings on the aspirations
Of bodhisattvas, nor on the bodhisattvas' conduct or thorough
    dedications.
Therefore, how could one become a bodhisattva through that
    vehicle? (4.90)

The topics on abiding in the bodhisattvas' conduct
Were not taught in the collection of sūtras [of the lower vehicles],

But were taught in the Mahāyāna .
Therefore, learned ones accept [the Mahāyāna]. (4.93)

This quotation demonstrates that it contradicts scripture and reasoning for a philosophical system to hold that the Mahāyāna is meaningless because phenomenal selflessness is taught in the vehicle of hearers. For, the Mahāyāna does not merely teach phenomenal selflessness. What does it teach? It teaches the bodhisattvas' grounds, perfections, aspirations, compassion, and so on, along with their complete dedications, their two accumulations, and the inconceivable true nature of reality.

THE SEVENTH SCRIPTURAL QUOTATION[162]

You taught that there is no liberation
Without realizing freedom from characteristics *(tsenma mepa/ mtshan ma med pa).*
Therefore, in the Mahāyāna,
You taught freedom from characteristics in a comprehensive way.

This quotation demonstrates that the Buddha taught phenomenal selflessness more extensively in the Mahāyāna . In the vehicle of hearers, only the afflictive obscurations are relinquished, and thus phenomenal selflessness was merely presented briefly. In the Mahāyāna, the cognitive obscurations are also relinquished.

The differences between the vehicles of the hearers and the Mahāyāna are explained in detail in this section of the *Ṭīkā,* which posits differences such as the brevity or extensiveness with which phenomenal selflessness is taught. Whether one is "extensive" or "brief" depends on whether or not one realizes the relationship that apparent phenomena have with phenomenal selflessness in every single instance of relative truth.[163]

2.2.2.1.1.1.2.2. THE PRIMARY QUALITY, THE PERFECTION
OF GENEROSITY
2.2.2.1.1.1.2.2.1. Generosity is foremost on this ground
2.2.2.1.1.1.2.2.2. The ancillary explanation of the praise to generosity
2.2.2.1.1.1.2.2.3. The difference between mundane and transcendent
generosity

2.2.2.1.1.1.2.2.1. GENEROSITY IS FOREMOST ON THIS GROUND
2.2.2.1.1.1.2.2.1.1. The actual explanation
2.2.2.1.1.1.2.2.1.2. How their generosity also highlights other qualities

2.2.2.1.1.1.2.2.1.1. THE ACTUAL EXPLANATION

> **At that time, the first cause of perfect buddhahood,**
> **Generosity, becomes preeminent. (1.9ab)**

At the time of attaining the first ground, from among the ten perfections, the causes of the enlightenment of perfect buddhahood, generosity *(dāna, jinpa/sbyin pa)*, the first, becomes vastly preeminent in those bodhisattvas, because the perfection of generosity is the first cause of omniscience. However, it is not the case that these bodhisattvas are devoid of the other perfections, such as discipline.

2.2.2.1.1.1.2.2.1.2. HOW THEIR GENEROSITY ALSO HIGHLIGHTS OTHER QUALITIES

> **They give even their flesh respectfully,**
> **Which provides a cause for inferring the unseen. (1.9cd)**

At that time, let alone giving ordinary things; the bodhisattvas are respectful even when cutting off their own flesh and giving it to beggars. This type of action becomes a cause for inferring the unseen essence and qualities of the first ground.[164] For if great compassion, which directly realizes that oneself and others are devoid of an inherent nature, was absent in one's mindstream, one would not be respectful about giving away one's own flesh.

2.2.2.1.1.1.2.2.2. THE ANCILLARY EXPLANATION OF THE PRAISE TO GENEROSITY
2.2.2.1.1.1.2.2.2.1. The reason why the Victorious One taught generosity first
2.2.2.1.1.1.2.2.2.2. Generosity produces temporary and ultimate happiness, even if the giver gives incorrectly
2.2.2.1.1.1.2.2.2.3. Generosity quickly produces happiness in bodhisattvas
2.2.2.1.1.1.2.2.2.4. A summary of the above topics
2.2.2.1.1.1.2.2.2.5. A special explanation of how generosity produces happiness in bodhisattvas

2.2.2.1.1.1.2.2.2.1. THE REASON WHY THE VICTORIOUS ONE TAUGHT GENEROSITY FIRST

All beings strongly desire happiness,
Yet for humans, there is no happiness without material
    enjoyments.
Knowing that enjoyments, in turn, come about through
    generosity,
The Sage spoke of generosity first. (1.10)

All ordinary beings—those who misperceive phenomena and dwell on a level below the third meditative concentration—strongly desire the happiness of saṃsāra, which is of the nature of suffering. Yet humans can only experience the feeling of happiness through the specific causes of that happiness: food, clothing, and so on, enjoyments which themselves involve causes of suffering. If humans have these enjoyments, happiness arises, and without them it does not. These enjoyments, in turn, come about through generosity. If one does not practice generosity they do not arise. Knowing this, the Sage spoke of generosity first, rather than speaking of discipline and so on.

2.2.2.1.1.1.2.2.2.2. GENEROSITY PRODUCES TEMPORARY AND ULTIMATE HAPPINESS, EVEN IF THE GIVER GIVES INCORRECTLY
2.2.2.1.1.1.2.2.2.2.1. How generosity serves as a cause for temporary happiness
2.2.2.1.1.1.2.2.2.2.2. How generosity serves as a cause for ultimate happiness

2.2.2.1.1.1.2.2.2.2.1. HOW GENEROSITY SERVES AS A CAUSE FOR TEMPORARY HAPPINESS

Even for those who are wanting in compassion, ill-tempered,
And focused exclusively on their own concerns,
The enjoyments they desire,
Which thoroughly pacify their suffering, arise from generosity.
    (1.11)

Some people give in a way that runs against the aim of benefiting others. They are wanting in compassion, the wish to free others from suffering.

They may also be ill-tempered in thought and deed, giving with only the thought, "If I give in this life, I will receive enjoyments in this and future lives," focusing solely on their own concerns. They do not strive for the results of generosity sought by the heirs of the victorious ones. In not doing so, they turn their backs on a rich banquet of generosity. Nevertheless, their conduct will produce results: the material enjoyments they desire, which thoroughly pacify their sufferings, such as hunger. These results arise due to regarding generosity as a good quality and regarding not giving as a fault.

2.2.2.1.1.1.2.2.2.2.2. HOW GENEROSITY SERVES AS A CAUSE FOR ULTIMATE HAPPINESS

> Even they, through an occasion of giving,
> Will one day come to meet a noble being.
> Perfectly cutting through the continuum of existence,
> They will attain the result and proceed to peace. (1.12)

Even those who have the disposition of hearers or solitary realizers, who do not have great compassion, through an occasion of giving motivated by desire to be free of the suffering of sickness and aging, will one day meet with a recipient of such generosity who is a noble being. This noble being will teach them the instructions on turning away from saṃsāra: they will teach them about good qualities, dedications, explaining the dharma, and so on.

Not long after obtaining these instructions, the giver will begin to see the shortcomings of saṃsāra. They will actualize the path of the noble ones, perfectly cutting through the continuum of existence. Through this, they will proceed to peace, the nirvāṇa of the hearers and solitary realizers that is the result of this path. Therefore, this attainment of nirvāṇa also arises due to generosity.

2.2.2.1.1.1.2.2.2.3. GENEROSITY QUICKLY PRODUCES HAPPINESS IN BODHISATTVAS

> Before long, those committed to benefiting beings
> Will achieve joy through giving. (1.13ab)

Those who hope for the karmic ripening of their generosity will not enjoy the results of generosity simultaneously with the giving itself. However, bodhisattvas, who are committed to benefiting beings, before long will continually enjoy the results of their generosity, even while they are giving. Thus they will attain joy.

2.2.2.1.1.1.2.2.2.4. A SUMMARY OF THE ABOVE TOPICS

Since it is for both those who are loving and not-so-loving in character,
The teaching on generosity is foremost. (1.13cd)

Generosity, as was explained above, is the cause for attaining the higher realms and definite goodness for those loving in character—the bodhisattvas—and for those not-so-loving in character—ordinary beings, hearers, and solitary realizers. Therefore, the teaching that praises generosity is foremost, and that is why it is given first.

2.2.2.1.1.1.2.2.2.5. A SPECIAL EXPLANATION OF HOW GENEROSITY PRODUCES HAPPINESS IN BODHISATTVAS
2.2.2.1.1.1.2.2.2.5.1. The actual explanation
2.2.2.1.1.1.2.2.2.5.2. Even if suffering arises, it is transformed into a cause for the further benefit of others

2.2.2.1.1.1.2.2.2.5.1. THE ACTUAL EXPLANATION

If the joy the heirs of the victors feel
Upon hearing "Please give to me"
Cannot be matched by the joy of the sages entering peace,
What need to mention their joy of giving everything? (1.14)

One may wonder, "What kind of joy do the bodhisattvas experience when they bring satisfaction to someone who has asked them for something?" If several beggars were to come to the door of a bodhisattva and cry out, "Please give this to me," asking for whatever enjoyments they desired, when the bodhisattvas first hear this cry they will first wonder, "Are they asking me or someone else?" When they realize it is they who are being asked, these heirs of the victorious ones experience a joy that cannot be rivaled even by the joy of the hearer and solitary realizer arhats when those sages enter into the pacification of all suffering. Therefore, what need is there to speak of the even greater joy and satisfaction that the bodhisattvas experience when they benefit others by giving away all inner and outer things?

2.2.2.1.1.1.2.2.2.5.2. EVEN IF SUFFERING ARISES, IT IS
TRANSFORMED INTO A CAUSE FOR THE FURTHER BENEFIT
OF OTHERS

> The suffering they experience when cutting off and giving their
> flesh
> Brings the sufferings of others in the hells and so forth
> Directly to the bodhisattvas' minds.
> They then swiftly apply themselves to ending that suffering. (1.15)

Do the bodhisattvas physically suffer when give their flesh and so forth away? There are two types of bodhisattvas: those without attachment and those with attachment. As to the first, it is impossible for them to experience suffering due to cutting off their own flesh, because they have realized that all phenomena are devoid of an inherent nature. Therefore their experience is just like the experience of someone cutting inanimate matter. In relation to this, the sūtra called the *Concentration of the Space Treasury (Namkha Dzö kyi Ting-nge Dzin/nam mkha' mdzod kyi ting nge 'dzin)* says:

> It is like this: If there were a large forest of sala trees to which a few people came and cut down one tree, the remaining trees would not think, "They cut that tree down; they did not cut me down!" They would have no attachment or anger. The patience of the bodhisattvas is like that. It is completely pure, supreme, and equal to space.

Therefore, noble beings have no suffering due to cutting off their flesh.

As for bodhisattvas with attachment, the suffering they experience in their body from cutting off and giving away their flesh causes them to infer, from their own torment, the incredibly great physical sufferings of other sentient beings in the three lower realms—the hells and so forth. Through fully experiencing their own suffering, they see that the sufferings of the lower realms are a thousand times more intense and intolerable. The bodhisattvas, therefore, do not view the suffering that arises from cutting off their flesh as merely suffering alone. Rather, in order to put an end to the continuum of suffering of the hells and so forth, they swiftly apply themselves to attain great enlightenment.

2.2.2.1.1.1.2.2.3. THE DIFFERENCE BETWEEN MUNDANE AND TRANSCENDENT GENEROSITY
2.2.2.1.1.1.2.2.3.1. Transcendent generosity
2.2.2.1.1.1.2.2.3.2. Mundane generosity

2.2.2.1.1.1.2.2.3.1. TRANSCENDENT GENEROSITY

Generosity that is empty of gift, recipient, and giver
Is known as a transcendent perfection. (1.16ab)

The term "perfection" is derived from words that mean "gone to the other shore."[165] What other shore does one travel to through generosity? The "other shore" is the state of buddhahood, in which the two obscurations are relinquished. This relinquishment is found on the "other shore" of saṃsāra.

If a given virtue can help one to travel to this other shore, it is called a "perfection." The actual quality that makes a virtue a perfection is the perfection of supreme knowledge, because one travels to the other shore through dedicating the generosity and so on that have been embraced by supreme knowledge to enlightenment. Supreme knowledge turns generosity and so on into "perfections."

Therefore, generosity that is empty of gift, recipient, and giver is taught to be a transcendent perfection in the *Lady Transcendent Conqueror* sūtras, because such generosity does not entail reification of the three spheres.

2.2.2.1.1.1.2.2.3.2. MUNDANE GENEROSITY

Generosity in which attachment to those three arises
Is taught to be a mundane perfection. (1.16cd)

Generosity in which there arises attachment to the gift, giver, and recipient, or in other words, generosity in which those three are observed, is taught to be a mundane perfection because observing things in that way is the view of the relative truth.

2.2.2.1.1.1.3. A CONCLUDING SUMMARY DESCRIBING THE GROUND'S QUALITIES

In this way they excellently abide in the mind of the heirs of the
victorious ones.
On the genuine support, they discover a beautiful light.
This joy is just like the water crystal jewel:
Completely dispelling the thick darkness, it is victorious. (1.17)

This completes the first bodhichitta generation from the *Entrance to the Middle Way*.

This verse praises the wisdom qualities of the first ground. The bodhisattvas on this ground excellently abide in the mind of the heirs of the victorious ones, who have attained all of the qualities described above. On the genuine support of relative bodhichitta, they discover the beautiful light of ultimate bodhichitta. This discovery is supremely joyful, and this ground, *Supreme Joy*, is like a full moon made from the water crystal jewel: just as the latter dispels darkness, this ground is victorious in completely dispelling the thick darkness of one's own individual obscurations.

This completes the explanation of the first bodhichitta generation, *Supreme Joy*, from the *Entrance to the Middle Way*.

⁞ Ground Two: The Stainless

2.2.2.1.1.2. THE EXPLANATION OF THE STAINLESS *(Nirmala, Drima Mepa/dri ma med pa)*
2.2.2.1.1.2.1. The brief teaching on its essence through explaining its pure discipline
2.2.2.1.1.2.2. The supplementary explanation of the praise to discipline
2.2.2.1.1.2.3. The summary that describes the precise meaning, ripening, and qualities of the ground

2.2.2.1.1.2.1. THE BRIEF TEACHING ON ITS ESSENCE THROUGH EXPLAINING ITS PURE DISCIPLINE
2.2.2.1.1.2.1.1. The actual explanation
2.2.2.1.1.2.1.2. The extensive explanation of how the discipline on this ground is pure

2.2.2.1.1.2.1.1. THE ACTUAL EXPLANATION

> Since they have the abundant qualities of discipline,
> They refrain from faulty discipline even in their dreams. (2.1ab)

As explained before, the term "ground" denotes the essence of wisdom, whose very nature is indivisible and singular. However, the differences of the grounds are clearly differentiated by the perfections that become supreme on them. The second ground, for instance, is presented due to the perfection of discipline *(shīla, tsultrim/tsul khrims)* becoming supreme.

Bodhisattvas abiding on this ground have the abundant qualities of this ground's discipline. Therefore, they refrain from faulty discipline even in their dreams. The word "even" in the second line indicates that one need not mention their conduct during waking life. The precise meaning *(nge-tsig/nges tshig)* of discipline is as follows: it is called "discipline" because through it one does not engage in the mental afflictions, one does not accumulate the misdeeds that result from mental afflictions, and, due to that, one's mind is satisfied and happy. Therefore, it is an object of reliance for genuine beings.

The essence of discipline is to relinquish the seven factors to be relinquished, and to possess the mind of the three virtues.[166] This, in short, is the tenfold path of virtue.

2.2.2.1.1.2.1.2.1.2. THE EXTENSIVE EXPLANATION OF HOW THE DISCIPLINE ON THIS GROUND IS PURE
2.2.2.1.1.2.1.2.1. The purity due to relinquishing nonvirtue
2.2.2.1.1.2.1.2.2. The purity of discipline due to supreme knowledge

2.2.2.1.1.2.1.2.1. THE PURITY DUE TO RELINQUISHING NONVIRTUE
2.2.2.1.1.2.1.2.1.1. The purity due to relinquishing the ten nonvirtues
2.2.2.1.1.2.1.2.1.2. How it is purer than the first ground
2.2.2.1.1.2.1.2.1.3. The illustration of its purity by way of example

2.2.2.1.1.2.1.2.1.1. THE PURITY DUE TO RELINQUISHING THE TEN NONVIRTUES

Because the movements of their body, speech, and mind are pure, They accumulate the actions of the genuine ones' tenfold path. (2.1cd)

Since the discordant stains of the movements of their body, speech, and mind have been purified, the bodhisattvas on this second ground naturally accumulate the actions of the tenfold path of the noble ones.[167]

2.2.2.1.1.2.1.2.1.2. HOW IT IS PURER THAN THE FIRST GROUND

This virtuous path in its tenfold aspect, though practiced before, Here becomes supreme and extremely pure. (2.2ab)

Do bodhisattvas who have generated the first level of bodhichitta also generate these ten virtuous paths? Indeed they do, but this virtuous path, in its tenfold aspect, becomes supreme and extremely pure in a bodhisattva who abides on the ground of the second level of bodhichitta. It is not this way for bodhisattvas who abide on the first bodhichitta level, because those bodhisattvas are devoid of the conduct that continually and without fail familiarizes them with the supreme knowledge that does not observe even discipline [as being truly existent].

2.2.2.1.1.2.1.2.1.3. THE ILLUSTRATION OF ITS PURITY BY WAY OF EXAMPLE

> Like an autumn moon, they are always pure
> And beautified by peaceful light. (2.2cd)

Just like an autumn moon unhindered by clouds, these bodhisattvas, who are pure, without the stains of faulty discipline, always control their sense faculties. Thus they are peaceful, like a vividly radiant light that beautifies their pure discipline.

2.2.2.1.1.2.1.2.2. THE PURITY OF DISCIPLINE DUE TO SUPREME KNOWLEDGE

2.2.2.1.1.2.1.2.2.1. If one has the view of real things, one's discipline is impure

2.2.2.1.1.2.1.2.2.2. The teaching on how the discipline of the victors' heirs is free of clinging to things

2.2.2.1.1.2.1.2.2.1. IF ONE HAS THE VIEW OF REAL THINGS, ONE'S DISCIPLINE IS IMPURE

> But if they viewed themselves as pure practitioners of discipline,
> For that reason their discipline would not be pure at all. (2.3ab)

If the persons who were guarding discipline viewed themselves as practitioners possessing a nature of pure discipline, for that very reason their discipline would not be pure at all, because they would have the stain of pretentious discipline.

2.2.2.1.1.2.1.2.2.2. THE TEACHING ON HOW THE DISCIPLINE OF THE VICTORS' HEIRS IS FREE OF CLINGING TO THINGS

> Therefore, these bodhisattvas are always perfectly free
> Of the movement of dualistic mind toward the three
>   spheres. (2.3cd)

Therefore, since their discipline is pure, the heirs of the victorious ones who abide on *The Stainless* are always perfectly free of the movement of the dualistic mind, which clings to things and nonthings, along with its movement toward the three spheres—the object toward which the discipline is aimed, the discipline itself, and the person who performs the discipline by refraining from a negative action.

2.2.2.1.1.2.2. THE SUPPLEMENTARY EXPLANATION OF THE PRAISE TO DISCIPLINE
2.2.2.1.1.2.2.1. The general praise of discipline
2.2.2.1.1.2.2.2. The particular praise of the discipline of bodhisattvas
2.2.2.1.1.2.2.3. The classifications of mundane and transcendent discipline

2.2.2.1.1.2.2.1. THE GENERAL PRAISE OF DISCIPLINE
2.2.2.1.1.2.2.1.1. The shortcomings of faulty discipline
2.2.2.1.1.2.2.1.2. The excellent qualities of discipline

2.2.2.1.1.2.2.1.1. THE SHORTCOMINGS OF FAULTY DISCIPLINE
2.2.2.1.1.2.2.1.1.1. How the results of generosity will be exhausted
2.2.2.1.1.2.2.1.1.2. The fault of not being able to gain liberation from the lower realms

2.2.2.1.1.2.2.1.1.1. HOW THE RESULTS OF GENEROSITY WILL BE EXHAUSTED
2.2.2.1.1.2.2.1.1.1.1. How one falls to the lower realms
2.2.2.1.1.2.2.1.1.1.2. The actual teaching on how the results of generosity will be exhausted

2.2.2.1.1.2.2.1.1.1.1. HOW ONE FALLS TO THE LOWER REALMS

> Having enjoyments, yet in the lower realms,
> Comes about due to the degeneration of the legs of discipline.
> (2.4ab)

It is taught that discipline yields greater results than generosity and is the support for all good qualities. This is so because if someone practices generosity while keeping good discipline, they will experience a wealth of enjoyments as a god or human. However, if one gives in a way that does not harmonize with discipline, one will receive enjoyments, yet they will be experienced in the lower realms, in a birth as a nāga and so on. This comes about due to the degeneration of the legs of discipline.

2.2.2.1.1.2.2.1.1.1.2. THE ACTUAL TEACHING ON HOW THE RESULTS OF GENEROSITY WILL BE EXHAUSTED

> **When both capital and interest become exhausted,**
> **One will not receive enjoyments again. (2.4cd)**

Will someone in the lower realms who has given without discipline still experience a continual stream of the results of their generosity? No, they will not. When the capital, the results of the generosity that they practiced in a god or human body, and the interest, the seed of generosity, become exhausted, they will not enjoy an uninterrupted stream of enjoyments as the result of generosity again. For, it is extremely rare for a being born in the lower realms to develop an aspiration towards virtuous activity.

2.2.2.1.1.2.2.1.1.2. THE FAULT OF NOT BEING ABLE TO GAIN LIBERATION FROM THE LOWER REALMS

> **At the time when one has freedom and favorable conditions,**
> **If one does not protect oneself,**
> **One will later fall into an abyss deprived of freedom.**
> **Who will lift one up from that state then? (2.5)**

Without discipline, not only will one not obtain enjoyments in the future, it will also be extremely difficult to gain liberation from the lower realms. At the time when one has the freedoms and advantages [of a precious human birth], one is like a warrior free from fear in a safe land. As a god or human, one does not need to depend upon others, but has the freedom and favorable conditions needed to practice virtue.

If beings in these situations do not protect themselves from the lower realms through the excellent conduct of discipline and so on, they will become like warriors bound by iron chains and cast away into mountain ravines: they will fall into the abyss of the lower realms. There they will be deprived of freedom and subject to karma and mental afflictions. Who will lift them out of the lower realms then? No one will, because it is impossible to gain freedom from the prison of negative karma unless the results of that karma have been exhausted. Furthermore, beings of the lower realms are not inclined to exert themselves in methods for attaining liberation. Even if one manages to take a human birth, one's life will be short, and one will not accumulate the karma of the pleasant existences.

2.2.2.1.1.2.2.1.2. THE EXCELLENT QUALITIES OF DISCIPLINE
2.2.2.1.1.2.2.1.2.1. The reason for the Buddha's teaching discipline after generosity
2.2.2.1.1.2.2.1.2.2. Discipline is the support for all good qualities
2.2.2.1.1.2.2.1.2.3. Discipline is the cause of the higher realms and the definite good for both ordinary and noble beings

2.2.2.1.1.2.2.1.2.1. THE REASON FOR THE BUDDHA'S TEACHING DISCIPLINE AFTER GENEROSITY

> **Therefore, the Victorious One followed his teaching on**
> **generosity**
> **With the teaching on discipline. (2.6ab)**

Faulty discipline produces many undesirables, such as meager results arising from generosity. Therefore, because discipline is what causes the results of generosity to flourish, the Victorious One followed his teachings on generosity with teachings in praise of discipline.

2.2.2.1.1.2.2.1.2.2. DISCIPLINE IS THE SUPPORT FOR ALL GOOD QUALITIES

> **By growing the seeds of qualities on the field of discipline,**
> **The enjoyment of their fruits will never cease. (2.6cd)**

Since discipline is the support for all good qualities, if on its field one plants the seeds of qualities (generosity and so on), when those seeds grow, the enjoyment of the fruits they bear will never cease.

2.2.2.1.1.2.2.1.2.3. DISCIPLINE IS THE CAUSE OF THE HIGHER REALMS AND THE DEFINITE GOOD FOR BOTH ORDINARY AND NOBLE BEINGS

> **For ordinary beings, those born of the victors' speech,**
> **Those set on solitary enlightenment,**

And heirs of the victors, the cause of definite goodness
And the higher realms is none other than discipline. (2.7)

For ordinary beings, the hearers born of the victors' speech, the solitary realizers set on their own enlightenment, and the bodhisattva heirs of the victorious ones, the liberation of definite goodness and the happiness of saṃsāra that comprises the higher realms are both, in this context of praising discipline as foremost, caused by discipline, the main quality of the second bodhisattva ground. There is no quality superior to discipline, because discipline is supreme among all qualities in terms of being the cause of [definite goodness and the higher realms].

2.2.2.1.1.2.2.2. THE PARTICULAR PRAISE OF THE DISCIPLINE OF BODHISATTVAS

Just as an ocean and a corpse do not remain together,
And just as something auspicious and inauspicious cannot
  coexist,
The great being who masters discipline
Does not remain together with depraved ethics. (2.8)

A great ocean cannot co-abide with a corpse,[168] and something auspicious cannot also be something inauspicious. In the same way, the great being of this ground, who has mastered the excellent qualities of discipline explained above, will not remain together with depraved ethics.

2.2.2.1.1.2.2.3. THE CLASSIFICATIONS OF MUNDANE AND TRANSCENDENT DISCIPLINE

If discipline involves observing the three spheres—
The relinquisher, the thing relinquished, and the being toward
  whom the relinquishing is performed—
That discipline is taught as a mundane perfection.
Discipline empty of attachment to those three is transcendent.
  (2.9)

It was taught in the sūtras that if discipline involves observing the three spheres—the individual doing the relinquishing, the thing relinquished, and the sentient being with respect to whom the relinquishing takes place—that discipline will be a mundane perfection. The discipline that has been embraced by supreme knowledge and is therefore empty of attachment to the three spheres is known as a transcendent perfection.

2.2.2.1.1.2.3. THE SUMMARY THAT DESCRIBES THE PRECISE MEANING, RIPENING, AND QUALITIES OF THE GROUND

> These heirs of the Victor, born of the moon, are not of cyclic
>   existence, yet they are the glory of cyclic existence.
> They are immaculate; this stainless ground,
> Like the light of an autumn moon,
> Dispels agony from the minds of beings. (2.10)

This completes the second bodhichitta generation from the *Entrance to the Middle Way*.

The heirs of the victorious ones on this bodhisattva ground are born of the moon. Since they are not within the domain of saṃsāra, they are not of cyclic existence *(sipa/srid pa)*, yet because of their abundant qualities they possess the causes for taking birth as the sovereigns of all four continents. Therefore, they are the glory of cyclic existence. They are immaculate, free of the stains of faulty discipline. This stainlessness is like the light of an autumn moon: just as it dispels the agony of beings, so the bodhisattva dispels the agony of faulty discipline from the minds of beings.

This completes the explanation of the second bodhichitta generation, known as *The Stainless*, from the *Entrance to the Middle Way*.

⋮ Ground Three: The Luminous

2.2.2.1.1.3. THE EXPLANATION OF THE LUMINOUS *(Prabhākari, Ö Jepa/'od byed pa)*

2.2.2.1.1.3.1. The brief teaching on the essence of the ground, the basis of its features

2.2.2.1.1.3.2. The extensive explanation of the features or qualities of the ground

2.2.2.1.1.3.3. The summary stating the qualities of the ground

2.2.2.1.1.3.1. THE BRIEF TEACHING ON THE ESSENCE OF THE GROUND, THE BASIS OF ITS FEATURES

> **Since the light of the fire that burns**
> **All the kindling of knowable objects arises**
> **On this third ground, it is called *The Luminous*.**
> **At that time, a brilliance like the sun or like copper dawns**
> **in the heirs of the sugatas. (3.1)**

Here the fire or light of wisdom that burns all the kindling of knowable objects without exception arises. Therefore this ground, where the third level of bodhichitta is generated, is called *The Luminous*, because at that time the brilliance of the wisdom of the heirs of the sugatas is like the rising sun or like copper.

2.2.2.1.1.3.2. THE EXTENSIVE EXPLANATION OF THE FEATURES OR QUALITIES OF THE GROUND

2.2.2.1.1.3.2.1. The qualities of the perfection of patience

2.2.2.1.1.3.2.2. The other qualities of relinquishment, realization, and activity

2.2.2.1.1.3.2.3. The support for this perfection, its corresponding accumulation, and its result

2.2.2.1.1.3.2.1. THE QUALITIES OF THE PERFECTION OF PATIENCE
2.2.2.1.1.3.2.1.1. How patience is foremost on this ground
2.2.2.1.1.3.2.1.2. The supplementary praise to patience
2.2.2.1.1.3.2.1.3. The classifications of transcendent and mundane patience

2.2.2.1.1.3.2.1.1. HOW PATIENCE IS FOREMOST ON THIS GROUND
2.2.2.1.1.3.2.1.1.1. Patience by way of compassion
2.2.2.1.1.3.2.1.1.2. Patience by way of supreme knowledge

2.2.2.1.1.3.2.1.1.1. PATIENCE BY WAY OF COMPASSION

> If someone, through unwarranted anger,
> Cut the flesh and bones from the body of a bodhisattva
> For a long time, ounce by ounce,
> The bodhisattva would engender patience, especially for the one
>   who is cutting. (3.2)

There is no time during which these bodhisattvas become angry, because they possess the excellent qualities that have been explained above, and because it is impossible for them to inflict harm on others through the actions of their three gates. When sustaining their altruistic attitude they are not motivated by any of the nine forms of tormented mind.[169] Therefore, if someone who was deeply agitated cut flesh and bones from the body of a bodhisattva, who is not an appropriate object of anger, for a long time, and moreover cut away methodically, ounce by ounce, the bodhisattva would still engender patience *(kṣhānti, zöpa/bzod pa)*, especially for the one who is cutting, because bodhisattvas pay close attention to the suffering of beings who possess the karma of negative actions.

2.2.2.1.1.3.2.1.1.2. PATIENCE BY WAY OF SUPREME KNOWLEDGE

> For bodhisattvas who see selflessness,
> All phenomena—what is cut, the cutter, the time of the cutting,
>   the method of cutting, and so on—
> Are seen to be a like a reflection.
> Therefore they have patience. (3.3)

Not only do the bodhisattvas have the patience described above, for a bodhisattva who sees all phenomena as selfless, the flesh and bones that are cut, along with the cutter, the time of the cutting, and the weapon used to do the cutting are met with patience. Why? Because the bodhisattvas see all phenomena of the three spheres to be like reflections—free of self and entities connected to the self and free of inherent nature. For this reason, the bodhisattvas have patience.

2.2.2.1.1.3.2.1.2. THE SUPPLEMENTARY PRAISE TO PATIENCE
2.2.2.1.1.3.2.1.2.1. The shortcomings of anger
2.2.2.1.1.3.2.1.2.2. The benefits of patience
2.2.2.1.1.3.2.1.2.3. The instruction to therefore relinquish anger and cultivate patience

2.2.2.1.1.3.2.1.2.1. THE SHORTCOMINGS OF ANGER
2.2.2.1.1.3.2.1.2.1.1. Anger is pointless in this world
2.2.2.1.1.3.2.1.2.1.2. Anger is contradictory to the aims of the next world
2.2.2.1.1.3.2.1.2.1.3. Further shortcomings connected to this life and the next

2.2.2.1.1.3.2.1.2.1.1. ANGER IS POINTLESS IN THIS WORLD

If you get angry at someone who does you harm,
Does your anger reverse what has already been done?
Therefore, anger is definitely pointless in this life
And is contradictory to one's aims in future lives as well. (3.4)

Patience is not only something to be practiced by bodhisattvas, it is also a most appropriate practice for other beings. If one gets angry at another person who has done one harm, does the anger toward them reverse the harm already done, such as the wounds on one's body? No, it does not. Therefore, being resentful and angry toward someone who does one harm is definitely pointless in this life, because the harmful action has already been committed. Not only that, if one holds on to anger towards someone who does one harm, this will also be contradictory to the aim of accomplishing happiness for future lives, because the cause of engendering anger ripens into unpleasant results.

2.2.2.I.I.3.2.I.2.I.2.I.2. ANGER IS CONTRADICTORY TO THE AIMS
OF THE NEXT WORLD
2.2.2.I.I.3.2.I.2.I.2.I.2.I. Anger ripens into unpleasant results
2.2.2.I.I.3.2.I.2.I.2.I.2.2. Anger is the cause for the exhaustion of long-
accumulated merit

2.2.2.I.I.3.2.I.2.I.2.I.2.I. ANGER RIPENS INTO UNPLEASANT RESULTS

> Patience is the very thing that is asserted
> To exhaust the results of previously committed nonvirtuous
> actions.
> Since harming and being angry toward others causes them
> suffering,
> Why lead yourself to the lower realms by planting such
> a seed? (3.5)

It is reasonable to have patience toward an enemy who stabs you with a
sharp weapon. [For the stabbing is undoubtedly a result of your own past
actions]—the result of one's own previous nonvirtuous actions of killing ripen as rebirth in the lower realms, and they also ripen in a causally
concordant way in this life. It is asserted that patience toward these situations is the very thing that exhausts such karmic results. Since harming
and being angry at another who has caused you harm make them suffer in
turn, if instead of cultivating patience toward the aggressor one responds
by harming them more, one plants the seed for bringing harm again upon
oneself. This will lead one to the lower realms. Why would one do that?
That would not be reasonable.

Just as it is reasonable to have patience toward a doctor who uses sharp
instruments in order to heal one's illnesses by removing the source of a
wound, it is also reasonable to cultivate patience toward the suffering that
purifies negative actions.

2.2.2.I.I.3.2.I.2.I.2.I.2.2. ANGER IS THE CAUSE FOR THE EXHAUSTION
OF LONG-ACCUMULATED MERIT

> Anger toward heirs of the victorious ones
> Destroys, in a single instant, the merit accumulated
> Through generosity and discipline during a hundred eons.
> Therefore, there is no greater misdeed than impatience. (3.6)

Not only does impatience ripen into suffering, it also causes the exhaustion of the roots of virtue one has accumulated for a very long time. If a bodhisattva, governed by mental afflictions, imputes a fault that is either true or false upon another bodhisattva, then, regardless of whether they knew that other person was a bodhisattva or not, this single instant of angry thinking will, right then and there, destroy the merit they had accumulated through generosity and discipline during a hundred eons. Therefore there is no greater misdeed than impatience, because impatience produces intense suffering and does great harm to virtue.

2.2.2.1.1.3.2.1.2.1.3. FURTHER SHORTCOMINGS CONNECTED TO THIS LIFE AND THE NEXT

Impatience makes one unattractive and casts one in bad
company.
It steals the intelligence that distinguishes between proper
and improper discipline,
And quickly propels one to the lower realms. (3.7abc)

If one loses patience yet does not have the ability to harm others, it will only be oneself who is defeated. However, if one is capable of harming others, one destroys both oneself and others. Impatience makes one unattractive—it produces tight wrinkles that come from frowning and other undesirable appearances. It casts one in bad company[170] because of one's engaging in behavior such as appropriating weapons.

Because of being submerged in anger, one becomes ignorant regarding what to adopt or reject. Impatience steals away the intelligence that distinguishes between proper and improper discipline. All of these are results of impatience that are observable in this life. When one's life force is exhausted, the karma of one's impatience will quickly propel one to the lower realms.

2.2.2.1.1.3.2.1.2.2. THE BENEFITS OF PATIENCE

Patience produces the opposite qualities to those just
explained— (3.7d)
Patience makes one beautiful, connects one with genuine
beings,
And gives one skill in distinguishing between

What is proper and improper.
Later, one will take birth as a god or human and see the
exhaustion of misdeeds. (3.8)

If impatience entails such faults, then what are the benefits of patience?
Patience produces the qualities opposite to those just explained, the unattractive form and others. What specifically are these qualities? For this life,
patience makes one appear beautiful the moment one is beheld by others,
causing others to have faith in one. Through not returning harm for harm
done, one will become connected with genuine beings. Through recognizing the genuineness of these beings, one will also be able to cause others
to have reverence and respect for them. One will become skilled in distinguishing between what ways are proper and what ways are improper. After
this life, one will take birth as a god or human and see the increase of one's
virtue and the exhaustion of one's misdeeds.

2.2.2.1.1.3.2.1.2.3. THE INSTRUCTION TO THEREFORE
RELINQUISH ANGER AND CULTIVATE PATIENCE

Ordinary beings and heirs of the victors,
Recognizing the faults of anger and the benefits of patience,
Should relinquish impatience and always quickly hold to
The patience praised by the noble ones. (3.9)

Ordinary beings and heirs of the victorious ones, recognizing the faults
of anger and the benefits of patience, should relinquish impatience and
always quickly hold to the patience praised by the noble ones.

2.2.2.1.1.3.2.1.3. THE CLASSIFICATIONS OF TRANSCENDENT
AND MUNDANE PATIENCE

Even if one's patience is dedicated to the enlightenment of
perfect buddhahood,
If it entails observation of the three spheres, it is a mundane
perfection.
If it is free from such observation, the Buddha has taught
Such patience to be a transcendent perfection. (3.10)

Even if one's patience is dedicated to the enlightenment of perfect buddhahood, if it entails observation of the three spheres—what is tolerated,
the person tolerating, and the sentient being toward whom the tolerance
is engendered—that perfection is a mundane perfection of patience. If it
is free from observation of the three spheres, the Buddha has taught such
patience to be a transcendent perfection.

2.2.2.1.1.3.2.2. THE OTHER QUALITIES OF RELINQUISHMENT, REALIZATION, AND ACTIVITY

> **On this ground, the bodhisattvas gain the concentrations and
>   higher cognitions,
> And completely exhaust attachment and aggression.
> They also become capable of continually
> Conquering worldly attachment toward desirables. (3.11)**

On this third ground, as these heirs of the victorious ones purify the perfection of patience, they also gain the four concentrations,[171] the four
absorptions of the formless realm,[172] the four limitless ones,[173] and the five
higher cognitions.[174] All of these are qualities of realization. Through their
realization of unmoving interdependence and the nondisintegration [of
interdependence],[175] they completely exhaust attachment, aggression, and
bewilderment. These are qualities of relinquishment. Due to the ripening
of the karma of the bodhisattvas on this ground, they are capable of taking birth as the ruler of the gods, yet they continually conquer the mundane attachment of craving the desirables, the sense pleasures. Thus they
gain the ability to extract themselves from the desire realm.

2.2.2.1.1.3.2.3. THE SUPPORT FOR THIS PERFECTION, ITS CORRESPONDING ACCUMULATION, AND ITS RESULT

> **The Sugata primarily taught
> The three dharmas of generosity and so on to laypeople.
> These three accomplish the accumulation of merit
> And are the causes for the buddhas' form kāyas. (3.12)**

At this time Chandrakīrti clearly describes the third ground's special support, the accumulation to which it corresponds, and the presentation of

its result. All bodhisattvas possess the support for the practices of all six perfections, yet out of the two categories of laypeople and monastics, the Sugata primarily taught the three dharmas of generosity and so on[176] to laypeople by praising them as something in which they should train. He did so because these three are easier to practice than the others.

For monastics, the Buddha praised diligence, concentration, and supreme knowledge as fields of training, not because the earlier perfections are not practiced, but because they will be brought to full completion simply as an incidental benefit of practicing the latter three. Of the two causes for buddhahood, the two accumulations, the accumulation of merit is accomplished by the first three perfections, and the accumulation of wisdom is accomplished by concentration and supreme knowledge. Diligence is a cause for both accumulations. The accumulation of merit serves as the cause for the supreme and inconceivable form kāyas of the buddhas, which are marked by one hundred merits.[177] The cause for the dharmakāya is the accumulation of wisdom.

2.2.2.1.1.3.3. The summary stating the qualities of the ground

> Here the heirs of the victors who dwell in the sun of
>   *The Luminous*
> First perfectly dispel their own darkness
> And then earnestly long to conquer the darkness of beings.
> Though on this ground they are very sharp, they do not get
>   angry. (3.13)

This completes the third bodhichitta generation from the *Entrance to the Middle Way.*

Here the heirs of the victorious ones abide on *The Luminous*, whose brilliance is like that of a sun disc. First, they perfectly dispel their own darkness, ignorance in their own mindstream, while it is arising. Then, they earnestly long to conquer the darkness of the obstructions that prevent beings from attaining the third ground. Through dispelling the darkness of faults that obscures this ground's qualities, the bodhisattvas' supreme knowledge becomes very sharp, like the rays of the sun. Nevertheless, they do not get angry at beings who have faults, because they have cultivated great patience and because their mindstreams have been moistened by compassion.

This concludes the explanation of the third bodhichitta generation, *The Luminous*, from the *Entrance to the Middle Way*.

⦙ Ground Four: The Radiant

2.2.2.1.1.4. THE EXPLANATION OF THE RADIANT *(Archiṣmati,*
Ö Trowa/'od 'phro ba)
2.2.2.1.1.4.1. The concise teaching on its essence by way of the
preeminence of diligence
2.2.2.1.1.4.2. The teaching on the name, meaning, and qualities of
the ground

2.2.2.1.1.4.1. THE CONCISE TEACHING ON ITS ESSENCE BY WAY OF THE PREEMINENCE OF DILIGENCE

> All good qualities without exception follow after diligence,
> The cause of the accumulations of both merit and knowledge.
> The ground on which diligence blazes
> Is the fourth, *The Radiant.* (4.1)

This verse describes the fourth bodhichitta generation, showing how, over and above the first three perfections, diligence *(vīrya, tsöndrü/brtson 'grus)* is preeminent on this ground. All good qualities without exception, whether mundane or transcendent, follow after diligence and do not arise without it, because if one has no delight in virtuous activity, it is impossible to engage in generosity and the other virtues. Furthermore, if one has such delight, one will attain the virtuous qualities one has not attained while expanding those one has already attained. Since diligence is the cause for the accumulations of both merit and knowledge,[178] the ground on which diligence blazes and becomes preeminent is the fourth bodhisattva ground, the one called *The Radiant.*

2.2.2.1.1.4.2. THE TEACHING ON THE NAME, MEANING, AND QUALITIES OF THE GROUND
2.2.2.1.1.4.2.1. The name and meaning of the qualities of realization
2.2.2.1.1.4.2.2. The teaching on the qualities of relinquishment

2.2.2.1.1.4.2.1. THE NAME AND MEANING OF THE QUALITIES OF REALIZATION

> On this ground, for the children of the Sugata
> There dawns a brilliance surpassing the glow of copper,
> Born from especially cultivating the factors of perfect enlightenment. (4.2abc)

On this, the fourth, ground, for the children of the Sugata there dawns the brilliance of wisdom that surpasses the glow of copper, an example that was explained previously[179] and is used again here. This wisdom is born from especially cultivating the dharmas of the thirty-seven factors of perfect enlightenment.[180] Therefore, since on this ground light from the fire of wisdom radiates, it is called *The Radiant*.

2.2.2.1.1.4.2.2. THE TEACHING ON THE QUALITIES OF RELINQUISHMENT

> Everything connected with the views of "me" and "mine" is completely exhausted. (4.2d)

This completes the fourth bodhichitta generation from *The Entrance to the Middle Way*.

On this ground, not only does wisdom arise due to cultivating the factors of enlightenment, additionally, all clinging to concepts of a creator as an external person—concepts that are connected to the views of "me" and "mine" (the self and entities connected to the self)—are completely exhausted.

This completes the explanation of the fourth bodhichitta generation, *The Radiant*, from the *Entrance to the Middle Way*.

⋮ Ground Five: Difficult to Overcome

2.2.2.1.1.5. The Explanation of Difficult to Overcome
(Sudurjayā, Jang Kawa/sbyang dka' ba)
2.2.2.1.1.5.1. The name of the ground and its meaning
2.2.2.1.1.5.2. The teaching on the ground's qualities

2.2.2.1.1.5.1. THE NAME OF THE GROUND AND ITS MEANING

The great beings on the ground *Difficult to Overcome*
Cannot be defeated by any of the māras. (5.1ab)

The great bodhisattva being that abides on this ground called *Difficult to Overcome* cannot be defeated by any of the devaputra māras[181] who live in the worldly realms. Therefore, what need to speak of whether they obey such māras? For that reason, this ground is given the name *Difficult to Overcome.*

2.2.2.1.1.5.2. THE TEACHING ON THE GROUND'S QUALITIES

Their concentration becomes preeminent, and their excellent intelligence
Becomes very skilled at thoroughly examining the nature of the truths. (5.1cd)

This completes the fifth bodhichitta generation from the *Entrance to the Middle Way.*

For bodhisattvas who abide on this ground, concentration *(dhyāna, samten/bsam gtan)*, from among the ten perfections, is preeminent. Their intelligence becomes excellent, because they attain great skill in examining the nature of the noble truths with precise and thorough supreme knowledge.

The four noble truths can be presented as two sets of cause and result: the afflictive set (what is to be relinquished), with the origin as the cause and suffering as the result, and the pure set (what is to be adopted), with the path as the cause and cessation as the result. However, these four truths can also be subsumed within the two truths of ultimate and relative. The truths of suffering, origin, and the path are relative truth, because they all entail the changes of conditioned phenomena at certain stages. The truth of cessation does not entail those changes, and therefore it is ultimate truth.

The above [paragraph] on how the four truths fit into the two truths, however, only represents the presentation of slight analysis from the perspective of others. Under thorough analysis, none of the four truths, which functionally depend on the other truths for their designation as truths, are suitable as ultimate truth. They are not truly established as either causes or results.

Other enumerations of truths can correlate with the two truths in a similar way.[182]

In the Ṭīkā, [Karmapa Mikyö Dorje] teaches that the assertion that the dharmadhātu is necessarily not the truth of cessation is untenable, and that the assertion that dharmatā is the truth of cessation is also untenable.

This completes the explanation of the fifth bodhichitta generation, *Difficult to Overcome*, from the *Entrance to the Middle Way*.

: Ground Six: The Manifest

2.2.2.1.1.6. The explanation of The Manifest (*Abhimukhi, Ngön du Gyurpa/mngon du gyur pa*)
2.2.2.1.1.6.1. The brief teaching on the essence of the ground, the perceiving subject
2.2.2.1.1.6.2. The extensive explanation of emptiness, the object
2.2.2.1.1.6.3. The concluding summary by way of stating the qualities of the ground

2.2.2.1.1.6.1. The brief teaching on the essence of the ground, the perceiving subject
2.2.2.1.1.6.1.1. The ground itself
2.2.2.1.1.6.1.2. The description of the greatness of the perfection of supreme knowledge, the ground's quality

2.2.2.1.1.6.1.1. The ground itself

> On *The Approach*, their minds abide in equipoise
> And they approach the qualities of perfect buddhahood.
> They see the suchness of dependent arising's mere conditionality,
> And, through abiding in supreme knowledge, will attain
>   cessation. (6.1)

The following explanation is from the perspective of the sixth bodhichitta generation. Because the bodhisattvas attained the completely pure perfection of concentration on the fifth ground, on the sixth ground, *The Approach*, their minds abide in equipoise. Through having focused on the truth of the path on the fifth ground, they closely approach the qualities of perfect buddhahood, the ten powers and so on. Therefore, this ground is also called *The Manifest*.

They see the profound suchness of phenomena's dependent arising through mere conditionality. The bodhisattvas abiding on this ground, through abiding in the completely pure perfection of supreme knowledge *(prajñā, sherab/shes rab)*, will attain the cessation that is the pacification of all elaborations and characteristics. This was not the case before, because supreme knowledge was not preeminent.

2.2.2.1.1.6.1.2. THE STATEMENT OF THE GREATNESS OF THE
PERFECTION OF SUPREME KNOWLEDGE, THE GROUND'S QUALITY

Just as someone with sight can easily lead
An entire group of blind people wherever they wish to go,
Knowledge takes the poor-sighted qualities
And leads them to the state of the victors. (6.2)

Just as a person with sight can easily lead an entire group of blind people to the place they wish to go, so here, because all qualities depend on the perfection of supreme knowledge, supreme knowledge embraces the qualities of generosity and so forth, which are likened to impaired vision. These qualities, which were not embraced by the perfection of supreme knowledge before, are embraced on this ground by the perfection of supreme knowledge. They are led to the state of the victorious ones, because the perfection of supreme knowledge distinguishes between what is a correct path and what is not.

2.2.2.1.1.6.2. THE EXTENSIVE EXPLANATION OF EMPTINESS, THE
OBJECT
2.2.2.1.1.6.2.1. The source of reliance for the explanation
2.2.2.1.1.6.2.2. The object toward which the explanation is directed
2.2.2.1.1.6.2.3. The dharma to be explained

2.2.2.1.1.6.2.1. THE SOURCE OF RELIANCE FOR THE EXPLANATION

Since how bodhisattvas realize sublime, profound suchness
Is taught by scripture and reasoning,
I will explain in a way that precisely accords
With the textual tradition of the noble Nāgārjuna. (6.3)

What is the suchness of dependent arising that will allow bodhisattvas to attain cessation? How do the bodhisattvas see it? Because the true nature of reality is not an object of our experience—it is rather the sphere of experience of the buddhas and bodhisattvas on the sixth ground and onward—these questions should be put to them.

Some may think that it is suitable to explain the answers to these questions based on the *Perfection of Supreme Knowledge* sūtras, the *Sūtra of the Ten Grounds*, and so on. To that suggestion [Chandrakīrti] would reply, "People like me who have not realized the meaning of such scriptures would not be able to teach them, because the meaning of the scriptures is difficult to realize. I have, nonetheless, studied the explanations in the treatises of an authoritative person[183] *(tseme kyebu/tshad ma'i skyes bu)*, treatises which clarify the meaning of the scriptures. Since those treatises precisely ascertain the intention of the scriptures, I am capable of answering the above questions."

Thus, verse [6.3] proclaims, "How the bodhisattvas who engage in the perfection of supreme knowledge realize the sublime, profound suchness of phenomena is taught, in the tradition of the genuine ones, using the scriptures and reasonings of the Tathāgata. The noble Nāgārjuna, knowing this way, founded an extremely clear textual tradition. I will teach here in a way that precisely accords with the scriptures, reasonings, and key instructions that are found in the noble Nāgārjuna's tradition."

One may ask, "How can we know that the noble Nāgārjuna possessed the unerring meaning of the scriptures?" This can be known from the prophecy of the Transcendent Conqueror himself in a sūtra called the *Descent into Laṅka*:

> In the southern land of Beta,
> There will be a monk known as Glorious[184]
> And called by the name of Nāgā.
> He will dismantle the positions of existence and nonexistence,
> And in this world will teach my vehicle,
> The unsurpassable Mahāyāna .
> Having accomplished the ground *Supreme Joy*,
> He will go to Sukhāvatī.

Thus Nāgārjuna was prophesied in many sūtras and tantras, which predict that he would realize the ultimate intention of the Mahāyāna's definitive meaning teachings and then elucidate that intention for others. In brief, those who purport to comment upon the ultimate intention of the Buddha, such as the proponents of the three lower philosophical systems, do not fully grasp the Buddha's intention.

2.2.2.1.1.6.2.2. THE OBJECT TOWARD WHICH THE EXPLANATION IS DIRECTED
2.2.2.1.1.6.2.2.1. The examination of the vessel that is the listener
2.2.2.1.1.6.2.2.2. The counsel to listen to these teachings

2.2.2.1.1.6.2.2.1. THE EXAMINATION OF THE VESSEL THAT IS THE LISTENER
2.2.2.1.1.6.2.2.1.1. The examination of the fortunate vessel by way of three signs
2.2.2.1.1.6.2.2.1.2. The explanation of the benefits of teaching emptiness to such vessels

2.2.2.1.1.6.2.2.1.1. THE EXAMINATION OF THE FORTUNATE VESSEL BY WAY OF THREE SIGNS

> Even when they are ordinary beings, when they hear about emptiness
> They experience supreme joy again and again inside,
> The tears from this supreme joy moisten their eyes,
>
> And the hairs on their bodies stand on end. (6.4)
> Ones like this have the seed of knowledge for perfect buddhahood.
> They are a vessel for in-depth teachings on suchness.
> They should be taught the ultimate truth. (6.5abc)

This way of interdependence and emptiness should not be taught to unworthy students, because even if they listen to such teachings their minds will engage them incorrectly—only a colossal waste will result. To give some examples of incorrectly engaging these teachings, we can first turn to some misguided Dzogchenpas. They hold the meaning of emptiness as nonexistence, thus denying all things. There was also Shar Tsongkapa, who maintained that emptiness exists and that therefore so does the nature of things, the supports for emptiness. Then there were the Jonang-pas and Shākya Chokden, who said that emptiness is truly existent, and that everything other than the ultimate, i.e., all relative phenomena, is nonexistent. These scholars, among others, are like patients whose doctors have given up on them. They hold views that the scriptures teach to be incurable.

Therefore, the teachers of this dharma should examine the worthiness of their students, and *then* teach them. The students' worthiness can be ascertained by their outer manner displayed at the time of hearing these teachings. Even when they are ordinary beings, when they hear the teachings on emptiness from others, they are not frightened; rather, they experience supreme joy and delighted faith again and again in their minds. The tears from this joy moisten their eyes, and the hairs of their body stand on end.

Ones like this have the seed of knowledge for perfect buddhahood: the seed of unsurpassable enlightenment, supreme knowledge free of obscurations. If they apply effort towards the attainment of omniscience, they will quickly attain buddhahood. Therefore these persons are vessels for in-depth teachings on the suchness of the precise nature. They should be taught the ultimate truth, because when so taught meaningful results will follow.

2.2.2.1.1.6.2.2.1.2. THE EXPLANATION OF THE BENEFITS OF TEACHING EMPTINESS TO SUCH VESSELS

They will gain the qualities that follow from that. (6.5d)

They always take up and abide by perfect discipline,
They give generously and rely on compassion.
They cultivate patience and, so that beings may be freed,
Fully dedicate their virtue to enlightenment. (6.6)

They respect the bodhisattvas who strive for perfect
enlightenment. (6.7a)

Not only will it not be a waste to teach these worthy students, when they are given teachings on emptiness, they will gain all of the qualities that follow from such an endeavor. How do they gain such qualities? They regard the teachings on emptiness like a newly discovered treasure. In order not to let their opportunity slip away, they always take up and abide by the perfect discipline that relinquishes all forms of nonvirtue, because faulty discipline causes rebirth in the lower realms, where the continuity of the view of emptiness would be severed.

However, even if due to discipline one takes birth in the pleasant existences, if one is impoverished, one will spend all of one's energy obtaining provisions. Bearing this in mind, these students give generously and rely on limitless compassion. For buddhahood is yielded by the view of emptiness being embraced by nothing other than compassion. Furthermore, they cultivate patience, because anger leads one to the lower realms and to taking on an awful color, due to which one will be unable to please the noble ones.

Since merit that is not dedicated to omniscience will not become a cause of buddhahood, these bodhisattvas fully dedicate all of their virtue to enlightenment, so that all beings without exception may be freed. Since no one other than bodhisattvas is capable of unerringly teaching dependent arising, these students deeply respect the bodhisattvas who strive for perfect enlightenment.

2.2.2.1.1.6.2.2.2. THE COUNSEL TO LISTEN TO THESE TEACHINGS

> **The one who is learned in the ways of the profound and vast**
> **Will gradually attain the ground of *Supreme Joy*.**
> **Therefore, those who strive to attain that ground should listen to**
> **teachings about this path. (6.7bcd)**

In this way, they quickly gather the accumulations of virtue. These beings, learned in the profound way of emptiness and in the vast way of generosity and so on, will gradually attain the ground of *Supreme Joy* after progressing through the paths of accumulation and juncture. Therefore, those who strive to attain the ground of *Supreme Joy* should listen to the teachings about this path given below.

2.2.2.1.1.6.2.3. THE DHARMA TO BE EXPLAINED
2.2.2.1.1.6.2.3.1. The explanation by way of the two types of selflessness
2.2.2.1.1.6.2.3.2. The explanation by way of the sixteen emptinesses

2.2.2.1.1.6.2.3.1. The explanation by way of the two types of selflessness
2.2.2.1.1.6.2.3.1.1. The individual explanations of the two types of selflessness
2.2.2.1.1.6.2.3.1.2. The summary of the two types of selflessness

2.2.2.1.1.6.2.3.1.1. The individual explanations of the two types of selflessness
2.2.2.1.1.6.2.3.1.1.1. The selflessness of phenomena
2.2.2.1.1.6.2.3.1.1.2. The selflessness of persons

2.2.2.1.1.6.2.3.1.1.1. The selflessness of phenomena
2.2.2.1.1.6.2.3.1.1.1.1 Scripture
2.2.2.1.1.6.2.3.1.1.1.2. Reasoning

2.2.2.1.1.6.2.3.1.1.1.1. Scripture
The first requisite for teaching the genuine, precise nature of phenomena is scripture. The following quotation is from the noble *Sūtra on the Ten Grounds (Dashabhūmikasūtra, Sa Chupey Do/sa bcu pa'i mdo)*:

> O children of the Victorious One! The bodhisattvas who completely perfect the path at the fifth bodhisattva ground will enter the sixth bodhisattva ground. They enter by [realizing] the ten types of equality of phenomena. What are these ten? They are as follows. All phenomena are equal in their absence of signs; they are equal in their absence of characteristics; they are equal in being free from arising; they are equal in being unarisen; they are equal in their voidness; they are equal in their primordial purity; they are equal in their absence of elaborations; they are equal in being free from adoption and rejection; they are equal in being like illusions, dreams, hallucinations, echoes, watermoons, reflections, and emanations; and they are equal in not being things or nonthings. When one excellently realizes the nature of all phenomena to be like this, one attains the sixth bodhisattva ground, *The Manifest*, through sharpness and through patience that harmonizes [with these forms of equality].

In this treatise the selflessness of phenomena is taught first, because when one realizes the suchness of all phenomena, one realizes that the basis for the confused view of the self of persons is devoid of inherent nature. Due to this, one relinquishes the two obscurations. For this reason the teaching on the selflessness of phenomena is said to be foremost.

One may think that since the selflessness of phenomena fulfills all objectives, it is not necessary to teach the selflessness of the person. However, that is not the case: the selflessness of persons is taught so that those of dull faculties can enter into the teachings gradually, and so that hearers and solitary realizers may gain liberation.

2.2.2.1.1.6.2.3.1.1.1.2. REASONING
2.2.2.1.1.6.2.3.1.1.1.2.1. The extensive refutation of arising from the four extremes
2.2.2.1.1.6.2.3.1.1.1.2.2. The teaching that arising in the relative truth is dependent arising
2.2.2.1.1.6.2.3.1.1.1.2.3. The explanation of the necessity of analysis through reasoning

2.2.2.1.1.6.2.3.1.1.1.2.1. THE EXTENSIVE REFUTATION OF ARISING FROM THE FOUR EXTREMES
2.2.2.1.1.6.2.3.1.1.1.2.1.1. The actual refutation of arising from the four extremes
2.2.2.1.1.6.2.3.1.1.1.2.1.2. Reconciling seeming contradictions in the refutation

2.2.2.1.1.6.2.3.1.1.1.2.1.1. THE ACTUAL REFUTATION OF ARISING FROM THE FOUR EXTREMES
2.2.2.1.1.6.2.3.1.1.1.2.1.1.1. The statement of the thesis of nonarising
2.2.2.1.1.6.2.3.1.1.1.2.1.1.2. The extensive explanation of the reasonings that refute arising from the four extremes
2.2.2.1.1.6.2.3.1.1.1.2.1.1.3. The above reasonings prove that phenomena have no inherent nature

2.2.2.1.1.6.2.3.1.1.1.2.1.1.1. THE STATEMENT OF THE THESIS OF
NONARISING

> **They do not arise from themselves; how could they arise from
> others?**
> **They do not arise from both; how could they arise causelessly?
> (6.8ab)**

From among the ten types of equality, the equality of all phenomena in
their freedom from arising is taught here by logical reasonings. Bearing in
mind that through teaching this first the other types of equality will be
taught with ease, the master Nāgārjuna said the following at beginning of
his *Treatise on the Middle Way*:[185]

> Not from themselves and not from others,
> Not from both nor causelessly—
> In things, of whatever type they may be,
> Arising never exists. (1.1)

First the four theses of nonarising will be stated, and then they will be
affirmed with reasoning. Things do not arise from themselves, as indicated
in the verse "They do not arise from themselves." They do not arise from
others, because if they do not arise from themselves, "how could they arise
from others?" They do not arise from both, because if they do not arise
from either themselves or others individually, they also do not arise from
both of those. They do not arise causelessly, as indicated in the verse "how
could they arise causelessly?"

One may wonder at this point, "Did not the master Nāgārjuna prove
these four theses already? What is the purpose of proving them again
here?" The master only taught the reasoning that refutes arising from
others, as in the following quotation *(Fundamental Wisdom)*:

> The nature of things
> Does not exist in conditions and so on. (1.3ab)

However, he did not teach the other three reasonings. In this treatise all four theses are proven in order to teach the three reasonings [that

Fundamental Wisdom did not teach] and in order to explain other reasonings that refute arising from others.

One may also wonder, "Why did the master not teach reasonings that refute arising from self and so on?" He did not because the reasonings that refute arising from self and other assertions of non-Buddhist schools had been previously refuted by our own schools.[186]

Does the refutation of arising from the four extremes apply to ultimate truth or to conventional truth? The Autonomists *(Svātantrika, Rang-gyüpa/rang rgyud pa)* assert that it only applies to the ultimate truth, but here, [in the Consequentialist system], arising from the four extremes is refuted in both truths. This is explained by this very treatise in the following and other verses:

> Reasonings prove that arising from self and other
> Are illogical in suchness.
> Since they also prove that arising is illogical conventionally,
> On what basis do you speak of "arising"? (6.36)

One may protest, "It follows that you deny the conventional arising of phenomena, because for you phenomena do not arise from the four extremes." It is true that we do not assert "conventional arising." However, to ensure that our presentation does not lapse from the worldly perspective renowned to others, and to avoid denying the connection between actions and results, we present conventional arising from the perspective of others. When doing so, we accept and proclaim—from the perspective of others—an arising resembling the arising of dreams and reflections. Arising in this context is synonymous with dependent arising, free from the four extremes. We describe arising, actions, results, and so on merely in accordance with what is accepted in the world.

Therefore, the consequence that arising would not exist even conventionally does not apply to us: when we speak of arising, we do so free of any logical analysis. When we analyze with logic, no arising is accepted. Since arising accepted in the context of analysis would definitely entail one of the four extremes, we do not accept any form of arising when enagaged in analysis.

Therefore, although Followers of the Middle Way do not accept arising even on the conventional level from their own perspective, they do accept arising and so forth on the conventional level from the perspective of others. There is no contradiction in doing this, because accepting something from the perspective of others is not an assertion of one's own position. It is, rather, a mere repetition of what others say, like an echo. This principle can be applied to all instances of accepting something provisionally.

According to Rendawa,[187] one should not refute arising on the conventional level if there has been no analysis, because the arising free of the four extremes is dependent arising. Furthermore, worldly people say things like "sprouts arise from seeds" and so on, and it is necessary to speak in harmony with the world. However, arising from any of the four extremes is not to be accepted even on the conventional level. It seems that on this topic there are no great contradictions between the position of Rendawa and that expressed here.

In sum, mere dependent arising, free from the four extremes, is emptiness. It is the path of the Middle Way, the antidote to all views. It is not a mistake, therefore, to accept arising conventionally from the perspective of others and at the same time say that there is no arising even conventionally. This is so because upon analyzing dependent arising it is seen to be free from all extremes. Therefore whoever propounds arising from any of the four extremes is not a proponent of dependent arising. The master Nāgārjuna, in a praise to the Buddha, said:

> Logicians imagine that
> Suffering is created by itself,
> By others, by both, or causelessly.
> You taught that it arises in dependence.

Those who speak of dependent arising are free of bias; in neither of the two truths do they fall into any of the four or eight extremes.[188] Since they are free of clinging to anything, they do not lapse from ultimate truth. Since they are free from error regarding any mundane or transcendent conventions, they also do not lapse from relative truth. For that reason, the master Nāgārjuna said (Fundamental Wisdom):

> For the one for whom emptiness is possible,
> Everything is possible.

For the one for whom emptiness is not possible,
Nothing is possible. (24.14)

One may ask, "Are the people who speak of dependent arising and who do not lapse from either of the two truths Followers of the Middle Way (*Umapa/dbu ma pa*)? Or are they not Followers of the Middle Way but something else?" Though the Autonomists do not assert such a proponent of interdependence in the ultimate truth, they do say that in conventional reality such a person claims to be a Follower of the Middle Way. But the degree to which they actually are a Follower of the Middle Way does not match the degree to which they claim they are.

The Consequentialists (*Prāsaṅgika, Talgyurwa/thal 'gyur ba*) say that others impute the name "Follower of the Middle Way" to the one who speaks of dependent arising, but for the Consequentialists themselves, regardless of the manner in which they need to address others, they do not assert that they are or are not a Follower of the Middle Way in either of the two truths. Therefore, according to the Consequentialists, not only are they not Followers of the Middle Way, they do not even claim to be.

Well, then, what is a Consequentialist? The name "Consequentialist" is a label given to Consequentialists by others. The Consequentialists themselves do not assert that they are Consequentialists. One may ask, "Why are they called 'Consequentialists'?" This is a label that *others* give them to separate them from others during debate; they simply repeat that label. When the debate, in which they are not defeated, is over, they do not make any statements such as "I am a Follower of the Middle Way," nor do they make such statements during the debate. The appearance of their making such statements is like the sound of a lute or an echo.[189]

You may object: "It follows that 'Consequentialists' are not established knowable objects even in conventional truth." However, we do not analyze the conventional truth; we simply repeat what accords with the worldly perspective, so what need is there to talk about being established or not established in conventional reality? This is as far as words can go. Thus, since we are free from notions about ourselves, about debating with you, and about providing answers, we have achieved the perfection of the inexpressible.

Here in the *Ṭīkā*, [Karmapa Mikyö Dorje] relates how, except for his guru, lord Sangye Nyenpa, very few individuals have truly comprehended this profound, unsurpassable secret.

There are some who say that the Buddha and the Followers of the Middle Way have theses because they have the theses of the four fearlessnesses,[190] and because they say that phenomena do not pass beyond dependent arising and emptiness. These people also point to the theses found in the textual traditions that refute the four extremes. Are these, they say, not all theses?

No, they are not. They were all spoken by the Tathāgata as a path for dispelling the deceptions, mistaken thoughts, and wrong expressions of others. Having taught in such a way, the Buddha called such teachings "undeceiving," and put forth a "thesis" of their being undeceiving. Such statements were mere imputations from the perspective of others. The Tathāgata himself is utterly free of theses and antitheses about fear and fearlessness.

Theses, positions, and assertions all involve attachment to one side or another. Therefore Followers of the Middle Way do not accept anything in either truth that arises from conceptualizing things. If they were to accept any such assertion, they would have attachment and fall into an extreme—they would not be Followers of the Middle Way at all. If one is a Follower of the Middle Way, it is not suitable to fall into bias toward any position.

The Followers of the Middle Way use mere conventional terms in order to reverse the misconceptions of those who propound arising from the four extremes and of those who cling to things. They use such terms from the confused perspective of others, like an echo. From their own perspective, they have no assertion of nonarising.

If it were the case that the Tathāgata and the Followers of the Middle Way had theses because they speak from the perspective of others, it would follow that all of their theses would have internal contradictions and would be susceptible to numerous refutations by reasoning. For the purpose of reversing the attachment of limitless beings to be tamed, they use limitless reasonings and gave limitless teachings on existence, nonexistence, both existence and nonexistence, and neither existence nor nonexistence. If they held those theses from their own perspective, their teachings could not dispel the confusion of others, since the theses' internal contradictions would be susceptible to refutation.

Therefore, Followers of the Middle Way do not have theses or positions.

They speak of existence, nonexistence, both, neither, dependent arising, emptiness, and so on from the perspectives of others and in a manner that is merely symbolic, nominal, and conventional. There is no contradiction in doing this: their style of communication is a method for helping others understand the profound reality that is utterly devoid of any bias or thesis. As the master Nāgārjuna himself said *(Fundamental Wisdom)*:

> We do not assert "emptiness."
> We do not assert "nonemptiness."
> We do not assert "both" or "neither."
> We use these only as labels. (22.11)

One may have the following doubt: "Do the reasonings that refute arising from the four extremes belong to oneself or to others? If they belonged to oneself, the nonarising established by reasoning would become the Follower of the Middle Way's own position. If they belonged to others, how could you refute someone else using their own reasoning?"

Those reasonings do not belong to the Followers of the Middle Way themselves because the latter do not have even the slightest position to be affirmed. Therefore they need no reasonings to affirm something. For them, others' positions to be refuted also do not truly exist. Therefore there is also no need for reasonings to refute anything. Nāgārjuna expressed this in his *Countering Objections (Vigrahavyāvartanīkārikā, Tsö-dok/rtsod bzlog)*:

> If I had a thesis,
> I would have a fault.
> Since I have no thesis,
> I am strictly faultless.

> If direct perception or any other form of valid cognition
> Were to observe some [truly existent] objects,
> It would be possible to engage in affirmation and refutation on the
>   basis of those.
> Since that is not the case, I have no argument.

And,

Since there is nothing whatsoever to be refuted,
I do not refute anything.
If you say, "You make refutations,"
It is you who are in denial.

This shows how the views of another are refuted by reasonings that are accepted by that same person.

The term "reasoning" refers to statements that are admissible to the common consensus and are written in treatises by proponents of philosophical systems. These philosophers relate to each other by refutations and proofs, accepting or rejecting various views. If one accepts any logic from one's own perspective, it will be impossible to be free from self-contradiction. And, even thought one's position will have many internal contradictions, they will not be seen by oneself. One will only see the internal contradictions present in the views of others. This is the very nature of all philosophies that hold to any given side. When dealing with systems such as these there will always be a mutual exchange of proofs and refutations, victories and defeats.

The Followers of the Middle Way, however, see the defects inherent in the confused approach of logicians who analyze the hypothetical features of nonexistent phenomena. When the Followers of the Middle Way reveal someone's internal contradictions in a way that can be seen by both parties through reasonings and through what is commonly accepted, their counterparts will see their own internal contradictions, and their clinging to their position will be reversed.

One may think that no one would respect the Followers of the Middle Way because they do not put forth proofs of their own system. This is not so. Disrespect toward the Followers of the Middle Way, who are free from all positions, will not arise in someone who has had their clinging to a certain view reversed. They will see that all presentations involving clinging to a particular side entail self-contradiction.

This supplementary explanation has been based on the thought of the master Nāgārjuna as elucidated in writings by Buddhapālita, Chandrakīrti, the excellent Dipaṃkara, Naktso Lotsawa, Dromtönpa, and others. In particular, it accords with the writings of Patsap Lotsawa and his four disciples. It seems that, in terms of the later masters of the Land of Snow, the only ones that presented this explanation in a manner faithful to the original language were Rendawa Shönu Lodrö and Lochen Kyapchok Pal-zang (*Lo chen skyabs mchog dpal bzang*, ca. fourteenth century).[191] There-fore, [Karmapa Mikyö Dorje], in the *Ṭīkā*, says that he presented the above as a quintessential key point of dharma, the heart of the eloquent explanations.

2.2.2.1.1.6.2.3.1.1.1.2.1.1.2. THE EXTENSIVE EXPLANATION OF THE
REASONINGS THAT REFUTE ARISING FROM THE FOUR EXTREMES
2.2.2.1.1.6.2.3.1.1.1.2.1.1.2.1. The way in which the Consequentialists and
Autonomists diverged with respect to the refutation of arising from the
four extremes
2.2.2.1.1.6.2.3.1.1.1.2.1.1.2.2. The extensive explanation of the reasonings
that refute arising from the four extremes

2.2.2.1.1.6.2.3.1.1.1.2.1.1.2.1. THE WAY IN WHICH THE
CONSEQUENTIALISTS AND AUTONOMISTS DIVERGED WITH
RESPECT TO THE REFUTATION OF ARISING FROM THE FOUR
EXTREMES[192]
2.2.2.1.1.6.2.3.1.1.1.2.1.1.2.1.1. The analysis of the intentions behind the
twofold division of Followers of the Middle Way into Autonomists and
Consequentialists
2.2.2.1.1.6.2.3.1.1.1.2.1.1.2.1.2. The way in which Consequentialists and
Autonomists related to each other through affirmations and refutations

2.2.2.1.1.6.2.3.1.1.1.2.1.1.2.1.1. THE ANALYSIS OF THE INTENTIONS
BEHIND THE TWOFOLD DIVISION OF FOLLOWERS OF THE
MIDDLE WAY INTO AUTONOMISTS AND CONSEQUENTIALISTS
2.2.2.1.1.6.2.3.1.1.1.2.1.1.2.1.1.1. How Tibetans of later years who claim to
be followers of the early Tibetan Consequentialists explain the intention
of the early Consequentialists inaccurately
2.2.2.1.1.6.2.3.1.1.1.2.1.1.2.1.1.2. To precisely comprehend and explain the
intention of the early Tibetan Consequentialists is to be in harmony
with the [Indian] Consequentialist and Autonomist masters
2.2.2.1.1.6.2.3.1.1.1.2.1.1.2.1.1.3. The Consequentialist-Autonomist
distinction imputed by later [Tibetans] is something the latter created
anew

2.2.2.1.1.6.2.3.1.1.1.2.1.1.2.1.1.1. HOW TIBETANS OF LATER YEARS
WHO CLAIM TO BE FOLLOWERS OF THE EARLY TIBETAN
CONSEQUENTIALISTS EXPLAIN THE INTENTION OF THE EARLY
CONSEQUENTIALISTS INACCURATELY
Some[193] [scholars inaccurately assert the following]: in harmony with the
presentations of Dignāga and Dharmakīrti—the refutations and proofs

of what is correct and what is seemingly correct—the Autonomists accept the direct and inferential valid cognitions of ordinary beings as correct valid cognition. Further, they accept the valid cognition of the power of things.[194] In taking these as their bases, they do not rely merely on the assertions of others. Rather, they rely on a valid cognition that is established by and accepted because of their own, autonomous experiences. Through this they affirm emptiness and refute those who oppose emptiness.

The Consequentialists, these scholars say, generally do not accept any type of valid cognition as a basis for refutations and proofs related to emptiness. Even if they did accept such a valid cognition, they would not accept the valid cognition of the power of things. Even if they accepted the valid cognition of the power of things, they would not accept autonomous valid cognition. However, they do rely on the valid cognition that is a basis for affirmations and refutations regarding the meaning of emptiness. Yet this is done only from the perspective of what is renowned to others.

Finally, these scholars claim that Consequentialists use a special presentation of proofs and refutations that is not possessed by the Proponents of Things. This presentation involves five types of logical methods: 1) inferences renowned to others[195] *(shen la drak gi jepak/gzhan la grags kyi rjes dpag)*, 2) consequences that highlight contradictions[196] *(galwa jöpe talgyur/'gal ba brjod pa'i thal 'gyur)*, 3) neutrality through equivalence[197] *(gyumtsen tsungpe gonyom/rgyu mtshan mtshungs pa'i mgo snyoms)*, 4) no proof because of the reason's equivalence to the probandum[198] *(drubje drubja dang tsungpe ma drubpa/sgrub byed bsgrub bya dang mtshungs pa'i ma grub pa)*, and 5) the absence of an autonomous thesis[199] *(rang-gyü kyi damcha mepa/rang rgyud kyi dam bca' med pa)*. The first four of these, they say, are like swords for defeating others, and the fifth is like the armor that protects one's own side.

The assertions above, along with those of Shangtang Sakpa *(zhang thang sag pa,* eleventh century), are examined in the great *Ṭīkā,* which describes them as "coarse assertions in need of further analysis." Detailed refutations and affirmations are found in the *Ṭīkā,* which should be consulted [for the remainder of this discussion].[200]

2.2.2.1.1.6.2.3.1.1.1.2.1.1.2.1.1.2. TO PRECISELY COMPREHEND AND EXPLAIN THE INTENTION OF THE EARLY TIBETAN CONSEQUENTIALISTS IS TO BE IN HARMONY WITH THE [INDIAN] CONSEQUENTIALIST AND AUTONOMIST MASTERS

In general, there is no difference between the basic thought of Consequentialists and Autonomists, since the object of their view is profound
dharmatā—emptiness or ultimate truth—and since, for both of them, the
mental state that realizes or engages dharmatā abides in peace, free from
all elaborations. In his *Blaze of Reasoning (Tarkajvālā, Tokge Barwa/rtog
ge 'bar ba)*, Bhāvaviveka[201] praised our Teacher, the Buddha, for demonstrating the indemonstrable—emptiness, the object of the view:[202]

> You showed that suchness cannot be imputed,
> Is not a knowable object, is not a basis,
> Is not demonstrable, is not a sign, is not an object of awareness,
> Is devoid of arising and disintegration, is beyond bliss,
>
> Is not an imputation, is devoid of appearance,
> Is free from characteristics and clarifiers,
> Is not a duality, is not the absence of duality,
> And is free from conceptualizations of peace.
>
> This reality, beyond words,
> You taught with words through your compassion.
> Unerring teacher,
> To you I respectfully bow.

Also, concerning the profound emptiness that is the object of the view:
though it is unseeable, it is conventionally labeled as an object of seeing.
From the same text:[203]

> It is not something imputed, is not a consciousness,
> Cannot be conceptualized, is without example,
> Is free of characteristics and free of appearance,
> And is free of thoughts and words.
> It is to be realized by the mind of the view.
> It is seen through the absence of seeing.

Thus, the Autonomists assert that not only is the Buddha free from conceptualization, he is also free of any movements or elaborations of nonconceptual wisdom. Many such assertions are made by the Autonomists.
As to the extensive elaborations of apparent phenomena, different pre-

sentations of the relative truth are made. These presentations of relative truth are used as a support for seeking out the suchness of ultimate truth. The relative phenomena posited conventionally are presented differently by the Consequentialists and Autonomists.

[The Proponents of Things],[204] on the other hand, engage and experience phenomena [thinking that they possess inherent] characteristics. They think, "Since these phenomena perform functions, they are truly existent things in and of themselves." In this way, not only do they engage in innate clinging, they also engage in imputed clinging.

Does a thing perform a function due to being real in and of itself? Or does the function appear to be performed due to imputations of confusion, even though the thing itself is not real? The Proponents of Things would assert that the former is true. However, both Consequentialists and Autonomists agree that a thing's performing a function due to holding its own power ultimately, and the valid cognition that establishes that function, do not exist in either of the two truths. Both say that no knowable object exists that performs a function and at the same time is ultimate truth. Their thoughts are harmonious in this regard.

Still, the Autonomists do present function-performing things that hold their own power in the relative truth and the valid cognition that establishes those things, even though they agree that neither of these exists ultimately. When presenting this, they posit the performance of functions by illusionlike relative phenomena that hold their own power and illusionlike valid cognition that establishes such phenomena. They posit all things of the relative truth from the perspective of their performing functions or bearing characteristics.

Positing the performance of functions and the bearing of characteristics, in turn, depends on things themselves, the performers of functions and bearers of characteristics—things that hold their own power. In the relative, therefore, the Autonomists accept the pleasant facade *(nyam gawa/nyams dga' ba)* of appearances—mere illusory, relative things that hold their own power—through a valid cognition of no analysis. Their intention in doing so is to clear away all poisonous clinging to inner and outer things.

Consequentialists, on the other hand, disagree with this approach: if there were relative things that held their own power in the relative truth and if they were established by valid cognition, they would necessarily be undeceiving. If they were undeceiving, they would be real, and it would absurdly follow that no phenomena of the relative truth are false. It is contradictory to accept that things are illusionlike and at the same time hold their own power as established by valid cognition. If an illusory horse were established due to holding its own power, it would not be an illusory horse at all. It would be a horse that is an autonomous thing.

[Having seen the faults of the Autonomist approach as explained above], one might assume that it is impossible to realize suchness on the basis of the Autonomist system. However, that is not so: [by using the Autonomist approach to reasoning] in connection with sprouts and so on, appearing subjects, one realizes the meaning of emptiness, what is to be proven, by such reasonings as "beyond one or many."

Such reasonings are used conventionally [by both the Autonomists and Consequentialists]. The only difference between Autonomists and Consequentialists is whether they say these proofs are established or not established in conventional reality. The clinging of Autonomists to conventional existence will later be counteracted naturally through their becoming familiar with the view of the Middle Way.

For Consequentialists, things that hold their own power and their valid cognitions do not exist even relatively. Nevertheless, Consequentialists repeat the mere relative truth that is accepted in the world and in the treatises. In this way, they dispel the assertions of those who cling to things: that phenomena established by the valid cognition of the power of things exist in either of the two truths.

The following is the heart of the matter: The Consequentialists, from their own perspective, are free from assertions of both objects and means of affirmation in both of the truths. Nevertheless, they present refutations and affirmations in accordance with worldly perspectives to dispel the imputations of others. The Autonomists, from their own perspective, are free from objects and means of affirmation regarding ultimate truth. Yet in relative truth, they dispel others' misconceptions using tenable objects and means of affirmation that encourage the discovery of suchness.

In sum, for the Consequentialists all relative things are, even in the relative truth, empty of performing their own functions. They are not established by valid cognition. For that reason, it is untenable to try to affirm things that hold their own power and their associated valid cognition. For the relative truth is merely something posited from the confused perspective of worldly beings who cling to it as real. When the realness of the relative is analyzed, it is impossible to find any valid cognition that establishes any entity in either of the truths. Superimposing tenability on the relative truth by saying that things that hold their own power are established in the relative by valid cognition is untenable. If it were tenable to do so, the relative truth would become ultimate truth.

Nevertheless, there is no fault when the master Nāgārjuna conventionally relies on presentations of the relative truth that accord with the worldly perspective and that are merely temporary supports for those who desire liberation to adopt what is beneficial and reject what is counterproductive. Such presentations vanquish all the misconceptions of the inferior Buddhist and non-Buddhist philosophical systems, which propound the existence of things. Nāgārjuna's approach is similar to having an executioner order his or her own execution.[205]

When Consequentialists engage in refutations and proofs based on this reasoning, they merely repeat statements that are accepted by their counterparts. In that way, they do use proofs, consequences, proof statements (drubngag/sgrub ngag), objects of affirmation, means of affirmation, inferences, and theses. But they do not become Autonomists for that reason alone: since they are Followers of the Middle Way, they do not, in either truth, posit objects and means of affirmation from their own perspective. No matter what means they use to undermine the internal contradictions and misconceptions of others' assertions, their reasons, predicates, and subjects will be in perfect accordance with the intentions and assertions of others. All contradictions in the Consequentialists' own refutations and proofs will then be liberated like a mirage in the sky.

Due to [the criticisms explained above of the logical approach of the early Autonomists], the later Autonomist masters held that, since it is impossible for subjects, predicates, and so on to be mutually established for both parties in a debate, the subjects to be employed must be the sprouts and the other phenomena that appear to the nonanalytical consciousnesses of both parties. The Consequentialists, in turn, would say that, since it is impossible for autonomously established subjects and predicates to exist in common between both debaters, one must simply repeat the worldly perspective.

Thus, when engaged in debate, both Consequentialists and Autonomists repeat what is accepted in the world. The Consequentialists and Autonomists differ in regard to the words they use to communicate, but their intentions are the same. The slight differences in their approaches are similar to a doctor treating different kinds of illnesses by administering sweet medicine to some and sour medicine to others: Consequentialists and Autonomists teach differently in order to eradicate sentient beings' different propensities to cling to the true existence of things.

In the context of the protector Nāgārjuna's refutation of arising from self in his root *Treatise*,[206] there arose a disagreement between Nāgārjuna's direct disciples[207] Buddhapālita and Bhāvaviveka. Buddhapālita held that it is not necessary to posit a subject of relative truth that is established by relative valid cognition for both contestants in a debate. Bhāvaviveka held that it is necessary to posit such a subject. Subsequently two distinct systems, the Autonomists[208] and the Consequentialists,[209] emerged.

However, the great master Chandrakīrti would later refute the affirmations and refutations of the Autonomists. From then on, since Chandrakīrti's refutations were directed at the view of Bhāvaviveka, they affected the approaches of Bhāvaviveka's followers such as Shāntarakṣhita. Shāntarakṣhita and others espoused the same approach as that of the Consequentialists [regarding commonly-appearing subjects established by valid cognition]: they let go of the view that when Followers of the Middle Way debate Proponents of Things they must employ subjects and so on that are commonly established by valid cognition for both contestants in the debate. Instead, they taught that this common establishment is not necessary.

It is impossible for subjects functioning as supports for affirmations and refutations to be commonly established for Proponents of Things and Followers of the Middle Way. In relation to the same basis, the Followers of the Middle Way would refute true existence using valid cognition renowned to others, while the Proponents of Things would posit and cling to true existence with claims of autonomous valid cognition.

There are many essential profound points that could be explained here related to the different assertions of the Consequentialists and Autonomists—their affirmations, refutations, and so forth—but, for fear of making this text too lengthy, they will not be elaborated upon here.

2.2.2.1.1.6.2.3.1.1.1.2.1.1.2.1.1.3. The Consequentialist-
Autonomist distinction imputed by later [Tibetans] is
something the latter created anew

The lord Tsongkapa's view of the divergence between the Consequentialists and the Autonomists was described by one of his foremost disciples,
Khedrub Je (*mkhas grub rje,* 1385-1438), as follows:

> For the Consequentialists, subjects in debate are established by
> valid cognition for both the defender and the challenger. Thus
> even in the system of the challenger,[210] subjects and so forth are
> assumed to be established by valid cognition,[211] and it is under
> this assumption that the challenger sets forth arguments. In this
> way, using only other-approved inferences and consequences,
> [the Consequentialists] generate [in the minds of their coun-
> terparts] the realization of the absence of true existence.
>
> For the Autonomists, the subject is also commonly estab-
> lished for both the challenger and the defender, yet it is under-
> stood to be an object of comprehension discovered by an
> unconfused consciousness and established by its own, objec-
> tively present characteristics. The Autonomists employ that
> subject [in dialogue with their counterparts] by setting forth
> predicates that they wish to have the defender infer [as a prop-
> erty of the subject] and reasons that affirm [those predicates].
> That is the meaning of an "autonomous reason."

And Gungru Gyaltsen Zangpo (*gung ru rgyal mtshan bzang po,* 1383-
1440) said:

> In the Autonomist system, one engages in refutations and affir-
> mations using subjects, predicates, and reasons (*tak chö dön
> sum/rtag chos don gsum*), the referent objects of which are com-
> monly established for both the defender and the challenger [in
> the debate]. This common establishment is discovered after
> one searches for the objects behind the labels [of subject, pred-
> icate, and reason]. In the Consequentialist system, there are no
> [subjects, reasons, or predicates] that can be verified as being
> established by valid cognition. However, all three are com-

monly established by *conventional* valid cognition for both the defender and the challenger. One engages in refutations and affirmations on the basis of this [type of common establishment].

These two spiritual brothers are certainly holders of Tsongkapa's teachings. However, their way of explaining the Consequentialist and Autonomist systems is a great misinterpretation that claims that the Consequentialist and Autonomist masters held views that, in fact, they did not even hold in their dreams. What could be more illogical than that?

Consequentialists never, in either of the two truths, assert subjects, predicates, and reasons that are commonly established by any kind of valid cognition for both the defender and the challenger. This is because the Consequentialists teach that subjects, predicates, and reasons are not established by ordinary beings' reasoning consciousnesses that analyze the ultimate truth, nor are they established by the valid cognition that is the noble ones' wisdom of meditative equipoise. Furthermore, "conventional valid cognition" is something that, for the Consequentialists, is not even valid cognition in either of the two truths.

The first reason[212] is established, because if reasons, predicates, and bases of debate were established by such [ultimate forms of valid cognition], those three would become the ultimate truth. The second reason[213] is also established: the Consequentialists do use the terms of subject, predicate, and reason. However, they use these dependent phenomena of the worldly relative truth in communication with worldly people—they employ these terms while not accepting them from their own side. [Tsongkapa and his followers], on the other hand, say that the things of the relative truth are established as function performers by conventional valid cognition. That is a position that Chandrakīrti not only avoided in the ultimate truth, he avoided it in the relative truth as well. He declares as much in his root text *(Entrance to the Middle Way)*:

> I do not accept relative truth
> In the way you assert the other-dependent nature to be a thing.
> For the sake of the result, I say, "things exist," even though they do
>   not.
> Thus I speak from the perspective of the world. (6.81)[214]

Furthermore, it has been extensively explained that Followers of the Middle Way do not posit relative phenomena that are established by the valid cognition of reasoning consciousnesses, conventional valid cognition, or anything else. It is rather the Proponents of Things whose view becomes untenable through positing such phenomena. Have the glorious Tsongkapa and his followers not ascertained this point? They need to think about what good there is in completely disregarding the teachings of Chandrakīrti, saying that the words of his commentary[215] are not his at all.

This and many other points about Tsongkapa's teaching system are presented in the *Ṭīkā*: how his reasoning contradicts [Chandrakīrti's presentation], how establishment by conventional or relative valid cognition is untenable, some further differences between the Consequentialists and Autonomists, several points about the philosophical systems, and other extensive refutations and affirmations.

2.2.2.1.1.6.2.3.1.1.1.2.1.1.2.1.2. THE WAY IN WHICH CONSEQUENTIALISTS AND AUTONOMISTS RELATED TO EACH OTHER THROUGH AFFIRMATIONS AND REFUTATIONS[216]

2.2.2.1.1.6.2.3.1.1.1.2.1.1.2.1.2.1. Showing how the master Buddhapālita is free from faults using the passage from *Lucid Words* that starts with "The master Buddhapālita said. . ." and ends with ". . . even the master Nāgārjuna himself, when authoring the commentary to *Dispelling Objections*, did not use probative arguments."

2.2.2.1.1.6.2.3.1.1.1.2.1.1.2.1.2.2. Showing how the assertions of Bhāvaviveka himself involve the faults of contradiction using the passage that begins with "Furthermore, this logician . . ." and ends with ". . . because he never mentioned vases and so on."

2.2.2.1.1.6.2.3.1.1.1.2.1.1.2.1.2.3. Showing how Chandrakīrti is free from the fault of contradiction using the passage that begins with "To all of these criticisms one may reply, 'The faults that you ascribe to the inferences of others . . .'" and ends with "Enough of this extensive elaboration."

2.2.2.1.1.6.2.3.1.1.1.2.1.1.2.1.2.1. SHOWING HOW THE MASTER BUDDHAPĀLITA IS FREE FROM FAULTS USING THE PASSAGE FROM *LUCID WORDS* THAT STARTS WITH "THE MASTER BUDDHAPĀLITA . . ." AND ENDS WITH ". . . THE MASTER NĀGĀRJUNA AS WELL, WHEN AUTHORING THE COMMENTARY

TO *DISPELLING OBJECTIONS*, DID NOT USE PROBATIVE
ARGUMENTS."

2.2.2.1.1.6.2.3.1.1.1.2.1.1.2.1.2.1.1. Setting forth the system of Buddhapālita

2.2.2.1.1.6.2.3.1.1.1.2.1.1.2.1.2.1.2. Stating the refutation of Bhāvaviveka

2.2.2.1.1.6.2.3.1.1.1.2.1.1.2.1.2.1.3. Chandrakīrti's explanation of how
Bhāvaviveka's refutation is untenable

2.2.2.1.1.6.2.3.1.1.1.2.1.1.2.1.2.1.1. SETTING FORTH THE SYSTEM
OF BUDDHAPĀLITA[217]
Chandrakīrti said *(Lucid Words,*[218] *Prasannapadā, Tsiksal/tshig gsal)*:

> The master Buddhapālita said,[219] "Things do not arise from
> themselves, because their arising would be pointless and
> because their arising would be endless.[220] Things that already
> exist by way of their own identity do not need to arise again. If
> they arose even though they already existed, there would never
> be a time at which they were not arising."

The meaning of that is as follows: It absurdly follows that, concerning
things, the subject, their arising would be pointless, because, [according
to the Enumerators, the proponents of arising from self], they are already
established at the time of their cause. If the Enumerators say that the reason is not included in the predicate,[221] Buddhapālita would continue with:
concerning things, the subject, their arising would be endless, because,
[according to you Enumerators], once they are established in their causes
they must arise again.[222]

2.2.2.1.1.6.2.3.1.1.1.2.1.1.2.1.2.1.2. STATING THE REFUTATION
OF BHĀVAVIVEKA[223]

> Some, [namely Bhāvaviveka], criticized that statement of con-
> sequences by saying,[224] "That refutation is not logical, because it
> does not employ arguments[225] or examples and because it does
> not dispel the countercriticisms of others. Since [Buddhapālita's]
> words are consequential, the opposite meanings of his proban-
> dum and of his reason are clearly implied. Thus [Buddhapālita
> unwittingly] implies that things arise from others, that arising

has meaning, and that arising has an end. In this way he contradicts the tenets of his own position."

To more extensively paraphrase Bhāvaviveka: the reasoning of the master
Buddhapālita that refutes arising from self, if spoken while assuming the
role of the defender, is a cause of the defender's defeat. For, when debating with an Enumerator *(Sāṃkhya, Drangchenpa/grangs can pa)* about
whether or not things arise from themselves, Buddhapālita does not state
arguments that affirm his own thesis, nor does he give examples [that demonstrate the inclusion of his reason in its predicate]. Further, his consequences do not dispel the countercriticisms of others, namely that they
entail contradiction and are not established.

As for the countercriticisms of others: when they hear the thesis,
"Things do not arise from themselves," the Enumerators will understand
it to mean, "Results that exist in an unclear way at the time of their causes
do not arise from themselves." Therefore, no matter what reason you use to
support the thesis, its inclusion[226] will have a contradictory effect.[227]

Furthermore, [the Enumerators may understand the latter portion of
his consequence] to mean, ". . . because things that are already established
due to being clearly manifest do not arise again."[228] By this Buddhapālita
will only affirm what is already established for the Enumerators, and his
intended subject-quality[229] will not be established. [Dharmakīrti's] *Logic
of Debate (Vādanyāya, Tsörik/rtsod rigs)* verifies that not stating faultless
reasons leads to defeat:

> Not stating the branches of affirmation[230]
> And not addressing the faults [that could be put forth as objections
>   by others]:
> Both of these are causes of defeat.

If Buddhapālita was the challenger, then [the question must be asked]:
does the consequence given to an Enumerator defender to refute arising
from self also imply an affirmation [of the absence of arising from self]?
If it does not, this lack of affirmation would become a cause of defeat for
the challenger. For, even though the challenger would have had the ability
to do so, he or she would not have stated a consequence that would have
placed within the awareness of the defender the three modes that are the

support for the latter's inferential valid cognition of a meaning opposite to his or her original thesis.

If it does imply an affirmation [of nonarising from self], the following meaning would also necessarily be implied: "Concerning things, the subject, it follows that their arising is pointless and endless, because they arise from themselves." It would then be necessary to accept a reversal of the predicate and reason. Buddhapālita would have to accept that arising was purposeful and had an end.[231] Thus his reasoning becomes a cause of his defeat as the challenger, because it involves stating refutations, in order to refute the thesis of the defender, that contain implications contradictory to the tenets of the challenger himself.

How does he contradict his own tenets? He accepts the arising of things in the context of using reasonings that analyze whether or not any of the four extreme types of arising exist. Since he would not assert that things arise from the other three extremes, he implicitly accepts arising from other. His explicit statements and the implicit meaning of his words contradict each other. Since he accepts arising in a context of reasoning, he contradicts the tenets of the noble and supreme Nāgārjuna himself.

Thus Bhāvaviveka criticized Buddhapālita's logic.

2.2.2.1.1.6.2.3.1.1.1.2.1.1.2.1.2.1.3. CHANDRAKIRTI'S EXPLANATION OF HOW BHĀVAVIVEKA'S REFUTATION IS UNTENABLE

2.2.2.1.1.6.2.3.1.1.1.2.1.1.2.1.2.1.3.1. Because we do not use autonomous reasonings that are established by any valid cognition of our own, there is no fault in our not stating examples or reasons

2.2.2.1.1.6.2.3.1.1.1.2.1.1.2.1.2.1.3.2. Because we do not set forth consequences that contain autonomous implications of their opposite meaning, we do not contradict ourselves

2.2.2.1.1.6.2.3.1.1.1.2.1.1.2.1.2.1.3.3. Because we do not state arguments and so on that are established by any valid cognition of our own, there is no need to clear away the faults involved in the theses and arguments we state to the defender

2.2.2.1.1.6.2.3.1.1.1.2.1.1.2.1.2.1.3.4. Although we do not have assertions of our own, we do use arguments, examples, and so on for the purpose of refuting others

2.2.2.1.1.6.2.3.1.1.1.2.1.1.2.1.2.1.3.5. The reversed meaning of consequences is connected to others, the Enumerators and so on, not to our position

2.2.2.1.1.6.2.3.1.1.1.2.1.1.2.1.2.1.3.6. Nāgārjuna himself, when refuting others, defeated them primarily by way of consequences

2.2.2.1.1.6.2.3.1.1.1.2.1.1.2.1.2.1.3.1. BECAUSE WE DO NOT USE AUTONOMOUS REASONINGS THAT ARE ESTABLISHED BY ANY VALID COGNITION OF OUR OWN, THERE IS NO FAULT IN OUR NOT STATING EXAMPLES OR REASONS[232]

This section corresponds to the section from *Lucid Words* that starts with "However, we see that such criticisms are themselves illogical . . ." and continues up until "Therefore, when the master [Bhāvaviveka] inappropriately uses [autonomous] inferences, he is merely showing his own affection for inferences, nothing more."

Its meaning is as follows. As to the reason "because it does not employ arguments or examples,"[233] it must be asked: does this refer to autonomous arguments and examples or to arguments and examples accepted by others? If it refers to autonomous arguments and examples, does your reason mean, "because Buddhapālita, having accepted the role of challenger, did not state arguments and examples that use consequences that imply affirmative statements that refute the theses of others"? Or, does it mean, "because Buddhapālita, having accepted the role of defender, did not state arguments and examples that would affirm his own thesis"?

In first case, when a challenger who is a Follower of the Middle Way is refuting the thesis of an Enumerator defender, the former will be focused on counteracting the misconceptions of arising from self held by the defender. She or he will not be focused on generating an inference in the mindstream of the defender that realizes the absence of arising from self. To counteract misconceptions, it is sufficient to merely use consequences that highlight the contradictions inherent in the counterpart's thesis—beyond that, the opposite meaning of the consequence has no residual effect.

Therefore, concerning the master Buddhapālita, the subject: it is suitable for him to set forth consequences that carry reversed meanings when he assumes the role of challenger and is refuting arising from self. He does not invite defeat by not using arguments and examples, because in this role he is refuting the wrong thought of arising from self. He is not setting forth an argument that tries to prove that there is no arising from self. That is what [Chandrakīrti] explained.

2.2.2.1.1.6.2.3.1.1.1.2.1.1.2.1.2.1.3.2. BECAUSE WE DO NOT SET FORTH
CONSEQUENCES THAT CONTAIN AUTONOMOUS IMPLICATIONS
OF THEIR OPPOSITE MEANING, WE DO NOT CONTRADICT
OURSELVES[234]

This is taught in the section of *Lucid Words* that begins with "It is unacceptable for a Follower of the Middle Way to use autonomous inferences
..." and ends with "Since that is not the case, I cannot be criticized."

When the master Buddhapālita, having accepted the role of defender,
affirms that things do not arise from themselves, he does not invite defeat
for the reason that he does not state autonomous arguments and examples.
For, when one is engaged in contemplating the true nature, it is not suitable
to accept any extreme elaboration, such as existence or nonexistence.[235]

[Buddhapālita could rightly say]:[236] If I, a Follower of the Middle Way,
had an inherent thesis about things and phenomena, such as that they are
established by valid cognition from my own perspective as existents or
nonexistents in either of the two truths, for that very reason I would have
the fault of not using reasons and examples. However, aside from the ultimate truth being free of all elaborations and the relative truth being mere
appearance, I do not conceive of anything being established by valid cog
nition. Since I thus hold no thesis of valid cognition in my own position
that affirms anything in either truth, I am strictly free from faults of not
setting forth reasons and examples to affirm the nonexistence of arising
from self.

If it were the case that anything could be observed as established by any
of the four types of valid cognition, such as direct perception, I would
be forced either to affirm it in my own system or to refute it. However,
since there is no such phenomenon, I, a Follower of the Middle Way, cannot be criticized for not stating reasons and examples that are my own
position.

2.2.2.1.1.6.2.3.1.1.1.2.1.1.2.1.2.1.3.3. BECAUSE WE DO NOT STATE
ARGUMENTS AND SO ON THAT ARE ESTABLISHED BY ANY VALID
COGNITION OF OUR OWN, THERE IS NO NEED TO CLEAR AWAY
THE FAULTS INVOLVED IN THE THESES AND ARGUMENTS WE
STATE TO THE DEFENDER[237]

This corresponds to the section of *Lucid Words* that begins with "Since
Followers of the Middle Way do not state autonomous inferences ..."

and concludes with "... it is not necessary for the master Buddhapālita to respond to such countercriticisms."

It is incorrect to say that the master Buddhapālita invited defeat by not removing the faults of contradiction and nonestablishment from an autonomous argument [that he implied as a means of] affirming that things do not arise from themselves. Nor did he need to do so. [In fact, he did not imply an autonomous argument at all.] For, when engaged in contemplating true reality's mode of abiding, it is not the approach of Followers of the Middle Way to set forth autonomous arguments.

Since Followers of the Middle Way do not propound any establishment of phenomena by any valid cognition in their own system, and since they do not state autonomous inferences, [there would be no benefit in stating an autonomous thesis, such as, "Things do not arise from themselves,"] to a counterpart such as an Enumerator. [If they did, they would incur the very] faults of the thesis and reason [that Bhāvaviveka ascribes to Buddhapālita]. This would happen in the following way.

[The Enumerators would say], "What is the meaning of your thesis, 'Things do not arise from themselves'? When you say, 'from themselves,' does that mean that things do not arise from their essential nature that is their result, or does it mean that things do not arise from their essential nature that is their cause? In the first case, you simply prove what is already established for us. What good is that? In the second case, your meaning will [merely] contradict [our assertion without revealing its illogicality]: for us, everything that has arising exists in the essential nature of its cause, and it is [from this essential nature] that results arise."

Bhāvaviveka, however, might say that it is necessary for Followers of the Middle Way to [use the autonomous thesis of nonarising from self and to follow that by] clearing away the faults that [the Enumerators] would describe as consequences [of that thesis]. However, it is not necessary for us to dispel such countercriticisms. What we do, instead, is say, "Things do not arise from themselves" as an undermining statement for the purpose of refuting someone who asserts, in reliance on their own system of valid cognition, that things arise from themselves. However, we do not posit "nonarising from self" to be established by valid cognition in our own system. In terms of our own position of valid cognition, we do not posit any phenomena, including arising from self, as being either existent or nonexistent.

For these reasons, Buddhapālita would not have to address any of the countercriticisms mentioned above, for they would not apply to him.

2.2.2.1.1.6.2.3.1.1.1.2.1.1.2.1.2.1.3.4. ALTHOUGH WE DO NOT HAVE ASSERTIONS OF OUR OWN, WE DO USE ARGUMENTS, EXAMPLES, AND SO ON FOR THE PURPOSE OF REFUTING OTHERS[238]

This is taught by the section of *Lucid Words* beginning with "[After hearing the above defenses of Buddhapālita . . .]" and ending with "There is nothing in what I have said that is not indicated [in Buddhapālita's original statements]."

One may think that Buddhapālita set himself up for defeat by not stating arguments and examples accepted by others. [To those who voice such criticisms, we pose the following question]: are you saying that when Buddhapālita accepted the role of challenger, and was primarily engaged in counteracting the misconceptions of an Enumerator defender, his not stating those becomes a basis for defeat? Or are you saying that when Buddhapālita accepted the role of defender, and was primarily engaged in generating a valid cognition [of the absence of arising from self] in the mindstream of an Enumerator challenger, his not stating those becomes a basis for defeat?

In the first case, when the master Buddhapālita was refuting an Enumerator defender, he did not invite defeat due the reasons that 1) it is necessary to generate valid cognition in the mindstream of the defender by way of correct other-approved arguments, and 2) that that is something he did not accomplish. He would certainly have invited defeat if, having accepted the role of defender, he did not set forth arguments that affirmed his thesis. Yet the master Buddhapālita, having accepted the role of challenger, is perfectly faultless, because as a challenger he prevented the defenders from proving their thesis.

In the second case, if Buddhapālita were to assume the role of defender, his primary endeavor would be to generate a valid cognition in the mindstream of the Enumerator challenger that realized the mere refutation of arising from self. In that situation, he would not have invited defeat by not stating arguments and examples that are accepted by others. For, [by way of implication], the master Buddhapālita definitely stated in a faultless way arguments and examples accepted by others. He set forth a five-part reasoning statement, as follows:[239]

1) Things, the subject, do not arise from themselves,
2) because they already exist by way of their own identity,
3) as in the case, for example, of a clearly manifest vase.
4) A clearly manifest vase that exists by way of its own identity has no need for arising. In the same way, a vase that exists by way of its own identity even at the stage of its production when it is a lump of clay
5) has, for the very reason of already existing, no need for arising.[240]

Therefore, since Buddhapālita used an argument[241] that was accepted by the Enumerators, he does not incur the fault of not countering the criticisms of others.[242] He is also free of the fault of affirming what is already established for the Enumerators. For, rather than affirming what the Enumerators already accept, he refutes the assertion of the Enumerators that the entity of the result exists in an unclear way in the cause. Further, his argument does not run contradictory [to what he wishes to affirm], because he uses an example that is accepted by the Enumerators to demonstrate the inclusion of the reason in the predicate.[243]

2.2.2.1.1.6.2.3.1.1.1.2.1.1.2.1.2.1.3.5. THE REVERSED MEANING OF CONSEQUENCES IS CONNECTED TO OTHERS, THE ENUMERATORS AND SO ON, NOT TO OUR POSITION[244]
This is taught by the section of *Lucid Words* beginning with "The reversed meaning of consequences is connected solely to our counterparts, not to us . . ." and ending with "The reversed meaning of the consequences does not follow."

The reversed meaning of a consequence is connected to the position of an Enumerator counterpart; it is not connected to us Followers of the Middle Way, because we do not posit any of the four theses of arising.[245] Nor do we posit any reasons, inclusions, or reverse inclusions (*salwa/bsal ba*) that would affirm those four theses or that we hold in our own system to be established by valid cognition. Therefore, how do we contradict our own philosophical system?

In response to the dispelling of objections expressed in the previous section [of this commentary], and in response to the meaning of the above quotation [from *Lucid Words*], we may imagine master Bhāvaviveka asking, "When Buddhapālita sets forth a consequence to an Enumerator, does the predicate of his consequence entail a reverse inclusion [as the principles of inferential] valid cognition [would dictate]?[246] If it does not, the consequence is not correct. If it does, then Buddhapālita must accept the reversed meaning of his consequence, and would thus be stained with the fault of contradicting his own philosophical system."[247]

However, the consequence that Buddhapālita employs is one that highlights the contradictions [inherent in the counterpart's thesis]. It therefore involves a reverse inclusion accepted by the Enumerator defender, not by Buddhapālita.[248] In this system [of Buddhapālita] all three modes of a reasoning statement are merely used for the purpose of voicing an absurd consequence of what the counterparts assert. It is this mere ability to refute the thesis of the counterpart that is the main purpose of consequences. We do not assert that one must set forth affirmations that prove the opposite of the thesis accepted by others.[249]

2.2.2.1.1.6.2.3.1.1.1.2.1.1.2.1.2.1.3.6. NĀGĀRJUNA HIMSELF, WHEN REFUTING OTHERS, DEFEATED THEM PRIMARILY BY WAY OF CONSEQUENCES[250]

This is taught by the section that begins with "Further, the master Nāgārjuna said . . ." and ends with ". . . even the master Nāgārjuna himself, when authoring the commentary to *Dispelling Objections*, did not use probative arguments."

Just as Buddhapālita dispelled the positions of others using consequences alone, so it was for the master Nāgārjuna (*Fundamental Wisdom*):

> Before the defining characteristics of space,
> Not even the slightest space existed.
> If space existed before its characteristics,
> It would absurdly follow that it had no characteristics. (5.1)

> If form existed without its cause,
> It would absurdly follow that form was causeless.
> But no object of perception whatsoever
> Is causeless. (4.2)

> Nirvāṇa is not a thing.
> For if it was, it would absurdly follow that it bears the characteristics of aging and death.

> There is no thing
> That does not have aging and death. (25.4)

Thus, the master Nāgārjuna mostly used consequences as the means to clear away the positions of others. "Mostly" means that on some occasions, in order to refute the [thesis of a counterpart], Nāgārjuna would take the meaning of a consequence as his probandum and correlate that [probandum] to the subject-quality and inclusion that the counterpart had already accepted.[251]

On this topic Zilungpa asserts that one should use autonomous assertions when engaging in the accumulation of merit via conduct, yet one should be free of autonomous assertions when engaging in [the accumulation of wisdom via view].[252] Thus there are many different assertions regarding this point. They are commented upon more extensively in the *Ṭīkā*, where [Karmapa Mikyö Dorje] says, ". . . though [such scholars as Zilungpa] may pretend to be detailed in hopes of being wise, how is his view different from saying, 'If the sun dries out the sky, do not assert that the sky has been washed; if the rain moistens the sky, assert that the sky has been washed'?"[253]

2.2.2.1.1.6.2.3.1.1.1.2.1.1.2.1.2.2. SHOWING HOW THE ASSERTIONS OF BHĀVAVIVEKA HIMSELF INVOLVE THE FAULTS OF CONTRADICTION USING THE PASSAGE THAT BEGINS WITH "FURTHERMORE, THIS LOGICIAN . . ." AND ENDS WITH ". . . BECAUSE HE NEVER MENTIONED VASES AND SO ON."

2.2.2.1.1.6.2.3.1.1.1.2.1.1.2.1.2.2.1. Stating the system of Bhāvaviveka
2.2.2.1.1.6.2.3.1.1.1.2.1.1.2.1.2.2.2. Stating that system's many faults
2.2.2.1.1.6.2.3.1.1.1.2.1.1.2.1.2.2.3. Bhāvaviveka has [in other contexts] acknowledged the faulty nature [of the approach he uses here]

2.2.2.1.1.6.2.3.1.1.1.2.1.1.2.1.2.2.1. STATING THE SYSTEM OF BHĀVAVIVEKA[254]

This is taught by the section beginning with "Furthermore, this logician, wishing merely to show others that he is very learned in the treatises of logic . . ." and ending with ". . . just as in the case, for example, of an existent consciousness."

Furthermore, this logician, Bhāvaviveka, wishing merely to show to others that he is very learned in the treatises of logic, accepts the view of the Middle Way, the emptiness and selflessness of all phenomena, yet, at the same time, in order to affirm that view, he insists on stating probative arguments that are autonomous, or in other words, established by a valid cognition in his own system. This approach can be seen as a wellspring of serious faults. First to explain why this is the case, I will quote his own phrasing of a probative argument: "Ultimately, the inner sense sources can be ascertained to not arise from themselves, because they exist, just as in the case, for example, of an existent consciousness."

2.2.2.1.1.6.2.3.1.1.1.2.1.1.2.1.2.2.2. STATING THAT SYSTEM'S MANY FAULTS[255]

This is taught by the section beginning with "Why did he apply the distinction 'ultimately' . . ." and ending with "It also has a basis that is not established."

Why did Bhāvaviveka apply the distinction "ultimately," and to what— the subject or the predicate—did he apply it?

If he applied it to the predicate, there are three faults.

THE FIRST FAULT

He may reply, "I applied the term 'ultimately' because the acceptance of arising from self in the worldly relative is not an object of refutation for Followers of the Middle Way. Further, if they refuted arising in the relative, Followers of the Middle Way would be undermined, since in the relative they accept mere arising from self."

That is incorrect. Followers of the Middle Way do not accept arising from self even in the relative truth. The *Rice Seedling Sūtra (Shālistambasūtra, Salu Jangpe Do/sa lu ljang pa'i mdo)* says:

When a sprout arises from its cause, a seed, it does not create itself; it is not created by others; it is not created by both; it is not created by Īshvara; it does not arise causelessly.[256]

When worldly people engage in their conventions about arising in the relative [truth], the Followers of the Middle Way simply repeat after them by using worldly conventions. Yet how [does he arrive at the conclusion] that worldly people assert arising from self on the level of the relative, and that [Followers of the Middle Way] do not refute mere arising of that type? When do Followers of the Middle Way ever assert arising from self in the relative? In sum, it is senseless to apply the term "ultimately" to the object of refutation.

THE SECOND FAULT

He might say, "I applied the distinction 'ultimately' based on the system of the Enumerators, who assert that arising from self on the level of the ultimate."

That is also unreasonable. Followers of the Middle Way do not accept the presentations of the Enumerators even in the relative. Thus it is also unreasonable to apply the distinction "ultimately" in dependence upon the systems of others.

THE THIRD FAULT

He may say, "Since we do not refute the assertions of arising from self made by worldly people whose minds have not been altered [by study of the philosophical systems], I applied the distinction 'ultimately.'"

However, not even worldly people conceive of arising from self. They do not analyze such notions as "arising from self" or "arising from other"; they merely think, "results arise from causes." For this reason, the way in which the master [Nāgārjuna] presented the two truths was to not analyze arising when engaging in the relative conventions of the world. In that context, he made presentations in accordance with the unanalyzed relative. Therefore it is clear that, from all perspectives, the distinction "ultimately" is meaningless.

[APPLYING "ULTIMATELY" TO THE SUBJECT]

Next it will be demonstrated how applying the term "ultimately" as a distinction to the subject is untenable. Bhāvaviveka may say that he applies the distinction "ultimately" to the *subject* of his probative argument, wishing to refute arising from self even in the relative, as follows: "The ultimately existent inner sense sources, the subject . . ."

In that phrasing, he would incur the fault of both a subject that was not established for himself and an argument or reason that was not established for himself. For Bhāvaviveka would not accept that the sense sources such as the eyes are established ultimately.

He might attempt to counter such criticisms by saying, "Since the eyes and so on exist relatively, the subject-quality is not faulty. Here, it is the *relative* eyes and so on that are the subject, while the term "ultimately" is used to refute [the assertion that the eyes and so on] arise ultimately. Thus it is ultimate arising that is being refuted."

That is also illogical. If he designates ultimate eyes and so on as the subject, it will not be established for him. If he designates relative eyes and so on as the subject, it will not be established for his counterparts, [the Enumerators]. He will not have relinquished the faulty subject-quality.

Here, I have not written about the many assertions of earlier and later masters that pertain to this topic.[257]

In summary, Bhāvaviveka takes as his basis for debate the mere relative-truth eyes and so on that are established by relative valid cognition. The great Chandrakīrti objects, saying, "To proceed in that manner contradicts both valid cognition and what you yourself accept. If you say that things exist in the relative truth as performers of functions, this statement contradicts instances when you accept that all phenomena—including all function-performing things—are empty of their own entities. No matter whether you assert a thing with the distinction of being ultimate or relative, or whether you assert the mere generality of a thing, such assertions of things will be undermined by direct valid cognition, not only that of noble beings, but of naïve, ordinary beings as well. Such things do not exist among knowable objects, and the Teacher himself extensively cleared away such misconceptions in the authoritative[258] scriptures of the Mahāyāna ."

This, [according to Chandrakīrti's] thought, represents the essential boundary line between the Autonomists and the Consequentialists.

2.2.2.1.1.6.2.3.1.1.1.2.1.1.2.1.2.2.3. BHĀVAVIVEKA HAS [IN OTHER CONTEXTS] ACKNOWLEDGED THE FAULTY NATURE [OF THE APPROACH HE USES HERE][259]

This is taught by the section that begins "As to why this is the case . . ." and ends ". . . because he never mentioned vases and so on."

It was explained above how Bhāvaviveka's reasoning entails bases for debate and reasons that are not established in common [for both parties of the debate] in either of the two truths. Not only do his reasonings involve these faults, the logician himself must admit that he has accepted [in his other writings that this logic is erroneous]! This will be explained below.

[Consider Bhāvaviveka's treatment of this probative argument set forth] by the hearers of our own Buddhist tradition: "The causes of the inner sense sources, name and form[260] and so on, are definitely existent, because the Tathāgata said that, due to the condition of name and form, the six sense sources' existence is established. The reason is included in the predicate: whatever is said to be so by the Tathāgata is just so, such as the statement, 'Nirvāṇa is peace.'"

To that reasoning of the hearers, Bhāvaviveka responded [in his *Lamp of Knowledge*], saying, "When you hearers use the reason of existence as taught by the Tathāgata, do you claim the true existence of the causes of the inner sense sources due to the Tathāgata's speaking of them in a relative sense, or due to his speaking of them in an ultimate sense? In the first case, the reason would not be established for you Proponents of Things, because you assert that the Teacher proclaimed the ultimate existence— not just the relative existence—of the inner sense sources.

"In the second case, it would be impossible for the Teacher to have said that about the inner sense sources in an ultimate sense. For he dispelled the notion of a result-producing cause or condition that bears the identity of existing, not existing, or both existing and not existing. So your probandum—the ultimate existence of the causes of the inner sense sources— and your means of affirmation—the statement by the Tathāgata—are not established ultimately. This means that if you hearers apply 'ultimately' to the reason, the reason will not be established. If you apply 'relatively' to the reason, the reason will be contradictory."[261]

Thus Bhāvaviveka himself clearly elucidated the fault of how one's own probative argument is not established for either oneself or others when joined with the distinctions of either of the two truths. [This is the very fault that Chandrakīrti now explains] that Bhāvaviveka committed [in the latter's refutation of arising from self]. Since Bhāvaviveka accepts that that approach is faulty, all of his criticisms fall back on no one other than himself. In particular, when Bhāvaviveka uses the reason "because they exist," that reason as well is unascertainable.[262]

2.2.2.1.1.6.2.3.1.1.1.2.1.1.2.1.2.3. SHOWING HOW CHANDRAKĪRTI IS FREE FROM THE FAULT OF CONTRADICTION USING THE PASSAGE THAT BEGINS WITH "TO ALL OF THESE CRITICISMS ONE MAY

REPLY, 'THE FAULTS THAT YOU ASCRIBE TO THE INFERENCES
OF OTHERS . . .'" AND ENDS WITH "ENOUGH OF THIS EXTENSIVE
ELABORATION."[263]
This is taught by the section beginning with "[To all of these criticisms],
one may reply: 'The faults that you ascribe to the inferences of others will
equally apply to your own inferences . . .'" and ending with "Enough of this
extensive elaboration."

One might think, "Whatever faults you ascribed to the inferences of
Bhāvaviveka will also apply in the same way to the inferences used by you,
Chandrakīrti. You will also have the faults of your inferences not being
established in common for both parties and of your reason not being
established, and so on."

That is not so. The faults of the basis for debate and the reason not
being established by valid cognition for both parties will be incurred only
by those people who state autonomous inferences in which the subject-
quality and the inclusion are presented as established in common by valid
cognition. We Consequentialists do not even use inferences that are established by *our own* valid cognition. Not even in our dreams would we ever
use autonomous inferences that we claim are established by a valid cognition held in common with the systems of others.

The inferences that we state are consequences to refute the theses and
misconceptions of others and to cut through others' superimpositions and
denials. As Followers of the Middle Way, from our own side, even when
we communicate in that way we are still free from all discursiveness of
wishing to express something to be understood or something that causes
understanding.

How is it, then, that we express these consequential inferences that
undermine the views of others? Followers of the Middle Way are, in their
own system, free from all speech, thought, and expression. Nevertheless,
they state consequential inferences in an echolike way to people who have
misconceptions and contradictory assertions, to show those people their
misconceptions and contradictions. Through this the Followers of the
Middle Way are actually capable of clearing away misconceptions. This
is because noble beings, though free of speech, thought, and expression
regarding existence and nonexistence or arising from the four extremes,
use the valid cognition system of their counterparts, who conceive of arising from the four extremes. Using such systems of valid cognition, they

refute conceptions of the four extremes. One may elaborate extensively.
Here it may also be said:[264]

Though the intention of glorious Nāgārjuna has a hundred colors,
The light of the moon[265] illuminated this world.
Once again a great light, the new morning sun, has shone—
The intelligence of the supreme, noble Karmapa.[266]

Through the blessings of that exalted one,
I as well have attained a slight taste of fearless confidence
In this dharma of profound interdependence.
Enjoy this nectar of deathlessness!

Nowadays the trees grow thick in the jungle of wrong views.
Consuming the fruit that grows there, many succumb to the strong
    poison[267] of clinging to true existence.
They are dazed by an array of colorful, yet misguiding,
    hallucinations.
I shall wake them from the sleep of their heedlessness!

2.2.2.1.1.6.2.3.1.1.1.2.1.1.2. THE EXTENSIVE EXPLANATION OF THE REASONINGS THAT REFUTE ARISING FROM THE FOUR EXTREMES
2.2.2.1.1.6.2.3.1.1.1.2.1.1.2.1. The extensive explanation of the refutation of arising from self
2.2.2.1.1.6.2.3.1.1.1.2.1.1.2.2. The extensive explanation of the refutation of arising from other
2.2.2.1.1.6.2.3.1.1.1.2.1.1.2.3. The extensive explanation of the refutation of arising from both
2.2.2.1.1.6.2.3.1.1.1.2.1.1.2.4. The extensive explanation of the refutation of causeless arising

2.2.2.1.1.6.2.3.1.1.1.2.1.1.2.1. THE EXTENSIVE EXPLANATION OF THE REFUTATION OF ARISING FROM SELF
2.2.2.1.1.6.2.3.1.1.1.2.1.1.2.1.1. The refutation in both truths
2.2.2.1.1.6.2.3.1.1.1.2.1.1.2.1.2. Other paths of refutation

2.2.2.1.1.6.2.3.1.1.1.2.1.1.2.1.1. THE REFUTATION IN BOTH TRUTHS
2.2.2.1.1.6.2.3.1.1.1.2.1.1.2.1.1.1. The refutation of arising from self ultimately
2.2.2.1.1.6.2.3.1.1.1.2.1.1.2.1.1.2. The refutation of arising from self conventionally
2.2.2.1.1.6.2.3.1.1.1.2.1.1.2.1.1.3. A summary of the refutation

2.2.2.1.1.6.2.3.1.1.1.2.1.1.2.1.1.1. THE REFUTATION OF ARISING FROM SELF ULTIMATELY
2.2.2.1.1.6.2.3.1.1.1.2.1.1.2.1.1.1.1. Arising from self is meaningless
2.2.2.1.1.6.2.3.1.1.1.2.1.1.2.1.1.1.2. Arising from self contradicts reasoning

2.2.2.1.1.6.2.3.1.1.1.2.1.1.2.1.1.1.1. ARISING FROM SELF IS MEANINGLESS

> **There is no purpose whatsoever to something arising from itself. (6.8c)**

The Enumerators claim that causes and results are of one entity: at the time of the cause, the result exists bearing its own identity, which is not clearly manifest; at the time of the result, it exists in a clearly manifest way.

This position is untenable. The sprout that performs the function of arising at the time of its arising does not originate or arise from a sprout that exists by way of its own identity in the seed, because if it did arise from itself, there would be no extra advantage or purpose whatsoever of having a result. The result's existence would already have been attained. A concordant example for this refutation is a clearly appearing vase.[268]

2.2.2.1.1.6.2.3.1.1.1.2.1.1.2.1.1.1.2. ARISING FROM SELF CONTRADICTS REASONING
2.2.2.1.1.6.2.3.1.1.1.2.1.1.2.1.1.1.2.1. Setting forth the thesis
2.2.2.1.1.6.2.3.1.1.1.2.1.1.2.1.1.1.2.2. Setting forth its tenability

2.2.2.1.1.6.2.3.1.1.1.2.1.1.2.1.1.1.2.1. SETTING FORTH THE THESIS

It is illogical for something that has arisen to arise again. (6.8d)

To provide an alternative refutation: it absurdly follows that an already-established seed arises from an already-established seed, because you accept [that results arise from their own essential nature in their cause]. If you say that the reason is not included in the predicate,[269] you then lose the position that the seed and sprout are of the same substance. If you accept the latter, it follows that the arising of seeds would be endless.[270] Therefore your assertion amounts to saying that a seed that has already arisen plants another seed, which in turn arises again. That is illogical.

2.2.2.1.1.6.2.3.1.1.1.2.1.1.2.1.1.1.2.2. SETTING FORTH ITS TENABILITY
2.2.2.1.1.6.2.3.1.1.1.2.1.1.2.1.1.1.2.2.1. The contradiction with what is commonly accepted and the consequence of endless arising
2.2.2.1.1.6.2.3.1.1.1.2.1.1.2.1.1.1.2.2.2. The untenability of arising from self shown by examining whether the defining characteristics of causes and results are the same or different
2.2.2.1.1.6.2.3.1.1.1.2.1.1.2.1.1.1.2.2.3. The consequence that seeds and sprouts would either equally appear or equally not appear

2.2.2.1.1.6.2.3.1.1.1.2.1.1.2.1.1.1.2.2.1. THE CONTRADICTION WITH WHAT IS COMMONLY ACCEPTED AND THE CONSEQUENCE OF ENDLESS ARISING

If you think that something arisen arises again,
It would be impossible to observe the arising of sprouts,

And seeds would arise in infinitude until the end of existence. Moreover, how would a sprout ever cause the disintegration of its seed? (6.9)

If it is possible, as you think, for an already-arisen sprout to once again arise, then it would be impossible to observe an opportunity for any result subsequent to the seed (such as sprouts, stems, blossoms, and so forth) to arise. Only seeds would arise from seeds! Regarding seed, sprout, stem, and so forth, the earlier stages would never cease, and one would never see the arising of the later stages. If seeds and so on arose from themselves, the conditions needed for their arising would never be incomplete, nor would there ever be any obstruction to their arising. There would never be a chance for the continuity of a seed to cease! Thus your position incurs the logical fault, among others, of seeds arising in infinitude until the end of existence—until saṃsāra becomes emptied.

You may respond, "The cooperative conditions of a sprout (water, time, and so forth) transform the seed, the sprout's cause, to produce the result that is the sprout. Since the sprout does not abide simultaneously with that which produced it, it is a cause that brings about the cessation of the seed, after which the result that is the sprout originates. Thus there is no fault of 'seeds until the end of existence,' and, since the seed and sprout are not different substances, arising from self is verifiable."

That is not acceptable. How would a sprout, which is the essential nature or identity *(dagnyi/bdag nyid)* of a seed, ever cause the disintegration of its seed, which is in turn the sprout's own essential nature? It could not, because according to you seeds and sprouts are not different substances. A concordant example for this argument is the essential nature of a seed itself.[271] If something caused its own disintegration, there would never be a time at which it was not disintegrating.

2.2.2.1.1.6.2.3.1.1.1.2.1.1.2.1.1.1.2.2.2. THE UNTENABILITY OF ARISING FROM SELF SHOWN BY EXAMINING WHETHER THE DEFINING CHARACTERISTICS OF CAUSES AND RESULTS ARE THE SAME OR DIFFERENT

For you, the sprout could have no shape, color, taste, potential, and ripening

> That were different from those of the seed, its enabling cause.
> If a thing loses its earlier attributes and becomes a different
>   entity,
> How could the later one be of the same nature as the previous?
> (6.10)

If sprouts and seeds were of the same nature, for you Enumerators there would be no long or round shapes, blue or yellow colors, sweet tastes, unique potential or energy, or any distinctive ripening of the sprout that were different from the shape, color, taste, potential, and ripening of the seed, which is the sprout's enabling cause. However, that is obviously not the case. A concordant example that illustrates this point is that plantain tree sprouts and so on are different from garlic seeds and so on.[272]

You may claim that the seed transforms into a sprout by attaining the shape and so on of a sprout, after abandoning its state of being a seed. If that were the case, and the seed loses its earlier attributes (its shape and so on from when it was a seed) and becomes a different entity (a sprout with its own shape and so forth), at that time the attributes of the sprout are a different entity, distinct from the seed. Therefore, how could the seed be the same in essence and not different from the sprout? It could not, because the seed relinquishes its previous entity of being a seed and attains a different state, namely that of a sprout.

If you reply, "Although the seed and sprout are of different shapes and so on, they are not different substances," that as well is not the case, for there are no other observable substances in these phenomena aside from their qualities—their shapes and so on.

2.2.2.1.1.6.2.3.1.1.1.2.1.1.2.1.1.1.2.2.3. THE CONSEQUENCE THAT SEEDS AND SPROUTS WOULD EITHER EQUALLY APPEAR OR EQUALLY NOT APPEAR

> If as you say seeds are not different from sprouts,
> Either a sprout would be imperceptible at the very stage of the
>   sprout, just like a seed is,
> Or, since the two are the same, a seed would be observable at the
>   time of the sprout.
> Therefore, we do not accept that seeds and sprouts are the
>   same. (6.11)

You who assert the self-arising of sprouts from seeds say that seeds are not different from sprouts. If that is the case, then just as the essential nature of a seed is imperceptible at the stage of the sprout, so the sprout would also be imperceptible at that stage. Or, since the two are the same, then just as the sprout can be observed, so the seed would also be observable. Since being observable and being imperceptible are contradictory in connection to the same instance of perception, those who do not wish to have this logical fault do not accept that seeds and sprouts are the same.

2.2.2.1.1.6.2.3.1.1.1.2.1.1.2.1.1.2. THE REFUTATION OF ARISING FROM SELF CONVENTIONALLY

**Since a result is seen only after the cessation of its cause,
Not even worldly people accept that the two are the same.
(6.12ab)**

Since the result produced by the cause that is a seed is only seen after the seed has ceased and thus become a sprout already, those who seek the suchness of liberation refute the arising from self asserted by the Enumerators. Since arising from self is also untenable from the worldly perspective, in which arising from self is not asserted, not even worldly people accept that seeds (causes) and sprouts (results) are the same.

2.2.2.1.1.6.2.3.1.1.1.2.1.1.2.1.1.3. A SUMMARY OF THE REFUTATION

**Therefore, this idea that things arise from themselves
Is illogical, both in suchness and in the world. (6.12cd)**

From both the worldly and transcendent perspectives, arising from self contradicts reasoning. Therefore, this idea of the Enumerators that things arise from themselves is illogical, both in suchness, the ultimate truth, and in the world, the relative truth.

Some scholars, such as Bhāvaviveka, say that it is necessary to apply "ultimately" as an excluding qualifier[273] *(namche/rnam bcad)* when refuting arising from the four extremes. This is untenable: such an excluding qualifier has already been refuted above, when it was explained that arising from self is not possible in Buddhist, non-Buddhist, or worldly systems. Further, the "ultimate" distinction is not tenable in the context of "conventional arising from others." This is so because if things conventionally arose from "others," it would absurdly follow that the continuity of each thing would be interrupted. With this consequence and in other ways, conventional arising from other is invalidated by the texts and reasonings of Nāgārjuna.[274]

2.2.2.1.1.6.2.3.1.1.1.2.1.1.2.1.2. OTHER PATHS OF REFUTATION

> For someone who asserts arising from self, that which is
>   produced, the producer,
> The action of producing, and the performer would all be the
>   same.
> Since they are not the same, arising from self is not to be
>   accepted,
> Because it entails the faulty consequences that have been exten-
>   sively explained. (6.13)

Arising from self involves still more faults. For someone who asserts that things arise from themselves, that which is produced, the producer, the action of producing, and the performer of the action would all be the same. However, these cannot logically be the same, because if they were, it would follow that father and son, fire and firewood, and the eye and the eye consciousness are also the same. Therefore those who wish to correctly realize the two truths should not accept that things arise from themselves, because as the master Nāgārjuna said *(Fundamental Wisdom)*:

> It is never tenable to posit
> Causes and results as the same. (20.19ab)

And,

> If causes and results were the same,
> What is produced and what produces it would be the same.
>   (20.20ab)

Thus the view of arising from self entails the faults or consequences that have been extensively explained in the treatises of the Middle Way.

2.2.2.1.1.6.2.3.1.1.1.2.1.1.2.2.2. THE EXTENSIVE EXPLANATION OF THE REFUTATION OF ARISING FROM OTHER[275]
2.2.2.1.1.6.2.3.1.1.1.2.1.1.2.2.2.1. The main refutation
2.2.2.1.1.6.2.3.1.1.1.2.1.1.2.2.2.2. The ancillary refutation of the system of the Proponents of Consciousness

2.2.2.1.1.6.2.3.1.1.1.2.1.1.2.2.2.1. THE MAIN REFUTATION
2.2.2.1.1.6.2.3.1.1.1.2.1.1.2.2.2.1.1. Stating the counterparts' position
2.2.2.1.1.6.2.3.1.1.1.2.1.1.2.2.2.1.2. Refuting the counterparts' position

2.2.2.1.1.6.2.3.1.1.1.2.1.1.2.2.2.1.1. STATING THE COUNTERPARTS' POSITION
There are those of our own Buddhist tradition who say, "It is logical to say that things cannot originate from themselves, but it is not logical to say that they do not arise from others. The *others* that produce things are the four types of condition: causal conditions, immediately preceding conditions, object conditions, and dominant conditions. Thus arising from other is to be accepted in reliance on what is taught in the scriptures.

"The following describes the 'four conditions': from among the six causes,[276] the five remaining after excluding the enabling cause are causal conditions. The observed objects of the six consciousnesses are object conditions. Primary mind and mental events, with the exception of the mind and mental events of the last type of arhat,[277] are the immediately preceding condition. The enabling cause is the dominant condition."

Still others say, "The definition of a 'cause' is 'that which accomplishes.' Accordingly, the definition of a causal condition is 'the producer of a given thing that abides as the entity of a seed.' Just as an old person stands up relying on a cane, so the primary minds and mental events arise in dependence upon an observed object. This observed object is the object condition.

"The just-ceased moment of a cause is the immediately preceding condition, which enables results to arise. The thing whose presence is required in order for a specific result to arise is the dominant condition. The conditions that arise together with or after any thing are included within these four conditions. Since Īshvara and so on are not conditions, there is no fifth condition."

2.2.2.1.1.6.2.3.1.1.1.2.1.1.2.2.1.2. REFUTING THE COUNTERPARTS'
POSITION
2.2.2.1.1.6.2.3.1.1.1.2.1.1.2.2.1.2.1. Refuting arising from other in both of the
two truths
2.2.2.1.1.6.2.3.1.1.1.2.1.1.2.2.1.2.2. The meaning that is established through
this refutation
2.2.2.1.1.6.2.3.1.1.1.2.1.1.2.2.1.2.3. Reconciling apparent contradictions in
the refutation of arising from other

2.2.2.1.1.6.2.3.1.1.1.2.1.1.2.2.1.2.1. REFUTING ARISING FROM OTHER IN
BOTH OF THE TWO TRUTHS
2.2.2.1.1.6.2.3.1.1.1.2.1.1.2.2.1.2.1.1. Refuting arising from other in the
precise nature
2.2.2.1.1.6.2.3.1.1.1.2.1.1.2.2.1.2.1.2. Refuting arising from other
conventionally

2.2.2.1.1.6.2.3.1.1.1.2.1.1.2.2.1.2.1.1. REFUTING ARISING FROM OTHER
IN THE PRECISE NATURE
   2.2.2.1.1.6.2.3.1.1.1.2.1.1.2.2.1.2.1.1.1. Stating the absurd consequences of
causes and results as different objects
2.2.2.1.1.6.2.3.1.1.1.2.1.1.2.2.1.2.1.1.2. Showing the impossibility of
causes and results being different as earlier and later moments or as
simultaneous occurrences
2.2.2.1.1.6.2.3.1.1.1.2.1.1.2.2.1.2.1.1.3. An examination of the four extremes
reveals the impossibility of there being a time at which a result depends
on a cause

2.2.2.1.1.6.2.3.1.1.1.2.1.1.2.2.1.2.1.1.1. STATING THE ABSURD
CONSEQUENCES OF CAUSES AND RESULTS AS DIFFERENT
OBJECTS
2.2.2.1.1.6.2.3.1.1.1.2.1.1.2.2.1.2.1.1.1.1. The absurd consequences themselves
2.2.2.1.1.6.2.3.1.1.1.2.1.1.2.2.1.2.1.1.1.2. The refutation of rebuttals

2.2.2.1.1.6.2.3.1.1.1.2.1.1.2.2.1.2.1.1.1.1. THE ABSURD CONSEQUENCES
THEMSELVES

If things arose in dependence upon other things,
Thick darkness would arise from a fire's flames

And everything would arise from everything,
Because all nonproducers would be equal to producers in being
different. (6.14)

Arising from other is untenable. In the abhidharma and other places, the Transcendent Conqueror taught—merely conventionally, for a specific purpose, and as a provisional meaning—that things arise from the four conditions. However, he did not teach about any phenomenon in either truth that is established by way of its own characteristics. He did not teach "arising from other": he merely taught interdependence, without saying anything about "arising from self" or "arising from other."

There are some from the factions of hearers who posit four conditions that are substantially established, but substantial establishment is not the thought of the Tathāgata—it contradicts scripture and reasoning. If in dependence upon some "other" cause an "other" result originated, thick darkness would originate from the flames of very bright fire. This is impossible, as the master Nāgārjuna said *(Fundamental Wisdom)*:

> It is never tenable to posit
> Causes and results as different. (20.19cd)

And,

> If causes and results were different,
> Causes and noncauses would be equivalent. (20.20cd)

Further, if things arose from other things, any result—whether it accorded with its cause or not—would arise from any cause—whether it accorded with its result or not. This would be so because, just as a seed and a sprout are different, all things that are not producers of rice sprouts, such as fire and charcoal, are equal to rice seeds in being *different* from rice sprouts. You may attempt to resolve this by simply accepting these consequences, but that position would be irreconcilable with what is established by direct perception.[278]

2.2.2.1.1.6.2.3.1.1.1.2.1.1.2.2.1.2.1.1.1.2. THE REFUTATION OF REBUTTALS
2.2.2.1.1.6.2.3.1.1.1.2.1.1.2.2.1.2.1.1.1.2.1. The rebuttals
2.2.2.1.1.6.2.3.1.1.1.2.1.1.2.2.1.2.1.1.1.2.2. The refutation of those

2.2.2.1.1.6.2.3.1.1.1.2.1.1.2.2.1.2.1.1.1.2.1. THE REBUTTALS

> You say, "Since their causes have the distinct ability to produce
> them, results can be identified definitively.
> Something that has the ability to produce, though different from
> its product, is still a cause.
> Causes and results are in the same continuum, and results arise
> only from specific producers.
> Therefore, the consequence that rice sprouts would arise from
> barley seeds and so on does not apply." (6.15)

You say, "Though causes and results are different from each other, this does not lead to everything arising from everything, because of the tangible definitiveness of causes and results. 'Definitiveness' means that a particular cause has the distinct ability to produce a particular result. Therefore that which is produced by a distinct cause can be identified precisely as the result of that cause.

"That which is able to produce a distinct result, although it is indeed other than the result itself, is a cause. Therefore causes and results are 'different' from each other in a very specific way. Simply being 'different' in a general sense does not [qualify two phenomena to have a cause-result relationship].

"Furthermore, causes and results are in one continuum: they are of a similar class of phenomena, just as rice seeds and rice sprouts are. Rice sprouts, moreover, arise subsequent to their producer, which exists in the previous moment. They do not arise from separate causes such as barley seeds, or from something that is of the same continuum yet is not a producer—for example, a previous moment does not arise from later moments. Therefore, the consequence that rice sprouts and so on would arise from barley seeds and so on does not apply [to our presentation of arising from other]."

2.2.2.1.1.6.2.3.1.1.1.2.1.1.2.2.1.2.1.1.1.2.2. THE REFUTATION OF THOSE

> You do not assert that barley, anthers, shellac, and so on
> Are producers of rice sprouts, because they have no capacity to
> produce rice,
> Because they are not part of the same continuum, and because
> they are not similar.

In the same way, the rice seed as well is not the rice sprout's producer, because it is *different* from the rice sprout. (6.16)

Your rebuttal is illogical. Where is this "definitiveness" to prove that the cause of the rice sprout is nothing other than the rice seed, and that the result produced by the rice seed is nothing other than the rice sprout? This is the first question that you proponents of [truly existent] causes and results need to address. If you respond by saying, "the definitiveness is perceptible," this is also illogical, because your reason will be equivalent with your probandum.[279]

If your response to the question, "Why is the definitiveness perceptible," is merely, "because the definitiveness is perceptible," you have not done anything to prove definitiveness. You are unable to even slightly eliminate the faults that we have just explained.

If you say, "The difference here is that we are not asserting a generality of otherness, but rather particular instances of otherness," that does not establish particular instances of otherness. For if the generality of otherness, the overarching category, is refuted, then it is impossible for a particular instance of otherness, a member of that category, to be established.

This is taught [in the root verse] as follows: you do not assert that barley, the anthers of a lotus, the shellac tree, and so on are the producers of rice sprouts, because they are different from rice sprouts, have no capacity to produce a rice sprout, are not part of the same continuum, and are not in a similar class of phenomena. In the same way, it would follow that the rice seed also is not the producer of the rice sprout, has no capacity to produce the sprout, is not part of the same continuum, and is not in a similar class of phenomena—because it is *different from* the rice sprout.

There are many assertions about this topic by the Tibetan masters of the earlier and later periods.[280]

In sum, if one asserts arising from other, one will have accepted arising in the context of analysis. Since Followers of the Middle Way never assert such arising, they do not accept causes and results to be either different substances or the same substance.

2.2.2.1.1.6.2.3.1.1.1.2.1.1.2.2.1.2.1.1.2. SHOWING THE IMPOSSIBILITY OF CAUSES AND RESULTS BEING DIFFERENT AS EARLIER AND LATER MOMENTS OR AS SIMULTANEOUS OCCURRENCES

2.2.2.1.1.6.2.3.1.1.1.2.1.1.2.2.1.2.1.1.2.1. Arising from other is untenable because different causes and results are not possible as earlier and later moments

2.2.2.1.1.6.2.3.1.1.1.2.1.1.2.2.1.2.1.1.2.2. Arising from other is untenable because it is impossible for causes and results to arise simultaneously

2.2.2.1.1.6.2.3.1.1.1.2.1.1.2.2.1.2.1.1.2.1. ARISING FROM OTHER IS UNTENABLE BECAUSE DIFFERENT CAUSES AND RESULTS ARE NOT POSSIBLE AS EARLIER AND LATER MOMENTS
2.2.2.1.1.6.2.3.1.1.1.2.1.1.2.2.1.2.1.1.2.1.1. The actual explanation of untenability
2.2.2.1.1.6.2.3.1.1.1.2.1.1.2.2.1.2.1.1.2.1.2. The refutation of the example through which the counterparts attempt to dispel faults

2.2.2.1.1.6.2.3.1.1.1.2.1.1.2.2.1.2.1.1.2.1.1. THE ACTUAL EXPLANATION OF UNTENABILITY

> A sprout does not exist simultaneously with its seed.
> Since their otherness does not exist, how could a seed be differ-
>   ent from a sprout?
> Therefore, since a sprout cannot be established as arising from its
>   seed,
> Let go of this position of arising from other. (6.17)

This verse shows that causes and results cannot be truly different. Some logicians who are Proponents of Things think, "Causes and results cannot possibly exist simultaneously, because if they did, they would be devoid of purpose and power. If a result was not established, its cause would not be established, and if a cause was established, its result would also—already—be established. Thus they could not exist in the mutual relationship of pro-ducer and produced."[281]

It is impossible for causes and results to be different from each other as that system claims. One can posit Maitreya and Upagupta as merely mutually dependent others, however those two cannot be established as causes and results that are different from each other.[282] A sprout does not exist simultaneously with its seed. Since without the seed changing there can be no sprout, those two do not exist as different. Since otherness itself is therefore impossible, how could a seed be something "other" than its sprout? Since otherness or difference does not exist, a sprout cannot be established as arising from a seed that is a "different" object. Therefore it is most reasonable to let go of this position holding that things arise from others.

2.2.2.1.1.6.2.3.1.1.1.2.1.1.2.2.1.2.1.1.2.1.2. THE REFUTATION OF THE EXAMPLE THROUGH WHICH THE COUNTERPARTS ATTEMPT TO DISPEL FAULTS

2.2.2.1.1.6.2.3.1.1.1.2.1.1.2.2.1.2.1.1.2.1.2.1. The example through which the counterparts attempt to dispel faults

2.2.2.1.1.6.2.3.1.1.1.2.1.1.2.2.1.2.1.1.2.1.2.2. The refutation of the example

2.2.2.1.1.6.2.3.1.1.1.2.1.1.2.2.1.2.1.1.2.1.2.1. THE EXAMPLE THROUGH WHICH THE COUNTERPARTS ATTEMPT TO DISPEL FAULTS

> **You say, "Just as one arm of a balance moves up**
> **At the same time that the other moves down,**
> **So it is with the arising and ceasing of the produced and**
> **producer." (6.18abc)**

You may say, "It is not reasonable to say that seeds and sprouts do not exist simultaneously. One arm of a balance moves up at the same time that the other moves down. It is the same for the produced, or result, and the producer, the cause. The arising of the result is simultaneous with the cessation of the cause. The sprout arises at the same time that the seed ceases. Therefore, since seeds and sprouts are both simultaneous and different, we are without fault."

2.2.2.1.1.6.2.3.1.1.1.2.1.1.2.2.1.2.1.1.2.1.2.2. THE REFUTATION OF THE EXAMPLE

2.2.2.1.1.6.2.3.1.1.1.2.1.1.2.2.1.2.1.1.2.1.2.2.1. The reason why the counterparts' example does not fit

2.2.2.1.1.6.2.3.1.1.1.2.1.1.2.2.1.2.1.1.2.1.2.2.2. The refutation of the counterparts' response

2.2.2.1.1.6.2.3.1.1.1.2.1.1.2.2.1.2.1.1.2.1.2.2.1. THE REASON WHY THE COUNTERPARTS' EXAMPLE DOES NOT FIT

2.2.2.1.1.6.2.3.1.1.1.2.1.1.2.2.1.2.1.1.2.1.2.2.1.1. Giving the reason

2.2.2.1.1.6.2.3.1.1.1.2.1.1.2.2.1.2.1.1.2.1.2.2.1.2. Explaining the reason

2.2.2.1.1.6.2.3.1.1.1.2.1.1.2.2.1.2.1.1.2.1.2.2.1.1. GIVING THE REASON

> **The arms of the balance are simultaneous, but causes and results
> are not; therefore your example does not fit. (6.18d)**

Causes and results cannot be realized to be simultaneous using your example of a scale, because the example and what is exemplified do not match.
Though in the example the higher and lower arms of a balance do exist
simultaneously, here, in what is exemplified, the arising and ceasing of the
result and cause do not happen at the same time. Therefore your response
falls short, because your example that does not fit.

2.2.2.1.1.6.2.3.1.1.1.2.1.1.2.2.1.2.1.1.2.1.2.2.1.2. EXPLAINING THE
REASON

> **We assert that something in the process of arising does not yet
> exist;**
> **Something that is in the process of ceasing has not yet ceased.**
> **So how are causes and results congruent to the example of a
> scale? (6.19abc)**

This verse teaches that the arising and ceasing of results and causes do not
exist simultaneously. A sprout that is in the process of arising is merely
approaching the actual stage of arising. Thus it does not exist in the present. A seed that is in the process of ceasing exists in the present and is
merely approaching the actual stage of dissolution. So how are the sup-
posedly simultaneous arising and ceasing of results and causes congruent
with the example of the higher and lower arms of a balance? It follows that
they are not.

2.2.2.1.1.6.2.3.1.1.1.2.1.1.2.2.1.2.1.1.2.1.2.1.2.2.2. THE REFUTATION OF
THE COUNTERPARTS' RESPONSE

> **This arising that you assert, devoid of a performer, is illogical.
> (6.19d)**

If you respond, "Though the phenomena of seeds and sprouts are not
simultaneous, the *actions* of the sprout's arising and the seed's ceasing *are*

simultaneous," this is also unacceptable. Actions cannot be observed apart from the phenomena that perform them. The performer of the action of a sprout's arising is the sprout itself. It is illogical for the sprout's arising to exist at the time of the seed's cessation if the sprout itself does not exist. During the action of arising, the performer, the sprout, is a future phenomenon, and does not exist. Devoid of the performer, the support, there can also be no action, the supported. Therefore the actions of the arising of the result and the cessation of the cause cannot be established as being simultaneous.

You may protest, "In the *Rice Seedling Sūtra*, the Buddha taught that, just as the arms of a balance move up and down, in the very moment that the seed ceases the sprout arises." The Buddha did say that, but not in order to teach arising from other or arising of a phenomenon's own characteristics. Rather, this teaching shows that simultaneity exists only as a dependent arising when there is no analysis, like a dream. As [Nāgārjuna explained when praising the Buddha] *(Praise of the Supramundane, Lokātītastava, Jigten Detö/'jig rten 'das bstod)*:

> Since sprouts do not originate
> Due to the disintegration or nondisintegration of their seeds,
> You taught that all arising
> Is like the arising of an illusion. (18)

2.2.2.1.1.6.2.3.1.1.1.2.1.1.2.2.1.2.1.1.2.2. ARISING FROM OTHER IS UNTENABLE BECAUSE IT IS IMPOSSIBLE FOR CAUSES AND RESULTS TO ARISE SIMULTANEOUSLY

> **If the eye consciousness exists separately from its producers that are simultaneous with it—**
> **The eye and so on and the discriminations that arise together with the eye consciousness—**
> **What purpose is there in an existent arising again?**
> **If you say the eye consciousness does not exist simultaneously with its producers, we have already explained the faults of that position. (6.20)**

Those who assert that causes and results are simultaneous, such as the Particularists *(Vaibhāṣhika, Jedrak Mawa/bye brag smra ba)*, think, "If seeds and sprouts were not simultaneous there would be no otherness, and thus arising from other would be illogical. Yet all things that exist simultaneously exist as different things. Therefore arising from other exists. For example, the eye consciousness and all that arises together with it—all primary minds and mental events such as feelings—are simultaneous causes and results.[283] The eye and so on,[284] forms and so on, and feelings and so on—all that arises together with the consciousnesses—produce the eye consciousness and so on while they are simultaneous with it. In the same way, eyes and so on and the mind, the eye consciousness, and so on, simultaneously, become the conditions for feelings and so on, the mental events."

That is not the case, because things that are simultaneous cannot logically exist as causes and results. This is what the root verse explains: if it were the case that the producers of the eye consciousness (which are simultaneous with it, the eye, forms, and so on), along with the discriminations and so on that originate together with the eye consciousness (the primary minds and mental events, which are simultaneous with the eye consciousness) existed as being different from the eye consciousness, then the eye consciousness would have to exist at that time as well. If it did not, there would be nothing to posit as "other."

If you answer "I accept," then an existent that has already been established as a result would need to arise again. What purpose is there in that? There is not even the slightest. The eye, discriminations, and so on would not function as producers.

If you say, "Since we do not assert that there is no arising, the eye consciousness does not exist [at the same time as its producers, the eye faculty and so on]," we have already explained the faults of that position, namely that the eye and so on cannot be something *different* from a nonexistent mind, the eye consciousness. When accepting arising from other, if things are established as other, they are not established as produced and producer. If they are not established as produced and producer, they are not established as others. Therefore, the position of arising from other is not reasonable.

2.2.2.1.1.6.2.3.1.1.1.2.1.1.2.2.1.2.1.1.3. AN EXAMINATION OF THE FOUR EXTREMES REVEALS THE IMPOSSIBILITY OF THERE BEING A TIME AT WHICH A RESULT DEPENDS ON A CAUSE

> If a producer is a cause that gives rise to a different product,
> The product must be either existent, nonexistent, both,
>   or neither.
> If it exists, what need for a producer? If it does not, what would a
>   producer do?
> And if it is both or neither, of what use would a producer be?
> (6.21)

This verse was taught to show that there is no time at which results depend on causes. If a producer, the cause, gives rise to a product that is an object different from itself, it must give rise to products that are either existent, nonexistent, both, or neither. In terms of causes producing results, there are no other permutations.

The Enumerators, Particularists, Differentiators (*Vaisheshika, Jedrakpa/ bye brag pa*), Sūtra Followers (*Sautrāntika, Dodepa/mdo sde pa*), Practitioners of Yogic Conduct (*Yogāchāra, Naljor Chöpawa/rnal 'byor spyod pa ba*), and Jains (*Cherbupa/gcer bu pa*)[285] variously assert that results arise as existents, nonexistents, or both.[286] The first of these positions is untenable: if the product exists already, what need is there for a producer? It is illogical for something already arisen to arise again. The second position is also unreasonable: without a product, what would a producer do? For the product would not exist, like the horns of a donkey. Āryadeva's *Four Hundred Verses* says:

> Pillars and so on for the ornamentation of houses
> Are meaningless
> To those who assert an existent result
> And to those who assert a nonexistent result. (11.15)

It is also not tenable for products to be both existent and nonexistent. What could any condition do in that case? The faults of each of the two previous positions will apply. Moreover, it is impossible for the two states of existence and nonexistence to exist simultaneously within one phenomenon. The *Treatise* says:

> How could nirvāṇa be
> Both a thing and a nonthing?

Those two cannot exist with regard to one instance,
Just as brightness and darkness. (25.14)

Also, what function could any condition perform in relation to a product that was neither existent nor nonexistent? There is no result that has relinquished both existence and nonexistence. If it were impossible to have either an existent or nonexistent object of refutation, then it would be impossible to have something that is neither to refute that. The *Treatise* says:

It has been taught that nirvāṇa
Is not a thing nor a nonthing.
Only if things and nonthings existed
Could nirvāṇa be said to exist in such a way. (25.15)

2.2.2.1.1.6.2.3.1.1.1.2.1.1.2.2.1.2.1.2. REFUTING ARISING FROM
OTHER CONVENTIONALLY

2.2.2.1.1.6.2.3.1.1.1.2.1.1.2.2.1.2.1.2.1. The counterparts' position

2.2.2.1.1.6.2.3.1.1.1.2.1.1.2.2.1.2.1.2.2. The refutation of the counterparts'
position

2.2.2.1.1.6.2.3.1.1.1.2.1.1.2.2.1.2.1.2.1. THE COUNTERPARTS' POSITION

> "Abiding in their natural view, worldly people assert that what
> they see is valid cognition,
> So what need is there to propound logic?
> Worldly people know that results arise from causes that are
> different—
> What need is there for logic to prove that arising from other
> exists?" (6.22)

[The hearers might give up defending their view logically] and say, "All
the reasonings we use to affirm arising from other are burned by the fire
of your intellect, like dry kindling sprinkled with butter. Well then, go
ahead and light the fire of your knowledge with the kindling of logic. You
may think that without using reasonings our aim of affirming arising from
other will not be accomplished, but that is not so. For when a reality is
established for worldly people, logic is not involved in any way whatever.
The perceptions of worldly people are very powerful.

"Worldly people do not follow logic. Their view consists simply in what
they see. Abiding in that natural view, they engage in, or reject, objects.
Through acting in this way they also gain results. That is why we say, 'the
direct perceptions of worldly people are very powerful.' Due to this, direct
perceptions are asserted to be valid cognition by the world.

"Therefore, when affirming the existence of arising from other, what
need is there to propound logic? For worldly people directly see and know
that results arise from causes, and that these causes and results are different from each other. There is no need to prove such perceptions with logic.
Arising from other is established as existing—why would we pointlessly
exert ourselves trying to prove arising from other using logical reasonings? Logic is suitable only in relation to things that cannot be perceived
directly; it does not apply to direct perception, [and direct perception is
what affirms the existence of arising from other]."

2.2.2.1.1.6.2.3.1.1.1.2.1.1.2.2.1.2.1.2.2. THE REFUTATION OF THE
COUNTERPARTS' POSITION
2.2.2.1.1.6.2.3.1.1.1.2.1.1.2.2.1.2.1.2.2.1. Even if arising from other were
established from the worldly perspective, it would not invalidate our
refutation of arising in the context of analyzing the precise nature
2.2.2.1.1.6.2.3.1.1.1.2.1.1.2.2.1.2.1.2.2.2. Arising from other is not even
established from the worldly perspective

2.2.2.1.1.6.2.3.1.1.1.2.1.1.2.2.1.2.1.2.2.1. EVEN IF ARISING FROM OTHER
WERE ESTABLISHED FROM THE WORLDLY PERSPECTIVE, IT
WOULD NOT INVALIDATE OUR REFUTATION OF ARISING IN THE
CONTEXT OF ANALYZING THE PRECISE NATURE
2.2.2.1.1.6.2.3.1.1.1.2.1.1.2.2.1.2.1.2.2.1.1. The ancillary presentation of the
two truths
2.2.2.1.1.6.2.3.1.1.1.2.1.1.2.2.1.2.1.2.2.1.2. The teaching on how the mundane
worldly perspective does not invalidate [our refutation of arising]

2.2.2.1.1.6.2.3.1.1.1.2.1.1.2.2.1.2.1.2.2.1.1. THE ANCILLARY
PRESENTATION OF THE TWO TRUTHS
2.2.2.1.1.6.2.3.1.1.1.2.1.1.2.2.1.2.1.2.2.1.1.1. The general teaching on the
classifications of the two truths
2.2.2.1.1.6.2.3.1.1.1.2.1.1.2.2.1.2.1.2.2.1.1.2. The extensive explanation of the
essence of each truth

2.2.2.1.1.6.2.3.1.1.1.2.1.1.2.2.1.2.1.2.2.1.1.1. THE GENERAL TEACHING
ON THE CLASSIFICATIONS OF THE TWO TRUTHS
2.2.2.1.1.6.2.3.1.1.1.2.1.1.2.2.1.2.1.2.2.1.1.1.1. The actual teaching on the
classifications of the two truths
2.2.2.1.1.6.2.3.1.1.1.2.1.1.2.2.1.2.1.2.2.1.1.1.2. The ancillary teaching on the
classifications of false seeing

2.2.2.1.1.6.2.3.1.1.1.2.1.1.2.2.1.2.1.2.2.1.1.1.1. THE ACTUAL TEACHING
ON THE CLASSIFICATIONS OF THE TWO TRUTHS

> Since all things can be seen genuinely or falsely,
> Every thing bears two natures.
> The Buddha taught that the object of genuine seeing is suchness
> And that false seeing is the relative truth. (6.23)

There are those who have not realized the meaning of the treatises that teach profound dependent arising. Beginningless saṃsāra's habitual tendencies of clinging to true existence have fully ripened in their minds. They cling strongly to things. Devoid of genuine friends, they babble about the worldly perspective invalidating the refutation of arising from other.

Without explaining to them the vast and manifold way things actually arise in the world, it is impossible to counteract their erroneous claims to invalidate our refutations by worldly perception. Therefore the presentation of the two truths will now be given to show what aspects of worldly perception can and cannot invalidate [the refutation of] arising from other.

The Transcendent Conqueror taught that all inner and outer things, such as sprouts, can be presented in terms of the two truths. The ultimate truth *(paramārthasatya, döndam denpa/don dam bden pa)* is the authentic object seen by the genuine wisdom of the noble ones. Even though it can be called an "object," it does not exist objectively via its own identity—it cannot be discovered by the conceptual mind *(lo/blo)*. The relative truth *(saṃvṛtisatya, kundzob denpa/kun rdzob bden pa)* is posited from the perspective of ordinary sentient beings, whose eyes of intelligence are covered by the cataracts of ignorance. Since the objects seen are false, the relative truth is posited as a mental state.

Thus every thing that could ever be discovered bears two natures: ultimate and relative. From among those, the object of genuine seeing is that which is free of all elaborations of extremes: existence and nonexistence, permanence and nihilism, knowable objects and knowers, and so on. It cannot be labeled by any convention and is realized by the wisdom of the noble ones, which abides within and is cognized by oneself. It is the suchness that is conveyed by the term "ultimate truth."

The objects of false seeing are imputed, or posited, as persons and phenomena by conventional expressions and thoughts. These include all phenomena from form through omniscience, and were described by the Teacher as relative truth.

Here the great Tsongkapa and others assert that the two truths are of one entity yet differ in terms of their conceptual isolates *(ngowo chik la dokpa tade/ngo bo gcig la ldog pa tha dad)*. By holding this assertion, they autonomously posit that the entities of the two truths are established by valid cognition. These and many similar assertions are untenable and contradict all the sūtras and tantras. For the sūtra *Unraveling the Thought* *(Saṃdhinirmochana, Gongpa Ngedrel/dgongs pa nges 'grel)* says:

> O Utterly Pure Intelligence! If the defining characteristics of formations *(duje/'du byed)* and the defining characteristics of the ultimate were not different, all naïve ordinary beings would see the [ultimate] truth.

And so on. Furthermore, if the two truths were one entity, the relative would be the same as the ultimate. That position has the fault that all formations would have no features or distinctions. The ultimate would also be the same as the relative—that position has the fault that the ultimate would be a completely afflicted phenomenon, and so on.

There are some who say that in the relative truth the two truths are one entity, while others say that in the relative truth they are different entities. Yet since these people speak from a point of view of analyzing the truths with reasoning, they do not transcend any faults. There are some others who say that if things are not established as existent, nonexistent, and so on by conventional valid cognition in [the relative truth], [one's view] will become nihilistic and deny causes and results. There are many such positions, and they are all untenable.

Zilungpa says:

> There are two [different contexts]: one in which Followers of the Middle Way accept a position of their own, and one in which they do not. In the middle stage of reversing the view of self, one refutes existence and accepts nonexistence ultimately. In the final stage of reversing all views, one refutes the existence of the self, the truths, and so on ultimately, yet one does not establish nonexistence. The latter phase is what makes the Consequentialists superior to the Autonomists.

This is also untenable, because it is not suitable for any Followers of the Middle Way, [including Autonomists], to accept either existence or nonexistence from their own perspective. Many refutations and positions related to this topic are to be found in full detail in the great *Ṭīkā*.

Thus the two truths are not one entity nor are they different entities: they are posited in dependence upon each other. When two things depend on each other they are not the same, because there would be no need for something to depend on itself. They are also not different, because if the depender is not established, nothing can be established as being different from the depender. If that is not established, there is no need for anything to depend or rely on a "different" thing. It is as the master Nāgārjuna said *(Fundamental Wisdom)*:

> When something originates in dependence upon something else,
> The [depender] is not the same as [the depended-on],
> Nor is it different from it.
> In this way, nihilism and permanence are transcended. (18.10)

One may ask, "In what way are the two truths posited in dependence upon each other?" Falsity is posited in dependence upon truth; truth is posited in dependence upon falsity.

In this section of the *Ṭīkā* there is an extensive presentation containing refutations and affirmations related to the assertions of the Riwo Gendenpas,[287] the Jonangpas, and Zilungpa and to the assertions of many scholars and siddhas from India and Tibet. These explanations correctly set the boundaries of the two truths.

2.2.2.1.1.6.2.3.1.1.1.2.1.1.2.2.1.2.1.2.2.1.1.1.2. THE ANCILLARY
TEACHING ON THE CLASSIFICATIONS OF FALSE SEEING
2.2.2.1.1.6.2.3.1.1.1.2.1.1.2.2.1.2.1.2.2.1.1.1.2.1. The actual classifications of
false seeing
2.2.2.1.1.6.2.3.1.1.1.2.1.1.2.2.1.2.1.2.2.1.1.1.2.2. The teaching on how the
worldly perspective does not invalidate suchness

2.2.2.1.1.6.2.3.1.1.1.2.1.1.2.2.1.2.1.2.2.1.1.1.2.1. THE ACTUAL
CLASSIFICATIONS OF FALSE SEEING
2.2.2.1.1.6.2.3.1.1.1.2.1.1.2.2.1.2.1.2.2.1.1.1.2.1.1. The classifications by way of
the subject
2.2.2.1.1.6.2.3.1.1.1.2.1.1.2.2.1.2.1.2.2.1.1.1.2.1.2. The classifications by way of
the object

2.2.2.1.1.6.2.3.1.1.1.2.1.1.2.2.1.2.1.2.2.1.1.1.2.1.1. THE CLASSIFICATIONS
BY WAY OF THE SUBJECT

> False seeing is also said to have two aspects:
> That with clear faculties and that with faulty faculties.
> In dependence upon consciousnesses endowed with good
> faculties,
> Consciousnesses endowed with faulty faculties are asserted to be
> wrong. (6.24)

Having posited the natures of the two truths, the *Entrance to the Middle Way* will now explain that false seeing is also classified into genuine and false. The objects and subjects of false seeing's two aspects will now be presented.

The first aspect is what is renowned in the world as the correct apprehension of objects: consciousnesses arisen from a clear faculty, which means any one of the six faculties that have not been damaged by faults such as diseased vision *(rab-rib/rab rib)*.[288] The second aspect is a consciousness arisen from one of the six faculties that have been adulterated by causes of confusion. The perceptions of someone with a consciousness of faulty faculties are asserted to be wrong, but only in dependence upon the perceptions of good consciousnesses—consciousnesses that are not arisen from any of the six adulterated faculties.

2.2.2.1.1.6.2.3.1.1.1.2.1.1.2.2.1.2.1.2.2.1.1.1.2.1.2. THE CLASSIFICATIONS
BY WAY OF THE OBJECT
2.2.2.1.1.6.2.3.1.1.1.2.1.1.2.2.1.2.1.2.2.1.1.1.2.1.2.1. The general classification of objects into true and false
2.2.2.1.1.6.2.3.1.1.1.2.1.1.2.2.1.2.1.2.2.1.1.1.2.1.2.2. The special classifications of false objects

2.2.2.1.1.6.2.3.1.1.1.2.1.1.2.2.1.2.1.2.2.1.1.1.2.1.2.1. THE GENERAL
CLASSIFICATION OF OBJECTS INTO TRUE AND FALSE

> What is apprehended by the undamaged six faculties
> Is known by the world
> And is true for the world.
> Everything else is held by the world to be false. (6.25)

This verse teaches that just as worldly seeing is classified into correct and incorrect, there are also two classifications of objects. Objects apprehended by the six faculties that are undamaged by any inner or outer conditions are known by the world and are true for the world. Worldly people cling to them as real because they appear and because they are undeceiving conventions.

These appearances are not true or real for noble ones, because in meditative equipoise the noble ones do not see anything, and in the postmeditation they call such things confused appearances. Everything else—the objects that appear via damaged faculties—is held by worldly people to be false in dependence upon the worldly presentation of what is true and what is false.

Even though the appearances of the damaged faculties appear to worldly people, worldly people do not cling to them as real. Some objects may be thought of even though they do not appear, but, due to their not appearing, they are not conventionally labeled in the common, worldly perspective for the purpose of adopting and rejecting.[289]

Some Tibetan scholars take the position that the difference between Consequentialists and Autonomists lies in whether or not they assert the terms of correct and incorrect from their own perspective even in the relative truth. Others say that even the Consequentialist system, from its own perspective, holds distinctions of correct and incorrect. Still others say that there are no [such distinctions for Consequentialists] even conventionally. All of these positions are untenable.

Even in the Autonomist system there is utterly no difference between the appearances of a dream and waking appearances of the present. What need is there to speak of whether there is a difference between correct and incorrect in the Consequentialist system? Nevertheless, if following the worldly perspective one does not posit a difference between correct and incorrect conventionally, one will contradict the three verses of [this] text [that deal with this topic], both the root text and the commentary.[290]

The Autonomists do state the classifications of the relative as correct and incorrect, but these are merely repeated in accordance with what is accepted in the world. They are not positions of the Autonomists themselves, because Autonomists as well are genuine Followers of the Middle Way.

One may think, "According to the Autonomists, the relative truth is established from a conventional perspective by conventional valid cognition. Since they assert that the horses and oxen that appear to a deceived eye due to the spells of a magician are established by the consciousness that apprehends them, how could it not be the case that they affirm the relative truth as a genuine object from their own perspective?"

The Autonomists do not make assertions in this way, because the above reason is not included in its predicate.[291] In order to show that there is no such inclusion, the Consequentialists would respond as follows: "If an Autonomist spoke in that way, not only would there be no inclusion, they would also be asserting an inclusion that proved the opposite *(galkyab/ 'gal khyab)*.[292] It is untenable to say that illusionlike relative truth is established on the conventional level by conventional valid cognition, or in other words by correct reasoning, because [all Followers of the Middle Way] say that all illusionlike, relative phenomena are devoid of genuine establishment, ultimately establishment, or true establishment."

If the Autonomists were to think, "Since we say that all phenomena are not genuinely or ultimately established, what need is there to say that phenomena are not established in the relative truth?," the Consequentialists would respond, "This is also untenable—phenomena's lack of genuine or ultimate truth is an overarching or pervading quality. Therefore, in conventional reality as well it is not possible for true existence to be established by valid cognition. This logic is illustrated by the example of the appearance of strands of hair to someone with diseased vision."[293]

Thus the Consequentialists refute the system of the Autonomists. Due to this, in this world the Middle Way tradition split into two groups: the Consequentialists and the Autonomists. This represents a key point regarding the differences between the tenets of the Consequentialists and Autonomists.

There are many different assertions among individual Autonomist masters regarding whether conventional phenomena, such as the all-basis, are established conventionally by valid cognition. Some say that such phenomena are so established; some say that they are not. The master Chandrakīrti extensively refuted the position that holds that they are. The position that holds that they are not accords with the position [of the Consequentialists]. There is no difference between the Autonomist assertion of the distinction of genuine and false relative truth and the Consequentialist assertion of the same distinction. If one does not analyze mere

appearances, both correct and incorrect relative truth exist; when analyzed, neither exists.

2.2.2.1.1.6.2.3.1.1.1.2.1.1.2.2.1.2.1.2.2.1.1.1.2.1.2.2. THE SPECIAL
CLASSIFICATIONS OF FALSE OBJECTS

> The essential nature that is conceived by tīrthikas,
> Who are carried away by the sleep of ignorance,
> And the conceptions of illusions, mirages, and so on
> Do not exist even from the worldly perspective. (6.26)

In their texts, Buddhist and non-Buddhist tīrthikas, who are carried away
by the sleep of ignorance, conceive of an essential nature of things. They
designate this essential nature variously as a self, primal matter *(tsowo/gtso
bo)*, subtle particles, the all-basis, and so on. Moreover, worldly people
conceive of the illusions and mirages that appear for defective faculties to
be horses, oxen, and so on. Since none of these exist even as worldly conventions, what need is there to speak of them existing ultimately? There
is no need, because worldly people do not use them in conventional communication.

One may respond, "Such conceptions of the proponents of Buddhist
and non-Buddhist tenet systems do not exist ultimately, but they must
exist conventionally." However, those who hold to such conceptions cast
away the position of the relative truth, which is accepted throughout the
world, and then engage in accepting and rejecting on the basis of phenomena that do not even exist in the world. This is similar to climbing a tree
and letting go of the first branch before you take hold of the second: you
fall into a ravine of bad views. This approach, which fails to see either of
the two truths, brings no results.

2.2.2.1.1.6.2.3.1.1.1.2.1.1.2.2.1.2.1.2.2.1.1.1.2.2. THE TEACHING ON HOW
THE WORLDLY PERSPECTIVE DOES NOT INVALIDATE SUCHNESS

> Just as the perceptions of diseased vision
> Do not invalidate the consciousnesses free from diseased vision,
> So the mind devoid of stainless wisdom
> Does not invalidate the stainless mind. (6.27)

The direct perceptions of the world do not invalidate the refutation of arising from other, because the refutation of arising from other is not strictly based on, and does not follow, worldly seeing. Rather, it is made from the perspective of the noble ones' seeing.

This is taught by the root verse: when strands of hair are seen by someone with diseased vision, the hairs that they see do not invalidate, and engender no confusion in, a consciousness free of diseased vision. In the same way, the minds of ordinary beings, devoid of the stainless, uncontaminated wisdom of the noble ones, "see" arising from other and so on due to confusion. But this seeing does not invalidate the minds of the noble ones, who have no stains of mental impurities (illustrated by diseased vision), by polluting them with mistakenness. The perceptions of ordinary beings, when beheld by the noble ones, are only a cause of laughter.

2.2.2.1.1.6.2.3.1.1.1.2.1.1.2.2.1.2.1.2.2.1.1.2. THE EXTENSIVE EXPLANATION OF THE ESSENCE OF EACH TRUTH
2.2.2.1.1.6.2.3.1.1.1.2.1.1.2.2.1.2.1.2.2.1.1.2.1. The explanation of the nature of the relative truth
2.2.2.1.1.6.2.3.1.1.1.2.1.1.2.2.1.2.1.2.2.1.1.2.2. The explanation of the nature of the ultimate truth

2.2.2.1.1.6.2.3.1.1.1.2.1.1.2.2.1.2.1.2.2.1.1.2.1. THE EXPLANATION OF THE NATURE OF THE RELATIVE TRUTH

> It is called the "relative" because ignorance obscures the true nature.
> It contrives things to seem real.
> Contrivance was taught by the Sage to be relative truth.
> All contrived things are relative. (6.28)

Having stated that all things are of the natures of the two truths, the *Entrance to the Middle Way* now teaches the relative truth of the world. Ignorance causes sentient beings to be deluded about the actual status of phenomena. It imputes the nature of things to be other than what it is. Due to this, it is named the "relative" because it refers to phenomena that obscure the perception of the abiding true nature.

This ignorance, the nature of the relative, clings to things as having a nature, even though in reality they do not. Phenomena appear to sentient beings to be real, even though that appearance does not correspond to objective reality. [The appearance of things as real] arises due to the interdependence of contrivance and imputation. That is why [such appearance] was taught by the Sage to be "relative truth."

[It is called relative "truth" because] reflections and so on, the incorrect relative, are false and are realized by ordinary beings to be false. Conversely, blue, yellow, and so on appear to sentient beings to be real or *true*. Their nature, emptiness, does not appear to sentient beings in an unobscured way.

The ultimate nature and the incorrect relative are not relative *truth*. The relative truth is composed of the afflictive ignorance that forms the link of becoming [from among the twelve links of dependent arising].

Keeping strictly to Chandrakīrti's autocommentary on the *Entrance to the Middle Way*, minds apprehending the relative truth are necessarily afflictive obscurations. In terms of phenomena appearing as real, the relative truth appears to naïve, ordinary beings, who have not eliminated the ignorance [that pervades saṃsāra up to] the peak of existence. Conversely, for noble beings, who *have* eliminated such ignorance, the relative truth does not appear. What appears for them is the *mere relative*. This is an important distinction. Therefore, clinging to true existence necessarily entails the afflictive obscurations.

[To explain further,] relative truth [only appears to sentient beings]. The contrived things that seem to appear for the hearers, solitary realizers, and bodhisattvas who have relinquished afflictive ignorance are posited as the mere relative. Since those noble beings are free from assumptions that they are real or true, those phenomena are not described as *truths* or *realities*.[294]

This mere relative appears in the postmeditation of noble beings whose experience entails appearances. This is because such noble ones are still in active relationship with the ignorance that defines the cognitive obscurations. However, the mere relative does not arise during the noble ones' meditative equipoise, which does not entail appearances. This equipoise does not entail appearances, because at that time all elaborations have been thoroughly pacified.

Zilungpa and his followers assert that the inclusion of clinging to true existence in the afflictive obscurations[295] is untenable, and that it is unreasonable to say that there is utterly no afflictive ignorance in the mindstreams of noble ones. They criticize this position by saying, "If that were the case, do the mindstreams of noble ones who have not yet attained the eighth bodhisattva ground involve afflicted minds *(yi/yid)* or do they not? If you say they do not, this contradicts the explanation that the grounds from the seventh and downwards are impure grounds. If you say they do, it follows that the mindstream of a noble one, the subject, is a mental affliction." Even though my own guru has uttered such criticisms, those criticisms are taught in the *Ṭīkā* to be like a crow eating excrement and then purposely smearing its beak on a clean plot of land.[296]

Further, the protector Nāgārjuna and his followers teach that without realizing the selflessness of such phenomena as the aggregates, the bases of imputation, it is impossible to realize the selflessness of the self of persons, the imputed quality. This is how they explain the ignorance that is the cause and root of saṃsāra and that is equivalent to clinging to true existence.

This reasoning establishes that clinging to true existence is necessarily absent from the mindstreams of noble ones. Clinging to true existence is posited as the afflictive obscurations in reference to its obstruction of liberation. In reference to its obstruction of omniscience, it is posited as the cognitive obscurations.

Relative phenomena never appear to buddhas, because buddhas are truly and completely enlightened from all perspectives, with respect to all phenomena—they have completely reversed the movement of primary minds and mental events. Therefore, due to being contaminated by afflictive or nonafflictive ignorance respectively, one is not liberated from saṃsāra and one does not attain omniscience.

Such ignorance is relinquished through realizing the selflessness of persons and phenomena. Since buddhas have perfected familiarity with both forms of selflessness, they have reversed ignorance, the cause. Through reversing such a cause, they are free from the apprehension of relative appearances, the result.

The Transcendent Conqueror taught the two categories of relative truth and the mere relative. The three lower noble ones[297] see the relative truth as the mere relative. In their postmeditation, they have mere appearances and they are free of clinging to true existence regarding those appearances. They see them as false, but they still apprehend them. This apprehension is the cognitive obscuration. The emptiness that is the true nature of the mere relative is, from the perspective of the meditative equipoise of the noble ones, ultimate truth. Neither the mere relative nor the relative truth appear to buddhas: since buddhas have abandoned the two types of ignorance, the causes, the two types of relative, the results, do not arise.

There are many key secrets regarding the earlier Tibetans' assertions about whether or not the mere relative appears to buddhas that could be added here, but they have not been elucidated because that would require too many words.

Tanakpa *(rta nag pa)*,[298] in his writings, asserts that phenomena of the relative truth are not necessarily existent, whereas phenomena of the conventional truth *are* necessarily existent. He also says that something that exists relatively does not necessarily exist, whereas something that exists conventionally necessarily exists.[299] These positions are untenable, because what he calls "not necessarily existent" has already been shown to be the incorrect relative. The incorrect relative is not acceptable as relative truth. The autocommentary to the *Entrance to the Middle Way* says:

> If something is false even in the relative, it is not relative *truth.*

It seems Tanakpa did not read that line even once. The conventions of genuine and incorrect are repeated in accordance with what is accepted in the world. Followers of the Middle Way do not accept anything whatsoever as a position of their own.

Karmapa Mikyö Dorje teaches in the *Ṭīkā* that by writing about this topic without understanding those key points, Tanakpa courts the great danger of shattering his vase [of the relative] and scattering it in a hundred directions.

2.2.2.1.1.6.2.3.1.1.1.2.1.1.2.2.1.2.1.2.2.1.1.2.2. THE EXPLANATION OF THE NATURE OF THE ULTIMATE TRUTH

> The mistaken entities that are conceived
> As hairs and so forth due to diseased vision
> Will be seen correctly by someone with clear vision.
> It should be understood that the suchness of ultimate truth is the
> same. (6.29)

Having described the first truth, the *Entrance to the Middle Way* now teaches the second truth, the ultimate. Because the ultimate is not a direct object for the rational mind *(yi/yid)* or for terms, it is taught in this verse using an example that may be directly experienced by ordinary beings.

People with diseased vision see mistaken entities such as hairs, which may appear to be in their food bowls. When such people hold their bowls in their hands, they first think that such mistaken entities are really there. Wanting to get rid of the hairs, they may tire themselves out shaking the bowl back and forth. But when someone with clear vision comes along, they see that there are no hairs in the bowl at all. Since there are no hairs as a basis for features, the person with clear vision would not conceive of features those hairs could possess, such as being things or being nothings, being hairs or being [something else], having a certain color, and so on.

So when someone with clear vision says to someone with faulty vision, "There are no hairs in this bowl," they are not denigrating anything. The true nature of the hairs and so on is seen only by people with clear vision who look at the bowl. What is seen by people with diseased vision is not the true nature of the hairs.

In the same way, understand that when analyzing the two truths, what is seen by naïve, ordinary beings (who are afflicted by the diseased vision of ignorance)—the entities of the aggregates, sense sources, and so on—is relative. Perfect buddhas, who are free from the diseased vision of ignorance, do not see the hairlike aggregates. They see the aggregates' true nature. That true nature is suchness, the ultimate truth.

Do the perfect buddhas see the hairlike aggregates and so forth? They see them in the manner of not seeing.

2.2.2.1.1.6.2.3.1.1.1.2.1.1.2.2.1.2.1.2.2.1.2. THE TEACHING ON HOW THE
MUNDANE WORLDLY PERSPECTIVE DOES NOT INVALIDATE [OUR
REFUTATION OF ARISING]

2.2.2.1.1.6.2.3.1.1.1.2.1.1.2.2.1.2.1.2.2.1.2.1. The reasons for which the
worldly perspective is not valid cognition

2.2.2.1.1.6.2.3.1.1.1.2.1.1.2.2.1.2.1.2.2.1.2.2. Therefore the worldly perspective
does not invalidate suchness

2.2.2.1.1.6.2.3.1.1.1.2.1.1.2.2.1.2.1.2.2.1.2.3. The ancillary teaching on the
objects invalidated by the worldly perspective

2.2.2.1.1.6.2.3.1.1.1.2.1.1.2.2.1.2.1.2.2.1.2.1. THE REASONS FOR WHICH
THE WORLDLY PERSPECTIVE IS NOT VALID COGNITION

> If worldly perceptions were valid cognition,
> Worldly people would perceive suchness.
> What need would there be for the other, noble beings, and what
>   would the noble path accomplish?
> The foolish are not suitable sources of valid cognition. (6.30)

In an analysis of the precise nature, if the perceptions of worldly people
were valid cognition, worldly people would perceive the validly established suchness of things. Since they will have relinquished ignorance,[300]
what need would there be for others, noble beings, to teach the precise
nature? Worldly people themselves would already be experts in the ways
of suchness.

One may think, "Worldly beings are already skilled in suchness, but
they still need to rely on the path of the noble ones in order to make suchness perfectly manifest. They also need to rely on others, noble beings,
who teach the methods of the noble path: discipline, hearing, and so on."

If that were the case, the valid cognitions of the eyes and so on of worldly
people would realize suchness. Since the realization of suchness is all that
is needed for attaining liberation, none of the noble paths would offer
anything different from the worldly perspective. Therefore, what need
would there be to exert oneself in the path of the noble ones, hearing and
so on? Applying oneself to it will yield no additional results.

One may respond, "The valid cognitions of worldly people see suchness, but this does not mean that worldly people are noble beings, because
worldly people have yet to relinquish ignorance." Yet if a given subject does

not realize its object, then that subject is not a valid cognizer.[301] Therefore the mind of a foolish, ignorant, worldly person cannot reasonably be said to be valid cognition. For example, someone who is not a jeweler will not be able to tell the difference between ordinary stones and jewels. The *King of Samādhi* sūtra says:

> The eye, ear, and the nose are not valid cognizers.
> The tongue, the body, and mind are not valid cognizers.
> If these faculties were valid cognizers,
> What effect would the noble path have on anyone?

> The sense faculties are not valid cognition.
> By their nature they are matter—neutral phenomena.
> Therefore, those who want the path to nirvāṇa
> Should take up the actions of the noble path.

One may say,[302] "The phrase 'If the seeing of worldly beings was valid cognition . . .' does not mean, 'If the perception of the suchness of things as established by valid cognition were valid cognition . . .' Rather it means, 'If the appearance of true existence that is to be refuted by logic that is seen by worldly valid cognition were valid cognition . . .'"[303] Yet since phenomena appear to be real in worldly valid cognition, that view involves the fault that what is to be refuted by logic would be established by valid cognition. There are many other faults that pertain to that view, but they will not be described here.

Some later Tibetans, namely Shar Tsongkapa and his followers, say that if something exists conventionally, it meets the standard *(go chö/go chod)* of "existence." They also do not accept that the arising and ceasing and so on of interdependence are free from the eight extreme elaborations. They assert that the involvement of elaborations in the relative truth meets the standard of "the involvement of elaborations," but that freedom from elaborations in the ultimate does not meet the standard of "freedom from elaborations." The refutations of these untenable assertions are found in full in the *Ṭīkā*.

2.2.2.1.1.6.2.3.1.1.1.2.1.1.2.2.1.2.1.2.2.1.2.2. THEREFORE THE WORLDLY PERSPECTIVE DOES NOT INVALIDATE SUCHNESS

**Since in all cases the worldly perspective is not valid cognition,
The worldly perspective does not invalidate analyses of suchness.
(6.31ab)**

For the reasons that have been explained, when analyzing the precise nature, in all cases the worldly perspective is not valid cognition. Therefore the worldly perspective does not invalidate analyses of the precise nature, just as the perceptions of a mistaken consciousness do not invalidate the perceptions of an unmistaken consciousness.

2.2.2.1.1.6.2.3.1.1.1.2.1.1.2.2.1.2.1.2.2.1.2.3. THE ANCILLARY TEACHING ON THE OBJECTS INVALIDATED BY THE WORLDLY PERSPECTIVE

**If, in conversation with worldly people, a worldly object was
denied by ultimate reasonings,
The ultimate reasonings would be invalidated by the worldly perspective, because the object refuted is renowned in the world.
(6.31cd)**

How does the worldly perspective invalidate ultimate reasonings? If, [in conversation with worldly people], a worldly object was denied by ultimate reasonings, the ultimate reasonings would be invalidated by the worldly perspective, because the object refuted is renowned in the world.

For example, someone could say, "Something of mine has been stolen." A logician might ask that person, "What was it?" The first person would reply, "A vase." The logician may attempt to reason with the victim, saying, "A vase is not a substantial thing *(dze/rdzas)*, because it is an object of comprehension—it is just like a vase in a dream." Such reasoning would be invalidated by the worldly perspective, because in the worldly perspective vases of the waking period are asserted to be real, whereas vases in dreams are not asserted to be real. The dream example would not match what it attempts to refer to.

Worldly people do not accept such detailed analyses and reasonings. However, when one abides in the perceptions of the noble ones, one becomes authoritative about what is valid cognition. Worldly perceptions would not invalidate one's perceptions at that time.

2.2.2.1.1.6.2.3.1.1.1.2.1.1.2.2.1.2.1.2.2.2. ARISING FROM OTHER IS NOT
EVEN ESTABLISHED FROM THE WORLDLY PERSPECTIVE

> **Because worldly people will merely plant a seed**
> **And say, "I produced this boy"**
> **Or think, "I planted this tree,"**
> **Arising from other does not even exist for the world. (6.32)**

This verse teaches that, although Followers of the Middle Way repeat what
worldly people say in accordance with worldly seeing, the worldly perspective does not invalidate the refutation of arising from other. When worldly
men merely plant the seed of their semen in the womb of a woman, and
later a child is born with a male organ, they say, "I produced this boy." Similarly, having planted a mere mango seed, the seed will mature into a great
tree, and worldly people will think and say to others, "I planted this tree."

Therefore, there is no need to even mention whether things arise from
others when analyzing the precise nature—"arising from other" does not
even exist for the world. Worldly people, apart from merely saying things
like "I produced this boy" and "I planted this tree," do not use any other
conventions, such as describing whether causes and results are different
from each other or whether things "arise from other." It is definitely clear
that when analyzed boys and trees are not seen as different from their
seeds. If they were different, it would be impossible for them to depend on
their seeds for production, just as in the case of persons and trees.[304]

2.2.2.1.1.6.2.3.1.1.1.2.1.1.2.2.1.2.2.2. THE MEANING THAT IS
ESTABLISHED THROUGH THIS REFUTATION[305]
2.2.2.1.1.6.2.3.1.1.1.2.1.1.2.2.1.2.2.2.1. The quality of dependent arising being
free from eternalism and nihilism
2.2.2.1.1.6.2.3.1.1.1.2.1.1.2.2.1.2.2.2.2. If things inherently existed, emptiness
would involve the fault of denial

2.2.2.1.1.6.2.3.1.1.1.2.1.1.2.2.1.2.2.2.1. THE QUALITY OF DEPENDENT
ARISING BEING FREE FROM ETERNALISM AND NIHILISM

> **Since sprouts are not different from seeds,**
> **At the time of the sprout the seed does not disintegrate.**
> **Since they are also not the same,**

We do not say that the seed exists at the time of the sprout. (6.33)

If sprouts and seeds were different from each other, a seed's continuum would be severed when the sprout arose, precisely because of their being different. It is just as in the following two examples: if a buffalo existed, the death of a cow would not interrupt the continuity of the buffalo's existence. The existence of an ordinary being does not prevent a noble being from passing into nirvāṇa.

Therefore, since sprouts are not different from seeds, the seed does not disintegrate and have its continuum severed when the sprout arises. This explanation avoids nihilism. Since sprouts are not the same as seeds, we do not say that the seed exists at the time of the sprout. This explanation avoids eternalism.

Neither seeds nor sprouts are established by way of their nature. They are both mere imputations. Like the seeds and sprouts of a dream, the nature of seeds and sprouts is neither sameness nor difference.

2.2.2.1.1.6.2.3.1.1.1.2.1.1.2.2.1.2.2.2. IF THINGS INHERENTLY EXISTED, EMPTINESS WOULD INVOLVE THE FAULT OF DENIAL

If things inherently arose due to their own characteristics,
Realizing emptiness would deny and destroy them.
But since it is illogical for emptiness to cause things' destruction,
We conclude there are no truly existent things. (6.34)

Thus, without any doubt, one should accept that things do not arise by way of their own characteristics. If that were not the case, things from form up through omniscience, rather than being mere conceptual imputations, would originate or arise in dependence upon causes and conditions by way of their own characteristics, entities, or natures.

It would then absurdly follow that when yogins saw that things are empty of nature, and realized that all phenomena are devoid of nature, their certainty in and realization of emptiness would deny the nature of things, a nature that was inherently arisen. Emptiness would destroy things, just as hammers destroy vases, and so on.

Since speaking of emptiness—saying that things lacked an inherent existence when, in fact, they do exist—would be a denial of true reality, it would destroy things. But that is illogical. Therefore the characteristics of

things, in all instances, do not exist. Thus one should not accept any arising of things. The *Heaps of Jewels (Könchog Tsegpa/dkon mchog brtsegs pa)*
sūtra says:[306]

> O Kāshyapa, furthermore, when one examines the path and
> qualities of the middle way, one discovers that emptiness does
> not render phenomena empty. Phenomena themselves are
> empty. Signlessness does not render phenomena signless. Phe-
> nomena themselves are signless. Wishlessness does not render
> phenomena wishless. Phenomena themselves are wishless. The
> absence of formative activity *(ngönpar dujepa mepa/mngon par
> 'du byed pa med pa)* does not render phenomena free from for-
> mative activity. Phenomena themselves are free from forma-
> tive activity. Nonarising does not render phenomena unarisen.
> Phenomena themselves are unarisen. Nonorigination does not
> render phenomena unoriginated. Phenomena themselves are
> unoriginated.

Some later Tibetans[307] have a different approach to explaining the way
in which all phenomena are empty of their own entities. They say that a
vase, rather than simply being empty of a vase, is empty of a *truly existent*
vase. That, they say, is the meaning of intrinsic emptiness *(rangtong/rang
stong)*.

That interpretation is tantamount to accepting the position of the
counterparts that is refuted by our very root text and its autocommentary. In this Middle Way tradition, all forms of quasi emptiness *(nyitsewe
tongnyi/nyi tshe ba'i stong nyid)* are thoroughly refuted by profound emptiness. The emptiness taught in this tradition is an all-pervading emptiness.
Tsongkapa and his followers, on the other hand, turn away from that tradition and propound its opposite.

They should be questioned in this manner: If what you assert is the
case, is a vase empty of its own entity or is it not? It would be impossible
for you to explain how it is not, because you accept that a Follower of the
Middle Way is someone who speaks of the nonexistence of entities. If you
say that a vase *is* empty of its own entity, what is the "entity of the vase"?
Is it the thing that has a bulbous belly, is thin at its bottom, and performs
the function of carrying water,[308] or is it the true existence inherent in the

very presence of the vase *(döluk kyi drubpe dendrup/sdod lugs kyis grub pa'i bden grub)*?

It is impossible for the entity of the vase to be the second one. Such true existence does not even exist among knowable objects! If you accept the first option—that the entity of the vase is the thing that carries water and so on—but do not accept that a vase is empty of this entity, you fail to qualify as a Follower of the Middle Way who speaks of the nonexistence of entities regarding all phenomena: for you, the entity of the vase is its defining characteristics, the bulbous belly and so on, but the vase is not empty of its own entity.

We, on the other hand, hope we would avoid ascribing the above assertions to the tradition that propounds the nonexistence of entities even in our dreams. Speaking as Tsongkapa and his followers do about this topic hinders the development of realization and contradicts the scriptures of the Transcendent Conqueror.

In the definitive meaning teachings, the Transcendent Conqueror went to great lengths to reject assertions claiming that vases, as opposed to simply being empty of vases, are empty of a phenomenon extraneous to the vases. The Buddha described those assertions as insufficient portrayals of emptiness. Tsongkapa, however, propounds the opposite. The *Heaps of Jewels* says:

> The emptiness of forms does not render forms empty; forms themselves are empty.

The *Ṭīkā* at this point continues to describe how Tsongkapa's view on this topic contradicts countless statements of the Buddha.

2.2.2.1.1.6.2.3.1.1.1.2.1.1.2.2.1.2.3. RECONCILING APPARENT CONTRADICTIONS IN THE REFUTATION OF ARISING FROM OTHER[309]

2.2.2.1.1.6.2.3.1.1.1.2.1.1.2.2.1.2.3.1. Reconciling apparent contradictions with the relative truth

2.2.2.1.1.6.2.3.1.1.1.2.1.1.2.2.1.2.3.2. Reconciling apparent contradictions with what is generally perceived

2.2.2.1.1.6.2.3.1.1.1.2.1.1.2.2.1.2.3.3. Reconciling apparent contradictions with regard to actions and results

2.2.2.1.1.6.2.3.1.1.1.2.1.1.2.2.1.2.3.1. RECONCILING APPARENT
CONTRADICTIONS WITH THE RELATIVE TRUTH
2.2.2.1.1.6.2.3.1.1.1.2.1.1.2.2.1.2.3.1.1. When the relative is analyzed it is not
an object of comprehension
2.2.2.1.1.6.2.3.1.1.1.2.1.1.2.2.1.2.3.1.2. When analyzed both truths are free
from elaborations

2.2.2.1.1.6.2.3.1.1.1.2.1.1.2.2.1.2.3.1.1. WHEN THE RELATIVE IS
ANALYZED IT IS NOT AN OBJECT OF COMPREHENSION

> When things are analyzed,
> Apart from the suchness that is their true nature
> No abiding thing can be found.
> Therefore, the world's conventional truth should not be
>   analyzed. (6.35)

One may think, "Phenomena are indeed free of arising ultimately, but
they do arise from other relatively. If they did not, there would be no arising even in the relative truth, and therefore there would be no distinction
between the two truths."

Granted that, ultimately, there are not two truths. Yet, conventionally,
the relative truth is not just confusion—it is also a method for realizing
the ultimate truth. Without analyzing whether relative phenomena arise
from themselves or from something different than themselves, the Followers of the Middle Way accept—from the perspective of others—whatever
is asserted by worldly people on the basis of worldly ways.

When one analyzes to find whether relative things—forms, feelings,
etc.—arise from themselves or other and so on, one cannot find any abiding thing apart from the suchness that is the true nature of those things.
This suchness itself is the ultimate truth, free of arising and ceasing. The
arising, ceasing, and so on of the relative truth cannot be found.

Therefore one should not analyze the conventional truth of the world
in terms of arising from self, other, and so on. Rather, simply rely on what
is seen by worldly people: "If this exists, that arises." The conventional
should be accepted based only on what is renowned to others.

When one engages in and accepts the conventional truth for a specific
purpose, one should not accept it *after* analysis. As explained above, when

analyzed, conventional reality is unfindable. This unfindability renders any presentation of the conventional inappropriate.

Anything posited *after* analyzing the conventional truth is mistaken: something found after analyzing conventional truth with reasonings will become an ultimate truth and therefore unsuitable as conventional truth. Anything *not* found after analysis would be empty of conventional existence and therefore become ultimate.

2.2.2.1.1.6.2.3.1.1.1.2.1.1.2.2.1.2.3.1.2. WHEN ANALYZED BOTH TRUTHS ARE FREE FROM ELABORATIONS

> **Reasonings prove that arising from self and other**
> **Are illogical in suchness.**
> **Since they also prove that arising is illogical conventionally,**
> **On what basis do you speak of "arising"? (6.36)**

Deluded people, who excessively cling to the phenomena of the conventional truth, may say, "Certain substances are causes for complete affliction and certain are causes for total purity. These substances must arise by way of their own characteristics in the relative."

Such statements are mere empty words. When analyzing for the ultimate, suchness, the reasonings that have been explained prove that the arising of things from self and the arising of things from other are illogical. These reasonings also prove that it is illogical for things to arise from self or other conventionally. On what basis—in either of the truths—do you speak of things arising by way of their own characteristics? Such arising does not exist.

Some, such as the great Shar Tsongkapa, say that what is to be refuted by logic *(rikpe gakja/rigs pa'i dgag bya)* is the true existence in which the entity of the object is established by way of its own presence *(döluk kyi drubpa/sdod lugs kyis grub pa)*. The establishment of things by conventional valid cognition, he says, is *not* to be refuted by logic, because if it were, one would fall into a greatly nihilistic view. By saying this, Tsongkapa in effect accepts as his own view the counterparts' position that Chandrakīrti refutes and then refutes what Chandrakīrti actually taught.

2.2.2.1.1.6.2.3.1.1.1.2.1.1.2.2.1.2.3.2. RECONCILING APPARENT
CONTRADICTIONS WITH WHAT IS GENERALLY PERCEIVED
2.2.2.1.1.6.2.3.1.1.1.2.1.1.2.2.1.2.3.2.1. It is not contradictory for causes and
results to appear even though they are free from elaborations
2.2.2.1.1.6.2.3.1.1.1.2.1.1.2.2.1.2.3.2.2. Therefore phenomena are free from
eternalism and nihilism

2.2.2.1.1.6.2.3.1.1.1.2.1.1.2.2.1.2.3.2.1. IT IS NOT CONTRADICTORY FOR
CAUSES AND RESULTS TO APPEAR EVEN THOUGH THEY ARE FREE
FROM ELABORATIONS

> Empty things, such as reflections,
> Depend on collections of causes and conditions and are
>   accepted in the world.
> For example, a consciousness can arise
> From an empty reflection and bear that reflection's aspect. (6.37)
>
> In the same way, though all things are empty,
> They arise vividly from empty things. (6.38ab)

One may wonder, "If in both truths things do not arise objectively, how is
it that worldly people come to observe events such as arising?" This verse
teaches that what appears for worldly people (arising, causes and results,
and so on) does not entail true existence.

The results that are empty things, such as reflections and illusions,
arise and are observed in dependence upon the collection of their causes
and conditions—mirrors, faces, wood, pebbles, spells,[310] and so on. These
results are accepted in the world. Although the results are not intrinsically
real, they appear to be real results in dependence upon causes and conditions. The causes and conditions, in turn, are also devoid of their own true
existence.

This is illustrated by the example of a reflection in a mirror. In that
example, the reflection is the object condition and is a cause that is empty
of inherent nature. The result that this cause produces is an eye consciousness perceiving the reflection. The eye consciousness arises bearing the
aspect of the reflection.

As the example demonstrates, both causes *and* results are devoid of
their own true existence. They are like emanations arising from emana-

tions.[311] Similarly, all things such as forms and feelings are empty of nature, in that their causes and results do not abide as separate things. However, due to their own empty causes and conditions, empty results vividly arise from the merely conventional, worldly perspective.

Learned ones understand that phenomena—causes and results—are like reflections and have no inherent nature. They observe causes and results knowing that though they appear to be separate, in reality they are not separate. When would it ever be logical to claim causes and results have an inherent nature? They appear to exist, but do not arise by way of an inherent nature. As it was said:

> In a completely clear mirror,
> Reflections appear,
> Though they bear no inherent nature.
> Druma,[312] understand that all phenomena are the same.

2.2.2.1.1.6.2.3.1.1.1.2.1.1.2.2.1.2.3.2.2. THEREFORE PHENOMENA ARE FREE FROM ETERNALISM AND NIHILISM

Since things have no nature in either of the two truths,
They transcend both eternalism and nihilism. (6.38cd)

Since things are empty of nature—just like the aspect of a reflection—they have no nature in the ultimate truth or in the relative truth. Therefore they transcend eternalism and nihilism.

The way in which the great, glorious Tsongkapa and his followers posit, from their own perspective, natures and defining characteristics in the two truths and the way they posit what is to be refuted by logic are refuted thoroughly [in the *Ṭīkā*].

Followers of the Middle Way do not posit any existent or nonexistent phenomenon from their own perspective. If they posited or accepted anything in that manner, they would fall into a great extreme of either eternalism or nihilism.

2.2.2.1.1.6.2.3.1.1.1.2.1.1.2.2.1.2.3.3. RECONCILING APPARENT
CONTRADICTIONS WITH REGARD TO ACTIONS AND RESULTS
2.2.2.1.1.6.2.3.1.1.1.2.1.1.2.2.1.2.3.3.1. The main teaching
2.2.2.1.1.6.2.3.1.1.1.2.1.1.2.2.1.2.3.3.2. The ancillary explanation that the
Buddha's teaching on the support for actions and results is provisional
meaning

2.2.2.1.1.6.2.3.1.1.1.2.1.1.2.2.1.2.3.3.1. THE MAIN TEACHING
2.2.2.1.1.6.2.3.1.1.1.2.1.1.2.2.1.2.3.3.1.1. Though causes and results have no
nature their connection is tenable
2.2.2.1.1.6.2.3.1.1.1.2.1.1.2.2.1.2.3.3.1.2. Establishing that meaning by way of
example
2.2.2.1.1.6.2.3.1.1.1.2.1.1.2.2.1.2.3.3.1.3. Eliminating the absurd consequence
of endlessness

2.2.2.1.1.6.2.3.1.1.1.2.1.1.2.2.1.2.3.3.1.1. THOUGH CAUSES AND RESULTS
HAVE NO NATURE THEIR CONNECTION IS TENABLE
2.2.2.1.1.6.2.3.1.1.1.2.1.1.2.2.1.2.3.3.1.1.1. Teaching our own system
2.2.2.1.1.6.2.3.1.1.1.2.1.1.2.2.1.2.3.3.1.1.2. Refuting the systems of others

2.2.2.1.1.6.2.3.1.1.1.2.1.1.2.2.1.2.3.3.1.1.1. TEACHING OUR OWN SYSTEM

> Actions do not inherently cease,
> And, although there is no all-base, results have the ability to arise
>   from them.
> Therefore, even though a long time might transpire after the end
>   of the action,
> It should be understood that a result correctly arises. (6.39)

The following presentation accords with what is taught in the *Ṭīkā*, where
in an extensive fashion the assertions of the non-Buddhists, Vatsīputrīyas
(Ne Mabupa/gnas ma bu pa), Particularists, Sūtra Followers, and those
who accept the all-base are stated and then refuted with reasonings.

These schools, it seems, without exception assert that the support for
actions *(le/las)* and results is substantially established. Since this view is
refuted by all reasonings, it cannot be the intention of Nāgārjuna and
his disciples. Since there is no inherent nature in either of the two truths,
Nāgārjuna and his followers cast far away the faults of eternalism and nihilism [regarding the connection between actions and their results]. More-

over, even though supports for actions and results such as the all-base do not exist, the connection between actions and results is tenable.

How is it that an action in the past that has long ceased yields a result? In response to this question, some think that an "all-base," which holds the habitual tendencies of past actions, connects actions with their results. Some think that it is another phenomenon called "nonwastage" *(chü mi zawa/chud mi za ba)*, which is like a promissory note placed on a debt. Others think that it is the continuum of consciousness that possesses the habitual tendencies of actions.

According to us, because actions do not inherently arise, they also do not inherently cease or disintegrate. Therefore, it is not impossible for results to originate from such actions. Although there are no intrinsically real things, such as the all-base, that support actions and results, future results have the ability to arise from past actions. Therefore, it should be understood that it is not contradictory for ripened results to correctly arise from actions that had been performed at specific places and specific times, even though a long time transpires after the actions cease.

There is no inherent nature that connects actions with their results. Such a nature is not formed from the cessation or the abiding of postdisintegration *(shikpa/zhigpa)* or the absence of disintegration *(ma shikpa/ma zhig pa)*, which some claim are functional agents of karma.[313] However, for the perspective of others, we [describe the connection between actions and results in the following way].

Such a connection has, from the outset, never arisen. Yet, in terms of the adventitious connection between actions and results that is posited through dependence, the imputation "nonwastage" does not abide as an object. It is a reality of the mere deceptive falsity that is accepted in the world. The reason, however, that the term "nonwastage" [can be correctly applied in the worldly sense is that], since actions have no inherent nature, they do not arise. Since they do not arise, they also do not cease or disintegrate. Therefore it is not possible for any type of wastage to pertain to anything.

Conventionally, there is a connection between actions and results. Though empty of arising and ceasing, causes and results appear to arise and cease. There is nothing that is untenable about that connection, from the perspective of false perceptions.

This is what we say from the perspective of others. We affirm absolutely *no* connection between actions and results as our own position. Since the arising and ceasing of things is not established by any logic or valid cognition of our own, we do not accept anything from our own perspective about them. Nevertheless, in terms of the deceived consciousnesses of the relative world, we do describe, in an echolike way, [the tenability of actions and their results] only to clear away the misconceptions that think, "actions and their results are untenable."

You may wonder, "If the noble ones do not see any connection between actions and their results, how is it that they dispel the misconceptions of others?" It is true that they do not see any phenomenon connecting actions and their results. However, those who have not realized this, due to a lack of insight *(gyatsom du/gya tshom du)*, deny actions and results, and engage in adopting and rejecting incorrectly. Through this, they fall into the abyss of the lower realms. [The noble ones, therefore, provisionally speak of a connection between actions and results] in order to prevent this.

Although Followers of the Middle Way do not accept a support for actions and results such as an all-base, it is not the case that they are unable to dispel the misconceptions of others. Since actions and results are free of the eight extremes, such as arising and ceasing, they do not cease, and therefore no action is wasted. Thus it is not contradictory for results to arise. Followers of the Middle Way are capable of causing others to understand this.

You may say, "It is fine for actions not to cease since they have not arisen. Yet how can a result originate from a nonarisen cause?" All results that can ever originate do so from phenomena that, by their nature, are empty and unarisen. This principle was taught above through examples such as the reflection and so on.[314] If actions inherently arose, that would contradict the relationship between actions and results; it would also contradict all conventions of the worldly relative truth. This is the unmistaken intention of the texts [of Nāgārjuna's tradition].

Here the great Shar Tsongkapa asserts that the uncommon feature of Chandrakīrti's Consequentialist system is the explanation of "postdisintegration," which is, for Tsongkapa, a thing that performs the function of supporting actions and results. In holding this view, he accepts as his own position that which Chandrakīrti has already refuted.

Chandrakīrti set forth his refutation: If you posit the existence of a nature of actions and their results that entails such characteristics as existence, nonexistence, arising, or ceasing, that is a view in which all things are either eternal or annihilated. In particular, when commenting on the thought of the master Nāgārjuna, Chandrakīrti explained that actions, results, the support that connects them, and so on are not established as things that bear an entity. Nevertheless, one must posit the deceiving phenomena of actions, results, the support that connects them, and so on from the perspective of false appearances and what is approved by others as mere dependent arising. This is what [Chandrakīrti] emphasized. Why would he ever assert that disintegrated actions are established as things with their own entities?

You may ask, "In that case, how does one posit the support that connects causes and results on a conventional level?" When analyzed, the connection between causes and results is free of all arising and ceasing. Thus we are free from contradiction in saying that, without analysis, a result arises from a cause (or action) that has not ceased or disintegrated. This is because arising appears to the untainted minds[315] of worldly people. Since there is nothing out of place in speaking of arising in the world, we merely repeat such descriptions when communicating with others.

Furthermore, Chandrakīrti himself simply said, "The connection in which results ripen from the undisintegrated potential or energy of causes or actions is completely tenable." His autocommentary states:

> Since actions do not arise by way of their own essential nature, they also do not cease. It is also possible for a result to originate from an action that has not disintegrated. Therefore, since actions do not disintegrate, the connection between actions and results is completely tenable.

On this topic Majawa Changchub Tsöndrü[316] (*rma bya ba byang chub brtson 'grus,* ca. twelfth century), in his annotations,[317] writes:

> Actions do not cease, and it is possible for a result to originate from an action that has not disintegrated.

Maja says that "actions do not cease and have not disintegrated," or in other words, actions and results ultimately are devoid of cessation and have not disintegrated. He correlates this with nonimplicative negation (*me-gak/med dgag*). Saying that actions and results, relatively, are devoid of cessation and have not disintegrated correlates, according to

Maja, with the implicative negation *(ma yin gag/ma yin dgag)* of what is accepted without analysis.[318] Thus, he says, one should apply either of these in accordance with the context [of whichever of the two truths one is discussing]. [This description by Maja of the two types of negation] is an excellent explanation.

From the perspective of ordinary worldly beings up to, [but not including, the perspective of] the pure postmeditation of the tenth bodhisattva ground, it is posited that the results of happiness and suffering originate, respectively, from the causes of virtuous and nonvirtuous actions, and that the results of saṃsāra and nirvāṇa originate from the two types of origin-of-all actions *(kunjung gi le nyi/kun 'byung gi las gnyis)*. However, when one asks, "When such-and-such result originated from such-and-such cause, did it originate from something that had disintegrated or that had not disintegrated?," one's question becomes analysis. To posit the causes and effects of the relative truth *after* analyzing is the system of the Proponents of Things. Followers of the Middle Way do not posit anything connected to the relative truth after analysis, because they do not accept that any phenomenon can withstand analysis.

When one analyzes, there is no origination of results from either a cause that has disintegrated or a cause that has not disintegrated. If a result were to originate after its cause had disintegrated, any result could arise from any cause. If results were to originate from a cause that had not disintegrated, no results would depend on conditions.

If you assume that a result arises following the postdisintegration state of its cause, that view entails nihilism: the continuity of the subsequent phenomena would be severed. If you assume that a result arises following its cause which had not disintegrated, that view entails eternalism: all things would have to exist simultaneously. Thus postdisintegration is not a suitable cause for phenomena, nor is nondisintegration.

When one analyzes, one cannot posit the connection between causes and results, their support, and so on in any way, including conventionally. Understanding this is the supreme way of this teaching system.

[2.2.2.1.1.6.2.3.1.1.1.2.1.1.2.2.1.2.3.3.1.1.2. REFUTING THE SYSTEMS OF OTHERS][319]
This section is a supplementary refutation of the assertion that the state of postdisintegration is a thing. [The next stage of our analysis] is the explana-

tion of how the affirmations [used by those who assert postdisintegration as a thing] are logically untenable. [This, however, will not be elucidated here. Rather] it is to be found in the *Ṭīkā*, which describes how, in general, the assertion of the disintegration or postdisintegration of things is the domain of worldly people and of scholars who are Proponents of Things, and even conventionally, postdisintegration cannot in any logical way be posited as a thing. Thus the *Ṭīkā*, in addition to many eloquent explanations on this topic, provides extensive affirmations and refutations.

The master Chandrakīrti taught that, in the context of no analysis, sprouts do not arise from anything disintegrated or not disintegrated. Nevertheless, in accordance with what is accepted in the world, the Followers of the Middle Way merely say, "sprouts arise." Yet, in the context of an analysis accepted by others, the Followers of the Middle Way refute even the mere existence of all three phases of disintegration: past disintegration, future disintegration, and present disintegration. Therefore what need is there to speak of whether or not the Followers of the Middle Way refute arising?

2.2.2.1.1.6.2.3.1.1.1.2.1.1.2.2.1.2.3.3.1.2. ESTABLISHING THAT MEANING BY WAY OF EXAMPLE

> Due to seeing certain objects in a dream,
> Lust will arise in fools, even after they wake up.
> In the same way, results exist even though they arise
> From actions that have ceased and have no inherent nature. (6.40)

One may think, "You say it is illogical for results to arise from actions that are devoid of inherent nature ultimately and that, in the relative truth, have ceased. If that is the case, the arising of actions on any level is certainly illogical if actions are both devoid of inherent nature and have ceased." That is not so: the meaning of the previous verse[320] will now be explained using an example.

Having seen pleasing observable objects in a dream—such as visions of making love to an attractive local woman—some fools will allow those objects to cause lust to arise, even after they wake up and even though those objects were nonexistent by nature and have already ceased.

In the same way, dreamlike results exist even though they arise from actions that have long since ceased and that have no inherent nature.

2.2.2.1.1.6.2.3.1.1.1.2.1.1.2.2.1.2.3.3.1.3. ELIMINATING THE ABSURD
CONSEQUENCE OF ENDLESSNESS

2.2.2.1.1.6.2.3.1.1.1.2.1.1.2.2.1.2.3.3.1.3.1. The actual teaching on eliminating
the absurd consequence of endlessness

2.2.2.1.1.6.2.3.1.1.1.2.1.1.2.2.1.2.3.3.1.3.2. Even though they are empty, causes
and results can be individually ascertained and are inconceivable

2.2.2.1.1.6.2.3.1.1.1.2.1.1.2.2.1.2.3.3.1.3.1. THE ACTUAL TEACHING ON
ELIMINATING THE ABSURD CONSEQUENCE OF ENDLESSNESS

> **Although false objects are equal in terms of not existing,**
> **Someone with diseased vision will see images of hairs**
> **But not the images of other false objects.**
> **In the same way know that results, once they ripen, do not ripen**
> **again. (6.41)**

One might say, "You accept that ripened results originate due to actions
that do not inherently arise and yet are inexhaustible. If that is the case, ripened results would originate again from actions that had already yielded
results. The origination of results would be endless." That is not so.

Objects such as falling hairs for people with diseased vision and a childless woman's son are equal in terms of not existing. Nevertheless, someone
with diseased vision sees images of hairs, which are not existent, but they
do not see the images of other false objects, such as the horns of a donkey,
a childless woman's son, and so on.

In the same way, actions, whether they have yielded a ripened result
or not, are equal in terms of not ceasing and not inherently existing.
Know that results only originate from actions that have not yielded ripened results, and results do not ripen again from actions that have already
ripened.

This is not something that we affirm as our own position. It is merely a
way to dispel misconceptions by employing in dialogue what is accepted
by others. We do not assert that "the horns of a rabbit, the childless woman's son, and so on are nonexistent," because if something is not established as existent, it is untenable for it to be nonexistent.

2.2.2.1.1.6.2.3.1.1.1.2.1.1.2.2.1.2.3.3.1.3.2. EVEN THOUGH THEY ARE EMPTY, CAUSES AND RESULTS CAN BE INDIVIDUALLY ASCERTAINED AND ARE INCONCEIVABLE

> Intelligent ones see that negative results ripen from negative
>   actions
> And that positive results ripen from positive actions;
> Knowing that both positive and negative actions do not exist,
>   they will become liberated.
> The Buddha halted speculation about actions and their results.
>   (6.42)

The example in the previous verse shows that ripened results are never indeterminate. Moreover, the ripened results of virtue and nonvirtue can be individually ascertained. Just as in the example of falling hairs, although the hairs and so on are devoid of nature, their perception by people with diseased vision occurs in a definite way.

Wise ones see that although virtuous actions and nonvirtuous actions have no inherent nature, unpleasant results ripen due to their cause, negative or nonvirtuous actions—they do not ripen from virtuous actions. Pleasant or positive results ripen due to virtuous actions, not due to nonvirtuous actions. Furthermore, wise ones, endowed with the intelligence that realizes the lack of inherent nature of both virtuous actions and nonvirtuous actions, will become liberated.

However, it is very difficult to realize the way in which actions that have no inherent nature can yield results. It is also very difficult to realize that the ripened results of such actions are individually definite. For these reasons, the Transcendent Conqueror saw that, without a complete understanding of actions and results, ordinary beings would deny actions and results and fall from a proper relationship with the relative truth. Bearing this in mind he taught that "the ripening of the results of actions is inconceivable."

In this way, the Buddha halted the speculation *(sempa/sems pa)* of naïve beings about the connection between actions and their results. He did this because ordinary or "near-sighted" beings are incapable of understanding "such-and-such result arises from such-and-such cause." The realization that actions and results do not exist by way of their nature, moreover, occurs due to the supreme knowledges of hearing, contemplating, and meditating. It does not occur at random.

Followers of the Middle Way do not, from their own perspective, affirm or accept any positive statements *(yongchö/yongs gcod)* about actions and results. Nevertheless, there is a danger in not saying anything at all about actions and their results to naïve, ordinary beings. Ordinary beings have not yet realized that actions and results have no inherent nature. Due to their lack of such intelligence, if they were not taught the difference between virtue and nonvirtue, they would come to deny actions and results. They would think incorrectly of virtue and nonvirtue, what to adopt and what to reject. Not conducting themselves properly, they would fall to the lower realms.

For that reason, the Followers of the Middle Way communicate the undeceiving presentation of actions and their results. When doing so, they speak from the conventional perspective of others, even though actions and results are not truly established.

Therefore the Followers of the Middle Way do not deny actions and results in the manner of proponents of nonexistence. Nor do they cling to or propound actions and results as real phenomena in the manner of the Proponents of Things. Their approach is to speak of the mere dependent arising that is free of all extremes.

2.2.2.1.1.6.2.3.1.1.1.2.1.1.2.2.1.2.3.3.2. THE ANCILLARY EXPLANATION THAT THE BUDDHA'S TEACHING ON THE SUPPORT FOR ACTIONS AND RESULTS IS PROVISIONAL MEANING
2.2.2.1.1.6.2.3.1.1.1.2.1.1.2.2.1.2.3.3.2.1. The teachings on the all-base and so on are provisional meaning
2.2.2.1.1.6.2.3.1.1.1.2.1.1.2.2.1.2.3.3.2.2. Everything that the Tathāgata taught as existent is provisional meaning

2.2.2.1.1.6.2.3.1.1.1.2.1.1.2.2.1.2.3.3.2.1. THE TEACHINGS ON THE ALL-BASE AND SO ON ARE PROVISIONAL MEANING

> "The all-base exists," "The person exists,"
> And "Only these aggregates exist"—
> These statements were made to those
> Who could not grasp the very profound meaning. (6.43)

Someone may have the following doubts: "Followers of the Middle Way say that actions and results have no inherent nature. If that is the case, what are we to think of the Buddha's statements in the noble *Descent into Lanka* and other sūtras? In those scriptures, the Buddha taught that the all-base consciousness (*ālayavijñāna, kunshi namshe/kun gzhi'i rnam shes*) is the basis for implanting seeds of the potential for limitless phenomena. He described it is as the cause for the arising of all things, like waves arising from an ocean. Are you saying that this all-base consciousness is nonexistent in *all* respects?"

It is not nonexistent in all respects for *some* individuals. The Buddha gave these teachings to people whose style of clinging made the idea of an all-base consciousness appealing to them. Such people were inclined to believe in its existence. However, this teaching was not literal. It was given for the specific purpose of taming students who had a disposition toward the idea of an all-base by teaching that it exists.

If that was the purpose for the teaching, what basis was he really thinking of *(gongshi/dgongs gzhi)*[321] when he made those statements? He was thinking only of emptiness. [In teaching the all-base, the Buddha was actually describing nothing other than emptiness], yet using language that describes an existent thing called the "all-base." He did this because these teachings allow students with certain potentials to get closer to the actual nature of things.

Thus in some sūtras the Buddha spoke of the all-base consciousness as an existing phenomenon that connected actions and results. To some disciples the Buddha also spoke of the person as an existing phenomenon. For example:

> Bhikṣhus, the five aggregates are the load; the carrier of the load is the person.

The Buddha also told some students, "Only these mere aggregates, which are devoid of a self, exist." All of these are merely statements made with a special intention.[322] What was the intention? Some disciples had habituated to the views of the tīrthikas for a long time and had developed views of truly existent things. These disciples would not have been able to grasp the very profound meaning of emptiness if they were taught it right away. Having become frightened upon hearing of emptiness, they would renounce the teachings of the Buddha.

So that such individuals could enter gradually into the teachings, the all-base and so on were taught to exist. In this way the disciples could consider the all-base to be a suitable support for actions and results—in a similar manner as the self, primal substance, and so on that were asserted by the tīrthikas. Having entered into the teachings of the Blissfully Gone One, these students will correctly realize the genuine meaning of his scriptures. They will, thereby, naturally come to relinquish their clinging to the all-base. This method of teaching a provisional meaning only brings about positive qualities. It is not the basis for anything negative. As Āryadeva said:

> Start out with what they like
> As a basis for analysis.
> This will in no way cause them
> To be corrupt vessels for the genuine dharma.

2.2.2.1.1.6.2.3.1.1.1.2.1.1.2.2.1.2.3.3.2.2. EVERYTHING THAT THE TATHĀGATA TAUGHT AS EXISTENT IS PROVISIONAL MEANING

Even though he was free of the view of the transitory collection,
The Buddha spoke of "I" and "mine."
In the same way, though things have no inherent nature,
The statement "They exist" is a provisional meaning. (6.44)

In order to guide disciples along the path of the supreme teachings, not only did the Buddha teach the all-base, for even though he had fully relinquished the view of the transitory collection and was free of all clinging to "I" and "mine," the Buddha used conventions such as "I" and "mine" in order to be understood by worldly people. He said things such as "At such and such a time, I . . ." In the same way, all phenomena from form through omniscience are not established by way of their own nature. However, in order for disciples to understand the profound meaning, the Buddha taught, as a provisional meaning, that phenomena from form through omniscience "exist." This principle can also be applied to the Buddha's teachings on the two truths, the four noble truths, the three natures, and so on.

The following verses harmonize with the view of the Eastern Mountain faction:[323]

If the guides of the world[324]
Did not act in ways that accord with the world,
No one would know what the Buddha's teachings were
Or who the Buddha was.
The Buddha knew that the aggregates,
Sources, and constituents are of one nature,
But nonetheless taught them separately to the beings of the three
    realms.
This is how he acted in accordance with the world.

He described phenomena, which are nameless,
Using an inconceivable variety of names
That he taught to sentient beings.
This too is acting in accordance with the world.

He taught about the nonexistence of things
And about how it accords with the nature of buddhas.
Yet there is no nonexistence of things in reality.
This too is acting in accordance with the world.

He saw no objects or nonobjects,
Yet he is the supreme of speakers
Who teach on cessation and genuine reality.
This too is acting in accordance with the world.[325]

Throughout the three times,
A nature of sentient beings cannot be observed.
Nevertheless, the Buddha taught about such a nature in this world
    realm.
This too is acting in accordance with the world.

What is the way to act in accordance with the world? The Followers of
the Middle Way describe all phenomena according to the minds of worldly
people. When not analyzing, they posit phenomena according to worldly
perceptions of truth and falsity. In harmony with that, they say, "The two
truths exist" as a repetition of what is commonly accepted.

However, it would be untenable to posit an object in accordance with the minds of worldly people *after* analysis, for there is no actual "truth of falsity" that is real. And there is no "truth of reality" established as an object. "False truth" and "true as a falsity" are not established as objects.

No phenomena of either of the two truths, whether they are things—from form through omniscience—or nonthings, are established by their own entities. Any positing of elaborations, such as existence or nonexistence, is simply acting in accordance with the perceptions of beings to be tamed. It is merely a repetition of the worldly perspective.

This repetition of the worldly perspective can also distinguish Consequentialists from Autonomists. The Autonomists accept as conventional valid cognition the refutations and affirmations that the world accepts as valid. In this way Autonomists act in accordance with the world and refute an inherent nature of things. For Consequentialists, the refutations and affirmations that are renowned as valid in the world are not valid cognitions, even conventionally. However, they do repeat worldly refutations and affirmations and, in that way, act in accordance with the world while debating. In this way they refute an inherent nature of things.

2.2.2.1.1.6.2.3.1.1.1.2.1.1.2.2.2. THE ANCILLARY REFUTATION OF THE SYSTEM OF THE PROPONENTS OF CONSCIOUSNESS (NAMRIK MAWA/RNAM RIG SMRA BA)

2.2.2.1.1.6.2.3.1.1.1.2.1.1.2.2.2.1. Their position

2.2.2.1.1.6.2.3.1.1.1.2.1.1.2.2.2.2. The refutation of their position

2.2.2.1.1.6.2.3.1.1.1.2.1.1.2.2.2.1. THEIR POSITION[326]

2.2.2.1.1.6.2.3.1.1.1.2.1.1.2.2.2.1.1. The presentation of the contents of the scriptures

2.2.2.1.1.6.2.3.1.1.1.2.1.1.2.2.2.1.2. The presentation of their system on the basis of those scriptures

2.2.2.1.1.6.2.3.1.1.1.2.1.1.2.2.2.1.1. THE PRESENTATION OF THE CONTENTS OF THE SCRIPTURES

2.2.2.1.1.6.2.3.1.1.1.2.1.1.2.2.2.1.1.1. The reasons for which the heirs of the victorious ones realize the three levels of existence to be merely consciousness

2.2.2.1.1.6.2.3.1.1.1.2.1.1.2.2.2.1.1.2. The teaching on the cause of consciousness despite the nonexistence of outer objects

2.2.2.1.1.6.2.3.1.1.1.2.1.1.2.2.2.1.1.1. THE REASONS FOR WHICH THE HEIRS OF THE VICTORIOUS ONES REALIZE THE THREE LEVELS OF EXISTENCE TO BE MERELY CONSCIOUSNESS

> Without an apprehended object, the apprehender cannot be
> seen.
> Excellently realizing the three realms to be merely consciousness,
> The bodhisattvas who abide in supreme knowledge
> Realize that suchness is mere consciousness. (6.45)[327]

Followers of the Middle Way and others teach the all-base and so on as provisional meaning and explain that all phenomena are devoid of inherent nature. The Proponents of Consciousness, however, do not accept that position. They have their own system, made up from their own thoughts. The following section is devoted to clarifying their position.

Due to the reasonings that will be explained, bodhisattvas realize that the apprehended objects of mind do not exist. Therefore, they also do not see the apprehender that depends upon those objects. For a long time they cultivate familiarity with the view that "These three realms are merely consciousness, devoid of outer objects." When their familiarity reaches its highest point, they excellently realize, in the manner of personally cognizing it for themselves, a mere, inexpressible consciousness, free of both apprehender and apprehended.

Therefore these bodhisattvas, who abide in the meditation of the perfection of supreme knowledge on the sixth ground, excellently realize the ultimate suchness, the nature of phenomena, to have the nature of mere consciousness. Since there is no form, they realize primary minds and mental events to be mere dependently arisen things. In this way they realize the precise nature to be mere consciousness.

2.2.2.1.1.6.2.3.1.1.1.2.1.1.2.2.2.1.1.2. THE TEACHING ON THE CAUSE OF CONSCIOUSNESS DESPITE THE NONEXISTENCE OF OUTER OBJECTS

> Just as when the wind blows on a great ocean
> Waves arise, in the same way
> From the "all-base," the seed of everything,
> Mere consciousness originates through the all-base's own
>   potential. (6.46)

If all appearances are mere consciousness without objects, how can a consciousness possessing the aspect of form arise, despite the nonexistence of external objects such as form? When the wind blows on a great ocean, small and large waves arise precisely according to their conditions. In the same way, that which is called the "all-base" consciousness is the seed of all completely afflicted phenomena. It has been active since beginningless time, and it maintains its continuity by arising anew from moment to moment.

When the habitual tendencies of clinging to apprehender and apprehended fully ripen, the things associated with the all-base attain their existence. During their cessation, they again plant specific habitual tendencies in the all-base. These habitual tendencies become causes for the arising of other consciousnesses that are congruent with them.

Thus, due to the full ripening of their own potential, mere impure, dependent *(paratantra, shenwang/gzhan dbang)* consciousnesses arise. These dependent consciousnesses are conceived to be apprehender and apprehended by naïve beings, even though an apprehended object that is different from consciousness does not even slightly exist. For example, those who propound Īshvara as the cause of all things say:

> Just as spiders cause spider webs,
> Water crystals bring forth water,
> And trees are the causes of their branches,
> Īshvara is the cause of all embodied creatures.

Thus they assert that Īshvara and so on are the creators of beings. In the same way, the proponents of the all-base consciousness say that the all-base itself is the cause of all things. The only difference between the two views is that Īshvara is said to be permanent, whereas the all-base is said to be impermanent.

2.2.2.1.1.6.2.3.1.1.1.2.1.1.2.2.2.1.2. THE PRESENTATION OF THEIR SYSTEM ON THE BASIS OF THOSE SCRIPTURES

> Therefore the entity of the dependent nature
> Is the cause for the imputed existence of things.
> It originates without outer apprehended objects,
> Exists, and has a nature that is not an object of elaborations.
> (6.47)

This section explains the proofs the Proponents of Consciousness set forth for the existence of the all-base, based on what they say is taught in the scriptures. The entity of the dependent nature, incorrect conception *(yangdak minpe kuntok/yang dag min pa'i kun rtog)*,[328] is the cause for the imputations of the existence of things—persons and phenomena. One must accept this, because the dependent nature is asserted to be the basis of all mistaken conception. Since there is no other basis for confusion, without it the mistakenness of the selves of persons and phenomena could not logically arise.

For example, in the case of mistaking a rope to be a snake, the cause of mistakenness is the rope: without it the mistake would not occur. Also, it is just as in the case of mistaking something to be a vase—the cause of this mistakenness is earth and so on. Earth and so on are what are to be relied upon as the causes of mistakenness, not space and so on.

244   FEAST FOR THE FORTUNATE – GROUND SIX: THE MANIFEST

To support their position, the Proponents of Consciousness use logical reasonings such as the following: "Given the cognition of blue and so forth despite the nonexistence of outer objects, the subject, its cause is the dependent nature, because the dependent nature is the cause of all completely afflicted and completely pure phenomena."

This dependent nature is said to have three qualities: 1) despite the nonexistence of external apprehended objects, it entails dualistic appearances due to its own habitual tendencies; 2) it exists as the substantial basis of those dualistic appearances and of the superimpositions of the two types of self; 3) and it exists in the nature of not being an object of any elaborations—terms or conceptions. The third quality applies to the dependent nature because all terms and conceptions are the sphere of experience of superimposition, and because the dependent nature is the sphere of experience of both the pure postmeditation phase and of worldly people.

Such are the assertions of the Proponents of Consciousness.

2.2.2.1.1.6.2.3.1.1.1.2.1.1.2.2.2.2. THE REFUTATION OF THEIR POSITION
2.2.2.1.1.6.2.3.1.1.1.2.1.1.2.2.2.2.1. The actual refutation
2.2.2.1.1.6.2.3.1.1.1.2.1.1.2.2.2.2.2. Reconciling apparent contradictions in the refutation

2.2.2.1.1.6.2.3.1.1.1.2.1.1.2.2.2.2.1. THE ACTUAL REFUTATION
2.2.2.1.1.6.2.3.1.1.1.2.1.1.2.2.2.2.1.1. The refutation of a consciousness without outer objects
2.2.2.1.1.6.2.3.1.1.1.2.1.1.2.2.2.2.1.2. The refutation of a dependent nature that is nondual and substantially established
2.2.2.1.1.6.2.3.1.1.1.2.1.1.2.2.2.2.1.3. The refutation of the dependent nature's existence as something that is beyond all conceptual elaborations
2.2.2.1.1.6.2.3.1.1.1.2.1.1.2.2.2.2.1.4. The refutation of the dependent nature's existence as the cause of relative appearances

2.2.2.1.1.6.2.3.1.1.1.2.1.1.2.2.2.2.1.1. THE REFUTATION OF A CONSCIOUSNESS WITHOUT OUTER OBJECTS
2.2.2.1.1.6.2.3.1.1.1.2.1.1.2.2.2.2.1.1.1. The refutation of the concordant example of the dream
2.2.2.1.1.6.2.3.1.1.1.2.1.1.2.2.2.2.1.1.2. The refutation of the concordant example of diseased vision

2.2.2.1.1.6.2.3.1.1.1.2.1.1.2.2.2.2.1.1.3. The refutation of the concordant example of skeletons

2.2.2.1.1.6.2.3.1.1.1.2.1.1.2.2.2.2.1.1.4. The refutation of other examples for mistakenness

2.2.2.1.1.6.2.3.1.1.1.2.1.1.2.2.2.2.1.1.5. The summary

2.2.2.1.1.6.2.3.1.1.1.2.1.1.2.2.2.2.1.1.1. THE REFUTATION OF THE CONCORDANT EXAMPLE OF THE DREAM

2.2.2.1.1.6.2.3.1.1.1.2.1.1.2.2.2.2.1.1.1.1. Mind is not established in dreams

2.2.2.1.1.6.2.3.1.1.1.2.1.1.2.2.2.2.1.1.1.2. If recollection established the existence of consciousness, it would also establish the existence of objects

2.2.2.1.1.6.2.3.1.1.1.2.1.1.2.2.2.2.1.1.1.3. The refutation of rebuttals

2.2.2.1.1.6.2.3.1.1.1.2.1.1.2.2.2.2.1.1.1.1. MIND IS NOT ESTABLISHED IN DREAMS

> **What is your example of a mind without an outer object?**
> **If you say, "It is like a dream," this must be investigated.**
> **For when I am dreaming, my mind does not exist.**
> **Thus your example does not apply. (6.48)**

The position of the Proponents of Consciousness is to be analyzed as follows. Since consciousness is defined as that which is aware of objects, it is impossible for there to be a consciousness without an object. Therefore the question is, "What is your example of a mind without an outer object?" In response, they say that in dreams there are no objects yet there is consciousness. For instance, they say, if one falls asleep in a small room and dreams of a herd of elephants gathered together, there are no objects at that time in the way they are dreamt. Even though elephants cannot fit in the room, there is a dream consciousness apprehending them. The dependent consciousness that does not have outer objects is just like that.

Whether there is a consciousness in dreams that is without objects is something to be investigated. Not only in waking life, but also when I, a Follower of the Middle Way, am dreaming, the mind endowed with the aspect of a herd of crazy oxen does not exist, for exactly the same reason that objects in a dream do not exist—because it is unarisen. Since there is no dream mind, the dream example of you Proponents of Consciousness is not applicable in connection with either waking life or dreams. Therefore there are no consciousnesses without outer objects.

2.2.2.1.1.6.2.3.1.1.1.2.1.1.2.2.2.2.1.1.1.2. IF RECOLLECTION
ESTABLISHED THE EXISTENCE OF CONSCIOUSNESS, IT WOULD
ALSO ESTABLISH THE EXISTENCE OF OBJECTS

> If the recollection of the dream while awake
> Establishes the existence of mind, outer objects in dreams would
>   be established in the same way.
> Just as you recall, "I saw something,"
> So the outer objects would exist. (6.49)

You may respond, "There is a mistaken consciousness at the time of dreams, because if there were not, one would not remember one's dream experiences after having awoken." However, that reason is not included in its predicate,[329] as will be explained below.

You say that a mistaken mental consciousness can be established as an existent phenomenon by the memory of the experience of the mistaken dream consciousness during the waking state. Yet the same reasoning applies to the outer objects of the dream—they would also be proven as existent.

In the waking state, you remember the consciousnesses that experienced your dreams and think, "I saw such and such." You assert the existence of the dream consciousness due to that recollection. In the same way, the experience of the elephants and so on, the outer objects of the dream, is also recalled. Therefore even the outer objects perceived during dreams would be existents according to your logic. If you say that the reason is not included in the predicate,[330] your response establishes that consciousness does not exist.

2.2.2.1.1.6.2.3.1.1.1.2.1.1.2.2.2.2.1.1.1.3. THE REFUTATION OF THE
REBUTTALS
2.2.2.1.1.6.2.3.1.1.1.2.1.1.2.2.2.2.1.1.1.3.1. The rebuttal
2.2.2.1.1.6.2.3.1.1.1.2.1.1.2.2.2.2.1.1.1.3.2. The refutation of the rebuttal

2.2.2.1.1.6.2.3.1.1.1.2.1.1.2.2.2.2.1.1.1.3.1. THE REBUTTAL

> You say, "It is impossible for there to be an eye consciousness
>   during sleep.
> It does not exist; there is only mental consciousness.

> Its images are clung to as external objects,
> And the waking state is just like this dream example." (6.50)

The Proponents of Consciousness put forth the following additional reason in order to establish their dream example. Sleep causes the eye consciousness and so on to dissolve, rendering the sense consciousnesses impossible. For that reason, in dreams outer objects of form and so on do not exist. What does exist is only the mental consciousness that appears as objects and has been adulterated by sleep. During dreams merely the images of that consciousness are clung to as external objects. Thus in dreams there are no objects yet there is consciousness. The waking state is the same.

2.2.2.1.1.6.2.3.1.1.1.2.1.1.2.2.2.2.1.1.1.3.2. THE REFUTATION OF THE REBUTTAL

2.2.2.1.1.6.2.3.1.1.1.2.1.1.2.2.2.2.1.1.1.3.2.1. The eighteen constituents in dreams are all false

2.2.2.1.1.6.2.3.1.1.1.2.1.1.2.2.2.2.1.1.1.3.2.2. That falsity also applies during the waking state

2.2.2.1.1.6.2.3.1.1.1.2.1.1.2.2.2.2.1.1.1.3.2.3. In both the example and in reality, objects and consciousness are either equally existent or equally nonexistent

2.2.2.1.1.6.2.3.1.1.1.2.1.1.2.2.2.2.1.1.1.3.2.1. THE EIGHTEEN CONSTITUENTS (DHĀTU, KHAM/KHAMS) IN DREAMS ARE ALL FALSE

> In the same way you hold that outer objects
> Are unarisen in dreams, so the mind of dreams is also unarisen.
> The eye, the object of the eye, and the mind generated by those:
> All three of these are false. (6.51)

> The triad of the ear and the other sensory triads are also
>   unarisen. (6.52a)

The position of the Proponents of Consciousness is not valid: it is impossible for a mental consciousness to arise in dreams. You Proponents of Consciousness assert in your system that outer objects do not arise in dreams.

In the same way, the mental consciousness also does not arise in dreams, because the reasons for which objects and consciousnesses arise or do not arise are equivalent. From the confused perspective of dreams both exist; in the waking state neither exist.

When one sees forms in the waking state, the eye, forms, and eye consciousness are observable. In the same way, from the confused perspective of the dream state, there is the semblance of the collection of the eye, the object of the eye, and the mind generated by those two. Yet if one analyzes, in the same way that the eye and forms do not exist in the dream, the dream mind also does not exist—all three are false.

In the same way the triad of the ear, sound, and ear consciousness— along with the other triads of object, faculty, and consciousness up through the mind faculty, mental phenomena, and the mental consciousness—does not arise. In terms of mere appearances, all of them are equally existent; when analyzed, all of them are empty. Since in dreams all eighteen constituents are false, it is illogical to say, "The mental consciousness truly exists."

In this section of the Ṭīkā, there is a brief presentation of proofs and refutations connected to the assertions of the Proponents of Consciousness.[331]

2.2.2.1.1.6.2.3.1.1.1.2.1.1.2.2.2.2.1.1.1.3.2.2. THAT FALSITY ALSO APPLIES DURING THE WAKING STATE

> Just as they are in dreams, so here in the waking state,
> Things are false, and mind does not exist.
> There are no objects of experience and also no faculties.
>   (6.52bcd)

This verse teaches that not only are the objects, faculties, and consciousnesses in dreams false, in the waking state also the three are not established. Just as those three are false in dreams, so here in the waking state all things that are objects, faculties, and consciousnesses—from form through omniscience—are false. There is no mind that observes those things, nor are there objects of experience that such a mind would observe. The faculties that are the support for such observations are also not established in either of the truths in the way that they appear and the way in which they are clung to. It is said in the sūtras:

Just as one can observe sentient beings in illusions,
Things appear, yet in suchness they are not genuine.
They are like illusions and dreams.
Such a dharma was taught by the Blissfully Gone One.

And,

The beings of existence are like dreams.
Here there is no one who dies and no birth either.
No sentient beings, names, nor life force can be found.
Thus all these phenomena are like foam on water and plantain trees.

2.2.2.1.1.6.2.3.1.1.1.2.1.1.2.2.2.2.1.1.1.3.2.3. IN BOTH THE EXAMPLE AND IN REALITY, OBJECTS AND CONSCIOUSNESS ARE EITHER EQUALLY EXISTENT OR EQUALLY NONEXISTENT

Just as the triad of perceptions exists while awake,
So the triad exists in dreams for as long as one is still dreaming.
Just as upon awakening from dreams the dream triad does not exist,
It is the same when waking from the sleep of ignorance. (6.53)

It has been explained how, in dependence upon the waking state, the entire triad of dream objects, faculties, and consciousnesses is unarisen. However in a dream, from the perspective of a dream consciousness, all three exist. In the worldly perspective beings are controlled by the sleep of ignorance. When they wake up from ordinary sleep, the triad of objects, faculties, and consciousnesses exists from their perspective.

In the same way, for as long as one is still dreaming,[332] the triad of dream objects, faculties, and consciousnesses will exist for the dreaming person. This is so because the three appear in the dream and they are clung to by the dreamer as being real. Nāgārjuna's *Commentary on the Heart of Awakening (Bodhichittavivaraṇa, Changchub Semdrel/byang chub sems 'grel)* says:

There is no difference between things in dreams and things in the waking state
In terms of their performance of functions.
All things are the same as things in a dream:

They are equal in terms of performing functions, but they have no inherent nature.

Thus the Transcendent Conqueror and the noble and glorious protector Nāgārjuna and his followers—all of the early masters—extensively taught that an entity of things cannot be observed. However these teachings were explained by some later scholars to mean that the entity of things is to perform a function. That is very mistaken. Here in the *Ṭīkā* there is a presentation of proofs and refutations related to the assertions of these later Tibetans.[333]

This text does not teach that conventionally the eighteen constituents of dreams and those of the waking state are equally existent. Rather it teaches that the eighteen constituents are, in actuality, between realness and falsity, equally false in both the waking and dream states. When one awakens from the small sleep of worldly sleeping, the triad of the dream state does not exist. Similarly, when one completely awakens from the great sleep of deluded ignorance, through uprooting it and realizing the dharmadhātu, it is just as when waking from a dream—there are no appearances of the triad of perception. Since there are no objects, it would be illogical for a consciousness to exist.

2.2.2.1.1.6.2.3.1.1.1.2.1.1.2.2.2.2.1.1.2. THE REFUTATION OF THE CONCORDANT EXAMPLE OF DISEASED VISION
2.2.2.1.1.6.2.3.1.1.1.2.1.1.2.2.2.2.1.1.2.1. The actual refutation
2.2.2.1.1.6.2.3.1.1.1.2.1.1.2.2.2.2.1.1.2.2. The refutation of the rebuttal

2.2.2.1.1.6.2.3.1.1.1.2.1.1.2.2.2.2.1.1.2.1. THE ACTUAL REFUTATION
2.2.2.1.1.6.2.3.1.1.1.2.1.1.2.2.2.2.1.1.2.1.1. Objects and consciousnesses are equally real or false
2.2.2.1.1.6.2.3.1.1.1.2.1.1.2.2.2.2.1.1.2.1.2. The consequence that if they were not equal, people with no diseased vision would also see strands of hair

2.2.2.1.1.6.2.3.1.1.1.2.1.1.2.2.2.2.1.1.2.1.1. OBJECTS AND CONSCIOUSNESSES ARE EQUALLY REAL OR FALSE

The eye consciousness arisen from a diseased eye faculty
And the hairs seen due to the disease itself

Are both real from the perspective of that consciousness,
But from the perspective of a person that clearly perceives
objects, both are false. (6.54)

You may say, "Outer objects do not exist but consciousness does, because someone with diseased vision can observe hairs and so on that do not exist." That is untenable, because this example is exactly like the example of a dream. A consciousness arisen from a diseased eye faculty perceives hairs and so on due to disease. In dependence upon this mistaken consciousness the image of hairs appears. Thus for just that person the subject and object are both real, because they appear in that way. From the perspective of the perception of a person who clearly perceives objects, free of the disease, both the subject and the object are false. A subject that does not have an object cannot be established.

2.2.2.1.1.6.2.3.1.1.1.2.1.1.2.2.2.2.1.1.2.1.2. THE CONSEQUENCE THAT
IF THEY WERE NOT EQUAL, PEOPLE WITH NO DISEASED VISION
WOULD ALSO SEE STRANDS OF HAIR

If mind existed without a knowable object,
Someone who looked at the same object as someone with dis-
eased vision
Would cognize hairs—even if they had no diseased vision.
Since that is not the case, your position is inadmissible. (6.55)

You must accept beyond doubt [the explanation of the previous verse]. If it were not like that, there would exist a mind to which a knowable object appeared, the vision of hairs produced by diseased vision, that did not exist. It would then follow that someone without diseased vision would see the hairs produced by diseased vision in locations such as basins and so forth, because the nonexistence of the hairs is the same for both. You might accept that consequence, but this contradicts what is generally perceived: a mind perceiving the appearance of hairs does not arise in someone who does not have diseased vision. Therefore a "perceiving consciousness that arises without an object" does not exist.

2.2.2.1.1.6.2.3.1.1.1.2.1.1.2.2.2.2.1.1.2.2. THE REFUTATION OF THE REBUTTAL
2.2.2.1.1.6.2.3.1.1.1.2.1.1.2.2.2.2.1.1.2.2.1. The refutation of the proofs for "potential"
2.2.2.1.1.6.2.3.1.1.1.2.1.1.2.2.2.2.1.1.2.2.2. The refutation of the philosophical tenets that are posited on the basis of such "potential"

2.2.2.1.1.6.2.3.1.1.1.2.1.1.2.2.2.2.1.1.2.2.1. THE REFUTATION OF THE PROOFS FOR "POTENTIAL"
2.2.2.1.1.6.2.3.1.1.1.2.1.1.2.2.2.2.1.1.2.2.1.1. The rebuttal
2.2.2.1.1.6.2.3.1.1.1.2.1.1.2.2.2.2.1.1.2.2.1.2. The refutation of the rebuttal

2.2.2.1.1.6.2.3.1.1.1.2.1.1.2.2.2.2.1.1.2.2.1.1. THE REBUTTAL

> **You say, "If a mind perceiving a given appearance does not arise,**
> **It is because that mind's *potential* to perceive it has not ripened,**
> **Not because there are no objects." (6.56abc)**

The Proponents of Consciousness say, "In general the existence of an object is the cause for the arising of consciousness. Nevertheless, in the terms of our unique explanation the causes for the arising or nonarising of consciousnesses are the ripening and nonripening of the habitual tendencies planted by previous consciousnesses.

"When the habitual tendencies of a previous consciousness to which hairs appeared fully ripen, a consciousness endowed with the image of hairs arises, even though there are no hairs. But for someone who has healthy eyes, there are no habitual tendencies planted by a previous consciousness to which hairs appeared. Thus there is no ripening of *potential* for a mind perceiving hairs to arise. Therefore for someone who has no diseased vision, the mind perceiving hairs does not arise, but it is not the case that such a mind does not arise due to there being no knowable object."

2.2.2.1.1.6.2.3.1.1.1.2.1.1.2.2.2.2.1.1.2.2.1.2. THE REFUTATION OF THE REBUTTAL
2.2.2.1.1.6.2.3.1.1.1.2.1.1.2.2.2.2.1.1.2.2.1.2.1. Presenting the refutation
2.2.2.1.1.6.2.3.1.1.1.2.1.1.2.2.2.2.1.1.2.2.1.2.2. Extensively explaining the refutation

2.2.2.1.1.6.2.3.1.1.1.2.1.1.2.2.2.2.1.1.2.2.1.2.1. PRESENTING THE
REFUTATION

> Since such potential does not exist, your rebuttal is not
> established. (6.56d)

You say that such a thing as "potential" exists, and the ripening or non-ripening of that potential yields the arising and nonarising of consciousness. Yet as the reasonings below will demonstrate, such potential does not exist. Your assertions are not established with any degree of definitiveness.

2.2.2.1.1.6.2.3.1.1.1.2.1.1.2.2.2.2.1.1.2.2.1.2.2. EXTENSIVELY EXPLAINING
THE REFUTATION
2.2.2.1.1.6.2.3.1.1.1.2.1.1.2.2.2.2.1.1.2.2.1.2.2.1. In general "potential" is
impossible in any of the three times
2.2.2.1.1.6.2.3.1.1.1.2.1.1.2.2.2.2.1.1.2.2.1.2.2.2. In particular it is impossible
in the past and in the future

2.2.2.1.1.6.2.3.1.1.1.2.1.1.2.2.2.2.1.1.2.2.1.2.2.1. IN GENERAL
"POTENTIAL" IS IMPOSSIBLE IN ANY OF THE THREE TIMES

> It is impossible for potential to exist in what has arisen.
> The unarisen is also devoid of potential. (6.57ab)

If you say that "potential" exists, do you assert that the potential is connected to consciousnesses of the present? Or is it connected to consciousnesses of the past and future?

In the first case, it is impossible for potential to exist in the consciousness of the present, which has already arisen. When you say "the consciousness *of* potential," you are using the sixth case, that of connection.[334] That implies that the consciousness and potential both exist now. Since according to you the potential is also not different from consciousness, you are saying that the resultant consciousness of the present moment is also a cause, i.e., a potential, but that is illogical.

If the consciousness of potential were connected to the consciousness of the present moment, it would follow that the arising of the consciousness of the present moment would be without cause, because the potential of the present is not suitable to be its own cause. Furthermore, the arising of consciousness would be causeless because the potential of a present consciousness is not different from the present consciousness itself. If you say that those two reasons are not established, you give up your claim that potential is connected to the present consciousness. If you accept the above two reasons, you must accept the absurd consequence that the consciousness of the present moment does not need to be produced.

According to the logic by which you claim that "potential" exists in the present consciousness, it would follow that, when a sprout arises its seed would not disintegrate. For the cause and the result would be the same entity.

You may attempt to use the fifth grammatical case, "the source" *(jungkung/'byung khungs)*, and say that consciousness originates *from* potential. However, it is not suitable for an already arisen consciousness to arise from potential: since the consciousness of the present moment already exists, it does not depend upon others to arise.

In the case of the second possibility,[335] there is no potential connected to a consciousness of the future, which has not yet arisen. Such a notion is invalidated by reasoning, as will be explained.

2.2.2.1.1.6.2.3.1.1.1.2.1.1.2.2.2.2.1.1.2.2.1.2.2.2. IN PARTICULAR IT IS IMPOSSIBLE IN THE PAST AND IN THE FUTURE

2.2.2.1.1.6.2.3.1.1.1.2.1.1.2.2.2.2.1.1.2.2.1.2.2.2.1. Potential is not possible in the future

2.2.2.1.1.6.2.3.1.1.1.2.1.1.2.2.2.2.1.1.2.2.1.2.2.2.2. Potential is not possible in the past

2.2.2.1.1.6.2.3.1.1.1.2.1.1.2.2.2.2.1.1.2.2.1.2.2.2.1. POTENTIAL IS NOT POSSIBLE IN THE FUTURE

2.2.2.1.1.6.2.3.1.1.1.2.1.1.2.2.2.2.1.1.2.2.1.2.2.2.1.1. The untenability of a featureless "basis of features"

2.2.2.1.1.6.2.3.1.1.1.2.1.1.2.2.2.2.1.1.2.2.1.2.2.2.1.2. The refutation of the rebuttal to that

2.2.2.1.1.6.2.3.1.1.1.2.1.1.2.2.2.2.1.1.2.2.1.2.2.2.1.3. The nonestablishment due to dependence

2.2.2.1.1.6.2.3.1.1.1.2.1.1.2.2.2.2.1.1.2.2.1.2.2.2.1.1. THE UNTENABILITY
OF A FEATURELESS "BASIS OF FEATURES"

> A featureless "basis of features" does not exist.
> If it did, it would follow that the childless woman's son would
>   have potential. (6.57cd)

You may also use the phrase "the potential of consciousness" and say it
means that consciousness is the distinctive feature and potential is the
basis for this feature. Yet without the future consciousness, the distinctive
feature, the potential that is the basis of the feature does not exist. Without apprehending a feature, it is impossible for any mind to cognize a basis
of the feature.

You may assert that the nonarisen consciousness itself is the potential.
However, if that were the case, it would follow that the sons of childless
women[336] also have potential, because they are equivalent to future consciousnesses in not having arisen!

2.2.2.1.1.6.2.3.1.1.1.2.1.1.2.2.2.2.1.1.2.? ? ? ? ?.1.2. THE REFUTATION
OF THE REBUTTAL TO THAT

> You assert potential because consciousnesses will arise in the
>   future.
> Yet there is no potential, and there is no consciousness that will
>   arise from it. (6.58ab)

Attempting to explain the potential by considering the consciousness that
will arise in the future, you might assert potential simply because consciousness *will* arise. You might say that this sense of potential is similar to
the commands "Cook some rice" or "Make a blanket out of this wool."[337]

That assertion is also not reasonable. If potential were to exist, the
future consciousness for which such potential was a basis would be perceptible. Yet the future consciousness does *not* exist. And thus there is no
potential that would make such future consciousness into the potential's
distinct feature.

Just as it is in the case of the sons of childless women, there is no potential, and there is no consciousness that will arise from potential. The reasonings explained here also refute the examples of cooking rice and so on.

2.2.2.1.1.6.2.3.1.1.1.2.1.1.2.2.2.2.1.1.2.2.1.2.2.2.1.3. THE NON-ESTABLISHMENT DUE TO DEPENDENCE

> **"Objects that are established through dependence on each other**
> **Are not established at all"—thus teach the genuine ones. (6.58cd)**

You may say, "Potential and consciousness are causes and results that mutually depend on each other. One serves as a cause for the other. In this way the result, consciousness, arises from the cause, potential."

Well then, from that logic it would follow that consciousness is not something that inherently arises and is not something that is inherently established, for objects that are established in dependence upon each other, such as "long and short" and "here and there," are not established at all by way of their own nature. Thus teach the genuine ones, who have seen that the nature of all phenomena is emptiness. Āryadeva echoes this point *(Four Hundred Verses)*:

> Without a result,
> There is no basis for the cause itself.
> Therefore it follows
> That all results are causes. (9.8)

And from Nāgārjuna's *Treatise*:

> For a thing to be established through dependence,
> Something else needs to depend on it.
> If the depender is also established through dependence,
> What is established in dependence upon what? (10.10)

In this context, the meaning of these quotations is: without the establishment of potential, consciousness is not established, because potential is what is asserted to be the cause of consciousness. Without the establishment of consciousness, potential is not established, because when it is said, "the potential of consciousness," potential is assumed to be a feature of the consciousness. Since there is no establishment of either member of the pair without the establishment of the other member, there is no establishment of an entity whatsoever. Thus there is no potential in the future.

2.2.2.1.1.6.2.3.1.1.1.2.1.1.2.2.2.2.1.1.2.2.1.2.2.2.2. POTENTIAL IS NOT POSSIBLE IN THE PAST

2.2.2.1.1.6.2.3.1.1.1.2.1.1.2.2.2.2.1.1.2.2.1.2.2.2.2.1. The absurd consequence of things arising from other

2.2.2.1.1.6.2.3.1.1.1.2.1.1.2.2.2.2.1.1.2.2.1.2.2.2.2.2. The refutation of the rebuttal to that

2.2.2.1.1.6.2.3.1.1.1.2.1.1.2.2.2.2.1.1.2.2.1.2.2.2.2.1. THE ABSURD CONSEQUENCE OF THINGS ARISING FROM OTHER

> If consciousness arose from the ripening of habitual tendencies
> planted by the ceased consciousness of the past,
> It would follow that consciousnesses arise from the potential of
> other consciousnesses.
> The moments of their continua would be different from each
> other,
> And it would follow that anything could arise from anything.
> (6.59)

This verse teaches that there is also no potential in the past. You Proponents of Consciousness may say, "A consciousness that has arisen and is in the process of ceasing will plant its distinctive feature, its 'potential,' in the all-base, in order to yield a result. Thus the subsequent consciousnesses arise due to the ripening of the potential of the ceased consciousnesses."

Those who accept the all-base would assert that consciousness originates from potential in the present moment; those who do not accept the all-base assert that consciousness originates from the potential of the past. If the latter were the case, consciousnesses would originate from the potential of consciousnesses that are other, because you accept that consciousness is an uninterrupted continuum of earlier and later moments. These earlier and later moments are different from each other in substance and exist separately from each other. If you accept arising from other in that way, that position is untenable. It has been extensively refuted above during the refutation of arising from other.

The view of arising from other has the absurd consequence that anything would arise from anything, since all phenomena are equally different from each other. Since this has already been explained during the section on the refutation of arising from other, the explanation will not be repeated here. There are some who say that the Consequentialists willingly claim as their own position that things such as sprouts arise from seeds, but that is untenable.

2.2.2.1.1.6.2.3.1.1.1.2.1.1.2.2.2.2.1.1.2.2.1.2.2.2.2.2. THE REFUTATION OF THE REBUTTAL TO THAT

2.2.2.1.1.6.2.3.1.1.1.2.1.1.2.2.2.2.1.1.2.2.1.2.2.2.2.2.1. The rebuttal

2.2.2.1.1.6.2.3.1.1.1.2.1.1.2.2.2.2.1.1.2.2.1.2.2.2.2.2.2. The refutation of the rebuttal

2.2.2.1.1.6.2.3.1.1.1.2.1.1.2.2.2.2.1.1.2.2.1.2.2.2.2.2.1. THE REBUTTAL

> If you say, "members of a continuum are different,
> But they are not of different continua.
> Therefore there is no fault," (6.60abc)

You say, "When a consciousness is part of a continuum, the earlier and later moments that are members of that continuum are indeed different from each other. However, these earlier and later moments are strictly one continuum, not different continua. Therefore there is no fault of anything arising from anything."

2.2.2.1.1.6.2.3.1.1.1.2.1.1.2.2.2.2.1.1.2.2.1.2.2.2.2.2.2. THE REFUTATION OF THE REBUTTAL

> That is beyond your ability to prove.
> It is illogical for instances of a continuum not to be different.
> (6.60cd)

> Phenomena that depend on each other, such as Maitreya and
>   Upagupta,
> Are not part of the same continuum, precisely because they are
>   different from each other.
> Phenomena that are separate by virtue of their own
>   characteristics
> Cannot be parts of the same continuum. (6.61)

If your defense involving members of a continuum were correct, you would surely avoid fault. But since that is not established, it is beyond your ability to prove. There is no logical basis for the earlier and later moments of consciousness—which are different substances—to be undifferentiated components of the same continuum.

Phenomena, such as Maitreya and Upagupta, that depend on each other for their existence cannot be parts of the same continuum, precisely because they are different from each other.[338] Similarly, the earlier and later moments of consciousness, which are separate by virtue of their own characteristics, cannot be parts of the same continuum: they are different from each other.

This refutation of the counterparts' rebuttal dispels the notion that the ripening or nonripening, respectively, of "potential" will yield the arising or nonarising of consciousness. The dictum "If there is no knowable object, there can be no knower" has been established.

2.2.2.1.1.6.2.3.1.1.1.2.1.1.2.2.2.2.1.1.2.2.2. THE REFUTATION OF THE PHILOSOPHICAL TENETS THAT ARE POSITED ON THE BASIS OF SUCH "POTENTIAL"
2.2.2.1.1.6.2.3.1.1.1.2.1.1.2.2.2.2.1.1.2.2.2.1. The counterparts' position
2.2.2.1.1.6.2.3.1.1.1.2.1.1.2.2.2.2.1.1.2.2.2.2. The refutation of that

2.2.2.1.1.6.2.3.1.1.1.2.1.1.2.2.2.2.1.1.2.2.2.1. THE COUNTERPARTS' POSITION
2.2.2.1.1.6.2.3.1.1.1.2.1.1.2.2.2.2.1.1.2.2.2.1.1. The presentation of faculties and objects
2.2.2.1.1.6.2.3.1.1.1.2.1.1.2.2.2.2.1.1.2.2.2.1.2. Although there are no objects, consciousness originates from potential
2.2.2.1.1.6.2.3.1.1.1.2.1.1.2.2.2.2.1.1.2.2.2.1.3. A further teaching via example

2.2.2.1.1.6.2.3.1.1.1.2.1.1.2.2.2.2.1.1.2.2.2.1.1. THE PRESENTATION OF FACULTIES AND OBJECTS

> "An eye consciousness perfectly arises
> Immediately upon the ripening of its own potential.
> The potential that is the support for a given consciousness
> Is known in the world as a 'physical eye faculty.'" (6.62)

Here the Proponents of Consciousness call the faculties and objects "potential." They say, "Although there are no physical objects or faculties, the referent by which we assert consciousness to arise is established.

"The potential of a future consciousness that will arise on the basis of the eye faculty is planted when a previous consciousness of a similar type is ceasing. Later, at the very moment when this potential ripens, an eye consciousness perfectly arises in precise accordance with the habitual tendencies for objects and faculties that were previously planted there.

"The potential of this consciousness comes from an unbroken continuum and is the support of the eye consciousness. From the worldly perspective, due to ignorance, it is known and labeled as a 'physical eye faculty.' However, there are no eye or ear faculties and so on that are different from consciousness. This process of arising applies to the other sense faculties as well."

2.2.2.1.1.6.2.3.1.1.1.2.1.1.2.2.2.2.1.1.2.2.2.1.2. ALTHOUGH THERE ARE NO OBJECTS, CONSCIOUSNESS ORIGINATES FROM POTENTIAL

"Consciousnesses that arise from sense faculties
Depend on their own potential, not on outer apprehended objects.
They are themselves the appearances of blue and so on.
Not realizing this, worldly beings think of and accept them as outer apprehended objects." (6.63)

After teaching that there are no faculties separate from consciousness, the Proponents of Consciousness will now teach about how objects as well are not separate from consciousness.

"Objects arisen with an aspect of red, such as *bhanduka* and *kingshuka* flowers, are just like colors in crystals: they do not depend upon colors in the crystal; rather they arise with an aspect of red due to their own causes. In the same way, consciousnesses that arise from the sense faculties, the eye and so on, do not depend on the outer apprehended objects of blue and so forth. They are connected to and are the expression of their own potentials, which are propelled by their own seeds, cultivated and passed down since beginningless time. These consciousnesses themselves are the appearances of objects: blue and so forth. Not realizing this, worldly people think and accept that outer apprehended objects are things that appear *to* consciousness.

"The appearance of consciousness as objects is just like the example of a jewel's reflection in water. If you hang a precious gem from a tree branch at the edge of a clear pond, it appears as though there really is a jewel in the water, even though there is not. In the same way reflections of objects appear to consciousness, but they are not objects separate from consciousness itself."

2.2.2.1.1.6.2.3.1.1.1.2.1.1.2.2.2.2.1.1.2.2.2.1.3. A FURTHER TEACHING VIA EXAMPLE

> "In dreams, mind with the aspect of form arises
> From the ripening of its own potential, not from any form as an
>   outer object.
> It is the same in the waking state:
> Mind exists without outer objects," so you say. (6.64)

"In dreams, mind with the aspect of objects such as form arises from the ripening of its own concordant potential. It does not arise from other, outer objects. It is the same in the waking state: mind or mental consciousness exists without outer objects," so [the Proponents of Consciousness] say.

2.2.2.1.1.6.2.3.1.1.1.2.1.1.2.2.2.2.1.1.2.2.2.2. THE REFUTATION OF THAT
2.2.2.1.1.6.2.3.1.1.1.2.1.1.2.2.2.2.1.1.2.2.2.2.1. There are refutations of their position
2.2.2.1.1.6.2.3.1.1.1.2.1.1.2.2.2.2.1.1.2.2.2.2.2. There are no proofs of their position

2.2.2.1.1.6.2.3.1.1.1.2.1.1.2.2.2.2.1.1.2.2.2.2.1. THERE ARE REFUTATIONS OF THEIR POSITION
2.2.2.1.1.6.2.3.1.1.1.2.1.1.2.2.2.2.1.1.2.2.2.2.1.1. The consequence that if consciousness arose due to potential, an eye consciousness would arise in a blind person
2.2.2.1.1.6.2.3.1.1.1.2.1.1.2.2.2.2.1.1.2.2.2.2.1.2. The equivalence of the presence or absence of objects and faculties in dreams

2.2.2.1.1.6.2.3.1.1.1.2.1.1.2.2.2.2.1.1.2.2.2.2.1.1. THE CONSEQUENCE THAT IF CONSCIOUSNESS AROSE DUE TO POTENTIAL, AN EYE CONSCIOUSNESS WOULD ARISE IN A BLIND PERSON

If in dreams a mental consciousness, without an eye faculty,
Arises as blue appearances and so on,
Why would an eye consciousness not arise in a blind person,
Who does not have an eye faculty, due to the ripening of that
    consciousness's seed? (6.65)

You say that in dreams a mental consciousness that resembles an eye consciousness appears in the form of blue objects and so on; it arises without eyes or forms due to the ripening of its own habitual tendencies. Well then, someone who has fallen asleep and a blind person are equal in not having functioning eye faculties. So why would it not be the case that a blind person would experience the arising of a mental consciousness apprehending the blue visual objects in the waking state, just as in dreams? That would be the inescapable consequence.

2.2.2.1.1.6.2.3.1.1.1.2.1.1.2.2.2.2.1.1.2.2.2.2.1.2. THE EQUIVALENCE OF THE PRESENCE OR ABSENCE OF OBJECTS AND FACULTIES IN DREAMS
2.2.2.1.1.6.2.3.1.1.1.2.1.1.2.2.2.2.1.1.2.2.2.2.1.2.1. When analyzed, "potential" in dreams is untenable
2.2.2.1.1.6.2.3.1.1.1.2.1.1.2.2.2.2.1.1.2.2.2.2.1.2.2. When not analyzed, the eye also exists in dreams

2.2.2.1.1.6.2.3.1.1.1.2.1.1.2.2.2.2.1.1.2.2.2.2.1.2.1. WHEN ANALYZED, "POTENTIAL" IN DREAMS IS UNTENABLE
2.2.2.1.1.6.2.3.1.1.1.2.1.1.2.2.2.2.1.1.2.2.2.2.1.2.1.1. The entity of potential is untenable
2.2.2.1.1.6.2.3.1.1.1.2.1.1.2.2.2.2.1.1.2.2.2.2.1.2.1.2. The cause of potential is untenable

2.2.2.1.1.6.2.3.1.1.1.2.1.1.2.2.2.2.1.1.2.2.2.2.1.2.1.1. THE ENTITY OF POTENTIAL IS UNTENABLE

According to you, the sixth consciousness's potential
Ripens in dreams but not in the waking state.
Yet if such potential does not ripen in the waking state,
Why would it not be illogical to say it does not exist in
    dreams? (6.66)

The Proponents of Consciousness think that the cause for the arising of a mental consciousness that has aspects such as blue is the ripening of potential. Outer objects, they say, do not exist. Furthermore we are told that such ripening of the mental consciousness's potential only occurs in dreams, due to the condition of sleep, but not in the waking state. This verse teaches how that view is untenable.

According to their perspective—a mere, illogical word game—the ripening of potential for the mental consciousness that has such aspects exists in dreams but not in the waking state. For this reason, they say, they avoid the logical faults explained above. We, however, explain the situation as follows.

If the potential for the sixth consciousness does not ripen in the waking state for a blind person, why is it illogical to say that such potential also does not ripen in their dreams? That indeed is what you would be forced to accept.

2.2.2.1.1.6.2.3.1.1.1.2.1.1.2.2.2.2.1.1.2.2.2.2.1.2.1.2. THE CAUSE OF POTENTIAL IS UNTENABLE

> The absence of an eye faculty is not a cause for a blind person to perceive visual objects.
> Similarly, sleep is not a cause for the ripening of potential during dreams. (6.67ab)

The absence of an eye faculty is not a cause for the ripening of potential for a waking-state mental consciousness of a blind person to perceive such things as blue visual objects. Similarly, sleep is not a cause for the ripening of the mental consciousness's potential during dreams, because the eye faculty is equally nonexistent in the waking state and in dreams.

2.2.2.1.1.6.2.3.1.1.1.2.1.1.2.2.2.2.1.1.2.2.2.2.1.2.2. WHEN NOT ANALYZED, THE EYE ALSO EXISTS IN DREAMS

> Therefore you should accept that, even in dreams,
> The eye is the false perceiving subject that causes cognition. (6.67cd)

Since what was just explained is accurate, you should accept that, even in dreams, the eye is the false perceiving subject that serves as a support for the visual consciousness in dreams. It is what causes cognition, because without faculties like the eyes the cognition of objects like form does not occur.

2.2.2.1.1.6.2.3.1.1.1.2.1.1.2.2.2.2.1.1.2.2.2.2.2. THERE ARE NO PROOFS OF THEIR POSITION

2.2.2.1.1.6.2.3.1.1.1.2.1.1.2.2.2.2.1.1.2.2.2.2.2.1. There are no proofs by way of reasoning

2.2.2.1.1.6.2.3.1.1.1.2.1.1.2.2.2.2.1.1.2.2.2.2.2.2. There are no proofs by way of scripture

2.2.2.1.1.6.2.3.1.1.1.2.1.1.2.2.2.2.1.1.2.2.2.2.2.2.1. THERE ARE NO PROOFS BY WAY OF REASONING

> **All the answers they give**
> **Are just repetitions of their thesis.**
> **Seeing that, we close this debate— (6.68abc)**

The Followers of the Middle Way say, "In the waking state, the triad of objects, faculties, and consciousnesses is empty of inherent nature, because it can be observed, just like the triad that appears in a dream." Their counterparts say, "The consciousness of the waking state is empty of objects, because it is a consciousness, just like a consciousness in dreams."

The Proponents of Consciousness also say, "The observed objects in the waking state are of a false nature, because they are objects, just like objects in a dream" and "Completely afflicted phenomena[339] and completely pure phenomena[340] could not exist without the consciousness of the dependent nature, because they would have no support: they would be just like the fur on a tortoise." They also use the example of diseased vision to prove that consciousness can exist without objects.

Whatever of these or other answers they provide, these answers are seen by the learned Followers of the Middle Way to be mere repetitions of their thesis. Their objects of affirmation, therefore, have no power.

We Followers of the Middle Way thus close these purposeless debates of the proponents of the true existence of consciousness. It is impossible to prove that consciousness is empty of outer objects and that objects are of a false nature using the examples of dream consciousnesses and diseased vision. Furthermore, [in ordinary waking life], when they say that objects are consciousness, or when they say that objects are the dependent nature consciousness, these assertions as well are merely repetitions of their thesis.[341]

2.2.2.1.1.6.2.3.1.1.1.2.1.1.2.2.2.2.1.1.2.2.2.2.2.2. THERE ARE NO PROOFS BY WAY OF SCRIPTURE

Nowhere did the buddhas teach that "things exist." (6.68cd)

Nor can the Proponents of Consciousness produce any scriptural quotations to invalidate our refutation of the true existence of consciousness. Nowhere—at no time and at no place—did the perfect buddhas ever teach that "things such as aggregates, constituents, and sources exist." The *Descent into Laṅka* says:

> The three existences are merely imputations.
> They do not have any nature of being things.
> It is merely logicians who wrongly conceive
> Of their actual existence.

And,

> There is no nature; there is no consciousness;
> There is no all-base; there are no things.
> Naïve, bad logicians,
> Lifelessly impute all of these.

2.2.2.1.1.6.2.3.1.1.1.2.1.1.2.2.2.2.1.1.3. THE REFUTATION OF THE CONCORDANT EXAMPLE OF SKELETONS
2.2.2.1.1.6.2.3.1.1.1.2.1.1.2.2.2.2.1.1.3.1. The whole triad of perception does not arise
2.2.2.1.1.6.2.3.1.1.1.2.1.1.2.2.2.2.1.1.3.2. The refutation of claims to the opposite

2.2.2.1.1.6.2.3.1.1.1.2.1.1.2.2.2.2.1.1.3.1. THE WHOLE TRIAD OF PERCEPTION DOES NOT ARISE

Through meditating on their masters' key instructions,
Yogins may see the entire earth to be filled with skeletons.

> **But the three components of this perception also do not arise—**
> **This perception was taught to be an incorrect mental engagement. (6.69)**

The Proponents of Consciousness may protest, "You claim that consciousness cannot exist without objects, but what about the visions of yogins who, through meditating on repulsiveness relying on the key instructions of their masters, see the entire earth to be filled with skeletons to its ocean shores?"

That meditative apparition merely arises due to conditions. Its three components—the object, the faculty, and the consciousness—also do not arise. For it was taught in the scriptures that the appearances of that samādhi are not a product of mentally engaging the precise nature of reality. Rather they arise due to mentally engaging what is incorrect.[342]

2.2.2.1.1.6.2.3.1.1.1.2.1.1.2.2.2.2.1.1.3.2. THE REFUTATION OF CLAIMS
TO THE OPPOSITE

> **If, as you say, the mental objects of repulsiveness meditation**
> **Were the same as the objects of sense consciousnesses,**
> **Everyone who directed their minds to the same place the yogins**
> **   were looking**
> **Would perceive skeletons, and the samādhi would not be false.**
> **   (6.70)**

One must, without a doubt, accept the meaning of the previous verse. If that were not the case, an absurd consequence would follow. When someone views the object of a sense consciousness such as a vase, an eye consciousness with the aspect of the vase arises for them. Similarly, everyone else who directs their eyes to that same vase will also have an eye consciousness arise with the same aspect.

If what you say is true, however, the mental objects of repulsiveness meditation, such as skeletons, would be real, not incorrect. Therefore just as the yogins practicing the meditation would see skeletons, those who were not yogins would also perceive skeletons by directing their minds to the same place the yogins were looking. The skeletons would be exactly the same as an ordinary sense object such as blue. Furthermore, the samādhi of repulsiveness would also not be false, i.e., an incorrect mental engagement.

2.2.2.1.1.6.2.3.1.1.1.2.1.1.2.2.2.2.1.1.4. THE REFUTATION OF OTHER
EXAMPLES FOR MISTAKENNESS

> The perception of a water-river as a pus-river by hungry ghosts
> Is equivalent to the perception of a faculty with diseased vision.
>   (6.71ab)

It is has been explained that, in the case of someone with a faculty with diseased vision, from their mistaken perspective both the objects, the strands of hair, and the consciousnesses perceiving them will appear to exist; from an unmistaken perspective both the consciousness and the objects do not appear to exist.

In an equivalent way, rivers such as the Ganges will appear to the minds of hungry ghosts as pus. In this case as well, due to the power of karma, the consciousnesses and objects will, from this confused and adulterated perspective, appear to exist in the aspect of pus. In the absence of confusion neither the consciousness nor the object will appear to exist.

The above explanation applies to all relative phenomena. When conditions come together to produce a formation or to produce defilement, the appearances of both the objects and the subjects that depend on those conditions will arise. Yet in the absence of those conditions, the elaborations of subjects and objects are pacified and unobservable. The subjects and objects that would depend on those conditions do not arise.

Thus if the ground of an object's appearance is not established as real, it will certainly be the case that the consciousness—the phenomenon to which the appearance manifests—is not established as real. This is a genuine and crucial, secret point to understand.

What, then, does it mean when it is said that "Hungry ghosts perceive a water-river as a pus-river"? If placed in the appropriate location without any impediments to perception, hungry ghosts and humans will simultaneously perceive a river of pus and a river of water, respectively. Yet it is not the case that the water-river of humans appears as pus to the hungry ghosts. Nor is it the case that the pus-river of hungry ghosts appears as water to the humans.

For there is no truly existent thing—a basis for either appearance—there in the first place. Nor are there separate phenomena that perform their own separate functions and have achieved their own separate status as real things. If there is no truly established basis of features—such as a water-river for humans—then it is automatically established that there can be no pus for hungry ghosts as a feature of the river, regardless of whether the pus or the water came first.[343]

Here the *Ṭīkā* presents refutations of the ways in which this topic is presented by the great Tsongkapa and by the great Gorampa.

2.2.2.1.1.6.2.3.1.1.1.2.1.1.2.2.2.2.1.1.5. THE SUMMARY OF THE REFUTATION OF CONSCIOUSNESS THAT HAS NO OUTER OBJECT

In sum, understand the following point:
Just as there is no knowable object, there is also no mind.
(6.71cd)

Having extensively explained the way in which there can be no consciousness if there is no knowable object, the summary is given. Understand that just as the knowable object does not exist by way of its nature, so the mind with the aspect of that object also does not exist by way of its nature. Objects and consciousnesses are posited in dependence upon each other. The *Praise of the Transcendent* says:

That which has not arisen is not a knowable object.
Without knowable objects, there can be no consciousness.
Therefore you taught that consciousness and knowable objects
Do not exist by way of their nature. (10)

2.2.2.1.1.6.2.3.1.1.1.2.1.1.2.2.2.2.1.2. THE REFUTATION OF A DEPENDENT NATURE THAT IS NONDUAL AND SUBSTANTIALLY ESTABLISHED
2.2.2.1.1.6.2.3.1.1.1.2.1.1.2.2.2.2.1.2.1. Since there are no proofs for it, the existence of a nondual dependent nature is untenable
2.2.2.1.1.6.2.3.1.1.1.2.1.1.2.2.2.2.1.2.2. The refutation of their proofs for self-awareness

2.2.2.1.1.6.2.3.1.1.1.2.1.1.2.2.2.2.1.2.1. SINCE THERE ARE NO PROOFS FOR IT, THE EXISTENCE OF A NONDUAL DEPENDENT NATURE IS UNTENABLE

If there existed an actual dependent consciousness
That were empty of both apprehender and apprehended,

> How would you cognize its existence?
> If you say, "It exists without being apprehended," that is
>   unacceptable. (6.72)

Having shown that without an external object consciousness is impossible, the text will now refute the notion that consciousness can exist merely as a thing that does not involve perceiver or perceived.

If the dependent nature—a thing empty of both apprehender and apprehended—existed ultimately, what consciousness would cognize or observe its existence? If you say that it is not apprehended by any other consciousnesses, your answer is both unacceptable and utterly absurd.

A consciousness apprehending itself is untenable. It is contradictory for something to perform its own action on itself, just as a fire does not burn itself. Nor is the dependent consciousness apprehended by other consciousnesses, such as a previous consciousness. That would contradict your own tenets. For if you claim that consciousness is the object of another consciousness, you would undermine your own assertion of "mere consciousness."

The Proponents of Consciousness assert a nondual consciousness that is devoid of apprehender and apprehended and is self-aware and self-illuminating. They call it the "perfectly established nature" and say that it is real.

Some scholars assert that the perfectly established nature is unconditioned and does not exist in ordinary beings. Some say it is conditioned, that it is the unerring perfectly established nature, and that therefore it is not ultimate. Some others say that although it is ultimate it is not ultimate *truth*. Still others say that the dependent nature, though existing in the relative, does not exist in the ultimate.

All of these views are merely products of not even beginning to turn one's attention to the ocean of Middle Way and Mind Only texts. All texts of the Proponents of Consciousness assert that dependent, nondual wisdom is the ultimate truth; all texts of the Middle Way refute that assertion.

There are many subschools, such as the Practitioners of Yogic Conduct and the Proponents of Consciousness, who hold different views about which of the three natures are substantially established and so on. One can elaborate.

2.2.2.1.1.6.2.3.1.1.1.2.1.1.2.2.2.2.1.2.2. THE REFUTATION OF THEIR
PROOFS FOR SELF-AWARENESS
2.2.2.1.1.6.2.3.1.1.1.2.1.1.2.2.2.2.1.2.2.1. The brief teaching
2.2.2.1.1.6.2.3.1.1.1.2.1.1.2.2.2.2.1.2.2.2. The refutation of memory as a proof
2.2.2.1.1.6.2.3.1.1.1.2.1.1.2.2.2.2.1.2.2.3. Showing other paths of refutation

2.2.2.1.1.6.2.3.1.1.1.2.1.1.2.2.2.2.1.2.2.1. THE BRIEF TEACHING

The dependent consciousness does not experience itself. (6.73a)

You may say that although consciousness does not apprehend other consciousnesses, it is apprehended only in the manner of self-awareness.

However, the dependent consciousness does not experience that very same dependent consciousness. To perform an action to one's own self-entity is contradictory. Even people who are well trained in gymnastics cannot ride on their own shoulders.

2.2.2.1.1.6.2.3.1.1.1.2.1.1.2.2.2.2.1.2.2.2. THE REFUTATION OF MEMORY
AS A PROOF
2.2.2.1.1.6.2.3.1.1.1.2.1.1.2.2.2.2.1.2.2.2.1. A nonexistent cannot prove the
existence of another nonexistent
2.2.2.1.1.6.2.3.1.1.1.2.1.1.2.2.2.2.1.2.2.2.2. Even if self-awareness did exist, it
could not be proven by memory

2.2.2.1.1.6.2.3.1.1.1.2.1.1.2.2.2.2.1.2.2.2.1. A NONEXISTENT CANNOT
PROVE THE EXISTENCE OF ANOTHER NONEXISTENT

**You may say that memory, arising in subsequent moments, is
what proves self-awareness.
But memory is nonexistent, and relying on it to prove another
nonexistent
Does not prove anything. (6.73bcd)**

Some Proponents of Consciousness, in the manner of the Followers of Sūtra, attempt to first establish self-awareness and then, on the basis of that, establish that the dependent consciousness experiences itself. They say that the entity of consciousness cognizes both itself *and* an object. To support this contention they use the example of fire: fire, they say, illuminates itself from the moment of its inception, and it also illuminates outer objects like vases. They also use the example of terms, which, they say, indicate themselves *and* the objects they represent.

Therefore, they continue, "Those who do not accept self-awareness must definitely accept it. For, if they did not, they would not have any memory of objects or perceiving consciousnesses with regard to recollections like 'I saw a form.' If memory is a perceiving subject that has the nature of experiencing things, it must also experience consciousness. But if you do not accept self-awareness, the memory of consciousness would be impossible.

"Furthermore, if there were no self-awareness, it would absurdly follow that consciousness could not experience itself. If consciousnesses were experienced by another consciousness, the process would be endless.[344] It is also impossible for two simultaneously occurring consciousnesses to be the objects and subjects of each other: it would absurdly follow that all consciousnesses would be nothing more than perceiving subjects of other consciousnesses and that all sentient beings would have the same continuum of consciousness. When many consciousnesses appear to arise simultaneously, it is like a stack of one hundred lotus leaves being pierced all the way through: each stage occurs discretely, but due to the speed of the process the confused appearance of simultaneity arises.

"Therefore, one must accept self-awareness in order to avoid the logical fault of endlessness. The subsequent memory, moreover, that perceives both the subject and object of an earlier cognition of form does indeed arise. For, if the previous consciousness perceiving form did not cognize itself, it would be unreasonable to posit a memory as its perceiving subject.

"In instances where we think, 'I saw form,' the memory that arises later as the perceiving subject of the subject and object of the original perception is caused by the experience of the object and consciousness. Thus self-awareness, which simply means *self-experience*, is established. Since it is established, the existence of the dependent nature is also easily understood."

Let us examine how you Proponents of Consciousness use the notion of memory to prove the substantial existence of the dependent nature. Self-awareness does not exist ultimately. The "memory" that is used as an attempted proof of self-awareness is the same: it does not exist ultimately. Therefore memory cannot prove anything about self-awareness, because memory itself is not ultimately existent; it does not arise from self, other, or any of the alternatives.

You may respond, "In the context of analysis, it is true that memory cannot be used as a proof for self-awareness ultimately. However, without analysis memory establishes self-awareness conventionally." Yet even conventionally memory does not establish self-awareness. Not only is self-awareness not the cause of memory conventionally, self-awareness itself does not even *exist* conventionally! Thus a memory that is the result of self-awareness cannot be established either. In conventional reality, even though there is no self-awareness, mere memory arises from its own mere conditions.

Thus, as the root verse explains, self-awareness does not exist in either of the two truths. Relying on another nonexistent, memory, to prove self-awareness will not prove anything about self-awareness. There is no causal connection between the two, just like impermanent sounds and things perceived by the eyes.

The above commentary represents one way of commenting on this section of the *Entrance to the Middle Way*.[345]

2.2.2.1.1.6.2.3.1.1.1.2.1.1.2.2.2.1.2.2.2.2. EVEN IF SELF-AWARENESS DID EXIST, IT COULD NOT BE PROVEN BY MEMORY
2.2.2.1.1.6.2.3.1.1.1.2.1.1.2.2.2.1.2.2.2.2.1. Self-awareness is not the object of memory because it arises in a different moment
2.2.2.1.1.6.2.3.1.1.1.2.1.1.2.2.2.1.2.2.2.2.2. Refuting claims that the above refutation applies equally to our own explanation of memory

2.2.2.1.1.6.2.3.1.1.1.2.1.1.2.2.2.1.2.2.2.2.1. SELF-AWARENESS IS NOT THE OBJECT OF MEMORY BECAUSE IT ARISES IN A DIFFERENT MOMENT

> Even if self-awareness did exist,
> It is illogical to say it is recalled by memory,
> Because it is different from memory, just like the self-awareness
> of someone else.
> The same reason will also defeat any further rebuttals. (6.74)

Leaving behind the above analysis for the time being, Chandrakīrti now entertains the position that self-awareness does exist, yet refutes the notion that its existence could be proven by memory. Thus, the verse teaches, let us for now assume that self-awareness, the consciousness that experiences both consciousness and objects, exists. Even if it did, it is illogical to say that memory of later moments recalls objects and consciousnesses from before, because the previous experience and the subsequent memory are two different substances.

Consider, for example, the memory in the mindstream of a person named Maitreya. That memory does not recall the self-awareness and the experience of objects that arise in the mind of another person named Upagupta. Upagupta's self-awareness is not known or recalled by Maitreya, precisely because Upagupta's self-awareness and Maitreya's memory are two different things.

You may reply, "Even though self-awareness and memory are different, memory still recalls self-awareness. Earlier experiences and later memories are included within the same continuum, and those two are things that perform functions and have a cause and result relationship."

However, the reason "because they are other" also defeats any further[346] rebuttals such as claims that experience and memory are part of the same continuum and have a cause and result relationship. Phenomena that are different from each other are never consciousnesses that experience each other, are never phenomena included in the same continuum, and are never involved in a cause and result relationship. They are just like the consciousnesses of two different people.[347]

In sum, any attempt at using memory to prove self-awareness should be thoroughly refuted by the following logic: "Later moments of recollection are different from earlier moments of self-awareness."

2.2.2.1.1.6.2.3.1.1.1.2.1.1.2.2.2.2.1.2.2.2.2.2. REFUTING CLAIMS THAT THE ABOVE REFUTATION APPLIES EQUALLY TO OUR OWN EXPLANATION OF MEMORY

A memory that is different
From a consciousness experiencing an object does not exist
   for us.
There is simply the memory, "I saw it."
This is just how conventions work in the world. (6.75)

You may protest, "Well, then, how do you Followers of the Middle Way explain the occurrence of a later memory recalling an earlier experience? For you, there could be no memory whatsoever, because 'the memory is different from the experience.'"

We Followers of the Middle Way, when analyzing the earlier experience and the later memory, do not set out to prove that later memory arises because of the existence of earlier self-awareness. Rather, we speak merely from the perspective of no analysis—what is accepted in the world.

Since, when analyzed, it is seen that earlier experiences and later memories do not exist as causally connected things that could be described as "the same" or "different," it is therefore possible for us to posit—*without* analysis—mutually dependent experiences and memories as causes and results. When positing causes and results without analysis, we merely repeat what is said by worldly people. This has already been clearly explained above in verses such as "Worldly people merely plant a seed . . ."[348]

There are some, such as Gorampa and Shākya Chokden, who say that this verse proves that Chandrakīrti holds, from his own perspective, that self-awareness exists conventionally. They also say that in Chandrakīrti's tradition the all-base, self-awareness, outer objects, and the person all exist conventionally, but they do not exist as "conventional phenomena that can withstand analysis."

These positions are untenable. The master Chandrakīrti does not, as his own position, accept any phenomenon as existent or nonexistent in either ultimate or conventional truth. What need is there to mention his position on the "existence" of self-awareness? Since the earlier and later consciousnesses are not different substances, it is possible to say, [repeating after worldly people], that what is experienced initially is also experienced by memory and that what is unique to that experience is also unique to its memory.

Thus a later consciousness can remember something by thinking, "I saw it before." Yet this relation between experience and memory is simply the way conventions work in the world. It is not to be thoroughly analyzed: worldly conventions are by nature false.

We speak in this manner to reverse the misconceptions of the Proponents of Things, who say that experience and memory are not impossible because they are different from each other. Nevertheless, the Followers of the Middle Way do not affirm these conventional descriptions of memory as a position of their own.

2.2.2.1.1.6.2.3.1.1.1.2.1.1.2.2.2.2.1.2.2.3. SHOWING OTHER PATHS OF REFUTATION

> Therefore, since self-awareness does not exist,
> What consciousness will perceive your dependent nature?
> Since agents, actions, and objects are not the same thing,
> For a consciousness to apprehend itself is unreasonable. (6.76)

For the reasons that have been explained above, self-awareness does not exist. Since other types of consciousness cannot apprehend your dependent nature either, how will it be apprehended? It is, in fact, unapprehendable, because it is illogical for it to be apprehended by itself or something different from itself.

Since agents, actions, and objects are not the same thing, it is illogical for a consciousness to apprehend itself. Consider the example of cutting a tree: the person who cuts the tree, the tree itself, and the action of cutting the tree are not the same thing. The *Descent into Laṅka* says:

> A sword does not cut its own blade.
> A fingertip does not touch itself.
> The same logic applies to the notion of a self-aware mind.

2.2.2.1.1.6.2.3.1.1.1.2.1.1.2.2.2.2.1.3. THE REFUTATION OF THE DEPENDENT NATURE'S EXISTENCE AS SOMETHING THAT IS BEYOND ALL CONCEPTUAL ELABORATIONS

> If the dependent nature, whose essential nature
> Is unarisen and unknowable, exists as a thing,
> Why would the childless woman's son not reasonably exist?
> What harm has he caused you? (6.77)

This verse teaches that a dependent nature that is an object of unfabricated wisdom and that is not an object of conceptual elaborations is untenable. It was explained above that the dependent nature does not arise from itself or others. It was also explained that it cannot be cognized by itself or other consciousnesses. If that is its essential nature, and if it is logical for a thing to exist in that way, beyond all conceptual elaborations, its mode of existence is certainly striking.

Based on the way you describe the dependent nature's existence, the childless woman's son would have equal status! So why do you insist on saying that one exists yet it is illogical for the other to exist? What harm has the childless woman's son inflicted on you Proponents of Consciousness? And what favors has the dependent nature performed for you?

You would do better to drop your prejudice and make the following assertion: "Just like the dependent nature, the childless woman's son, because it is free from elaborations, is the object of the wisdom of the noble ones and exists inexpressibly."

The *Ornament of Great Vehicle Sūtras* teaches how the dependent nature *is* an object experienced by the wisdom of the noble ones:[349]

> In the absence of [the imaginary nature],
> One clearly perceives [the dependent nature free of imagination].
> Similarly, when there is transformation,
> One perceives incorrect conception. (12.17)

> In the world, people act as they please
> In relation to the cause [of an illusion] from which confusion has
>   been removed.
> In the same way, the disciplined ones, following transformation,
> Act as they please, free from confusion. (12.18)

And:

> [The bodhisattvas] see the conditioned phenomena of the three
>   realms
> In a nondualistic manner
> As incorrect conception
> With their very pure wisdom. (15.32)

It may appear at first glance that the Middle Way system contradicts the above scripture on this point, since it describes the dependent nature as not being an object for genuine wisdom. There is, however, no contradiction: the systems of the Middle Way and Mind Only are distinct. Followers of the Middle Way highlight the way the dependent nature of false imagination *(yangdak minpe kuntok/yang dag min pa'i kun rtog)* is not an object for the noble ones' wisdom during meditative equipoise. The Proponents of Consciousness, on the other hand, teach that the depen-

dent nature that is mere perception is an object for both meditative equipoise and postmeditation. There is no contradiction between these two
explanations.

2.2.2.1.1.6.2.3.1.1.1.2.1.1.2.2.2.2.1.4. THE REFUTATION OF THE
DEPENDENT NATURE'S EXISTENCE AS THE CAUSE OF RELATIVE
APPEARANCES
2.2.2.1.1.6.2.3.1.1.1.2.1.1.2.2.2.2.1.4.1. By claiming that the dependent
nature exists, one lapses from the relative truth
2.2.2.1.1.6.2.3.1.1.1.2.1.1.2.2.2.2.1.4.2. By lapsing from the two truths, one
cannot attain liberation
2.2.2.1.1.6.2.3.1.1.1.2.1.1.2.2.2.2.1.4.3. Explaining the reasons why

2.2.2.1.1.6.2.3.1.1.1.2.1.1.2.2.2.2.1.4.1. BY CLAIMING THAT THE
DEPENDENT NATURE EXISTS, ONE LAPSES FROM THE RELATIVE
TRUTH
2.2.2.1.1.6.2.3.1.1.1.2.1.1.2.2.2.2.1.4.1.1. A nonexistent is not suitable as a
cause
2.2.2.1.1.6.2.3.1.1.1.2.1.1.2.2.2.2.1.4.1.2. The contradiction with the worldly
perspective

2.2.2.1.1.6.2.3.1.1.1.2.1.1.2.2.2.2.1.4.1.1. A NONEXISTENT IS NOT
SUITABLE AS A CAUSE

> If the dependent nature does not even slightly exist,
> What type of dependent nature could be the cause of the
>   relative? (6.78ab)

You say, "It is logical for the dependent nature, which is the cause for the
imputed existence of things, to exist," but that is illogical. Since there
are no proofs for it, but there are refutations of it, the dependent nature
does not even slightly exist. Therefore what kind of dependent nature
could be the cause of relative things? It does not function as a cause in
the slightest.

   It is said in the older texts that commenting on this verse as if it were a
description of the counterparts' position contradicts the intention of the
root text and its commentary.[350]

2.2.2.1.1.6.2.3.1.1.1.2.1.1.2.2.2.2.1.4.1.2. THE CONTRADICTION WITH
THE WORLDLY PERSPECTIVE

> **Attachment to the idea of substantial existence**
> **Destroys even the presentations of what is renowned in the**
> **world. (6.78cd)**

The Proponents of Mind Only assert that the cause of the conventional
relative is the dependent nature. Due to this, they fail to accept the actual
causes of worldly conventions and are rendered incapable of presenting
what is renowned in the world. How sad!

Devoid of supreme knowledge, they cling to the all-base consciousness
as being the cause of all phenomena—the completely afflicted and the
completely pure. In this way they call "existent" what does not exist substantially at all. Through this attachment they pour waterlike conventions
into the leaky vase of the dependent nature. They destroy the conventions
of the world through the bad ways of their own intellects.

They also destroy the commands of "stay" and "go" and the phenomena of forms, feelings, and so on, which are accepted by all worldly people,
including even shepherds. The reason this happens is because the concepts
of "staying" and "going," if presented in light of the dependent nature, cannot possibly be used by worldly people. Therefore, the approach of the
Proponents of Consciousness produces only decline. Through relying on
it one will be incapable of attaining even the higher existences—never
mind liberation!

2.2.2.1.1.6.2.3.1.1.1.2.1.1.2.2.2.2.1.4.2. BY LAPSING FROM THE TWO
TRUTHS, ONE CANNOT ATTAIN LIBERATION

> **Those who dwell outside the path of the master Nāgārjuna**
> **Have no method for accomplishing peace.**
> **They lapse from the two truths, the relative and suchness,**
> **And, by so lapsing, do not achieve liberation. (6.79)**

There are those who dwell outside the path of the master Nāgārjuna's presentation of the two truths. Under the influence of their mundane thoughts
and with the hope of attaining liberation, they talk about consciousness,
subtle particles, persons, primal matter, and so on. These people—from
the Proponents of Mind Only down to the Chārvākas *(Gyangphenpa/
rgyang 'phen pa)*[351]—have no method for accomplishing peace.

Why? Set aside logical analyses of the Proponents of Consciousness and others—even from the worldly, conventional perspective, they posit phenomena in their systems that cannot coincide with the common consensus of the world. Since they have nothing in common with the worldly perspective, they lapse from the relative truth. Since they have nothing in common with the wisdom vision of the noble ones, they lapse from the precise nature, the ultimate truth. Since they fall from the two truths, they do not achieve liberation.

2.2.2.1.1.6.2.3.1.1.1.2.1.1.2.2.2.2.1.4.3. EXPLAINING THE REASONS WHY

The conventional truth is the method;
The ultimate truth is what arises from the method.
Those who do not know the distinctions between these two
Will, due to wrong thinking, follow inferior paths. (6.80)

This verse explains the reasons why falling from the two truths will make attaining liberation impossible. The conventional truth refers to the interdependent phenomena—aggregates, constituents, and sources—taught by the perfect Buddha as methods for realizing the ultimate truth. The teaching on the ultimate truth is what arises from such methods. The ultimate truth is taught in dependence upon the conventional truth. And through comprehending the ultimate truth, one attains the ultimate, that is, nirvāṇa. The *Treatise* says:

Without relying on conventions,
One cannot realize the ultimate.
Without realizing the ultimate,
One cannot attain nirvāṇa. (24.10)

In this context, the following are synonyms: that which arises from methods, the result, that which is to be attained, that which is to be realized, the object that is to be seen by the wisdom of meditative equipoise, and nonabiding nirvāṇa.

Unlike the Followers of the Middle Way, those who do not understand the distinctions between the two truths (such as the Proponents of Mind Only), will, due to their wrong thinking, follow inferior paths. They incorrectly interpret the intention of the Transcendent Conqueror.

The way of positing the two truths is presented extensively in the

noble sūtra *The Samādhi That Definitively Shows the Precise Nature*
(Tattvanirdeshasamādhi, Dekonanyi Ngepar Tenpe Ting-nge Dzin/de kho
na nyid nges par bstan pa'i ting nge 'dzin) in these thirteen verses:[352]

> The Knower of the World, not listening to others,
> Taught the dharma by way of these two truths,
> The relative and the ultimate—
> There is no third truth.

> Beings generate faith in the Sugata
> For the sake of happiness.
> The Victorious One, for the sake of beings,
> And to benefit the world, taught the relative truth.

> When the Buddha taught about the six realms of beings—
> The realms of hell, animals, hungry ghosts,
> Demi-gods, humans, and gods—
> They were all relative imputations made by the Lion of Humans.

> Low classes, high classes,
> Rich households and poor ones too,
> Servants and slaves,
> Men, women, and neuters—

> Whatever distinctions among beings there are,
> You, the peerless one, taught about this in the world.
> Being skilled and thoroughly knowledgeable in the relative truth,
> You taught about it to humans for the benefit of the world.

> Sentient beings who are fond of saṃsāra
> Will, in their circling, engage in the eight worldly dharmas:
> Gain and loss, fame and disrepute,
> Praise and criticism, and joy and sorrow.

> In times of gain their attachment will surge.
> Loss will, in turn, disturb their minds.
> The rest of these eight illnesses are the same:
> They will continuously harm beings.

Know that whoever propounds the relative as the ultimate
Is of erring intellect.
There will be those who speak of the unpleasant as pleasant, suffer-
ing as happiness,
The selfless as a self,

And impermanent phenomena as permanent.
Whoever is taken in by the elaborations of those teachings
Will, upon hearing the teachings of the Sugata,
Become frightened; not understanding them, they will renounce
them.

Having abandoned the teachings of the Sugata,
These sentient beings will undergo the unbearable sufferings of the
hells.
Even though they seek out misguided forms of happiness,
The immature will only be pounded by a hundred sufferings.

Whoever has a mind that can stay with and quickly understand
The teachings that benefit the world
Will, like a snake shedding its old skin, free themselves of all bonds.
Transcending all existence, they will attain peace.

"All phenomena are devoid of inherent nature.
They are empty and free of characteristics—this is the ultimate."
Whoever hears this and gives rise to joy
Will attain unsurpassable enlightenment.

Victorious One, you see the aggregates as hollow *(wenpa/dben pa)*,
And you see the constituents and the sources in the same way.
You see the fortress of the faculties to be void of traits.
You, the Sage, see all phenomena precisely in this way.

This quotation appears in Chandrakīrti's autocommentary and is extensively explained there. Its meaning [for our context here] is that, first, Consequentialists refute the ways in which the Proponents of Things and the
Autonomists posit the two truths. Then, they perfectly teach the presentation of the two truths using mere statements renowned to others. They do

this because all phenomena of both truths are devoid of inherent nature and free from elaborations. When using conventions in conventional reality, rather than fitting their descriptions to the views of philosophical systems, they describe the relative in precisely the way it is renowned in the world for all beings, high and low, of the six realms.

2.2.2.1.1.6.2.3.1.1.1.2.1.1.2.2.2.2.2.2. RECONCILING APPARENT
CONTRADICTIONS IN THE REFUTATION
2.2.2.1.1.6.2.3.1.1.1.2.1.1.2.2.2.2.2.1. Reconciling seeming contradictions with the relative truth
2.2.2.1.1.6.2.3.1.1.1.2.1.1.2.2.2.2.2.2. Reconciling seeming contradictions with scripture

2.2.2.1.1.6.2.3.1.1.1.2.1.1.2.2.2.2.2.1. RECONCILING SEEMING
CONTRADICTIONS WITH THE RELATIVE TRUTH
2.2.2.1.1.6.2.3.1.1.1.2.1.1.2.2.2.2.2.1.1. The relative is accepted for a purpose
2.2.2.1.1.6.2.3.1.1.1.2.1.1.2.2.2.2.2.1.2. We do not accept that which does not appear in the world
2.2.2.1.1.6.2.3.1.1.1.2.1.1.2.2.2.2.2.1.3. It is impossible to refute the relative in the world

2.2.2.1.1.6.2.3.1.1.1.2.1.1.2.2.2.2.2.1.1. THE RELATIVE IS ACCEPTED FOR
A PURPOSE

> I do not accept relative truth
> In the way you assert the dependent nature to be a thing.
> For the sake of the result I say, "Things exist," even though they
>   do not.
> Thus I speak from the perspective of the world. (6.81)

A Proponent of Consciousness might say, "If you Followers of the Middle Way are willing to boldly refute our position about the dependent nature, I, a Proponent of Consciousness, will also not accept your view. You use reasonings, such as the refutation of arising from self and other, to refute everything. But what will you do when you are forced, with the same reasonings, to refute the relative truth that you yourselves accept?"

We Followers of the Middle Way state emphatically that the reasonings of the Middle Way are only used to refute the world's relative truth *after* analyzing it. You, however, *posit* the dependent nature *after* analyzing the relative with reasonings. We do not posit the relative truth after analyzing it with reasoning. Rather, we posit it from the unanalyzed perspective of what is commonly accepted.

Thus, as the root verse explains, I, a Follower of the Middle Way, do not, out of my own will and from my own perspective, accept the relative as established in the same way you assert the dependent nature to be a thing that, being free from elaborations, is something to be realized by the wisdom of the noble ones.

How do I express the presentation of the relative truth? For the sake of the result, or purpose of engaging with the world, in strict keeping with what is approved in the world, I say that "things exist" even though relative things actually do not exist. I speak only from the perspective of the world. Repeating after the world, moreover, is done to *counter* the assertion that such relative phenomena are genuinely established. The Transcendent Conqueror said:

> The world may debate with me, but I do not debate with the world. Whatever is asserted to exist in the world, I will also assert to exist. Whatever is asserted not to exist in the world, I will also assert not to exist.

2.2.2.1.1.6.2.3.1.1.1.2.1.1.2.2.2.2.2.1.2. WE DO NOT ACCEPT THAT WHICH DOES NOT APPEAR IN THE WORLD

For an arhat who has abandoned the aggregates and entered peace,
The relative does not exist.
In the same way, if something does not exist in the world,
I do not say that it exists in the world. (6.82)

Are there times when Followers of the Middle Way say that phenomena do not even exist on the worldly level? Absolutely. For arhats who, having completely abandoned the aggregates, have entered the peace of nirvāṇa, the relative does not exist. In the same way, if something does not even exist in the world, I will treat it the same way as the aggregates of an arhat and say that it does not exist.

In some contexts I will not, even in reliance on what is renowned in the world, speak of something existing. When worldly people, without analysis, speak of the relative existing conventionally, we simply repeat after them. But we are free from accepting existence or nonexistence as our own position, even in a relative, conventional sense.

2.2.2.1.1.6.2.3.1.1.1.2.1.1.2.2.2.2.2.1.3. IT IS IMPOSSIBLE TO REFUTE
THE RELATIVE IN THE WORLD

> If the worldly perspective poses no threat to your views,
> Then go ahead—refute it!
> Debate with the worldly people about what relative truth is,
> And I will side with whoever comes out the strongest. (6.83)

Why do the Proponents of Mind Only chide us, saying our refutations of arising from self and other leave no room for any presentation of relative truth? This suggestion is meaningless. We Followers of the Middle Way do not posit any existence from our own perspective in either of the two truths, but we accept the relative merely from the worldly perspective.

Your criticisms of our presentation of the relative, therefore, apply to none other than worldly people themselves. If you want to do away with our utterances about the relative, it is the relative truth of worldly people that you will have to contend with. Followers of the Middle Way, who have achieved the wisdom of the noble ones, have no need to dispel the relative truth. The noble ones do not abide in any characteristics of the relative. This point is taught by the root verse as follows.

We Followers of the Middle Way find that, when analyzed, the phenomena of the worldly relative do not exist. Nevertheless, sentient beings mistakenly think they exist. Therefore, we work hard out of compassion to reverse their confusion. If you Proponents of Mind Only, when attempting to engage with the world, are not defeated by what the world accepts, then go ahead— refute the unanalyzed relative truth of the world. We will support you!

If worldly views defeat your own, it is best for you to give up your biases. But do proceed with the debate, and see what happens. Debate the worldly folks about what exists and what doesn't exist for the common consensus of no analysis. If your side wins, we will side with you and abandon the worldly relative altogether. But if the worldly perspective defeats you, we will side with worldly people, the strongest of all.

The truth of the matter is that Proponents of Consciousness cannot refute the world. They have no reasonings to prove the freedom from elaborations of mere appearances; their reasonings that try to prove that appearances are mind are incapable of refuting the worldly relative. Instead, they pile more clinging to true existence *on top of* the worldly perspective by insisting that appearances are mind!

However, worldly people are not completely incapable of relating to logic. If they were, it would be impossible to help any worldly person engage in methods to realize the true nature of reality. Without accepting reasonings, they would not have any chance of turning around and facing the true nature. There are several refutations and affirmations based on this point in the *Ṭīkā*, but I will not write about them here.

Thus the Followers of the Middle Way, seers of the ultimate, dwell in the state in which all thoughts of logic or illogic have been thoroughly pacified. From within that state, they advance reasonings that are accepted in the world, to students in the world. Through these very reasonings, they clear away the students' misconceptions and teach the true nature of reality, which transcends the worldly perspective.

You might think, "It is impossible to refute the worldly relative using reasonings accepted by the world itself. The relative is accepted as real in the world, and it would contradict worldly thinking if one used what is commonly accepted to undermine what is commonly accepted."

It is true that we use worldly conventions to undermine worldly conventions, but it is not the case that this approach is fruitless. For the relative that is accepted as real is false, even *in the relative*. It would be illogical, therefore, to try to prove as real what is in itself false. And with regard to invalidating the worldly perspective with reasonings accepted by the world, the view invalidated is the worldly view. We Followers of the Middle Way are not invalidated at all, because we do not posit the worldly consensus as our own position. Why would it matter to us if the worldly view is rendered invalid?

You may retort, "Reasonings accepted by the world cannot refute the worldly relative, because mere appearances and mere illusions cannot be refuted." That is not so. First, through the supreme knowledges of hearing and contemplating, and later, through the supreme knowledge born of meditating, fixation on illusions and dreams as being real is gradually reversed. The habitual tendencies to perceive illusions as real are then themselves uprooted. Finally, even the mere illusory appearances are purified.

"How then," you may ask, "do you communicate about mere appearances for others to people who have not pacified their fixation on mere appearances?" In harmony with the appearances of those who perceive things to be real, we speak of the undeceiving quality of actions and results. Yet when even that undeceiving quality is analyzed it is found not to exist as an entity. Undeceiving actions and results are empty of their own entity. Therefore, it is reasonable to apply the refutation and dispelling of relative appearances for as long as one remains in the worldly perspective, in which those appearances have not been reversed. However it is not that way for Followers of the Middle Way, who are free from the reference points of any phenomenon.

You may further ask, "Why do you accept conventions of the unanalyzed world from the perspective of others, but shun the conventions of the philosophical systems?" The conventions of the philosophical systems are imputed by logicians. The logicians invent many terms that do not exist in the unanalyzed worldly perspective. We do not use such conventions in general when communicating with worldly people.

However, we do make statements that accord with the philosophical systems when engaged in communication with philosophers of other systems, when attempting to refute their conceptual imputations. In this way, we use what is accepted by others to refute them. In this process, moreover, we do not incur any undesired fault of our consequences' reverse meaning applying to ourselves. This method of dismantling the assertions of others is a great declaration of the Consequentialist tradition that was well founded by Buddhapālita and Chandrakīrti.

Nevertheless, repeating the logic of others in this way does not constitute an logical position of our own. Nor is there any fault in merely repeating the claims of philosophical systems for the purpose of guiding students along the path. The Followers of the Middle Way may indeed make presentations of the five bases of knowable objects,[353] the all-base, and so on. But they never posit such phenomena as part of their own system.

2.2.2.1.1.6.2.3.1.1.1.2.1.1.2.2.2.2.2.2. RECONCILING SEEMING
CONTRADICTIONS WITH SCRIPTURE
2.2.2.1.1.6.2.3.1.1.1.2.1.1.2.2.2.2.2.2.1. Reconciling seeming contradictions with the contents of the *Sūtra on the Ten Grounds*

2.2.2.1.1.6.2.3.1.1.1.2.1.1.2.2.2.2.2.2.2. Reconciling seeming contradictions with the contents of other sūtras

2.2.2.1.1.6.2.3.1.1.1.2.1.1.2.2.2.2.2.2.1. RECONCILING SEEMING CONTRADICTIONS WITH THE CONTENTS OF THE *SŪTRA ON THE TEN GROUNDS*
2.2.2.1.1.6.2.3.1.1.1.2.1.1.2.2.2.2.2.1.1.1. The explanation of how the term "only" carries the meaning of refuting other creators
2.2.2.1.1.6.2.3.1.1.1.2.1.1.2.2.2.2.2.1.2. The explanation of how mind is foremost in comparison with form
2.2.2.1.1.6.2.3.1.1.1.2.1.1.2.2.2.2.2.1.3. The teaching that form and mind are equivalent with respect to their existence or nonexistence

2.2.2.1.1.6.2.3.1.1.1.2.1.1.2.2.2.2.2.1.1. THE EXPLANATION OF HOW THE TERM "ONLY" CARRIES THE MEANING OF REFUTING OTHER CREATORS
2.2.2.1.1.6.2.3.1.1.1.2.1.1.2.2.2.2.2.1.1.1. The explanation of the intention of the sūtra
2.2.2.1.1.6.2.3.1.1.1.2.1.1.2.2.2.2.2.1.1.2. The teaching on how that is established by other sūtras

2.2.2.1.1.6.2.3.1.1.1.2.1.1.2.2.2.2.2.1.1.1. THE EXPLANATION OF THE INTENTION OF THE SŪTRA

> When it is said that the bodhisattvas on the approach of
> *The Manifest*
> Realize the three existences to be only consciousness,
> The meaning is that their realization refutes a permanent
> creator such as the self.
> They realize that the creator is only mind. (6.84)

A Proponent of Consciousness might say, "You Followers of the Middle Way do not have any reasonings to refute the relative. Furthermore, your refutations are undermined by the worldly perspective itself. Since you do not have your own presentation of the unanalyzed relative, you should accept that all relative phenomena are mind. For the Buddha, in the *Sūtra on the Ten Grounds*, said, 'The three realms are mind only.'"

However, the intention of that sūtra is not what they hold it to be. This point is taught in the root verse: the bodhisattvas who are approaching the dharmadhātu by attaining the sixth ground, *The Manifest*, are said to realize that the three existences are only consciousness. That statement means that from the mere conventional perspective, in accord with what is generally accepted and established in the world, the creator of phenomena is posited to be mind only.

The bodhisattvas' realization thus refutes ideas of a creator—such as a permanent self or permanent primal matter—imputed by others. From the conventional perspective of others, the bodhisattvas realize that the cause or creator of the three existences is only mind. This realization is valid because, if one analytically searches for any other causes and conditions of the three existences, one does not find anything. Even from the perspective of what is renowned without analysis in the world, nothing aside from mind can be observed as the cause of phenomena. The *Essence of the Middle Way (Madhyamakahridaya, Ume Nyingpo/dbu ma'i snying po)*[354] says:

> The teachings on "mind only" in the sūtras
> Were given to refute the creator and the experiencer.

Also, the sūtras say *(Sūtra on the Ten Grounds)*:[355]

> Thoroughly examine the links of interdependent origination in their sequential order. Reflect on how the aggregates of suffering and the results of suffering are in every sense free from creators and experiencers. Reflect on how clinging to notions of a creator produces actions. Reflect on how actions, free from a creator, are ultimately unobservable. Reflect on how these three realms are mind only. The twelve links of becoming, excellently taught by the Tathāgata, are all completely dependent on mind.

One should understand the meaning that is expressed in this and other quotations.

2.2.2.1.1.6.2.3.1.1.1.2.1.1.2.2.2.2.2.1.1.2. THE TEACHING ON HOW
THAT IS ESTABLISHED BY OTHER SŪTRAS
2.2.2.1.1.6.2.3.1.1.1.2.1.1.2.2.2.2.2.1.1.2.1. Referring to the sūtra
2.2.2.1.1.6.2.3.1.1.1.2.1.1.2.2.2.2.2.1.1.2.2. Explaining its meaning

2.2.2.1.1.6.2.3.1.1.1.2.1.1.2.2.2.2.2.1.1.2.1. REFERRING TO THE SŪTRA

> Therefore, to increase the intelligence of the wise bodhisattvas,
> The All-Knowing One, in the *Descent into Laṅka Sūtra*,
> Conquered the mountain peaks of tīrthika views with the vajra
>   of his speech
> In order to clarify his intention. (6.85)

The meaning taught [in the *Sūtra on the Ten Grounds*] is also corroborated
by other sūtras. Since only mind is the creator, to increase the intelligence
realizing selflessness of the wise bodhisattvas, the All-Knowing One, in
the *Descent into Laṅka Sūtra*, conquered the high mountain peaks of the
tīrthikas' wrong views. (Their views include those of the self, primal matter, and so on.) With the firelike and lightninglike vajra of his speech, he
taught, for example, as follows:

> The person, the continuum, and the aggregates;
> Conditions, and likewise particles;
> Primal matter and Īshvara—
> I teach that all of these creators are only mind.

By teaching verses such as these, the Buddha clearly identified what his
intention was with respect to his statements about "mind only."

2.2.2.1.1.6.2.3.1.1.1.2.1.1.2.2.2.2.2.1.1.2.2. EXPLAINING ITS MEANING

> In their own treatises, the tīrthikas
> Spoke of the person and so on as creators.
> Not seeing them as creators,
> The Victorious One taught the creator of the world to be mind
>   only. (6.86)

This verse further explains the meaning of the *Descent into Laṅka Sūtra*.
In the treatises that discuss their philosophical systems, the tīrthikas spoke

of the person, primal matter, and so on as creators. Those of our own Buddhist faction also imputed such things as attainment, nonwastage, and the all-base as creators.[356] The Victorious One, not seeing any of these as creators even conventionally, taught that nothing other than mind—and mind only—is the creator of the world.

That is the meaning of the *Descent into Laṅka Sūtra*. The term "only" in the phrase "mind only" is also explained by Bhāvaviveka in his *Blaze of Reasoning (Tarkajvala, Tok-ge Barwa/rtog ge 'bar ba)*[357] to mean refuting creators that are other than mind.

The term "tīrthika,"[358] which appears in the above root verse, can rightly be applied to all logicians who assert that things are creators. The term applies to non-Buddhist philosophers whose comprehension of things is incorrect and runs counter to the meaning of the Buddha's teachings. Moreover, "tīrthika" can also apply to the Proponents of Things of the Buddhist tradition. According to Chandrakīrti, the Proponents of Things are not part of this dharma tradition.[359]

Furthermore, in Tibet there are followers of this dharma tradition who assert an entity called buddha nature. They say it is uncompounded, the creator of all of saṃsāra and nirvāṇa. Some others assert that the person, the support for actions and results, is a creator. Others assert a thing called postdisintegration as a creator that is established by conventional valid cognition and supports continuity between actions and results. Still others assert the entity of the indestructible, subtle bindu, endowed with three distinct features, as a creator that is simultaneously the essential nature, the pervader, the emanator, and the dissolver of all phenomena of saṃsāra and nirvāṇa.

Some people have said that the term "tīrthika" applies in a completely precise way—in terms of its meaning, application, and explanation—to all of those assertions. One may then be inclined to ask, "What is it that establishes someone, whether Buddhist or non-Buddhist, as a tīrthika because of what they say?" The answer has been provided by the scriptures of our Teacher, the perfect Buddha, and by the writings of his heirs such as Nāgārjuna. The Buddha's *Descent into Laṅka* says:

> Whoever conceives of things produced by conditions
> To be existent or nonexistent
> Is someone who holds the view of a tīrthika.
> Know that they are a long distance from my teachings.

And:

> In the future, there will appear
> Some who refute my teachings
> Even while wearing the saffron robe.
> They will propound the existence and nonexistence of results.

Nāgārjuna's *Precious Garland* says:

> Ask those who propound the person as the aggregates,
> Worldly people, the Enumerators, the Vaisheṣhikas,
> And the Jains,
> If the Tathāgata exists or not after nirvāṇa.

> The buddhas, for their part,
> Taught the deathless state
> That is the profound transcendence of existence and nonexistence.
> Know that this is the profundity of the dharma.[360]

2.2.2.1.1.6.2.3.1.1.1.2.1.1.2.2.2.2.2.1.2. THE EXPLANATION OF HOW MIND IS FOREMOST IN COMPARISON WITH FORM
2.2.2.1.1.6.2.3.1.1.1.2.1.1.2.2.2.2.2.1.2.1. The brief teaching
2.2.2.1.1.6.2.3.1.1.1.2.1.1.2.2.2.2.2.1.2.2. The extensive explanation
2.2.2.1.1.6.2.3.1.1.1.2.1.1.2.2.2.2.2.1.2.3. The conclusion

2.2.2.1.1.6.2.3.1.1.1.2.1.1.2.2.2.2.2.1.2.1. THE BRIEF TEACHING

> "Expansion *(gye)* into suchness" indicates "buddhahood" *(sangye)*.
> In the same way, when the Buddha taught worldly beings about "mind only" in the sūtras,
> The meaning is that mind is foremost.
> Negating form is not the intended meaning of those sūtras.
> (6.87)

This verse teaches how the term "only" in "mind only" refutes the idea of a creator other than mind. However, this term definitely does not indicate the existence of consciousness as a refutation of the existence of external objects.

An expansion of mind *(gye/rgyas)* into the suchness of the precise nature indicates the state of buddhahood *(sangye/sangs rgyas)*,[361] even without explicitly using the first syllable, *sang*. In the same way, the Buddha taught worldly beings that the creator of the three realms is mind only in the sūtras. This meant that mind is foremost.[362] Yet in this explanation he did not explicitly refute the notion that other phenomena, forms and so on, are creators as well. However, that "Mind and only mind is what exists, and form does not exist," is *not* the refutation that those sūtras intended.[363]

2.2.2.1.1.6.2.3.1.1.1.2.1.1.2.2.2.2.2.1.2.2. THE EXTENSIVE EXPLANATION

2.2.2.1.1.6.2.3.1.1.1.2.1.1.2.2.2.2.2.1.2.2.1. It contradicts the sūtras to say that mind truly exists yet form does not

2.2.2.1.1.6.2.3.1.1.1.2.1.1.2.2.2.2.2.1.2.2.2. The reasons why mind only is foremost

2.2.2.1.1.6.2.3.1.1.1.2.1.1.2.2.2.2.2.1.2.2.3. The reasons why form is not foremost

2.2.2.1.1.6.2.3.1.1.1.2.1.1.2.2.2.2.2.1.2.2.1. IT CONTRADICTS THE SŪTRAS TO SAY THAT MIND TRULY EXISTS YET FORM DOES NOT

If the Buddha knew that the three realms are mind only
And refuted form in the sūtra,
Why would that great being, in the same sūtra,
Say that mind arises from ignorance and karmic actions? (6.88)

This verse teaches that the meaning of the sūtras should be explained just as we Followers of the Middle Way explain it. According to your system, the three realms are mind only, and mind is a phenomenon that is truly and ultimately established. If the Buddha knew this and refuted form in the *Sūtra on the Ten Grounds*, then why in that same sūtra would the great being, the perfect Buddha, again say that consciousness or mind arises from bewildered ignorance and the karmic actions of formations?

Illogical consequences would follow if you held that mind is truly existent. If consciousness were ultimately established by its own entity, it would not need to depend on the causes and conditions of ignorance and formations. Therefore mind does *not* inherently exist, because its presence and absence are concurrent with the presence and absence of its conditions, manifestations of confusion such as ignorance and formations. It is the same with the appearance of strands of hair, whose presence and absence are concurrent with the presence or absence of diseased vision.

The section of the *Sūtra on the Ten Grounds* that deals with the way consciousness or mind originates from ignorance and formations begins with:[364]

> In this way bodhisattvas should excellently examine interdependent origination in its forward sequence.

And ends with:

> . . . this also uproots the cause of the endless stream of ignorance.

The meaning of that quotation was taught extensively in the autocommentary.

There is also a small ancillary section here in the *Ṭīkā*.[365]

2.2.2.1.1.6.2.3.1.1.1.2.1.1.2.2.2.2.2.2.1.2.2.2. THE REASONS WHY MIND ONLY IS FOREMOST

Mind itself sets up varieties of sentient beings, worlds,
And worldly environments.
All beings are taught to arise from actions,
And when mind is relinquished there is no karma. (6.89)

This verse teaches that mind is foremost. Mind itself, due to gathering karma and mental afflictions, causes persons to attain all the phenomena of saṃsāra. It sets up great varieties of worlds of sentient beings, from the hells to the peak of existence, and worldly environments, the wind maṇḍala up through Akaniṣṭha.[366] As was said:

> Sentient beings, due to karma,
> Take birth in timely ways due to negative actions.
> For example, in hell and in the higher realms,
> There are weapons and jewel trees, respectively.

Thus all inner and outer beings were taught to arise from common and uncommon karma. Karma is something that is accumulated only by the mind, and when mind is relinquished, there is no accumulation of karma.[367]

2.2.2.1.1.6.2.3.1.1.1.2.1.1.2.2.2.2.2.1.2.2.3. THE REASONS WHY FORM IS NOT FOREMOST

Form does indeed exist conventionally,
But it is not a creator like mind is. (6.90ab)

Conventionally, like mind, form as well exists, but it is not a creator like mind is. Mind accumulates the karma that is the cause of beings. Since form is equivalent with matter, it does not perform the functions of mind.

2.2.2.1.1.6.2.3.1.1.1.2.1.1.2.2.2.2.2.1.2.3. THE CONCLUSION

Therefore creators other than mind
Are refuted, but form itself is not. (6.90cd)

Some assert the self, primal matter, and so on as creators; others assert the creator to be mind. But there is no debate about the fact that form is not a creator. Therefore creators other than mind—such as primal matter—are refuted, but form as a creator does not need to be refuted. Therefore, since primal matter and mind—whatever one may assert to be a creator—both rely on form, it is illogical to refute form. From the unanalyzed, conventional perspective, form exists.

2.2.2.1.1.6.2.3.1.1.1.2.1.1.2.2.2.2.2.1.3. THE TEACHING THAT FORM AND MIND ARE EQUIVALENT WITH RESPECT TO THEIR EXISTENCE OR NONEXISTENCE

2.2.2.1.1.6.2.3.1.1.1.2.1.1.2.2.2.2.2.1.3.1. In both truths, form and mind are equivalent with respect to their existence and nonexistence
2.2.2.1.1.6.2.3.1.1.1.2.1.1.2.2.2.2.2.1.3.2. When the two truths are dismantled there is no substantial establishment
2.2.2.1.1.6.2.3.1.1.1.2.1.1.2.2.2.2.2.1.3.3. The conclusion

2.2.2.1.1.6.2.3.1.1.1.2.1.1.2.2.2.2.2.1.3.1. IN BOTH TRUTHS, FORM AND MIND ARE EQUIVALENT WITH RESPECT TO THEIR EXISTENCE AND NONEXISTENCE

2.2.2.1.1.6.2.3.1.1.1.2.1.1.2.2.2.2.2.2.1.3.1.1. Form and mind are to be either equally proved or equally disproved when using reasoning
2.2.2.1.1.6.2.3.1.1.1.2.1.1.2.2.2.2.2.2.1.3.1.2. Form and mind are either equally proved or equally disproved in the scriptures

2.2.2.1.1.6.2.3.1.1.1.2.1.1.2.2.2.2.2.2.1.3.1.1. FORM AND MIND ARE TO BE EITHER EQUALLY PROVED OR EQUALLY DISPROVED WHEN USING REASONING
2.2.2.1.1.6.2.3.1.1.1.2.1.1.2.2.2.2.2.2.1.3.1.1.1. Form and mind are equivalent in the perceptions of both ordinary and noble beings
2.2.2.1.1.6.2.3.1.1.1.2.1.1.2.2.2.2.2.2.1.3.1.1.2. Form and mind are equivalent on both levels of analysis and no analysis

2.2.2.1.1.6.2.3.1.1.1.2.1.1.2.2.2.2.2.2.1.3.1.1.1. FORM AND MIND ARE EQUIVALENT IN THE PERCEPTIONS OF BOTH ORDINARY AND NOBLE BEINGS

> For someone abiding in a worldly outlook,
> The five aggregates, which are accepted in the world, exist.
> For someone in whom the wisdom realizing suchness has
>   dawned,
> For that yogin, the five will not originate. (6.91)

Proponents of Consciousness, when you say that outer objects do not exist yet consciousness does, are you referring to the perceptions of ordinary beings? Or are you referring to the seeing of the noble ones?

If you choose the first, your assertion is not tenable. As was taught above, those who dwell in the worldly outlook accept the existence of all five aggregates in a person, because, for them, all five aggregates exist. The second choice is also untenable: for a yogin in whom the wisdom that realizes suchness has dawned, none of the five aggregates arises. This is because such yogins have completely pacified all characteristics of elaboration.

2.2.2.1.1.6.2.3.1.1.1.2.1.1.2.2.2.2.2.2.1.3.1.1.2. FORM AND MIND ARE EQUIVALENT ON BOTH LEVELS OF ANALYSIS AND NO ANALYSIS

> When form is found not to exist, do not cling to the existence
>   of mind!

> **When mind is cognized as existent, do not cling to the nonexistence of form! (6.92ab)**

It is never tenable for an instance of mind to exist while form does not exist. If, when analyzing, you realize form to be nonexistent, you should realize that the existence of both form *and* mind is untenable. Do not cling to the existence of mind! If, when not analyzing, you cognize mind's existence, do not cling to the nonexistence of form! Both form and mind are accepted to exist in the world.

2.2.2.1.1.6.2.3.1.1.1.2.1.1.2.2.2.2.2.2.1.3.1.2. FORM AND MIND ARE EITHER EQUALLY PROVED OR EQUALLY DISPROVED IN THE SCRIPTURES

> **In the sūtras on the way of supreme knowledge, the Buddha relinquished them equally.**
> **In the abhidharma, he described them equally as existent.**
> **(6.92cd)**

No matter what the context is—be it the scriptures of definitive meaning or those of provisional meaning—it is never tenable for mind to exist at the same time that form does not exist. For, with regard to form and mind, the Buddha, in the sūtras on the way of the perfection of supreme knowledge, relinquished them equally:[368]

Subhūti, form is empty of inherent nature.

Up until:

Consciousness is empty of inherent nature.

And in the teachings of the abhidharma, through the detailed classifications of the specific and the general, the Buddha described all five aggregates[369] equally as existent.

2.2.2.1.1.6.2.3.1.1.1.2.1.1.2.2.2.2.2.2.1.3.2. WHEN THE TWO TRUTHS
ARE DISMANTLED THERE IS NO SUBSTANTIAL ESTABLISHMENT

Holding your position will destroy the presentation of the two
truths.
And, since we have refuted it, your "substance" will not be established. (6.93ab)

Saying that mind exists while form does not is a meaningless waste of
energy. If you hold that position, the stages of the two truths, renowned
in scripture and reasoning, will be destroyed. Furthermore, since we have
refuted the "substance" that is your dependent nature, it will not be established.

2.2.2.1.1.6.2.3.1.1.1.2.1.1.2.2.2.2.2.2.1.3.3. THE CONCLUSION

Through these stages of explanation, know that all things
primordially
Do not arise in suchness yet arise for the world. (6.93cd)

Due to the stages of scriptures and reasonings that were explained above,
know that all inner and outer things primordially do not arise in suchness,
yet arise in the mere conventions of the worldly perspective.

2.2.2.1.1.6.2.3.1.1.1.2.1.1.2.2.2.2.2.2.2. RECONCILING SEEMING
CONTRADICTIONS WITH THE CONTENTS OF OTHER SŪTRAS
2.2.2.1.1.6.2.3.1.1.1.2.1.1.2.2.2.2.2.2.2.1. The teachings from the sūtras on
"mind only" are provisional meaning
2.2.2.1.1.6.2.3.1.1.1.2.1.1.2.2.2.2.2.2.2.2. The explanations of the scriptures
and reasonings that prove that
2.2.2.1.1.6.2.3.1.1.1.2.1.1.2.2.2.2.2.2.2.3. The ancillary teaching on the
classifications of definitive and provisional

2.2.2.1.1.6.2.3.1.1.1.2.1.1.2.2.2.2.2.2.2.1. THE TEACHINGS FROM THE
SŪTRAS ON "MIND ONLY" ARE PROVISIONAL MEANING

The sūtras that teach that outer appearances do not exist
But that mind appears as all varieties
Were taught for those who are extremely attached to form.

They refuted form only for that purpose, and are provisional meaning. (6.94)

At this point a Proponent of Consciousness may say, "The meaning of the *Sūtra on the Ten Grounds* may very well match your explanations above. Nevertheless, the principle of 'mind only,' as *we* explain it, is corroborated by other scriptures. The *Descent into Lanka*, for instance, says:

> Outer appearances do not exist;
> Mind appears as all varieties.
> I explain that what appears
> As bodies, enjoyments, and abodes is mind only.

"'Bodies' refers to faculties such as the eye, 'enjoyments' to objects such as form, and 'abodes' to world environments. Since there is no outer object apart from mind, mind—and mind only—appears as bodies, enjoyments, and so on. Phenomena simply *appear* to arise external to and separate from mind. Therefore the three realms are indeed mind only."

However, when the *Descent into Lanka* and other sūtras say, "Outer appearances do not exist," this statement regarding outer appearances being nonexistent and mind appearing as the varieties of bodies, enjoyments, and so on is a statement that bears an ulterior intention *(gongpa chen/dgongs pa can)*. In making that statement, the Buddha was thinking of people who, due to their excessive attachment to form, accrue great misdeeds in their relationship with form. Form becomes a condition for their attachment. Due to misdeeds, their accumulations of merit and wisdom diminish.

Bearing these beings in mind, the Transcendent Conqueror taught methods for relinquishing the mental afflictions whose condition is form, such as desire. Among these methods is the visualization of skeletons and so on. The Buddha's teachings on "mind only" follow the same principle: they are not genuine, definitive meaning teachings, yet their refutations of form help some beings to overcome their attachment to it. Therefore these "mind only" teachings do *not* teach about a "mind only" that exists without any form existing. Sūtras such as the *Descent into Lanka* were given only as provisional meaning teachings.

2.2.2.1.1.6.2.3.1.1.1.2.1.1.2.2.2.2.2.2.2.2. The explanations of the
scriptures and reasonings that prove that
2.2.2.1.1.6.2.3.1.1.1.2.1.1.2.2.2.2.2.2.2.2.1. The proofs via scripture
2.2.2.1.1.6.2.3.1.1.1.2.1.1.2.2.2.2.2.2.2.2.2. The proofs via reasoning

2.2.2.1.1.6.2.3.1.1.1.2.1.1.2.2.2.2.2.2.2.2.1. THE PROOFS VIA SCRIPTURE
2.2.2.1.1.6.2.3.1.1.1.2.1.1.2.2.2.2.2.2.2.2.1.1. The proofs that this sūtra is
provisional meaning
2.2.2.1.1.6.2.3.1.1.1.2.1.1.2.2.2.2.2.2.2.2.1.2. Therefore other sūtras like this
one are also provisional meaning

2.2.2.1.1.6.2.3.1.1.1.2.1.1.2.2.2.2.2.2.2.2.1.1. THE PROOFS THAT THIS
SŪTRA IS PROVISIONAL MEANING

> **This was taught by the Teacher as none other than provisional
> meaning,
> And it is also logical that it is provisional meaning. (6.95ab)**

In this very sūtra, the *Descent into Laṅka*, the Teacher said that the sūtra is
none other than provisional meaning, as will be explained. Furthermore,
it is also logical that it is provisional meaning, as will be explained.

2.2.2.1.1.6.2.3.1.1.1.2.1.1.2.2.2.2.2.2.2.2.1.2. THEREFORE OTHER SŪTRAS
LIKE THIS ONE ARE ALSO PROVISIONAL MEANING

> **Scriptures clarify that other similar sūtras
> Are provisional meaning. (6.95cd)**

This sūtra is provisional meaning. Not only that, let us consider the other
sūtras that are asserted as definitive meaning by the Proponents of Consciousness, such as the *Noble Unraveling of the Intention*, which teach using
the terms of "self" and "true existence." Such sūtras say:

> The imputed nature does not exist; the dependent nature exists;
> and the perfectly established nature exists.

And:

> The appropriating consciousness is profound and subtle.
> In it all seeds flow like a river.

I do not teach it to immature beings
Because they would think of it as a self.

These quotations, interpreted literally, accord with the tenets of the Proponents of Consciousness. However, consider the following quotation:

To different sick people
A doctor will give different medicine.
In the same way, the Buddha taught
"Mind only" to certain sentient beings.

This quotation clarifies that the teachings on "mind only" were none other than provisional meaning. The Teacher spoke of "mind only" based on the distinct attitudes of different disciples. Teaching in this way is like the example of a doctor treating different patients: when ministering to a variety of illnesses, a doctor might sometimes prescribe even poison as medicine.

If the Buddha refuted the existence of *all* things when he taught beings who held the view of the true existence of things, those beings would not become engaged with the Buddha's teachings. To avoid this, the Buddha spoke as if an inherent nature of things existed. In particular, the Buddha's descriptions of buddha nature as being permanent, substantial, and real have all three criteria of provisional meaning: ulterior intentions, purposes, and refutations.[370]

Furthermore, since the Buddha taught buddha nature as provisional meaning, it can also be understood that the all-base consciousness is provisional meaning. Quotations from the *Descent into Laṅka* clearly demonstrate that all scriptural references to the ultimate definitiveness of the threefold enumeration of the vehicles, to other-emptiness *(shentong/gzhan stong)*, and to self-awareness are provisional meaning.

There is more tangential discussion on this point in the *Ṭīkā*, but I will not write about it here.

2.2.2.1.1.6.2.3.1.1.1.2.1.1.2.2.2.2.2.2.2.2.2. THE PROOFS VIA REASONING

**"If there are no knowable objects, consciousness is also refuted—
This is easy to understand," so teach the buddhas.**

> Since the nonexistence of knowable objects also refutes the exis-
> tence of consciousness,
> The Buddha refuted knowable objects first. (6.96)

The above three scriptural quotations, among others, clearly demonstrate
that all of the scriptures asserted by the Proponents of Mind Only to be
definitive meaning are provisional meaning. The *Entrance to the Middle
Way* will now explain how those scriptures are provisional meaning using
logical reasoning.

"If there is no knowable object, the perceived, consciousness, the perceiver, is also refuted—this is easy to understand," so teach the buddhas,
the transcendent conquerors. The reason why they teach in this way is
because knowers and knowables, objects and subjects, are posited in
mutual dependence. Once the selflessness of knowable objects is cognized, the refutation of the self of consciousness is easily established.

Therefore the Buddha, who presented the accumulation of merit as a
preliminary and as a method for entering into the accumulation of wisdom, first made statements such as:

Outer appearances do not exist.

In this way he refuted knowable objects first.

2.2.2.1.1.6.2.3.1.1.1.2.1.1.2.2.2.2.2.2.2.3. THE ANCILLARY TEACHING ON THE CLASSIFICATIONS OF DEFINITIVE AND PROVISIONAL

> In this way, know the background of any given scripture.
> Understand that sūtras that teach about something other than
> suchness
> Are provisional meaning; quote them for appropriate students.
> Understand that sūtras that teach emptiness are definitive
> meaning. (6.97)

Those who possess supreme knowledge should analyze the topics of the
definitive and provisional just as they were explained. After that analysis,
they should gain extensive knowledge of the backgrounds of scriptures of
the definitive and provisional meanings.

They should understand that a sūtra is provisional meaning if it does not directly clarify the suchness of interdependence free of the eight extremes of arising and so on. The sūtras of provisional meaning teach explicitly about arising, ceasing, true existence, and so forth. They were taught so that students could enter into the profound meaning. Having clearly understood those sūtras, those who possess supreme knowledge should quote such scriptures to students who will be tamed by those teachings and lead[371] them to the ultimate truth.

In the same way, correctly understand that sūtras that directly teach about interdependence— emptiness free from the eight extremes—are the definitive meaning, because the meaning of those sūtras cannot be interpreted[372] in any other way. Concerning the presentation of the definitive and provisional, the noble *King of Samādhi* sūtra says:

> Emptiness as explained by the Sugata
> Should be understood to belong to the category of definitive
>   meaning sūtras.
> Sūtras where sentient beings, persons, and individuals are taught
> Are all the dharma of provisional meaning.

And,

> In the thousands of world realms,
> The sūtras that I have taught
> Have different words but one meaning.
> Nevertheless, not all of them can be proclaimed to everyone.
>
> If you contemplate one teaching,
> You will become familiar with all my teachings.
> The many teachings of all buddhas
> Which were taught thoroughly in the worlds
>
> Come down to nothing other than the selflessness of all
>   phenomena.
> Those people who are skilled in this meaning
> Should train in its vital point.
> The qualities of the Buddha will not be difficult for them
>   to achieve.

And also, from the *Teaching of Inexhaustible Intelligence (Pagpa Lodrö Mizepa Tenpa/ 'phags pa blo gros mi zad pa bstan pa):*[373]

> What is a sūtra of the provisional meaning? A sūtra in which the relative truth is taught is provisional meaning. What is a sūtra of the definitive meaning? A sūtra that was taught so that the ultimate truth could be realized is definitive meaning. Sūtras that teach about great varieties of words and letters are provisional meaning; sūtras that teach about what is profound, difficult to see, and difficult to comprehend are definitive meaning. Sūtras that teach about the self, the sentient being, the life force, the rejuvenator, the person, the individual, the one born of strength, the strong one, the performer, and the experiencer are provisional meaning: these sūtras use a variety of linguistic methods to assume the existence of an owner in cases where there is actually no owner. Sūtras that teach emptiness, signlessness, wishlessness, freedom from formation, nonorigination, nonarising, the absence of things, the lack of sentient beings, the lack of life force, the lack of person, the lack of self, and the doors to liberation are sūtras of the definitive meaning.

The meaning of that quotation is that a sūtra whose explicit teaching can be refuted by reasoning is provisional meaning. The reason why such sūtras are provisional meaning is because they allow students to first enter the path. So that their mindstreams may be ripened, the sūtras use words and letters that harmonize with the students' thoughts. Although these sūtras mostly teach relative truth and are susceptible to refutation in terms of what they explicitly teach, they are still methods for leading students along the path in a gradual manner.

Sūtras that are the opposite of the above are definitive meaning, because they enable students to engage the result. Their meaning is vast and difficult to fathom, and they teach the ultimate truth in a way that is commensurate with the wisdom of the noble ones. They are not susceptible to refutation in terms of what they explicitly teach; comprehending them leads to the attainment of liberation.

One may protest, "Why did the Buddha in the sūtra *Unraveling the*

Intention say that the sūtras that teach the lack of essence of all phenomena are provisional meaning and that the sūtras that teach that the imputed nature does not exist and the dependent and perfectly established natures exist are definitive meaning?" Followers of Mind Only assert this sūtra in a literal way. We Followers of the Middle Way hold that even *Unraveling the Intention* teaches nothing other than our own approach. It does not teach what the Proponents of Consciousness claim.

The explicit teachings of sūtras that classify the three natures as existent or nonexistent are provisional meaning. They cannot be taken literally. The definitive teaching of these sūtras is that all three natures are devoid of their own entities. Therefore these sūtras cannot be held to be "sūtras that teach mind only."

There are some, such as Zilungpa, who say that the individual positions of each of the four philosophical systems are correctly established as the Middle Way. This is untenable: if that were the case, the lower philosophical systems would be irrefutable by the higher ones. One would be incapable—even conventionally—of positing differences regarding which systems are more accurate and which are deficient.

Therefore the middle turning of the wheel is definitive meaning. The final turning of the wheel has elements of both provisional and definitive: statements about the lack of essence of all phenomena are definitive meaning; statements about the dependent nature, the all-base, self-awareness, the self, permanence, nonemptiness, the cut-off potential, the definite potential, and so on are provisional meaning. They are provisional because it is impossible to accept them in a literal way.

You might ask, "Why did the Buddha, in some sūtras, say that the middle turning is provisional and that the final turning is definitive?" He did say that to some students, but that presentation of the differences between provisional and definitive is itself not the final thought of the Buddha. Thus our presentation of what is definitive and what is provisional is free of fault.

The Buddha turned the first wheel of dharma, the four truths, for students who are uniquely disposed to the lower vehicles. He turned the second wheel of dharma, freedom from characteristics, for those who are uniquely disposed to the Mahāyāna. And for students who are disposed to a variety of vehicles he turned the final wheel of dharma, the three natures and other topics.

Following the Buddha's teaching in that way, those who clung to the view of truly existent things wishfully conceived of the provisional meaning as the definitive meaning. They tried to establish the real definitive meaning teachings as provisional meaning and commented upon the intention of the Transcendent Conqueror in that way. However, those who did not have any clinging to truly existent things did not hold the provisional meaning to be definitive meaning. Rather, they held the definitive meaning itself to be definitive, and they commented upon the intention of the Transcendent Conqueror in that way.

Nevertheless, our Teacher bestowed the authoritative teachings of the provisional and definitive meanings in the context of the three dharma wheels, and those teachings, just as they were given, are all, without any exceptions, methods by which students of the three vehicles may obtain the higher realms and definite excellence. *All* of those scriptures are supreme causes of liberation.

What is the meaning of the teachings on the three natures from the middle and final turnings? We Followers of the Middle Way explain it as follows. The dependent nature is the apparent phenomena that are qualified by ultimate reality. It is the conditioned phenomena of dependent arising. Though these phenomena do not exist, sentient beings imagine[374] them to exist. The perception of their existence is indeed imaginary: if things truly existed, their nature would, rather than being contrived and conditioned, be an uncontrived nature that held its own ground—and that is not the case.

In this way we explain the many assertions of the Proponents of Consciousness to be untenable. When we Followers of the Middle Way analyze, we do not even describe emptiness—the ultimate truth—as something that possesses an unconditioned nature. If we spoke in that way, we would contradict the extensive refutations of a nature existing in either of the two truths. If the lack of nature were held as a nature, that position would be the same as asserting the absence of rabbit horns as rabbit horns.

This is the way to posit the three natures in an unanalyzed way from the perspective of others: the dependently arisen relative is the dependent nature. It is commonly accepted, on the conventional level, to arise in dependence upon causes and conditions. Natures, abiding reality *(neluk/gnas lugs)*, the way things really are *(yinluk/yin lugs)*, the uncontrived essence, consciousness *(namrik/rnam rig)*,[375] and so on are all the imaginary nature. They are superimpositions made with regard to relative, interdependent phenomena. Emptiness, the ultimate truth, is the perfectly established nature. For, in terms of what is commonly accepted, if the relative is considered contrived and conditioned, the ultimate must be considered to be what is uncontrived and unconditioned. In this way, we Followers of the Middle Way explain the intention of the sūtras in a way that merely does not contradict what is commonly renowned in the world.

Also, when the sūtras say that the imaginary nature is essenceless, that the dependent nature has no essence of arising, and that the perfectly established nature has no ultimate essence, all these statements are tenable for Followers of the Middle Way, who speak of the lack of essence. The imaginary nature is like the horns of a rabbit: it is not established by valid cognition, even conventionally. The dependent nature is like an illusion: by its very identity it does not arise. It depends on causes and conditions. The perfectly established nature is empty of nature even conventionally. Since it is undeceiving, it is ultimately established.

When it is said, "It is ultimately established because it is undeceiving," that statement is merely made from the unanalyzed, relative perspective of others. When analyzed, the ultimate is devoid of being either deceiving or undeceiving. Therefore, it is impossible for the ultimate truth to be ultimately established.

2.2.2.1.1.6.2.3.1.1.1.2.1.1.2.1.1.2.3. THE EXTENSIVE EXPLANATION OF THE
REFUTATION OF ARISING FROM BOTH SELF AND OTHER
2.2.2.1.1.6.2.3.1.1.1.2.1.1.2.3.1. The logic of the refutation
2.2.2.1.1.6.2.3.1.1.1.2.1.1.2.3.2. The concluding summary
2.2.2.1.1.6.2.3.1.1.1.2.1.1.2.3.3. The teaching on other paths of refutation

2.2.2.1.1.6.2.3.1.1.1.2.1.1.2.3.1. THE LOGIC OF THE REFUTATION

> It is also illogical for phenomena to arise from both themselves
> and others,
> Because all the faults explained before would apply to that asser-
> tion. (6.98ab)

The Jains *(cherbupa/gcer bu pa)*[376] say, "Outer and inner things arise from
both self and other: it may be asserted that a vase arises from mounds of
clay, staffs, wheels, craftspeople, and so on. From among the vase's causes,
clay is not different from the vase, so the vase, in part, arises from itself.
Yet since the craftsperson, wheel, and so on *are* different from the vase, the
vase also arises from other.

"All other outer and inner things similarly arise from both self and other
because all things abide within the 'nine principles of word and meaning.'[377] Maitreya[378] takes birth only because his life force existed in other
lives too. This life force arises from itself, because Maitreya and Maitreya's
life force are not two different things. Maitreya also arises from other, such
as his parents, dharma, nondharma,[379] persons, and so on. Therefore the
refutations of arising from self and arising from other do not negate our
view. For we do not accept arising strictly from self or other."

The following is an explanation of how the assertions of the Jains are
illogical. It is illogical for phenomena to arise from both self and other,
because all of the faults explained before would apply to the assertion of
arising from both. Arising from self and arising from other have already
been refuted in the *Entrance to the Middle Way*, in lines such as:

> There is no purpose whatsoever to something originating from
> itself. (8c)

And,

> If things arose in dependence upon other things,
> Thick darkness would arise from a fire's flames

And everything would arise from everything,
Because all nonproducers would be equal to producers in being
different. (6.14)[380]

2.2.2.1.1.6.2.3.1.1.1.2.1.1.2.3.2. THE CONCLUDING SUMMARY

**We do not make this assertion in the world, nor do we make it
regarding suchness. (6.98c)**

We do not make this assertion of arising from both self and other regarding arising in the relative world, nor do we make it regarding arising in the precise nature of suchness. We refute arising from self and other in both of the two truths.

2.2.2.1.1.6.2.3.1.1.1.2.1.1.2.3.3. THE TEACHING ON OTHER PATHS OF REFUTATION

**Why? Because arising from either of them individually is not
established. (6.98d)**

Not only do the refutations that were taught above apply, consider this example. If one sesame seed can yield sesame oil, many seeds together can wield yield a large amount of oil. Yet if a grain of sand cannot yield sesame oil, many grains of sand together will not be able to yield any oil either.

In the same way, if self and other individually could produce any phenomena, they could produce even more phenomena by acting together. But arising from either of them individually is not established, so bringing them together yields no further results.

2.2.2.1.1.6.2.3.1.1.1.2.1.1.2.4. THE EXTENSIVE EXPLANATION OF THE
REFUTATION OF CAUSELESS ARISING
2.2.2.1.1.6.2.3.1.1.1.2.1.1.2.4.1. The refutation of the Proponents of Entity
2.2.2.1.1.6.2.3.1.1.1.2.1.1.2.4.2. The refutation of mental activity arising
from the elements

2.2.2.1.1.6.2.3.1.1.1.2.1.1.2.4.1. THE REFUTATION OF THE
PROPONENTS OF ENTITY
2.2.2.1.1.6.2.3.1.1.1.2.1.1.2.4.1.1. The refutation in both of the two truths
2.2.2.1.1.6.2.3.1.1.1.2.1.1.2.4.1.2. The refutation using the logic of
nonobservation

2.2.2.1.1.6.2.3.1.1.1.2.1.1.2.4.1.1. THE REFUTATION IN BOTH OF THE
TWO TRUTHS

> If things arose without any causes at all,
> Everything would always arise from everything.
> Worldly people would not have to go through hundreds of
> hardships to engage causes,
> Such as planting seeds, to make results arise. (6.99)

The Proponents of Entity *(Ngowonyi Mawa/ngo bo nyid smra ba)*[381] say, "If
things arose from causes, they would have to arise from themselves, others,
or both. Since we do not accept arising from causes, however, the criticisms of those three views do not apply to us. All outer and inner things
arise from their own entities, as in the following example.

"The stems and leaves of lotuses, and their corresponding rough and
soft qualities, are not created by any causes. Nevertheless, they arise, taking precisely the forms in which they appear. Peacocks and seagulls, moreover, are free from causes that arrange their particular shapes and colors
and so on. Yet, inevitably, those shapes and colors originate from their very
own entities."

If all outer and inner things arose at random without any causes at all,
all results would always arise from everything—causes and noncauses.
For example, the panasa[382] tree would not be the cause of panasa fruit,
and therefore panasa fruit could arise even from mango trees, because
mango trees and panasa trees would be equivalent in not being causes of
panasa fruit.

Similarly mangos, which are seasonal, and other phenomena that depend on special times would, according to the view of causeless arising, exist at all times, because they would not need to rely on time as a cause. All beings, moreover, would be born everywhere and at all times. But these scenarios simply do not take place.

If, through your clinging, you insist that such things do occur, not only is your assertion illogical, it also contradicts direct perception. Therefore it is untenable to claim that things arise from their own entities. For, if it were tenable, worldly people would not have to exert themselves in hundreds of hardships, planting seeds and the like in order to make results arise. But they *do* undergo such hardships. Therefore the arising of things does not occur due to things' own entities.

2.2.2.1.1.6.2.3.1.1.1.2.1.1.2.4.1.2. THE REFUTATION USING THE LOGIC OF NONOBSERVATION

> If beings were empty of causes, then, just like the scent and color
> Of utpala flowers in the sky, they would be imperceptible.
> Yet the world, in all its intense brilliance, *is* perceptible.
> Therefore, just like your own mind, understand that the world
>   arises due to causes. (6.100)

Furthermore, if beings were empty of causes, they would be just like the scent and color of utpala flowers in the sky:[383] they would be imperceptible, incapable of being apprehended at all. Yet inner and outer worlds, in all their intense brilliance, are indeed perceptible by the consciousnesses that are the perceiving subjects of each individual. It is just like the minds of you Chārvākas *(Gyangpenpa/rgyang 'phen pa)* apprehending blue and so on: these minds would not arise without objects that were blue and so on. Mental states arise due to specific objects. In the same way, understand that the inner and outer worlds originate only because of causes.

2.2.2.1.1.6.2.3.1.1.1.2.1.1.2.4.2. THE REFUTATION OF MENTAL ACTIVITY ARISING FROM THE ELEMENTS
2.2.2.1.1.6.2.3.1.1.1.2.1.1.2.4.2.1. If one is bewildered regarding this world, it is contradictory to assume anything about the world beyond
2.2.2.1.1.6.2.3.1.1.1.2.1.1.2.4.2.2. The thought that there is no world beyond is a wrong view

2.2.2.1.1.6.2.3.1.1.1.2.1.1.2.4.2.1. IF ONE IS BEWILDERED REGARDING
THIS WORLD, IT IS CONTRADICTORY TO ASSUME ANYTHING
ABOUT THE WORLD BEYOND

> The elements do not have the essential nature
> That you think they possess.
> Since you are so deeply ignorant of this world,
> How could you correctly realize anything about the world
>   beyond? (6.101)

The Proponents of the Elements as the Cause[384] say, "Primary minds and
mental events are caused by the elements. That they are so caused is undis-
putable because such causation is directly perceivable. Furthermore, if that
were not the case, many logical faults would accrue. All outer and inner
things are produced by earth, water, fire, and wind. Furthermore, a 'subsequent world,' in which the results of one's virtuous and nonvirtuous
actions will ripen, does not exist in the slightest."

The way to refute this view is presented extensively in other sources,
and will therefore be presented here in brief. The elements, earth and so
on, do not have the essential nature that you Chārvākas think they possess.
In particular, they do not have a nature that is the cause of consciousness.
When you say that the elements *are* the cause of consciousness, you are displaying a deep ignorance of this world: you are speaking incorrectly about
things of this world that you can directly perceive. Therefore how could
you correctly realize anything about the world beyond, which can only be
perceived by the extremely subtle perceptions of gods and humans? Such
realization is utterly impossible.

2.2.2.1.1.6.2.3.1.1.1.2.1.1.2.4.2.2. THE THOUGHT THAT THERE IS NO
WORLD BEYOND IS A WRONG VIEW
2.2.2.1.1.6.2.3.1.1.1.2.1.1.2.4.2.2.1. The statement of the inference accepted
by others
2.2.2.1.1.6.2.3.1.1.1.2.1.1.2.4.2.2.2. The establishment of the example

2.2.2.1.1.6.2.3.1.1.1.2.1.1.2.4.2.2.1. THE STATEMENT OF THE
INFERENCE ACCEPTED BY OTHERS

> When you refute a world beyond,
> You should understand that you are incorrectly viewing the
>   nature of knowable objects,

Because your view is based on the body.[385]
It is the same when you assert the true existence of the elements'
essential nature. (6.102)

The Chārvākas have two types of clinging: they cling to the elements as
being real and to the world beyond as nonexistent. These forms of clinging should be addressed as follows: when you Chārvākas refute a world
beyond, saying that it does not exist, you should understand that you are
incorrectly viewing the knowable objects of the worldly relative truth.
This is because your view is based on the body.[386]

It is the same when you assert the true existence of the elements' essential nature: you do so with reference to the body, a knowable object which
you view incorrectly.

2.2.2.1.1.6.2.3.1.1.1.2.1.1.2.4.2.2.2. THE ESTABLISHMENT OF THE
EXAMPLE

The nonexistence of the elements has already been explained
In a general way during the sections that refuted
Arising from self, other, both, and no causes.
Although they are not refuted extensively here, the elements do
    not exist. (6.103)

You might say, "You Followers of the Middle Way have not reversed the
view that the elements such as earth are truly existent, nor have you engendered any doubts about their true existence. Your example—possessing a
body—does not establish that the elements are not real."

However, we do not need to establish a concordant example for the
lack of true existence and lack of arising of the elements. We have already
explained that those elements do not exist and have no inherent nature. In
fact, all things were refuted in a general way above during the sections on
arising from self, other, both, and no causes. We have, therefore, refuted
these elements in a general way, even though we have not refuted them
extensively or made reference to their particular lack of inherent nature.
The elements cannot in even the slightest way support a view of true existence. Our example of the body, therefore, is established.

Philosophers who deprecate the Omniscient One, who say that things
exist, who say that things do not exist, or who assert Īshvara, time, parti-

cles, inherent natures, or essences to truly exist—in short, all the logicians from the Chārvākas through the Proponents of Consciousness—engage in wrong thinking. Know them for what they are—people who have incorrect thoughts and, due to those thoughts, propound wrong views.

We Followers of the Middle Way, on the other hand, are never susceptible to undesirable consequences of our statements, either on the level of no analysis, regarding what is renowned about the two truths, or on the level of analysis. We transcend all faults because, when we engage the conventions of the world, we speak in a way that accords with what the world accepts; when we contemplate the true nature, we do not accept any position of nonexistence after refuting existence, nor do we accept any position of existence after refuting nonexistence. Therefore we are free from all objections.

Wise ones can use the above two verses to transcend all positions asserted by Buddhist and non-Buddhist logicians. Since these verses refute the entire network of conceptions, they clarify the wisdom of the ultimate.

If you claim that the faults that we highlight in others also apply to us, that is not the case: in all situations we correctly realize the abiding mode of things. Therefore it is impossible to cite our examples as being incorrectly established.

In particular, the first of the above two preceding verses may be adapted in the following way:

> When we cognize a world beyond,
> It should be understood that we are genuinely viewing the nature of
>   knowable objects,
> Because our view is based on the body.
> It is the same when we assert that we realize selflessness.

2.2.2.1.1.6.2.3.1.1.1.2.1.1.3. THE ABOVE REASONINGS PROVE THAT
PHENOMENA HAVE NO INHERENT NATURE[387]

> Since there is no phenomenon that arises from self, other, both,
> Or that does not depend on causes, all things are devoid of inher-
> ent nature. (6.104ab)

"If things do not arise from self, other, both, or causelessly, how do they
arise?" If things had any nature, there would be no other way their arising
could occur. Thus phenomena, if they are to arise, must arise from one of
these four extremes. Yet, as was explained above, things do not arise from
themselves, others, both, or through not depending on causes. Therefore
all things are devoid of inherent nature.

2.2.2.1.1.6.2.3.1.1.1.2.1.2. RECONCILING APPARENT
CONTRADICTIONS IN THE REFUTATION[388]
2.2.2.1.1.6.2.3.1.1.1.2.1.2.1. Reconciling apparent contradictions with what
is seen
2.2.2.1.1.6.2.3.1.1.1.2.1.2.2. Responding to the objection that if things lack
an inherent nature, it is contradictory for them to exist conventionally

2.2.2.1.1.6.2.3.1.1.1.2.1.2.1. RECONCILING APPARENT
CONTRADICTIONS WITH WHAT IS SEEN
2.2.2.1.1.6.2.3.1.1.1.2.1.2.1.1. The way in which the unwise see due to
ignorance
2.2.2.1.1.6.2.3.1.1.1.2.1.2.1.2. The way in which things do not appear for the
wise

2.2.2.1.1.6.2.3.1.1.1.2.1.2.1.1. THE WAY IN WHICH THE UNWISE SEE
DUE TO IGNORANCE
2.2.2.1.1.6.2.3.1.1.1.2.1.2.1.1.1. The actual teaching
2.2.2.1.1.6.2.3.1.1.1.2.1.2.1.1.2. Reconciling the apparent contradiction of
seeing things that do not exist

2.2.2.1.1.6.2.3.1.1.1.2.1.2.1.1.1. THE ACTUAL TEACHING

> Worldly people are covered by the thick darkness of ignorance,
> like the sky covered by clouds.

> **For them, things exist; therefore objects appear in an incorrect**
> **way. (6.104cd)**

"Things such as the color blue do not arise by their nature and thus are not true objects. Since they are not perceptible as true objects, why is it that they appear again and again before us?"

The perceptions of worldly people are covered by ignorance. Ignorance is like rain clouds that block one from seeing the true color of the sky. The thick darkness of ignorance prevents worldly beings from seeing the emptiness nature of phenomena, which is like the blueness of the sky. For this reason, things exist for worldly people. These immature, worldly beings do not see the nature of objects such as the color blue. When they see objects, they perceive them in a way that does not match their nature. Due to worldly beings' clinging, objects appear in an incorrect way.

2.2.2.1.1.6.2.3.1.1.1.2.1.2.1.1.2. RECONCILING THE APPARENT
CONTRADICTION OF SEEING THINGS THAT DO NOT EXIST
2.2.2.1.1.6.2.3.1.1.1.2.1.2.1.1.2.1. The example
2.2.2.1.1.6.2.3.1.1.1.2.1.2.1.1.2.2. The meaning of the example

2.2.2.1.1.6.2.3.1.1.1.2.1.2.1.1.2.1. THE EXAMPLE

> **Due to diseased vision, some people will incorrectly perceive**
> **strands of hair, double moons,**
> **Eyes on peacocks' feathers, and bees. (6.105ab)**

If the obscurations of ignorance cause sentient beings not to see the true nature of things—emptiness—how is it that incorrect seeing happens? Why do sentient beings see anything at all? In response, the above verse teaches by way of example how ignorance causes things to appear in a way that does not correspond to what they really are.

When people are afflicted with diseased vision, they will erroneously perceive such things as strands of hair, double moons, eyes on peacocks' feathers, and bees, even though they utterly do not exist, and even though by their very nature they have never arisen.

2.2.2.1.1.6.2.3.1.1.1.2.1.2.1.1.2.2. THE MEANING OF THE EXAMPLE

In the same way, due to the problem of ignorance, the unwise
Perceive the variety of conditioned phenomena by conceptualiz-
ing them. (6.105cd)

In a manner equivalent to the diseased vision example, beings, due to the
problem of ignorance, do not see the true nature of phenomena. They are
unwise in the sense that they do not realize the reality that is phenomena's true nature. Due to this lack of realization, they accumulate karma
in its meritorious, nonmeritorious, and unmoving[389] varieties. Through
their concepts, they perceive the variety of conditioned phenomena—the
realms, beings, environments, and inhabitants of saṃsāra—to exist.

2.2.2.1.1.6.2.3.1.1.1.2.1.2.1.2. THE WAY IN WHICH THINGS DO NOT
APPEAR FOR THE WISE

"Actions arise due to bewilderment; without bewilderment,
Actions would not arise—" this is definitely something to be
realized only by the unwise.
The wise ones whose sun of excellent intelligence clears away the
thick darkness of ignorance
Will comprehend emptiness and gain liberation. (6.106)

In the context that assumes the true existence of arising and ceasing,
inherently existent actions arise due to inherently existent bewilderment.
"Without a substance known as bewilderment, the substance that is karmic formations will not arise"—this principle is definitely something to be
realized only by naïve, unwise beings. For, it is the unwise who fail to realize that both bewilderment and actions are primordially unarisen. Through
this lack of realization, they cling to the arising of actions due to ignorance
and to the nonarising of actions due to the absence of ignorance.

The wise ones, however, have the excellent intelligence of supreme
knowledge, which sees the suchness that is beyond existence and nonexistence.[390] The sun of this intelligence clears away the thick darkness of
bewilderment. The wise ones comprehend that when karmic formations
arise due to the condition of ignorance, they are devoid of nature and are
emptiness. They relinquish ignorance and, from that point onward, do
not take on more formations, because they have relinquished the cause of

appropriating them. By being free from karmic formations, they will gain full liberation from saṃsāra.

2.2.2.1.1.6.2.3.1.1.1.2.1.2.2. RESPONDING TO THE OBJECTION THAT IF THINGS LACK AN INHERENT NATURE, IT IS CONTRADICTORY FOR THEM TO EXIST CONVENTIONALLY
2.2.2.1.1.6.2.3.1.1.1.2.1.2.2.1. The objection
2.2.2.1.1.6.2.3.1.1.1.2.1.2.2.2. The response

2.2.2.1.1.6.2.3.1.1.1.2.1.2.2.1. THE OBJECTION

> "If things do not exist in suchness,
> They cannot exist conventionally either, like the childless
>   woman's son.
> Yet since phenomena do exist conventionally,
> They therefore exist inherently." (6.107)

"If things such as form do not exist in the suchness of the precise nature, i.e., ultimately, they cannot exist conventionally either. They are just like the childless woman's son.[391] Relative phenomena, according to your reasoning, would not exist even relatively. Yet that is illogical: relative phenomena *do* exist on the level of the relative. Since form and other things exist, they must exist inherently or ultimately as well."

2.2.2.1.1.6.2.3.1.1.1.2.1.2.2.2. THE RESPONSE
2.2.2.1.1.6.2.3.1.1.1.2.1.2.2.2.1. Showing the lack of definitiveness in the example
2.2.2.1.1.6.2.3.1.1.1.2.1.2.2.2.2. The counterparts' argument does not apply to Followers of the Middle Way
2.2.2.1.1.6.2.3.1.1.1.2.1.2.2.2.3. It is unreasonable for other Buddhist schools to debate with us

2.2.2.1.1.6.2.3.1.1.1.2.1.2.2.2.1. SHOWING THE LACK OF DEFINITIVENESS IN THE EXAMPLE
2.2.2.1.1.6.2.3.1.1.1.2.1.2.2.2.1.1. The lack of definitiveness as shown by the diseased vision example
2.2.2.1.1.6.2.3.1.1.1.2.1.2.2.2.1.2. The lack of definitiveness in the counterparts' position itself

2.2.2.1.1.6.2.3.1.1.1.2.1.2.2.2.1.1. The lack of definitiveness as shown by the diseased vision example

> The objects, such as strands of hair,
> Perceived by people with diseased vision are unarisen.
> Therefore debate first with people with diseased vision;
> Then take the same approach with beings who have the diseased
>   vision of ignorance. (6.108)

This verse expresses the response of the Followers of the Middle Way to the above objection. The objects, such as strands of hair, of the minds of those with diseased vision are equal to the sons of childless women in being unarisen. So why don't our counterparts debate first with people who have diseased vision? Ask them, "Why can't you see the childless woman's son if you can see strands of hair that do not exist?"

Then, take the same approach with ordinary beings, whose eyes of intelligence are afflicted by the diseased vision of ignorance. Ask them, "Why can't you see the childless woman's son if you can see forms that are unarisen?" Debate with and examine them in this way.

Do not, however, try to debate with or examine us. We simply explain to others how yogis and yoginīs see things. We encourage others who wish to attain the wisdom of yogis and yoginīs to engender devoted interest in the nature of phenomena explained in the treatises. In this way we base ourselves on scripture when explaining the lack of inherent nature of things.

However, we do not rely on our own consciousnesses when teaching in this way, for our consciousnesses are obscured by the diseased vision of ignorance. We would not be able to establish the lack of inherent nature strictly in reliance on our own perceptions.

In sum, the strands of hair for someone with diseased vision are equal to the childless woman's son in being unarisen. However, strands of hair appear to people with the corresponding disease; sons of childless women appear to no one. It is the same with conventional phenomena. They are, even conventionally, equal to the sons of childless women in being unarisen. Yet, at the same time, forms, for example, can become objects of an ordinary person's mind, whereas the sons of childless women cannot. There is nothing contradictory about this fact.

2.2.2.1.1.6.2.3.1.1.1.2.1.2.2.2.1.2. THE LACK OF DEFINITIVENESS IN
THE COUNTERPARTS' POSITION ITSELF
2.2.2.1.1.6.2.3.1.1.1.2.1.2.2.2.1.2.1. The lack of definitiveness in reasoning
2.2.2.1.1.6.2.3.1.1.1.2.1.2.2.2.1.2.2. The lack of definitiveness in scripture

2.2.2.1.1.6.2.3.1.1.1.2.1.2.2.2.1.2.1. THE LACK OF DEFINITIVENESS IN
REASONING

> You can perceive what is unarisen, such as dreams, cities of
>   gandharvas,
> Mirage water, hallucinations, and reflections.
> Since these are equal to the childless woman's son in not existing,
> Why do you not see the childless woman's son? Your view is
>   illogical. (6.109)

Now set aside debating those with diseased vision—you need to have a
debate with yourselves for a while. You can perceive what is unarisen, such
as dreams, cities of gandharvas with their walls, the water of mirages, hallucinations, reflections, echoes, and emanations. None of these phenomena inherently arise. Since they are equal to the childless woman's son in
being nonexistent in reality, why do you not see the childless woman's son
like you see dreams and the others?

First examine yourselves in this way, and then come debate with us. It
is illogical to claim that since form and so on are without inherent nature
they are equally existent or nonexistent as the childless woman's son.

2.2.2.1.1.6.2.3.1.1.1.2.1.2.2.2.1.2.2. THE LACK OF DEFINITIVENESS IN
SCRIPTURE

> In suchness things do not arise.
> Yet, unlike the childless woman's son,
> They can be perceived by the world.
> Therefore your position has no definitiveness. (6.110)

In the suchness of the precise nature, things such as forms are just like
dreams: they do not arise. Nevertheless, they are unlike the childless woman's son because they *can* be perceived by the world. They are objects of
perception for sentient beings. Therefore we are justified in saying that
your position that things are equal to the sons of childless women in

terms of their status of existence or nonexistence has no definitiveness. The sūtras say:[392]

Beings are taught to be like dreams.
They are not presented as the true nature.
There is no true existence in dreams,
Aside from the clinging of mistaken minds.

Cities of gandharvas appear,
But they cannot be found in any of the ten directions or elsewhere.
These cities are designated by names alone.
The Sugata looks upon beings in the same way.

People looking at a mirage with the thought of water
Will see water even though there is none.
In the same way beings, stirred by conception,
Conceive the unpleasant as pleasant.

In a completely clear mirror,
Reflections appear,
Though they bear no inherent nature.
Druma, understand that all phenomena are the same.

2.2.2.1.1.6.2.3.1.1.1.2.1.2.2.2.2. THE COUNTERPARTS' ARGUMENT
DOES NOT APPLY TO FOLLOWERS OF THE MIDDLE WAY
2.2.2.1.1.6.2.3.1.1.1.2.1.2.2.2.2.1. We do not contradict reasoning
2.2.2.1.1.6.2.3.1.1.1.2.1.2.2.2.2.2. We do not contradict scripture

2.2.2.1.1.6.2.3.1.1.1.2.1.2.2.2.2.1. WE DO NOT CONTRADICT
REASONING

The childless woman's son does not arise by way of its essential
    nature
In suchness, nor does it exist in the world.
In the same way, all things are devoid of arising by way of their
    essence
In the world and in suchness. (6.111)

You have no grounds for opposing us, the Followers of the Middle Way. We do not accept that things, such as form, inherently arise in the relative; nor do we refute such a notion on the ultimate level. Why? Consider once more the example of the childless woman's son. Such a phenomenon does not arise by way of its own nature in suchness or ultimately; it is also devoid of any conventional existence in the world.

In the same way, things such as form do not arise by way of their own nature: not in suchness, or ultimate reality, nor in the world, or relative reality. For, when analyzed, all things are free from conceptual elaborations in both truths. The notion of "inherent arising" refers to an arising of the very characteristics of phenomena themselves, an arising that exists independent of the conceptual mind. There is no such arising in either of the truths.

2.2.2.1.1.6.2.3.1.1.1.2.1.2.2.2.2.2. WE DO NOT CONTRADICT SCRIPTURE

> Therefore the Teacher said that all phenomena
> Are primordially peace, free of arising,
> And perfect nirvāṇa by nature.
> Therefore never is there any arising. (6.112)

Due to the reasonings just explained, the Teacher, the Buddha, when turning the wheel of dharma, said *(Clouds of Jewels, Könchog Trin/dkon mchog sprin)*:

> Primordially peace, unarisen,
> Naturally nirvāṇa.
> Protector, you taught all phenomena to be like that.

He taught that all phenomena, from form through omniscience, are primordially peace, free from arising, and perfect nirvāṇa by their nature. With such scriptural corroboration, we can correctly state that all phenomena are always devoid of arising in both of the two truths.

Further, since wisdom is an object of peace, all phenomena are peace. Why are all phenomena peace? Because they do not inherently arise. For the same reason, all phenomena are also naturally nirvāṇa.

There are further discussions in this section of the *Ṭīkā* on the assertions of Bodong [Chogle Namgyal] and others, but I will not write about them.

2.2.2.1.1.6.2.3.1.1.1.2.1.2.2.2.3. IT IS UNREASONABLE FOR OTHER BUDDHIST SCHOOLS TO DEBATE WITH US

> **Vases and so on do not exist in suchness,**
> **But they exist in terms of what is thoroughly renowned in the**
> **world.**
> **All other things are the same way,**
> **So the consequence that they are like the childless woman's son**
> **does not apply. (6.113)**

The Particularists and Sūtra Followers of our own Buddhist tradition say, "If things do not exist ultimately, they must also not exist conventionally." They have no grounds for opposing us in this way, because there is an example from their own tenet systems that disproves their refutations.

According to them, vases, forests, and so on are imputed existents of the relative. They say that such phenomena do not exist in ultimate reality, yet they are renowned as existing in the world. Thus the Particularists and Sūtra Followers accept those phenomena as coarse, imputed existents.

In the same way, form and all other things do not exist when analyzed. Yet, from the first-glance *(nyam gawa/nyams dga' ba)* unanalyzed perspective of what is approved in the world, they appear. Therefore the consequence that phenomena, because of not existing ultimately, are utterly nonexistent and equal to the childless woman's son does not apply to our presentation.

You may object, "Your explanation does not speak to the criticisms that we have made. The imputations of vases and other things are supported by the elements and so on, which substantially exist. Since the elements function as causes, the imputed vase, the relative phenomenon, arises as a tenable result. However, you Followers of the Middle Way think that all phenomena are imputed and that there are utterly no substances that would serve as the causes of imputation. You have not dealt with the logical consequence that would befall your explanations: according to your logic, all phenomena are just like the childless woman's son."

That objection is unreasonable because it is impossible to establish the bases for imputation, earth and so on, as anything substantial. The *Four Hundred Verses* says:

Just as vases do not exist
Without forms and so on,
Forms as well do not exist
Without wind and so on. (14.14)

The *Precious Garland* says:

Earth, water, fire, and wind
Do not exist as their own entities.
If one became devoid of the other three, that one could
not exist.
Without that one, the other three also could not exist.
Without three, the one does not exist.
If without one the three do not exist,
None of them can exist individually.
Therefore, how would a collection of them truly arise?

Extensive explanations about this can be found in other sources.

2.2.2.1.1.6.2.3.1.1.1.2.2. THE TEACHING THAT ARISING IN THE
RELATIVE TRUTH IS DEPENDENT ARISING[393]
2.2.2.1.1.6.2.3.1.1.1.2.2.1. The actual teaching on how arising in the relative
truth is dependent arising
2.2.2.1.1.6.2.3.1.1.1.2.2.2. The benefits of realizing dependent arising

2.2.2.1.1.6.2.3.1.1.1.2.2.1. THE ACTUAL TEACHING ON HOW ARISING
IN THE RELATIVE TRUTH IS DEPENDENT ARISING

Since things do not arise causelessly,
Nor through the causes of Īshvara and so on,
Nor from self, other, or both,
Therefore they excellently arise *in dependence.* (6.114)

You may ask, "If you refute arising from the four extremes, how can you
ascertain relative arising: the arising of consciousness due to ignorance
and karmic formations, the arising of sprouts from seeds, and so on?"

The answer is that we speak in a way that does not destroy the world's
conventions that are accepted on the level of no analysis. As we have previously explained, things do not arise causelessly, from their own entities.

Nor do things arise, in either of the two truths, from Īshvara, time, particles, inherent natures, persons, Narayana, or other such causes.

Rather, results such as sprouts excellently arise in dependence upon all the causes and conditions, such as seeds, that are necessary for the result to appear. Furthermore, the Transcendent Conqueror said:

> The hallmark of all phenomena is this: if this exists, that arises.
> If this arises, that arises. Through the condition of ignorance,
> formations arise . . .

The *Treatise*, the *Precious Garland*, and others teach extensively in the same way. They repeat after the world about the process of conditionality. This presentation of the arising of mere conditionality refutes the ways of arising and ceasing proclaimed by the realist proponents of incorrect philosophical systems. However, it does not contradict the ways of arising and ceasing that are generally renowned in the world.

The conventions used by the Followers of the Middle Way are in harmony with the relative truth of the world. Not only that, they are used in a way that they can become a stepping stone to the ultimate truth. This is the Followers of the Middle Way's "harmonious engagement with the world." Even though it accords with what is generally accepted in the world, it is the only method that can serve as a stepping stone from the interdependent relative to the genuine reality that is the ultimate.

Furthermore, this approach to the relative truth, in which the worldly perspective is simply repeated, word for word, regarding dependently arisen phenomena, is only practiced by the Followers of the Middle Way. It is not presented in other philosophical systems, from the Proponents of Consciousness down.

These lower systems' presentations of the relative truth are not only unsuitable supports for entering into ultimate reality, they are also full of imputations of utter nonexistents, imputations that are purported to be the grounds for adopting what is beneficial and shunning what is harmful. That is why these systems are untenable. Even though the Middle Way approach to the relative is the only approach that is free of fault, it is still not posited by the Followers of the Middle Way as their own system.

The Followers of the Middle Way posit the relative truth from others' perspective as interdependent phenomena. Although the term "interdependence," which is also posited by the Proponents of Things, is employed, it does not carry the same meaning as when used by them. The Proponents of Things hold interdependent phenomena to be established in and of themselves, whereas Followers of the Middle Way do not claim any level of existence—even conventional—for any things or nothings in their own system. For Followers of the Middle Way, there is no choice but to present interdependent phenomena in the way they are accepted in the world.

How, then, do they use the presentation of interdependent, relative phenomena to guide students to realize that, in the ultimate truth, causes and results are empty of their own entities? They do so by explaining how all dualistic opposites depend on each other for their existence. "Dualistic opposites" refers to such phenomena as performers and actions, the self and the aggregates *(nyerlen/nyer len)*, causes and results, viewers and the viewed, expressers and the expressed, parts and wholes *(yenlak chen/yan lag can)*, features and bases of features, characteristics and things that illustrate characteristics *(tsenshi/mtshan gzhi)*, truth and falsity, saṃsāra and nirvāṇa, and the permanent and the impermanent. Since every one of these phenomena depends on its counterpart, there is no phenomenon that is established in and of itself, independent of anything else. By realizing this, students will gain liberation from the extremes of eternalism and nihilism.

It is untenable, moreover, to hold as one's own position that the causes, results, and so on of those interdependent phenomena are the same or different, or that they bear any other such qualities. The ones who view them as being the same or different are naïve, *(jipa/byis pa)*, ordinary beings, not the noble ones.

When we use the term "mere conditionality" *(kyen dipa tsam/rkyen 'di pa tsam)*, we include what is tenably considered causes and results. We posit whatever causes and results are renowned in the world, but concepts such as Īshvara, which do not even appear in the world, are simply imputations made by others. We do not posit them as causes or results.

Followers of the Middle Way thus present the relative truth from the perspective of others in the world and before analysis. They describe arising, ceasing, causes, and results based on what is renowned in the world. Through this very approach they are capable of refuting the four extremes of arising. They are also capable of refuting the views by which the Proponents of Things assert arising and ceasing.

This process of reasoning reveals a logical method that establishes all phenomena as being unarisen. Through it one can realize that anything dependently arisen is, by necessity, emptiness. However, even *these* conclusions about interdependence being equal to emptiness and so forth are true *(drup/grub)* only for those who abide in what is seen as tenable from a relative, worldly point of view. They are not true for a Follower of the Middle Way from his or her own point of view. When Followers of the Middle Way, from their own point of view, engage in analysis, they do not find *any* interdependent, relative phenomena to be tenable.[394]

When the logical arguments involving the arising and ceasing of other-approved, dependently arisen phenomena are used to refute the four extremes of arising and ceasing, from a strictly literal perspective there occurs the paradox of "arising and ceasing" being used to refute "arising and ceasing." However, there is nothing contradictory in the use of such language. Witness, for instance, the times in which what is arisen through conditions is described as unarisen.[395] This is a case of "not relying on the words but relying on their meaning."[396] As was said:

Anything that arises due to conditions does not arise.
This is what the supreme one, who knows reality, taught.

One may ask, "Do you use the reason of dependent arising to establish relative arising and so forth conventionally?" By describing dependent arising in the way explained above, we posit relative arising and ceasing and relative causes and results at the time of no analysis. If we were to affirm relative arising and so on *after* analysis using the reasoning of interdependence, we would contradict what has been explained through many reasonings: that, in both truths, arising and so on are to be refuted and transcend all speech and expression.

There is no difference between someone who reifies arising and ceasing by superimposing arising from the four extremes and someone who reifies the same concepts by relying on dependent arising. If one uses interdependence to establish arising and ceasing after analysis, such arising and ceasing would exist ultimately; that would be untenable. Anyone can establish that ultimately there is no arising and ceasing.

Even from a relative perspective, establishing the existence of arising and ceasing by dependent arising is untenable. If one goes beyond repeating the world's view of arising and ceasing, which does not involve analysis, and posits arising and ceasing *after* having analyzed, such arising and ceasing would become truly existent and irrefutable. Positing arising and ceasing after analysis would mean that arising and ceasing are phenomena that can withstand analysis. If any phenomenon existed that could withstand analysis, it would not be tenable in either of the two truths. One would be forced to include such phenomena in a third category, yet no such category exists.

Therefore, Followers of the Middle Way posit dependently arisen causes and results from the perspective of no analysis. They do so merely to avoid superimpositions or denials regarding the merely appearing relative truth of the world. They do so in order not to denigrate the connection between actions and results on the worldly level.

They speak in a way that does not take anything away from nor add anything to precisely what is accepted in the world. After analysis, interdependent arising and ceasing are not posited in either of the two truths. If one affirms interdependent relative phenomena after analysis, this will become a denial of ultimate truth, for one will be attempting to establish something that does not exist.

This way of explaining mere conditionality from the perspective of no analysis is in stark contrast with the reification of asserting arising from the four extremes. The method Followers of the Middle Way use to draw distinctions between the two truths is far superior to that of others. They speak in a way that does not contradict what is accepted in the world. They do not contradict what is conventionally known by anyone, from buddhas to sentient beings. By proceeding in this way, they are able to refute and clear away concepts of arising from the four extremes. They are also able to establish the reality that is their ultimate intention.

There are many different critical examinations presented in this section of the *Ṭīkā*.

2.2.2.1.1.6.2.3.1.1.1.2.2.2. THE BENEFITS OF REALIZING DEPENDENT ARISING
2.2.2.1.1.6.2.3.1.1.1.2.2.2.1. Dependent arising is the antidote to all bad views
2.2.2.1.1.6.2.3.1.1.1.2.2.2.2. The reasons why

2.2.2.1.1.6.2.3.1.1.1.2.2.2.1. DEPENDENT ARISING IS THE ANTIDOTE TO ALL BAD VIEWS

Since all things perfectly arise dependently,
All wrong conceptions are rendered powerless.
Therefore this reasoning of dependent arising
Cuts through the net of all bad views. (6.115)

Through explaining, as above, the dependent arising of mere condition-ality, not only are conceptions of causeless arising and so on reversed, this simple reasoning, "all things arise in a manner of one depending upon the other," establishes, at the level of no analysis, that arising, ceasing, causes, and results exist as they are renowned in the world. However, it does not prove anything beyond that.

It renders all dualistic conceptions about permanence, nihilism, things, nonthings, and so on powerless—not only ultimately but also convention-ally. This reasoning of the mere conditionality of dependent arising cuts through the net of all bad views that cling to extremes. We do not assert anything to exist inherently: although we posit mere dependent arising of conditionality, we do not posit anything else. As was said in Nāgārjuna's *Sixty Stanzas on Reasoning*:

Whatever arises dependently
Does not arise in terms of its own entity.
Regarding what does not arise in terms of its own entity—
Why say it "arises"?

The *Treatise* says:

That which arises dependently
Is explained to be emptiness.
It is an imputation dependent on causes.
This is the path of the middle way.

The sūtras say *(Sūtra Requested by Anavatapa, Ma Dröpe Shupe Do/ma dros pas zhus pa'i mdo)*:

That which arises due to conditions does not arise.
It does not have the nature of arising.

That which depends on conditions is taught to be empty.
The one who knows emptiness is heedful.

As these quotations demonstrate, no bad views arise in the mindstream of a proponent of the absence of inherent nature.

2.2.2.1.1.6.2.3.1.1.1.2.2.2.2. THE REASONS WHY

Conceptions will occur if things are held to exist,
But how things do not exist has been thoroughly analyzed.
When things are seen not to exist, conceptions about their
existence will not arise,
Just as fire will not burn without fuel. (6.116)

If things are held to be objects and phenomena that exist, conceptions of their being self, other, permanent, or extinct will occur. As Ajita *(Abhi-samayālaṃkāra, Ngön Tok Gyen/mngon rtogs rgyan)* says:[397]

Others say that phenomena exist
While at the same time the Teacher's obscurations
Connected to knowable objects are exhausted.
I find this very strange.

The logic already explained has thoroughly analyzed how things are devoid of nature. The noble ones, therefore, see in the manner of not seeing. For those who do not see any thing or subtle particle in any phenomenon whatsoever, conceptions about things such as form will not occur. This is just as in the example of fire not burning if it has no fuel.

2.2.2.1.1.6.2.3.1.1.1.2.3. THE EXPLANATION OF THE NECESSITY OF ANALYSIS THROUGH REASONING
2.2.2.1.1.6.2.3.1.1.1.2.3.1. The actual result of analysis
2.2.2.1.1.6.2.3.1.1.1.2.3.2. Analysis as an expression of the compassionate activity of Nāgārjuna

2.2.2.1.1.6.2.3.1.1.1.2.3.1. THE ACTUAL RESULT OF ANALYSIS

Ordinary beings are bound by conception,
And yogins, free from conception, are liberated.

The wise ones teach that the reversal of conception
Is the result of analysis. (6.117)

Ordinary beings, who do not know or comprehend dharmatā, the emptiness of nature of all phenomena, are bound by their own conceptions,
like a spider trapped in its own web. Yogins, noble ones who comprehend
suchness and are free from conceptions of any elaboration, are liberated.
Thus the wise ones, such as the master Nāgārjuna in his *Treatise on the
Middle Way*, teach that the reversal of all conceptions that cling to the
extremes is the result of analysis. As it is said:

> If things existed by way of their nature,
> What good quality would lie in seeing emptiness?
> Conception is what binds our seeing,
> And is what comes to cessation when suchness is seen.

There are some who say that the position of not asserting any level of
existence or nonexistence is an unconscious, nihilistic view of utter nothingness. Others say that all relative phenomena exist but no ultimate
phenomena exist, and that relatively everything exists while ultimately
everything is nonexistent. Others say that the conventional existence of
phenomena suffices as existence but the ultimate nonexistence of phenomena does not suffice as nonexistence. They say that phenomena that
are established bases exist for noble ones but do not appear in a dualistic
way. Still others say that the ultimate exists but all relative phenomena do
not exist.

All of these views are outside the scope of the Buddha's teachings. If
what they propound were accurate, all phenomena included within the
two truths would be bound by conceptual elaborations. In both truths,
they would hold their own status as existent or nonexistent, permanent
or extinct. Everyone who desires liberation, therefore, must relinquish
clinging to both existence and nonexistence—whatever one is clinging to.
Without relinquishing such clinging, it is impossible to attain liberation.

Here the *Ṭīkā* presents further explanation on the meaning of the
above, as well as affirmations and refutations connected with the assertions of some later Tibetans.

2.2.2.1.1.6.2.3.1.1.1.2.3.2. ANALYSIS AS AN EXPRESSION OF THE
COMPASSIONATE ACTIVITY OF NĀGĀRJUNA
2.2.2.1.1.6.2.3.1.1.1.2.3.2.1. The actual teaching
2.2.2.1.1.6.2.3.1.1.1.2.3.2.2. Rejecting rebuttals
2.2.2.1.1.6.2.3.1.1.1.2.3.2.3. It is best to analyze after having overcome
attachment and aversion toward views

2.2.2.1.1.6.2.3.1.1.1.2.3.2.1. THE ACTUAL TEACHING

> Nāgārjuna did not present analysis in his treatise because he
> was fond of debate.
> Rather, he taught about suchness so that beings could attain
> liberation. (6.118ab)

You should understand that the master Nāgārjuna did not present extensive analyses and collections of reasonings in his treatise because he was
fond of debate and wanted to deride and prevail over others. Rather, he was
thinking that nothing else would suffice other than for beings to analyze,
whereby they will come to comprehend the precise nature of dharmatā
and attain liberation. To this end, Nāgārjuna taught about the suchness of
the precise nature in his *Treatise on the Middle Way* so that beings could
attain liberation.

2.2.2.1.1.6.2.3.1.1.1.2.3.2.2. REJECTING REBUTTALS

> But if when suchness is explained
> The texts of others fall apart, there is no fault in that. (6.118cd)

You may say, "The author of the *Treatise* simply writes what others think
and then refutes their views. The purpose of the *Treatise*, therefore, is
nothing other than debate. How can you claim that its result is only the
reversal of conception?"

Analysis is not engaged in simply for the purpose of debate. Nevertheless, when explaining the precise nature of suchness by way of analysis, the
texts of others will naturally be seen as weak, because they are untenable.
Their adherents will not be able to sustain their assertions, just like darkness when the morning is fast approaching. If the assertions in these texts
fall apart due to the vajra mountain of our analysis, there is no fault on our
part. The *Four Hundred* says:

This dharma was not taught by the tathāgatas
In order to engage in debate.
Nevertheless, it burns our counterparts' views
Like fire burns kindling.

2.2.2.1.1.6.2.3.1.1.1.2.3.2.3. IT IS BEST TO ANALYZE AFTER HAVING OVERCOME ATTACHMENT AND AVERSION TOWARD VIEWS

Attachment to one's own view and
Aversion to the views of others are nothing more than
  conception.
Therefore, if you first overcome attachment and aggression
And *then* analyze, you will be liberated. (6.119)

If this dharma were taught for the purpose of debate out of fierce attachment towards one's own position and aversion towards the positions of others, it would be impossible for it to reverse misconceptions. Therefore attachment to one's own view and a disturbed mind of aversion towards the views of others are nothing more than thoughts that reify things.

Conceptions that are not reversed cause one to be bound and are antithetical to liberation. This dharma was not taught for the sake of debate. Therefore you should first overcome attachment to your own position and aversion toward the positions of others. If after that those who wish to realize the precise nature analyze the abiding mode, they will be swiftly liberated. The *Sixty Stanzas on Reasoning* says:[398]

Genuine beings who are free from debate
Have no position of their own.
For those who have no own-position,
How could a position of others exist? (50)

The *Four Hundred* says:

If you become attached to your own position
And averse to the positions of others,
You will not attain nirvāṇa
Nor will your conduct become free of duality.

The sūtras say:

Those who study a teaching and become attached to it
Will become angry when they hear something that is not that
teaching.
Their pride and conceit will defeat them
And lead them only to suffering.

Those who desire liberation must first let go of their clinging to positions. They will then be capable of relying on the teachings of Nāgārjuna,
which explain the nature of reality in a way that harmonizes with what is
generally accepted in the world. They should train in the essential point
that all phenomena are merely dependently arisen. This training itself will
become the cause of their liberation.

From the perspective of analysis, and from the perspective of the noble
ones, even interdependence and the liberation that its realization causes
are inexpressible. Nothing is attained, and no one attains anything. At the
time of realizing this, one does not even say that such things "do not exist."
One does not attempt any description using words such as "exist," "does
not exist," "both," or "neither."

At that time, one does not conceive of anything. One does not fixate
on anything. One does not apply any effort. One does not do anything.
In this great state of no action itself, one rests uncontrived, loosely, and
evenly.

When resting in that way, all appearances of the sixfold collection of
consciousness are appearance-emptiness, sound-emptiness, awareness-
emptiness. Look nakedly. Rest in their naked liberation.

This is the supreme view and meditation of the Middle Way. It is what
has dawned in the minds of the great beings of the glorious Takpo Kagyü.
This is their stainless oral instruction.

It is the approach of some people[399] to refute the four extremes of existence, nonexistence, and so on in a different way in each of the two truths.
They say that the relative truth is established by valid cognition, that there
is a common locus for confusion and valid cognition, and that things validly perform functions. For them, moreover, all things of the relative truth
are, in the relative, real in their own place. Therefore, they say, apprehending things of the relative truth as being things does not constitute reifica-

tion or clinging to true existence. They say that the "true existence" in the context of determining the "lack of true existence" refers to something that cannot possibly be a knowable object. To this they add that in order to realize the lack of true existence one must identify true existence itself.

These scholars, furthermore, describe "postdisintegration" to be, even conventionally, an uncompounded phenomenon that connects the causes and results of things. They say that all the different confused appearances of the six kinds of beings are "confused truth," perform functions, and are established by valid cognition. Rather than explaining existence and non-existence in the context of all phenomena of the two truths, they make separate presentations of what exists and what does not exist by separating the two truths from each other.

Many such explanations have been attempted, but all of them are untenable. The approach of those scholars is to allow the refutation of existence to imply an affirmation of nonexistence. Yet their refutations of nonexistence will then become implicit affirmations of existence! Similarly, they claim that the refutation of "being both" implies an affirmation of "being neither" and so on. Their words, in the end, wind up refuting each other! Due to this, all the meanings they convey lie outside the realization of emptiness.

Followers of the Middle Way, therefore, do not affirm nonexistence through refuting existence. Nor do they affirm or accept "being neither" through refuting "being both." The refutations of existence, being both, being neither, and so on are simply words used to undermine the wrong thinking of others. They are accepted merely as statements from the perspective of other, worldly beings. Relying on them as such, the Followers of the Middle Way reverse others' misconceptions. They do *not* refute anything or affirm anything as their own system. They simply speak in accordance with the following quotation from Shāntideva's *Entrance to the Conduct of Bodhisattvas*:

All analyses depend
On simply what is renowned in the world. (9.108cd)

Limitless such statements have been made. More extensive and critical examinations on this topic are to be obtained from other sources.

2.2.2.1.1.6.2.3.1.1.2. THE SELFLESSNESS OF PERSONS

2.2.2.1.1.6.2.3.1.1.2.1. The reasons why it is necessary to refute the self of persons

2.2.2.1.1.6.2.3.1.1.2.2. The extensive explanation of the reasonings of the refutation

2.2.2.1.1.6.2.3.1.1.2.3. The teaching subsequent to the refutation on how the person is a mere dependent imputation

2.2.2.1.1.6.2.3.1.1.2.1. THE REASONS WHY IT IS NECESSARY TO REFUTE THE SELF OF PERSONS

> **Seeing with their intelligence that all mental afflictions and**
> **problems**
> **Arise from the view of the transitory collection,**
> **And realizing that the self is the object of that view,**
> **Yogis and yoginīs refute the self. (6.120)**

The *Entrance to the Middle Way* has taught the selflessness of phenomena by presenting scriptural quotations, key instructions, and reasonings. It will now present the selflessness of persons.

All mental afflictions, such as attachment, and all problems, such as birth, aging, sickness, death, and misery, arise from the view of the transitory collection *(jiktsok la tawa/'jig tshogs la lta ba)*. The defining characteristic of this view, an afflicted form of supreme knowledge, is fixation toward the self *(dak/bdag)* and entities connected to the self *(dak giwa/ bdag gi ba)*.[400]

Yogis and yoginīs see with their intelligence that the above problems arise due to the view of the transitory collection. Therefore, they understand that it is appropriate to refute that view. They also see that without addressing the object of that view, the view itself will remain. Therefore, realizing that the self is the observed object of the view of the transitory collection, and realizing that self-fixation *(dak-dzin/bdag 'dzin)* is the perceiving subject of the self, yogis and yoginīs, wishing to abandon all mental afflictions and problems, treat the view of the transitory collection as something to relinquish.

Since they know that comprehending the selflessness of persons will lead to relinquishing the view of the transitory collection, yogis and yoginīs who are dedicated to liberation refute the self that is that view's object. They therefore see it appropriate to analyze this object. The sūtras say:

> Regarding all mental afflictions, the view of the transitory collection is their root. The view of the transitory collection is their cause. The view of the transitory collection is their origin.

From the view of the transitory collection arise formations and so on. The wheel of existence of dependent arising, pervaded by the three mental afflictions,[401] turns fiercely for a long time. Therefore this analysis of personal selflessness, which relinquishes the view of the transitory collection, is the unsurpassable method for accomplishing liberation.

Now, in the context of teachings on the two forms of selflessness, what is the self of persons? What is the self of phenomena? What are the reasonings that refute both of them? In what manner do these types of self not exist?

First, the self of persons is the referent object *(shen yul/zhen yul)* of the view of the transitory collection, which fixates on the self and entities connected to the self. It is renowned as the self, the sentient being, the person, the individual, the experiencer *(tsorwapo/tshor ba po)*, and so on. This self is of two types: the object of the connate *(lhen kye/lhan skyes)* view of the transitory collection and the object of imagination *(kuntak/kun brtags)*.

The first type of self is conceived of due to habitual tendencies, gathered since beginningless time, toward fixating upon the self and entities connected to the self. In observing the aggregates, one thinks, "I," "me," and "mine." This type of mental engagement or self-fixation *(dakdzin/bdag 'dzin)*, known as "the connate view of the transitory collection," occurs in all sentient beings—from birds and beasts upward. The object of this view is the "self," which, since its view is connate, is not an imputation of philosophical systems.

The second type of self is conceived of by those, such as non-Buddhist philosophers, who create superimpositions of the self as separate from the aggregates, permanent, singular, independent, and so on. The Saṃmitīyas[402] *(Mangkurwa/mang bkur ba)*, moreover, claim that the self is the aggregates or the mind-in-itself. The Vātsīputrīyas[403] view the self as being neither the same as nor different from the aggregates. Still others[404] describe a self that is different from the self that is to be refuted by logic:

they assert a self that is an imputed existent, is established by conventional valid cognition, and is imputed on the basis of the aggregates.

All of these views fall under the category of the imagined view of the transitory collection. As opposed to being present due to beginningless habitual tendencies alone, they are wrong fabrications created anew with the help of bad teachers and incorrect philosophies. The imagined self, therefore, is the object viewed by all forms of the imagined view of the transitory collection.

The self of phenomena is conceived of in relation to all phenomena from form through omniscience that are not the person yet are included within the aggregates, constituents, and sources. Worldly people and proponents of philosophical systems impute these phenomena to exist by way of their own entities. They superimpose qualities of being permanent, impermanent, and so on upon phenomena.

As for the reasonings that refute those forms of the self, the root text of the *Entrance to the Middle Way* will lead us through the stages of logic that refute the self of persons asserted by non-Buddhists, Saṃmitīyas, and Vātsīputrīyas. The text has already explained the reasonings that refute the self of phenomena.

The mere imputed self, the object of the connate view of the transitory collection, does not actually exist. Nevertheless, when not analyzed this mere, imputed self *does* exist from the perspective of what is accepted conventionally by others. It can be said to exist in this way because it is clearly seen that sentient beings cling to "I," "me," "mine," and so forth, along with using these terms.

The self that is the object of imagination, however, does not exist on any level. It is a mere imputation made by people who cling to incorrect philosophies. The terms and so on of these philosophies are not renowned in the world. The conventions for such a self do not appear in common to everyone; therefore such a self does not exist even in the relative truth.

Thus the self imputed by non-Buddhists does not exist even conventionally. However, the basis of imputation for the self that is asserted by the Saṃmitīyas[405] exists conventionally, because worldly people do not fixate upon a self that is different from the aggregates, and because sentient beings fixate upon a self when observing the aggregates.

You may think, "If you accept the self asserted by the Saṃmitīyas to exist conventionally, it would follow that the self of the Vātsīputrīyas also exists: worldly people do not analyze or speak of whether the self is the same as or different from the aggregates, or whether the self is permanent, impermanent, and so on." However, that is not correct: the Vātsīputrīyas assert the aggregates as the support for self-fixation *after* logical analysis. They then assert that the self is inexpressible in terms of being the same as or different from the aggregates. Once such a notion of self is examined, its existence is found to be impossible, even conventionally. Such a self, moreover, is not renowned in any way in the world.

Worldly people do not conceive of such assertions through relying on logical analysis. Thus there is no contradiction in accepting the aggregates as the basis for self-fixation on the level of no analysis. We accept this merely in a context of not analyzing whether the self is the same as the aggregates or different. Worldly people do not assert the self to be real due to being "inexpressible."

When logically analyzed, no form of the self, whether an object of the imaginary view or an object of the connate view, exists. None exists because all are invalidated by the reasonings to be explained by this text.

The connate self is imputed in dependence upon the aggregates. It is an imputed existent in the same manner that a vase is an imputed existent. Though we do not refute its conventional, relative existence on the level of no analysis, when we analyze, we refute its inherent, true existence in both truths. Such a refutation is appropriate because the self's perceiving subject, the connate view of the transitory collection, is the source of all mental afflictions and problems. Furthermore, the noble ones, when resting in meditative equipoise, do not see such a self even conventionally.

The imaginary, or imputed, self[406] is refuted in both truths. It does not accord with the perceptions of either noble ones or worldly beings, and its perceiving subject, the imaginary view of a self, further entrenches the connate view of a self. Clinging to the imaginary self will also make it impossible to definitively travel the paths to liberation and omniscience and the path of the Middle Way that relinquishes the two extremes.

Since the root of saṃsāra is the connate form of self-fixation, you might wonder, "Why does the *Entrance to the Middle Way* not present reasonings that refute the self that is the object of the connate view? It only presents reasonings that refute the imputed form of a self."

Not so. The self, person, and so on, the objects of the connate view, are not to be refuted on the conventional, nonanalytical level. There is no need to refute them on that level, and refuting them on that level, furthermore, would be impossible. When the objects of the connate view are refuted, they are refuted *after* analysis. In that context, the reasonings that refute the imputed self also become reasonings that will refute the connate self. This is so because the reasonings needed to refute the connate self do not pass beyond the three methods of analysis presented in this text.[407]

Therefore, the reasonings that refute the imputed self also refute the connate self. The *Entrance to the Middle Way* refutes all objects of the twenty peaks[408] of the mountain of the view of the transitory collection. It is not the case that the connate self is not refuted.

As to the self of phenomena, most phenomena from form through omniscience are conceived of by sentient beings to possess an essence. These phenomena exist conventionally, from the mere perspective of confusion. Most of the distinct features of these phenomena that sentient beings cling to also exist conventionally from the confused perspective. These phenomena are either renowned in the world or are suitable to be renowned in the world. An instance of the latter category is the scriptures of the Tathāgata that were spoken conventionally to his students.

The conceptual imputations of Buddhist and non-Buddhist tīrthikas, however, do not exist even conventionally. They are not renowned in the world, nor were they taught by the Tathāgata. Examples of such conceptual imputations are: the six or nine principles of word and meaning regarding knowable objects;[409] partless particles;[410] hidden outer objects;[411] the nondual and truly existent dependent nature;[412] the all-base consciousness;[413] buddha nature as an unconditioned phenomenon adorned with the major and minor marks of enlightenment;[414] the valid establishment of conventional phenomena;[415] and the notion that the lack of true existence, ultimate truth, is a basis that is established in individual instances of phenomena.[416]

You may protest by saying that our Teacher, the Buddha, *did* teach conventionally about the all-base consciousness. Yet such statements by the Buddha, made on the level of no analysis, must be categorized as either provisional or definitive, even conventionally. The Buddha's statements about the all-base consciousness were, even on the conventional level, provisional meaning. The Buddha made them with an ulterior intention in mind. Nevertheless, there are some from our own Buddhist tradition who cling to those statements and say, "He did teach the all-base consciousness conventionally!" But on the conventional level those statements were not definitive meaning. On the other hand, everything that the Buddha said *following* analysis—in the relative truth or in the ultimate truth—is definitive meaning and not provisional meaning.

In sum, all superimpositions made regarding the features and entities of all phenomena, from form through omniscience, are, in both truths, emptiness by nature. This point is the sublime life force of this dharma system of the Middle Way.

What objective, then, is accomplished by explaining the dharma in the manner of the Followers of the Middle Way? Let us examine first the response of some others to that question.[417] There are some who say that although the Particularists, Sūtra Followers, Proponents of Mind Only, Autonomists, and so on present many reasonings that refute the self of persons, none of them succeed in refuting that self.

These scholars say, "The systems from the Autonomists down fail to identify the self of persons as a unique object of logical refutation. Since they do not identify the self of persons, they are incapable of refuting it. The Consequentialist system is the only system that entertains the hypothetical possibility *(si ta kakpa/srid mtha' bkag pa)* of the existence of the self and, on that basis, refutes the hypothetical self of persons."

They continue, "Thus it is impossible to reverse the view of the self without relying on the Consequentialist system. Similarly, although the Proponents of Consciousness refute such notions as subtle particles, hidden outer objects, form as an outer object, and so on, they still cannot refute the nature of those phenomena. This is due to the same reasons. The reification of phenomena can only be halted by relying upon the tradition of the Consequentialists."

They add, "The view of the transitory collection and the view of a self have four permutations in their relationship."[418]

However, all of these assertions are utterly absent in the Consequentialist system.

Furthermore, regarding the connate self-fixation that is present in the mindstreams of all of us nearsighted beings, these same scholars refuse to posit it as an object of refutation by logic. Rather, they claim that such self-fixation is the support for actions and results and that, in a way that does not contradict analysis, exists and is established by "conventional valid cognition."

This position is illogical. The great master Chandrakīrti has already refuted it in his writings, and, in doing so, treated it as something to be refuted by logic!

The lower vehicles use the Transcendent Conqueror's scriptures and his reasonings, the content of the scriptures, to establish the selflessness of both persons and phenomena. If these lower-vehicle scriptures and reasonings were incapable of refuting the self and true existence, consider the implications: his teachings on personal and phenomenal selflessness in the lower philosophical systems, given in accordance with the capabilities of his disciples, would be rendered meaningless. All his refutations of the self and of true existence would have, in the end, refuted nothing at all, for his teachings would not have lived up to the function they had been stated to perform.

If you[419] agree with that, it follows that most of the lower-vehicle teachings are not teachings of the Buddha, which help students relinquish their reification of the self of persons and the self of phenomena. For those teachings do not help students comprehend emptiness and selflessness. If you agree, it follows that all the students of the three vehicles who look to you with hope are, along with their followers, engaging in meaningless actions when they relate to the Buddha's teachings from the Autonomist philosophical system down. This is precisely the consequence of what you agreed with above.

According to us, there is no disagreement between the main Buddhist philosophical systems, from the Particularists through the Consequentialists, regarding the basis of the view of the self of persons, the self that is the object of that view, and the reasonings that help students relinquish the view of a self. Moreover, the view of the self of persons and the view of the transitory collection are synonyms. We posit the self merely as a referent object, conceived by imputations toward the appropriated aggregates of "sentient being" and "self." Therefore, apprehending this self is to be known as "the view of the transitory collection" or "the view of a self."

When we teach reasonings to refute the view of a self, we ask questions such as, "If the sentient being or the self exist substantially, are they of the same substance as the aggregates? Or are they of a different substance?" Accordingly, Chandrakīrti's autocommentary states:

The view of the transitory collection is an afflicted form of prajñā and manifests in the aspect of thinking "me" and "mine."

This quotation confirms that the view of the self consists of the thoughts —of the sentient being, the self, "me," and "mine"—that arise in observation of the aggregates.

There are basic similarities between the Particularists and the Followers of the Middle Way regarding the way they refute the self: both systems agree that the self is a conventional imputation made on the basis of the aggregates. They also both refute the notion of a substantially existent self, while holding the self to be a mere imputed existent. Furthermore, both schools treat connate fixation on a substantially existent self as something to be refuted by logic.

However, there are differences between the two schools' approaches to the self as well. Particularists hold the imputedly existent self to exist when analyzed and assert that it has an inherent nature of being an imputedly existent thing. Consequentialists, on the other hand, do not hold the imputedly existent self to exist when analyzed, nor do they view that self to have an inherent nature of being an imputedly existent thing, even on the conventional level of no analysis.

Furthermore, the Particularists hold personal selflessness, which is empty of the self of persons, to be a substantially existent thing, a knowable object that forms part of the truth of suffering. The Consequentialists do not posit such things at all. Rather, they describe selflessness and emptiness to be free of all traits of being a knowable object, a nonknowable, a thing, a nonthing, a substance, or an imputation.

The Consequentialists also recognize the necessity of explaining the dependently posited, unanalyzed self to be free of inherent nature and empty of its own entity in both truths. Others, conversely, posit the emptiness or nonemptiness of the self's inherent nature based on whether or not it is established by way of its own presence. This approach is pointless, because no one besides the tīrthikas—those who propound the entity of things as a cause—speaks of any phenomenon being established or arisen by way of its own presence or established by way of its own entity.

Some try with great effort to establish that the Consequentialists, when explaining the selflessness of persons, do not regard the self apprehended by connate fixation as something to be refuted. Instead, they say, the Consequentialists hold such a self to be the supporting connection between actions and their results. However, that approach amounts to claiming that all statements in the three vehicles that "The self of persons does not exist" are simply deceitful refutations.

If that self really were not an object of refutation, it would follow that it is also not a factor to be relinquished.[420] For, according to you, the self that is the object of connate self-fixation, on the basis of which ordinary sentient beings confusedly engage in adopting and rejecting, exists, without analysis, in a manner that matches the way it is apprehended, and is the support for actions and results.[421]

You say that, when analyzed, the self is not taught as an object of refutation in the scriptures and reasonings of the three vehicles. Yet even if you were to claim such a self, the support for actions and results, was *not* the self that is to be refuted, consider this: a presentation of something *other* than the self that you explain, such as "a self that is to be refuted by logic," "a self established from its own side," "the term 'self of persons,'" "the hypothetical self," and so on is to be found nowhere in the ocean of scriptures of the three vehicles—not even one letter.[422] No one has ever heard or seen such statements in the scriptures.[423]

If you accept the first reason but say that the second reason is not established, that is absurd. You need to demonstrate a source. The inclusion of both reasons is established, and you cannot but accept the main consequence.[424] If the self actually were as you describe it, even the Buddha would not have had any way to relinquish it. Such a self would exist in the mindstream of the Buddha, because it is the support for actions and their results and because it is not a factor to be relinquished.

If you accept that, it follows that the Buddha possesses the view of a self and the view of the transitory collection. If you accept that, it follows that the Buddha is not liberated from saṃsāra, because the Buddha possesses the view of the transitory collection! If you accept that, what greater disregard for the Buddha could be shown? It is the case that having the view of the transitory collection entails not being free from saṃsāra: the view of the transitory collection necessarily entails a mindstream that is afflicted and not at peace. Thus, if one's mindstream is afflicted by such a view, one is necessarily not liberated from saṃsāra.

Furthermore, there is no scripture that describes the view of the transitory collection and the view of a self as having a relationship with four permutations. If they did have such a relationship, it would be necessary to delineate four permutations in the relationship between flour and dough by citing examples such as barley flour and wheat dough—the process would be endless.[425]

If clinging to phenomena that are entities connected to the self—the eyes, ears, and so on—is not also the view of the transitory collection, it would follow that the eyes, and so on were not part of the transitory collection. In fact, they would become unconditioned phenomena! And, if viewing another person as a self were not the view of the transitory collection, that would not even be an instance of a view of the person. For, without viewing the transitory collection of the other person, it is impossible to develop a view of the self of the other person.

Some also say that the Consequentialists identify the self that is to be refuted by reasons in the context of personal selflessness, whereas the Autonomists do not. They say that, due to this difference, the Consequentialist view is superior to that of the Autonomists. That position is untenable. Not only is that position untenable, the same scholars also assert a thing called "postdisintegration" as a support for actions and results, in addition to asserting a self that supports actions and results. They thus assert two supports for actions and results. Therefore we must ask: Are these two supports for actions and results the same, or are they different?

If they are the same, it would follow that all things are persons that support the connection between actions and results, for the following two reasons. First, all disintegration and postdisintegration of things are things. Second, if the thing called postdisintegration is a person that supports the connection between causes and results, the same status would apply to all disintegrating[426] things: no logic could refute that status, and the proofs of that status are equal to those you use to prove the status of postdisintegration.

You already accept the first reason, and the second reason is established by valid cognition. If you accept the root consequence,[427] it would follow that all things are persons!

If you say that the two supports for actions and results are different from each other, it would follow that when one person commits an action of killing he would gather two actions and the seeds for two results in his mindstream. For he would accumulate the action separately on the basis of the self that supports actions and results and on the basis of the thing called postdisintegration. The results, then, would also ripen separately.

You may protest that the above reasoning does not apply to your system by saying, "When a person accumulates actions, the two supports for actions and results work together so that only one action, not two, is accumulated at a time." Well then, are such actions partless or do they have parts?

You could not claim that the actions are partless. It is impossible for an action to arise through two supports for actions and results working together. For, this would contradict the very notion of the action being partless![428] If you agree, you will lose the position that actions are created by two different supports. If you asserted that actions have parts, it would follow that individual actions are not singular, because they are created by two different supports that exist separately from each other.

You say that, in the Followers of the Middle Way's own system, there are two types of self: one that must be accepted and one that must be refuted by logic. No one in our own Buddhist tradition, however, except for you, the Vātsīputrīyas, and the Saṃmitīyas, speaks in that way. You, moreover, purport to be Mahāyānists! No Mahāyānist preceding you—in India or Tibet—has ever asserted an existence of the self. The dictum "Anything established as a base of knowledge is necessarily selfless" is a statement held in common by all Buddhist philosophical systems. Nevertheless, you insist on positing a system of your own that contradicts it. Alas! How sad!

Another consequence of your logic: you would have to accept a common locus between existents and that which does not exist among knowable objects. For, firstly, you have accepted that there two types of self: one that is a basis of refutation and one that is a basis of affirmation. And, secondly, you assert that the self that is to be refuted does not even exist among knowable objects! You accept both reasons, and their inclusion in the predicate is established by valid cognition. Consider the implications!

You may retort, "The self that is to be refuted is not a phenomenon." Well then, it follows that such a self to be refuted does not bear the characteristic of producing self-fixation.[429] For, firstly, something is posited to be or not be a phenomenon based on whether or not it bears its own characteristics. And, secondly, the self to be refuted is not established as a phenomenon bearing the characteristic of producing a consciousness apprehending itself. If you accept, then regarding the self to be refuted by reasons, the subject, it follows it is not something to be refuted by reasons. For, firstly, it is not a phenomenon that produces self-fixation. And, secondly, objects of refutation by reasons are necessarily phenomena that produce self-fixation.

All ordinary beings hold as valid cognition the conceptually imputed phenomena that serve as supports for actions and results. You, however, are not satisfied with merely describing such supports as imputed existents. Instead, you claim that the unique mode of analysis of the Consequentialists consists of searching for the referent object behind those conceptual imputations, which thus becomes an analysis of the true nature of reality.

If that were the case, the activities of the bodhisattvas would become meaningless. According to you, the dependent arising of the world's relative truth is renowned to everyone; therefore there would be no need for buddhas and bodhisattvas to help sentient beings, through stainless scriptures and reasonings, understand the dependent arising of the world's relative truth in the context of the conventional teachings about the two truths by Nāgārjuna and his disciples. Such activity by the buddhas and so forth would become meaningless because, firstly, the relative truth of dependent arising is a phenomenon that arises in dependence upon conceptual imputation. And, secondly, even ordinary beings, from their own perspective, cognize the functions of conceptually imputed supports for actions and results. They are satisfied with their nonanalytical understanding, and thus they do not seek out the reality of the Middle Way, nor do they look for the referent object behind their imputations. If you accept, your position contradicts your earlier claims that only the omniscient ones, not ordinary beings, realize interdependence.

If, as you agree, there are no phenomena other than those conceptually imputed, is the object of refutation by reasons a conceptual imputation or is it not? If it is, it is just like the other phenomena of the relative: it exists conventionally. For, firstly, it is a phenomenon that is posited by imputation. And, secondly, being posited by imputation is sufficient to achieve existence. You have no choice but to accept!

As a result of this logic, it also follows that the object of refutation by reasons is a phenomenon that is imputed even though it does not even exist conventionally, because *it exists conventionally*!

If it is not a conceptual imputation, it follows that the object of refutation by reasons, a substantial object established from its own side, exists among knowable objects. For it must exist either as a substantial phenomenon or as an imputed phenomenon, and it is not an imputed phenomenon.

If you say that it does not have to exist as either a substantial phenomenon or an imputed phenomenon, it follows that it cannot be taken as an object of mind. For, the object of refutation by reasons does not exist as a phenomenon that is imputed or substantial. If you say the reason is not included in the predicate,[430] then regarding the object of refutation by reasons, the subject, it follows that it exists among knowable objects, because it can be taken as an object of mind. If you then say that the reason is not included in the predicate, you lose your original position.[431]

If you accept the root consequence,[432] it follows that it is indeed possible for substances and objects that are established objectively *(rang ngö ne/ rang ngos nas)*[433] to exist among knowable objects. For the object of refutation by reasons is precisely that—a substance or object established from its own side—and it is also a knowable object. But it is very undesirable for you to accept that consequence!

If you assert that the object of refutation by reasons is not suitable to be taken as an object of mind, the consequence of your assertion is that the connate clinging to true existence—that which apprehends the object of refutation by reasons—utterly does not arise in sentient beings. If you agree, then it would absurdly follow that all sentient beings would gain liberation without effort.

The self that is to be refuted by reasons does not exist in any way, yet it is thought to exist by sentient beings. Thus it is conceptually imputed. In the context of the Middle Way, all objects of affirmation by reasoning, along with all objects of refutation by reasoning, are imputed existents.

According to you, however, the objects of *affirmation* as well do not exist among knowable objects. For, if the objects of refutation utterly do not exist, it would only be equal logic to say that the objects of affirmation utterly do not exist. All objects of affirmation and refutation exist in no other way than being dependent imputations. If you agree to that, you would also be forced to accept that emptiness—the ultimate truth—does not exist among knowable objects, but that is not a position of yours.

This notion that you espouse—that what is to be refuted by reasons, or correct logic, is *not* an imputation of false conception—is the very downfall of your tenet system.

It is renowned to everyone that, when affirming the impermanence of sound using the reason of production,[434] the object of refutation by reasons is permanent sound, the opposite of the impermanent sound that is affirmed. Even though "permanent sound" is an imputation of incorrect conception, it is not asserted to exist as an object of incorrect conception. When we treat the object of refutation in this way—on the unanalyzed, conventional level—we are in perfect harmony with the worldly perspective.

For you, however, the status of the object of refutation by reasons' being a mere conceptual imputation is grounds for seeking out the referent object behind the imputation. This, for you, is the way in which one must affirm the emptiness of phenomena. Yet, according to this logic, the object of refutation by reasons itself is not even an object of refutation by reasons! For, once it has been identified, its own referent object must be found and treated as an object of refutation by reasons, in relation to which emptiness must once again be established![435]

If you accept the reason but say that it is not included in the predicate,[436] objects of refutation by reasons would be produced in infinity. It would be impossible to ever arrive at a time of final refutation.

If you say that the object of refutation by reasons is *not* a conceptual imputation, you would contradict your explanation that it is impossible to find the object of refutation by reasons upon searching for it.

In sum, even though the self in general does not exist, worldly people impute the existence of a mere self. Therefore, when engaged with worldly people, we repeat their statements that the self exists. Yet, in our own system, there is no self. We have no position about the self whatsoever. In the context of slight verbal engagement with the world, the self is an imputed existent: it does not exist actually, but is imputed to exist by worldly people.

2.2.2.1.1.6.2.3.1.1.2.2. THE EXTENSIVE EXPLANATION OF THE
REASONINGS OF THE REFUTATION
2.2.2.1.1.6.2.3.1.1.2.2.1. The refutation of the self involving a fivefold analysis of the aggregates
2.2.2.1.1.6.2.3.1.1.2.2.2. The refutation of the self that cannot be expressed as being the same as or different from the aggregates
2.2.2.1.1.6.2.3.1.1.2.2.3. The concluding summary of the refutation

2.2.2.1.1.6.2.3.1.1.2.2.1. THE REFUTATION OF THE SELF INVOLVING
A FIVEFOLD ANALYSIS OF THE AGGREGATES

2.2.2.1.1.6.2.3.1.1.1.2.2.1.1.1. The refutation of the self that is different from the aggregates

2.2.2.1.1.6.2.3.1.1.1.2.2.1.1.2. The refutation of the self that is of the same entity as the aggregates

2.2.2.1.1.6.2.3.1.1.1.2.2.1.1.3. The refutation of the self that exists in a relationship of supporter-supported with the aggregates

2.2.2.1.1.6.2.3.1.1.1.2.2.1.1.4. The refutation of a self that possesses the aggregates

2.2.2.1.1.6.2.3.1.1.1.2.2.1.1.5. The summary of the refutation by expressing it in the form of the antidotes to the twenty extreme views of the transitory collection

2.2.2.1.1.6.2.3.1.1.1.2.2.1.1.1. THE REFUTATION OF THE SELF THAT IS DIFFERENT FROM THE AGGREGATES

2.2.2.1.1.6.2.3.1.1.1.2.2.1.1.1.1. The statement of the counterparts' position

2.2.2.1.1.6.2.3.1.1.1.2.2.1.1.1.2. The refutation of the counterparts' position

2.2.2.1.1.6.2.3.1.1.1.2.2.1.1.1.1. THE STATEMENT OF THE COUNTERPARTS' POSITION

> The tīrthikas assert that the self is an enjoyer, is a permanent thing,
> Is not a creator, has no qualities, and is inactive.
> Based on subtle differences regarding those assertions,
> Different tīrthika systems arose. (6.121)

What is the nature of the self that is the object of the view of the self?[437] In addressing this question, we shall first examine the nature of the self imputed by others. The following is an explanation of the assertions of the Enumerators, beginning with their imputations as summarized in the following verse:

> The root nature is not a manifestation.
> The seven factors[438] such as the Great One are both natures and manifestations.
> The sixteen[439] are only manifestations.
> The person[440] is neither a nature nor a manifestation.

"Nature" comes from the Sanskrit *prakṛti*, which carries a meaning of "thorough creation." At the time when a person wishes to enjoy objects, the nature yields the things such as sound that are to be enjoyed by the person.[441] Therefore, it is called "nature" in light of the etymology just explained.

The way the nature yields things to be enjoyed by the person is as follows. From the nature arises the Great One *(mahat, chenpo/chen po)*, which is also called intelligence *(buddhi, lo/blo)*. From the Great One arises the I-principle *(ahaṃkāra, nga-gyal/nga rgyal)*. From the latter arises the collection of sixteen.[442] From the five subtle objects (such as sound)[443] of those sixteen, the five elements[444] arise.

The root nature is strictly a cause—it is not a manifestation like the Great One and so forth. The seven factors—the Great One, the I-principle, and the five subtle objects—are both causes and results: in comparison to their own manifestations they are natures, and in comparison to the root nature they are manifestations. The ten faculties,[445] the intellectual faculty, and the five elements—totaling sixteen—are strictly manifestations: they arise from causes, but they do not produce results. The person is neither a nature nor a manifestation: it does not arise from causes, nor does it produce results.

The stages outlined above explain how all manifestations arise. The following will explain how a person becomes an enjoyer *(zapo/za po)* in whom desire arises.

Intelligence clings to the objects, such as sound, that are apprehended by the faculties, such as the ear, which are influenced[446] by the intellectual faculty. The person then mentally engages the objects to which intelligence clings. Since the person or self enjoys objects in this way, it is called an "enjoyer." The entity of the person is the mental engagement oriented towards enjoying objects, as was just explained. This phase is called "saṃsāra."

After the self has enjoyed objects out of desire, the person becomes free of attachment to objects. At that time, through cultivating concentration *(samten/bsam gtan)* in a progressive fashion, the person attains the divine visions *(lha mik/lha mig)*. When the divine visions view the nature, the nature becomes embarrassed, like another man's wife.[447] From that point onward, the manifestations do not gravitate towards the self.

Instead, the manifestations begin withdrawing in the order reverse to that in which they arose. The primal matter *(tsowo/gtso bo)*[448] becomes unclear and crippled in a dormant state.[449] The person becomes isolated[450] and is liberated. Because the person or self does not become crippled in the same way that the manifestations do, it is a permanent thing. Since the self is indifferent with regard to activities, it is not a creator. Since it lacks the characters of motility *(rajas, dul/rdul)*, darkness *(tamas, munpa/mun pa)*, and lightness *(sattva, nying-top/snying stobs)*, it is devoid of qualities. Since it is all-pervasive, it is free of actions such as coming and going. Such are the features of the person.

As stated previously, the nature is the creator. Of the nature's manifestations, some are creators and some are not creators. In exploring which of the manifestations are creators and which are not, let us now examine the nature's three qualities: motility, darkness, and lightness.[451] Motility has an essential nature that makes mind move toward objects and engage with others. Darkness has an essential nature that covers the body and so on with heaviness and ignorance. Lightness has an essential nature that makes the body and so on light, lucid, and clear. Happiness, suffering, and ignorance also correspond with these three qualities.[452]

The time at which the three qualities exist in equal measure with each other is called "primal matter," a state in which the three qualities are predominant in the nature. The nature's manifestations are completely crippled. At this time the nature is free from manifestations.

Manifestations arise as follows. From the nature arises the Great One, which is synonymous with intelligence. From the Great One arises the I-principle. The I-principle then takes on three different aspects: the I-principle based on motility[453] and possessed of suffering, the I-principle based on lightness and possessed of happiness, and the I-principle based on darkness and possessed of indifference.

From the first I-principle arise the five subtle objects: forms, sounds, and so on. From the five subtle objects arise the five elements: earth and so on.

From the second I-principle eleven types of phenomena arise: the five action faculties (speech, arms, feet, anus, and genitalia), the five mental faculties (the eyes, ears, nose, tongue, and skin), and the intellectual faculty, which has a nature that is both mental and physical.

FEAST FOR THE FORTUNATE – GROUND SIX: THE MANIFEST

The third I-principle, the I-principle based on darkness, activates the other two I-principles.

These are the assertions or imputations of the Enumerators, who are tīrthikas. Based on subtle differences regarding those assertions about the self, different tīrthika systems arose. The Differentiators *(Vaisheṣhika, Jedrakpa/bye brag pa)*, for example, say that the self has nine qualities: intelligence, happiness, suffering, desire, aversion, effort, dharma, nondharma, and the energy of the conditioned. They say that these nine qualities respectively perform the functions of apprehending objects, experiencing a desirable object, experiencing an undesirable object, engendering hope for something one wants, pushing away what one does not want, being skilled in maintaining resolve to complete a goal, accomplishing the higher realms and definite goodness, accomplishing the opposite of the higher realms and definite goodness, and serving as both the cause for consciousness and the result that arises from consciousness.

They say that for as long as those nine qualities exist in the self, the person will perform positive and negative actions. Therefore, they say, that phase is called "saṃsāra." When it is realized that the entities connected to the self of the person, such as the faculties,[454] are of the nature of suffering, the qualities such as intelligence are eliminated together with their roots. The self then becomes isolated and free from all qualities. That phase is called "liberation."

They say that the self is permanent, is not a creator, is an enjoyer, has qualities, has a nonmental nature, and is all-pervasive. For these reasons, they say, the self is not active. Some Differentiators say that the self does perform the actions of contracting and extending.

There are various assertions, however, about the nature of the self. The Vedavādins *(Rikje Mawa/rig byed smra ba)*, for example, say that the self is like the space inside different vases: it is singular, but the bodies it inhabits are different.

The Enumerators, Vedāntins *(Rikje Tapa/rig byed mtha' pa)*, Guhyakas *(Sangwapa/gsang ba pa)*, Jains, Mīmāṃsakas *(Chöpawa/dpyod pa ba)*, Jaiminis *(Gyalpokpa/rgyal dpog pa)*, and so on assert that the self is consciousness. The Differentiators and the Naiyāyikas *(Rikpa Chenpa/rig pa can pa)*, however, assert that the self is matter. The Chārvākas say that the self is permanent from birth to death but becomes extinct after death.

2.2.2.1.1.6.2.3.1.1.2.2.1.1.2. THE REFUTATION OF THE
COUNTERPARTS' POSITION
2.2.2.1.1.6.2.3.1.1.2.2.1.1.2.1. The refutation of the entity of the self
2.2.2.1.1.6.2.3.1.1.2.2.1.1.2.2. The refutation of its features
2.2.2.1.1.6.2.3.1.1.2.2.1.1.2.3. It is not tenable for the self to be different
from the aggregates
2.2.2.1.1.6.2.3.1.1.2.2.1.1.2.4. Such a self is not the support for the
conception of "I"

2.2.2.1.1.6.2.3.1.1.2.2.1.1.2.1. THE REFUTATION OF THE ENTITY OF
THE SELF

> Since, like the childless woman's son, it does not arise,
> Such a self does not exist.
> It is not the support for the conception of "I,"
> And we do not assert its existence even relatively. (6.122)

None of the forms of self described by any of the various tīrthika systems
arise: they are like the childless woman's son. Such a self, therefore, which
was explained to be permanent, an enjoyer, and so on, does not exist. It is
also illogical for such a self to be the support or object of the worldly conception of "I" *(ngar-dzin/ngar 'dzin).*[455] For, since it does not arise, it is like
the childless woman's son. And, not only do we not assert such a self to
exist as the object of the conception of "I" ultimately, we do not make such
assertions even relatively. For, it cannot be observed as the support for the
conception of "I." Thus in both truths we describe the self asserted by the
tīrthikas to be like the horns of a rabbit. It is, in both truths, contradictory
to direct perception and inferential reasoning.

2.2.2.1.1.6.2.3.1.1.2.2.1.1.2.2. THE REFUTATION OF ITS FEATURES

> All of the self's features that were taught
> By the tīrthikas in their various treatises
> Are invalidated by the reason of nonarising, which the tīrthikas
>   themselves accept.
> Therefore none of those features exist. (6.123)

Not only is it the case that it is inadmissible for the self to exist in either of the two truths as the support for the conception of "I," furthermore, all of the self's features (such as being an enjoyer, being a permanent thing, not being a creator, and so on) that were taught by the tīrthikas in their various treatises are invalidated by the inferential reasoning that the tīrthikas themselves approve—nonarising.[456] Therefore none of the features of such a self exist. The self is not permanent, because it is nonarisen, like the childless woman's son—since the asserted features of the self are invalidated by this pairing of reason and example, they are untenable.

2.2.2.1.1.6.2.3.1.1.2.2.1.1.2.3. It is not tenable for the self to be different from the aggregates

> Therefore there is no self that is different from the aggregates,
> Because, apart from the aggregates, there is no way the self could
>   be apprehended. (6.124ab)

Therefore, there is no self that is different from the aggregates. If the self existed separately from the aggregates, it would be possible to apprehend the aggregates and the self as distinct entities. However, there is no avenue other than the aggregates through which such a self, which would bear the features of permanence and so on, could be apprehended.

2.2.2.1.1.6.2.3.1.1.2.2.1.1.2.4. Such a self is not the support for the conception of "I"
2.2.2.1.1.6.2.3.1.1.2.2.1.1.2.4.1. The teaching
2.2.2.1.1.6.2.3.1.1.2.2.1.1.2.4.2. The explanation

2.2.2.1.1.6.2.3.1.1.2.2.1.1.2.4.1. The teaching

> Nor do we assert such a self to be the support for the worldly
>   conception of "I."
> For even those who do not perceive it have a view of self.
>   (6.124cd)

Not only is it the case that there is no self separate from the aggregates, we also do not assert such a self—a possessor of the features of permanence and so on—to be the support for the worldly conception of "I," the innate view of the transitory collection. For even naïve beings, who do not perceive a self that is permanent and so forth, have the views of self and entities connected to the self due to their clinging.

2.2.2.1.1.6.2.3.1.1.2.2.1.1.2.4.2. THE EXPLANATION

Moreover, those who have spent many eons as animals
Have never seen this unarisen, permanent self,
Yet they are still seen to engage in the conception of "I."
Therefore a self that is different from the aggregates does not
exist at all. (6.125)

One may think, "Even though one may not be able to distinguish the features of such a self (permanence, nonarising, and so on), one would still possess the conception of "I," which is that self's perceiving subject, due to familiarity with such a self from one's past lifetimes and so on." The root verse here teaches how that is not the case.

There are sentient beings, such as animals, who have taken successive births in the lower realms for many eons and who will not be free from such births for a long time. They will spend their time in such births as animals and hell beings. These sentient beings, as well, have never seen the self that is unarisen and permanent, as asserted by the tīrthikas.

Nor have they ever seen the self that is an imputed existent established by conventional valid cognition—the self that is the support for actions and results. They have never perceived the self that is an object of refutation by reasons—the self that cannot be found after, due to dissatisfaction with a mere imputation, one searches for the object behind the imputation.

Yet those animals and the others are still seen to engage in the conception of "I" in relation to the aggregates. Therefore, those endowed with supreme knowledge see that it is impossible to posit the self asserted by the tīrthikas as the support for the conception of "I." A self that is different or separate from the aggregates does not exist at all.

Since those endowed with supreme knowledge see in this way, it is illogical to say that the self that is the support for the conception of "I" is a conceptually imputed phenomenon that is an object of conventional direct valid cognition. Such notions are not renowned in the world or in the treatises. They are, themselves, conceptual imputations!

2.2.2.1.1.6.2.3.1.1.2.2.1.2. THE REFUTATION OF THE SELF THAT IS OF THE SAME ENTITY AS THE AGGREGATES
2.2.2.1.1.6.2.3.1.1.2.2.1.2.1. The statement of the counterparts' position
2.2.2.1.1.6.2.3.1.1.2.2.1.2.2. The refutation of the counterparts' position

2.2.2.1.1.6.2.3.1.1.2.2.1.2.1. THE STATEMENT OF THE COUNTERPARTS' POSITION
2.2.2.1.1.6.2.3.1.1.2.2.1.2.1.1. The basic assertion
2.2.2.1.1.6.2.3.1.1.2.2.1.2.1.2. The classifications

2.2.2.1.1.6.2.3.1.1.2.2.1.2.1.1. THE BASIC ASSERTION

> "Because the self is not established as different from the
> aggregates,
> The focal object for the view of the self is strictly the aggregates."
> (6.126ab)

The Saṃmitīyas and others of our own faction say that, due to the reasoning explained above, the self is not established as a different object than the aggregates. Therefore, they say, the focal object for the view of the self or the view of the transitory collection is strictly the aggregates. In this way they assert that the self is only the mere aggregates.

2.2.2.1.1.6.2.3.1.1.2.2.1.2.1.2. THE CLASSIFICATIONS

> Some say that all five aggregates are the support
> Of the view of the self; others assert that such a support is only
> the mind. (6.126cd)

From among those of our own faction who assert the self to be the aggregates, some assert that the self that is the support or focal object of the view of the self is all five aggregates, including form. Others assert that the focal object of the view of the self is a self that is only mind.

2.2.2.1.1.6.2.3.1.1.2.2.1.2.2. THE REFUTATION OF THE
COUNTERPARTS' POSITION
2.2.2.1.1.6.2.3.1.1.2.2.1.2.2.1. The actual refutation
2.2.2.1.1.6.2.3.1.1.2.2.1.2.2.2. The conclusion via the consequence that the
view of the self would not be relinquished

2.2.2.1.1.6.2.3.1.1.2.2.1.2.2.1. THE ACTUAL REFUTATION
2.2.2.1.1.6.2.3.1.1.2.2.1.2.2.1.1. The statement of the refutations
2.2.2.1.1.6.2.3.1.1.2.2.1.2.2.1.2. The refutation of their proofs
2.2.2.1.1.6.2.3.1.1.2.2.1.2.2.1.3. The person is dependently imputed

2.2.2.1.1.6.2.3.1.1.2.2.1.2.2.1.1. THE STATEMENT OF THE
REFUTATIONS
2.2.2.1.1.6.2.3.1.1.2.2.1.2.2.1.1.1. Refutation by reasoning
2.2.2.1.1.6.2.3.1.1.2.2.1.2.2.1.1.2. Refutation by scripture
2.2.2.1.1.6.2.3.1.1.2.2.1.2.2.1.1.3. Refutation by the perceptions of yogins

2.2.2.1.1.6.2.3.1.1.2.2.1.2.2.1.1.1. REFUTATION BY REASONING
2.2.2.1.1.6.2.3.1.1.2.2.1.2.2.1.1.1.1. The consequence of there being several
selves and so on
2.2.2.1.1.6.2.3.1.1.2.2.1.2.2.1.1.1.2. The consequence of extinction and so on
2.2.2.1.1.6.2.3.1.1.2.2.1.2.2.1.1.1.3. The concluding summary

2.2.2.1.1.6.2.3.1.1.2.2.1.2.2.1.1.1.1. THE CONSEQUENCE OF THERE
BEING SEVERAL SELVES AND SO ON

If the aggregates were the self,
There would be several selves, because there are several
    aggregates.
The self would be substantial, and viewing it would constitute
    engaging in a substance.
The view of a self would therefore not be erroneous. (6.127)

The above verse is given in response to the counterparts' position. If the
aggregates really were the self, as the counterparts hold, there would be
several selves—or individuals, sentient beings, or persons—in the same
continuum. For the aggregates—form, feeling, and so on—are many in
number.

If strictly the mind were the self, the same consequence would apply. There are many classifications of consciousness, and consciousness also involves many discrete moments of arising and ceasing. The self would be as numerous as all of these.

These logical faults apply to those who assert the aggregates or the mind to be the self. More faults also apply to these positions, and these will be explained below. These faults should be described, therefore, to those who hold either position: that the aggregates are the self or that the mind is the self.

Saying that there are many selves, moreover, is untenable. Such a contention contradicts the worldly dictum, "When birth occurs, only one person is born."

Furthermore, an "aggregate" is a named used to refer to an aggregation of forms and other substances of the three times. If you accept that such an aggregate is the self, it would follow that the self is substantially established, but it is impossible to assert that. As the scriptures say:

> Bhikṣhus, these five are mere names, mere terms, and mere imputations. They are past time, future time, space, nirvāṇa, and the person.

And,

> Just as something is called a chariot
> In dependence upon the collection of its parts,
> In the same way, in dependence upon the aggregates,
> The name "relative sentient being" is given.

Thus your assertion would contradict those two quotations.

If the self were a substance, the view of the transitory collection that perceived that self would be engaging in a substantially existent object. It would therefore not be erroneous. It would be just like a consciousness perceiving blue, yellow, and so on. Even though one perceived true reality, one would still be incapable of relinquishing the origin of suffering, the view of the transitory collection, in a manner analogous to cutting a rope. One would be thus incapable of relinquishing the factors to be relinquished on the path of seeing, because one would have only relinquished the desire connected to observing the self.

If you accept, it absurdly follows that there is no point in seeing true reality. One's realization would be just like the realization attained in the form and formless realms: it relinquishes the mental afflictions to be relinquished on the path of meditation, but it does not relinquish the view of self.

Another absurd consequence is that the view of the transitory collection would be a factor to be relinquished by the path of meditation, since it is a factor to be relinquished *and* cannot be relinquished by the path of seeing. "Seeing true reality" would be nothing more than a vacuous phrase.

2.2.2.1.1.6.2.3.1.1.2.1.2.2.1.1.1.2. THE CONSEQUENCE OF EXTINCTION AND SO ON
2.2.2.1.1.6.2.3.1.1.2.1.2.2.1.1.1.2.1. The actual consequences
2.2.2.1.1.6.2.3.1.1.2.1.2.2.1.1.1.2.2. The refutation of the rebuttal

2.2.2.1.1.6.2.3.1.1.2.1.2.2.1.1.1.2.1. THE ACTUAL CONSEQUENCES

> At the time of attaining nirvāṇa, the self would be severed.
> In the moments before nirvāṇa, the self would arise and
>   disintegrate.
> Since there would be no agent, there would be no karmic results,
> And one would experience the results of actions accumulated by
>   others. (6.128)

More absurd consequences would apply if the self were of the nature of the aggregates. When arhats pass into nirvāṇa without the remainder of the aggregates the self would have to be severed, since all five aggregates' continua are severed at that time. For the self is of the nature of the aggregates and the aggregates, when an arhat passes into nirvāṇa, are severed.

Yet accepting this would entail holding an extreme view of nihilism. For you hold views of eternalism and nihilism in relation to that which the view of the transitory collection apprehends as a self.[457] Your position also contradicts the notion of the self passing into nirvāṇa without remainder.

Furthermore, because the self was of the nature of the aggregates, it would arise and disintegrate in every moment preceding the attainment of nirvāṇa, just as the aggregates, before nirvāṇa, arise and disintegrate in every moment.

And, at the time of future births, the self that had performed actions in previous lives would have already disintegrated. Since the self, the support, would be gone, that which it supports—its actions, the results of those actions, and the connection between those two—would also be gone. For, just like the aggregates, the self would have disintegrated following its birth.

This absurd consequence, when spoken to our counterparts, does not carry an affirmative proof statement of its own. For, if one posits actions and results, it does not amount to affirming, as a position of one's own, the existence of a self as a support for those actions and results. In stating this absurd consequence, we simply repeat what is renowned to others: conventionally, if one uproots the view of the self, one will no longer take birth in saṃsāra. Similarly, if the self, the support, is severed, actions and results, the supported, cannot remain on their own.

The great Shar Tsongkapa asserts that the postdisintegration of things is itself a thing. If that were the case, it would be suitable to say that the extinction of the self is the self, and that that position is the unique feature of the Consequentialist system. For those two positions are based on the same essential point of reasoning. Tsongkapa's position seems to be a new transmission, not available before, that he received from the noble Mañjushrī.

Also, if the self were of the nature of the aggregates, it would follow that individuals would experience the results of actions performed by others. Results of actions performed in previous moments are experienced in subsequent moments, but, according to you there would be two separate selves corresponding to the earlier and later moments. If you accept, it would follow that actions, once performed, could be wasted,[458] and that one would meet with the results of actions one had not performed.

The above logical faults apply to the assertion that causes and results are different from each other. However, this is not the case for Followers of the Middle Way, who do not say anything about actions and results or previous and subsequent persons in terms of whether they are identical or different.

In sum, the assertion that the aggregates are the self is illogical.

2.2.2.1.1.6.2.3.1.1.2.2.1.2.2.1.1.1.2.2. THE REFUTATION OF THE
REBUTTAL

If the continuum existed in suchness, such faults would not
apply.
But the faults of the continuum have already been explained in
earlier analyses. (6.129ab)

You may say, "Although previous and subsequent moments are different
from each other, they are of the same continuum. Therefore, the above-
mentioned faults do not apply to our position." If the continuum existed
in suchness, such faults would indeed not apply. Yet, the continuum was
analyzed before in this text, in verses such as:

> Phenomena that depend on each other, such as Maitreya and
> Upagupta,
> Are not part of the same continuum, precisely because they are dif-
> ferent from each other.
> Phenomena that are separate by virtue of their own characteristics
> Cannot be parts of the same continuum. (6.61)[459]

When this analysis is applied, there are faults, which have already been
explained, in saying that previous and subsequent moments are of one
continuum. Therefore your position is inadmissible.

2.2.2.1.1.6.2.3.1.1.2.2.1.2.2.1.1.1.3. THE CONCLUDING SUMMARY

Therefore the aggregates and the mind are untenable as the self,
(6.129c)

Because of the logical refutations explained above, it is untenable for either
the aggregates or the mind to be the self.

2.2.2.1.1.6.2.3.1.1.2.2.1.2.2.1.1.2. REFUTATION BY SCRIPTURE

Since the end of the world and so on do not exist. (6.129d)

Not only is it that the aggregates and the mind are completely untenable as
the self because of the logical flaws explained above, there are more reasons
why this view is untenable. The end of the world and so on, the fourteen

things that left unspoken by the Buddha,[460] were all asserted not to exist by those of the factions of hearers. Therefore, it is inadmissible to say that the aggregates or the mind are the self.

As for the fourteen things that were left unspoken by the Buddha, they are as follows:

> Whether the world is permanent, impermanent, both, or neither,
> Whether the world has an end and so on, the four,
> Whether the Teacher exists or not after passing away—those four,
> And whether the body and life force are one or different phenom-
>   ena that support each other—
> These are the fourteen things that were left unspoken.

The above verse is a mere summary; for an extensive explanation one should look elsewhere.

2.2.2.1.1.6.2.3.1.1.2.2.1.2.2.1.1.3. REFUTATION BY THE PERCEPTIONS OF YOGINS
2.2.2.1.1.6.2.3.1.1.2.2.1.2.2.1.1.3.1. The consequence that the aggregates would not appear to someone who has cognized selflessness
2.2.2.1.1.6.2.3.1.1.2.2.1.2.2.1.1.3.2. The consequence that one would not relinquish the mental afflictions even if one had cognized selflessness

2.2.2.1.1.6.2.3.1.1.2.2.1.2.2.1.1.3.1. THE CONSEQUENCE THAT THE AGGREGATES WOULD NOT APPEAR TO SOMEONE WHO HAS COGNIZED SELFLESSNESS
2.2.2.1.1.6.2.3.1.1.2.2.1.2.2.1.1.3.1.1. The actual teaching
2.2.2.1.1.6.2.3.1.1.2.2.1.2.2.1.1.3.1.2. The refutation of rebuttals

2.2.2.1.1.6.2.3.1.1.2.2.1.2.2.1.1.3.1.1. THE ACTUAL TEACHING

> According to you, when a yogin sees selflessness
> Things would definitely become nonexistent. (6.130ab)

Furthermore, if the aggregates or mind were the self, then, according to you, when a yogin sees reality, or, when they have the insight, "all phe-nomena are selfless," an insight that accompanies the perception of the selflessness aspect of the truth of suffering,[461] at that time things such as forms would definitely become nonexistent or extinct. For form and so on, the five aggregates, are the self, and the yogin has realized that the self does not exist.

2.2.2.1.1.6.2.3.1.1.2.2.1.2.2.1.1.3.1.2. THE REFUTATION OF REBUTTALS

If you assert that the idea of a permanent self is what is relinquished,
Your aggregates or mind could not be the self. (6.130cd)

You may retort, "In the context of the teaching on the connection between actions and results, the term 'self' applies only to the aggregates. In the context of yogins cognizing selflessness, the term 'self' applies to notion of a person as an internal creator, which is an imputation by other philosophical systems. Thus, when yogins see selflessness, they do see the mere five aggregates that are formed by causes and conditions. They see these aggregates as being free of an internal creator. How could it be that yogins would see forms and so on as being utterly nonexistent?"

If, in the context of yogins perceiving selflessness, you use the term "self" to refer to a permanent self-entity and say that it is the idea of this self that the yogins relinquish, you can no longer maintain your original position, which was that the mind or the aggregates is the self. Your own position will be diminished.

If you do not accept that the term "self" applies to the aggregates in the context of the phrase "all phenomena are selfless," you must also refrain from asserting that the term "self" applies to the aggregates in other contexts. If you assert in other contexts that the term "self" applies to the aggregates, you must also assert the same thing here.

2.2.2.1.1.6.2.3.1.1.2.2.1.2.2.1.1.3.2. THE CONSEQUENCE THAT ONE WOULD NOT RELINQUISH THE MENTAL AFFLICTIONS EVEN IF ONE HAD COGNIZED SELFLESSNESS

When your yogins cognized selflessness,
They would not see the true nature of form and other phenomena.
Attachment and other afflictions would arise in them when they engaged forms,

Because they would not have realized the essence of the aggregates. (6.131)

In the system of our counterparts, seeing the true nature of reality is restricted to a mere perception of the nonexistence of a self that is an internal creator separate from the aggregates. If that were really the case, it would follow that when yogins cognized selflessness, they would cognize phenomena such as forms as merely being free of a permanent self.

They would not completely perceive the true nature of form and so on. They would fail to realize the suchness of form and the other aggregates. What benefit would come of their realization?

Furthermore, attachment, the view of the self, and other mental afflictions would arise in those yogins when they engaged in objects such as form. For they would be engaging such objects while observing them to have a truly existent entity. They would be lacking in the realization of the aggregates' own essence, which is emptiness, and of the selflessness of the person. This, I think, resembles the situation of the non-Buddhists!

2.2.2.1.1.6.2.3.1.1.2.2.1.2.2.1.2.2. THE REFUTATION OF THEIR PROOFS
2.2.2.1.1.6.2.3.1.1.2.2.1.2.2.1.2.2.1. The statement of the former position
2.2.2.1.1.6.2.3.1.1.2.2.1.2.2.1.2.2.2. The refutation of the former position

2.2.2.1.1.6.2.3.1.1.2.2.1.2.2.1.2.2.1. THE STATEMENT OF THE FORMER POSITION

You say, "The Teacher said that the aggregates are the self; Therefore we assert the same." (6.132ab)

You say, "We take scripture as an authoritative source of valid cognition. Thus we are not harmed by the inferences of logicians. Furthermore, even the scriptures teach the aggregates as the self. The Teacher said,

> Bhikṣhus, whether it be a monk or a Brahmin, when a person comes to have a fully developed view that thinks, "I," they are viewing none other than these appropriated aggregates.

Thus the Buddha taught that none other than the aggregates is the self. Therefore we assert that the aggregates are the self."

2.2.2.1.1.6.2.3.1.1.2.2.1.2.2.1.2.2.2. THE REFUTATION OF THE FORMER POSITION

2.2.2.1.1.6.2.3.1.1.2.2.1.2.2.1.2.2.2.1. The intended meaning of the scriptures is that the aggregates are *not* the self

2.2.2.1.1.6.2.3.1.1.2.2.1.2.2.1.2.2.2.2. Even if the aggregates were the self, their collection could not logically be the self

2.2.2.1.1.6.2.3.1.1.2.2.1.2.2.1.2.2.2.3. The appropriator cannot be the appropriated

2.2.2.1.1.6.2.3.1.1.2.2.1.2.2.1.2.2.2.1. THE INTENDED MEANING OF THE SCRIPTURES IS THAT THE AGGREGATES ARE NOT THE SELF

2.2.2.1.1.6.2.3.1.1.2.2.1.2.2.1.2.2.2.1.1. The teaching

2.2.2.1.1.6.2.3.1.1.2.2.1.2.2.1.2.2.2.1.2. The explanation

2.2.2.1.1.6.2.3.1.1.2.2.1.2.2.1.2.2.2.1.1. THE TEACHING

> That statement was made to refute a self that is different from the
> aggregates.
> It was taught in other sūtras how form and so on are not the self.
> (6.132cd)

That sūtra did not teach that the aggregates are the self. Then what did it mean to say? The statements in that sūtra were made in order to *refute* a self. Its meaning is, "The self imputed by Buddhist and non-Buddhist factions as separate from the aggregates does not exist."

The Buddha, therefore, taught, "It is only the aggregates that are viewed as a self. The self cannot be conceived in relation to something separate from the aggregates."

From a relative truth point of view, statements such as these were given in order to refute the tīrthikas. And, in order to clarify the correct understanding of the relative truth, it was said, from a unanalyzed perspective, that the object of the view of the self is the aggregates. As the Transcendent Conqueror said:

> The view of the self is the view of the transitory collection.

You may ask, "How can we be sure that these sūtra teachings refute a self that is separate from the aggregates?" You can be sure because the

Buddha, in other sūtras, said, "Form is not the self" and so on. Thus the notion of form and so on being the self has already been refuted.

2.2.2.1.1.6.2.3.1.1.2.2.1.2.2.1.2.2.1.2. THE EXPLANATION

> It was taught in other sūtras that forms and feelings are not the self,
> That discriminations are not the self, that formations are not the self,
> And that consciousnesses are not the self.
> Therefore, the teaching of the above-mentioned sūtra did not assert that the aggregates are the self. (6.133)

This verse explains further the statement made in the previous verse. It was taught in other sūtras, sūtras that are renowned to and accepted by the hearers, that forms are not the self, feelings are not the self, discriminations are not the self, formations are not the self, and consciousnesses are not the self. Therefore the teaching of the above-mentioned sūtra was definitely given only in order to refute a self that is different from the aggregates It did not assert that the aggregates are the self.

The intention of the above-mentioned sūtra was to teach that, in the relative truth, the self that is imputed on the basis of the aggregates is the object of the view of the transitory collection. A self that is separate from the aggregates, therefore, is to be refuted. Other sūtras teach that, when analyzing and contemplating the precise nature, one first refutes the notion that form and so on are the self. Following that, one refutes even the dependently imputed self, the object of the view of the transitory collection, that arises from the aggregates, which support the appropriation [of the concept of self].

The sūtras teach that if the aggregates do not exist as the cause of appropriating [the concept of] self, then the result, the self, could not exist as what is appropriated. Therefore [these sūtras were taught] with the intention that [students] free themselves from the attachment that conceives of the self as form and so on.

There are some who say, "Some Buddhists, namely the Saṃmitīyas, assert the self to be the aggregates themselves. The Vātsīputrīyas, meanwhile, assert an inexpressible self. Both of those schools assert the self to be substantially existent. The schools from the Particularists through the Autonomists assert that the aggregates are the basis of imputation of the self and that the self is an imputed existent. The Consequentialists say that the aggregates are the cause of the imputation of the self, but they do not assert them to be either the basis of imputation of the self or the basis of illustration of the self."

However, there is no definitive certainty as to whether both of the first two traditions[462] assert the self to be a substantial existent. The second of the above-mentioned positions[463] can be accepted as tenable. The third,[464] however, is utterly untenable. The Consequentialists refute, using limitless scriptures and reasonings, the notion that the aggregates are the causes of the appropriator while the self is the result of appropriation. Even if one reads just once the refutations in the above root verse (which reads, for instance, ". . . forms and feelings are not the self") and their explanation in the autocommentary, one will see that there is no contradiction with what has just been said. Therefore, it is most appropriate to give up saying that in the Consequentialist system the aggregates are the cause of the self.

2.2.2.1.1.6.2.3.1.1.2.2.1.2.2.1.2.2.2. EVEN IF THE AGGREGATES WERE THE SELF, THEIR COLLECTION COULD NOT LOGICALLY BE THE SELF
2.2.2.1.1.6.2.3.1.1.2.2.1.2.2.1.2.2.2.1. The refutation of the collection as the self
2.2.2.1.1.6.2.3.1.1.2.2.1.2.2.1.2.2.2.2. The ancillary refutation of shape as the self

2.2.2.1.1.6.2.3.1.1.2.2.1.2.2.1.2.2.2.1. THE REFUTATION OF THE COLLECTION AS THE SELF
2.2.2.1.1.6.2.3.1.1.2.2.1.2.2.1.2.2.2.1.1. The collection is not substantially established
2.2.2.1.1.6.2.3.1.1.2.2.1.2.2.1.2.2.2.1.2. Therefore it is not suitable as a protector and so on
2.2.2.1.1.6.2.3.1.1.2.2.1.2.2.1.2.2.2.1.3. The refutation of rebuttals

2.2.2.1.1.6.2.3.1.1.2.2.1.2.2.1.2.2.2.1.1. THE COLLECTION IS NOT SUBSTANTIALLY ESTABLISHED

When you say that the aggregates are the self,
You are referring to the collection of the aggregates, not to the

entities of the aggregates. (6.134ab)

Furthermore, you cannot use the mode of proof of the previous sūtra to show that the aggregates are the self. For example, when you say that trees are the forest, you are referring to the collection of trees as the forest, but not to the entities of the trees themselves. If you were referring to the latter, it would follow that each tree is a forest.

In the same way, when you say that the aggregates are the self, you are referring to the collection of the aggregates as the self, but you are not referring to the entities of the aggregates themselves as the self. For, if you were, it would follow that each aggregate would be a self.

2.2.2.1.1.6.2.3.1.1.2.2.1.2.2.1.2.2.2.1.2. THEREFORE IT IS NOT SUITABLE AS A PROTECTOR AND SO ON

> The collection of the aggregates is not a protector, nor is it a tamer or witness.
> Since the collection does not exist, it cannot be the self. (6.134cd)

The collection of the aggregates is not substantially established. It is nothing whatsoever. Therefore it is not suitable as a protector and so on. The Transcendent Conqueror said,

> I[465] am my own protector;
> I am also my own enemy.
> I am my own witness
> To my positive and negative actions.

In those cases he taught the self as a protector and a witness.

> Through well taming themselves,
> The wise ones gain the higher realms.

Thus the Buddha spoke of the self as what is to be tamed. The mere collection of the aggregates, however, does not exist substantially and thus cannot be a protector, one who is tamed, or the witness. For the collection itself does not exist. Therefore the collection of the aggregates is not the self.

2.2.2.1.1.6.2.3.1.1.2.2.1.2.2.1.2.2.2.1.3. THE REFUTATION OF
REBUTTALS
2.2.2.1.1.6.2.3.1.1.2.2.1.2.2.1.2.2.2.1.3.1. The example
2.2.2.1.1.6.2.3.1.1.2.2.1.2.2.1.2.2.2.1.3.2. The meaning of the example

2.2.2.1.1.6.2.3.1.1.2.2.1.2.2.1.2.2.2.1.3.1. THE EXAMPLE

**At that time, the parts of a chariot that form a collection
Would become the chariot, and the chariot and the self are
equivalent. (6.135ab)**

You may think, "The collection is not separate from its components. It can
be cognized that results such as the protector come about due to the components of a collection. Therefore the protector, the one to be tamed, and
the witness are logical."

That is not the case. It has already been explained how individual phenomena cannot together form single units or the self. Furthermore, if you
claim that the aggregates are the self and imply that the components of
the aggregates' collection are the self, your approach would be equal to the
following example. Calling a collection of vehicle parts a "chariot" would
mean that the individual members—like the axle—of the parts' collection
would themselves become the chariot. That is illogical. It will be explained
below that the parts of the chariot cannot be the chariot.

Since the chariot and the self are equivalent in the context of this logic,
the individual members of the aggregates' collection cannot logically be
the self. As the sūtras say:[466]

> O mind of māra saying conceiving of a "self,"
> You are a wrong view.
> This assembly of aggregates is empty.
> There is no sentient being here.
> Just as a chariot is expressed in dependence upon the collection of
>   its parts,
> In the same way, in dependence upon the aggregates,
> Relatively the label "sentient being" is given.

2.2.2.1.1.6.2.3.1.1.2.2.1.2.2.1.2.2.2.1.3.2. THE MEANING OF THE
EXAMPLE

> The sūtras taught that the self is an imputation made on the basis
> of the aggregates.
> Therefore the mere assembly of the aggregates is not the self.
> (6.135cd)

As in the teaching of the sūtras that was just mentioned, the self, the sentient being, and the person are imputations made on the basis of the aggregates. Therefore the mere assembly of the aggregates is not the self.

2.2.2.1.1.6.2.3.1.1.2.2.1.2.2.1.2.2.2.2. THE ANCILLARY REFUTATION
OF SHAPE AS THE SELF

> If you say that shape is the self, shape is physical.
> For you, physical phenomena could be the self,
> But the collection of consciousness and so on could not be the
> self,
> Because those aggregates do not have any shape. (6.136)

You may say, "The mere collection of wheels and so on is not the chariot.
When the wheels and the other parts are arranged so that they take on a
particular shape, the resultant collection only then takes on the name of
a 'chariot.' In the same way, the mere collection of forms and the other
aggregates is not the self. Rather, the arrangement of the *shape* of form and
the other aggregates is the self."

That is not so. Shape exists within the phenomenon of form. Therefore,
for you, physical phenomena could be called "the self," but the collection
of consciousness[467] and so on, the four mental aggregates,[468] could not be
the self, because those aggregates do not have the shape that forms do-
they are not physical phenomena.

2.2.2.1.1.6.2.3.1.1.2.2.1.2.2.1.2.2.3. THE APPROPRIATOR CANNOT BE
THE APPROPRIATED
2.2.2.1.1.6.2.3.1.1.2.2.1.2.2.1.2.2.3.1. The actual teaching
2.2.2.1.1.6.2.3.1.1.2.2.1.2.2.1.2.2.3.2. The refutation of the object of action
devoid of a performer

2.2.2.1.1.6.2.3.1.1.2.2.1.2.2.1.2.2.3.1. THE ACTUAL TEACHING

It is illogical for the appropriator to be the same thing as the appropriated.
If they were the same, objects of action would be the same thing as their performers. (6.137ab)

There are further faults to be explained regarding the position that the self is the same as the appropriated aggregates. It is illogical for the appropriator, the self, to be the same thing as the aggregates that it appropriates. For, if it were, objects of action would be the same as their performers. Yet that cannot be asserted. If you attempted to assert that position, it would absurdly follow that the causal constituents of a vase, the vase itself, and the craftsperson who makes the vase would all be the same thing. As the *Treatise* says:

> If the wood were fire,
> Performers and their objects of action would be the same. (10.1ab)

2.2.2.1.1.6.2.3.1.1.2.2.1.2.2.1.2.2.3.2. THE REFUTATION OF THE OBJECT OF ACTION DEVOID OF A PERFORMER

If you think there are objects of action devoid of performers,
That is not the case, because without performers there are no objects of action. (6.137cd)

You may think, "There is no performer who is the appropriator, but there are objects of action that are appropriated—the mere assembly of appropriated form[469] and so on." That is not the case, because without performers, the cause, objects of action will also become nonexistent. The *Treatise* says:

> Thus the self is not different from the appropriated,
> Nor is it the appropriated itself.
> The self is not devoid of the appropriated,
> Nor can it be ascertained as strictly nonexistent. (27.8)

Thus the statement, "Though the performer is not observable, actions exist, as do their ripening," should be understood to refute the true existence of the performer.[470]

2.2.2.1.1.6.2.3.1.1.2.2.1.2.2.1.3. THE PERSON IS DEPENDENTLY IMPUTED

> The Sage taught the self to be imputed in dependence
> Upon the six elements—earth, water, fire, wind, consciousness,
>   and space—
> And upon the six supports for contact,
> The eye and so on. (6.138)
> He also definitively taught that the self is imputed
> Through apprehending primary minds and mental events.
> Therefore the self is not those phenomena, nor is it their mere
>   collection.
> Those phenomena cannot logically be the objects of the conception of "I." (6.139)

In the sūtras *(Sūtra on the Meeting of Father and Son, Pitiputrasamigama-sūtra, Yap Se Jalwe Do/yab sras mjal ba'i mdo)*, the Sage said:

> Great king, the person or individual is the six elements, the six sources of contact, and the eighteen movements of mind.

Thus the Buddha taught the self to be imputed in dependence upon the six elements of earth, water, fire, wind, consciousness, and space, and on the six supports of contact—the contact via assembly of elements in relation to the eye up through the mind. He also definitively taught that the self is imputed through apprehending primary minds and mental events, which in turn depend upon the eighteen movements of mind: the six movements of happy mind, the six movements of suffering mind, and the six neutral movements.

Therefore the self is not those phenomena, nor is it the mere collection of those phenomena. Since those phenomena are not suitable as the self, they cannot logically be the objects of the conception of "I."

Since they do not observe the self as being of a nature of the aggregates or something different from the aggregates, yogins understand that the self and entities connected to the self do not exist. They cut the continuum of the five appropriated aggregates and pass into nirvāṇa without them. This analysis of selflessness, therefore, is very beautiful.[471]

2.2.2.1.1.6.2.3.1.1.2.2.1.2.2.2. THE CONCLUSION VIA THE CONSEQUENCE THAT THE VIEW OF THE SELF WOULD NOT BE RELINQUISHED

2.2.2.1.1.6.2.3.1.1.2.2.1.2.2.2.1. The untenability of a factor to be relinquished and an antidote that are not connected
2.2.2.1.1.6.2.3.1.1.2.2.1.2.2.2.2. A clarifying example

2.2.2.1.1.6.2.3.1.1.2.2.1.2.2.2.1. THE UNTENABILITY OF A FACTOR TO BE RELINQUISHED AND AN ANTIDOTE THAT ARE NOT CONNECTED

> You say that when yogins realize selflessness they relinquish the
>   view of a permanent self,
> But you do not even assert such a self as the support for the
>   conception of "I."
> Your description of how the cognition of selflessness
> Uproots the view of a self is marvelous indeed! (6.140)

This verse teaches that if the objects of the conception of "I" are the aggregates and the mind, then for as long as the aggregates arise, the conception of "I" will also be active, because one will possess a mind that fixates upon the self.

If a permanent self were the object of the conception of "I," one would become free of the conception of "I" through realizing the nonexistence of such a self. And, according to you, when yogins realize selflessness they realize just this nonexistence, or selflessness, of a permanent self. They relinquish the view, you say, that such a self could exist. However, *you* do not even assert such a self to be the support for the worldly conception of "I"—you assert the *aggregates* as the support for the conception of "I."

Therefore your description of the cognition of selflessness is quite marvelous indeed: you say that, through cognizing the nonexistence of a permanent self, separate from the aggregates, yogins uproot the seeds of the view of the self that takes the aggregates as its object. What an amazing feat of exposition you have accomplished—those two forms of self have nothing to do with one another!

To explain the meaning of the above further, all sentient beings innately view the aggregates as the self. Philosophers, additionally, make various imputations regarding the object of that view of self. They label the self with such terms as compounded and uncompounded, permanent and impermanent, and so on.

The imputed self can be refuted by reasonings by investigating such questions as "Regarding the innate and imaginary selves, if they truly exist, is their support permanent or impermanent? In what phenomena do they exist?" The same investigations can be used to refute the innate self. This is so because, if the innate self truly existed, it would need to be either permanent or impermanent, conditioned or unconditioned, and so on. When an imputed self with such qualities is not found when analyzed, that nonfinding mirrors the discovery that the innate self does not exist as a thing. This relationship is similar to how the refutation of the imputed arising (arising from the four extremes) of sprouts, etc. resembles the refutation of the innate arising of sprouts, etc.

Even though there are such resemblances between the refutations of the imputed self and the innate self, the Saṃmitīyas are still singled out by the *Entrance to the Middle Way* as being mistaken in their approach. Their mistake relates to two basic assertions: firstly, the assertion of the self as a permanent, singular, and independent entity separate from the aggregates; and, secondly, the assertion of the self or sentient being as an impermanent phenomenon equivalent with the aggregates.

The Saṃmitīyas say that, by simply refuting the first assertion, one will have done away [completely] with the second assertion.[472] This notion of the Saṃmitīyas is ridiculed in the root verse above.

Even though the Saṃmitīyas do not explicitly claim that through refuting the first type of self one will have refuted the latter, their philosophical system is still mistaken. No matter how one describes the process of refuting the self, it will still be the case that, in the worldly perspective, the realization of selflessness depends on putting to a stop the pattern of viewing the aggregates as the self. It is not the case that realizing selflessness depends in any way on whether or not one refutes something separate from the aggregates as the self. The same applies to viewing phenomena separate from the aggregates as the self and entities connected to the self. One should understand the explanation given here as the most tenable.

2.2.2.1.1.6.2.3.1.1.2.2.1.2.2.2.2. A CLARIFYING EXAMPLE

> While looking at a snake's nest in the hole of your house's wall,
> To dispel anxiety you say, "There is no elephant there."
> This is how you try to pacify the fear of snakes.
> Oh dear, how others will laugh! (6.141)

The fault of unconnectedness explained above will now be illuminated further using an example. Some people might look at a snake's nest in a hole of their house's wall and act as if they did not see any danger present. Not attempting any meaningful solution, they say, "There is no elephant there" to relieve the anxiety of the house's occupants. In this way they try to pacify the fear of snakes. Oh dear, how the discerning ones will laugh!

Why is this behavior so laughable a response? An unsuspecting person, who, having heard the announcement about the elephant, will believe there is no snake in the wall. The snake, therefore, will have a chance to attack and harm that person. The same danger lies in the approach of those who assert the self as the aggregates or the mind. Those people say that yogins, when realizing selflessness, will relinquish the view of a permanent self but will be unable to relinquish the view of a self that takes the aggregates as its object. Yogins following their approach will remain cycling in the karma and mental afflictions of saṃsāra.

Furthermore, [verse 6.140] can be altered in the following way to apply to those who assert the self that is the object of refutation by reasons:

> You say that when a yogin realizes selflessness they relinquish the
> view of a primordially established self,
> But you do not even assert such a self as the support for the conception of "I."

2.2.2.1.1.6.2.3.1.1.2.2.1.3. THE REFUTATION OF THE SELF THAT EXISTS IN A RELATIONSHIP OF SUPPORTER-SUPPORTED WITH THE AGGREGATES

> The self does not exist in the aggregates
> And the aggregates do not exist in the self.
> You may think of them as different,
> But they are not different, so any relationship between them of

support and supported is merely a conceptual imputation. (6.142)

Having proven that the self is not established as being the same as or different from the aggregates, Chandrakīrti now describes how the self does not exist in a support-supported relationship with the aggregates. The self, the supported, does not exist in the aggregates, the support. Nor do the aggregates, the supported, exist in the self, the support. For, in this context of examining the relationship between the aggregates and the self, you may think that they are different from each other, like yogurt and a bowl that holds the yogurt. In other words, you may think of them as support and supported. But the self and the aggregates are not separate from each other. Therefore a relationship between them of support and supported is merely a conceptual imputation.

2.2.2.1.1.6.2.3.1.1.2.2.1.4. THE REFUTATION OF A SELF THAT POSSESSES THE AGGREGATES

We do not assert that the self possesses form—since the self does not exist,
No meaning of "possession" is applicable.
Extrinsic possession is as in "Devadatta has a cow"; intrinsic possession is as in "Devadatta has a body,"
But the self is not the same as or different from form. (6.143)

This verse shows that the self also does not exist as something that possesses the aggregates. We do not assert that the self possesses the aggregates such as form—since the self does not exist, no meaning of "possession" is applicable to the relationship between the "self" and the aggregates.

The meaning of "possession" in the sense of extrinsic possession is exemplified by the sentence, "Devadatta has a cow." The meaning of "possession" that is intrinsic is exemplified by the sentence, "Devadatta has a body." But in terms of the self and the aggregates such as form, the self is not the same thing as or a different thing than form. The possibilities of sameness and difference have already been refuted.

2.2.2.1.1.6.2.3.1.1.2.2.1.5. THE SUMMARY OF THE REFUTATION BY EXPRESSING IT IN THE FORM OF THE ANTIDOTES TO THE TWENTY EXTREME VIEWS OF THE TRANSITORY COLLECTION

2.2.2.1.1.6.2.3.1.1.2.2.1.5.1. The list of how to engage the reference points of the view of the transitory collection in reverse

2.2.2.1.1.6.2.3.1.1.2.2.1.5.2. The way in which vajra wisdom conquers the view of the transitory collection, presented in connection with scripture

2.2.2.1.1.6.2.3.1.1.2.2.1.5.1. THE LIST OF HOW TO ENGAGE THE REFERENCE POINTS OF THE VIEW OF THE TRANSITORY COLLECTION IN REVERSE

> Form is not the self; the self does not possess form;
> The self does not exist in form; form does not exist in the self.
> These four statements should be understood to apply to all the aggregates.
> The reversals of these statements represent the twenty views of the self. (6.144)

Now Chandrakīrti summarizes the meaning of the refutations that have already been made by giving the list of the ways of engaging in reverse the reference points of the view of the transitory collection. Form is not the self, because form does not have the same defining characteristics as the self. Furthermore, if form were the self, it would absurdly follow that actions and the performers of actions would be the same.

The self does not possess form, like a person possessing a necklace, because the self and form cannot be expressed as being the same or different. The self, the supported, does not exist in form, the support, in the manner of engaging or abiding in it, like a lion in the forest; nor do form and so on, the supported, exist in the self, the support, in a manner of being controlled by it, like a group of trees on a snowy mountain. For the self and form are not inherently different from each other.

In this manner, these four statements should be understood to apply to all of the other aggregates of feeling and so on, the four name aggregates. These statements should be understood to indicate the selflessness of those other aggregates. The view of the transitory collection apprehends the five aggregates, which are devoid of self, in a way that is the reverse of the above statements, which correctly describe the relationship between the self and the aggregates.

The four incorrect ways of apprehending the self apply to each of the five aggregates. They are therefore asserted to be the twenty extremes of the view of the self or the view of the transitory collection.

You may protest: "In the *Treatise*, it says,

The Tathāgata is not the aggregates; the Tathāgata is not different from the aggregates. (22.1a)

"In that way Nāgārjuna taught an additional view of the self related to each
aggregate—that of the self being different from the aggregates. Therefore
the total amount of views of the transitory collection should be twenty-
five."

That teaching from the *Treatise* was indeed a fifth axis of analysis,
taught in order to refute some tīrthikas who viewed the self as being different from the aggregates. However, as the sūtras teach, it is impossible
for the view of the transitory collection to apprehend the self without
apprehending the aggregates. Therefore the view of the transitory collection engages the five aggregates in sets of four for each aggregate—there is
no fifth mode of engagement.

The *Ṭīkā*, at this section, presents refutations and affirmations connected to the assertions of the great Gorampa and others.

2.2.2.1.1.6.2.3.1.1.2.2.1.5.2. THE WAY IN WHICH VAJRA WISDOM
CONQUERS THE VIEW OF THE TRANSITORY COLLECTION,
PRESENTED IN CONNECTION WITH SCRIPTURE

When the vajra that is the realization of selflessness
Conquers the mountain of views of the transitory collection,
The twenty high peaks on that massive mountain
Disintegrate, together with the self. (6.145)

The sūtras say,

By conquering the twenty high peaks on the mountain of the
view of the transitory collection with the vajra of wisdom, one
actualizes the result of stream-enterer.

The root verse at this section of the *Entrance to the Middle Way* teaches
the meaning of the above scriptural quotation. When the vajra of wisdom
that is the realization of selflessness conquers the mountain of the views of
the transitory collection, the twenty high peaks of the view of the transi-

tory collection, the perceiving subject, disintegrate together with the self, the perceived object.

If the vajra of the wisdom of the noble ones does not descend upon this mountain, the mountain's rocky cliffs—the mental afflictions of beginningless saṃsāra—grow higher and higher every day. This massive mountain extends through the three realms of saṃsāra and was born from the golden ground of ignorance.[473] Its high peaks are these twenty views that were explained above.

Some assert the twenty views to be the imaginary nature, but they are not. Since they are factors to be relinquished on the path of seeing, they act as a basis for confusion, but they are not imaginary. Imaginary phenomena are imputed in the short term and on the basis of philosophies. Therefore they do not exist for all sentient beings. But the twenty views of the transitory collection, on the other hand, are habits of all sentient beings, active since beginningless time, of viewing the aggregates as the self and entities connected to the self.[474]

2.2.2.1.1.6.2.3.1.1.2.2.2. THE REFUTATION OF THE SELF THAT CANNOT BE EXPRESSED AS BEING THE SAME AS OR DIFFERENT FROM THE AGGREGATES
2.2.2.1.1.6.2.3.1.1.2.2.2.1. The statement of the counterparts' position
2.2.2.1.1.6.2.3.1.1.2.2.2.2. The refutation of the counterparts' position

2.2.2.1.1.6.2.3.1.1.2.2.2.1. THE STATEMENT OF THE COUNTERPARTS' POSITION

> **Some assert the person as a substantial existent**
> **That cannot be expressed in terms of being the same as or different from the aggregates or in terms of being permanent or impermanent, and so on.**
> **They assert it to be an object of knowledge of the six consciousnesses**
> **And the basis for the conception of "I." (6.146)**

The *Entrance to the Middle Way* will now dispel the assertion that the person is a substantial existent.

The Vātsīputrīyas[475] say that the person cannot be different from the aggregates, because the person is not established for worldly people through any other means than the aggregates. They also say that the person is not of the nature of the aggregates themselves, because if it were, it would absurdly follow that the self arises and disintegrates. Thus, they say, the self is not expressible in terms of being the same as or different from the aggregates. In the same way, the Vātsīputrīyas say that the self cannot be said to be permanent or impermanent and so on, because such descriptions would entail eternalism and nihilism.

They assert that such a self of person is also substantially existent, because it is called a creator and an enjoyer in the world and because it is inextricably connected to saṃsāra and nirvāṇa and to bondage and liberation.

For the Vātsīputrīyas, the person is not a knowable object in terms of its entity. However, it is an object that is knowable by the six consciousnesses. For the person is known due to form and so on, the six sense sources, being taken as objects for the mind.

Finally, the Vātsīputrīyas assert the person to be the object or basis of the worldly conception of "I."

2.2.2.1.1.6.2.3.1.1.2.2.2.2. THE REFUTATION OF THE COUNTERPARTS' POSITION
2.2.2.1.1.6.2.3.1.1.2.2.2.2.1. The refutation of a substantially existent self
2.2.2.1.1.6.2.3.1.1.2.2.2.2.2. The self is an imputed existent
2.2.2.1.1.6.2.3.1.1.2.2.2.2.3. The self is not established because it does not have the qualities of a thing

2.2.2.1.1.6.2.3.1.1.2.2.2.2.1. THE REFUTATION OF A SUBSTANTIALLY EXISTENT SELF

> Just as mind is not seen as inexpressible in relation to form,
> No existent thing is cognized as inexpressible.
> If the self is an established thing,
> Then, like mind, it could not be inexpressible. (6.147)

If you say that the self is substantially established, it is illogical to say that it is also inexpressible. Mind, for example, is not inexpressible in terms of whether it is the same as or different from form. In the same way, no existent thing is cognized as inexpressible in terms of being the same as or different from another thing. For, if something is substantially established, it cannot transcend being one of those two.

If the self, as you say, is a substantially established thing, then, like mind and form, it could not be cognized as inexpressible in terms of being the same as or different from the aggregates.

2.2.2.1.1.6.2.3.1.1.2.2.2.2.2. THE SELF IS AN IMPUTED EXISTENT

According to you, a vase is not established as a thing
And its entity is inexpressible in relation to its form and so on.
Just so, since the self is inexpressible in relations to the
**   aggregates,**
It is impossible to cognize its own existence as being established.
**   (6.148)**

If the self is not expressible as the same as or different from the aggregates, it is necessarily an imputed existent. According to you, a vase is a mere imputed existent that is not established as a thing. For that reason, the entity of the vase is inexpressible in terms of whether it is the same as or different from its form and so on. In the same way, since the self is inexpressible in terms of being the same as or different from the aggregates, it is impossible to cognize it as being substantially existent by way of its entity. Like a vase, it should be understood to be an imputed existent.

2.2.2.1.1.6.2.3.1.1.2.2.2.2.3. THE SELF IS NOT ESTABLISHED BECAUSE IT DOES NOT HAVE THE QUALITIES OF A THING

You do not assert that consciousness is different from its own
**   entity.**
You do assert it as a thing that is different from form and so on.
Things, therefore, must be seen to have those two qualities.
The self does not exist, because it is devoid of these qualities of a
**   thing. (6.149)**

The previous two root verses refuted the substantial existence of the self and proved its imputed existence, respectively. The *Entrance to the Middle Way* will now state that sameness and otherness are the very supports for the establishment of a thing and refute the self by revealing how the self does not meet these prerequisites.

According to you,[476] the self substantially exists. However, you do not assert that consciousness is different from its own entity. You do assert consciousness as a thing that is different from form and so on. The self, [by your own admission, does not meet these two prerequisites of being a thing]: it is not something that is the same as its own entity and different from that of others.

Since substantially existent things must be seen to have these two qualities, sameness and difference, the self does not substantially exist. For, it is devoid of these qualities of a thing, just as in the case of vases. The self also cannot tenably be a knowable object of the six consciousnesses.

2.2.2.1.1.6.2.3.1.1.2.2.3. THE CONCLUDING SUMMARY OF THE REFUTATION

> Therefore the support for the conception of "I" is not a thing,
> Is not different from the aggregates, is not the entity of the
>   aggregates,
> Is not the support of the aggregates, and does not possess the
>   aggregates. (6.150abc)

Under the above analyses, the person cannot logically be a substantial existent. Therefore the support or object for the conception of "I," when definitively contemplated, is not a substantially existent beyond expression in terms of sameness or difference. It is not different from the aggregates, nor is it the entity of the aggregates. It is not the support of the aggregates, and it is not logical for the self to possess the aggregates.

2.2.2.1.1.6.2.3.1.1.2.3. THE TEACHING SUBSEQUENT TO THE REFUTATION ON HOW THE PERSON IS A MERE DEPENDENT IMPUTATION

2.2.2.1.1.6.2.3.1.1.2.3.1. The brief teaching
2.2.2.1.1.6.2.3.1.1.2.3.2. The extensive explanation by way of example and correspondent meaning
2.2.2.1.1.6.2.3.1.1.2.3.3. Therefore all other phenomena of the same type are merely imputations

2.2.2.1.1.6.2.3.1.1.2.3.1. THE BRIEF TEACHING

> It is established merely in dependence upon the aggregates.
>   (6.150d)

One may ask, "Since you have refuted the existence of the person through various reasonings as above, are we to conclude that the person is utterly nonexistent?" The Buddha said, "In dependence upon this, that arises." He made that statement merely not to render extinct the presentation of relative truth and to affirm that things do not arise without causes and so on. Similarly, when we analyze the self, the substantially existent self is refuted because of the logical faults that were explained above.

The self, therefore, is merely an imputation made in dependence upon the aggregates. Worldly people simply use the term "self" as a way of abiding by the conventions of the world.

2.2.2.1.1.6.2.3.1.1.2.3.2. THE EXTENSIVE EXPLANATION BY WAY OF EXAMPLE AND CORRESPONDENT MEANING
2.2.2.1.1.6.2.3.1.1.2.3.2.1. The example that illustrates the meaning
2.2.2.1.1.6.2.3.1.1.2.3.2.2. The meaning illustrated by the example

2.2.2.1.1.6.2.3.1.1.2.3.2.1. THE EXAMPLE THAT ILLUSTRATES THE MEANING
2.2.2.1.1.6.2.3.1.1.2.3.2.1.1. The teaching
2.2.2.1.1.6.2.3.1.1.2.3.2.1.2. The explanation

2.2.2.1.1.6.2.3.1.1.2.3.2.1.1. THE TEACHING

> A chariot is not asserted to be different from its parts.
> It is not the same as its parts, nor does it possess them.
> It does not depend on its parts, nor do its parts depend on it.
> It is not its parts' mere assembly, nor is it their shape. (6.151)

Having taught that the self is a mere imputation, the *Entrance to the Middle Way* will now use an external example to clarify the meaning of this principle.

A chariot is not asserted to be different from its parts such as its nails. For, aside from those parts, the chariot cannot be perceived. It is not the same as its parts,[477] because, if it were, the performer and the object of action would be the same—it would absurdly follow that there would be a chariot in each of the parts, thus making many chariots.

The chariot does not possess its parts: since it is inexpressible in terms of being the same as or different from them, the meaning of "possession" is inapplicable. The chariot does not depend on its parts, nor do its parts depend on it, because the chariot and its parts are not inherently different from each other.

The chariot is not the mere assembly of its parts—the faults of that position have already been explained. The shape is also not the chariot, because that position will be invalidated by the reasonings explained below. When this sevenfold analysis is applied, the chariot cannot be found. [The self and the aggregates] are the same way.

2.2.2.1.1.6.2.3.1.1.2.3.2.1.2.2. THE EXPLANATION
2.2.2.1.1.6.2.3.1.1.2.3.2.1.2.2.1. The refutation of parts
2.2.2.1.1.6.2.3.1.1.2.3.2.1.2.2.2. The refutation of part-possessors without parts

2.2.2.1.1.6.2.3.1.1.2.3.2.1.2.2.1. THE REFUTATION OF PARTS
2.2.2.1.1.6.2.3.1.1.2.3.2.1.2.2.1.1. The general refutation of the last two properties
2.2.2.1.1.6.2.3.1.1.2.3.2.1.2.2.1.2. The special refutation of shape

2.2.2.1.1.6.2.3.1.1.2.3.2.1.2.2.1.1. THE GENERAL REFUTATION OF THE LAST TWO PROPERTIES[478]
2.2.2.1.1.6.2.3.1.1.2.3.2.1.2.2.1.1.1. The refutation of the mere collection
2.2.2.1.1.6.2.3.1.1.2.3.2.1.2.2.1.1.2. The general refutation of shape

2.2.2.1.1.6.2.3.1.1.2.3.2.1.2.2.1.1.1. THE REFUTATION OF THE MERE COLLECTION

If the mere collection of parts were the chariot,
A chariot would exist in every single one of its parts. (6.152ab)

The *Entrance to the Middle Way* has already refuted the first five positions[479] related to the sevenfold analysis—sameness, difference, and so forth. It will now provide the proofs that will refute the two remaining positions, namely the collection and shape. If the mere collection of parts were the chariot, a chariot would exist in every single one of its parts such as the nails, because the collection is not different from its constituents, the members of the collection.

2.2.2.1.1.6.2.3.1.1.2.3.2.1.2.1.1.2. THE GENERAL REFUTATION OF SHAPE

> Since there are no parts without something to possess them,
> Mere shape as well cannot be the chariot. (6.152cd)

There are no parts without something to possess the parts, because those two are established through mutual dependence. Therefore the mere shape of the collection of parts cannot logically be the chariot. The words "as well" of the last line indicate that the mere collection of the parts is also not tenable as the chariot.

2.2.2.1.1.6.2.3.1.1.2.3.2.1.2.1.2. THE SPECIAL REFUTATION OF SHAPE
2.2.2.1.1.6.2.3.1.1.2.3.2.1.2.1.2.1. The refutation of shape as a substantial existent
2.2.2.1.1.6.2.3.1.1.2.3.2.1.2.1.2.2. If shape is an imputed existent, it has the same status as all other imputed existents
2.2.2.1.1.6.2.3.1.1.2.3.2.1.2.1.2.3. Dispelling the notion that we contradict the conventional world

2.2.2.1.1.6.2.3.1.1.2.3.2.1.2.1.2.1. THE REFUTATION OF SHAPE AS A SUBSTANTIAL EXISTENT
2.2.2.1.1.6.2.3.1.1.2.3.2.1.2.1.2.1.1. The refutation of the shape of the parts
2.2.2.1.1.6.2.3.1.1.2.3.2.1.2.1.2.1.2. The refutation of the shape of the collection

2.2.2.1.1.6.2.3.1.1.2.3.2.1.2.1.2.1.1. THE REFUTATION OF THE SHAPE OF THE PARTS
2.2.2.1.1.6.2.3.1.1.2.3.2.1.2.1.2.1.1.1. The refutation of the chariot as the shape of the parts that maintains its original features
2.2.2.1.1.6.2.3.1.1.2.3.2.1.2.1.2.1.1.2. The refutation of the chariot as the shape of the parts that has relinquished its original features

2.2.2.1.1.6.2.3.1.1.2.3.2.1.2.1.2.1.1.1. THE REFUTATION OF THE CHARIOT AS THE SHAPE OF THE PARTS THAT MAINTAINS ITS ORIGINAL FEATURES

> If for you the shapes of the parts when they form the chariot
> Are exactly the same as the shapes before the chariot's assembly,

> **Then just as there was no chariot in the discrete parts before,**
> **There is also no chariot now. (6.153)**

It is untenable for you to assert that mere shape is the chariot. If for you the features of the shapes of the parts, such as the wheels, at the time when they form the chariot,[480] are exactly the same as the shapes of each of the parts before the chariot's assembly, there was no chariot in the discrete and individual parts before. And, similarly, there is also no chariot now, when the chariot has been formed. For there is no difference in the shapes of the wheels and so on in their two stages: before the chariot's formation and after.

2.2.2.1.1.6.2.3.1.1.2.3.2.1.2.1.2.1.1.2. THE REFUTATION OF THE CHARIOT AS THE SHAPE OF THE PARTS THAT HAS RELINQUISHED ITS ORIGINAL FEATURES

> **Now, when the chariot has been formed,**
> **If the wheels and so on had shapes that are different from the ear-**
> **lier shapes,**
> **The new shapes would be perceptible—but they are not.**
> **Therefore the chariot is not merely shape. (6.154)**

Now, when the chariot has been formed and achieved full existence, if the wheels, axles, and so on—bearing individual shapes of round, long, etc. before the chariot was formed—had shapes that are different than the shapes that are now the chariot's form, these new shapes would be perceptible, but they are not. For that reason, the chariot cannot logically be the mere shape of its parts.

2.2.2.1.1.6.2.3.1.1.2.3.2.1.2.1.2.1.2. THE REFUTATION OF THE SHAPE OF THE COLLECTION

> **Since your "collection" does not even slightly exist,**
> **There can be no shape of a collection of parts.**
> **How could you give the label of "shape"**
> **To nothing at all? (6.155)**

You may say, "The chariot is the distinct shape of the collection of parts, such as wheels." That is not so. If a substantial thing called a "collection" even slightly existed, only then could you give the label "shape" to the support of the label, the collection. However, the "collection" you assert has not even the slightest substantial existence.

Therefore the shape of the chariot cannot depend on the "collection" of its parts. How could you give the label of shape to a collection that is nothing at all? The collection does not exist whatsoever! You could not give such a label, because a label or imputation can only be accepted to *depend on* something substantially existent. The label in itself is not substantial.

2.2.2.1.1.6.2.3.1.1.2.3.2.1.2.1.2.1.2.2. IF SHAPE IS AN IMPUTED EXISTENT, IT HAS THE SAME STATUS AS ALL OTHER IMPUTED EXISTENTS
2.2.2.1.1.6.2.3.1.1.2.3.2.1.2.1.2.2.1. The actual teaching
2.2.2.1.1.6.2.3.1.1.2.3.2.1.2.1.2.2.2. The shapes of vases and so on are untenable
2.2.2.1.1.6.2.3.1.1.2.3.2.1.2.1.2.2.3. The shapes of form and so on are untenable

2.2.2.1.1.6.2.3.1.1.2.3.2.1.2.1.2.2.1. THE ACTUAL TEACHING

It is just how you assert it to be:
If the aspect of a result arises in dependence upon an unreal cause,
That result is also not real.
Know that this is so regarding all things. (6.156)

You may assert, "Though the shape of a mere collection is unreal, still in dependence upon collections there are unreal shapes." It is just how you assert it to be: if the aspects of results arise in dependence upon unreal causes such as ignorance and seeds, those results, such as formations and sprouts,[481] will also, by their nature, not be real. Know that this is so regarding all things. It is illogical to engender the desire to eat in relation to an optical illusion of a deer. Even through hundreds of hardships you will not be able to consume its meat. In the same way, what benefit is there in clinging to things?

2.2.2.1.1.6.2.3.1.1.2.3.2.1.2.1.2.2.2. THE SHAPES OF VASES AND SO ON
ARE UNTENABLE

> The chariot example shows that it is illogical for a mental state
>   apprehending a vase
> To arise in dependence upon particles of form and other such
>   phenomena. (6.157ab)

The chariot example shows that it is illogical for a mental state apprehending a vase, wherein the vase is a substantially established thing, to arise
in dependence upon form and other phenomena of a similar type (i.e.,
phenomena formed through the arrangement of the eight substances of
particles). The reason such arising is illogical is because the phenomena
perceived by such mental states are themselves equally refutable by the
analysis of the chariot.

2.2.2.1.1.6.2.3.1.1.2.3.2.1.2.1.2.2.3. THE SHAPES OF FORM AND SO ON
ARE UNTENABLE

> Since they are free of arising, form and so on do not exist either.
> Therefore they too are untenable as shape. (6.157cd)

It has already been explained how form and so on are free of arising. Due
to that freedom from arising, form and so on do not inherently exist either,
and therefore they are also untenable as the causes of imputations such as
"vase." Since it is illogical to assert vases as the possessors of substances, we
can conclude that they cannot bear the identity of possessing the features
of shape, form, and so on.

2.2.2.1.1.6.2.3.1.1.2.3.2.1.2.1.2.3. DISPELLING THE NOTION THAT WE
CONTRADICT THE CONVENTIONAL WORLD
2.2.2.1.1.6.2.3.1.1.2.3.2.1.2.1.2.3.1. Though the chariot cannot be found in
either of the two truths, it is imputed *without* analysis in dependence
upon its parts
2.2.2.1.1.6.2.3.1.1.2.3.2.1.2.1.2.3.2. We accept all conventions associated
with the chariot because they are renowned in the nonanalytical world
2.2.2.1.1.6.2.3.1.1.2.3.2.1.2.1.2.3.3. Through this approach to conventional
reality one can fathom the depth of the precise nature

2.2.2.1.1.6.2.3.1.1.2.3.2.1.2.1.2.3.1. THOUGH THE CHARIOT CANNOT
BE FOUND IN EITHER OF THE TWO TRUTHS, IT IS IMPUTED
WITHOUT ANALYSIS IN DEPENDENCE UPON ITS PARTS

The sevenfold reasoning shows that the chariot[482]
Is not established in suchness or in the world.
Yet, without analysis, here in the world
The chariot is imputed in dependence upon its parts. (6.158)

One may protest, "If one searches in those seven ways, one finds that there is no chariot. It follows, therefore, that the use of the term 'chariot' would, according to your analysis, become extinct in the world! However, one *can* see the use of phrases such as 'Get that chariot!' Therefore the chariot exists."

However, the consequence that the term "chariot" would become extinct in the world applies only to you, not to us. We only fail to discover the chariot *after* analysis. But you *posit* the chariot after analysis. You do not have any way to discuss the chariot except for positing it after analysis. So the question should rather be put to you: how would phrases like "Get that chariot" be established?

We, however, are not at fault. As we explained above, the sevenfold analysis reveals that the chariot is not established in suchness, the ultimate truth, or in the world, the relative truth. Yet, without such analysis we follow worldly consensus, just as in the case with the color blue. The chariot is imputed in dependence upon its own parts, such as its wheels.

We accept the dependent arising of mere conditionality. On the level of no analysis, conventions are not destroyed. Therefore, when you use conventions, you should do so in the way we prescribe.

2.2.2.1.1.6.2.3.1.1.2.3.2.1.2.1.2.3.2. WE ACCEPT ALL CONVENTIONS
ASSOCIATED WITH THE CHARIOT BECAUSE THEY ARE
RENOWNED IN THE NONANALYTICAL WORLD
2.2.2.1.1.6.2.3.1.1.2.3.2.1.2.1.2.3.2.1. The actual teaching
2.2.2.1.1.6.2.3.1.1.2.3.2.1.2.1.2.3.2.2. The untenability of the nonexistence of
a part-possessor and so on

2.2.2.1.1.6.2.3.1.1.2.3.2.1.2.1.2.3.2.1. THE ACTUAL TEACHING

> It is common for beings to refer to a chariot as something that
> has parts and sections,
> And to say that it is a performer.
> The chariot is also established for people as an appropriator.
> (6.159abc)

Not only do we use the convention "chariot" from the perspective of what is renowned in the world, we also accept that, at the time of no-analysis, it is necessary to communicate in a way that accords with the world and to use the conventions that are the names of the chariot's features as well.

It is common for beings to refer to a chariot, in dependence upon its parts such as wheels, as a part-possessor. It is also common for them to refer to a chariot as a section-possessor, in dependence upon the chariot's sections. And, in dependence upon the action of its taking on that which to be appropriated—the nails and so forth—beings call the chariot a performer. The chariot is renowned to people, on the basis of its appropriated phenomena, as an appropriator of its parts.

2.2.2.1.1.6.2.3.1.1.2.3.2.1.2.1.2.3.2.2. THE UNTENABILITY OF THE
NONEXISTENCE OF A PART-POSSESSOR AND SO ON

> Do not destroy the relative that is renowned in the world.
> (6.159d)

There are some Buddhist factions who say, "The mere collection of parts exists, but the part-possessor does not exist from any perspective. Sections, actions, and the mere appropriated aggregates exist, but section-possessors, performers, appropriators, and so on do not exist."

These factions turn away from the relative renowned in the world and speak incorrectly. Yet according to their very own logic, not even mere parts exist—parts and part-possessors are posited in dependence upon each other, and they say that part-possessors do not exist!

We refute them by highlighting the fact that it is their assertion, not ours, that entails the fault of nihilism. Therefore do not destroy the relative that is renowned in the world, in which parts and part-possessors are accepted. Since we posit those two as being mutually dependent, both of them exist conventionally, but neither of them exists when analyzed.

2.2.2.1.1.6.2.3.1.1.2.3.2.1.2.1.2.3.3. THROUGH THIS APPROACH TO CONVENTIONAL REALITY ONE CAN FATHOM THE DEPTH OF THE PRECISE NATURE

> "How can the chariot exist, since when it is analyzed in these
> seven ways it is seen not to exist at all?"
> Thus the yogis and yoginīs do not find the existence of the
> chariot.
> Through this they also easily engage in suchness,
> But, in the relative, the existence of the chariot should be
> accepted in accordance with the world. (6.160)

When analyzed things do not exist, but when not analyzed, they exist. These are the stages by which yogis and yoginīs abide. Through analyzing in this way, the yogis and yoginīs, at an utterly swift pace, come to fathom the depths of suchness.

They analyze as follows: "If a chariot is to inherently exist, its entity must be discoverable in the context of the sevenfold analysis. Yet how can it exist, since, when sought in those seven ways, it is seen not to exist at all?" In this way the yogis and yoginīs do not find the existence of the chariot.

The "chariot," in fact, is merely an imputation made by the eyes of the intellect that have been blurred by the cataracts of ignorance. The ones who realize how the chariot is empty of its own entity will easily enter into the reality that is suchness. The word "also" in the third line of the root verse indicates that these yogis and yoginīs also will avoid lapsing from the relative.

In the unanalyzed relative, the existence of the chariot should be accepted in accordance with worldly consensus. For, accepting such worldly consensus does not entail any faults and is endowed with advantages.

2.2.2.1.1.6.2.3.1.1.2.3.2.1.2.2. THE REFUTATION OF PART-POSSESSORS WITHOUT PARTS
2.2.2.1.1.6.2.3.1.1.2.3.2.1.2.2.1. The actual meaning
2.2.2.1.1.6.2.3.1.1.2.3.2.1.2.2.2. A clarifying example

392   FEAST FOR THE FORTUNATE – GROUND SIX: THE MANIFEST

2.2.2.1.1.6.2.3.1.1.2.3.2.1.2.2.1. THE ACTUAL MEANING

> **When the chariot does not exist,**
> **Both the part-possessor and its parts are nonexistent. (6.161ab)**

You may object, "It is agreed that the yogis and yoginīs do not observe the chariot. However the mere collection of the chariot's parts does exist." You, who search for yarn in the ashes of a burned woolen cloth, are laughable. As has been explained, when the chariot does not exist, its parts also do not exist, because the part-possessor that depends on the existence of the chariot does not exist.

You may think, "If after the chariot is destroyed the parts are still observable, at that time the part-possessor does not exist but the parts do." But that is not the case—due to concepts from seeing a chariot before, one thinks of the discrete parts like wheels as "the parts of the chariot" when one sees them. But, in any other case, someone who did not know of the connection these parts had to a chariot would not think of those things as "the parts of the chariot."

2.2.2.1.1.6.2.3.1.1.2.3.2.1.2.2.2. A CLARIFYING EXAMPLE

> **Just as in the example of both the chariot and its parts getting**
> **burnt,**
> **When the fire of intelligence burns the part-possessor, the parts**
> **are burned as well. (6.161cd)**

The meaning of the above should be understood through the following example. When a chariot is burnt by fire its parts are also burned and rendered nonexistent. When one rubs the sticks of analysis together there the fire of intelligence arises. When this fire burns the chariot, the part-possessor, in its entirety, the fire of supreme knowledge definitely burns the parts as well. It does not allow the parts of the chariot to retain their identity.

2.2.2.1.1.6.2.3.1.1.2.3.2.2. THE MEANING ILLUSTRATED BY THE EXAMPLE
2.2.2.1.1.6.2.3.1.1.2.3.2.2.1. The teaching on how the self is imputed dependently
2.2.2.1.1.6.2.3.1.1.2.3.2.2.2. The benefit of understanding that: the reversal of all views

2.2.2.1.1.6.2.3.1.1.2.3.2.2.3. The liberation that comes from realizing the nonexistence of self and entities connected to the self

2.2.2.1.1.6.2.3.1.1.2.3.2.2.1. THE TEACHING ON HOW THE SELF IS IMPUTED DEPENDENTLY
2.2.2.1.1.6.2.3.1.1.2.3.2.2.1.1. How the self is conventionally imputed in dependence upon the aggregates and so on
2.2.2.1.1.6.2.3.1.1.2.3.2.2.1.2. The way of explaining the conventions of objects of action and performers

2.2.2.1.1.6.2.3.1.1.2.3.2.2.1.1. HOW THE SELF IS CONVENTIONALLY IMPUTED IN DEPENDENCE UPON THE AGGREGATES AND SO ON

> Similarly, worldly consensus asserts
> That the self is an appropriator in dependence
> Upon the aggregates, the six constituents, and the six sources;
> (6.162abc)

In the example, the imputation of the chariot was made in dependence upon its wheels and so on. In that case, the wheels and so on are asserted as the appropriated, and the chariot is asserted as the appropriator. In the same way, from the perspective of what is accepted in the world and in order to present the relative truth without eliminating its conventions, it is taught that the self is imputed in dependence upon the five aggregates, the six inner constituents, and the six sources of form and so on. Therefore worldly consensus asserts that the aggregates and so on are that which is appropriated by the self and that the self is the appropriator of the aggregates.

2.2.2.1.1.6.2.3.1.1.2.3.2.2.1.2. THE WAY OF EXPLAINING THE CONVENTIONS OF OBJECTS OF ACTION AND PERFORMERS

> That the appropriated are the objects of action; and that the self is their performer. (6.162d)

In the example of the chariot, the presentations of the appropriated and the appropriator were made in accordance with what is accepted and communicated in the world. The principles of actions and performers concerning the self are expressed in the same way.

The appropriated—the aggregates and so on—are objects of action.

The self is the performer of those actions. This is what is posited conventionally and without analysis. For it is expressed conventionally that the self appropriates the aggregates of the three realms due to accumulating meritorious, nonmeritorious, and unmoving actions.

A small minority of Buddhist factions assert the person as a substantial existent. Leaving them aside, I will now explain the triad of basis of imputation, purpose, and refutation in actual fact[483] in relation to the assertion of the sentient being or person as an imputed existent. The sections under which these topics are presented are as follows.[484]

A. THE BASIS OF IMPUTATION
B. THE PURPOSE
C. THE REFUTATION IN ACTUAL FACT

A. THE BASIS OF IMPUTATION
A.I. The common presentation from the general scriptures of the greater and lesser vehicles
A.II. The uncommon presentation from the scriptures of the Vajrayāna

A.I. THE COMMON PRESENTATION FROM THE GENERAL SCRIPTURES OF THE GREATER AND LESSER VEHICLES
The Particularist and Sūtra-Follower traditions label the continuum of any of the five aggregates the person. The *Ultimate Verses (Döndampe Tsigche/ don dam pa'i tshigs bcad)* says:

The continuum is called the person;
That which bears its own characteristics is called a phenomenon.
In these, there is no saṃsāra at all;
And no one passes into nirvāṇa.

The Practitioners of Yogic Conduct hold that, if the individual aggregates were the imputed person, it would absurdly follow that form and so on would become persons. Also, they say, if the person were the collection of the aggregates, it would absurdly follow that there is no basis of imputation for the person in the formless realm or in the five states devoid of mind[485] and so on. Therefore the Practitioners of Yogic Conduct impute the person on the basis of the continuum of the all-base consciousness.

Ascertaining the Three Continua (Gyü Sum Nam-nge/rgyud gsum rnam nges) says:

> If one labels the individual aggregates or the collection of aggregates the person,
> The continuum of the five aggregates
> Could not be the person. Therefore,
> We assert the continuum of the seedlike all-basis consciousness
> To be the person.

Some say that the above view entails the absurd consequence that the Buddha would not be a person, but that consequence is untenable. For, in the Yogic Conduct tradition, mirrorlike wisdom is the continuum of the all-basis.

There are also some Proponents of Mind only who make the imputation of self in dependence upon the perfectly established dharmadhātu, which they say is the dependent nature empty of the imputed nature. Maitreya's *Distinguishing the Middle from the Extremes (Madhyāntavibhāga, Ü Ta Namje/dbus mtha' rnam 'byed)* says:

> The dharmadhātu has three aspects:
> Impure, both impure and pure,
> And completely pure—it can correlate with either three.
> It is asserted that the person is posited
> As any one of these three.

And, *Distinguishing Phenomena from True Reality (Dharma-dharma-tāvibhāga, Chö dang Chönyi Namje/chos dang chos nyid rnam 'byed)* says:[486]

> There are four faults involved in having a lack of transformation: 1) the fault of not having a support for refusing engagement with the mental afflictions, 2) the fault of not having a support for engaging the path, 3) the fault of not having a basis for the imputation of the person who has attained nirvāṇa, and 4) the fault not having a basis for the imputation of the distinctions between the three types of enlightenment. Through

having transformation one attains four benefits that are the opposite of the four above faults.

Thus, these Proponents of Mind Only say that the imputation of the person who has passed into nirvāṇa is made in dependence upon the transformed, uncontaminated expanse.

In terms of calling the dharmadhātu—emptiness that is free from elaborations—the support for the self and the support for accomplishment, the *Ornament of Clear Realization (Abhisamayālaṃkāra, Ngön Tok Gyen/ mngon rtogs rgyan)* says:

> The foundation of accomplishment
> Is the nature of dharmadhātu . . . (6cd)

The Proponents of Mind Only teach this above-mentioned dharmadhātu to be the nondual consciousness that is self-aware and self-illuminating. The Followers of the Middle Way teach it to be freedom from elaborations itself: naturally pure emptiness, the interdependence that cannot be expressed in terms of sameness or difference and in the manner of which, conventionally, all of saṃsāra and nirvāṇa can suitably arise.

A.II. The uncommon presentation from the scriptures of the Vajrayāna

The phenomenon that followers of the Vajrayāna take as the basis for the imputation of the person is buddha nature—the coemergent, stainless kāyas and wisdoms that are present continually through the phases of ground, path, and result. It is on the basis of this buddha nature that they impute the convention of self. From the unanalyzed perspective of what is commonly accepted, when one enters the activities of the Vajrayāna path, that mere imputation of buddha nature is posited as the cause, support, and accomplisher of all of saṃsāra and nirvāṇa.

This buddha nature is also what is posited as the pride of the creation and completion stages. When one engages in the yogas of creation and completion, all impure, confused phenomena do not even exist in a worldly, conventional sense. Rather, they are purified as emptiness.

This stainless buddha nature, the vajra of wisdom, is, even from a mere conventional perspective, something different from the tenability of emptiness as interdependent arising. And it is this very buddha nature that, through Vajrayāna pride, is given the names "I" and "me." As it was said:

> I am the explainer, I am the dharma,
> I am my own audience listening,
> I am the mundane and the supramundane,
> I am the teacher of the world, and I am what is to be accomplished.

Limitless such statements have been made. There are also the presentations such as:

> Sentient beings themselves are buddhas.

Bearing this type of "person" in mind, a great many sublime beings have spoken of "the original, all-pervasive lord," "Vajradhara," "the heruka at the time of the cause," "the original buddha," and so on. Many noble yogis and yoginīs, during the impure stages of ground and path, have skillfully used these conventions. They cannot be defeated by debates from dharma lectures.

The same meaning was also taught in a concealed manner in the Middle Way scriptures that teach the definitive meaning of the sūtras. The noble Maitreya said *(Highest Continuum)*:

> Those who are impure,
> Both pure and impure, and completely pure
> Are referred to as sentient beings, bodhisattvas,
> And buddhas, respectively.

And Nāgārjuna said:

> When one is covered by the mesh of mental afflictions,
> One is called a "sentient being."
> When the same one is free from the mental afflictions,
> He or she is called a "buddha."

Such statements are made in limitless sūtras and tantras. The meaning of those quotations is also detailed extensively in *The Great Single Intention (Gong Chik Chenmo/dgongs gcig chen mo).*[487]

Some also apply the term "the subtle, indestructible bindu endowed with three distinctions" to this buddha nature as it is taught in the Secret Mantra. They say that not only from the perspective of nonanalysis, but also when analyzed, this bindu is the self. However, they continue, when thoroughly analyzed, it is not established as a true self, because this non-establishment is the intention of Chandrakīrti, the master free from extremes.

Though there is no contradiction in applying terms such as "subtle" to buddha nature, it is not tenable to posit it in the context of analysis as the self or to say that it exists in a certain way even when analyzed. If it were tenable to do so, it would absurdly follow that the self can withstand analysis. What could be worse than pretending to first refute the selves of persons and phenomena and then positing them in the end? Furthermore, who would place any trust in the statement, "Under thorough analysis, there is no establishment of a true self: this is the system of the Middle Way as asserted by Chandrakīrti"?

We do posit the causal, coemergent buddha nature as the person from the unanalyzed perspective. However, we also accept that buddha nature is not established as the person or the self in either of the two truths. You, on the other hand, say that buddha nature is established as the self in the relative truth. Therefore you hold a view of self.

When the noble beings of the Vajrayāna engage in the unanalyzed, worldly, relative truth, they use the terms of "person" and "self" in reference to buddha nature. Using terms in this way can only be done by those who have realized the objects of knowledge of the Vajrayāna—the uncommon presentation of the worldly relative truth, which consists of cause, path, and result. Using terms in this way is not to be attempted by those who have not comprehended these points. The use of the label of "self" in reference to buddha nature is not within the sphere of experience of the proponents of relative truth who abide on a worldly plain. This includes ordinary beings whose minds have not been changed by the philosophical systems, non-Buddhists, and Buddhists up to and including the followers of the Pāramitāyāna.

In the context of the Vajrayāna approach, the mode of apprehending of the view of the self takes on two forms: one in which a view of the self arises in dependence upon the aggregates and another in which a view of the self arises in dependence upon buddha nature. Nevertheless, it does not follow that there will be two persons in the mindstream of the viewer of the self. For, when one holds a view of the self in dependence upon the transitory collection, one observes all five aggregates. Yet five persons will not be present in the continuum of the person holding that view.

The following summarizes the way in which the Consequentialist tradition explains how the person is imputed in dependence upon the aggregates, constituents, and sources. Other than those three categories of phenomena, there is no other conventional object of the conception of "I." The person is spoken of in this way in order to present the relative truth on the unanalyzed level. For worldly people fixate on the self in reference solely to the aggregates.

The other explanation of how the person is imputed—the explanation involving the imputation on the basis of true reality—is given to highlight a distinction between realization and nonrealization: when one realizes that persons and all other phenomena are completely bereft of all elaborations and signs, one is posited as a buddha. When one does not realize this, one is posited as a sentient being.

B. The purpose

The master [Shāntideva], the heir of the victorious ones, teaches that the imputation of the person is made so that conventions would be easy to use, even though the person does not substantially exist; so that one may speak in a way that accords with the world; so that sentient beings would not be frightened by the teachings; and so that oneself and others may be described as possessing faults and qualities. The *Ornament of the Sūtras* says:

> The person is taught
> Through the distinctions of the phases of engaging
> The thoroughly afflicted and the completely pure,
> And through the distinctions of entrance and stream.

Buddha nature is posited as the pride of self on the level of no analysis in the Vajrayāna of the great secret. The term "self" is used in this context in order to provide for an unbroken continuity regarding the phases of ground, path, and result.

C. The refutation in actual fact

In both truths, those bases of imputation are *not* the self that would correspond to the imputations placed upon them. When analyzed with reasonings, the person is not established. In particular, if you were to say that buddha nature is the self, you would contradict the ocean of the scriptures of Secret Mantra, in which the self was not spoken of as an existent. For example *(Saying the Names of Mañjushrī, Mañjushrīnāmasaṃghiti, Jampal Tsen Jö/'jam dpal mtshan brjod)*:

> You possess the lion's roar of selflessness.

And:

> Perfect selflessness, suchness . . .

And:

> Complete purity, the dharma of selflessness . . .

The approach of accepting that there is one type of self that exists and another type of self that does not exist was adopted by Indian schools such as the Saṃmitīyas and the Vātsīputrīyas, and by Tibetans such as Bodongwa, the Gelukpas, and the Jonangpas. All of their views in this regard are untenable.

In this Land of Snows, furthermore, some have said that, although the self does not even exist conventionally, the individual, the sentient being, and the person are substantially existent. Some have said that, even though the self is not substantially established, its functioning as the support for actions and their results is not undermined by the valid cognition of reasoning consciousnesses. Some say the self is established by conventional valid cognition. Still others claim that the self is permanent and exists separately from the aggregates. The individual, the sentient being, and so on, they say, are nonexistent.

These positions are contradictory to all the tenets of the Buddhist systems, from the Particularists through the Followers of the Middle Way. If the self did not even exist conventionally, it would be nonsensical to speak of dependent imputation. Such a notion also contradicts both scripture and the worldly perspective. And, as to a notion of the self being substantially existent, if the Particularists do not even assert this, what need is there to mention the higher philosophical systems? Vasubandhu's autocommentary to the *Treasury of Abhidharma (Abhidharmakosha, Chö Ngönpa Dzö/chos mngon pa mdzod)* says:

> Thus the person is an imputed existent, just as in the case of the aggregates and continua.

If the self imputed by the conventional valid cognition of ordinary beings is unassailably established as a support for actions and their results, it would absurdly follow that such a self can withstand analysis. For, it cannot be invalidated by valid reasoning consciousnesses and, furthermore, it can withstand the analysis of conventional valid cognition.

It follows, then, that you accept the existence of an analysis-withstanding self as the support for actions and results. If you accept, it would further follow that it is illogical to refute the self of person when analyzing!

Furthermore, your assertion that the innate self (which exists when not analyzed) is established by conventional valid cognition is illogical. For, firstly, conventional valid cognition is the apprehension by worldly minds of the correct relative truth. And, secondly, although worldly people hold what appears to their minds as real to be valid cognition, it is, in fact, not valid at all. For, in this tradition of the Middle Way, it is held that all minds apprehending the relative are necessarily arisen from deluded ignorance.

The Jonangpas say that the self of ultimate truth exists and is permanent, whereas the relative imputation of the self is, like the horns of a rabbit, utterly nonexistent. In this way they refute even on the conventional level the mere self of no analysis renowned in the relative truth. They also affirm through analysis something that is, actually, utterly nonexistent: a self of the ultimate truth. They commit superimpositions and denigrations in relation to both of the two truths.

Zilung Shākya Chokden asserts that nondual consciousness is the self and that it becomes the self of genuine wisdom at the level of buddhahood. He also says that the Proponents of Mind Only label the dependent nature the "self." Further, he says that there is no confusion in viewing something that is the self as the self. This perception, he says, will not produce obscurations or any other factors to be relinquished. He continues by saying that confusion comes about only when viewing something that is not the self as the self. At that time, the consciousness does not accord with its object. This discord produces obscurations and other factors to be relinquished.

He continues, saying that the imaginary five aggregates—the subjects and objects of the relative—are not the self. Taking them to be the self is the root of saṃsāra. However, ultimate, nondual wisdom is the self, and viewing it as the self is the unsurpassable cause of enlightenment and liberation. Further, the attainment of liberation is equivalent to achieving the status of the genuine self. For scriptural support, he relies on quotations such as the following (*Highest Continuum* and *Ornament of Sūtras*):

> Free of the elaborations of self and selflessness,
> It is the genuine self.

And,

> When emptiness is pure,
> One attains the supreme self of selflessness.
> Since one thus attains the pure self of buddhahood,
> One becomes the self of great self.

Your position is untenable. Those scriptural quotations explain the way of realizing selflessness. They reference the Buddha's actualization of selflessness with the terms such as "actualizing the self." When the genuine beings fully comprehend the freedom from elaborations, the freedom from elaborations is sometimes labeled with the term "self." You, however, simply did not understand this point.

If an ultimate self existed, sentient beings would either have no chance whatever of gaining liberation from saṃsāra or would gain liberation without any effort at all. One of those two situations would absurdly follow. For, firstly, due to the ultimate existence of the self, some beings would be bound in saṃsāra while others would be liberated in nirvāṇa—desire to change this would be impossible. And, secondly, the ultimate self is perceived, according to you, by the perception of a correct consciousness, unlike the self of the relative. Your assertion resembles that of Īshvara!

If a self existed ultimately, this existence would contradict all of the

Transcendent Conqueror's teachings about the selflessness of all phenomena of saṃsāra and nirvāṇa. If, ultimately, nondual wisdom were the self, someone holding the view of a relative self would not view the ultimate self as a self. The nondual wisdom that is the ultimate self would itself be liberation; it could not serve as a *cause* for liberation. Also, one who held the view of a relative self would not be able to even conventionally attain liberation, because there would be no self conventionally. Since you assert nondual wisdom as the paths and grounds, it follows that there is a common locus for persons and paths. It also follows that the traversed is also the traverser. If that nondual wisdom were primordially established as the self, what bigger foolishness could there be in the world than to say that a buddha newly attains his or her buddha-self?

In sum, when explaining this textual tradition one must understand that, in the confused perspective of no analysis, the person, sentient being, and so on exist. In the same way, the mere imputed self exists in a way that is approved by others. When analyzed, however, the self does not exist. And, in the same way, the individual and so on do not exist either. Furthermore, just as vases, sweaters, forests, and so on exist merely conventionally, the imputed self exists in an other-approved way. When analyzed, the self does not exist. All phenomena are like this—they transcend conceptual elaborations.

2.2.2.1.1.6.2.3.1.1.2.3.2.2.2. THE BENEFIT OF UNDERSTANDING THAT: THE REVERSAL OF ALL VIEWS

> Since it is not a thing, the self is not stable or unstable;
> It does not arise or disintegrate;
> It is not permanent, impermanent, both, or neither,
> And is not the same as or different from the aggregates. (6.163)

Phenomena that depend on imputations can in no way be valid supports for conceptions of stability, nonstability, and so on. Therefore the conceptions related to such notions, such as permanence and impermanence, are easy to reverse.

Since the "self" is dependently imputed, it does not inherently exist and is not a thing. Therefore the self is not something stable that had arisen in the past. Nor is it something unstable, born from an unarisen phenomenon in the past. The self does not arise nor does it cease. None of the four properties—permanence, impermanence, and so on,[488]—applies to the self. The self, moreover, is not the same as or different from the aggregates. The following scriptural quotations[489] prove the meaning of the above as follows. The *Treatise* says:

> It is untenable to say
> That the self arose in the past.
> That which arose in the past
> Is not the self of the present. (27.3)

> You think that what arose then is the self
> And that the appropriated are different from it.
> But if your self is not the appropriated,
> What is it?[490] (27.4)

And,

> It did not arise from the unarisen.
> That position involves faulty consequences:
> Either the self would be a product
> Or its arising would be causeless. (27.12)[491]

And,

> The appropriated are not the self,
> For they arise and disintegrate.
> How could that which is appropriated
> Become the appropriator? (27.6)[492]

And,

> Permanence, impermanence, and so on, the four:
> Where are they in this peace?
> Finite, infinite, and so on, the four:
> Where are they in this peace? (22.12)

> There are some who think, "the Tathāgata exists"
> And cling thereto with dense fixation.
> Their thinking imputes,
> "The Tathāgata does not exist in nirvāṇa." (22.13)

Concerning what is naturally empty,
If you think that the Buddha
Does or does not exist after nirvāṇa,
Your thoughts are untenable. (22.14)[493]

And,

If the aggregates were the self,
The self would arise and disintegrate.
If the self were different from the aggregates,
It would not have their defining characteristics. (18.1)[494]

The meaning of those statements is as follows. The attributes such as stability, nonstability, and so forth would arise if they had a real basis for attributes, and they could not arise without such a basis. Since no such basis exists, the self is not a thing. The sūtras teach:

The four inexhaustible phenomena
Were taught by the Protector of the World.
They are sentient beings, space, bodhichitta,
And the qualities of buddhas.

If they existed substantially,
They would be fully exhaustible.
Since they do not, they are inexhaustible.
Therefore they were taught to be inexhaustible.

2.2.2.1.1.6.2.3.1.1.2.3.2.2.3. THE LIBERATION THAT COMES FROM REALIZING THE NONEXISTENCE OF SELF AND ENTITIES CONNECTED TO THE SELF
2.2.2.1.1.6.2.3.1.1.2.3.2.2.3.1. Self and entities connected to the self are merely imputed due to ignorance at the level of no analysis
2.2.2.1.1.6.2.3.1.1.2.3.2.2.3.2. The way of liberation through realizing that those two do not exist

2.2.2.1.1.6.2.3.1.1.2.3.2.2.3.1. SELF AND ENTITIES CONNECTED TO THE SELF ARE MERELY IMPUTED DUE TO IGNORANCE AT THE LEVEL OF NO ANALYSIS

The conception of "I" is always present in beings.
It arises in connection with
The supports for the imputation of the self.
The self that is its object exists only in the ignorant, nonanalyti-
cal perspective of the world. (6.164)

Even though the self cannot be found when analyzed in the seven ways, what is the self that, in the absence of self, circles in saṃsāra due to the view of the transitory collection produced by ignorance? Non-Buddhists cling to the self as being different from the aggregates. Those of our own faction apprehend the self as being either the same as the aggregates or inexpress-ible as the same or different.

The Transcendent Conqueror taught that the mind merely imputes the self on the basis of the aggregates. Other than that, the self has no inher-ent nature. It is in this simple way that the Buddha used the convention of the "self."

The conception of "I," which fixates on such a self, is always present in beings—humans, animals, and all other beings who possess ignorance. The referent object for that conception of "I" is the self, and that which the self controls—the bases upon which it is imputed—are inner phenomena such as the eyes and outer, enjoyed phenomena such as forms. The con-ception of "I" fixates on the self in observation of these phenomena. The self that is the object of that fixation exists in the unanalyzed, ignorant per-spective of what is renowned in the world—it is not established from its own side, by its own entity.

2.2.2.1.1.6.2.3.1.1.2.3.2.2.3.2. THE WAY OF LIBERATION THROUGH REALIZING THAT THOSE TWO DO NOT EXIST

There are no objects of action without performers.
Therefore there are no entities connected to the self without a
self.
Viewing self and entities connected to the self as empty,
Yogis and yoginīs gain complete liberation. (6.165)

Conventions of the self are used despite the fact that the self does not inherently exist. Realizing this, the yogis and yoginīs do not observe the self. Since they do not observe the self, they also do not observe entities connected to the selves, which depend on the self. The yogis and yoginīs, therefore, gain liberation from saṃsāra, for they do not observe any things. As the *Treatise* teaches:

> If thinking of the inner and the outer
> As "me" and "mine" is exhausted,
> Appropriation will cease.
> When that is exhausted, birth is also exhausted. (18.4)

How is it that, since the self does not exist, entities connected to the selves are also nonexistent? Without a craftsperson there can be no clay vase. Accordingly, without a performer there are no objects of action, for the objects of action are labeled as such in dependence upon the objects toward which the performer's actions are directed.

Therefore there are no entities connected to self without the self existing as a performer. For this reason the yogis and yoginīs view the aggregates as being empty of self and entities connected to self. Since in this way they do not observe saṃsāra, these yogis and yoginīs gain complete liberation. Since they do not see forms and so on, they have no thoughts of attachment and so on toward those phenomena. In this context the hearers and solitary realizers pass into nirvāṇa free from the appropriated aggregates. The bodhisattvas, even though they realize selflessness, maintain the continuity of their existence out of compassion.

2.2.2.1.1.6.2.3.1.1.2.3.3. THEREFORE ALL OTHER PHENOMENA OF THE SAME TYPE ARE MERELY IMPUTATIONS
2.2.2.1.1.6.2.3.1.1.2.3.3.1. All things are imputed in dependence
2.2.2.1.1.6.2.3.1.1.2.3.3.2. The special examination of causes and results

2.2.2.1.1.6.2.3.1.1.2.3.3.1. ALL THINGS ARE IMPUTED IN DEPENDENCE
2.2.2.1.1.6.2.3.1.1.2.3.3.1.1. Things, although unfindable when analyzed, are posited through mere imputation
2.2.2.1.1.6.2.3.1.1.2.3.3.1.2. No conventions are in contradiction with the two truths

2.2.2.1.1.6.2.3.1.1.2.3.3.1.1. THINGS, ALTHOUGH UNFINDABLE WHEN ANALYZED, ARE POSITED THROUGH MERE IMPUTATION

> Vases, sweaters, canvases, armies, forests, rosaries, trees,
> Houses, chariots, hotels, and so on—
> All these things should be accepted in the way they are labeled by
>   beings,
> Because the Lord of Sages did not dispute with the world. (6.166)

The self and its appropriated aggregates are equivalent to the analysis of the chariot and its constituent parts. This verse teaches how all other things follow the same logic. Vases, sweaters, canvases, armies, forests, rosaries, trees, houses, chariots, hotels, and so on—all the things there are—do not exist when analyzed in the seven ways, just as in the case of the chariot. Apart from that nonexistence, these things are posited to exist by worldly consensus in dependence upon the collection of their parts.

For this simple reason, phenomena should be posited without analysis in a way that accords with how beings employ conventions in the world. For the Lord of Sages did not dispute or engage in polemics with the world. As he said:

> The world may dispute with me, but I do not dispute with the
> world.

This quotation explains how, on the conventional level, the consensus of the world should not be refuted.

2.2.2.1.1.6.2.3.1.1.2.3.3.1.2. NO CONVENTIONS ARE IN CONTRADICTION WITH THE TWO TRUTHS

> Parts, qualities, desire, characteristics, firewood, and so on
> And part-possessors, quality-possessors, desirous ones, bases of
>   characteristics, fire, and so on,
> If analyzed in seven ways as in the case of the chariot, do not
>   exist.
> Apart from that, they exist by way of what is renowned in the
>   world. (6.167)

Parts, qualities, desire, characteristics, firewood, and so on correspond respectively with part-possessors, quality-possessors, desired ones, bases of characteristics, fire, and so on. All of these, when analyzed in seven ways as in the case of the chariot, do not exist. Apart from that analysis, that is, in the unanalyzed perspective of what is renowned in the world, the conventions of all of these phenomena exist.

In that unanalyzed perspective, a vase is a part-possessor, and dirt and so on are its parts. A vase is a quality-possessor, and drawings of flames, the color of light blue, and so on are its qualities. A vase is a basis of characteristics, and the bulbous belly, high aperture, long neck, and so on are its characteristics. Similar distinctions can be drawn with regard to the sweater and so forth.

Desire is a mental event that features strong clinging. The desirous one is the mind or person that is the support for such desire. Fire is that which burns and firewood is what is burnt. If something among these phenomena acts as a cause for its parts, it is labeled as the part-possessor. The label "part" is given in turn in dependence upon the part-possessor. All these properties are equivalent to the chariot example.

Fire is posited as fire in dependence upon firewood; firewood is posited as firewood in dependence upon fire. All things in between are the same. Similarly, all phenomena imputed dependently—subject and object, phenomena and their true reality, and so on—are merely worldly conventions. They cannot withstand the analysis of reasoning. Therefore, understand that none of these phenomena contradict the two truths.

2.2.2.1.1.6.2.3.1.1.2.3.3.2. THE SPECIAL EXAMINATION OF CAUSES AND RESULTS
2.2.2.1.1.6.2.3.1.1.2.3.3.2.1. Causes and results are merely mutually dependent
2.2.2.1.1.6.2.3.1.1.2.3.3.2.2. The refutation of the substantial establishment of causes and results

2.2.2.1.1.6.2.3.1.1.2.3.3.2.1. CAUSES AND RESULTS ARE MERELY MUTUALLY DEPENDENT
2.2.2.1.1.6.2.3.1.1.2.3.3.2.1.1. The actual teaching
2.2.2.1.1.6.2.3.1.1.2.3.3.2.1.2. The illogicality of causes and results not being mutually dependent

2.2.2.1.1.6.2.3.1.1.2.3.3.2.1.1. THE ACTUAL TEACHING

> Something is a cause only if it produces a result,
> And if it does not, there is no reason for it to be called a cause.
> Results, as well, arise only if they have causes. (6.168abc)

Just as parts and so on are established in dependence, causes and results are also established in dependence. Something is a cause only if it produces a result. If a cause does not produce a result, then, since its result is nonexistent, the term "cause" will not apply. If something could be a cause without having a reason to posit it as a cause, it would follow that everything would be a cause. Whether or not something is a cause follows after whether or not it produces a result.

Results, as well, arise only if they have causes. Without causes, they do not arise. Therefore, causes and results are posited in mutual dependence: they do not exist by way of their own individual natures.

2.2.2.1.1.6.2.3.1.1.2.3.3.2.1.2. THE ILLOGICALITY OF CAUSES AND RESULTS NOT BEING MUTUALLY DEPENDENT

> Therefore, state which would arise from which, and which would be the prior support for which! (6.168d)

If you think that causes and results are established by their own entities, which would be established first—the cause or the result? Which would arise later? Which would be the prior support for the other? State your response! Since you cannot possibly have a response, understand that the imputations of causes and results are just as they were explained in the case of the chariot example. Causes and results do not exist in their own entities.

2.2.2.1.1.6.2.3.1.1.2.3.3.2.2. THE REFUTATION OF THE SUBSTANTIAL ESTABLISHMENT OF CAUSES AND RESULTS
2.2.2.1.1.6.2.3.1.1.2.3.3.2.2.1. The actual teaching
2.2.2.1.1.6.2.3.1.1.2.3.3.2.2.2. Relinquishing objections that our critiques equivalently apply to us

2.2.2.1.1.6.2.3.1.1.2.3.3.2.2.1. THE ACTUAL TEACHING
2.2.2.1.1.6.2.3.1.1.2.3.3.2.2.1.1. The refutation through examining contact versus noncontact

2.2.2.1.1.6.2.3.1.1.2.3.3.2.2.1.2. Causes without a basis for the positing of causes are untenable

2.2.2.1.1.6.2.3.1.1.2.3.3.2.2.1.3. Followers of the Middle Way do not incur the fault of contradiction

2.2.2.1.1.6.2.3.1.1.2.3.3.2.2.1.1. THE REFUTATION THROUGH EXAMINING CONTACT VERSUS NONCONTACT

> If, for you, causes produced results by contacting them,
> Since the two would have the same potential, there would be no
> difference between the producer and its result.
> If causes did not contact results, they would be undifferentiable
> from noncauses.
> There is no third concept that could apply to the relationship.
> (6.169)

Let us investigate the connection between causes and results further. If causes inherently produce results, do they produce results through coming into contact with the results? Or do they not contact the results at all?

In the first case, if for you causes produced results by contacting them, those two would be, like a river flowing into the ocean, inseparable. The causes and results would have the same potential. It would be impossible to classify them separately, saying, "This, the cause, is the producer, whereas this, the result, is what was produced."

In the second case, if causes and results did not come into contact, but rather a result arose from the situation of the two being separate, either no results would be produced at all (just like a rice seed does not produce a barley sprout because it does not come into contact with that sprout) or, alternatively, all causes and noncauses would produce all results and nonresults. For, all of these situations are equivalent with respect to their not entailing any contact. Causes, therefore, would become equivalent with noncauses.

Yet those consequences are not what you assert. And, furthermore, if causes and results are to inherently exist, they must exist in one of these two contexts: either the produced and the producer come into contact with each other or they do not. There is no third concept that could apply to the relationship.

In conclusion, production does not take place in a context of inherently existent causes and results.

2.2.2.1.1.6.2.3.1.1.2.3.3.2.2.1.2. Causes without a basis for the positing of causes are untenable

If your causes do not produce results, there is nothing to call a "result."
Therefore there is no cause devoid of a result. (6.170ab)

If your causes do not produce results, that which is called a "result" would not exist. Since the result would not exist, a cause, devoid of a "result," would be devoid of reason for the term "cause." For the application of the term "cause" arises in dependence upon the presence of results. There are no existent causes that do not have a reason for achieving such status. Causes and results, therefore, do not exist inherently.

2.2.2.1.1.6.2.3.1.1.2.3.3.2.2.1.3. Followers of the Middle Way do not incur the fault of contradiction

Since both causes and results are like illusions,
These faults do not apply to us, and, for the worldly perspective, things exist. (6.170cd)

In the Middle Way system, how does a cause produce a result? The above analyses are to be applied to those who speak of inherently existent causes and results. According to us, however, all things are produced due to erroneous imagination. Both causes and results are devoid of arising, like illusions.

Nevertheless, one should not analyze the things that are the objects of beings' conceptions and are like the strands of hair seen by those with blurry vision. For this reason, the faults revealed by the analysis of the contact versus the noncontact of causes and results do not apply to us Followers of the Middle Way. The unanalyzed appearances of things in the world, moreover, exist for others. Saying that things exist in this way is irrefutable.

2.2.2.1.1.6.2.3.1.1.2.3.3.2.2.2. Relinquishing objections that our critiques equivalently apply to us
2.2.2.1.1.6.2.3.1.1.2.3.3.2.2.2.1. The counterparts' position
2.2.2.1.1.6.2.3.1.1.2.3.3.2.2.2.2. The response

2.2.2.1.1.6.2.3.1.1.2.3.3.2.2.2.1. THE COUNTERPARTS' POSITION
2.2.2.1.1.6.2.3.1.1.2.3.3.2.2.2.1.1. Their description of the equivalence
2.2.2.1.1.6.2.3.1.1.2.3.3.2.2.2.1.2. Their conclusion that ours is not a valid refutation
2.2.2.1.1.6.2.3.1.1.2.3.3.2.2.2.1.3. Their claims about other faults of ours

2.2.2.1.1.6.2.3.1.1.2.3.3.2.2.2.1.1. THEIR DESCRIPTION OF THE EQUIVALENCE

"Does your refutation refute its intended target through
contacting it, or does your refutation involve no contact?
The faults you ascribe to us equally apply to your own logic."
(6.171ab)

Our counterparts might retort: "You ask, 'Do causes and results arise through contact or through noncontact,' but your logic applies equally to yourselves! You Followers of the Middle Way use a means of refutation that attempts to refute the notion that causes and results are established by their own entities. Yet do your means of refutation come into contact with what is to be refuted? Or do they refute the target of refutation by not contacting it?

"If you choose the first option, the means of refutation and the target of the refutation would have the same potential; they would not be separate. In the second option, the object of refutation and the means of refutation would not come into contact. Therefore it would either be impossible to refute the object of refutation or everything would refute everything.

"The faults that you have ascribed to us, therefore, would also become undesired consequences for you. For, just as you have said, apart from the two concepts of contact and noncontact, there is no third concept that could apply to the relationship between the object of refutation and the means of refutation."

2.2.2.1.1.6.2.3.1.1.2.3.3.2.2.2.1.2. THEIR CONCLUSION THAT OURS IS NOT A VALID REFUTATION

"When arguing in that way, you defeat only your own position.
You are incapable of refuting your desired object of refutation."
(6.171cd)

"When arguing in that way, asking whether causes and results are produced through contact or noncontact, your debates that analyze causes and results become equally applicable to your own method of debate, as we have explained above. You defeat only your own position, the means of refutation you use to refute your desired object of refutation.

"You Followers of the Middle Way are incapable of refuting your desired object of refutation—inherently existent causes and results—with your chosen means of refutation. Since you refute your own means of refutation of the opposite, we can conclude that causes and results are established inherently."

2.2.2.1.1.6.2.3.1.1.2.3.3.2.2.2.1.3. THEIR CLAIMS ABOUT OTHER FAULTS OF OURS

> "Your words, which contain consequences that equally apply to you, express frivolous arguments.
> With them, you illogically denigrate all things.
> Therefore, noble beings will not accept you,
> Because you are just quibblers with no position of your own."
> (6.172)

"There are further faults. The words of refutation of you Followers of the Middle Way express frivolous arguments and are merely seeming refutations. They contain consequences (the analysis of contact versus noncontact) that equally apply to your logic.

"With these words, you illogically denigrate all things by analyzing whether causes and results, which exist as things, come into contact or not. It is untenable for you to say, 'Causes that do not contact their results could produce any result randomly, because random results would be equivalent with respect to not contacting their causes.' For, although all things are equivalent in not coming into contact with each other, production does happen distinctly, as in the following examples.

"Magnets attract metals that are in their vicinity and suitable to be attracted by them. Eyes apprehend forms that are in their vicinity and suitable to be apprehended by the eyes. Similarly, causes produce results without coming into contact with them, but they do not produce everything with which they have no contact. Rather, causes only produce the results that are specifically suitable to them.

"Since you Followers of the Middle Way illogically denigrate all things, noble beings will not accept you. Not only that—you are quibblers[495] *(sun chi chin du golwa/sun ci phyin du rgol ba)* because you have utterly no position of your own but rather endeavor only to defeat the positions of others. Someone who cannot posit their own position yet argues only to defeat the positions of others is called a 'quibbler.' Your arguments will cause only laughter and will end up being fruitless efforts."

2.2.2.1.1.6.2.3.1.1.2.3.3.2.2.2.2.2. THE RESPONSE
2.2.2.1.1.6.2.3.1.1.2.3.3.2.2.2.2.2.1. The reasons why our consequences do not equally apply to us
2.2.2.1.1.6.2.3.1.1.2.3.3.2.2.2.2.2.2. Proving by example how a refutation can accomplish its intended purpose, even though it is devoid of inherent nature
2.2.2.1.1.6.2.3.1.1.2.3.3.2.2.2.2.2.3. It is unreasonable to refute the assertions of others if you have not understood what those assertions are
2.2.2.1.1.6.2.3.1.1.2.3.3.2.2.2.2.2.4. It is unreasonable to invalidate the worldly perspective by casting away a good path and taking up a bad one
2.2.2.1.1.6.2.3.1.1.2.3.3.2.2.2.2.2.5. There are a great many other ways to refute your position

2.2.2.1.1.6.2.3.1.1.2.3.3.2.2.2.2.2.1. THE REASONS WHY OUR CONSEQUENCES DO NOT EQUALLY APPLY TO US

> When you ask, "When your refutation refutes its intended
>   object, does it contact it or not,"
> The fault that you ascribe to us
> Will only apply to those who hold a definite position;
> Since we do not hold such a position, it is impossible for this
>   consequence to apply to us. (6.173)

We provide the following response to the above objections of our counterparts.

You asked, "When your refutation refutes its intended object, does it contact it or not," adding that our words contain consequences and frivolous arguments that apply equally to ourselves. However, the fault that you ascribe to us will only apply to those who hold a definite position, in which the refutation and the object of refutation are both held to be inherently existent.

We Followers of the Middle Way do not hold any position of the primordial existence of the refutation and its intended object. Therefore it is impossible for the consequences of our own words to apply equally to us. We neither say nor think that refutations accomplish their intended purpose with regard to their targets by way of coming into contact or not coming into contact. This point is taught in the sūtras:[496]

> "Venerable Subhūti, will an unarisen attainment be attained due to an arisen quality, or will an unarisen attainment be attained due to an unarisen quality?"

> "Venerable Shāriputra, I do not assert that unarisen attainments will be attained due to arisen qualities, nor do I assert that unarisen attainments will be attained due to unarisen qualities." To this, Shāriputra replied,

> "Venerable Subhūti, is it the case that there are no attainments, and that there are no clear realizations?" Subhūti answered,

> "Venerable Shāriputra, indeed attainments exist, and clear realizations exist. But they do not exist in the manner of duality. Venerable Shāriputra, attainments and clear realizations exist as worldly conventions, and stream enterers, once-returners, nonreturners, arhats, solitary realizers, and bodhisattvas exist as worldly conventions. Ultimately, there are no attainments, and there are no clear realizations."

Since such extensive statements have been made, we refute the attainment or nonattainment and the arisen or unarisen qualities in both truths. Nevertheless, we allow for the mere appearance of things from the unanalyzed, first-glance perspective. In worldly conventions, the term "attainment" is used with regard to mere false appearances and deceiving phenomena. Those phenomena are not established by the valid cognition of the noble ones' wisdom, nor are they established by the valid cognition of reasoning consciousnesses.

Accordingly, there is no truly existent refutation that either contacts or does not contact its object. Yet from the worldly, conventional, unanalyzed perspective, a means of refutation refutes an object of refutation. Thus, we posit our refutations in dependence upon worldly convention.

It is necessary to understand that this manner of refutation is like an emanation refuting an emanation, an illusion refuting an illusion, logic in a dream refuting that which is illogical in a dream, and brightness dispelling darkness.

There are some who have not realized this profound mode of dharma of the Middle Way. They say that deceiving, confused, and false phenomena (objects of the eyes such as forms, pillars, and so on), which are similar to the two moons seen by someone with impaired vision, are real in the sense that they are established by conventional valid cognition. Apprehending them as real, moreover, is not clinging to true existence; it is the correct view of the Middle Way. Clinging to true existence, they say, is different from that: in order to cling to true existence, one must cling to the true existence that does not exist among knowable objects.

The view of these scholars is a long distance from the dharma of the Middle Way. Oh my! If you are dedicated to liberation, it would be better to first exert yourself in purifying misdeeds and gathering the two accumulations!

At this section of its commentary, the great *Ṭīkā* presents verses that summarize the topics of the objects of refutation by reasons, the two truths, and so on. They begin with the following verses:[497]

> If the objects of refutation by reasons—the self and true
>   existence—
> Did not exist among knowable objects, the appearance of self and
>   true existence as knowable objects
> And the perception of them would not be relative truth.
> Therefore, the objects of refutation by reasons—
> The self and true existence—would not exist even in the worldly
>   perspective.
>
> If you accept that, it follows that all worldly people
> Effortlessly realize the view of the Middle Way.

They conclude with the following verses:

If the mind becomes confused regarding an object that utterly does
    not exist,
The horns of a rabbit would also become the observed objects of
    the confusion of sentient beings.
Since the objects of refutation, the self and true existence, exist for
    the confused perspective when there is no analysis,
There is no self and no true existence in either of the truths that
    exist free from confusion.

I feel compassion for you, who, losing sight of what to hold as your
    own Middle Way tenets,
Wind up not knowing what to say at all.

One should consult those verses, which speak to some important points
and are the essence of eloquent explanations.

2.2.2.1.1.6.2.3.1.1.2.3.3.2.2.2.2.2. PROVING BY EXAMPLE HOW A REFUTATION CAN ACCOMPLISH ITS INTENDED PURPOSE, EVEN THOUGH IT IS DEVOID OF INHERENT NATURE

When the sun is reflected in a pool of water, its attributes,
Such as eclipses, are clearly seen in the reflection.
Although it is illogical for the sun and its reflection to have con-
    tact or no contact,
The mere convention of "the reflection" arises in a dependent
    way. (6.174)

Even though it is not real, a reflection can help beautify one's
    face.
In the same way, in order to clean the face of supreme knowledge,
Arguments are used whose ability to refute or affirm can be
    witnessed.
Although they lack ultimate tenability, understand that these
    arguments can help us realize an object of affirmation. (6.175)

The meaning above will now be clarified by two examples.
    The sun in the sky, with attributes such as an eclipse, can be reflected in
a clear pool of water. In the reflection as well one can clearly see the attri-

butes of the original sun, such as the eclipse. It is illogical, nevertheless, for the sun and the water upon which the reflection depends to have contact or no contact.

If they met when the reflection arose, it would absurdly follow that there would be no sun in the sky. If they did not meet, that is, if the reflection arose without a connection to the sun, it would absurdly follow that there would need to be some other, intermediary substance to make the connection between the sun and the reflection. Therefore, when analysis is applied, not the slightest "reflection" can be found. When analyzed, the existence of the reflection is illogical.

Nevertheless, when there is no analysis, there does arise the mere convention of a "reflection." This convention arises in dependence upon the conditions of clear water and the celestial body of the sun. Even though the reflection has no nature of being a sun, one can still definitely cognize the sun's reflection, along with the eclipse and so on.

In harmony with the above example, even while the means and object of refutation are not established at all in terms of having contact or no contact, it is renowned in the conventional world that a means of refutation can refute an object of refutation. There is a second example that can clarify this point further.

A face appearing in a mirror does not truly exist as a face. Nevertheless, one may depend on a mirror to beautify one's face. This is the way in which the reflection of the face exists when there is no analysis. Similarly, in this context of refuting the assertions of others using the very assertions that they accept, the face of the opponent's supreme knowledge is dirty with the stains of ignorance. To purify those stains there are other-approved arguments that possess tangible abilities.

These means of refutation, which are empty by nature, can refute objects of refutation from the perspective of others. We can also see the ability of certain means of affirmation, which are empty by nature, to affirm certain objects of affirmation. Such arguments are devoid of the ultimate tenability of having inherently established modes of logic. Yet it should be understood that one can affirm and realize an object of affirmation by relying on something devoid of inherent nature.

As to the use of the example of reflections in a mirror to illustrate the lack of inherent existence of all phenomena, there are some, such as Shar Tsongkapa, who say that such an example is not used to illustrate that things are empty of being established bases that perform functions. Rather, he says, the example shows the emptiness of the objects of refutation by reasons. He says that although reflections are established as entities of reflections, the reflection of a face is not established as a face. This reflection's lack of being a face, he concludes, is what is illustrated by the mirror example.

However, his interpretation has been thoroughly refuted by those who possess the eyes of dharma. The master Bhavabhaḍa, in his *Commentary to the Vajra Ḍākinī (Dorje Kandrö Drelpa/rdo rje mkha' 'gro'i 'grel pa)*,[498] says:

> Reflections and so on, as well, are not suitable as things.[499]

Since we Followers of the Middle Way do not accept either the inherent establishment of a means of refutation or that of an object of refutation, there are no contradictions in the words we use. Further, we merely posit the means and objects of refutation as imputations from the perspective of no analysis. If you pretentiously attempt to respond to a Follower of the Middle Way by saying, "In your refutations, do the object and means of refutation, which are both substantially established, contact each other, or do they not contact each other," you will not have much of a chance. For as Āryadeva said:

> Since we do not have a position
> Of existence, nonexistence, or both,
> Even if this is the case for a long period of time,
> One still will not be able criticize us.

And, the *Treatise* says:

> When debating against the view of emptiness,
> Whatever answers one provides
> Will not run counter to our position.
> Rather, they will be equivalent to our object of affirmation.

The first of the above verses shows that Followers of the Middle Way are free of faults. The second verse shows that it is impossible to respond successfully to the Followers of the Middle Way in debate, and that the Followers of the Middle Way are able to dispel all misconceptions of others. The Followers of the Middle Way are free from positions, theses, and assertions; this has already been extensively explained.

That which brings about understanding of the refutation of an object of refutation, or in other words, an object of clarification, is a "clarifier." Furthermore, in terms of whether the object and means of refutation have contact or no contact, if one analyzes, one finds that both are devoid of inherent nature. Yet, when there is no analysis, the action of refutation is tenable. This process is taught to be similar to the process of a cause producing a result: if one analyzes whether the cause and result have contact or no contact, one finds that they are devoid of inherent nature. Yet, when there is no analysis, the cause and production are considered tenable.

Bhāvaviveka takes a different approach to responding to the debates of the Proponents of Things. He says, "The *Treatise on the Middle Way* deals here with the context of analyzing the causes and results of production by asking whether the two contact each other or not. The task of this analysis is to refute an inherent nature of causes and results.

"However, it is different for causes that are clarifiers as opposed to causes that are producers. Clarifiers merely refute and reverse wrong conceptions. They have no direct role in production, as in the case of a cause producing a result.

"Therefore, the analysis of contact or no contact does not apply in an equivalent way to Middle Way reasonings. The Proponents of Things claim that this analysis applies in an equivalent way, but the analysis, in actuality, only applies to causes that have direct roles in production. There is no opportunity, therefore, for the Proponents of Things to accuse me, Bhāvaviveka, of spurious arguments."

However, Bhāvaviveka has failed to shut the door of opportunity for his dialectical counterparts, the Proponents of Things. His counterparts analyze the causes and results of production with the thought in mind that those two inherently exist. In the same way, they will equally analyze the causes of clarification with the thought in mind that they inherently exist.

The Proponents of Things assert, as part of their own system, that both the means and the objects of refutation are real in themselves. Responding to them in the manner of Bhāvaviveka, therefore, will not relinquish their claims to fault, namely that Middle Way refutations are spurious because they equally apply to themselves. They will simply say, "Your response attempting to relinquish faults is illogical."

For us Consequentialists, on the other hand, the means and objects of refutation have no inherent nature under analysis. Nevertheless, when there is no analysis, we posit them. In this way it is never possible for us to be refuted by claims of our own spuriousness.[500]

Furthermore, Bhāvaviveka misses the key purpose of the *Treatise*: to refute the misconceptions of others using arguments that are approved by worldly people. Instead, he claims that the "theses" of the *Treatise* must be affirmed using arguments from one's own system. He proceeds to defend his reasons, and the inclusion of his reasons in their predicates, from the counterparts' claims of falsehood.

His approach is nothing more than a target for the refutations of the Proponents of Things. For he asserts that, conventionally and in his own system, his reasons, examples, and so on are established by valid cognition. By so asserting, he does a great deal of harm to his endeavor of establishing that all phenomena are free from elaborations—whatever proofs and probanda he uses, since they come from his own system conventionally, will become elaborations that he does not pacify.

In the approach of we who follow Chandrakīrti, it is impossible, even conventionally, for our arguments and so on to be established by any valid cognition of our own system. Nevertheless, for others, and in order to refute the extreme elaborations, we use the valid cognition approved without analysis in the world, such as the argument of beyond one or many. Through this, we refute truly existent arising. This approach alone is beautiful, for none of our counterparts can refute it, and, since we posit no system of our own, we remain free from any contradictions.

The following, then, summarizes the distinction between the Consequentialist and Autonomist Followers of the Middle Way. The Consequentialist approach is, on the conventional level, to explain, debate, and write about the scriptures of the victorious ones, such as the scriptures that teach the Middle Way, in order to reverse the misconceptions of others. When doing so, the scriptures and reasonings used to effect such reversals do not have an inherent nature even conventionally. However, the Consequentialists repeat the valid cognition that is accepted in the world. The result of this is that not only ultimately but in the worldly relative as well the genuine existence of all phenomena is refuted.

The Autonomist approach is the opposite of that. The arguments used to reverse misconceptions about the ultimate have no ultimate nature of being established by valid cognition. Nevertheless, they say, if one does not accept conventionally the establishment by valid cognition of the reasons and so forth, one will be incapable of reversing the misconceptions of the Proponents of Things.

The above, and only the above, represents the distinction between the Consequentialists' and the Autonomists' Middle Way tenets. Others have claimed differences between the two schools in terms of the way they posit conventional reality when there is no analysis. But their explanations of conventional reality in that regard are not grounds for claiming a separation between their tenets. There are other, more profound, distinctions.

Those who propound the distinctions related to the two schools' positions on the status of conventional reality have no logic to back their arguments. For, their explanations contradict all of the teachings on the worldly relative of all of the past masters of the Consequentialist and Autonomist traditions.

2.2.2.1.1.6.2.3.1.1.2.3.3.2.2.2.2.3. IT IS UNREASONABLE TO REFUTE THE ASSERTIONS OF OTHERS IF YOU HAVE NOT UNDERSTOOD WHAT THOSE ASSERTIONS ARE

> If the arguments that produce the understanding of our objects
>   of affirmation were established as things,
> And if the objects of affirmation actually existed as something to
>   be understood,
> The reasonings of contact and so on would be applicable to us.
> But since they do not exist, your complaints bring about only
>   your own dejection. (6.176)

Furthermore, if our arguments, which produce an understanding of the objects of affirmation in our system, were established as things, and if those objects of affirmation were objectively and inherently established as objects with the potential to be understood, only then would the reasonings of contact, no contact, and so on be applicable. Only then would those arguments actually refute our reasonings.

Yet for us inherently established reasons and so on do not exist. You rely on the illogicality of your own system to criticize as illogical something

424 FEAST FOR THE FORTUNATE – GROUND SIX: THE MANIFEST

that is free from fault. Your complaints will bring about only your own dejection. For example, the strands of hair of those with diseased vision do not invalidate the visual perceptions of those with healthy eyes. Since we, who posit causes and results when not analyzing an inherent nature, ascribe faults to you, who propound inherently existent causes and results, how could we be refuted?

When the Proponents of Things attack the Followers of the Middle Way, they prop themselves up with the delusion of their own thoughts. They think the Followers of the Middle Way must definitely hold assertions that mirror their own. They think that, just as they do, the Followers of the Middle Way must hold their own objects of affirmation, means of affirmation, objects of refutation, and means of refutation. Since this is the outlook with which they debate us, they fail completely to understand their opponents. They set up an imaginary opponent of their own conceptual creation and refute him instead!

For this reason it is also reasonable to refute the Proponents of Things' examples—such as those of the eye and the magnet—of instances of non-contact that still yield results. Our consequences apply equally to those examples. For, as the *Treatise* says:

> If a candle flame dispels darkness
> Without contacting the darkness,
> It would follow that the darkness of the entire world
> Could be dispelled by this one candle.

And, from the *Reversal of Objections*:

> If fire dispels darkness
> Without contacting it,
> This fire here
> Would dispel the darkness of the entire world.

2.2.2.1.1.6.2.3.1.1.2.3.3.2.2.2.2.4. IT IS UNREASONABLE TO INVALIDATE THE WORLDLY PERSPECTIVE BY CASTING AWAY A GOOD PATH AND TAKING UP A BAD ONE

Our examples are able to easily bring about the realization
That all things are nothings.

> Yet you have no method by which you can conveniently cause
> others to understand that things possess an inherent nature.
> Why entrust worldly people to the web of your bad logic? (6.177)

The examples of illusions, dreams, reflections, and so on, which are established for worldly people themselves, have an ability to easily bring about the realization that all things are nothings. You, on the other hand, have no method by which you can easily produce in others the understanding that things possess an inherent nature. For you do not have an example to prove that thesis that is accepted by both worldly people and yourselves.

It does not matter who sent you here to invalidate what is renowned in the world. You ensconce yourselves in the cocoon of the innate mental afflictions, and, on top of that, you wrap yourselves in the sturdy mesh of the imputed ignorance of bad logic. Why should anyone entrust worldly people to you? By trusting you, they will only add to their misconceptions which existed previously in relation to the nature of things. Even if they do not trust you, they will still be bound by their beginningless fixation on the conceptual elaborations. By these elaborations they are driven crazy, tossed about in cycles on the violent waves of saṃsāra's ocean of suffering. Both they and you are objects of compassion.

Since your claims to the spuriousness of our logic are themselves illogical, you should abandon them.

2.2.2.1.1.6.2.3.1.1.2.3.3.2.2.2.2.5. THERE ARE A GREAT MANY OTHER WAYS TO REFUTE YOUR POSITION

> Having understood the rest of the refutations taught above,
> Employ them in response to the positions of contact and so on.
> How it is that we who are not quibblers
> Should be understood from our position as it was just explained.
> (6.178)

Many refutations have been presented above by this text. They speak to those who assert an inherent existence of things. To teach the selflessness of phenomena, the text presented dependent arising. To teach the selflessness of persons, the text presented dependent imputation. The text also explained the refutation of the four extreme types of the arising of things and the sevenfold analysis as well.

One should understand and remember these refutations. Then, in response to the objections of others who say, "Do the causes and results [of your refutations] contact each other, or do they have no contact," one should respond as follows: "The means and objects of refutation do not arise in any of the four extreme ways. Nor can they be discovered under the sevenfold analysis. Nor can any genuine refutation be observed under the analysis of contact or no contact. However, without analysis and in order to reverse the misconceptions of others, a refutation takes place." This is the way in which you should refute those objections.

Under the examinations of the four extremes, the sevenfold analysis, contact or no contact, and so on, arising, discovering, and refutations are not established. Nevertheless, there is no contradiction in employing the conventions of arising, discovering, and refutations on the level of no analysis.

How is it that we are not quibblers? We simply reverse the incorrect thoughts of others; we do not posit our own position and then dispel the position of someone else. For, we do not observe even the slightest thing to dispel. We Followers of the Middle Way are not quibblers: we do not simply refrain from positing our own position even though we have one, nor do we believe that the positions of others which we refute exist.

Through extra refutations that have been just explained one may understand our position: that we have no position, and therefore our consequences are not reflexively applicable to ourselves.

2.2.2.1.1.6.2.3.1.2. THE SUMMARY OF THE TWO TYPES OF SELFLESSNESS[501]

So that beings may be liberated, the Buddha taught two types of selflessness:
The selflessness of phenomena and the selflessness of persons.
(6.179ab)

The verses beginning with

Things do not arise from themselves; how could they arise from others? (8a)

and ending with

... And then analyze, you will be liberated. (119d)

have clearly explained the selflessness of phenomena. The verses beginning with

> Seeing with their intelligence that all mental afflictions and
> faults... (120a)

and continuing up to this point have extensively clarified the selflessness of persons. After concluding such extensive explanations, Chandrakīrti now wishes to summarize the teaching on selflessness in general and state the two classifications of emptiness.

Thus, to summarize this selflessness: so that his students, sentient beings, could be liberated from the mental afflictions and the cognitive obscurations, the Transcendent Conqueror taught two classifications of selflessness: the selflessness of phenomena and the selflessness of persons. He taught the selflessness of persons in order to liberate the hearers and solitary realizers, and, so that the bodhisattvas may attain omniscience, he taught both forms of selflessness.

You may ask, "Is it not the case that hearers and solitary realizers as well realize the selflessness of phenomena?" Hearers and solitary realizers do see the mere conditionality of dependent arising. Nevertheless, they have not gained complete familiarity with the selflessness of phenomena. This is so because they do not take up the benefit of sentient beings and because they do not fully realize knowable objects.

Through habituating themselves for a short time in the phenomenal selflessness of the aggregates, constituents, and sources of their own continua, they relinquish merely the mental afflictions related to engagement in the three realms. They have, on the other hand, cultivated complete familiarity with the selflessness of persons.

Bodhisattvas, over many countless eons, train in the limitless qualities of relative bodhichitta, which is a cause for the attainment of buddhahood. These qualities are mixed inseparably to be of one taste with the phenomenon of ultimate bodhichitta, also a cause for the attainment of buddhahood. Through training in those two forms of bodhichitta, their familiarity with selflessness increases, because they gather the accumulation of merit in a way that equals the number of phenomena involved in the two bodhichittas.

As the end result of this familiarity, the bodhisattvas attain the vast and profound dharmakāya of the Buddha. The hearers and solitary realizers, on the other hand, do not unite their understanding of selflessness with the vast and profound phenomena that are the factors of enlightenment and that bring about the attainment of genuine, perfect buddhahood. Cultivating the two bodhichittas in a fragmented way, they enter into the expanse of liberation. Even though [from a cognitive standpoint] they arrive at the pinnacle of the realization of phenomenal selflessness, they do not attain even one quality of the dharmakāya.

2.2.2.1.1.6.2.3.2. THE EXPLANATION BY WAY OF THE SIXTEEN
EMPTINESSES[502]
2.2.2.1.1.6.2.3.2.1. Making the link
2.2.2.1.1.6.2.3.2.2. Explaining the meaning

2.2.2.1.1.6.2.3.2.1. MAKING THE LINK

The Teacher again taught these two types of selflessness
To students by dividing them into many different types.
(6.179cd)

Thus the teacher again taught these two types of selflessness to students by
dividing them into many types: four, sixteen, and so on.

2.2.2.1.1.6.2.3.2.2. EXPLAINING THE MEANING
2.2.2.1.1.6.2.3.2.2.1. The brief teaching
2.2.2.1.1.6.2.3.2.2.2. The extensive explanation
2.2.2.1.1.6.2.3.2.2.3. The summary

2.2.2.1.1.6.2.3.2.2.1. THE BRIEF TEACHING

In elaborate fashion, the Buddha explained the sixteen
emptinesses.
Abbreviating that explanation,
He again taught four.
These are asserted to belong to the Mahāyāna . (6.180)

Here the master Chandrakīrti explains the meaning of the sūtras' teaching on the sixteen emptinesses and the four emptinesses. The intention
behind those teachings was to present the sixteen emptinesses as the elaborate explanation and to present the four emptinesses as the condensed
explanation.

> Subhūti, furthermore the Mahāyāna of the bodhisattvas is as
> follows: the emptiness of the inner, the emptiness of the outer,
> the emptiness of the outer and inner, the emptiness of emp-
> tiness, the emptiness of the great, the emptiness of the ulti-
> mate, the emptiness of the conditioned, the emptiness of the
> unconditioned, the emptiness of what is beyond extremes, the

emptiness of the beginningless and endless, the emptiness of what is not to be discarded, the emptiness of nature, the emptiness of all phenomena, the emptiness of defining characteristics, the emptiness of nonobservation, and the emptiness of the entities of nonthings.

Thus in an elaborate fashion, the Buddha explained the sixteen emptinesses.

Subhūti, furthermore, things are empty of things; nonthings are empty of nonthings; natures are empty of natures; other things are empty of other things.

Thus, abbreviating the above explanation, he again taught four emptinesses. These twenty emptinesses are asserted to belong to the path of the Mahāyāna, because they extensively teach the selflessness of phenomena as the antidote to the cognitive obscurations.

In sum, the extensive division is that of sixteen, the abbreviated is four, and the very abbreviated is the two selflessnesses. These classifications are of the domain of the worldly relative—if analyzed, there is not the slightest phenomenon from among those emptinesses that is not empty. The Buddha taught these classifications of emptiness as relative phenomena— just like forms and so on—merely to communicate with the different ways of thinking of sentient beings to be trained. The *Treatise* says:[503]

If there were the slightest phenomenon that was not empty,
There would be that much existence of emptiness.
Since there is not the slightest phenomenon that is not empty,
How could emptiness exist? (13.7)

And,

We do not assert "emptiness."
We do not assert "nonemptiness."
We do not assert "both" or "neither."
We use these only as labels. (22.11)

A great variety of similar statements have been made.

2.2.2.1.1.6.2.3.2.2.2.2. THE EXTENSIVE EXPLANATION
2.2.2.1.1.6.2.3.2.2.2.2.1. The elaborate explanation, the sixteen emptinesses
2.2.2.1.1.6.2.3.2.2.2.2.2. The abbreviated explanation, the four emptinesses

2.2.2.1.1.6.2.3.2.2.2.2.1. THE ELABORATE EXPLANATION, THE SIXTEEN EMPTINESSES[504]
2.2.2.1.1.6.2.3.2.2.2.2.1.1. The emptiness of the inner
2.2.2.1.1.6.2.3.2.2.2.2.1.2. The emptiness of the outer
2.2.2.1.1.6.2.3.2.2.2.2.1.3. The emptiness of the outer and inner
2.2.2.1.1.6.2.3.2.2.2.2.1.4. The emptiness of emptiness
2.2.2.1.1.6.2.3.2.2.2.2.1.5. The emptiness of the great
2.2.2.1.1.6.2.3.2.2.2.2.1.6. The emptiness of the ultimate
2.2.2.1.1.6.2.3.2.2.2.2.1.7. The emptiness of the conditioned
2.2.2.1.1.6.2.3.2.2.2.2.1.8. The emptiness of the unconditioned
2.2.2.1.1.6.2.3.2.2.2.2.1.9. The emptiness of what is beyond extremes
2.2.2.1.1.6.2.3.2.2.2.2.1.10. The emptiness of the beginningless and endless
2.2.2.1.1.6.2.3.2.2.2.2.1.11. The emptiness of what is not to be discarded
2.2.2.1.1.6.2.3.2.2.2.2.1.12. The emptiness of nature
2.2.2.1.1.6.2.3.2.2.2.2.1.13. The emptiness of all phenomena
2.2.2.1.1.6.2.3.2.2.2.2.1.14. The emptiness of defining characteristics
2.2.2.1.1.6.2.3.2.2.2.2.1.15. The emptiness of nonobservation
2.2.2.1.1.6.2.3.2.2.2.2.1.16. The emptiness of the nonexistence of things

2.2.2.1.1.6.2.3.2.2.2.2.1.1. THE EXTENSIVE EXPLANATION OF THE EMPTINESS OF THE INNER

Since its nature is emptiness,
The eye is empty of the eye.
In the same way, the ear, nose, tongue,
Body, and mind are explained to be emptiness. (6.181)

They do not stay together[505]
And do not disintegrate.
Therefore, the eyes and the rest of the six faculties
Lack an inherent nature—this lack of inherent nature
Is asserted to be the *emptiness of the inner*. (6.182)

The sūtras say:

What are the inner phenomena that are the reference points for the emptiness of the inner? The "inner phenomena" are the eye, ear, nose, tongue, body, and mind. Regarding the eye, it does not stay together and it does not disintegrate. Therefore the eye is empty of the eye. Why is this so? Because that is the nature of the eye.

The meaning of that quotation is as follows. Since the nature of the eye is emptiness, the eye is empty of the entity of the eye. In the same way, the ear, nose, tongue, body, and mind are also explained to be emptiness. That very emptiness is the nature of inner phenomena, because, without a doubt, for a thing to possess an inherent nature it must be eternal and irreversible. Things that arise from causes and conditions, things that depend on others, and things that change into other things are not suitable as natures.

"Do not stay together" in the root verse is a translation from Sanskrit of the term *akūṭastha*. *Kūṭa* means "collection," that is, a collection of causes and conditions. *Stha* means "to abide," and *a* is a negating particle. Thus the term carries a basic meaning of "not remaining as a collection" *(tsok-par nepa mepa/tshogs par gnas pa med pa)*.

Therefore the nature of emptiness that is the eye's emptiness of its own entity does not abide as a collection. It is not contrived by causes and conditions, it does not depend on other things, and it does not disintegrate, or, in other words, it is not impermanent.

Therefore, emptiness is, conventionally, tenable as the nature of all phenomena and as the nature of dharmatā. This is so because all phenomena are empty of all phenomena. Such a nature was not newly created, nor will it, in the end, change into something else. Such a nature never moves from that very state.

Thus the eyes and so on, the six inner sources, are primordially empty of their own entities. This lack of inherent nature, the emptiness of the inner, can be said to be a nature. This nature is posited when explaining the mutual dependence of the two truths in accordance with worldly renown and on the level of no analsysis.

The Followers of the Middle Way, who speak precisely about interdependence, are known as "the ones who conduct themselves in accordance with what is renowned in the world." Without analysis, they employ the terms of conventional renown when discussing the existence or nonexistence of a nature in the two truths. It is seen, moreover, that they posit as a "nature" the very lack of nature of the eye and the rest of the six faculties. They speak of this nature as the emptiness of the six faculties' own entities.

Did the master Nāgārjuna, in his *Treatise*, accept a special nature that bears the traits of being uncontrived and not dependent on anything? Nāgārjuna engaged in conventions in order to counter the wrong assertions of others. Some people held wrong views—not only regarding the ultimate, but regarding the conventional as well—about the nature of phenomena such as the eyes. They said that the eyes and so on are things that are real in and of themselves (i.e., *not* empty of their own entities) and bear a nature that produces the consciousnesses by which they are perceived. Nāgārjuna, to counter notions of this erroneous nature, spoke of how the eyes and so on are empty of themselves. On the interdependent, relative level, and in accord with what is renowned in the world, he spoke of this emptiness as the unerring "nature" of those phenomena.

In this way, Nāgārjuna abided in the worldly perspective. The terms he used, moreover, were those that were already clarified by the Transcendent Conqueror. At the level of no analysis, he spoke of the natures of the two truths as supports for the conventions of bondage, liberation, and so on. In the context of repeating what is said from the worldly perspective in this way, he did teach about a nature that had special traits: he gave the name "ultimate truth" to the very lack of true nature of the relative truth. He posited the very lack of nature as the unerring nature of both of the two truths.

However, he also said that an inherently established nature is not suitable as the nature of either of the two truths, whether the relative or the ultimate. Nāgārjuna's statements in this regard are, themselves, nonexistent when analyzed. Yet, on the level of no analysis, he spoke of the lack of nature as a nature, following after the tenable worldly perspective of dependent arising. Using this contemplation, he undermined the assertions of worldly people who do not accept dependent arising—assertions that held a truly existent nature as a nature of phenomena. In this way Nāgārjuna avoided contradicting the worldly perspective of the dependently arisen relative.

Explaining things in this way does not annihilate the continuity of worldly conventions—dependently arisen phenomena, the two truths, saṃsāra and nirvāṇa, and so on. So there is no need to become anxious and frightful, thinking, "The Followers of the Middle Way, by speaking of emptiness as the true nature of reality, speak of everything as being primordially nonexistent!"

As to speaking of emptiness as the true nature of reality, the Transcendent Conqueror said (Descent into Laṅka):

> Whether the tathāgatas arise or not, the true nature of phenomena abides.

This quotation states the existence of "the true nature of reality." Also, in the noble Cloud of Jewels (Ratnamegha, Könchok Trin/dkon mchog sprin):[506]

> Child of noble family, the ultimate is free from arising, free from cessation, free from disintegration, free of coming, free of going, inexpressible by letters, unexplainable by letters, unrealizable by elaborations. Child of noble family, it does not matter whether the tathāgatas arise or not: why would the bodhisattvas shave the hair on their heads and faces, wear saffron robes, and, out of genuine faith, leave home and become homeless? They do so for the sake of this dharma. They exert themselves as if their hair or their clothing had caught fire. The dharma for which they exert themselves is free of disintegration. Child of noble family, if there were no ultimate, it would be pointless to practice the vows of pure conduct,[507] and it would be pointless for the tathāgatas to arise. Because the ultimate exists, the bodhisattvas are called "skilled in the ultimate."

Some may protest, "You do not assert the slightest nature of things, but you do assert a nature of emptiness that is uncontrived and independent—this is contradictory." These people have not understood [Nāgārjuna's approach in the Treatise].[508] If dependently arisen phenomena such as the eyes, as they are perceived by ordinary beings, were natures, the practices of pure conduct and so on would become pointless. For those objects are cognizable even by erroneous consciousnesses. Since such objects are not natures, the practices such as pure conduct can be meaningful.

When Chandrakīrti calls the lack of nature (the emptiness of own-entity) of the eyes and so on a "nature," he is not positing a nature that is established by the reasonings and analyses of our own Middle Way system. He does, however, speak of emptiness as being the true nature of reality, uncontrived and independent, in accordance with the analyses approved by others—those who speak in accordance with the interdependent relative truth of the world.

The nature seen by ordinary beings is a contrived nature. Compared to an uncontrived nature, it is not an authentic nature. Chandrakīrti uses the argument that the uncontrived nature cannot be seen by ordinary beings in order to refute those who speak in a way that does not accord with the interdependent relative truth of the world.

Through this mere other-approved argument, to others he conventionally describes emptiness—the lack of nature—as a nature. He does so for a specific purpose. But when such a nature is described, it is possible for beings to develop extra clinging to an elaboration of a "nature." To counter such clinging, Chandrakīrti again relies on reasonings that are approved by those who speak correctly of the interdependent, worldly relative. When the "nature" that is a lack of nature is itself analyzed, he teaches, it is emptiness—it has no status of being a thing, nonthing, or any other designation. For, since by its very nature it is peace, it is like fire burning wood: the fire not only burns the wood, it burns itself as well. Both fire and wood are reduced to nothing more than dust.

Emptiness that is described in this way as a nature is not inherently existent and is not inherently nonexistent. Since the contrived nature of the relative truth is not truly existent, even more lacking in true existence is the uncontrived nature of the ultimate. However, there comes a time when yogis and yoginīs who are Followers of the Middle Way must skillfully use concepts to clear away other, more inaccurate, concepts. The process by which they do this is described as follows.

First, there are sentient beings with concepts that do not harmonize with the interdependence of the worldly relative. They erroneously think that, beyond being an illusion, the relative truth possesses a nature that truly exists. This conception arises due to beings' very thick ignorance. To help beings become free of such incorrect notions, the Followers of the Middle Way communicate with beings using concepts that *are* harmonious with the interdependence of the worldly relative. They frame logical arguments such as the following: "The nature of the relative truth is not truly existent, because the nature of forms and so on is to be produced by causes and conditions. Therefore, the nature of such relative phenomena is merely an illusion—their nature is established as emptiness, in which no inherent nature is observable."

Again, the label "nature" given to the ultimate lack of nature is not something that exists for the Followers of the Middle Way, nor is it something they affirm from their own side. If they did affirm it from their own side, they would become "Followers of the Middle Way who affirm illusions using reasoning." Furthermore, if the emptiness that is the illusory nature of the relative existed, it would have to be observable among the objects and perceiving subjects on either the path of training or the path of no training.[509] Yet, from the perspective of the beings who abide on those paths, there is not even the slightest nature of either of the two truths to be seen. Therefore you, our counterparts, may hope that we contradict ourselves, but where is there any contradiction?

The yogis and yoginīs, therefore, speak of a nature that is the opposite of the nature clung to by ordinary beings. Even though the nature of which they speak is not established as a nature, they label it a nature for the purpose of countering the nature clung to by ignorant beings. Statements like these bear an ulterior intention, because, apart from such statements, there is no nature in the two truths at all. The *Treatise* says:

> We do not assert "emptiness."
> We do not assert "nonemptiness."
> We do not assert "both" or "neither."
> We use these only as labels. (22.11)

And Jñānagharba *(Yeshe Nyingpo/ye shes snying po)* says:

> From the standpoint of the genuine, there is no duality.
> Therefore, the genuine is not emptiness.
> It is not nonemptiness, nor does it exist or not exist.
> It is not nonarisen, nor is it arisen.
> Such is the teaching of the Transcendent Conqueror.

Thus if the ultimate truth is not even established as emptiness, it follows that the nature of emptiness is not findable. The *Commentary to the Two Truths (Den nyi Drelpa/bden gnyis 'grel pa)* says:

> Therefore the nature of even relative things is definitely a long way from eternalism or nihilism. What need, therefore, to speak of the ultimate?
>
> > For an entity that never arose,
> > How could there be eternalism or nihilism?
> > Conceptions made about the particulars of phenomena
> > Are made in relation a phenomenon's entity.
>
> > Just as no one
> > Can write letters on the sky,
> > It is the same with conceiving things,
> > Which have never arisen, as phenomena.

And, from the *Treatise*:

> How could there be things
> That are neither themselves nor others?
> If there were sameness or otherness,
> Things would be established. (15.4)

> Since things are not established,
> How could nonthings be established? (15.5ab)

In the context of making statements that bear ulterior intentions in response to the varieties of students' misconceptions, Followers of the Middle Way will make various statements. To some students they will say, "There is no nature." To some they will say, "The nature is emptiness." To others they will say, "The nature is not emptiness." To others still they might say, "Things exist," and, to others, "Things do not exist."

They could make any of the above statements to fulfill a certain purpose. But, regardless of what they say, the Followers of the Middle Way do not posit any elaborations whatsoever of existence, nonexistence, and so on from their *own* perspective of the two truths. They never wane from the way of not holding any positions and not forming any theses. Regarding the way of being free from internal contradictions by not holding any position, the master Āryadeva said:

> The alternatives of existence, nonexistence, both existence and
>   nonexistence,
> And neither were taught in different contexts.
> From the perspective of the sicknesses they treated,
> Are not all of them medicines?
>
> That which benefits others for a while is "truth."
> That which does not is the opposite, "falsity."

And,

> Against someone who does not hold any position
> Of existence, nonexistence, or both existence and nonexistence,
> One cannot prevail in argument,
> Even if [one tries] for a long time.

The Consequentialists absolutely do not, even conventionally, posit either of the two truths or any natures of the two truths in their own system of analysis. When they do posit the truths, their natures, and so on, they do so in dependence upon untenable worldly conventions—they use tenable other-approved conventions to refute misconceptions. They do so in a manner of merely repeating after others to address a specific need.

Yet they are completely free from their own intention of asserting "emptiness" or a "nature." Since, in both truths, the elaborations of a nature of phenomena—whether they be elaborations of objects or elaborations of expressions about objects—are not established by valid cognition. Since all these elaborations are pacified for Followers of the Middle Way, the latter do not delight in speaking of a nature that is the indestructible mode of abiding.

There are some, such as the glorious Shākya Chokden, who say, "In the Consequentialists' own system, the nature of the relative truth does not suffice as a nature. The genuine nature is the emptiness nature of the ultimate truth, and the Consequentialists accept that this nature truly exists. At the intermediate level of reversing the view of a self,[510] one must accept such an ultimate nature, for, if one did not, one would not realize the ultimate truth: the nature of emptiness in which the self and true existence do not exist. However, at the level of reversing all views,[511] the Consequentialists do not accept that the nature of the ultimate truth truly exists."

That description is untenable. When the Consequentialists analyze suchness, they emphasize that, regardless of who makes the assertion, no reality or nature exists even conventionally with respect to either of the two truths. This is the correct explanation of how the self and true existence are refuted in relation to the person and phenomena.

According to your approach, however, at the level of reversing views of the self, the self and true existence are refuted with respect to relative phenomena, the subject. In the wake of that refutation, the self and true existence are affirmed with respect to the ultimate truth, the qualifier of the subject!

There are, however, utterly no grounds for saying that the above is the assertion of the Consequentialists at the level of refuting the view of the self. If they held that assertion, they would be accepting, word for word, the tenets of the False Aspectarian Proponents of Mind Only. If at that level the nature of the ultimate truth existed, it would be impossible for the same nature to be nonexistent at the level of reversing all views. And, if you held that at the level of reversing the view of a self the nature does not exist, viewing a nature of selflessness in that context would be a wrong view. Even though you attempt to affirm the true existence of the nature of the ultimate truth, it is not established by valid cognition. By what means do you try to establish it?

The master Chandrakīrti said:[512]

> With respect to the persons, phenomena, and so on that are identified in the relative truth, due to beginningless, innate ignorance beings conceive, in dependence upon the aggregates, of a nature of the person that functions as the support for actions and results. They also conceive of a nature of form and so on, in dependence upon the elements such as earth. They mistakenly believe that this latter nature produces the consciousnesses that apprehend form and so on. This incorrect mode of apprehension, which assumes the true existence of the natures and self-entities of persons and phenomena, is the object of refutation of

correct reasonings arisen from hearing and contemplation. The mere apprehension of those things is the object of refutation by the path—the yogic direct valid cognition that arises from meditation. Therefore, in terms of the objects of refutation of reasoning and the path, these are none other than the objects of the incorrect view that conceives of a "nature" or "true existence" of the relative truth, which does not truly exist.

Even while witnessing clear explanations such as these from the root text and commentary, the great Shar Tsongkapa and others still search elsewhere for the object of refutation by reasons. They are like someone looking for the footprints of a thief on the near side of the mountain even though the thief was on the mountain's far side.

In relation to the way in which clinging to true existence is identified, Tsongkapa says things like, "It is too narrow a description to say that the view of true existence entails fixation toward the qualities of being uncontrived, independent, and unchanging. The Proponents of Mind Only, for example, consider things to be arisen from causes and conditions. If you held to the above-mentioned description of the view of true existence, it would absurdly follow that Followers of the Middle Way would not need to affirm the lack of true existence for the Proponents of Mind Only."

That is untenable. The Proponents of Mind Only and others assert that a cause that is a thing produces a result that is a thing. Nevertheless, they view the discrete causes and results involved in production to be in and of themselves uncontrived, independent, unchanging, autonomous, and truly existent. They say things like, "If a cause is not real in and of itself, it is incapable of producing a genuine result."

In response to such statements, the Followers of the Middle Way instill certainty in their counterparts about how all causes and results lack true existence. It appears that you have not paid adequate attention to their approach. Fixation toward those qualities of being uncontrived and so on is present in all sentient beings of the three realms. Whatever major and minor sufferings sentient beings undergo in saṃsāra, they do so on the basis of this very fixation. Since as much is perceptible, you have no need to be fraught with worries that such a description of the view of true existence is too narrow.

Some followers of the Shangpa (shangs pa) Kagyü tradition have a unique interpretation of the following lines from the *Treatise on the Middle Way*:[513]

> "Natures" must be uncontrived
> And not dependent upon others. (15.2cd)
> Since natures are nonexistent,
> How could there be "other" things? (15.3ab)

They say, "The intention of that quotation, and of the rest of that section of the *Treatise*, is to proclaim that if a nature existed, it would have to exist in both truths. Yet such a nature does not exist in the relative truth, nor does it exist in the ultimate. If it did exist, it would be a permanent thing that was uncontrived and independent, yet such a phenomenon is impossible.

"Therefore, in the own-system of the Followers of the Middle Way, stainless reasonings are used to refute a nature in both of the two truths. In our own system, not only when analyzing, but when there is no analysis as well, we refrain from positing a nature in either of the two truths. Any such position would be confusion. Knowable objects cannot have one true nature."

That is a depraved assertion. The Teacher, in the scriptures on the Middle Way, spoke about how at the level of no analysis both truths exist. The Followers of the Middle Way simply repeat this. Even though the Buddha did not say the same at the level of analysis in his own system, he did speak in accordance with the interdependence of the worldly relative. At that time, he used tenable arguments that were approved by others to teach that the nature of the relative is not tenable as a true nature. Furthermore, he taught that the nature of the ultimate is tenable as a true nature by employing the other-approved analysis of mutual dependence: at the conventional level of no analysis, the relative and ultimate truths bear natures of falsity and truth, respectively. In dependence upon truth, falsity is established as not being acceptable as a true nature. This logic is accepted in the world.

The Followers of the Middle Way communicate that way on the worldly level. Nevertheless, when they place special emphasis on the genuine nature of suchness, their analysis reveals that there is no nature of either of the two truths established as either existent or nonexistent. It is impossible to deliver this lack of establishment to the systems of others, and it is equally impossible to pull this lack of establishment into our own system. One cannot transform that which is free from elaborations into an elaboration.

Those who say that, "even when the Followers of the Middle Way speak conventionally they do not describe any natures of the two truths in their own system" are like a crow giving a lofty discourse: they attempt to speak from a high and exalted standpoint, but really their position is inferior.

Not only did the master Nāgārjuna accept this "nature that is emptiness" on the nonanalytical, conventional level; he was also capable of making his students accept it. Therefore such a nature must, in that context, pertain to both [truths]. For, the heat and so on of fire are not suitable as the nature of fire. Since they are interdependent, they are contrived and dependent on others. There is no such thing as a heat of fire that is uncontrived and independent. Nor can an uncontrived heat be observed as a superior nature that is emptiness.

Nevertheless, in the abhidharma sūtras and so on, it was taught that "in the relative, the nature of fire is the aspect of heat and so on." The Teacher made this statement in harmony with the relative truth of ordinary beings. He did not say, "since the relative nature of fire is interdependent, it is not suitable as a nature; and since the nature of the ultimate is not interdependent, it is tenable as a nature." This is the meaning of what he said: "From among the two interdependent truths, the nature of the relative truth is, in an interdependent way, false. In dependence upon that falsity, the nature of the ultimate truth is true or real. This is a tenable description of the natures of the two truths in the context of interdependence."

When it is said that the eye is empty of the eye and so on, emptiness is clearly referring to everything. This emptiness is not an emptiness of one thing from another, as in the case of the hearers (who say that "emptiness" refers merely to the absence of an internal creator) and of the Proponents of Mind Only (who say that "emptiness" refers merely to the absence of an essential nature composed of the duality of apprehender and apprehended).

As just intimated, those who follow this dharma of the Buddha have different ways of discussing emptiness. The factions of hearers who assert the existence of the person identify the person, the aggregates, and so on as the bases of emptiness. They say that these bases are empty of the two extremes of eternalism and nihilism. They are empty of the extreme of eternalism in that they lack the permanent, singular, and independent self imputed by the non-Buddhists. They are empty of the extreme of nihilism in that they lack the nonexistence of actions and their results, past and future lives, and so on.

In terms of the factions of hearers who do not assert the person, the Particularists identify the conditioned phenomena of the three times (the aggregates, sources, and constituents) and unconditioned phenomena as the bases of emptiness. They say that these bases are empty of the extremes of eternalism and nihilism imputed by the non-Buddhists and by the hearers who assert the existence of the person. They also say that the five bases of knowable objects, which are empty of those extremes, inherently exist.

The Followers of Sūtra identify the aggregates, sources, and constituents of the present moment—which include forms, primary minds, and mental events—as the bases of emptiness. They say that these bases are empty of the self and of the extremes of eternalism and nihilism asserted by the non-Buddhists and by the hearers who assert the person. They also assert that the same bases are empty of the substantial existents of the past and future imputed by the Particularists and of the substantial existents that are nonassociated formations. They say that partless particles and indivisible moments of consciousness, which are empty of the aforementioned imputations, are real.

The True Aspectarian Proponents of Mind Only identify the momentary cognition of the present, along with its aspects of objects, as the basis of emptiness. They say that this basis is empty without exception of the selves of phenomena and persons imputed by the tīrthikas and by the hearers. They also say that the dependent nature and its aspects, which are empty of those imputations, are *not* empty of the perfectly established nature—self-illuminating self-awareness.

The False Aspectarian Proponents of Mind Only identify the dependent nature—clarity-awareness, mere experience—as the basis of emptiness. They say it is empty of all the forms of self imputed by the tīrthikas and the hearers. They also assert it to be empty of the impurities of aspects imputed by the True Aspectarians. They say that the dependent nature of mere cognition, empty of all of the above, is substantially established. They assert that the perfectly established nature—true, nondual reality—

ultimately exists but exists in a way that is not identical to or different from mere cognition.

The great Tsongkapa says that things established by conventional valid cognition are empty of the entities that are to be refuted by reasons. He asserts that such emptiness exists as a base that is established in the particular instances of phenomena that it qualifies.

The Autonomist Followers of the Middle Way, when using the analyses that investigate the ultimate, do not find even the slightest basis of emptiness. Nor do they find any quality of which that basis is empty, or anything such as emptiness, nonemptiness, phenomena, or the true nature of phenomena. All phenomena are completely pacified of all elaborations and traits. Nevertheless, the reasonings that investigate conventional reality cannot refute certain objects and appearances of the mind. These illusionlike phenomena are, conventionally, taken as the bases of emptiness. The Autonomists say that these phenomena are ultimately empty of all phenomena imputed by the Buddhist and non-Buddhist Proponents of Things.

The Autonomists describe how all phenomena are empty of their own entities. Genuinely, or, in other words, in the meditative equipoise of the Mahāyāna noble ones, all elaborations and traits are pacified. Therefore, the emptiness of the Autonomists is by far superior in comparison with the emptiness of the Proponents of Things. However the Autonomist presentation of emptiness in this way does involve some faults: if appearances of objects and minds conventionally arose in the noble ones' equipoise, they would become things that withstand analysis—they would become the ultimate. Either that would be the case or the noble ones' equipoise would have to be posited as confusion.

If such appearances did not arise conventionally in the noble ones' equipoise, it would be the case that phenomena are not empty conventionally but are made empty by that equipoise. There would be the logical fault that the noble ones' equipoise denigrates conventional phenomena.

According to the Consequentialist Followers of the Middle Way, the emptiness of all phenomena is not a case of conceptually fabricated emptiness, wherein all phenomena are actually not empty but are meditated upon by the intellect as being empty. Nor is emptiness a principle wherein phenomena are not empty without analysis but become empty when analyzed, like a hammer destroying a vase. Nor is it that phenomena are not empty before the wisdom of the noble ones has arisen in one's mindstream but become empty after such wisdom has arisen. Emptiness is not a state in which phenomena exist before and then become nonexistent later, like the snuffing of a candle flame. It is not an emptiness of other objects to be negated, like a vase being empty of water. Nor is emptiness, like the horns of a rabbit, an utter nonexistence.

All of these approaches to emptiness are, in contrast to phenomena being empty of their own entities, forms of emptiness that are fabricated by the intellect. They are nihilistic, or partial, emptinesses. They are unsuitable as supports for the path of liberation or as antidotes to the two obscurations.

What, then, *is* emptiness? All phenomena from form through omniscience are, from the outset, not established whatsoever as any extreme elaboration such as existent, nonexistent, arisen, ceased, permanent, impermanent, empty, not empty, true, or false. To that lack of establishment, mere conventional terms such as "emptiness" and "suchness" are given. It is nothing more than that.

This emptiness—that conventionally all phenomena are empty of their own entities—is the natural being *(rang bab/rang babs)*, the abiding mode, of all knowable objects. Resting in equipoise within it is the antidote to all obscurations. It is the sun that conquers the darkness of wrong views, the supreme medicine that clears away the snake venom of reification, the essential nectar of the Buddha's teachings. Everyone who sincerely desires liberation and omniscience should engage it through applying great effort in hearing, contemplating, and meditating.

The great Dolpopa[514] says that the Middle Way system asserted by Chandrakīrti is inferior, quoting the following statement of the Transcendent Conqueror, which, according to Dolpopa, prophesies Chandrakīrti's system and also refutes it *(Kālachakra Tantra)*:

> The emptiness of analyzing the aggregates
> Is, like a banana tree, without pith.[515]

Chandrakīrti's system, Dolpopa continues, is a teaching from the age of dispute *(tsö dü/rtsod dus)*.[516] He asserts that his own Middle Way system is the great, supreme dharma of the age of perfection *(dzogden/rdzogs ldan)* of the Rigdens of Shambhala.[517]

In Dolpopa's system, some phenomena are interdependent and other phenomena are not interdependent. The ultimate truth is known as "the supreme other" and is not suitable as an interdependent phenomenon. It is isolated because it does not rely on any relative phenomena, which are intrinsically empty or self-empty *(rangtong/rang stong)*. The true nature of reality, ultimate truth, is unconditioned. Even in relation to this ultimate truth dichotomies exist: the two truths, phenomena and their true nature, saṃsāra and nirvāṇa, existence and nonexistence, truth and falsity, emptiness and nonemptiness, and faults and qualities. The same sets of dichotomies exist in relation to the relative truth, apparent phenomena.

Phenomena that are empty of other *(shentong/gzhan stong)*, he continues, are real in the way that they appear to the mind. Self-empty phenomena are not real in the way that they appear to the mind. Therefore relative phenomena are contradictory and faulty. It is necessary for that reason to accept truth and falsity as being distinct from each other in the context of the relative. Since ultimate phenomena have no fault of contradiction, the ultimate is free from all contradictions between truth and falsity. It is the equality of one taste, free from classifications.

He says that, furthermore, when the Buddha described all phenomena as being equality, he was referring not to the equality of self- and other-empty phenomena, but rather to the pairings of phenomena and true-nature-of-phenomena as they are present *distinctly* in *each* of the two truths. Moreover, since the ultimate truth is permanent, it dispels the extreme of nihilism. And, since the relative truth is impermanent, it dispels the extreme of eternalism.

This way of transcending the two extremes, he says, is the view of the extreme-free Middle Way that is like the view of an eagle soaring through the sky. The analyses of others, he says, are like a flock of moths.

His system is untenable. It is unsuitable for a Follower of the Middle Way to speak of a nature of phenomena with no apparent phenomenon to qualify. Furthermore, phenomena and their true nature are both free from the elaborations of existence, nonexistence, and so on. The notion that there could be a true nature of reality without apparent phenomena to be qualified does not even hold muster in the system of the Proponents of Things. For, in that system, both phenomena and true natures exist.

Moreover, this notion cannot even withstand the logic of your own system. For you say that dichotomies (phenomena and true nature, saṃsāra and nirvāṇa, faults and qualities, etc.) exist in the ultimate but do not exist in the relative.

You interpret the above quotation, "The emptiness of analyzing the aggregates . . .," as a refutation of the validity of determining the emptiness of phenomena such as the aggregates using reasonings. If your interpretation were accurate, it would also follow that the *Trilogy of Bodhisattva Commentaries*[518] *(Sem Drel Kor Sum/sems 'grel skor gsum)* and limitless other tantric texts are useless. For, in those texts, reasonings are used to determine the state of emptiness as well.

What that quotation actually teaches is this: the emptiness to be determined in both sūtra and tantra is the same. There is no difference between sūtric emptiness and tantric emptiness with respect to profundity. Nevertheless, if one employs in analysis only the prajñās of hearing and contemplating—be it in a sūtric *or* a tantric context—the emptiness one arrives at will merely be a generality of emptiness.

In the Vajrayāna, one employs the special interdependence of binding the body and mind. The prajñā born of that meditation directly experiences emptiness. The analyses of hearing and contemplating, on the other hand, do not possess such a vital essence—*that* is the intended meaning of your quotation. How could it be a refutation of the notion that analytical meditation on the aggregates and so forth can help one to determine emptiness and thus become the path to liberation?

Furthermore, your contention that the great master Chandrakīrti is a paṇḍita of the age of dispute contradicts even your own system! The following are your own words *(The Fourth Council, Ka Du Shipa/bka' bsdu bzhi pa)*:[519]

> I will now thoroughly explain the two sets of four ages.
> The four great ages *(dü/dus)* concern the quality of the ages of an
> eon *(kalpa/bskal pa).*
> The four lesser ages concern the quality of the teachings.
> The first set of ages
> Lasts for 4,320,000 years,
> A quarter of which being called a "foot."
> One, two, three, and four feet, respectively,
> Are called the age of dispute,
> The twofold, the threefold, and the age of perfection.

The four lesser ages, those that concern the quality of the teachings,
Last for 21,600 human years,
A quarter of which being the duration of each age.
The dharma that is faultless and perfected in qualities is that of the
    age of perfection.
When a quarter has passed it is the first half of the threefold age.
When another half has passed it is the last half of the threefold age.
The remainder, when three quarters have passed, is the twofold.
When there is not even a quarter, it is the age of dispute.
The dharma of that era is taught to be that of evil, jealous-god
    barbarians.

With regard to the duration of the lesser ages, the length of each age,
according to Dolpopa, would be 5,400 years (one quarter of 21,600). Yet,
according to the sūtras, the teachings of the present Buddha will remain
for no longer than five thousand years. According to the calculations of
the *Kālachakra*, moreover, our present time is one in which just over two
thousand years have passed since the Buddha's parinirvāṇa. Since the age
of dispute is to take place 16,200 years[520] after the parinirvāṇa, the master
Chandrakīrti, according to the sūtras, would need to be alive a very long
time after the Buddha's passing in order to be a teacher during that age.

Yet we see in the histories that the protector Nāgārjuna taught four
hundred years after parinirvāṇa. And, according to the glorious lord Atisha, the glorious Chandrakīrti relied on the protector Nāgārjuna in person. Your assertion that Chandrakīrti was a master in the noble land of
India during the age of dispute, therefore, means that the age of dispute
would have occurred *before* the age of perfection was finished! With your
own words you have excellently refuted your very own thesis.

You say that your philosophical system is the dharma of the Rigdens
of Shambhala from the age of perfection. Yet, before you, this system was
not known to anyone in Tibet or in India—it was not even known to your
own guru, Yönten Gyamtso *(yon tan rgya mtsho)*. Therefore, you need to
explain whether you went away to join the Rigdens or the Rigdens came
to join you!

It was said just above that Chandrakīrti was a direct disciple of Nāgārjuna, whereas earlier in this commentary it was said that that was not so.
One must examine which of these two presentations is most tenable by

consulting the biographies and so forth. Due to the different perceptions of the various students, there are many different explanations given concerning the biographies and ways of teaching of the genuine beings. These explanations should not be thought of as contradictory.

Back to the analysis of Dolpopa's views: it follows that phenomena of the relative truth are extrinsically empty, because the undeceiving quality of karmic causes and results conventionally is true in the manner that it appears to the minds of ordinary beings.[521] If you say that the reason is not established, it follows that it is not necessary for ordinary beings conventionally to correctly engage in adopting and rejecting, because of the reason not being established.[522]

If you say that the reason is not included in the predicate,[523] it follows that it is necessary for ordinary beings conventionally to exercise caution so that they do not fall off a ladder made of the horns of a rabbit. For, firstly, according to you, conventionally those two[524] are equivalent in not being true in the way that they appear to the mind. And, secondly, you say it is reasonable to engage in adopting and rejecting with respect to causes and results.

Another consequence: it follows that all ultimate phenomena are intrinsically empty. For, firstly, the ultimate truth appears to the minds of worldly beings.[525] And, secondly, it is not true in the manner that it appears.

You may say, "The first reason is not established." It then follows that you are incapable of demonstrating the ultimate truth—which bears the features of being extrinsically empty, unconditioned, permanent, and so on—as an object of mind to your worldly students. For, it is utterly impossible for such an ultimate truth that bears those features to appear to a worldly mind. If you accept, all the energy you put into your dharma system is pointless.

Another consequence: concerning the perceiving subjects of the relative, the subject: it follows that they are not confused. For, single and multiple phenomena are real in the way that they appear to worldly consciousnesses. If you say the reason is not established, it follows that the separateness of 21,600 moving karmic prāṇas of worldly beings on the one hand and the movement of the 675 wisdom prāṇas on the other are not real in the way that they appear. For you said the earlier reason was not established, and that reason equivalently applies to the reason here.[526]

If you accept, it follows that it is meaningless to try to stop the many movements of the impure prāṇas and to try to establish through effort the movements of the pure prāṇas. For the movements of those prāṇas, appearing as either single or multiple, are completely nonexistent and unreal.

Next, it follows that all perceiving subjects of the ultimate are confused, because in order for worldly beings to engage the ultimate as an object they must engage it via appearances of one or many—but those appearances are not real in the way they appear. You may respond by saying, "It is impossible for worldly beings to engage the ultimate as an object." Well then, what about your claim that you have instructed many of your worldly disciples in the practices of the six applications *(jor druk/sbyor drug)*? You say that they have engendered many experiences and realizations of the special intellect that engages the ultimate as an object. Your contention that worldly beings cannot engage the ultimate as an object is in contradiction with this.

Another consequence: it follows that everything that appears as confusion is real. For the relative is rife with faults of contradiction—from its own perspective, existence, nonexistence, and so on are contradictory and real in their own place. Furthermore, it follows that everything that appears to unconfused minds is false. For the ultimate is free from the faults of contradiction—from its perspective, even though existence and nonexistence are contradictory, they exist in a manner of not being real in their own places. According to you, in that context existence is also nonexistence, and nonexistence is also existence, and so on.

Further, it follows that the distinctions between the two truths regarding which one is empty of faults and which one is empty of positive qualities are untenable. For the two truths of the extrinsically empty ultimate are empty of faults and not empty of positive qualities.

It is also untenable to posit the two truths as intrinsically empty and extrinsically empty because, according to you, the true nature of both is extrinsic emptiness, and extrinsic emptiness is free from the distinctions of self and other.

It also follows that there is no difference between buddhas and sentient beings with respect to whether or not they possess qualities such as the ten powers. For sentient beings also possess all the ultimate, unconditioned qualities such as the ten powers. And even the buddha that is the ultimate truth does not possess the relative qualities such as the conditioned ten powers.

It follows that the inequality of saṃsāra and nirvāṇa is untenable. For the saṃsāra and nirvāṇa of the relative are both untenable, and the saṃsāra and nirvāṇa of the ultimate are an inseparable unit.

It follows that the inequality of all phenomena is untenable. For in the ultimate all phenomena are free from contradictions—it makes no difference whether you say they are equal or not! The reason is included in the predicate because, from among the relative and the ultimate the ultimate is more powerful. The ultimate is a permanent entity that accords with the mode of being of reality.

It follows that, according to your system, half of knowable objects holds the extreme of eternalism and the other half holds the extreme of nihilism. For, firstly, the ultimate truth dispels the extreme of nihilism by upholding the extreme of eternalism. And, secondly, the relative truth dispels the extreme of eternalism by upholding the extreme of nihilism. You have no choice but to accept.

It then follows that it is impossible for there to be an instance of anything performing a function in the context of the interdependence between the two truths, because nothing eternalistic or nihilistic can perform a function.

The Jonangpas have a unique interpretation of the following quotation from the *Perfection of Supreme Knowledge in Five Hundred Verses (Pañcha-shati-prajñā-pāramitā, Sherchin Ngabgyapa/sher phyin lnga brgya pa)*:

> When I, the Transcendent Conqueror, said that form is free
> of nature—free of arising, free of ceasing, primordially peace,
> and naturally nirvāṇa—I said that those statements do not bear
> an ulterior intention and are literal. This characterization was
> made in dependence upon [the views of philosophers] outside
> [of my teachings] and of ordinary beings.

The Jonangpas say that the meaning of that quotation is that the final turning of the wheel of dharma teaches that the teachings from the middle turning that describe the true nature of reality as intrinsic emptiness are not literal. However, that is not the case: the meaning of that quotation, as has been explained by Nāgārjuna, is that when permanent form is refuted impermanent form is not affirmed. When nonemptiness is refuted emptiness is not affirmed. If you take emptiness, nonarising, and so on to be literal and essentially existent, you will be adopting a tīrthika position—that is the meaning of the above quotation. That emptiness, nonarising, and so on are, themselves, empty of their own entities should be understood to be the literal, definitive meaning.

Let us examine more assertions of Dolpopa and his followers. They say that, on the one hand, the two truths are different from each other because they possess the difference that refutes sameness. This is so, they say, because the relative truth does not actually exist, while the ultimate truth actually exists. Since existence and nonexistence cannot be called the same, the ultimate truth, which exists, is established as being different from the relative truth, which does not.

On the other hand, they say, the two truths are the same because they possess the sameness that refutes difference. This is so, they continue, because the essence of the relative truth does not exist separately from the ultimate truth. And, furthermore, since there is no relative aside from the ultimate truth, the two truths are singular; that is, they are not established as the opposite of singular, which is a plurality. And, of course, the two truths are not utterly nonexistent.

Yet the logic of Dolpopa can be used equally to refute his own positions. The two truths are not different because they are the sameness that refutes difference. They are not the same because they are the difference that refutes sameness. Not only are your own words contradictory in this regard, they create further problems for your own view.

If you hold that the relative truth is utterly nonexistent even conventionally, how are you to make conventional presentations of the relation between the two truths? Since you have already denied both sameness and difference regarding the two truths, you have rendered useless your earlier statement, "The two truths are not utterly nonexistent." It becomes illogical for you to even ask the question, "Conventionally, are the two truths the same or different," or to attempt an answer. If the relative truth, in the context of even the relative, is utterly nonexistent, it would be impossible for someone who possesses realization to ever be in doubt about whether it is the same as or different from the ultimate truth conventionally. One would not, for example, analyze whether the horns of a rabbit are the same as or different from the ultimate truth.

I see nothing in your style of denying sameness and difference regarding the two truths apart from a great exhibition of the superimpositions and denigrations of wrong thoughts. For all you say is that the ultimate truth is permanently existent and that the relative truth is utterly unobservable.

We do not distinguish between the sameness or difference of the two truths at the level of no analysis. In that context, and when engaging in adopting and rejecting in relation to worldly or transcendent objectives, the relative truth, the subject, does not discard the ultimate truth, the qualifier. When analyzing, we refute both sameness and difference and refrain from viewing the two truths as being either the same or different. In this mode we engage in view and meditation.

You, on the other hand, must always refute one extreme and hold on to the other. You engage in view and meditation via the mode of clinging to the extremes. Why do you feel so fond of the garbage of view and meditation when the pleasant sensations of this fondness turn around to torment you in the end?

Then there is Shar Tsongkapa, who, due to a transmission from the noble Mañjushrī, divided the supreme tradition of Chandrakīrti in a way that had not been done before. He says, "The bases of emptiness are the person and phenomena. Yet in order to realize the nonexistence of the self and true existence, respectively, in relation to those bases, one must first identify the opposite of such nonexistence. That opposite is called 'the object of refutation by reasons.'

"This object of refutation by reasons does not exist as a knowable object. However, the emptiness that refutes it does exist among knowable objects. Therefore the ultimate truth exists within the relative truth, but does not so exist in the manner of *being* the ultimate truth. One must ensure that existence and being (in the equative sense)[527] are not confused.

"The bases of emptiness—the person, the aggregates, and so on—are established by conventional valid cognition as things that perform functions in an undeceiving way. When conventional valid cognition cognizes this, the valid cognition of the reasoning consciousness also, as an aftereffect, cognizes the true nature of those bases. It cognizes the emptiness that is free from the self and true existence and, furthermore, it cognizes such emptiness as an established base."

Tsongkapa's system clings to the two truths in a way in which each truth is isolated from the other. The followers of that system speak in a way that does not accord with interdependent knowable objects. The question must be asked of them: does your object of refutation by reasons (true existence), which does not exist among knowable objects, function among knowable objects as something to be refuted by reasons?

If you say it does, then concerning knowable objects, the subject: it follows that the object of refutation by reasons (true existence) exists among them. For the object of refutation by reasons is refuted by reasons within the frame of reference of knowable objects. The reason *is* included in the predicate,[528] for if true existence is refuted in the frame of reference of knowable objects, one must refute either the true existence that exists among knowable objects or the true existence that does not exist among knowable objects.

If one refutes the true existence that exists among knowable objects, the refutation will be equivalent to affirming the true existence that does not exist among knowable objects. According to your system, understanding the natural implication of the two negatives[529] *(gakpa nyi kyi nalma/dgag pa gnyis kyi rnal ma)* is crucial to the process of reasoning. When supreme knowledge refutes [the object of refutation by reasons that does not exist among knowable objects], there is no choice but to posit [an object of refutation by reasons] that exists among knowable objects.

You may retort, "We perform our refutation by entertaining the hypothetical possibility of true existence. We say, 'If it were to exist among knowable objects . . .' and proceed with the refutation in that way. Therefore the consequence that we would affirm the existence among knowable objects of true existence does not follow."

Well then, just as such true existence is a mere hypothetical possibility that cannot exist actually, it follows that the lack of true existence that depends on it is also a mere hypothetical possibility that cannot exist among knowable objects. This is so because, firstly, you insist that in order for the lack of true existence to exist one must definitely identify its opposite, true existence, in the manner of entertaining a hypothetical possibility. In dependence upon the nonexistence of that true existence, you posit the lack of true existence. And, secondly, that true existence is only held to hypothetically exist among knowable objects—according to you, it does not exist among knowable objects at all.

You may say that the first reason is not included in its predicate, but it is.[530] For, the lack of true existence and the nonexistence of the self depend on the objects of negation, true existence and the self. The two sets are mutually dependent. If one is utterly impossible, the same would follow for the other.

You may attempt a rebuttal by saying, "The object of refutation by reasons does not exist *among* knowable objects, but it does exist *as* a knowable object," but you would not be employing any meaningful grammatical distinction.[531]

If you say that the object of refutation by reasons does not function among knowable objects as something to be refuted by reasons, your claim to the nonexistence of the object of refutation is affirmed within knowable objects themselves. Do not argue against what is directly evident.

Another consequence—let us examine your refutation (in the frame of reference of knowable objects) of true existence, the object of refutation that does not exist among knowable objects. It follows that it would be logical to accept the existence of the lack of true existence as an object of refutation by reasonings that exists among knowable objects. For it is you who constantly proclaims the necessity of understanding the natural implication of a double negation.

If you accept, consider this. Concerning the lack of true existence as the object of refutation by reasons that exists among knowable objects, the subject: it follows that it is not different from the bases of refutation, the aggregates and so on. For it is a knowable object that lacks true existence. If you accept, we conclude that, if conventionally there is no object of refutation, it is a deprecation of interdependence to say that the emptiness that refutes it exists conventionally.

The glorious protector Nāgārjuna, as well, upheld the principle of interdependence in the same way when he elucidated the intention of the perfect Buddha: on the level of no analysis, the object, means, and action of refutation—all three—are posited in dependence upon each other. When analyzed, the same triad is free from all the extremes of conceptual elaboration.

In contrast to Nāgārjuna's approach to fulfilling the intention of the Buddha, your system says that, when analyzed, the object of refutation is not established as a knowable object, but the means and the action of the refutation *are* established. In effect, therefore, you are accepting that the means and action of refutation are ultimate truths that can withstand analysis. Those of you who accumulate [the karma of espousing this approach to logic] should consider your actions well.

You say that it harmonizes with interdependence to describe the ultimate truth as not being existent in the ultimate truth, but that is untenable. According to you it would follow that the ultimate truth is not real in the relative. For the ultimate truth is not ultimately real either.

If you think, "The reason is not included in the predicate," in this system it is: if something is not real in the ultimate, it must also not be real in the relative. And, if something is real in the relative, it must also be real in the ultimate. This other-approved, conventional approach to reasoning is the feature that makes [the Consequentialist system] superior to the Autonomist system.

Another consequence—concerning the emptiness that is empty of the object of refutation by reasons, which does not exist among knowable objects, the subject: it follows that it is *not* the emptiness that is the inseparable nature of phenomena from form through omniscience. For, firstly, it is an emptiness that is empty of true existence, and true existence does not exist among knowable objects. Secondly, it is not an emptiness that is empty of a self or true existence that exists as a thing among knowable objects.

If you say that the second reason is not established, it then follows that the self to be refuted *exists* among knowable objects. For you accept an emptiness that is empty of the self and true existence as things that exist among knowable objects.

Our approach is as follows. When analysis is applied, there is no such thing as a knowable or nonknowable object that truly exists in either a substantial or an imputed way. However, when there is no analysis the innate ignorance of worldly beings apprehends and clings to the self and true existence in relation to individual knowable objects. Yet those phenomena are, according to you, established by conventional valid cognition and not refuted by reasoning consciousnesses—therefore you assert that they are *not* objects of refutation by reasonings. So, even if you say that all phenomena, from form through omniscience, are not emptiness, what are we to do?

The following consequence applies to your approach. Concerning the relative truth, which you describe as being the objects and subjects perceived by worldly people that are established by conventional valid cognition, the subject: it follows that it is logical to accept it as being the emptiness free from the self and true existence. For its phenomena are not empty of themselves, but you do describe them as emptiness. If you accept, it follows that the objects and subjects of the relative truth, which are not empty of themselves, are themselves selflessness, the lack of true existence, and emptiness, because of what you just accepted.

If that is the case, it follows that emptiness devoid of a self and true existence—the emptiness that refutes the self and true existence in relation to the true nature—is not established. For the self and true existence are themselves selflessness and the lack of true existence! If you accept, you will be forced to say that the self is selflessness and that true existence is the lack of true existence!

You cling to the notion that, after the true existence that is refuted by reasonings is refuted, the person, the aggregates, and other things still perform their own functions and are real. Clinging to them in that way, moreover, does not constitute clinging to characteristics and is therefore not refuted.

This description of realizing emptiness is not that of the emptiness of the Followers of the Middle Way. For it is impossible to accept the realness of the person, the aggregates, and so on in performing their own functions as the emptiness that is empty of the individual entities of phenomena. Instead, you take a "true existence" that you say does not exist among knowable objects and then make it existent by entertaining its hypothetical possibility. Phenomena's emptiness of this "true existence," you assert, is the unsurpassable nectar of emptiness.

Let us now turn to some points you make about the two truths. You say, "The two truths are of the same entity, but they themselves are not the same." The idea you are clinging to when you say this is that of the ultimate truth, emptiness, being different from the things of the relative such as form. However, trying to prove the status of the two truths in this way entails faults of both words and meaning. Let us first examine the faults connected to your words.

It follows that, conventionally, there is a third choice which is neither sameness nor difference. For "the sameness in entity of the two truths" does not carry the meaning of the sameness of the two truths. And it also does not carry the meaning of a difference between the two truths. You accepted the reasons, and the inclusion is established by the valid cognition of what is approved by others.

If you accept, then concerning the sameness in entity of the two truths that is the third choice, which is neither sameness nor difference, the sub-ject: it follows that it is impossible to determine its lack of inherent exis-tence using the reasoning of "beyond one or many." For, in this context, there is no apparent phenomenon in the reasoning that could qualify as either single or multiple.

Another consequence: it follows that, conventionally there is a third category between sameness and difference. For the two truths have the sameness that is the sameness in entity and the difference that is the dif-ference in terms of isolates. You accepted the reason, and the inclusion is established by what is approved by others. If you accept, it follows that sameness and difference are not contradictory!

Another consequence: it follows that the two truths are the same, because they are the same in entity. If you say the reason is not included in the predicate, it is, because difference in entity is necessarily difference.

Another consequence: it follows that it is impossible for the two truths to be the same in entity, because it is impossible for the two truths to be the same. If you say the reason is not included in the predicate, it is, because if you refute sameness, the overarching quality, you must also refute same-ness in entity, which is subsumed by sameness.

Let us now examine the faults in your assertion of the two truths' same-ness in entity with regard to meaning. If the two truths were the same in entity, it would be utterly impossible for anyone to realize the entities of forms and so on as emptiness. For you assert emptiness to be something different from the entities of forms and so on. And it is impossible to real-ize a quality without relying on what is qualified. If you accept, it would, for you, be impossible to reverse thoughts of attachment and so on in rela-tion to an attractive form, even if one observed the emptiness that is the suchness of form. For you, the attractiveness would be established as the entity of the form.

Furthermore, forms and so on would not be empty of their own enti-ties. Instead, they would be empty of something else, namely the object of refutation by reasons. If that really sufficed as the emptiness of form's own entity, it would also follow that form's emptiness of the horns of a rab-bit would be the emptiness of the own-entity of form. For, firstly, form is not empty of form, and the emptiness of form is form's emptiness of true existence, the object of refutation by reasons. And, secondly, the horns of a rabbit and the object of refutation by reasons are equal with regard to their nonexistence among knowable objects. If you accept, you will also be accepting that the horns of a rabbit are the entity of form and that the emptiness of rabbit horns is the true reality of form.

In this way you explain emptiness as phenomena's being empty not of themselves but of something else. From among the twenty types of emptiness, you only explain the emptiness of other, or extrinsic emptiness. For you, other-emptiness is the meaning of self-emptiness.

You may ask us, "In relation to form, what about the emptiness of form? Do you assert that it exists? Or do you say it does not exist?" At the time of no analysis, when we Followers of the Middle Way engage people who do not like interdependence in conversation, we use the terms of either existence or nonexistence—whatever the need may be—to help the person to whom we are talking relinquish his or her fear. We make such statements as provisional meanings and for a specific purpose. When we talk to people who like interdependence, we say, "It is beyond all elaborations of existence and nonexistence." At the time of analysis, however, since such emptiness is not established in any way, the Followers of the Middle Way do not think or say anything about it.

Here is another question for you: if, for you, emptiness (the absence of true existence) exists in relation to things that are themselves not emptiness, things such as form, is the relation of emptiness to those things one of contradiction or connection?[532] If emptiness exists in a way that is contradictory to the phenomena it qualifies, that is unreasonable, because contradiction cannot suffice as existence. If it is connected to the phenomena it qualifies, the connection must be one of identity or causality.[533] However, it is impossible for the absence of true existence to have a connection of identity or causality with the phenomena it qualifies.

You might say, "Emptiness, the absence of true existence, is supported by things such as form." Well then, space and the children of childless women would also be supported by form. Go ahead and fill the vase, the support, with its supported phenomena: the corn of the past and future, or, perhaps, flowers that grow in the sky!

According to you, the Proponents of Mind Only are correct when they posit emptiness as the nonestablishment of the imputed nature, which is something other than the other-dependent nature, in the other-dependent nature. For the five aggregates, created by the causes and conditions of the other-dependent nature, are not empty of their own entities. Rather, they are empty of something else, the object of refutation by reasons which is separate from the aggregates. For the Proponents of Consciousness—and, it seems, for you as well—this is the unsurpassable emptiness.

Those who focus on the two truths as being either the same in entity or different in terms of isolates, along with those who cling to true existence as being either real or unreal, will not only be devoid of antidotes to the two forms of self and to the two obscurations. They will also see the increase of clinging to the two selves and of the two obscurations. Their clinging to the establishment by conventional valid cognition of the relative causes them to fixate on the emptiness that is different from things, which for them are not empty of their own entities. Through reifying that emptiness as being either real or unreal, their clinging will only increase.

The Transcendent Conqueror himself derided such incorrect interpretations of emptiness as incomplete forms of emptiness, in the same way he derided the emptiness asserted by the non-Buddhists. The *Descent into Lanka* says:[534]

> Great Intelligence, the emptiness in one thing of another thing
> is an inferior emptiness. You should abandon it.

The *King of Samādhi Sūtra (Samādhirājasūtra, Tingdzin Gyalpö Do/ ting 'dzin rgyal po'i mdo)* says:

> Children of the victors, all disintegrating things
> And all existence are emptiness.
> Do not debate with the tīrthika scholars,
> Who propound an incomplete emptiness.

The *Great Transcendence of Misery Sūtra (Mahā-parinirvāṇa-sūtra, Yong su Nya-ngen le Depa Chenpö Do/yongs su mya ngan las 'das pa chen po'i mdo)* says:

> Child of noble family, all phenomena are empty of inherent nature. If you ask why, it is because the inherent nature of all phenomena cannot be observed.

And,

Since the bodhisattva mahāsattvas possess five qualities, they see that the nature of phenomena is, from the outset, empty, peace. Child of noble family, if a bhikṣhu or Brahmin[535] sees any phenomenon as not being empty of inherent nature, they are not a bhikṣhu. They are not a Brahmin. They have not obtained the perfection of transcendent knowledge. They have not gone beyond all misery. They do not directly see the buddhas and bodhisattvas. They are the retinue of māras. Child of noble family, all phenomena are empty of inherent nature. When bodhisattvas meditate on emptiness, they will see the emptiness of all phenomena.

Thus those who assert that the final turning is the literal, definitive meaning, and that the ultimate truth is not empty of its own entity, should reflect deeply on the quotations above. Moreover, those who assert that ultimate truth, not empty of the lack of true existence, is an established base by way of its entity should also think about those quotations.

Even if you assert that the middle turning is the literal, definitive meaning, [you still have no grounds for asserting "conventional valid cognition."] For the *Mother* scriptures say:

In the perfection of supreme knowledge one observes neither the permanence of form nor the impermanence of form. If one does not observe form, how could one observe its permanence or impermanence? The same principle should be understood to apply to all phenomena through omniscience.

Thus, in the manner of a prophecy,[536] the Buddha extensively refuted the assertions that form is established by conventional valid cognition, that it is not empty of its own entity, and that it is not an object of refutation by reasons.

2.2.2.1.1.6.2.3.2.2.2.1.2. THE EXTENSIVE EXPLANATION OF THE EMPTINESS OF THE OUTER

Because its nature is emptiness,
Form is empty of form.

Sound, smell, taste, tangible objects,
And mental objects are the same way. (6.183)

The lack of inherent nature of form and so on
Is asserted to be the *emptiness of the outer*. (6.184ab)

If you ask, "What is the emptiness of the outer," this refers to form
and so on. As to that, since it does not stay together and does not
cease, form is empty of form, because its nature is emptiness.*

The meaning of that quotation is as follows. The six outer sense-sources
are also empty of their own entities. Since the nature of form is emptiness,
form is empty of the entity of form. Sound, smell, taste, tangible objects,
and mental objects are also, in the same way, empty of their own entities.
The lack of inherent nature itself of form and so on, the six outer sources,
is asserted to be the emptiness of the outer.

2.2.2.1.1.6.2.3.2.2.2.1.3. THE EXTENSIVE EXPLANATION OF THE
EMPTINESS OF THE OUTER AND INNER

The lack of inherent nature of both outer and inner
Is the *emptiness of the outer and inner*. (6.184cd)

The lack of inherent nature, or emptiness of own-entity, of both the outer
and the inner sources is the emptiness of the outer and inner. *Distinguishing the Middle from the Extremes* asserts "outer and inner" as what is inside
the body and what is outside the body, respectively. The tradition of the
master Haribhadra[537] asserts "outer and inner" as the faculties and their
supports. The explanation found here, however, follows the sūtras.

2.2.2.1.1.6.2.3.2.2.2.1.4. THE EXTENSIVE EXPLANATION OF THE
EMPTINESS OF EMPTINESS

The wise explain the lack of phenomena's inherent existence
To be "emptiness."

---

* George Churinoff's translation of Chandrakīrti's autocommentary indicates that this
quotation, along with the quotations that appear in the beginning of the commentaries
to the root verses on the following emptinesses, is drawn from a "Prajñaparamita Sutra."
(Chandrakīrti 2004, pp. 143-159)

This emptiness is also asserted to be empty
Of the entity of emptiness. (6.185)

The emptiness of what is called "emptiness"
Is asserted to be the *emptiness of emptiness.*
It was taught in order to reverse the fixation
Of those who think of emptiness as a thing. (6.186)

If you ask, "What is the emptiness of emptiness," that which is empty of the emptiness of all phenomena is the emptiness of emptiness.

The topic of that quotation, the emptiness of emptiness, is taught by all of the dharma teachings of the tantras, by the tradition of Haribhadra, by the tradition associated with *Distinguishing the Middle from the Extremes,* and so on. However, here the master Chandrakīrti teaches in precise accordance with sūtra. The wise explain that conditioned phenomena, unconditioned phenomena, and so on lack an inherent nature or entity of their own. That lack of inherent nature, moreover, is "emptiness." Nāgārjuna's *Commentary on Bodhichitta (Bodhichittavivaraṇa, Changchub Sem kyi Drelpa/byang chub sems kyi 'grel pa)* says:

The nonarising of phenomena
Is excellently explained to be emptiness.

This emptiness is also asserted to be empty of its own entity of emptiness. If apparent phenomena even slightly existed as bases of refutation that are not empty, emptiness as a means of refutation would also exist. However, due to the reasonings explained above, there is not even the slightest phenomenon that is not empty. It is untenable for emptiness, therefore, to be an existent or an established base. Thus the emptiness of emptiness's own entity is asserted to be the emptiness of emptiness.

Apart from that, there are some scholars who think that emptiness is established as a basis that is either a thing or a nonthing. They say that this established base performs a function, in either a real or an unreal way.

However, the emptiness of emptiness was taught in order to reverse the fixation of people who think in such ways. Nāgārjuna's *Praise of the Supramundane* says:

To vanquish all conceptual imagination,
You taught the nectar of emptiness
And denounced fixation upon it.

And, from the *Sūtra Requested by Kāshyapa*:[538]

Kāshyapa, concerning those who conceptually fixate on emptiness due to their observation of emptiness: I say that they have fallen far from my teachings. Kāshyapa, it is permissible to dwell in the view of the person, which is similar in stature to Mount Meru. But that is not the case regarding those who, possessing flagrant pride, espouse the view of emptiness. Why? Kāshyapa, since emptiness is what uproots all views, I teach that espousing the view of only emptiness cannot be cured. For example, Kāshyapa, if a sick person is administered medicine, and that medicine exacerbates her illnesses, Kāshyapa, what do you think? If that medicine does not leave her stomach, will she gain freedom from what ails her?

Kāshyapa responded: O Blessed One, no she will not. If the medicine that exacerbates her illnesses does not leave her stomach, her illnesses will become all the more severe.

The Blessed One spoke: Kāshyapa, in the same way, emptiness is what uproots all views. Kāshyapa, I teach that one who espouses a view of only emptiness will be incurable.

And, from the *Thickly Arrayed Ornaments (Ghanavyūha, Gyen Tukpo Köpa/rgyan stug po bkod pa)*:[539]

One will not be harmed by the view of the self,
Which is merely the equivalent of Mount Meru.
Yet one will be harmed by the view of emptiness
If one espouses pride and false imagination.

Yogis and yoginīs who practice emptiness
Should not use it in an inappropriate way.

If they use it in an inappropriate way,
Its vital nectar will turn into poison.

Whatever views there are,
Whatever views embodied beings have,
Emptiness was taught
To help beings relinquish those views.

Some people may hear the view of emptiness
And then fail to dismantle emptiness itself as a view.
Their views will then be incurable,
Like a patient forsaken by the doctor.

Those quotations speak to the approaches of those such as the Jonang-pas and the Gendenpas *(dge ldan pa)*,[540] who cling to emptiness as being real and assert extrinsic emptiness as their view. These types of scholars are explained to be like patients forsaken by their doctors, for they espouse views that cannot be cured by the nectar of genuine dharma taught by the great doctor, the perfect Buddha, who endeavors to clear away all illnesses of the two obscurations.

2.2.2.1.1.6.2.3.2.2.2.1.5. THE EXTENSIVE EXPLANATION OF THE EMPTINESS OF THE GREAT
2.2.2.1.1.6.2.3.2.2.2.1.5.1. The explanation of the greatness that is the support or subject
2.2.2.1.1.6.2.3.2.2.2.1.5.2. The explanations of the way in which it is empty and of the purpose of this category

2.2.2.1.1.6.2.3.2.2.2.1.5.1. THE EXPLANATION OF THE GREATNESS THAT IS THE SUPPORT OR SUBJECT

Since they pervade without exception
The worlds of sentient beings' environments,
And since the example of the limitless ones shows their infinitude,
The directions are "great." (6.187)

What is the emptiness of the great? The eastern direction is empty of the eastern direction.

Other texts, such as *Distinguishing the Middle from the Extremes*, teach that the meaning of that quotation about the emptiness of the great refers to the environment of the world. Here, however, Chandrakīrti teaches in accordance with the *Mother* sūtras.

Beyond the ten directions—all of space—there are no worlds consisting of environments and inhabitants. Sentient beings and all environments and worlds are pervaded by these ten directions. Furthermore, these directions are completely included within the meditations of the limitless ones—loving-kindness and so on. Meditating on the four limitless ones means to be completely inclusive of all of space in one's meditation. Thus the example of limitlessness embodied in those practices shows the infinitude of the directions. Therefore, the ten directions are indeed "great."

2.2.2.1.1.6.2.3.2.2.2.1.5.2. THE EXPLANATIONS OF THE WAY IN WHICH IT IS EMPTY AND OF THE PURPOSE OF THIS CATEGORY

> The ten directions'
> Emptiness of themselves
> Is the *emptiness of the great.*
> It was taught in order to reverse fixation on greatness. (6.188)

These ten directions are empty of the directions' own entity. This emptiness is the emptiness of the great. It was taught in order to reverse the fixation on greatness that is held by people such as the Vaisheshikas, who think, "The directions are a substantial entity that pervades in a limitless way all of the particulars and so on of phenomena."

2.2.2.1.1.6.2.3.2.2.2.1.6. THE EXTENSIVE EXPLANATION OF THE EMPTINESS OF THE ULTIMATE

> Since it is the supreme objective,
> Nirvāṇa is the ultimate.
> Its emptiness of itself
> Is the *emptiness of the ultimate.* (6.189)

> In order to reverse the fixation
> Of those who think nirvāṇa is a thing,
> The Knower of the Ultimate
> Taught the emptiness of the ultimate. (6.190)

What is the emptiness of the ultimate? That which is called the ultimate is nirvāṇa. *Distinguishing the Middle from the Extremes* and other texts explain this emptiness to mean that since nirvāṇa is unchanging and does not cease, it is empty of nirvāṇa. There are many such ways of explanation, but here Chandrakīrti teaches in accordance with the *Perfection of Supreme Knowledge* sūtras. Nirvāṇa is the supreme objective of all beings. Therefore, it is the ultimate *(döndam/don dam)*.

As to that, "ultimate" renders the Sanskrit *paramārtha*, of which *parama* means "genuine" *(dam)* or "supreme," and *artha* means "objective" or "meaning" *(don)*. Thus, nirvāṇa is the ultimate—the most supreme objective. The emptiness of that nirvāṇa of nirvāṇa is the emptiness of the ultimate. Nirvāṇa is empty of itself because it is free from the four possibilities of being a thing, a nonthing, both, or neither.

The Particularists assert that instances of cessation through analysis are substantial entities that are equal in number to the instances of separation from the impure mental events.[541] The Practitioners of Yogic Conduct, on the other hand, assert that nirvāṇa is a thing that is established as the truth of cessation.

In order to reverse such fixation and bad views of those who think of and cling to nirvāṇa as being a real thing, the Buddha, the Knower of the Ultimate, taught the emptiness of the ultimate.

2.2.2.1.1.6.2.3.2.2.2.1.7. THE EXTENSIVE EXPLANATION OF THE
EMPTINESS OF THE CONDITIONED

> Because they arise from conditions, the three realms
> Are definitively described as being conditioned.
> The three realms' emptiness of themselves
> Is taught to be the *emptiness of the conditioned.* (6.191)

What is the emptiness of the conditioned? "Conditioned" refers to the three realms. As to that, the desire realm is empty of the desire realm.

The meaning of that quotation is asserted in various ways, but here Chandrakīrti teaches in accordance with the *Perfection of Supreme Knowledge* sūtras. Since they arise from causes and conditions, the three realms are definitively described in the sūtras as being conditioned. The three realms' emptiness of their own entity is taught to be the emptiness of the conditioned.

2.2.2.1.1.6.2.3.2.2.2.1.8. THE EXTENSIVE EXPLANATION OF THE EMPTINESS OF THE UNCONDITIONED

Phenomena free from
Arising, abiding, and impermanence are unconditioned.
Their emptiness of their own entity
Is the *emptiness of the unconditioned.* (6.192)

What is the emptiness of the unconditioned? "Unconditioned" means to be free from arising, free from cessation, free from disintegration, and free from changing from the state of abiding into something else. The unconditioned is empty of the unconditioned.

The meaning of that quotation is explained here in accordance with the sūtras. That which is free from the three defining characteristics of conditioned phenomena—arising in the beginning, abiding in the middle, and impermanence in the end—is unconditioned. Unconditioned phenomena's emptiness of themselves is the emptiness of the unconditioned. The teaching about this emptiness reverses fixation towards unconditioned phenomena, such as space, as being permanent.

2.2.2.1.1.6.2.3.2.2.2.1.9. THE EXTENSIVE EXPLANATION OF THE EMPTINESS OF WHAT IS BEYOND EXTREMES

That which does not have an extreme
Is called "beyond the extremes."
Its emptiness of precisely itself
Is explained as the *emptiness of what is beyond extremes.* (6.193)

What is the emptiness of that which is beyond extremes? "Extremes" refers to the extreme of eternalism and to the extreme of nihilism. That which does not have an extreme is "beyond the extremes." What is beyond the extremes is empty of what is beyond the extremes.

The meaning of the above is explained here according to the sūtras. That which does not have an extreme of eternalism or nihilism but is rather free from these two extremes is the path of the Middle Way, which is called "beyond the extremes." The state of what is beyond the extremes being empty of precisely itself is explained as the "emptiness of what is beyond extremes." This section of text refutes the assertion of some that the path beyond the extremes is a permanent thing.

2.2.2.1.1.6.2.3.2.2.2.1.10. THE EXTENSIVE EXPLANATION OF THE EMPTINESS OF THE BEGINNINGLESS AND ENDLESS

Since it is free
From a beginning at the start and an end at the finish,
Saṃsāra is described as being beginningless and endless.
Since it is free from coming and going, (6.194)

Cyclic existence, like an illusion, is devoid of its own entity.
This is the *emptiness*
Of the beginningless and endless.
It was definitively explained in the treatises. (6.195)

What is the emptiness of the beginningless and endless? That which has no observable beginning or end is free from coming and going. Since it does not stay together and does not cease, it is free from beginning, end, and middle.

The meaning of the above quotation is as follows. That which is free from beginning and end is saṃsāra. Since saṃsāra is free from a beginning at the start and an end at the finish, it is described as being beginningless and endless.

Here, the phrase "free from beginning, end, and middle" does not refer to a freedom from beginning and end from the confused perspective of the relative. Rather, it refers to saṃsāra's inherent nature—saṃsāra is free from arising, abiding, and disintegration.

Since this state of being free from beginning, end, and middle does not go somewhere else later, and since it does not come from some place it was before, cyclic existence is like an illusion. It is devoid of its own entity. This is the emptiness of the beginningless and endless. It was definitively explained in the treatises of the perfection of supreme knowledge, which possess the qualities of transformation and protection.

2.2.2.1.1.6.2.3.2.2.2.1.11. THE EXTENSIVE EXPLANATION OF THE EMPTINESS OF WHAT IS NOT TO BE DISCARDED

> "To discard" is definitively explained
> As "to cast away" or "to abandon."
> What should not be discarded
> Is that of which one should never let go. (6.196)
>
> What is not to be discarded
> Is empty precisely of itself.
> Therefore, this emptiness is called
> The *emptiness of what is not to be discarded.* (6.197)

What is the emptiness of what is not to be discarded? To discard is to cast away, to abandon, or to empty. What is not to be discarded is empty of what is not to be discarded.

The meaning of the above is explained in many ways, but here its meaning is explained as follows. "To discard" is definitively expressed as "to cast away" or "to abandon." That which is not to be discarded refers to that of which, conventionally, one should not let go. What should not be discarded is not an object of relinquishment and should in no way be abandoned. It is, rather, what should be adopted: the virtue of the two accumulations,[542] such as generosity. Those very things that are not to be discarded are empty of what is not to be discarded. Therefore, this emptiness is called the emptiness of what is not to be discarded.

2.2.2.1.1.6.2.3.2.2.2.1.12. THE EXTENSIVE EXPLANATION OF THE EMPTINESS OF NATURE

> The essence of conditioned phenomena and so on
> Is not created by the students—the solitary realizers
> And bodhisattvas—or by the Buddha himself.
> Therefore the essence, emptiness, of conditioned phenomena
> (6.198)
>
> And so on
> Is explained to be their nature.

Its emptiness of itself
Is the *emptiness of nature*. (6.199)

What is the emptiness of nature? The nature of phenomena is not created, nor was it conditioned. It was not created by the hearers . . .

The meaning of the above is as follows. The essence or nature of conditioned and unconditioned phenomena is something that neither students of the Buddha—the hearers, solitary realizers, and heirs of the victorious ones—nor the Tathāgata himself created through knowing it or seeing it.

Regardless of whether these individuals arrive or do not arrive in the world, the nature of phenomena is emptiness—phenomena are primordially empty. Since this was not created by any of these individuals, the essence, or emptiness, of conditioned phenomena and so on is explained to be their nature. This is a case of giving the name "nature" to the lack of nature.

You may think, "According to this symbolism of the Middle Way scriptures, it would be logical to express the qualities of fire, heat, and so forth as a nature. For those qualities were not created by noble beings and the like."

It is true that without analysis such a nature would not be refuted. However, even though heat and so forth were not created by noble ones, it is still illogical for those qualities to be natures from the perspective of other-approved reasonings. This is so because a nature is something that is uncontrived and nondependent upon others, whereas heat and so forth, though not created by noble ones, *are* created by ignorance and the other [links of dependent arising].

Emptiness, on the other hand, is not realized at the time of being an ordinary being, yet it is seen directly by noble beings. For this reason it is possible for ordinary beings to be doubtful regarding whether emptiness was created by noble beings. To address such doubts, the Buddha taught that emptiness was not created by the noble ones.

Since no cause or condition for emptiness apart from the noble ones' perception can be found, and since the noble ones as well did not create emptiness, emptiness can be tenably described as a "nature" that is uncontrived and independent. Such a nature's emptiness of itself is "the emptiness of nature."

The Jonangpas assert that the nature of all phenomena, the ultimate truth, is permanent and stable, and is not empty of its own entity. Their position is well refuted here, using the teaching that the empty nature of all phenomena is empty of its own nature.

The great Tsongkapa refutes the nature of phenomena (such as form) that is their emptiness of their own entities. He proposes instead that if the object of refutation by reasons (which has never existed among knowable objects) were to exist, it would be refuted by the nature that he calls emptiness. However, for him that emptiness is not empty of itself—it is empty of, again, the object of refutation by reasons, which does not exist among knowable objects.

His positions are refuted, however, in the *Mother* sūtras on the perfection of supreme knowledge. In those scriptures, the Buddha teaches how, in an interdependent and other-approved way, emptiness is the nature and essence of phenomena such as form. He also teaches how the emptiness nature of phenomena is itself emptiness. For, if form and so on were not empty of their own entities, emptiness would not be established in any way as the nature of all phenomena.

You assert a nature of emptiness that is empty of something that has never existed among knowable objects. That emptiness, moreover, is not empty of itself, but it is empty yet again of the object of refutation by reasons. According to you, the empty nature of phenomena would, rather than being emptiness, have an inherent nature of its own. Your emptiness would not be the emptiness of form and so on, which is empty of emptiness.

You may respond, "The nature of emptiness does have a nature of its own, but there is no fault, because that nature is an ultimate nature."

The Transcendent Conqueror taught emptiness as an antidote to views that regard any phenomenon as not being empty. If you view emptiness as something that is not empty of its own entity but instead has a nature of being an established base, what greater form of reification than that view could there be? Your approach is similar to doubting the ability of water to extinguish fire and then having the water itself blaze as fire—you will be left without any way to extinguish the water.

[Let us now examine another incorrect view]: When the Buddha spoke of natural nirvāṇa, or "the nirvāṇa that is the only truth," he described the relative truth as being "real in the sense of being primordially unreal." The meaning of that statement is that, from the outset, the relative possesses no reality whatsoever. From the standpoint of the supreme tradition of the Consequentialists, the purpose of those statements was not to declare that natural nirvāṇa is real in certain contexts.

Some scholars, however, interpret those statements as proof that the relative truth is not real even conventionally but the ultimate truth is truly existent, even conventionally. In particular, the great Zilungpa asserts that, even in the system of the Consequentialists, there are times when it is appropriate to assert the nature of the ultimate as being truly existent.

There can be no greater deprecation of the Consequentialist tradition than this. For, in this context of the teachings on the emptiness of nature, there is no split approach by which sometimes the nature is considered empty of itself and sometimes not—it is taught to apply universally that the nature is empty of itself.

2.2.2.1.1.6.2.3.2.2.2.1.13. THE EXTENSIVE EXPLANATION OF THE EMPTINESS OF ALL PHENOMENA

"All phenomena" refers to the eighteen constituents, the six types of contact,
The six feelings that arise from contact,
Physical phenomena, nonphysical phenomena,
And conditioned and unconditioned phenomena. (6.200)

All of these phenomena are void of their own entity.
This emptiness is the *emptiness of all phenomena*. (6.201ab)

What is the emptiness of all phenomena? "Phenomena" include the conditioned, the unconditioned . . .

The meaning of the above quotation is explained in many different ways, but here is explained in accordance with the sūtras. "All phenomena" refers to the eighteen constituents: the inner constituents (the eye and so on), the outer constituents (form and so on), and the consciousness constituents; the six types of contact: contact of the eye that meets with its objects through contact of the mind that meets with its objects; the six feelings that arise from those forms of contact; physical phenomena; nonphysical phenomena; conditioned phenomena; and unconditioned phenomena.

All phenomena are void of their own entity. This emptiness is the emptiness of all phenomena. Although the six types of contact and the six feelings are included within the eighteen constituents, the reason for teaching the six types of contact and the six feelings as foremost is because they are the direct causes of desire.

Also included in the eighteen constituents are physical phenomena and nonphysical phenomena, as well as conditioned phenomena and unconditioned phenomena. The reason for teaching these separately is because, in an elaborate classification scheme, one may speak of eighteen constituents, but if those classifications are condensed, they may be condensed into either of these two latter pairings.

2.2.2.1.1.6.2.3.2.2.2.1.14. THE EXTENSIVE EXPLANATION OF THE EMPTINESS OF DEFINING CHARACTERISTICS
2.2.2.1.1.6.2.3.2.2.2.1.14.1. The brief teaching of the essence
2.2.2.1.1.6.2.3.2.2.2.1.14.2. The extensive explanation of the subjects
2.2.2.1.1.6.2.3.2.2.2.1.14.3. The summary of the supports and the summary of the mode of emptiness

2.2.2.1.1.6.2.3.2.2.2.1.14.1. THE BRIEF TEACHING OF THE ESSENCE

"Suitable as form" and so on are not things.
This is *the emptiness of defining characteristics.* (6.201cd)

What is the emptiness of defining characteristics?[543] The defining characteristic of form is to be suitable as form. The defining characteristic of feeling is to experience. The defining characteristic of discrimination is to apprehend. The defining characteristic of formation is to form. The defining characteristic of consciousness is to be aware. Because they do not stay together and do not cease, the defining characteristics of phenomena—of conditioned phenomena and of unconditioned phenomena—are empty of their own defining characteristics.

The meaning of the above quotation is as follows. The defining characteristic of form, "suitable as form," through the defining characteristic of omniscience, "to actualize" *(ngön du jepa/mngon du byed pa)*, are not real things. This is the emptiness of defining characteristics.

2.2.2.1.1.6.2.3.2.2.2.1.14.2. THE EXTENSIVE EXPLANATION OF THE
SUBJECTS
2.2.2.1.1.6.2.3.2.2.2.1.14.2.1. The explanation of the defining characteristics
of the thoroughly afflicted
2.2.2.1.1.6.2.3.2.2.2.1.14.2.2. The explanation of the defining characteristics
of the completely pure

2.2.2.1.1.6.2.3.2.2.2.1.14.2.1. THE EXPLANATION OF THE DEFINING
CHARACTERISTICS OF THE THOROUGHLY AFFLICTED
2.2.2.1.1.6.2.3.2.2.2.1.14.2.1.1. The defining characteristics of the aggregates
and constituents
2.2.2.1.1.6.2.3.2.2.2.1.14.2.1.2. The defining characteristics of the sources
2.2.2.1.1.6.2.3.2.2.2.1.14.2.1.3. The defining characteristics of
interdependence

2.2.2.1.1.6.2.3.2.2.2.1.14.2.1.1. THE DEFINING CHARACTERISTICS OF
THE AGGREGATES AND CONSTITUENTS

> Form bears the defining characteristic of "suitable as form."
> Feeling is of the character of "experience."
> Discrimination apprehends characteristics;
> Formation refers to "forming." (6.202)

> Individually cognizing objects
> Is the defining characteristic of consciousness.
> The aggregates' defining characteristic is suffering.
> The character of the constituents is that of a poisonous snake.
> (6.203)

What are the defining characteristics of form and so on? The following
explanation is given in order to elaborate extensively on those characteristics. The definition of form is "that which is suitable as form," because
when physical phenomena contact each other, they are suitable to produce a transformation.

The definition of feeling is "that which experiences" the results of virtue
and misdeeds—satiation and agony, and so on. Discrimination is defined
as that which apprehends the uncommon characteristics of phenomena.
Formation is defined as the mind that forms things and moves in relation

to objects. The definition of consciousness is that which individually cognizes objects such as form. The defining characteristic of the appropriated aggregates is any one of the three kinds of suffering.[544] The definition of the constituents is identified by using the example of a similar phenomenon: poisonous snakes.[545]

2.2.2.1.1.6.2.3.2.2.2.1.14.2.1.2. THE DEFINING CHARACTERISTICS OF THE SOURCES

The Buddha taught that the sources
Are the doors for the arising of suffering. (6.204ab)

The Buddha taught that the twelve sources are the doors for the arising or origination of suffering.

2.2.2.1.1.6.2.3.2.2.2.1.14.2.1.3. THE DEFINING CHARACTERISTICS OF INTERDEPENDENCE

The defining characteristics of dependent arising
Are assembly and contact. (6.204cd)

Since dependent arising takes place due to the coming together and assembling of causes and conditions, its defining characteristics are assembly and contact.

2.2.2.1.1.6.2.3.2.2.2.1.14.2.2. THE EXPLANATION OF THE DEFINING CHARACTERISTICS OF THE COMPLETELY PURE
2.2.2.1.1.6.2.3.2.2.2.1.14.2.2.1. The defining characteristics of the path
2.2.2.1.1.6.2.3.2.2.2.1.14.2.2.2. The defining characteristics of the result

2.2.2.1.1.6.2.3.2.2.2.1.14.2.2.1. THE DEFINING CHARACTERISTICS OF THE PATH
2.2.2.1.1.6.2.3.2.2.2.1.14.2.2.1.1. The defining characteristics of the perfections, the concentrations, and so on
2.2.2.1.1.6.2.3.2.2.2.1.14.2.2.1.2. The defining characteristics of the factors of enlightenment
2.2.2.1.1.6.2.3.2.2.2.1.14.2.2.1.3. The defining characteristics of the three gates of liberation

2.2.2.1.1.6.2.3.2.2.2.1.14.2.2.1.4. The defining characteristics of the eight forms of liberation

2.2.2.1.1.6.2.3.2.2.2.1.14.2.2.1.1. THE DEFINING CHARACTERISTICS OF THE PERFECTIONS, THE CONCENTRATIONS, AND SO ON

> The perfection of generosity is giving;
> Discipline is to be without torment;
> Patience is to be free from anger;
> Exertion is to be without nonvirtue. (6.205)

> Concentration is to draw together;
> Supreme knowledge is to be free from attachment—
> These are held to be the defining characteristics
> Of the six perfections. (6.206)

> The Perfect Knower taught
> That the concentrations,
> The limitless ones, and the formless states
> Bear the definition "free of disturbance." (6.207)

From among the six perfections, to give to sentient beings one's body, enjoyments, and positive results is the perfection of generosity. Since through discipline one abandons harming others and instead of harming them helps them, the defining characteristic of discipline is to be without the torment of the mental afflictions. The definition of patience is to be free from anger towards those who do harm.

The definition of exertion is to be free from nonvirtue, since exertion is of the nature of fully taking hold of virtue. The definition of concentration is to draw together all positive qualities. The definition of supreme knowledge is to be free from attachment, since through supreme knowledge one travels to the state of nirvāṇa. These are stated to be the defining characteristics of these six perfections.

The victorious Perfect Knower, the Buddha, taught that the four concentrations,[546] the four limitless ones,[547] and the four formless states[548] bear the definition "free of disturbance," or free of anger, because all of them are attained through the relinquishment of attachment and aversion in relation to the desirable.

2.2.2.1.1.6.2.3.2.2.2.1.14.2.2.1.2. The defining characteristics
of the factors of enlightenment

The thirty-seven factors of enlightenment
Bear the defining characteristic of "that which brings deliverance." (6.208ab)

Because they are the cause by which one transcends saṃsāra, the thirty-seven factors of enlightenment[549] bear the defining characteristic of "that which is able to bring deliverance into liberation."

2.2.2.1.1.6.2.3.2.2.2.1.14.2.2.1.3. The defining characteristics
of the three gates of liberation

The defining characteristic of emptiness is voidness,
Since in emptiness there is no observation of things. (6.208cd)

The absence of characteristics is peace,
And the definition of the third gate
Is to be free from suffering and ignorance. (6.209abc)

The three gates of liberation[550] will now be defined. The defining characteristic of emptiness is voidness. For, since in emptiness there is no observation of things, it is not corrupted by the stains of thoughts.

The absence of characteristics bears the defining characteristic of being the peace that is the nonobservation of characteristics. Wishlessness, the third of the three gates of liberation, bears the defining characteristic of being free from suffering and ignorance. It is free of those qualities because, when its supreme knowledge examines the nature of the all-pervasive suffering of formations, it does not engender wishfulness in relation to that suffering.

2.2.2.1.1.6.2.3.2.2.2.1.14.2.2.1.4. The defining characteristics
of the eight forms of liberation

The eight forms of liberation
Bear the defining characteristic of causing liberation. (6.209cd)

The eight forms of liberation bear the defining characteristic of causing liberation, because they bring about liberation from the obscurations to absorption *(nyom juk/snyoms 'jug)*.

The eight are as follows. The first form of liberation is that of form-possessors viewing forms. The second is to view external forms with the outlook that internal forms do not exist. The third is the pleasant liberation, which is of the nature of the fourth concentration. The remaining five are the four formless liberations and the liberation that is the cessation of discriminations and feelings.

A more extensive explanation will now be provided. As to the first form of liberation, in order to become free from the obscurations to emanation, the yogins, relying mainly on the practice of concentration, assume an outlook towards themselves as being possessors of form. They then engage in a samādhi and a supreme knowledge that enable them to imagine the forms of others to be variously pleasant and unpleasant and of greater and lesser sizes.

The second is the same as the first, except for the one difference that, in it, the yogins dismantle the outlook towards themselves as possessors of form.

During the third, in order to gain liberation from the obscurations of desire to emanate pleasant forms and the lack of desire to emanate unpleasant forms, the yogins, relying on the fourth concentration, dismantle the outlook of form toward themselves, and then focus on pleasant, unpleasant, and neutral forms. They engender an outlook of mutual dependence, an outlook of connectedness, and, finally, they imagine that all forms are of one taste in being of a pleasant nature. This is accompanied by the concordant factors of the shamatha and vipashyanā meditative samādhis, as well as supreme knowledge.

The four formless liberations are engaged for the purpose of gaining freedom from craving toward one's own state of absorption. First is the liberation known as limitless space.[551] At the time of approaching it, one imagines, "Space is limitless." At the time of the main practice, one attains the full culmination of the experience of clear appearance connected to limitless space. This experience is accompanied by the concordant factors of the shamatha and vipashyanā samādhis and by supreme knowledge. Through attaining it, one gains liberations from craving one's own absorption.

This process is also applied in a correspondent way to the three other formless states: limitless consciousness, utter nonexistence, and the outlook of not existence, not nonexistence.

As for the eighth form of liberation, in order to gain liberation from the obscurations to the cessation of discriminations and feelings, the yogins rely on the mental state of the peak of existence. Through this they attain the absorption that entails the cessation of coarse discriminations and feelings.

2.2.2.1.1.6.2.3.2.2.2.1.14.2.2.2.2. THE DEFINING CHARACTERISTICS OF THE RESULT
2.2.2.1.1.6.2.3.2.2.2.1.14.2.2.2.2.1. The defining characteristics of the powers
2.2.2.1.1.6.2.3.2.2.2.1.14.2.2.2.2.2. The defining characteristics of the fearlessnesses
2.2.2.1.1.6.2.3.2.2.2.1.14.2.2.2.2.3. The defining characteristics of the correct and discerning awarenesses
2.2.2.1.1.6.2.3.2.2.2.1.14.2.2.2.2.4. The defining characteristics of great loving-kindness and so on
2.2.2.1.1.6.2.3.2.2.2.1.14.2.2.2.2.5. The defining characteristics of the unshared qualities of the Buddha
2.2.2.1.1.6.2.3.2.2.2.1.14.2.2.2.2.6. The defining characteristics of the knowledge of all aspects

2.2.2.1.1.6.2.3.2.2.2.1.14.2.2.2.2.1. THE DEFINING CHARACTERISTICS OF THE POWERS

The powers were taught to be of the nature
Of decisive resolution. (6.210ab)

The ten powers, which will be explained,[552] were taught to be of the nature of decisive resolution *(ten la bebpa/gtan la 'bebs pa)*. Due to this decisive resolution, they are unobstructed.

2.2.2.1.1.6.2.3.2.2.2.1.14.2.2.2.2.2. THE DEFINING CHARACTERISTICS OF THE FEARLESSNESSES

The fearlessnesses of the Protector
Are of the essence of utter stability. (6.210cd)

The fearlessnesses of the Protector are as follows. The Buddha is fearless regarding the realization connected to benefit for self. When he proclaims, "I have gained true enlightenment regarding all phenomena," no one, such as a bhikṣhu, Brahmin, god, māra, or Brahma could oppose that by saying,

"you have not gained enlightenment with respect to this phenomena."
The Buddha is fearless regarding the relinquishment connected to benefit for self. When he proclaims, "I have exhausted all defilements," no one can oppose that by saying, "You have not exhausted such-and-such aspect of defilement."

The Buddha is fearless in terms of teaching the phenomena of obscuration, a teaching that is connected to the benefit of others. When he teaches certain phenomena as obstacles for the hearers, no one can oppose that by saying, "Those will not become obstacles."

And the Buddha is fearless in terms of teaching the path of definite deliverance, which is connected to the benefit of others. When he teaches the path that brings definite deliverance from suffering, no one can oppose this teaching by saying, "Even through relying on those, one will not gain definitive deliverance from suffering."

These four fearlessnesses are of the essence of utter stability, because no one whosoever is capable of changing them into something else.

2.2.2.1.1.6.2.3.2.2.2.1.14.2.2.2.3. THE DEFINING CHARACTERISTICS OF THE CORRECT AND DISCERNING AWARENESSES

The correct and discerning awarenesses, confidence and so on,
Bear the defining characteristic of being unceasing. (6.211ab)

Regarding the four correct and discerning awarenesses,[553] which are to be explained,[554] the four factors of the awareness of confidence and so on bear the defining characteristic of being unceasing or unobstructed, because they are free from hindrances in relation to the four objects that they engage.

2.2.2.1.1.6.2.3.2.2.2.1.14.2.2.2.4. THE DEFINING CHARACTERISTICS OF GREAT LOVING- KINDNESS AND SO ON[555]

To thoroughly accomplish the benefit of beings
Is called "great loving-kindness." (6.211cd)

To fully protect those who are suffering
Is great compassion; joy
Is defined by utter joy, and impartiality
Bears the defining characteristic of being unadulterated. (6.212)

That which bears the defining characteristic of thoroughly accomplishing temporary and ultimate benefit for all sentient beings is called "the great loving-kindness of the Buddha." To fully protect those who are suffering is the great compassion of the Buddha. The great joy of the Buddha bears the defining characteristic of utter joy in all sentient beings never, at any time, being separate from happiness. Great impartiality, since it is free from attachment, anger, and so on, bears the defining characteristic of being unadulterated.

2.2.2.1.1.6.2.3.2.2.2.1.14.2.2.2.5. THE DEFINING CHARACTERISTICS OF THE UNSHARED QUALITIES OF THE BUDDHA

> The unshared qualities of the Buddha
> Are asserted to number eighteen.
> Since the Teacher cannot be deprived of them,
> Their defining characteristic is undeprivability. (6.213)

The unshared qualities of the Buddha are asserted to number eighteen. There are six associated with conduct: 1) his body is free of error, 2) his speech is free of idle chatter, 3) he is not forgetful of the needs of sentient beings, 4) there is no time at which his mind is in a state of nonequipoise, 5) he is free from discriminations of viewing saṃsāra and nirvāṇa as being separate objects, with one to reject and the other to adopt, and 6) he is free from the indifference by which he would neglect beings to be tamed without having analyzed them.

There are six qualities associated with realization; these are the Buddha's being free of decline in relation to aspiration, exertion, mindfulness, samādhi, supreme knowledge, and complete liberation.

There are three qualities associated with deeds; these are the Buddha's actions in body, speech, and mind being preceded by and following after wisdom.

There are three qualities associated with wisdom; these are the Buddha's wisdom visions that see without any impediment the knowable objects of the three times.

The Teacher cannot be deprived of these eighteen, for, since he is free from error, there is no chance for deprivation. Therefore these qualities of the Buddha are undeprivable and unconquerable. They bear the defining characteristic of undeprivability.[556]

2.2.2.1.1.6.2.3.2.2.2.1.14.2.2.2.6. THE DEFINING CHARACTERISTICS
OF THE KNOWLEDGE OF ALL ASPECTS

The wisdom of the knowledge of all aspects
Is asserted to have a defining characteristic of directness.
Others, which are only partial knowledges,
Are not asserted to be direct. (6.214)

The wisdom of the knowledge of all aspects is asserted to bear the defining characteristic of precisely and directly perceiving the mode of abiding
of all phenomena included within the aggregates, sense-sources, and constituents. Others, i.e., the knowledges of hearers and solitary realizers, are
only partial knowledges of knowable objects. Those forms of knowledge
are not asserted to be direct knowledges of all aspects.

2.2.2.1.1.6.2.3.2.2.2.1.14.3. THE SUMMARY OF THE SUPPORTS AND
THE SUMMARY OF THE MODE OF EMPTINESS

The defining characteristics of conditioned phenomena
And the defining characteristics of unconditioned phenomena
Are empty precisely of themselves.
This is the *emptiness of defining characteristics.* (6.215)

The defining characteristics of conditioned phenomena and the defining
characteristics of unconditioned phenomena are empty precisely of their
own entities. This is the emptiness of defining characteristics.

2.2.2.1.1.6.2.3.2.2.2.1.15. THE EXTENSIVE EXPLANATION OF THE
EMPTINESS OF NONOBSERVATION

The present does not abide;
The past and future do not exist.
The state in which these are unobservable
Is called "nonobservation." (6.216)

Nonobservation is void
Of its own entity.
Since it is unchanging and does not cease,
It is the *emptiness of nonobservation.* (6.217)

What is the emptiness of nonobservation? Since it does not stay together and does not cease, nonobservation is empty of nonobservation.

The meaning of the above quotation is as follows. The present is momentary. This momentariness, when analyzed in terms of its beginning, middle, and end, does not abide even for a moment. Since the past has ceased and the future has not arisen, neither the past nor the future exists. Therefore, the state of the three times in which the three times cannot be observed is called "nonobservation." Nonobservation is devoid of its own entity, since it does not stay together and does not cease. This state is called the emptiness of nonobservation.

2.2.2.1.1.6.2.3.2.2.2.1.16. THE EXTENSIVE EXPLANATION OF THE EMPTINESS OF THE NONEXISTENCE OF THINGS

Since they arise from conditions,
An entity of their assembly does not exist.
The emptiness of that nonexistence
Is the *emptiness of the nonexistence of things*. (6.218)

What is the emptiness of the entities of nonthings? The entities of qualities that arise from conduct do not exist, because they are dependently arisen. Since it does not stay together and does not cease, juncture is empty of juncture . . .

The meaning of the above quotation is as follows. Since they arise from causes and conditions, things have no entity of consisting in an assembly arisen from a collection of causes and conditions. The assembled and that which arises from the assembled are empty of their own entities. The emptiness of the nonexistence of such entity is the emptiness of the nonexistence of things.

There are many lineages of explanation of the sixteen emptinesses, such as the *Vajra Garland (Vajravalī, Dorje Trengwa/rdo rje phreng ba)*, the later Sambuta tantras, the root text, commentaries, and explanations of [Maitreya's] *Distinguishing the Middle from the Extremes*, and the root text and commentary to [Dignāga's] *Summary of the Eight Thousand Lines (Gye Tong Dön Du/brgyad stong don bsdu)*. The methods of teaching of all of these are for the most part in harmony with each other. However, to obtain an explanation of the definitive meaning, one must keep strictly to what is explained here in this context of the Middle Way teaching tradition.

2.2.2.1.1.6.2.3.2.2.2.2.2. THE ABBREVIATED EXPLANATION,
THE FOUR EMPTINESSES
2.2.2.1.1.6.2.3.2.2.2.2.2.1. The emptiness of things
2.2.2.1.1.6.2.3.2.2.2.2.2. The emptiness of nonthings
2.2.2.1.1.6.2.3.2.2.2.2.3. The emptiness of phenomena's own entities
2.2.2.1.1.6.2.3.2.2.2.2.4. The emptiness of other entities

2.2.2.1.1.6.2.3.2.2.2.2.1. THE EMPTINESS OF THINGS

The term "thing" refers, in brief,
To the five aggregates.
The emptiness of those five aggregates of themselves
Is explained to be the *emptiness of things*. (6.219)

What is the emptiness of things? The term "thing" refers to the appropriated aggregates.

To summarize the meaning of the above sixteen emptinesses, the *Entrance to the Middle Way* will now describe the four emptinesses. The term "thing" refers, in brief, to the five aggregates. The emptiness of those aggregates of themselves is the emptiness of things.

2.2.2.1.1.6.2.3.2.2.2.2.2. THE EMPTINESS OF NONTHINGS

In brief, "nonthing"
Refers to unconditioned phenomena.
Nonthings' being empty of themselves
Is the *emptiness of nonthings*. (6.220)

What is the emptiness of nonthings? "Nonthing" refers to unconditioned phenomena.

To summarize the meaning of the above quotation, the expression "nonthing" refers to unconditioned phenomena such as space and nirvāṇa. The emptiness of nonthings of themselves is called "the emptiness of nonthings."

2.2.2.1.1.6.2.3.2.2.2.2.3. THE EMPTINESS OF PHENOMENA'S OWN
ENTITIES

> The absence of an essential nature
> Is the *emptiness of nature*.
> Since it was not created by anyone,
> It is called "nature." (6.221)

> What is the emptiness of own-essence? Own-essence is not cre-
> ated through being known or seen. Therefore it is the unerring
> nature.

The meaning of the above is as follows. The nature of phenomena—
the nonexistence of any phenomenon's own entity—is the emptiness of
nature. Since it was not created by the hearers and so on by their knowing
or seeing the nature of phenomena, it is called "nature."

2.2.2.1.1.6.2.3.2.2.2.2.4. THE EMPTINESS OF OTHER ENTITIES

> Whether buddhas arise
> Or not, in reality
> The emptiness of all things remains.
> Therefore it is excellently proclaimed to be an "other entity."
> (6.222)

> This emptiness, which is also called "the perfect limit" and
>   "suchness,"
> Is the *emptiness of other entities*. (6.223ab)

The sūtras say:

> What is the emptiness of other entities? Whether the tathāgatas
> arise or do not arise, the dharmatā of phenomena abides. The
> dharmadhātu, the definitive dharma, suchness, the suchness
> that is not other, and the perfect limit—all of these abide,
> because they are not created by others.

The meaning of the above is as follows. Whether buddhas arise or not,
in reality the abiding mode and the suchness of all things is emptiness.

Conventionally, it always exists while not being established as any kind of entity. Therefore, since it is an object of realization of sublime wisdom, it is excellently proclaimed to be an "other entity."

Alternatively, it is called "the perfect limit": since it is beyond saṃsāra, and exists on the "other side" of saṃsāra, it is an "other entity." Since it does not change in its manifestation, it is "suchness." These descriptors, which bear the defining characteristic of emptiness, refer to the emptiness of different things.

The following is a description of how the four emptinesses encompass the sixteen emptinesses. The first of the four emptinesses includes all emptiness that involve conditioned phenomena. The second emptiness includes all emptinesses that involve ultimate, unconditioned phenomena. The third emptiness includes the emptinesses of nature, and the fourth includes the emptiness of emptiness. The fourth emptiness was taught in order to dispel the misconception of asserting suchness, the perfect limit, and so on to be an extrinsic emptiness that is not empty of its own entity. Therefore, it should be understood that the sixteen emptinesses are included in these latter four.

The *Ṭīkā* here presents extensive refutations, positions, and critical analyses.

2.2.2.1.1.6.2.3.2.2.3. THE SUMMARY

These emptinesses were excellently proclaimed
In the teachings of the perfection of supreme knowledge.
(6.223cd)

These emptinesses which were just explained, the elaborate categorization of sixteen and the brief categorization of four, were excellently proclaimed in the sūtras falling under the category of the mother of all victorious ones—the perfection of supreme knowledge.

2.2.2.1.1.6.3. THE CONCLUDING SUMMARY BY WAY OF STATING THE QUALITIES OF THE GROUND[557]

2.2.2.1.1.6.3.1. The way of entering into cessation through the supreme knowledge that realizes the two truths

2.2.2.1.1.6.3.2. The way in which, out of compassion, the bodhisattvas do not abandon sentient beings

2.2.2.1.1.6.3.3. The way in which the bodhisattvas outshine the other noble ones when they achieve the higher grounds

2.2.2.1.1.6.3.4. The way in which the two benefits will be perfected through realizing the two truths

2.2.2.1.1.6.3.1. THE WAY OF ENTERING INTO CESSATION THROUGH THE SUPREME KNOWLEDGE THAT REALIZES THE TWO TRUTHS

> Thus the light rays of the bodhisattvas' intelligence bring forth the brilliance of suchness.
> Just like a myrobalan fruit in the palm of the hand,
> The bodhisattvas realize that the three realms without exception have been unborn from the outset.
> Through the power of conventional truth, they proceed to cessation. (6.224)

The *Entrance to the Middle Way* will now describe the sublime, unique qualities of the bodhisattvas who abide in the perfection of supreme knowledge. In doing so it will bring the chapter on supreme knowledge to completion.

Through engaging in the analyses that were explained above, the bodhisattvas develop an intelligence whose light rays vanquish all the darkness that stands in the way of their seeing the true nature of reality. These bodhisattvas thoroughly illuminate the brilliance of the true nature that is suchness.

To give an example of the clarity of their perceptions at this stage we may turn to the myrobalan fruit.[558] When holding that fruit in the palm of one's hand, everything—outside and inside—is seen clearly and directly, without impediment. With the same level of clarity, the bodhisattvas at this stage realize that the entirety of the three realms of existence are primordially unarisen.

Ultimately the bodhisattvas do not enter into the state of absorption. Nevertheless, through the power of engaging in the conventional truth of the world, they move in the direction of, or realize, the entrance into the natural cessation that is suchness free from all elaborations.

2.2.2.1.1.6.3.2. THE WAY IN WHICH, OUT OF COMPASSION, THE
BODHISATTVAS DO NOT ABANDON SENTIENT BEINGS

Though they always possess the aspects of mind that are
    commensurate with cessation,
They also generate compassion for beings without a protector.
    (6.225ab)

Having actualized cessation, do these bodhisattvas cast away the benefit
of others? No, they do not. The bodhisattvas at this stage attain the ability to always enter into the absorption of cessation. Therefore, during the
phase of the main practice, they possess the superior aspects of mind that
are commensurate with nirvāṇa.

However, during the preparation and the subsequent phase, their minds
are full of love towards all beings included within saṃsāra. Therefore they
also generate great compassion for the beings of cyclic existence who are
without a protector.

2.2.2.1.1.6.3.3. THE WAY IN WHICH THE BODHISATTVAS OUTSHINE
THE OTHER NODLE ONES WHEN THEY ACHIEVE THE HIGHER
GROUNDS

On higher grounds, the bodhisattvas conquer with their
    intelligence
All of those born from the Sugata's speech and also the middling
    buddhas. (6.225cd)

On grounds that are higher than this sixth bodhisattva ground, the seventh ground and upward, the bodhisattvas' intelligence, through the
power of its supreme knowledge, conquers without exception the hearers, who are born from the speech of the Sugata, and the solitary realizers,
the middling buddhas.

2.2.2.1.1.6.3.4. THE WAY IN WHICH THE TWO BENEFITS WILL BE
PERFECTED THROUGH REALIZING THE TWO TRUTHS

Spreading the vast immaculate wings of the relative and suchness,
These sovereign swans fly ahead to lead the flock of beings.
Through the powerful winds of virtue,

They proceed to the other shore of the victorious ones' qualities. (6.226)

This completes the sixth bodhichitta generation from the *Entrance to the Middle Way*.

The bodhisattvas on this ground spread their vast wings of the qualities of the relative—generosity and the other perfections, as well as the close placements of mindfulness and so on—which now blaze even brighter than before. They also spread their wings of suchness, the ultimate truth.

Since these wings are free from conceptions and free from the stains of self-centered concern, they are immaculate. These sixth-ground bodhisattvas are like the sovereigns of swans—through their many sublime qualities, they fly out in front of the flock of the beings who are to be tamed by them. Through the powerful winds of the two accumulations' virtues, they lead those beings to the other shore of the ocean of the qualities of the victorious ones, an inexhaustible ocean of unfathomable depth.

This completes the explanation of the sixth bodhichitta generation, called *The Manifest*, from the *Entrance to the Middle Way*.

⫶ Ground Seven: Gone Far Beyond

The explanation of Gone Far Beyond
(Dūraṃgamā, Ringdu Songwa/ring du song ba)

> Here on *Gone Far Beyond*, the bodhisattvas
> Can enter into cessation in every moment.
> They also attain the perfection of methods, which greatly
> blazes. (7.1)

This completes the seventh bodhichitta generation from the *Entrance to the Middle Way*.

An explanation from the perspective of the seventh bodhichitta generation will now be given. The mind of the bodhisattva abiding here on *Gone Far Beyond*, the seventh bodhisattva ground, enters into and arises from, in every moment, the absorption of the cessation that was attained on the sixth ground. However, it is not the case that the bodhisattvas on this ground fully actualize cessation. The sūtras say:[559]

> O children of the Victorious One! The bodhisattvas on the sixth ground and upwards enter into the absorption of the cessation of bodhisattvas. On the seventh bodhisattva ground, the bodhisattvas, in each and every moment of mind, enter into and arise from cessation. However, do not understand this to mean that they fully actualize cessation.

Thus, the mere *label* "cessation" is used to describe the bodhisattvas' absorption at this stage. The meaning of the noble ones' absorption is asserted by the faction of the hearers to refer to the cessation of the sixfold collection of consciousnesses. The Particularists assert it to be a nonassociated formation that is substantially established. The Followers of Sūtra assert it to be an imputed existent. The noble Asaṅga says *(Abhid-harmasammucchaya, Chö Ngönpa Kuntü/chos mngon pa kun btus)*:[560]

> What is the absorption of cessation? When one becomes free from the desire connected to the perceptual state of utter non-existence, one employs the mental engagement that involves the discrimination of calm abiding and arises after one begins to move upward from the peak of existence. Through the practitioner's employing this mental engagement, some unstable primary minds and mental events, along with even some that *are* stable, cease. This cessation is labeled "the absorption of cessation."

In that way Asaṅga asserted the absorption of cessation to be the calm abiding of coarse feelings and discriminations of the noble ones who have attained the mental state of the peak of existence. He thus teaches it to be a nonassociated formation imputed[561] upon the phase of the aggregates in which the sevenfold collection, along with its accompanying factors, has ceased.

Here, the noble Nāgārjuna and his followers assert [such] absorption to be the suchness that is free from all elaborations.

The autocommentary says:

> To enter the absorption of cessation is to enter the absorption of the perfect limit[562] *(yangdakpe ta/yang dag pa'i mtha')*. Therefore suchness is called "cessation," because, when one enters into or engages in suchness, all elaborations come to their cessation.

The hearers and solitary realizers remain for a long time in the absorption of cessation, because they are extremely fond of peace. Since the bodhisattvas do not want peace and are skilled in methods, from the seventh ground onward they enter into and arise from cessation in every instant. In this way, through the power of their intelligence, they outshine the hearers and solitary realizers.

The above statement that the bodhisattvas enter into and arise from cessation refers to the capability of the bodhisattvas to enter cessation in every instant and to arise from cessation in every instant. In other contexts, many moments would have to elapse with regard to the distinct actions of entering into cessation and arising from cessation.[563]

On the eighth ground, there is, just as on the seventh, a momentary entrance into the absorption of cessation. However, there is also, on the eighth ground, a phase in which the bodhisattvas do not arise from cessation in every moment. This is so because the bodhisattvas of the eighth ground have a greater ability to rest evenly in suchness, since they are free from effort and free from the apprehension of characteristics.

Since the bodhisattvas of the seventh ground are able to enter into and arise from cessation with each moment, they attain the perfection of methods *(upāya, tap/thabs)*, which excellently blazes for them in a completely pure way. When supreme knowledge takes on special appearances it becomes methods, powers, aspirations, and wisdom.[564] At those times it is called "methods" and so on; but the methods and so on are none other than supreme knowledge.[565]

This completes the explanation of *Gone Far Beyond*, the seventh bodhichitta generation from the *Entrance to the Middle Way*.

⫶ Ground Eight: The Immovable

2.2.2.1.1.8. The explanation of The Immovable
(*Achala, Miyowa/mi gyo ba*)
2.2.2.1.1.8.1. The brief teaching on the essence of the ground
2.2.2.1.1.8.2. The extensive explanation of its qualities

2.2.2.1.1.8.1. THE BRIEF TEACHING ON THE ESSENCE OF THE GROUND

> In order to repeatedly attain virtues greater than before,
> On this ground the great beings become irreversible
> And enter into *The Immovable*. (8.1)

Now an explanation from the perspective of the eighth bodhichitta generation will be given. In order to repeatedly attain virtue that exceeds the virtue of the two accumulations gathered on the seventh ground and lower, the bodhisattvas of the eighth ground now attain forbearance in relation to the nonarising of phenomena. Through this forbearance, their path to the wisdom of buddhahood becomes irreversible.

These great beings thus enter into *The Immovable*. There is a reason for their repeatedly attaining virtues that exceed those attained on the seventh ground—the sūtras say *(Ten Grounds)*:[566]

> O, children of the Victor, let me begin with an example: if you set out on land with a large ship to sail the great ocean, you must work very hard to carry the ship until you reach the water's edge. Once you reach the ocean, however, the ship's sails pick up the wind, and the ship moves rapidly without any effort. Moreover, the distance you will travel during just one day of sailing in this

way could not possibly be covered in even one hundred years by
traveling with the ship as you did before, on land.

O, children of the Victor, it is the same way regarding the bodhisattvas' steadfast accumulation of merit, gathered through
genuinely practicing the great vehicle. Here, the bodhisattvas'
conduct arrives at the ocean: due to spontaneously present wisdom, even an instant of their experiencing the wisdom of omniscience will far outrival all the bodhisattvas' previous actions of
one hundred thousand eons.

Thus, the grounds preceding the eighth ground entail effort. Once one
attains the eighth ground, one engages effortlessly and naturally in the
wisdom of buddhahood. Thus there is a great distinction possessed by this
ground in terms of the bodhisattvas' rapidity of progress and in terms of
the manner in which they attain further positive qualities.

2.2.2.1.1.8.2. The extensive explanation of its qualities
2.2.2.1.1.8.2.1. The qualities of the perfection of aspirations and of being
guided by the buddhas
2.2.2.1.1.8.2.2. Though unsurpassable in the three realms, they still have
yet to accomplish the qualities of buddhahood
2.2.2.1.1.8.2.3. Though saṃsāra has stopped for them, they bring the
qualities of buddhahood to perfection through the ten masteries

2.2.2.1.1.8.2.1. The qualities of the perfection of aspirations and of being guided by the buddhas

Their aspirations become extremely pure,
And they are roused from cessation by the victorious ones. (8.2)

The aspirations (*praṇidhāna, mönlam/smon lam*) of these bodhisattvas,
ten sexdecillion[567] of which were made on the first ground, at this time
become extremely pure. Through the perfection of aspirations, their qualities become superior. This ground is posited as the ground of the youthful
children of the victorious ones: on the ninth ground one attains the state
of victorious regent, while on the tenth ground one receives the empowerments of the victorious ones in the manner of a Chakravartin king.
  Since on this ground all mental afflictions without exception are relin-

quished, one enters without effort into the dharmadhātu. Therefore at this time the victorious ones must encourage the bodhisattvas to arise from their absorption, for their not arising from absorption would sever in an untimely way the continuity of the benefit they bring to others. The victorious ones address them as follows:

> You do not have the wisdom, powers, and other qualities of
>   buddhahood that we have.
> In order to attain these, hold fast to exertion!

In this way the victorious ones rouse them from cessation, making them accomplish the qualities and vast wisdom of buddhahood. The sūtras say (*Ten Grounds*):[568]

> O, children of the victorious ones! The bodhisattvas abiding on this *Immovable* bodhisattva ground develop the full power of their aspirations.

Up until:

> ... the continuity of the activities for all sentient beings would be severed.

The nirvāṇa from which the bodhisattvas are roused at this time is explained in the following quotation from the *Brilliance of the Sun (Nyi Nang/nyi snang)*:[569]

> This nirvāṇa is not the nirvāṇa of the hearers. For the bodhi-sattvas cast far away the mental engagements of the hearers from the time they engender bodhichitta onward. Nor is it the nirvāṇa of the buddhas. For this nirvāṇa does not relinquish all of the factors to be relinquished by meditation. What is this nirvāṇa? In general one can speak of eight types of nirvāṇa: 1) the nirvāṇa that follows the attainment of the peak stage [of the path of juncture] and is a transcendence of the severance of the roots of virtue; 2) the nirvāṇa that follows the attainment of the patience stage and is a transcendence of the lower realms; 3) the nirvāṇa that follows the attainment of concen-

tration and is [itself] a branch of concentration; 4) the nirvāṇa of the stream-enterer that transcends the eighth level of existence; 5) the nirvāṇa of the once-returner that transcends the two desirous existences; 6) the nirvāṇa of the nonreturner that transcends the desire realm; 7) the nirvāṇa of arhats, which takes on the forms of being with and without remainder; and 8) the nirvāṇa bearing an ulterior intention. Of these eight, the nirvāṇa referred to here is the last. It is posited as a form of nirvāṇa by bearing in mind the potential severance of benefit to others.

2.2.2.1.1.8.2.2. THOUGH UNSURPASSABLE IN THE THREE REALMS, THEY STILL HAVE YET TO ACCOMPLISH THE QUALITIES OF BUDDHAHOOD

Since the mind that is free from attachment does not coexist with faults,
On the eighth ground the impurities and their roots are thoroughly pacified.
Though the mental afflictions are exhausted and they become unsurpassable in the three realms,
They are not able to attain what buddhas possess in a limitless way, similar to space. (8.3)

As was explained above, the bodhisattvas on the eighth ground are roused from cessation. Due to their being roused in that way, they become stainless: just as brightness and darkness cannot exist in the same place, the mind that is free from attachment due to the rising of the sun of nonconceptual wisdom does not coexist with the dark faults of the mental afflictions.

On the eighth ground, therefore, the stains that are the causes for birth in the three realms of saṃsāra—the mental afflictions that had arisen before—are thoroughly pacified at their very root. Since the bodhisattvas here exhaust and relinquish the mental afflictions without exception, they now become free from attachment toward the three realms. They become unsurpassable[570] in the three realms.

Nevertheless, the bodhisattvas at this stage are unable to attain the qualities of buddhas. They cannot attain the qualities that buddhas, in a manner limitless as space, possess. Since this is the case, the bodhisattvas must apply themselves all the more energetically in order to attain those qualities.

2.2.2.1.1.8.2.3. THOUGH SAṂSĀRA HAS STOPPED FOR THEM,
THEY BRING THE QUALITIES OF BUDDHAHOOD TO PERFECTION
THROUGH THE TEN MASTERIES

Even though saṃsāra has stopped for them, they attain the ten masteries, and through these
They display their own essential nature in many different ways to the beings of cyclic existence. (8.4)

This completes the eighth bodhichitta generation from the *Entrance to the Middle Way*.

How do these bodhisattvas relinquish all of the mental afflictions and bring the qualities of buddhahood to perfection? For them, taking birth in saṃsāra due to mental afflictions or due to actions—be they virtuous or nonvirtuous, contaminated or uncontaminated—has stopped. However, they do attain the ten masteries *(wang chu/dbang bcu)*, which will be explained below.

Through these ten masteries, they display for the benefit of others their own essential character to the beings of cyclic existence via bodies that are of a mental nature. They manifest in a variety of ways: sometimes they display bodies to the six realms of saṃsāra; sometimes they display nirvāṇic bodies to worldly pure realms.

They create such displays through emanation and also through nonemanation by relying on the principal *(rang-gyü/rang rgyud)* body they have taken on. Through making such displays, they perfect without exception the accumulations and purifications. The "mental body" mentioned here is explained to be similar to a state in which one is able to go wherever one thinks of without any impediment.[571]

As to the ten masteries, the bodhisattvas attain:

1) mastery over life, because they can bless their life [spans to endure] for an inexpressible number of eons;

2) mastery over mind, because they enter into states of absorption through limitless avenues of samādhi;

3) mastery over accoutrements *(yo-je/yo byad)*, because they are able to continually bless and display many arrays of ornaments in all world realms;

4) mastery over actions, because, through the blessings of the karma they have accumulated, they can display any birth desired[572] in accordance with the capabilities of disciples;

5) mastery over birth, because they are able to display any birth in accordance with the capabilities of disciples in all of the world realms;[573]

6) mastery over aspirations, because they can be born in whatever buddha realm they like, at whatever time they like, and display themselves as buddhas;

7) mastery over imagination *(möpa/mos pa)*, because they can display all of the world realms as being utterly filled with buddhas;

8) mastery over miracles, because they are able to continually display all of the miraculous deeds that appear in all of the buddha realms;

9) mastery over wisdom, because they continually display the qualities of the tathāgatas, such as the powers; and

10) mastery over phenomena, because they continually display the appearances of the gateways of dharma that are beyond center or fringe.[574]

This completes the explanation of the eighth bodhichitta generation, *The Immovable*, from the *Entrance to the Middle Way*.

: Ground Nine: Excellent Intelligence

2.2.2.1.1.9. THE EXPLANATION OF EXCELLENT INTELLIGENCE
(*Sādhumatī, Lekpe Lodrö/legs pa'i blo gros*)

> On the ninth, the bodhisattvas' powers, though needless to
> mention, become completely pure.
> They also attain the completely pure form of the correct and
> discerning awarenesses, qualities that have been theirs all
> along. (9.1)

This completes the ninth bodhichitta generation from the *Entrance to
the Middle Way*.

Now, an explanation from the perspective of the ninth bodhichitta generation, *Excellent Intelligence*, will be given.

On this ninth bodhisattva ground, the bodhisattvas' perfection of powers *(bala, top/stobs)*, though needless to mention, becomes pure in a full
and complete way due to analysis and familiarization, causing them to
attain all the powers. They also attain the completely pure form of the
four correct and discerning awarenesses, which had been their own qualities all along, but here they become completely purified.

These four are the correct and discerning awarenesses of phenomena,
meanings, contextual etymologies, and confidence. The first of these correct and discerning awarenesses, that of phenomena, excellently cognizes
the defining characteristics of all phenomena. The second, that of meanings, excellently cognizes the classifications of all phenomena. The third,
that of contextual etymologies, excellently cognizes how to teach all phenomena in an unmixed way. The fourth, that of confidence, excellently

cognizes how to provide in an unimpeded way answers to questions that accord with the dharma.

This completes the explanation of the ninth bodhichitta generation, *Excellent Intelligence*, from the *Entrance to the Middle Way*.

⦂ Ground Ten: Cloud of Dharma

2.2.2.1.1.10. The explanation of Cloud of Dharma
(*Dharmameghā, Chökyi Trin/chos kyi sprin*)

> On the tenth ground, the bodhisattvas receive the most sublime
> empowerments from the buddhas of all directions,
> And their wisdom also becomes utterly supreme.
> Just as water flows from rain clouds,
> From these bodhisattvas a spontaneously present rain of dharma
> falls down for the harvest of beings' virtue. (10.1)

This completes the tenth bodhichitta generation from the *Entrance to
the Middle Way*.

Now, an explanation from the perspective of the tenth bodhichitta generation will be given. These bodhisattvas who abide on the tenth bodhisattva ground, *Cloud of Dharma*, receive the most sublime empowerments
via great rays of light from the buddhas of all of the ten directions. They
become regents of the victors, the kings of dharma. The sūtras add:[575]

> At the end of one octodecillion[576] samādhis, the bodhisattvas
> make manifest a samādhi that is called "that which possesses
> the empowerment of being inseparable from the wisdom of the
> omniscient ones."

Up until:

> ... the bodhisattvas sit there, and are empowered by the bud-
> dhas who have assembled there from all of the buddha realms
> by means of light rays emanating from their foreheads.

At this time, their perfection of wisdom *(jñāna, yeshe/ye shes)* also becomes utterly supreme. Just as limitless water flows from rain clouds, from these children of the victorious ones a spontaneously present rain of genuine dharma falls down for the harvest of beings' virtue. That is why this ground is called *Cloud of Dharma.*

This completes the explanation of the tenth bodhichitta generation, *Cloud of Dharma,* from the *Entrance to the Middle Way.*

⦂ Qualities of the Bodhisattva Grounds

2.2.2.1.2.1. THE EXPLANATION OF THE QUALITIES OF THE FIRST GROUND

At the time of the first ground, the bodhisattvas see a hundred buddhas
And realize those buddhas' blessings.
They are able to remain for a hundred eons,
And correctly engage the beginnings and ends of those ages.
(11.1)

These intelligent ones are able to enter into and let go of one hundred samādhis;
They can cause one hundred worlds to quake, and they can illuminate one hundred realms.
Through their miracles, they ripen one hundred sentient beings,
And, in keeping with the number one hundred, can go to that many buddha realms. (11.2)

These children of the Lord of Sages open one hundred gates of dharma;

They can display one hundred bodhisattvas in their own body,
Each bodhisattva beautified by a retinue and enjoyments,
And each in turn being surrounded by one hundred
    bodhisattvas. (11.3)

Now the *Entrance to the Middle Way* will provide an explanation of the numbers of qualities attained by the bodhisattvas, beginning with the first bodhichitta generation.

At the time of attaining the first ground, the children of the victorious ones see one hundred buddhas in an instant or brief moment. These bodhisattvas also realize and comprehend the blessings of those buddhas. The bodhisattvas remain for one hundred eons and they correctly engage in the wisdom vision that sees the end and beginning of those ages.

These intelligent bodhisattvas, in one instant, can enter into and let go of, or arise from, one hundred samādhis. They are able to cause one hundred worlds, such as the *Unafraid (Mi Jepa/mi mjed pa)*,[578] to quake, and can also illuminate one hundred realms. They can ripen one hundred sentient beings through their miracles, and, in keeping with the number one hundred, can travel to one hundred pure realms.

These children of the Lord of Sages can open one hundred gates of dharma and can also display in their own bodies the forms of one hundred bodhisattvas. Each of these hundred bodhisattvas is beautified by his or her own retinue and enjoyments, and each of them in turn is surrounded by one hundred bodhisattvas.

2.2.2.1.2.2. THE EXPLANATION OF THE QUALITIES OF THE
SECOND GROUND

By abiding on *Supreme Joy*, the intelligent bodhisattvas attain
    the qualities explained.
In the same manner, those who abide on *The Stainless*
Attain the thousandfold manifestation of those qualities.
    (11.4abc)

By abiding on the ground of *Supreme Joy*, the intelligent bodhisattvas attain the hundredfold manifestation of the twelve qualities that were explained above.[579] In the same manner, the bodhisattvas abiding on the second ground, *The Stainless*, attain the thousandfold manifestation of those twelve qualities. This is so because the qualities of these second-ground bodhisattvas are that much greater than those of first-ground bodhisattvas.

2.2.2.1.2.3. THE EXPLANATION OF THE QUALITIES OF THE THIRD THROUGH SEVENTH GROUNDS

On the next five grounds, the bodhisattvas attain those qualities (11.4d)

In their hundred thousandfold, billionfold,
Ten billionfold, trillionfold,
And sexillionfold
Manifestations, respectively. (11.5)

As to the next five grounds, the bodhisattvas on the third bodhichitta generation attain the above-mentioned twelve qualities in their hundred thousandfold manifestation. Those abiding on the fourth attain them in their billionfold manfestation. The bodhisattvas on the fifth ground attain them in their ten billionfold manifestation. On the sixth, they attain them in their trillionfold manifestation. On the seventh, they attain them in their sexillionfold[580] manifestation.[581]

2.2.2.1.2.4. THE EXPLANATION OF THE QUALITIES OF THE EIGHTH GROUND

The bodhisattvas who abide on *The Immovable* are free from thoughts.
They attain qualities that are equal in number
To the number of atoms that exist
In one hundred trillion worlds. (11.6)

The qualities of the bodhisattvas who dwell on grounds higher than the seventh are uncountable using numbers; therefore they are explained using the analogy of atoms contained in world realms. The bodhisattvas who abide on the eighth bodhichitta generation of *The Immovable* are free from thoughts. They attain qualities that are equal in measure and number to the number of atoms that exist in one hundred trillion worlds.

2.2.2.1.2.5. THE EXPLANATION OF THE QUALITIES OF THE
NINTH GROUND

> The bodhisattvas abiding on the ground
> Of *Excellent Intelligence* attain the qualities
> That were explained before, in a number
> That equals that of the atoms in one hundred vigintillion worlds.
> (11.7)

The bodhisattvas abiding on the ninth bodhichitta generation of *Excellent Intelligence* attain the qualities that were explained before, in a number that equals that of the atoms in one hundred vigintillion[582] worlds.

2.2.2.1.2.6. THE EXPLANATION OF THE QUALITIES OF THE
TENTH GROUND
2.2.2.1.2.6.1. The enumerations of the qualities explained before
2.2.2.1.2.6.2. The teaching on the limitless other qualities

2.2.2.1.2.6.1. THE ENUMERATIONS OF THE QUALITIES
EXPLAINED BEFORE

> Moreover, on the tenth ground, the bodhisattvas' qualities
> Go far beyond what can be expressed verbally.
> Nevertheless, to summarize them, their qualities become equal
>   in number
> To however many atoms there are in the inexpressible number
>   of buddha realms. (11.8)

Here on the tenth ground, the qualities of these children of the victorious ones go far beyond what can be expressed verbally. Thus, though they are not an object of verbal expression, to summarize them their qualities become equal in number to however many atoms there are in the inexpressibly inexpressible number[583] of buddha realms. The word "moreover" *(re shik/re zhig)* of the first line indicates that the qualities explained above are not exhausted with merely what was explained in relation to the ninth ground. It also indicates the progressive order of the topics to be taught.

2.2.2.1.2.6.2. THE TEACHING ON THE LIMITLESS OTHER QUALITIES

> In each pore of their bodies, they can display,
> In a single instant, bodhisattvas together with
> Countless buddha forms.
> They can also display gods, demigods, and humans. (11.9)

Bodhisattvas abiding on the tenth bodhichitta generation can, at the same time as being free from thoughts, display in each pore of their bodies inestimable numbers of bodhisattvas who, as a retinue, abide together with countless forms of perfect buddhas. These bodhisattvas are able to display such appearances in various different forms with each passing instant.

They can also display in a clear and distinct way beings that are different from the ones described above: gods, demigods, humans, and other inhabitants of the five realms of saṃsāra[584] in each pore of their body. The word "also" in the fourth line indicates that these bodhisattvas are capable of assuming the forms of Indra, hearers, and so on. By doing this they can, in a spontaneously present way, teach the dharma to beings that can be tamed by the teachers whose forms they assume.

⁝ The Resultant Ground of Buddhahood

2.2.2.2. THE EXPLANATION OF THE RESULT, THE GROUND OF
BUDDHAHOOD[585]
2.2.2.2.1. The place in which buddhas attain enlightenment
2.2.2.2.2. The manner in which they become enlightened
2.2.2.2.3. The presentation of the kāyas, the essence of enlightenment
2.2.2.2.4. The teaching of one enlightenment as three is a teaching that
bears an ulterior intention
2.2.2.2.5. The teaching of the time of enlightenment and the time of
remaining

2.2.2.2.1. THE PLACE IN WHICH BUDDHAS ATTAIN
ENLIGHTENMENT

> To be just like the full moon in a stainless sky, lighting the way
> for all,
> Once again you apply effort to achieve the ten powers within
> your reach.
> In Akaniṣṭha you attain that most exalted form of peace,
> The unexcelled rank of buddhahood with the fullest extent of
> qualities. (12.1)

Having explained the abundantly perfect cause, the bodhisattva grounds,
along with their qualities, Chandrakīrti now wishes to explain in a brief
manner the abundantly perfect result that follows such a cause—the
ground of buddhahood and its qualities. He does so in the manner of
praising the Buddha, the Transcendent Conqueror.

When the full moon, the moon of the fifteenth day of the lunar month,
appears in a stainless sky, it has the potential to clear away darkness and light

the way for all beings. In the same way, bodhisattvas on the tenth ground become aware of their potential to attain buddhahood. They attained the tenth ground by purifying the darkness of that which obscures the attainment of the qualities of buddhahood. Now they become aware of the fact that they possess the ability to actualize those qualities completely.

Once again they apply effort to attain the ten powers of the completely perfect state of buddhahood, the state of the Transcendent Conqueror. In the palace of Akaniṣṭha they attain the most exalted form of peace: the unsurpassed wisdom that is the pacification of all elaborations. This state possesses the ten powers and all other qualities in their fullest extent. It is unexcelled because there is no rank higher than this.

The Akaniṣṭha mentioned here is identified in various different ways in the sūtras, tantras, and commentaries. An extensive discussion of this issue is available in the seventh chapter, on the result stage, of the *Single Intention (Gong Chik/dgongs gcig)*. The *Descent into Laṅka*, moreover, refutes the notion that this Akaniṣṭha is the Akaniṣṭha of the Pure Places.[586] Yet the same sūtra also states that the buddhas do *not* attain enlightenment in an Akaniṣṭha *outside* of the form realms. These two separate points are made, in order, in the following quotations from the *Descent into Laṅka*:

> They relinquish the Pure Places
> And, in the pleasant place of Akaniṣṭha,
> The perfect buddhas awaken—
> The emanators will awaken here.

And,

> The buddhas will not awaken
> In the desire or formless realms.
> In the Akaniṣṭha of the form realm
> You, the one free of desire, will awaken.

Basing himself on these [seemingly contradictory] quotations, Lochen Kyapchok Palzang[587] [attempts to reconcile the two descriptions] by asserting that there must be another Akaniṣṭha in the form realm which is not a Pure Place. The *Ṭīkā*, however, [expresses doubt about this suggestion].

2.2.2.2.2. THE MANNER IN WHICH THEY BECOME ENLIGHTENED
2.2.2.2.2.1. The actual teaching
2.2.2.2.2.2. Relinquishing objections

2.2.2.2.2.1. THE ACTUAL TEACHING

Differences in containers do not produce differences in the space
they contain.
In the same way, no distinctions of things exist in suchness.
In your mind, you genuinely integrate the equal taste of all
phenomena.
Perfect knower, in an instant you comprehend all knowable
objects. (12.2)

When the buddhas truly and fully awaken in the place specified above,
they, the Transcendent Conquerors, attain the wisdom of omniscience in
a single instant.

Containers, such as vases and bowls, do not obscure the space inside
them. Therefore, though containers may be different, the space inside them
has no differences or distinctions. In the same way, worldly people and
philosophers make all kinds of superimpositions of difference—be they
about a difference in entity or a difference in distinct features—regarding
phenomena from form through omniscience. Nevertheless, those conventional terms do not exist in terms of suchness, the true nature of the phenomena that bear the trait of freedom from arising. For all phenomena are
free from the conceptual elaborations.

For buddhas, all these elaborations of superimposition have been pacified. They are of equal taste. The buddhas genuinely integrate this equal
taste in their minds. The Transcendent Conquerors, the perfect knowers,
comprehend all knowable objects in a single instant of their omniscient
knowledge—they attain the wisdom of omniscience.

The wisdom of the buddhas is posited in this way from the perspective
of the worldly relative. This presentation accords with interdependence
on the level of no analysis and is free from confusion, because when using
other-approved descriptions that accord with interdependence, one does
not commit any superimpositions or deprecations.

Nevertheless, our presentation of the buddhas' wisdom knowing all knowable objects does not, at any time, harmonize with the presentations of the non-Buddhists and of the Buddhists from the Particularists through the Autonomists. This is so because the knowledge of all objects as they assert it is not even established for the worldly relative—the nonanalytical perspective that accords with interdependence. Since it does not even exist on that level, it is impossible to use other-approved reasonings to rightly affirm it in any context.

You may think, "The Consequentialists do not posit the knowledge of knowable objects as part of their own system, but instead say 'knowledge happens from the perspective of others.' If this is so, how do they repeat after others about the way the buddhas' knowledge works?"

There are two different approaches Consequentialists can take when communicating with students. The first is an uncommon approach. It involves repeating what others accept from a worldly, nonanalytical standpoint that accords with the interdependence of the relative. The second is a common approach. It involves repeating what others accept from a worldly, nonanalytical standpoint that does *not* accord with the interdependence of the relative.

When we take the first approach we say that the Transcendent Conqueror-to-be cultivates familiarity *(gom/goms)*[588] again and again with the abiding mode of all phenomena—the elaborations and characteristics of all phenomena are, from the very outset, completely pacified. Due to this cultivation, the time comes when all the elaborations—in their manifest, seedlike, and dormant forms—become completely pacified, even conventionally. We call that state "complete and true awakening in relation to all phenomena" or "the attainment of the wisdom of enlightenment."

We apply labels such as these because, at that time, the buddhas have relinquished all nonrealization, misconceptions, and doubt regarding all knowable objects. Further, we apply such labels because, when buddhas attain enlightenment, the way of being of phenomena and the way they are cognized by wisdom are no longer separate or differentiable. Realization cannot be enhanced any further.

Thus, when taking this first approach, we say that such wisdom and cognition *exist* for buddhas. We voice other-approved statements like this in a way that accords with interdependence. Even though the three spheres of omniscience—the objects of cognition, the cognizers, and the action of cognition itself—do not exist for us, the voicers of these statements, we voice them nonetheless as repetitions of others. We do so only to address specific needs. For when refuting the assertions of the Buddhist and non-Buddhist tīrthikas and of the Autonomists about how omniscience knows things, conventionally there is nothing else we can say.

In the system of the Followers of the Middle Way themselves, no such statements could apply: no special "wisdom of omniscience" can be observed as existing, not existing, and so on. When the systems of others are analyzed, omniscience as they describe it is found not to be established in either of the two truths. Therefore in the nonanalytical, conventional context that accords with interdependence, we refute wrong systems and describe the wisdom of omniscience in a way that repeats what others accept. There is nothing else we can do.

When we take the second approach mentioned above, we use similar labels to convey enlightenment. We describe enlightenment as a purification and an expansion with regard to knowable objects. The knowable objects involved are phenomena from form through omniscience: the contaminated, the uncontaminated, the conditioned, the unconditioned, the substantial, the imputed. The suchness *(ji tawa/ji lta ba)* of those phenomena is the two forms of selflessness. The variety *(ji nyepa/ji snyed pa)* of those phenomena is included within the two truths.[589] When one is liberated from all that obscures the knowledge of the entities and divisions of those phenomena, we call this state "complete and true awakening in relation to all phenomena" or "the attainment of the wisdom of omniscience."

The purification *(sang/sangs)*[590] aspect of this enlightenment consists of cleansing the ignorance of the obscurations that block the attainment of omniscience. The expansion *(gye/rgyas)* aspect consists in the blossoming of the intelligence that comprehends all knowable objects. When enlightenment is attained, the function of the two accumulations—to effect such purification and expansion—is perfectly completed. Descriptions like this are renowned among the Buddhist factions.

The above represents the style of communication of the Followers of the Middle Way in the context of mere other-approved analyses. Yet what do the Followers of the Middle Way assert in terms of their own, thorough analysis?

When thoroughly analyzing, it is like this: regarding the statement, "In our own system we do not speak of the buddhas' wisdom as being existent or nonexistent," we do not say even that! Therefore when the Proponents of Things criticize us, saying, "Refraining from asserting either existence or nonexistence is itself your own system," their criticisms do not apply.

Further discussion on the existence versus nonexistence of the buddhas' wisdom is available in the *Ṭīkā*. There is found a wondrous and eloquent explanation of the heart of the scriptures' intended meaning, together with some affirmations and refutations. Also, a discussion on this topic is available in the first chapter of the *Single Intention*. [Those who wish to continue their research] may consult those texts.

2.2.2.2.2.2. RELINQUISHING OBJECTIONS
2.2.2.2.2.2.1. The objections
2.2.2.2.2.2.2. The response

2.2.2.2.2.2.1. THE OBJECTIONS

> "If the pacification of elaborations is the suchness of all
>   phenomena, it could not be engaged by mind.
> It is definitely illogical for a perceiving subject to arise without
>   having engaged its knowable object.
> How can something unknowable be known? That is a
>   contradiction.
> Since there is no omniscient knower, how do you teach others,
>   'The Buddha comprehends reality'?" (12.3)

Someone may object, "You say that nonarising and the pacification of all elaborations are the suchness of phenomena such as form. You also say that such freedom from elaborations is cognized by wisdom. However, it would be impossible for a mind to cognize such freedom from elaborations.

"The convention of 'cognizing an object' is employed in connection with a consciousness arising with the aspect of an object. If the mind were to engage suchness, nonarising, it would not take on an aspect of anything. Emptiness does not have an aspect, so it would be impossible for any mind to engage emptiness.

"It is definitely illogical for a perceiving subject to arise without having engaged its knowable object.[591] So how can this emptiness of yours be known?

"It will be illogical for you to reply that the buddhas fully cognize the emptiness that cannot be cognized. For, how can unknowable be known? That would be a contradiction. For the notions of being known and being unknowable are mutually exclusive when applied to the same subject.

"Furthermore, according to your logic the buddhas would have no mind. Without an omniscient knower, how is it that you Followers of the Middle Way can say, 'The buddha comprehends such-and-such a reality'? That as well is illogical."

2.2.2.2.2.2.2. THE RESPONSE

2.2.2.2.2.2.2.1. Rejecting claims of illogic connected to the realization of the precise nature

2.2.2.2.2.2.2.2. Rejecting claims of illogic connected to the buddhas teaching worldly beings about suchness

2.2.2.2.2.2.2.1. REJECTING CLAIMS OF ILLOGIC CONNECTED TO THE REALIZATION OF THE PRECISE NATURE

In the context of nonarising being the suchness of all
  phenomena, the mind that perceives that suchness is also free
  from arising.
In dependence upon the aspect of nonarising, the seeming
  realization of suchness is posited.
Just as it is commonly described that a mind fully knows its
  object when it takes on the object's aspect,
Here, in dependence upon conventions, wisdom is posited as
  knowing the precise nature. (12.4)

In the context of nonarising being the suchness of all phenomena, the mind of the yogin, the perceiving subject of suchness, is also free from arising. The wisdom that seemingly[592] realizes suchness is posited in dependence upon the aspect of nonarising.

The Followers of Sūtra and others say that a mind fully cognizes its objects, blue and so on, through taking on the aspects of blue and so on. Just like that example, wisdom is posited as cognizing the precise nature in dependence upon other-approved conventions. It is not the case that in reality certain objects are identified by certain perceiving subjects—both object and subject are free from arising.

The basic meaning of the above verse and commentary is as follows. The Followers of the Middle Way do not speak of any existence or non-existence of the wisdom of the Buddha as their own position. However, when repeating what others accept in a worldly, nonanalytical context that accords with interdependence, they do say that the movements of the arising and ceasing of consciousness exist for sentient beings, because sentient beings possess the causes of confusion in a complete way. The buddhas do not possess those causes, so the wisdom of buddhas, from the buddhas' own perspective, does not arise or cease.

From the perspective of disciples, the wisdoms, powers, and so on of the buddhas appear to exist. This is so because those qualities are the undeceiving result of the cause that is the accumulation of wisdom. They are mere dependent arising.

Does it then follow that the wisdom of the buddhas is a specifically characterized thing? No, it does not. All of the causes and results spoken of in relation to wisdom are themselves merely phenomena that are posited through imputation.

2.2.2.2.2.2.2.2. Rejecting claims of illogic connected to the buddhas teaching worldly beings about suchness
2.2.2.2.2.2.2.2.1. Buddhas teach the precise nature to sentient beings even though all elaborations are pacified for them
2.2.2.2.2.2.2.2.2. The example of how the buddhas spontaneously benefit others even though all elaborations are pacified for them

2.2.2.2.2.2.2.2.1. Buddhas teach the precise nature to sentient beings even though all elaborations are pacified for them

> By the blessings of the Buddha, the sambhogakāya resulting from merit,
> The nirmāṇakāya, and the sounds of space and other things
> Can teach the suchness of phenomena.
> Beings in the world can receive these teachings and realize suchness. (12.5)

Without a truly existent knower, who can buddhas teach? The verse above provides a response to this question. It is true that when the dharmakāya is actualized all primary minds and mental events are pacified. However, it is not impossible for buddhas to teach about suchness in the world.

The sambhogakāya is the form kāya in which the buddhas actualize the dharmakāya. It is the result of the perfection of merit. It is also the cause by which bodhisattvas enjoy the genuine dharma. By the blessings of the buddhas, whoever hears the sounds of dharma arisen from the sambhogakāya will definitely become a receptacle for the teachings.

Not only that; also through the blessings of the buddhas the nirmāṇakāyas teach the dharma. Disciples can also realize suchness on the basis of those teachings. Similarly, the buddhas can bless phenomena that do not possess the movements of mind—space, trees, plants, rocks, and so on—so that whatever sounds arise from them teach the suchness of phenomena. Through these teachings as well, beings in the world can realize suchness.

2.2.2.2.2.2.2.2.2.2. THE EXAMPLE OF HOW THE BUDDHAS SPONTANEOUSLY BENEFIT OTHERS EVEN THOUGH ALL ELABORATIONS ARE PACIFIED FOR THEM

> A strong craftsperson will first
> Apply effort for a long time to get their wheel to spin.
> Later, without any further effort needed,
> The wheel spins on its own to make vases and so on. (12.6)

> Just so, without any current effort to make it arise,
> The activity of the buddhas, who engage the dharmakāya,
>   extends to the reaches of space.
> It is a result of the virtue of beings and of aspirations.
> The special causes and results of buddhahood are utterly
>   inconceivable. (12.7)

Someone may inquire as follows: "You say that it is impossible for buddhas of the present to engage in any activities that are of a conceptual nature or that involve primary minds and mental events. So what is the cause of their activity?"

The response to that question will first be approached using an external example. A strong craftsperson must begin their work by exerting a great amount of energy, using sticks and so forth, to get their wheel to spin. Later, the wheel spins on its own due to the previous efforts of the craftsperson. It can be seen that this spinning wheel, even while effortlessly spinning, becomes a cause for the production of several containers such as vases.

Just so, the buddhas, at present, are free from any efforts produced by thoughts in their three gates. Nevertheless, even while they are free of such effort, and even while they remain engaged in the dharmakāya, their activity extends to the reaches of space.

This activity has as one of its causes the ripening of the virtuous actions of sentient beings, such as listening to the buddhas' dharma. It is also caused by the previous aspirations of the buddhas made during the time of performing bodhisattva conduct. These aspirations can take forms such as the following: "Just as wish-fulfilling jewels benefit beings without thoughts, may I, in a timely way, fulfill the needs and desires of beings to be tamed by me without ever moving from the wisdom of dharmadhātu."

This activity is thus the result of special causes. The causes and results involved in perfect buddhahood are utterly inconceivable.

2.2.2.2.3. THE PRESENTATION OF THE KĀYAS, THE ESSENCE OF ENLIGHTENMENT

2.2.2.2.3.1. The dharmakāya, the abundant benefit for oneself
2.2.2.2.3.2. The form kāyas, the abundant benefit for others

2.2.2.2.3.1. THE DHARMAKĀYA, THE ABUNDANT BENEFIT FOR ONESELF

When the firewood of knowable objects is burned completely,
The peace that emerges is the dharmakāya of the victorious ones.
It has no arising and no ceasing.
When mind ceases, the buddhas make the kāya manifest. (12.8)

With the moisture of longstanding clinging removed from the now dried firewood of knowable objects from form through omniscience, the latter is burned completely by the fire of wisdom. This kāya, of the nature of wisdom, does not exist as a knowable object that arises. Therefore its consciousness as well is free from arising—all elaborations are thoroughly pacified. This is the dharmakāya of the victorious ones. About it the scriptures have said (Diamond Cutter Sūtra, Vajrachchhedikā-sūtra, Dorje Chöpe Do/

rdo rje gcog pa'i mdo):

Buddhas see the dharmatā.
The perfect guides are the dharmakāya.
Dharmatā is not a knowable object;
It cannot be known.

When the dharmakāya is actualized, it is not the case that it was not present before but arises anew. Nor is it the case that what was present before has ceased. Rather, all phenomena are free from arising and ceasing from the outset. It is this freedom from arising and ceasing that is realized in a final and perfect way. Mundane forms of death and birth are inconceivably transformed, and buddhas gain liberation from all death and birth. The sūtras say:

Mañjushrī, "free from arising and free from cessation" is an epithet of the Tathāgata.

Thus the object of wisdom, suchness, is in no situation ever engaged by a perceiving subject composed of primary mind and mental events. Such perceiving subjects have ceased. Therefore it is posited conventionally that the dharmakāya is actualized only by the sambhogakāya.

The phrase "mind and mental events cease" does not refer to something existent before that now becomes nonexistent. If it did, this would entail the extremes of eternalism and nihilism. For, if something existed before, it could not be nonexistent later. It is also untenable to say "that which has not existed from the beginning is nonexistent later." What actually happens here is that the fixation of primary minds and mental events dissolves. The confused appearances of ignorance disappear. The conventional term "cease" is merely a conventional label given to this outcome.

On this point, some Tibetans say that until the continuum's end[593] the pure wisdom that arises due to analysis exists, yet on the ground of buddhahood it does not exist. They say that this assertion is the uncommon system of the Consequentialists. Others say that the Consequentialists in their own system do not debate over the names "mind" or "mental events" on the ground of buddhahood, but they do accept that the wisdom that sees the entities and features of objects exists. They say that it exists because masters such as Nāgārjuna spoke extensively of the existence of qualities such as the ten powers.

These positions are untenable. As was explained above, one must harmonize with what is accepted by others when speaking on the nonanalytical level in order to be in accord with the interdependence of knowable objects. In this context we say that wisdom exists on the ground of buddhahood. After analysis, there is absolutely no time at which the Followers of the Middle Way say from their own perspective that such wisdom exists or does not exist.

Moreover, the above claims are untenable because, in general, all knowable objects are primordially free from the elaborations of existence, nonexistence, and so on. Failing to understand that, those who put forth the claims above debate only about whether the wisdom of the buddhas exists. Both existence and nonexistence are refuted in all of the Buddha's scriptures and in the scriptures of Nāgārjuna and his heart disciples.

If the obscurations inherently existed, it would be impossible to relinquish them. Equally impossible, therefore, would be the attainment of liberation. If the obscurations inherently existed before but then became inherently nonexistent later, it would be untenable even conventionally to speak of sentient beings and saṃsāra. If you say that [even conventionally wisdom] did not inherently exist, all positive mundane and transcendent qualities would be rendered nonexistent.

If you say that wisdom exists until the continuum's end but does not exist after that, your view would entail the extremes of eternalism and nihilism. It is untenable to say that the two obscurations and the impure aggregates, sources, and constituents exist for sentient beings and then say that the phenomena that depend on those—wisdom and the qualities of transformation—do not exist for buddhas. If wisdom did not exist for buddhas,[594] the positive qualities of the higher realms and definite liberation would also become nonexistent. The *Perfection of Supreme Knowledge* scriptures say:[595]

> If wisdom did not exist, it would be impossible to increase positive
>   qualities, and there would be no enlightenment.
> The oceanlike buddhadharma would also become nonexistent.

Those who debate about existence or nonexistence miss the wisdom
of the buddhas. Instead, they identify wisdom as the arising and ceasing
of the primary minds and mental events and as the illusionlike confused
appearances.

What *is* wisdom? It is as explained in the perfection of supreme knowledge teachings: all phenomena are free from elaborations, and when the
perceiving subject as well becomes equally free from elaborations, that is
wisdom. In particular, the wisdom of the buddha consists in the pacification of the elaborations and their habitual tendencies in relation to suchness. It is the inseparability of the expanse and wisdom. It is free from
singularity and multiplicity, quality and qualified. It realizes the nonduality of subjects and objects. In it all phenomena—saṃsāra and nirvāṇa,
faults and qualities, and so on—are always undifferentiable and equal.
Outside of that, there is no way to posit wisdom.

Some Tibetans have not understood this. Some of them say that the
essence kāya *(svabhāvikakāya, ngowo nyi ku/ngo bo nyid sku)* is not buddhahood. Others say that the buddhas do not cognize knowable objects.
These views are untenable. If all phenomena are free from elaborations,
the perceiving subject of buddhas must also be free from elaborations. So
there is no reference point for statements of "realizing" or "not realizing"
knowable objects.

In a nonanalytical context of repeating what others accept, we Followers of the Middle Way describe knowable objects as existing. The wisdom
of the buddhas is the same. Since we speak of all phenomena as existing
from the perspective of others (even though from our own perspective
they are free of the elaborations of existence and nonexistence), it is unreasonable to debate solely about the existence or nonexistence of the wisdom of buddhas.

Just as we posit form through omniscience as existing for the confused
perspective of the world, we also posit the wisdom of the buddhas as being
existent. When analyzed—and from the perspective of the tathāgatas
themselves—just as the wisdom of the buddhas is free from all elaborations of existence and nonexistence, so all phenomena are free from all
elaborations. Since this is an important point, I have made it not once but
several times, and will continue to make it!

At this section of the *Ṭīkā*, Karmapa Mikyö Dorje says that he has based his writings on this topic on the explanations Tropu Lotsawa (*khro phu lo tsʾa ba,* b. twelfth century), which he sees as tenable.

2.2.2.2.3.2. THE FORM KĀYAS, THE ABUNDANT BENEFIT FOR OTHERS

2.2.2.2.3.2.1. The sambhogakāya
2.2.2.2.3.2.2. The kāyas of natural outflow
2.2.2.2.3.2.3. The nirmāṇakāya

2.2.2.2.3.2.1. THE SAMBHOGAKĀYA

> **The peaceful sambhogakāya is brilliant like a wish-fulfilling tree;**
> **It is free of thoughts like a wish-fulfilling jewel;**
> **It remains permanently, until beings are liberated, so that they**
> **   may attain the endowments of freedom and happiness;**
> **It appears only to those who are free from elaborations. (12.9)**

The sambhogakāya is the kāya in which the buddhas actualize the dharmakāya. It is of a peaceful nature, because it is free from all primary minds and mental events. Even though it is peaceful, it is brilliant: it acts for the benefit of beings just like a wish-fulfilling tree. Like a wish-fulfilling jewel it is free of thoughts; yet, at the same time, it accomplishes the wished-for aims of beings.

This kāya remains permanently: it remains until all beings are liberated, until saṃsāra is emptied, so that beings of the world may attain the endowments of the freedom of definite liberation and the happiness of the higher realms. It remains for as long as space endures.

The sambhogakāya appears only to those who are free from the elaborations: tenth-ground bodhisattvas who, through their gathering the two accumulations, have obtained the mirror of stainless supreme knowledge.

The sambhogakāya is endowed with the five certainties: the certainty of place, Akaniṣṭha; the certainty of entity, the adornments of the major and minor marks; the certainty of retinue, tenth-ground bodhisattvas; the certainty of time, uninterruptedly; and the certainty of enjoyments, the enjoyment of only the dharma of the Mahāyāna. As is said:[596]

> The form kāyas of the buddhas
> Excellently blaze with the major and minor marks.

They hold various forms due to
The personal interests of beings.

The sambhogakāya arises due to
An immeasurable accumulation of merit.
The tenth-ground heirs of the victors
Can perceive it.

It is only to be experienced by bodhisattvas,
Because it is the enjoyment of the perfect form of dharma.
When a perceiving subject abides only
In the nature of phenomena, that state is called buddhahood.

It is asserted that buddhahood is actualized
In the palace of Akaniṣṭha.

Many earlier and later Tibetans, such as Zilung Chokden, have developed assertions connected to passages such as the following:[597]

Just as reflections of bodies of great devas
Appear on a pure ground of lapis lazuli,
On the pure ground of beings' minds
Shines the reflection of the form of the Muni.

And:

Ordinary beings do not know
That [the form kāyas] are an appearance of their own minds.

And,

Virtue arises and disintegrates.
The form [kāyas] of the Buddha arise and disintegrate.
Indra arises and disintegrates.
Unlike those, the dharmakāya of the Sage has no arising or
    disintegration.

Zilungpa and the others also base themselves on the *Great Commentary on the Eight Thousand Lines (Gyetong Drelchen/brgyad stong 'grel chen)* when they say, "The form kāyas are not the buddha. Furthermore, they are not tangible matter—the genuine form kāyas must be posited to be bodies of consciousness."

Those statements are untenable. The following is the meaning of the above scriptural quotations. The dharmakāya is what is supported. It is the freedom from elaborations that is to be realized, seen, touched, or comprehended by the buddhas themselves with their individual wisdoms. The form kāyas are the support. The elaborations of their activities and qualities are perceptible in the pure mirrors of the minds of disciples who have engaged in accumulation and purification. Beings can hear the speech of the form kāya buddhas; they can also take the essence of those buddhas' intentions, the taste of the genuine dharma, as an object of their minds through hearing, contemplating, and meditating.

The dharmakāya, however, is not like that. Even the buddhas, when they actualize the dharmakāya, see it in a manner of not seeing anything. What need, therefore, to speak of sentient beings perceiving the dharmakāya or taking it as an object?

The meaning of the above quotations is *not* that the forms kāyas that appear to disciples are not the buddha. If the form kāyas were not the buddha, the genuine dharma spoken by those buddhas would not be the speech of the buddha. The teachings connected to putting that speech into practice would not be the teachings of the buddha. Those who follow such form kāyas—the four pairs or eight individuals,[598] the twenty types of saṅgha members,[599] and so on—would not be the saṅgha.

Furthermore, if fire is hot and if form is suitable as form, it is contradictory to say that the form kāyas are not form. If the form kāyas that disciples directly rely on were not the buddha, what are we to think of the aspirations of bodhisattvas? For the bodhisattvas make aspirations such as, "May I attain the kāya by which I will be perceptible even to evildoers who have not purified even a little bit of their obscurations." The karmic result of such aspirations, along with the practices that accompany them, would go to waste.

The genuine form kāyas must, you say, be posited as consciousness as opposed to form. That is illogical. If you consult the infinite scriptures of the Transcendent Conqueror, you will see that the kāyas of the buddhas that are connected to the benefit of others are the form kāyas, which are the objects of sentient beings' five sense consciousnesses. The terms "mind kāya" or "consciousness kāya" do not appear in print even once.

If you assert the major and minor marks to be distinctive features of consciousness, it would follow that consciousness is of the entity of shape and color, since the buddhas' fingernails are the color of copper, their hair is black like a bumble bee, and so on. It would also become necessary to divide the collection of consciousnesses beyond the eightfold collection.

Furthermore, the form kāyas are the buddha because, relatively, the kāyas and wisdoms of the buddha are just that: they are of the buddha; they are not the kāyas and wisdoms of sentient beings. The buddhas' disciples as well perceive no other kāyas and wisdoms than those of the buddhas.

If there are some scriptures stating that the form kāyas are not the buddha, they are speaking from the same perspective as those that teach emptiness as the nature of fire. In other words, they are employing ultimate analyses. The scriptures that speak of the dharmakāya and the form kāyas as the buddha are similar to the scriptures that teach hotness to be the nature of fire. They are speaking from a nonanalytical, relative perspective.

The dharmakāya and essence kāya are posited to be free from the elaborations of arising and ceasing. The form kāyas are posited to entail the elaborations of arising and ceasing. These are how the two truths are presented in dependence upon the perspective of disciples. From the perspective of buddhas themselves, there are no distinctions whatsoever in which, from among the form kāyas, the dharmakāya, and the essence kaya, one is ultimate and the other is relative, or one is buddha and others are not buddha.

You may protest that the kāyas were split into the categories of the two truths in instances such as the following passage from the *Highest Continuum*:

> The kāyas are two; the benefit for self and benefit for others, respectively:
> The ultimate kāya and, what depends on it, the relative kāya.

That passage merely represents the presentation in which the buddhakāyas are described as qualifier and qualified. It is a conventional, other-approved description. From that perspective, the dharmakāya is the qualifier or true nature, the ultimate truth, and the form kāyas are the qualified or the apparent phenomena, the relative truth.

However, the dharmakāya cannot be categorically proclaimed to be the true nature or ultimate truth, free of arising and ceasing. For, there are also explanations of dharmakāya in which it is presented as relative truth. There, the dharmakāya is taught to be omniscience and to entail the arising and ceasing of the powers possessed by the twenty-one types of uncontaminated wisdom and so on. There are also contexts in which the form kāyas are posited as ultimate truth. The Vajrayāna, in a great many instances, speaks of the ultimate form kāyas of definitive meaning as being none other than Vajradhara. Therefore, it is important to understand the presentations of the kāyas in their distinct settings and not become attached to only one position.

There are some who say that the essence kāya exists separately from the form kāyas. Some others say that none other than the form kāyas are the wisdom of the buddha. It seems that those scholars have not remembered the key point that the two truths are inexpressible as being the same or different. As a result, they allow such careless prattle to spill from their mouths. An extensive critical analysis can be found here in the *Ṭīkā*.

2.2.2.2.3.2.2. THE KĀYAS OF NATURAL OUTFLOW[600] *(gyu tünpe ku/ rgyu mthun pa'i sku)*
2.2.2.2.3.2.2.1. Abundant form
2.2.2.2.3.2.2.2. Abundant mastery of intention
2.2.2.2.3.2.2.3. Abundant qualities

2.2.2.2.3.2.2.1. ABUNDANT FORM
2.2.2.2.3.2.2.1.1. The sublime power to display depictions of previous lifetimes
2.2.2.2.3.2.2.1.2. The sublime power to display depictions of conduct

2.2.2.2.3.2.2.1.1. THE SUBLIME POWER TO DISPLAY DEPICTIONS OF PREVIOUS LIFETIMES

> In a single form kāya that is the natural outflow of the other two
> And in a single moment, the lords of sages
> Can clearly and unerringly display the details of all their previous
>   births,
> Even though those lifetimes have already ceased. (12.10)

After the dharma and form kāyas of the Buddha have been produced, another kāya, the natural outflow of those two, arises for the benefit of disciples through the other two kāyas' power. The *Entrance to the Middle Way* will now explain how these kāyas are also endowed with inconceivable powers.

In a single form kāya that is the natural outflow of the other two kāyas and in a single moment, the lords of sages can display the details of all their births in beginningless saṃsāra, before they attained buddhahood, even though those births have already ceased. They can display such details clearly, distinctly, unerringly, and completely, with the clarity of viewing one's face in the mirror.

2.2.2.2.3.2.2.1.2. THE SUBLIME POWER TO DISPLAY DEPICTIONS OF CONDUCT

2.2.2.2.3.2.2.1.2.1. The power to depict conduct in one kāya

2.2.2.2.3.2.2.1.2.2. The power to depict conduct in a single pore

2.2.2.2.3.2.2.1.2.1. THE POWER TO DEPICT CONDUCT IN ONE KĀYA

2.2.2.2.3.2.2.1.2.1.1. The power to display histories of generosity

2.2.2.2.3.2.2.1.2.1.2. The power to display histories of the other five perfections

2.2.2.2.3.2.2.1.2.1.1. THE POWER TO DISPLAY HISTORIES OF GENEROSITY

In a single kāya, buddhas can display without exception
The details about the buddha realms they lived in, the sages that
    inhabited them,
The types of powers, forms, and conduct those sages had,
The number of members of the saṅgha of hearers present and
    their qualities, (12.11)

The different forms the bodhisattvas had,
The types of dharma taught there and the types of births they
    took,
The types of trainings they engaged in after hearing the dharma,
And the types of generosity they offered. (12.12)

The buddhas can display details about the situations they were in when practicing the perfection of generosity: the buddha realms, with their lapis lazuli, padma raga trees, and other attributes seen as beautiful by sentient beings; the lords of sages in those buddha realms; the births and so on of those sages; the sublime powers, forms, and conduct those buddhas possessed; the number of members of the saṅgha of hearers those buddhas had as their retinue; the qualities those hearers displayed in working out their own salvation with diligence; the bodhisattvas in those buddha realms and the features of their forms such as the major and minor marks; the clothing and food they enjoyed; the types of dharma that they taught, such as one or three vehicles; the births they themselves took in that buddha realm, such as that of a Brahmin, monk, or lay person; the types of trainings and vows they took on after hearing the dharma, such as the abbreviated trainings entailing remainders (the novice monastic vows) or the extensive trainings without remainders (the monastic vows of full ordination); the types of generosity—food, clothing, precious ornaments, and so on—they extended to buddhas, bodhisattvas, and the saṅgha of hearers; and other details such as the time spans such generosity involved. The buddhas can display all of these details without exception in a single kāya.

2.2.2.2.3.2.2.1.2.1.2. THE POWER TO DISPLAY HISTORIES OF THE OTHER FIVE PERFECTIONS

> Similarly, in a complete way they can display in one kāya
> The details of previous times when they were practicing discipline,
> Patience, diligence, concentration, and supreme knowledge—
> ... (12.13abc)

Just as they are able to relay details about when they practiced generosity, they can similarly display in a complete way and in a single kāya all the details of previous times when they were practicing discipline, patience, diligence, concentration, and supreme knowledge. The specific details about these times correlate with those of the above verse on generosity.

2.2.2.2.3.2.2.1.2.2. THE POWER TO DEPICT CONDUCT IN A SINGLE PORE

2.2.2.2.3.2.2.1.2.2.1. Displaying their own conduct in a single pore

2.2.2.2.3.2.2.1.2.2.2. Displaying the conduct of all buddhas of the three times in a single pore

2.2.2.2.3.2.2.1.2.2.3. Displaying the conduct of other noble and ordinary beings in a single pore

2.2.2.2.3.2.2.1.2.2.1. DISPLAYING THEIR OWN CONDUCT IN A SINGLE PORE

> . . . all their forms of conduct
> They can display clearly in a single pore of their body. (12.13cd)

Not only can they display the details of their conduct in a single kāya; they can also display in a complete way all of their conduct of the six perfections clearly in a single pore of their body.

2.2.2.2.3.2.2.1.2.2.2. DISPLAYING THE CONDUCT OF ALL BUDDHAS OF THE THREE TIMES IN A SINGLE PORE

> A buddha can display the deeds of past and future buddhas
> And also the deeds of the buddhas of the present,
> Who dwell in the world to relieve beings to the limits of space
>   oppressed by suffering
> By teaching the dharma in high, melodic tones. (12.14)

> From the time of the buddhas' first generating bodhichitta to
>   their going to the essence of enlightenment,
> A buddha can display all their deeds clearly,
> In one moment, in a single pore of his or her body,
> Knowing the nature of these deeds to be like a magical illusion.
> (12.15)

Not only can a buddha display his or her own deeds, he or she can display the deeds of past and future buddhas and also the deeds of the buddhas of the present. The buddhas of the present are those who dwell in the world to relieve beings to the limits of space oppressed by suffering. They do so by teaching the dharma in high, melodic tones such as the melody of Brahma. From the time of the buddhas' first generating bodhichitta to their going to the essence of enlightenment, a buddha can, in one moment, display all their deeds—just like he or she is capable of displaying his or

her own deeds—clearly in a single pore of his or her body, knowing the
nature of these deeds to be like a magical illusion. Since the transcendent
conquerors know all phenomena to be like a magical illusion, they have
mastered the ability to teach others that all phenomena are that way.

2.2.2.2.3.2.2.1.2.2.3. DISPLAYING THE CONDUCT OF OTHER NOBLE
AND ORDINARY BEINGS IN A SINGLE PORE

> Similarly, in one moment they can display in a pore of their body
> All of the deeds of the bodhisattvas,
> The noble solitary realizers, and the hearers of the three times.
> They can also display all deeds performed during the phase of
>   being an ordinary being. (12.16)

Just as they can display their own and other tathāgatas' deeds in a single
pore, similarly, in one moment they can display in a pore of their body all
of the deeds of the bodhisattvas, the noble solitary realizers, and the hearers of the three times. They can also display all deeds performed during the
phase of being an ordinary being.

2.2.2.2.3.2.2.2. ABUNDANT MASTERY OF INTENTION
2.2.2.2.3.2.2.2.1. Mastery of intention concerning spatiality
2.2.2.2.3.2.2.2.2. Mastery of intention concerning time

2.2.2.2.3.2.2.2.1. MASTERY OF INTENTION CONCERNING
SPATIALITY

> These pure ones, by simply directing their intention,
> Can display worlds to the reaches of space in the area of one
>   atom,
> And make an atom pervade the space of limitless worlds,
> But without enlarging the atoms or shrinking the worlds. (12.17)

These buddhas, who are pure in their relinquishment and realization, can,
through merely directing their intention, display worlds to the reaches of
space in the area of one atom, and make an atom pervade the space of limitless worlds. Even though that is the case, they still do not need to enlarge
the atoms or shrink the worlds.

2.2.2.2.3.2.2.2.2. MASTERY OF INTENTION CONCERNING TIME

You, who are free from thoughts, can, in each instant
Until the end of existence, display various types of conduct
Whose number is not equaled
By all the atoms in Jambudvīpa. (12.18)

You, our Teacher free from thoughts, can, in each instant until the end of existence, display various types of conduct such as the twelve deeds, conduct that embodies the methods for taming beings. The number of these types of conduct is not equaled even fractionally by the subtlest atoms in all of Jambudvīpa.

2.2.2.2.3.2.2.3. ABUNDANT QUALITIES

2.2.2.2.3.2.2.3.1. The explanation of the ten powers, the foremost of the qualities

2.2.2.2.3.2.2.3.2. The buddhas' qualities are limitless and cannot be fathomed by anyone other than buddhas

2.2.2.2.3.2.2.3.3. All qualities are included within the profound and the vast

2.2.2.2.3.2.2.3.1. THE EXPLANATION OF THE TEN POWERS *(top chu/ stobs bcu)*, THE FOREMOST OF THE QUALITIES

2.2.2.2.3.2.2.3.1.1. The teaching

2.2.2.2.3.2.2.3.1.2. The extensive explanation

2.2.2.2.3.2.2.3.1.1. THE TEACHING

The powers of the knowledge of bases and nonbases;
The awareness of the ripening of actions;
The comprehension of various higher interests;
The knowledge of the various dhātus; (12.19)

The knowledge of supreme and nonsupreme faculties;
The knowledge of the paths and their respective destinations;
The awareness of the concentrations, liberations,
Samādhis, absorptions, and so on; (12.20)

The knowledge that recalls previous states;
The awareness of deaths and births;
And the knowledge of the exhaustion of contaminants—
These are the ten powers. (12.21)

Some scholars explain the ten powers as being accompanied by congruent mental events, such as samādhi and supreme knowledge. This is the style of explanation of the abhidharma, but it contradicts the explanation of our text here, which states that all primary minds and mental events are pacified upon the attainment of buddhahood. The ten powers are an appearance for others, but they are posited from a nonanalytical perspective. Therefore, they do not need to be correlated with any of the mental events.

2.2.2.2.3.2.2.3.1.2. THE EXTENSIVE EXPLANATION
2.2.2.2.3.2.2.3.1.2.1. The power of knowledge of bases and nonbases
2.2.2.2.3.2.2.3.1.2.2. The power of knowledge of actions and their ripening
2.2.2.2.3.2.2.3.1.2.3. The power of knowledge of various higher interests
2.2.2.2.3.2.2.3.1.2.4. The power of knowledge of various dhātus
2.2.2.2.3.2.2.3.1.2.5. The power of knowledge of supreme and nonsupreme faculties
2.2.2.2.3.2.2.3.1.2.6. The power of knowledge of all paths and their respective destinations
2.2.2.2.3.2.2.3.1.2.7. The power of knowledge of concentrations, liberations, samādhis, absorptions, and so on
2.2.2.2.3.2.2.3.1.2.8. The power of knowledge that recalls previous states
2.2.2.2.3.2.2.3.1.2.9. The power of knowledge of deaths and rebirths
2.2.2.2.3.2.2.3.1.2.10. The power of knowledge of the exhaustion of contaminants

2.2.2.2.3.2.2.3.1.2.1. THE POWER OF KNOWLEDGE OF BASES AND NONBASES *(ne dang ne ma yinpa kyenpe top/gnas dang gnas ma yin pa mkhyen pa'i stobs)*[601]

Specific results arise with precision from specific causes.
The buddhas know and teach about the bases of all these arisings.
The absence of such precision is called a nonbasis.

**The freedom from obstruction to the knowledge of these is
explained to be the first power. (12.22)**

Specific results arise from their own, specific causes. In relation to any
arisen result, the buddhas know and can teach about its basis. There is
an unerring basis, for example, for the ripening of pleasant and unpleasant results from the causes of virtuous actions and nonvirtuous actions,
respectively.

The opposite of those scenarios is called a nonbasis: the [wrong thought]
of a result [having the capacity] to arise from something that is not its own
specific cause. For example, there is no basis for the ripening of an unpleasant result from a cause that is a virtuous action.

The buddhas are free from impediments to the knowledge of all knowable objects that fall into the categories of bases and nonbases. This is
explained to be the Teacher's first power: the knowledge of bases and
nonbases.

2.2.2.2.3.2.2.3.1.2.2. THE POWER OF KNOWLEDGE OF ACTIONS AND
THEIR RIPENING (*le dang nam-min/las dang rnam smin*)

**The buddhas' knowledge can individually engage without
impediment
The four types of actions—desirable, undesirable, mixed actions,
and exhausting actions—
Along with their ripening, in all their great variety.
This knowledge, which pervades all objects of the three times, is
asserted to be the second power. (12.23)**

The four types of actions are as follows: desirable actions, whose ripening
is a pleasant result; undesirable actions, whose ripening is an unpleasant
result; the opposite of those, i.e., mixed actions that cannot be categorically labeled virtuous or nonvirtuous; and exhausting or uncontaminated
actions, which bring actions to their exhaustion. The sūtras say:

> One type of action is bright; one is dark; others are a mixture
> of bright and dark; others are uncontaminated actions, which
> are the cause for the exhaustion of actions. Thus there are four
> types of action.

Thus, this explanation is given from the perspective of those sūtras.

Jayānanda's[602] *Commentary on the Entrance to the Middle Way* speaks of "actions that are the entity of nonexhaustion." It posits the entity of nonexhaustion as the cause for the attainment of nirvāṇa. However, such statements are made in accord with the lower systems, which assert nirvāṇa as a substantial existent. The [Mahāyāna] sūtras and the Mahāyāna abhidharma texts explain this point more accurately: it is the absence of contamination that causes exhaustion.

From among the four types of action, uncontaminated actions are unique in that they do not have a ripened result. Therefore, the buddhas' knowledge of "the ripening of actions" pertains only to the other three types.

These actions occur in a great variety of ways, and the buddhas have the power to know all of them, and their ripening, in terms of entity and classifications. They engage this ability without impediment at the right times and in the right places for the benefit of their disciples. The perceiving subject of these actions, which pervades all knowable objects of the three times, is asserted to be the Teacher's second power: the knowledge of actions and their ripening.

2.2.2.2.3.2.2.3.1.2.3. THE POWER OF KNOWLEDGE OF VARIOUS HIGHER INTERESTS *(möpa natsok/mos pa sna tshogs)*

> Due to desire and so on,
> A great variety of wishes for the good arise in lesser, middling,
> and superior forms.
> These higher interests in turn may become covered by other
> factors.
> The buddhas' knowledge of all of this, pervading all beings of the
> three times, is the third power. (12.24)

Due to seeds of desire and other mental afflictions such as aggression, and due to seeds of virtuous qualities such as faith (the latter qualities being indicated by the phrase "and so on" in the first line of the root verse), a great variety of wishes for the good, or higher interests, arise in lesser, middling, and superior forms. These wishes and interests may in turn become covered or veiled by beings' engagement in other, coarse mental afflictions such as passion. The buddhas have knowledge of all these phenomena in their basic entities and in their classifications. This knowledge, pervading all beings of the three times, is the buddhas' third power: the knowledge of various higher interests.

2.2.2.2.3.2.2.3.1.2.4. THE POWER OF KNOWLEDGE OF VARIOUS DHĀTUS *(kam natsok/khams sna tshogs)*

> The perfect buddhas, skilled in the dhātus' divisions,
> Teach the nature of the eye and so on to be a dhātu.
> Their limitless knowledge that, at all times,
> Engages the distinct features of the dhātus is the fourth power.
> (12.25)

The buddhas are skilled in the divisions of the emptiness of the dhātus.[603] They teach the nature or essence—which is emptiness[604]—of the eye and so on[605] to be a dhātu. The perfect buddhas know the inner emptinesses and so on along with their classifications. Their knowledge is limitless since it pervades all of the different types of dhātu. It engages without impediment the distinct features of the emptinesses of the dhātus. This is the buddhas' fourth power: the knowledge of the various dhātus.

2.2.2.2.3.2.2.3.1.2.5. THE POWER OF KNOWLEDGE OF SUPREME AND NONSUPREME FACULTIES *(wangpo chok dang chok min/dbang po mchog dang mchog min)*

> Regarding the faculties of conceptualization and so on, those
>   that are very sharp are asserted to be supreme,
> And the middling and dull are taught to be nonsupreme.
> The buddhas possess fully developed knowledge of the eye and
>   so on and of how the faculties assist each other in producing
>   results.
> This unimpeded knowledge is their fifth power. (12.26)

The faculties of conceptualization *(kuntok/kun rtog)* are the faculties of the mental afflictions. For they wield control over the production of desire and so on. The phrase "and so on" of the first line refers to faith and so on, which are completely pure *(namjang/rnam byang)* faculties, since they wield control over the production of virtuous qualities. Regarding these faculties, those that are very sharp are asserted to be supreme or sublime.

The middling phase and the dull or lesser faculties are taught to be non-supreme.

All of these faculties are known by the buddhas. The buddhas also possess knowledge of the entities of the twenty-two faculties such as the eye.[606] They are also aware of how the faculties mutually assist each other in the production of results: for example, the objects to be appropriated by the eye can also become simultaneous conditions for the nose when they produce an eye consciousness.

The buddhas' knowledge is completely purified and developed with respect to these objects. Its ability to engage them at all times in an unimpeded way is the buddhas' fifth power: the knowledge of supreme and nonsupreme faculties.

2.2.2.2.3.2.2.3.1.2.6. THE POWER OF KNOWLEDGE OF ALL PATHS AND THEIR RESPECTIVE DESTINATIONS *(tamche du drowe lam/ thams cad du 'gro ba'i lam)*

> Some paths lead to buddhahood; some lead to the enlightenment
> of solitary realizers;
> Others lead to the enlightenment of hearers or to the hungry
> ghost realm,
> The animal realm, the realms of gods, humans, and hell beings,
> and other destinations.
> The limitless and unimpeded knowledge of these is the sixth
> power. (12.27)

Some paths are asserted to lead to victorious buddhahood itself; some paths are asserted to lead to the enlightenment of solitary realizers, while some are asserted to lead to the enlightenment of hearers. Some others lead to the realms of hungry ghosts, animals, gods, humans, hell beings, and other destinations. There are a great many paths that lead to a variety of destinations. The perceiving subject that engages in the knowledge of all of these in a limitless and unimpeded way is asserted to be the Teacher's sixth power: the knowledge of all paths and their respective destinations.

2.2.2.2.3.2.2.3.1.2.7. THE POWER OF KNOWLEDGE OF CONCENTRATIONS, LIBERATIONS, SAMĀDHIS, ABSORPTIONS, AND SO ON *(samten namtar ting-dzin nyomjuk sok/bsam gtan rnam thar ting 'dzin snyoms 'jug sogs)*

> Yogis and yoginīs in the limitless worlds experience different
> meditative states:
> The concentrations, the eight liberations, the states of shamatha,
> And the nine distinct absorptions.
> The unobstructed knowledge of these is explained to be the
> seventh power. (12.28)

The power of the knowledge of the concentrations, liberations, samādhis, absorptions, completely afflicted phenomena, and completely pure phenomena will now be explained. The yogis and yoginīs who dwell in the limitless world realms are different from each other regarding the distinctions of their mindstreams. Some abide in the world, some have transcended the world; some have sharp faculties, and some have dull faculties. Therefore these limitless differences correlate to differences in the meditative states that these yogis and yoginīs experience.

For example, there are the four concentrations, the eight forms of liberation, and the samādhi of shamatha, the essence of which is to place one's mind one-pointedly on a virtuous object. There is also the categorization scheme of the nine distinct and successive absorptions: the four concentrations, the four formless realm states, and the cessation of discriminations and feelings.

The causes for all these states, such as concentration, are limitless and manifold: some causes are completely afflicted phenomena, some are completely pure phenomena.

The buddhas know all of these phenomena in an unimpeded way. This is their seventh power: the knowledge of the concentrations and so on and of completely afflicted and completely pure phenomena.

2.2.2.2.3.2.2.3.1.2.8. THE POWER OF KNOWLEDGE THAT RECALLS PREVIOUS STATES *(ngön gyi ne je su drenpa/sngon gyi gnas rjes su dran pa)*

> Buddhas remember all of the births they took in cyclic existence
> due to ignorance;
> They also know the births of others—all sentient beings—
> And the bases and locations of these births.
> Such unobstructed knowledge is explained to be the eighth
> power. (12.29)

The power of knowledge that recalls previous states will now be explained. The objects cognized by this power are the beginningless births beings take due to beginningless ignorance. The buddhas recall their own births, taken previously when they abided in saṃsāra. They also can recall the individual births others—all sentient beings—have taken in all the limitless world realms. The buddhas also know the bases and locations of these previous births. This unobstructed awareness of the transcendent conquerors is explained to be their eighth power: the knowledge that recalls previous states.

2.2.2.2.3.2.2.3.1.2.9. THE POWER OF KNOWLEDGE OF DEATHS AND REBIRTHS *(chi powa dang kye ne/'chi 'pho ba dang skye gnas)*

> Buddhas know the deaths and births of each and every sentient being
> In all world realms as limitless as space.
> They know these in all of their variety in a single instant,
> In an unattached, completely pure, and limitless way—this is asserted to be the ninth power. (12.30)

The power of knowledge of deaths and rebirths will now be explained. The buddhas know the deaths and births of each and every sentient being in all world realms without exception—they know the disintegration of their aggregates as well as their [subsequent] conception [in the womb and so on]. They know all of these forms of death and birth in all their great variety—all of the worlds as limitless as space, and all of the different situations created by different kinds of karma.

The knowledge of the transcendent conquerors can engage correctly in these objects in a single instant. The transcendent conquerors' wisdom is not attached to any of those objects—it engages them always in a completely pure way. Therefore it is limitless and unobstructed. This is asserted to be the teachers' power of knowledge of death and rebirths.

2.2.2.2.3.2.2.3.1.2.10. THE POWER OF KNOWLEDGE OF THE EXHAUSTION OF CONTAMINANTS *(zakpa zepa/zag pa zad pa)*

> Through the power of their omniscient knowledge, the victorious ones rapidly

Cognize the dissolution of mental afflictions and habitual
tendencies.
They also know how the intelligence of their students causes the
cessation of mental afflictions.
This limitless and unattached knowledge is asserted to be the
tenth power. (12.31)

The power of knowledge of the exhaustion of contaminants will now be
explained. Through the power of their omniscient knowledge of all knowable objects, the victorious ones rapidly cognize the disintegration and
cessation of the mental afflictions and habitual tendencies of the three
realms of saṃsāra. The "habitual tendencies" are phenomena that, due to
ignorance and so on, corrupt and obscure the mind. Furthermore, "the
limit of the mental afflictions," "habituation," "root," and "habitual tendency" are synonyms.

The buddhas also are aware of how the intelligence or discriminating
prajñā of their students, the hearers and others, causes the cessation of the
mental afflictions. Though the hearers can bring the mental afflictions to
their end, they cannot stop the habitual tendencies. This is similar to the
example of a vase being emptied of the flowers or oils that it contained yet
still holding the scent of those contents.

Since the arhats still possess the habitual tendencies despite having
relinquished the mental afflictions, they perform such actions as jumping
around because of having been a monkey, or talking to female servants in
certain ways because of having been a Brahmin. Even the buddhas themselves cannot reverse these tendencies of arhats.

The habitual tendencies of ignorance are an obstruction to the complete knowledge of knowable objects. The habitual tendencies of desire
and so on are the causes of shortcomings in the body and speech of hearer
and solitary realizer arhats. The perfect buddhas are the only ones who
have vanquished those habitual tendencies. They are not vanquished by
anyone else.

It is also important here to understand that Chandrakīrti teaches that
the mental afflictions' habitual tendencies fall into the category of the cognitive obscurations.

The buddhas have unimpeded knowledge of the relinquishment of all
the mental afflictions' habitual tendencies and of all the mental afflictions

that those tendencies produce. The limitless engagement of this knowledge is the buddhas' tenth power: the knowledge of the exhaustion of contaminants.

2.2.2.2.3.2.2.3.2. THE BUDDHAS' QUALITIES ARE LIMITLESS AND CANNOT BE FATHOMED BY ANYONE OTHER THAN BUDDHAS
2.2.2.2.3.2.2.3.2.1. The buddhas' qualities are not in the range of experience of other noble ones who are not buddhas
2.2.2.2.3.2.2.3.2.2. Though they are not in the range of experience of naive beings, they have been described slightly in reliance on the master Nāgārjuna

2.2.2.2.3.2.2.3.2.1. THE BUDDHAS' QUALITIES ARE NOT IN THE RANGE OF EXPERIENCE OF OTHER NOBLE ONES WHO ARE NOT BUDDHAS

> Birds do not return because the sky is exhausted;
> They return because the strength of their wings is drained.
> In the same way, the heirs of the buddhas, along with the hearers,
> Return, not having expressed the buddhas' skylike, limitless
>   qualities. (12.32)

Even if the Buddha himself devoted countless, inconceivable eons to describing the buddhas' qualities, very quickly and without engaging in other enlightened activity, the Buddha would still not be able to explain them all. What need, therefore, is there to ask if the bodhisattvas, hearers, or solitary realizers would be able to understand or express them? The root verse here clarifies this principle using an example.

The kings of birds do not return to the place from which they started because they ran out of sky after their wings ran out of energy. Rather, they return because the strength of their wings has exhausted and because their power to conquer others has been drained.

In the same way, there is no need to mention whether the students such as the hearers are able to describe the qualities of the Buddha: not even the heirs of the buddha who are tenth-ground bodhisattvas are able to describe those qualities. After attempting to offer descriptions, they must return to their own vantage point, not having been able to describe fully the buddhas' qualities, which are limitless like the sky.

2.2.2.2.3.2.2.3.2.2. THOUGH THEY ARE NOT IN THE RANGE OF
EXPERIENCE OF NAIVE BEINGS, THEY HAVE BEEN DESCRIBED
SLIGHTLY IN RELIANCE ON THE MASTER NĀGĀRJUNA

Therefore, what need to speak of my ability to understand
Or describe the buddhas' qualities?
Nevertheless, since they were briefly elucidated by the noble
  Nāgārjuna,
I have left behind qualms and described merely a fraction.
  (12.33)

Since the above-mentioned beings are incapable of describing the genuine qualities of the buddhas, what need is there to mention my own ability
to understand or describe them? For, to myself and those like me, beings
blinded by ignorance, the completely pure qualities of the buddhas are a
hidden phenomenon. Nevertheless, the noble Nāgārjuna has briefly elucidated these qualities. I therefore follow after him here without hesitation.
Leaving behind qualms of inadequate confidence to speak about them, I
have, through the power of my faith, raised a few words as a brief description of a mere fraction of the buddhas' qualities.

2.2.2.2.3.2.2.3.3. ALL QUALITIES ARE INCLUDED WITHIN THE
PROFOUND AND THE VAST

The profound is emptiness;
The other qualities are the vast.
By knowing the ways of the profound and vast,
These qualities will be attained. (12.34)

In sum, this treatise teaches the ways of two types of quality: the vast and
profound qualities of the buddhas. "Profound" refers to the true nature of
reality that is emptiness. For the depth of emptiness is difficult to fathom.
"Vast" refers to the other, temporary qualities connected to cause and
effect. For the limits of those qualities are difficult to realize. The benefit of understanding these two qualities is that by knowing the ways of the
profound and vast and by putting them into practice, these qualities will
be easily attained.

2.2.2.2.3.2.3. The nirmāṇakāya

Once again you arrive in the three existences in an unwavering
kāya.
Through emanations, you display the deeds of descending, birth,
enlightenment, and turning the dharma wheel of peace.
Compassionately, you lead all worldly, deceptive beings, who are
bound in the nooses of hope,
To the ground of nirvāṇa. (12.35)

The nirmāṇakāya will now be explained. After performing the benefit of
the pure disciples by way of the sambhogakāya, you once again assume a
kāya that never wavers from the dharmakāya and arrive in the three existences, even though you have already transcended them. Harmonizing
with the perceptions of your disciples, you take on many emanations and
display yourself in relationships of having a father, mother, son, and so on.

In a way that accords with the world, you descend into the womb of
your mother from the abode of Tushita, take birth from that womb, attain
enlightenment in the vajra seat of Bodhgayā, and, in accordance with the
faculties of your students, turn the three stages of dharma wheels, which
pacify all suffering.

Worldly beings engage in the conduct of deception, the eighty-four
thousand classes of mental afflictions and so on. They are bound tightly in
the many nooses of their cravings and hopes. Compassionately, you, the
Transcendent Conqueror, lead all these beings to the ground of nirvāṇa,
free from the desire for fame or return favors.

2.2.2.2.4. The teaching of one enlightenment as three is a teaching that bears an ulterior intention
2.2.2.2.4.1. That there is one vehicle is a definitive meaning teaching
2.2.2.2.4.2. That there are three vehicles is a provisional meaning teaching

2.2.2.2.4.1. That there is one vehicle is a definitive meaning teaching

To dispel all impurities, there is no antidote to apply apart from
knowing the suchness of phenomena.

Suchness does not rely on the divisions of phenomena's
    manifestions,
And the intelligence that perceives suchness is also not
    multiple.
Therefore, you taught the unequalled and inseparable vehicle
    to sentient beings. (12.36)

Having presented the kāyas of the transcendent conquerors, the *Entrance
to the Middle Way* will now prove how the teaching of one vehicle is a
teaching that bears an ulterior intention. In this world, to dispel all the
impurities—both the afflictive and the cognitive obscurations—there is
no antidote to apply apart from knowing just as it is the suchness of all phenomena. For it is the very lack of knowledge of suchness that leads to the
inability to relinquish the obscurations. This [first line of the root verse,
therefore,] teaches that there is only one vehicle regarding the path—[the
realization of suchness].

Nonarising—the suchness of phenomena that qualifies all things—
is equally nonarising in all instances [of qualifying individual phenom-
ena]. Therefore it does not rely on the different divisions of manifestations
of phenomena. Suchness itself is not categorized into different groups;
this has already been explained. This [second line of the root verse, therefore,] teaches that there is only one vehicle regarding the basis of knowable objects.

Different resultant perceptions arise due to hearing, contemplating, or
meditating; but suchness does not have any divisions or manifestations.
Suchness does not change its aspect. Therefore the perceiving subject—
intelligence or wisdom—that realizes suchness as it is has no separations.
Its nature is singular. If wisdom had multiple natures, it could not realize
suchness, because it would not realize the nature of suchness just as it is.
This [third line of the root text, therefore,] teaches that there is only one
vehicle regarding the result that is realization.

Since suchness, the object, is singular, wisdom, the subject, is not multiple. Therefore you, the Transcendent Conqueror, accordingly taught
beings the one, unequalled vehicle that is inseparable from the vehicle of
the buddhas, since there is no other vehicle. The three vehicles do not
exist—the sūtras say:

Kāshyapa, when one realizes all phenomena as equality, one attains nirvāṇa. This nirvāṇa is singular; there are not two or three nirvāṇas.

The meaning of that statement is as follows. Suchness, the object realized, has no divisions. If the path one traverses does not realize suchness, one will be incapable of dispelling the impurities. Since the realization of suchness also has no divisions, the vehicles of the path traversed and the result, or destination, of that path are singular.

Here the existence of only one vehicle is taught to be the definitive meaning. This assertion accords with the explanation that the hearers and solitary realizers, in the end, attain enlightenment in reliance on the Mahāyāna. Those who assert that the hearers and solitary realizers do not realize phenomenal selflessness say that, in the short term, the enumeration of the vehicles as three is definitive. However, even for them, all paths must enter the Mahāyāna in the long term.

For those who assert that the hearers and solitary realizers do realize phenomenal selflessness, suchness and the hearers' wisdom that realizes it have no divisions. The wisdom of the hearers dispels all impurities. The vehicle of the hearers, therefore, is part of the singular vehicle of the buddhas. The division into three vehicles was explained to be provisional meaning in the *Chapter on the Great Assembly (Düpa Chenpö Le-u/'dus pa chen po'i le'u)*, in Nāgārjuna's *Praise to That for Which There Is No Example (Pe Mepar Töpa/dpe med par bstod pa)*, and so on.

Since there are no divisions in the wisdoms of the hearers and solitary realizers or in the object of those wisdoms, suchness, there is only one vehicle. However, how can the vehicles of hearers and solitary realizers rightly be called vehicles of the buddha? "Buddha" is a term applied to one who has relinquished completely the two obscurations and their habitual tendencies. Apart from unerringly realizing suchness, there is no antidote by which one may relinquish the two obscurations. And the hearers and solitary realizers, moreover, realize suchness. There are differences between buddhas and hearers, etc., however, with regard to faculties and with regard to methods. These differences dictate the rapidity or slowness by which [suchness is fully realized and, consequently, the two obscurations are relinquished].

You may protest, "Your explanation of the vehicles of hearers and solitary realizers as vehicles of the buddha contradicts the teaching that their paths are hindrances to enlightenment!" For those of lesser faculties, it is impossible to attain enlightenment without first proceeding through the lower vehicles. Nonetheless, the same disciples, through progressing gradually through the paths of hearers and solitary realizers, will attain unsurpassable enlightenment. Because at first they are lacking in methods, and because of their lesser faculties, they first enter the lower vehicles. Through cultivating themselves there, they eventually become capable of dispelling all impurities. For that reason those vehicles as well were taught to be vehicles of the buddha.[607]

If students with sharp faculties who have high interest in the profound and the vast apply themselves to the lower vehicles, their attainment of enlightenment will be delayed for a long time. In that context the lower vehicles were taught to be a hindrance.

2.2.2.2.4.2. THAT THERE ARE THREE VEHICLES IS A PROVISIONAL MEANING TEACHING

2.2.2.2.4.2.1. In the final analysis, the teaching of three vehicles bears an ulterior intention
2.2.2.2.4.2.2. A clarifying example

2.2.2.2.4.2.1. IN THE FINAL ANALYSIS, THE TEACHING OF THREE VEHICLES BEARS AN ULTERIOR INTENTION

Since worldly beings are afflicted by the pollutants that give
  rise to shortcomings,
They do not enter the deep sphere of experience of the buddhas.
Nevertheless, you, the sugatas, do not give up on them, for
  you possess excellent knowledge together with the method,
  compassion,
And because, before, you made the promise, "I will liberate
  sentient beings." (12.37)

If nirvāṇa is nothing other than singular, how can the vehicles of the hearers and solitary realizers be taught to lead to nirvāṇa? The teaching that those vehicles [alone] lead to nirvāṇa is a teaching that bears an ulterior intention.

Worldly beings are afflicted by the five pollutants (*nyikma nga/snyigs ma lnga)*[608] that give rise to shortcomings or deficiencies in body and mind. The five pollutants are the pollutants related to sentient beings, eons, mental afflictions, views, and life spans. These five cause beings to be beset mainly by the mental afflictions. These pollutants would prevent sentient beings from obtaining the wisdom of the buddhas even if beings wanted to obtain it. Therefore worldly beings do not enter the deep sphere of the buddhas' wisdom experience, which is difficult to fathom.

Nevertheless, you, the sugatas, do not give up on the possibility of those sentient beings' gaining liberation simply because at present those beings are unsuitable vessels for the teachings. This is so because you possess the omniscient knowledge of how to tame disciples in other ways. You also possess the method, compassion. Furthermore, previously, at the time when you engaged in bodhisattva conduct, you made the promise, "I will liberate all sentient beings." With your previous aspirations lighting the way, you seek out ways to liberate beings without being lazy. For, without a doubt, one must accomplish what one has promised to do.

2.2.2.2.4.2.2. A CLARIFYING EXAMPLE

> Just like the skillful guide who emanated a pleasant city
> In order to dispel the fatigue of travelers on their way to a jewel island,
> You teach the lower vehicles and have your students apply their minds to the way of total peace.
> Later on, you teach voidness separately to the ones whose minds are trained. (12.38)

There are many obstructions that prevent beings from entering the Mahāyāna, and worldly beings as well must be established in nirvāṇa. Therefore, the buddhas teach the lower vehicles first. The following example illustrates how they do so.[609]

Once a skillful travel guide was leading a group of people to a jewel island. In order to dispel the fatigue they incurred while traveling, and to make them feel refreshed, the guide emanated an attractive city for the travelers before they arrived at the island. He relieved them temporarily of their fatigue so that they could continue on. After a while he again led them on the path, and in the end they all arrived at the island of jewels.

In the same way, the transcendent conquerors lead beings fatigued by their travels in saṃsāra to the ground of buddhahood by skillfully teaching them the vehicles of the hearers and solitary realizers. In the beginning, they have students who have the aptitude of hearers and solitary realizers apply their minds to the way of complete peace. Later, they teach them with voidness—nonabiding nirvāṇa.

In this way the buddhas teach the Mahāyāna separately to the hearers and solitary realizers whose minds are trained because of having relinquished the mental afflictions of saṃsāra. Those disciples in turn exert themselves in the Mahāyāna activities of purifying and gathering, through which they too, in the end, attain unsurpassable enlightenment.

2.2.2.2.5. THE TEACHING OF THE TIME OF ENLIGHTENMENT AND THE TIME OF REMAINING

2.2.2.2.5.1. The time of manifesting enlightenment
2.2.2.2.5.2. The time of remaining

2.2.2.2.5.1. THE TIME OF MANIFESTING ENLIGHTENMENT

> However many subtle atoms there are
> In all the pure realms without exception that are the lands
>   of buddhas,
> For that many eons do the sugatas go to supreme, excellent,
>   genuine enlightenment.
> However, they do not share this secret with everyone.
> (12.39)

For how long do the buddhas gain the true enlightenment of the dharmakāya, which is the cause for the buddhas' form kāyas? The measure of such time will now be explained. However many subtle atoms there are in all the pure realms without exception that are the lands of buddhas, for that many eons do the sugatas go to supreme, excellent, genuine enlightenment regarding all phenomena. This going to enlightenment of the buddhas, however, is a "secret," because it is difficult for beings who have previously not accumulated virtue to feel a higher interest in it. Therefore the buddhas do not reveal this secret to those of dull faculties.

Nevertheless, this principle will be explained here, in order to provide for the accumulation of a boundless amount of merit for those who have the appropriate interest. Since the dharmakāya of the buddhas does not have the slightest of divisions, it is impossible for anyone to measure when it began.

This principle was not taught to those of dull faculties because of the potential for misconceptions arising due to misinterpretations of its meaning. Some people of lesser intelligence may think, "If there is only one buddha, it is meaningless for anyone else to try and gather the two accumulations!" Some Indian and Tibetan Buddhist philosophers[610] assert that the first buddha, Changeless Light, was enlightened from the outset, without ever engaging in purification or accumulation. The Jonangpas say that the permanent, unconditioned buddha is primordially attained, but buddhahood is newly attained from the relative, mere provisional perspective of disciples. Some say that, just as in the tīrthika assertion of the self as being permanent and singular, the dharmakāya is of the character of singularity and permanence. All of these are wrong thoughts, and the above "secret" of the buddhas was not shared with those of lesser faculties to avoid these misinterpretations. The *White Lotus of Genuine Dharma* says:

> Since a time that cannot even be measured
> By a billion inconceivable eons,
> I have attained supreme, excellent enlightenment
> And have always excellently taught the dharma.

2.2.2.2.5.2. THE TIME OF REMAINING
2.2.2.2.5.2.1. The buddhas remain for as long as saṃsāra lasts due to their supreme knowledge and compassion
2.2.2.2.5.2.2. They do not pass into nirvāṇa due to the abundant nature of their compassion
2.2.2.2.5.2.3. They do not pass into nirvāṇa because beings in all worlds are the objects of their compassion

2.2.2.2.5.2.1. THE BUDDHAS REMAIN FOR AS LONG AS SAṂSĀRA LASTS DUE TO THEIR SUPREME KNOWLEDGE AND COMPASSION

The victorious ones remain for as long as all worldly beings have not gone to supreme, excellent peace. For as long as space has not disintegrated,

You, borne by the mother of supreme knowledge and nurtured
by the nanny of loving compassion, remain.
Thus how could you depart to peace? (12.40)

Having briefly expressed the time frame of manifest, complete enlightenment, the text will now explain the time of the buddhas' remaining in the
world. The lifespan of the victorious ones endures for as long as all worldly
beings have not gone to the supreme, excellent peace of the dharmakāya—
for as long as they have not attained buddhahood.

For as long as space has not disintegrated, you, the transcendent conquerors, borne by the mother, the perfection of supreme knowledge,
and nurtured by the nanny of loving compassion, remain for as long as
saṃsāra. Thus, how could you depart to peace? One who relies on the
mother of supreme knowledge and the nanny of loving compassion
would never do so.

2.2.2.2.5.2.2. THEY DO NOT PASS INTO NIRVĀṆA DUE TO THE
ABUNDANT NATURE OF THEIR COMPASSION

You regard worldly beings, who consume poisonous food due to
the fault of ignorance,
As members of your own family.
The love you feel for them is not even rivaled by that of a mother
whose only child has eaten poison.
Therefore, protector, you do not pass into supreme, excellent
peace. (12.41)

What does the buddhas' compassion—which accomplishes the benefit
of all sentient beings and nourishes them through time without limits—
resemble? The compassion of the buddhas, which helps beings through all
time, is as follows.

Worldly beings are obscured by the fault of ignorance. They engage the
five sense objects while clinging to them as being real. This is similar to
eating food that has been poisoned—it will produce the vast sufferings of
saṃsāra. The Sage takes personal care of these beings who consume such
poisonous food and treats them like his own family members.

The love the buddhas have for these beings, and the concern the buddhas feel about their suffering, cannot be rivaled even by the love and

concern a mother whose only child is in danger of becoming poisoned feels. The buddhas, protectors that they are, born of great compassion, will therefore not pass into nirvāṇa. They do not depart for supreme, excellent peace.

2.2.2.2.5.2.3. THEY DO NOT PASS INTO NIRVĀṆA BECAUSE BEINGS IN ALL WORLDS ARE THE OBJECTS OF THEIR COMPASSION

> Unskillful beings cling to existence and nonexistence,
> By which they fall prey to the sufferings of birth, death, losing
>   the pleasant, meeting with the unpleasant,
> And negative actions—every being in all the worlds there are is
>   an object of your loving compassion.
> Therefore, transcendent conquerors, you feel no fondness for
>   peace and instead choose not to pass into nirvāṇa. (12.42)

Since the transcendent conquerors have turned away from the desire for nirvāṇa, they see worldly beings as being vulnerable to a great host of sufferings. Naïve, unskillful beings cling to existence and nonexistence, things and nonthings. Their clinging to existence leads them to births as gods and humans because of their trust in cause and effect, but they will still be prey to birth, death, losing what they find pleasant, and meeting with what they find unpleasant. They will experience a great variety of those sufferings.

Their clinging to nonexistence will lead them to commit great negativities, which will in turn propel them into births in the hell realms and so on. There, they will experience the sufferings mentioned above, beginning with birth.

For the buddhas, therefore, every being in all the worlds there are, to the limits of space, is an object of their loving compassion. Bearing these suffering beings in mind, the transcendent conquerors feel no fondness for peace. Instead, they choose not to pass into nirvāṇa for as long as space endures.

⠿ Conclusion

2.2.3.1. THIS TREATISE, WHICH FEATURES SCRIPTURAL QUOTATIONS, REASONINGS, AND KEY INSTRUCTIONS, IS UNIQUE

This system has been expressed by the bhikṣhu Chandrakīrti
By drawing on the *Treatise on the Middle Way*
And in precise accordance with scripture
And key instructions. (13.1)

Just as there are no treatises that teach the dharma of emptiness
In the way the *Treatise on the Middle Way* does,
Learned ones should ascertain that there is no other treatise
    among Nāgārjuna's followers
That teaches his system like this one. (13.2)

This system, which clarifies in an unerring way the meaning of the two truths, has been expressed by Chandrakīrti, a bhikṣhu who was fully ordained by way of the four rituals.[611] The text has been composed in consultation with the main points from the *Treatise on the Fundament Wisdom of the Middle Way,* composed by the great, glorious Nāgārjuna, and other treatises. Chandrakīrti has spoken in harmony with reasoning and in precise accordance with profound and vast scriptural quotations from the *Ten Grounds*, the *Perfection of Supreme Knowledge* sūtras, the *Descent into Laṅka*, the *King of Samādhi*, and so on. In particular, he has expressed this system in precise accordance with the key instructions of the noble master Nāgārjuna.

Just as "emptiness" is not taught anywhere apart from the *Treatise on the Middle Way* in such an unerring fashion, there is also no other treatise from among the followers of Nāgārjuna like this one of Chandrakīrti, an elucidation that not only explains emptiness but also includes rebuttals to opponents' objections. Wise ones should ascertain this fact now, and they should also use their abundant mindfulness and supreme knowledge to deepen this ascertainment in the future.

The early lines of the above verses[612] teach that the Proponents of Things do not realize emptiness and that the Followers of the Middle Way do. They also teach that the Autonomists are Followers of the Middle Way. The closing lines of the above verses[613] teach that the system of the master Chandrakīrti is superior to that of the Autonomists.

The Autonomists say that what is posited as ultimate truth by the Particularists and Sūtra Followers is posited as relative truth by the Followers of the Middle Way. That statement is untenable. Transcendent dharmas and mundane dharmas cannot be held as equivalent. Furthemore, if you make such statements after contemplating the ultimate of Nāgārjuna, you have made something unconfused and unelaborate into something confused and elaborate.

The factions of hearers assert such things as partless particles to be ultimate truth. If you turn around and assert those things as relative truth, you will be using those schools' wrong imputations as the basis for the relative. Yet worldly people do not even take such phenomena as bases for adopting and rejecting. If a Follower of the Middle Way were to accept them as relative truth, what greater error could there be?

[The above two paragraphs] refute two assertions: the assertion of some that the Followers of the Middle Way who conduct themselves in accordance with worldly renown[614] present the relative in accordance with the Particularists, and the assertion of others that there are no Followers of the Middle Way who make presentations of the relative in accordance with the Particularists.[615]

Due to the chronology of the masters' lifetimes, Chandrakīrti did not directly refute the Practitioners of Yogic Conduct such as Shāntarakṣhita in the *Entrance to the Middle Way*. However, in terms of content, the latter's view was refuted during the refutation of the Proponents of Consciousness. Therefore, Shāntarakṣhita's system, in comparison with that of the Consequentialists, does not possess the full body of the Middle Way.

Thus, there are four ways in which the Followers of the Middle Way posit the conventional relative: three that accord with the three lower philosophical systems and the methods of those who conduct themselves in accordance with worldly renown.

The Jonangpas say that neither the Autonomist approach nor the Consequentialist approach is the Middle Way because in order for something to be the Middle Way it must be the dharmatā. They say that, since the Autonomist approach and the Consequentialist approach are conditioned phenomena, they both fall into the extreme of existence.

Their claims are untenable. If they were accurate, it would follow that the final turning of the wheel of dharma, the profound tantras, the treatises of Maitreya, and the treatises of Asaṅga, Asaṅga's brother,[616] Dignāga, Dharmakīrti, and so on are all dharmatā, because, [for you], they are the Middle Way. Furthermore, it is contradictory for you to say that the Consequentialists and Autonomists fall into the extreme of existence and at other times call them proponents of nothingness or deprecators.

If you retort by saying, "In the final turning of the wheel of dharma and so on, both conditioned phenomena and unconditioned phenomena exist; therefore those faults do not apply to our view," that is incorrect. For in the latter turning of the wheel of dharma and so on, there is utterly no unconditioned aspect to phenomena that are produced by causes and conditions. Therefore to speak as you do goes beyond the ways of logic and does not lie within the possible framework of knowable objects.

2.2.3.2. IT HAS BEEN COMPOSED BECAUSE IT TEACHES THE PROFOUND MEANING ABANDONED BY OTHERS
2.2.3.2.1. The actual teaching
2.2.3.2.2. The reasons why the Middle Way has been abandoned by others and the counsel to have affection for the path of the Middle Way alone

2.2.3.2.1. THE ACTUAL TEACHING

> Frightened by the vast, dark ocean of Nāgārjuna's mind,
> Some have cast his excellent tradition far away.

Now, his verses, like flower pistils waiting to open, have fully
  bloomed
Due to the water of Chandrakīrti, who thus perfectly fulfills the
  hopes of disciples. (13.3)

The ocean of the great, noble master Nāgārjuna's mind is difficult to
fathom in its limits and its depths. His wisdom of nonarising and emptiness is like a vast, dark ocean. Some, not realizing his teaching, become
fearful at even seeing the words in his texts. These timid scholars of the
Buddhist literature from years past have cast far away Nāgārjuna's excellent tradition that teaches the true, transcendent dharma.

Left[617] thus unattended, the night-blooming flowers of his verses in
the *Fundamental Wisdom of the Middle Way*, born from the waters of
his mind's ocean, languished. Their pistils have been all but closed, waiting for all these years to open. Now, they have fully bloomed due to the
cooling light rays of Chandrakīrti's intelligence.[618] With eloquent explanations of the two truths, the fine water possessing the eight qualities,[619]
Chandrakīrti thus perfectly fulfills and makes prosper the earnest hopes
of disciples to realize the reality of the way things are.

One may ask, "Did elders of the past, authors such as Vasubandhu,
Dignāga, Dharmakīrti, Dharmapāla, and so on, completely relinquish
Nāgārjuna's teachings, which unerringly explain dependent arising, due
to the fear they felt at merely having seen the words?" It is has been said
that they did.

Bhāvaviveka says that even Asaṅga did not comprehend the meaning of
the Middle Way. His *Blaze of Reasoning* says:

> Others, such as the Mahāyāna masters Asaṅga and Vasu-
> bandhu, pull students away from the Mahāyāna meaning that
> was perfectly realized by the noble Nāgārjuna, who attained the
> ground of Supreme Joy and was prophesied by the Tathāgata.
> Shamelessly and arrogantly, they pretend to understand and
> be learned in meanings that they do not understand. They say
> things like, "The nectar of suchness has been excellently taught
> only by us, not by the Followers of the Middle Way."

However, we do not make the same claims about Asaṅga. The master

Asaṅga was indeed a noble being, but he taught the system of Mind Only to some students in order to tame them. We do not assert that for the latter reason alone he was not a Follower of the Middle Way. It is clear, for example, that the noble Maitreya also composed Mind Only treatises.

2.2.3.2.2. The reasons why the Middle Way has been abandoned by others and the counsel to have affection for the path of the Middle Way alone

The suchness explained above, profound and frightening, will be realized
Through beings' previous habituation—it will not be comprehended by those who merely have done extensive hearing.
Therefore, just as the conceptually fabricated systems that propound a self should be relinquished,
So should all fondness be forsaken for the systems outside the way of Nāgārjuna. (13.4)

How is the way explained above realized? The suchness explained above is the profound emptiness and dependent arising. If those who do not possess an adequate amount of good fortune merely hear it, they will be frightened. What they are frightened about, suchness, will only be realized through previous habituation. It seems that only by planting habitual seeds of emptiness and by gathering accumulations of virtue can beings realize emptiness.

If one possesses the power of such accumulated causes, even if one is a tīrthika, one will be able to understand that one's tīrthika system is illogical and realize with definitiveness the depths of emptiness. Tīrthikas who have no habitual tendencies of emptiness may be able to relinquish some of the mental afflictions of the three realms; they may be able to forge a connection with other philosophical systems, but they will not be able to genuinely realize emptiness. For just as they are not highly interested in the teachings of the Sage, they will not engender high interest in profound emptiness, even if they study about it extensively. Devoid of this seed of higher interest, it will be impossible for them to comprehend emptiness fully.

It is for this reason that those who desire liberation should relinquish the systems of the tīrthikas that proclaim the existence of the self. For those systems do not accord with the worldly or transcendent truths, and they are the conceptual fabrications of those who create them.

In the very same way, all fondness should be forsaken for the other systems that lie outside the way of Nāgārjuna—those, for example, of the hearers and the Proponents of Mind Only. These systems are not amazing in that conventionally they posit conceptual imputations as bases for correct adopting and rejecting, even though those imputations do not accord with knowable objects. The Middle Way, because it accords with knowable objects, is amazing.

2.2.3.3. DEDICATING THE VIRTUE OF THIS COMPOSITION TO ENLIGHTENMENT, THE PERFECT BENEFIT OF OTHERS

> May the merit I have gained through explaining the good system of master Nāgārjuna pervade space in all directions.
> With the blue hue of the mental afflictions becoming a brilliant autumn star in mind's sky,
> And with the jewel hood-ornament beautifying the snake of the mind,
> May the beings in all worlds realize suchness and swiftly proceed to the ground of the sugatas. (13.5)

Chandrakīrti concludes with a dedication: through explaining the good tradition of the unerring two truths as envisioned by the master Nāgārjuna, may the merit of I, Chandrakīrti, pervade space in all directions. With the blue hue, the stains, of the adventitious mental afflictions becoming as brilliant as an autumn star in the cloudless sky of the mind of emptiness, and with the jewel hood-ornament beautifying the snake of the mind of mental afflictions and thoughts—may this merit be especially directed toward the beings in all worlds without exception: may they realize the suchness of all phenomena and quickly proceed to the ground of the sugatas, the blissfully gone ones.

I will now discuss briefly the essential explanation of dependent arising that arose from the oceanic intelligence of the venerable lord of victorious ones, the Eighth Karmapa. This explanation, a wish-fulfilling jewel, holds the wisdom vision of Nāgārjuna and his heart disciples. It is the excellent way free of the extremes.

The Consequentialists refute the assertions of others in connection with the two truths and with how the two truths apply to the stages of ground, path, and fruition. How do they do this, and how do they posit their own positions following their refutations? Let us discuss this.

Bhāvaviveka says that [any objective notion of] things holding their own power does not apply to the ultimate truth, either relatively or ultimately. However, he says, the relative truth does, on the mere relative, conventional level (though not on the ultimate level) involve things that hold their own power. One must conduct presentations of existence and nonexistence, logic and illogic, in light of this. The existence and nonexistence, adopting and rejecting, and so on of the relative must be analyzed with the conventional valid cognition of the power of things. Whatever is logical under that analysis must be posited in one's own system; that which is illogical is to be refuted. The logical stages of reasons and so on are, in the relative, things that hold their own power. These are the tools that must be used, he says, to establish the reality of emptiness. The ones who uphold this approach are known as "Autonomist Followers of the Middle Way."

The great masters Buddhapālita and Chandrakīrti agree with the Autonomists that in both truths there is no ultimate existence of any objectivity of the power of things. In terms of the relative, however, for the Consequentialists not only does it not entail things that hold their own power in an ultimate sense; it is also devoid of such objectivity on the level of the relative. Such objectivity would be untenable, because, if it did exist, there would be leftover phenomena from among the two truths, phenomena that were not empty and not unarisen. Yet such "leftovers" do not exist in any context, in any place, in any time.

[The above paragraph] represents the way in which the Consequentialists extensively refute the illogical aspects of the Autonomist system.

How, then, do the Consequentialists deal with relative truth notions of existence and nonexistence, logic and illogic, and so on? There are two different contexts: the first is relating to the relative truth of mundane beings and engaging in adopting and rejecting from the worldly perspective. The second is relating to the mere relative and engaging in adopting and rejecting in that context.

For the first, they simply utter such repetitions as "relinquish killing" and "practice virtue" in a nonanalytical and other-approved way. For the second, they accept, without analysis and as approved by others, merely that all phenomena are unreal and illusionlike. They say, "We defeat illusionlike objects of refutation with illusionlike reasonings" and utter such repetitions as "relinquish nonvirtue, which lacks inherent existence," and "practice virtue, which lacks inherent existence."

They say, "When such relative truth, the basis for affirming and refuting, is analyzed, there is no existence even conventionally of things that hold their own power." They set forth unwanted consequences to those who do not accept this. Those who uphold this approach are renowned in this world as "Consequentialists."

The followers of this Middle Way tradition not only refrain from positing the relative truth as part of their own system when analyzing, they also refrain from positing even the mere relative. In order to relate with some people whose views do not accord with interdependence and who thus assert the existence of things that hold their own power in the relative, the Consequentialists will use other-approved reasonings that accord with interdependence. They will refute the incorrect assertions of their counterparts and speak of the mere relative. They say things like, "The relative is like an illusion—it has no inherent existence." When they do this, the statements they make are mere repetitions that are spoken for the special purpose of refuting misconceptions. This description of the mere relative is not made when analyzing. From the perspective of their own logical analyses, the mere relative also is not established, even conventionally.

Some people doubt that approach, thinking, "You cannot refute the illogic of others using other-approved reasonings, because the reasonings used are not one's own." The reason is not included in the predicate, so their doubts are unfounded.

Our approach to reasoning reflects the basic principles of mutually dependent designation. If something is renowned as illogical, something else can be renowned as its refutation. This is perfectly possible.

"Well then," you may continue, "How does a reasoning that accords with interdependence refute a misconception of true existence that does not accord with interdependence?"

Our reasonings, which are other-approved and pertain to the nature of phenomena, cut through elaborations of true existence with respect to isolates of apparent phenomena in the relative truth. Once those elaborations are cut, the ultimate truth is automatically comprehended. This is how we speak in accord with interdependence in a way that is approved by others. Yet even that approach is not established when analyzed. For when arising is refuted on the relative level, nonarising is not affirmed on the ultimate level. If there is no arising relatively, "nonarising" ultimately is of course untenable. In this way, the earlier stages of our approach to reasoning will disintegrate on their own.

The true nature of reality, the ultimate truth, or the isolate of "freedom from elaborations" is not an object of analysis for the refutations or affirmations of other-approved reasonings, because those whose views accord with interdependence do not refute or affirm them when engaging in analysis. Not only that; even when accepting the mere relative in a context of analysis, the ultimate truth and so on are not refuted or affirmed.

For example, when Mañjushrī, in the context of not even analyzing the relative as illusionlike, asked the noble Licchavī Nirmala about the ultimate truth, Licchavī did not say anything in response. Furthermore, the ultimate truth and so on cannot be taken directly as objects by the prajñās of hearing, contemplating, and meditating or by worldly prajñā. If one tried to affirm the ultimate as either existing or not existing, such efforts would not accord with the way things are. They would only be inaccurate conceptions.

The relative truth is not like that. It can be taken directly as an object of affirmation or refutation. Other-approved reasonings can be used to refute or affirm something, and the result of such refutation or affirmation accords with interdependent knowable objects on the mere nonanalytical level. This accordance is, on that level, indisputable, even with regard to the mere relative.

However, those who speak in accordance with interdependence do not, even in a context of no analysis, try to divide the isolate of the ultimate truth into included (yong chö/yongs gcod) or excluded (nam che/rnam bcad) aspects. The ultimate truth does not have an essence or entity, so it is not renowned as a perceptible thing to either ordinary or noble beings. The relative truth is merely proclaimed to exist for the confused perspective of ordinary beings.

Nevertheless, some logicians still insist on making incorrect imputations, such as existence, nonexistence, and so forth, upon the ultimate truth—emptiness free from elaborations. In response to this the Followers of the Middle Way are capable of dispelling their counterparts' mistaken thoughts using other-approved reasonings. But even when they dispel such wrong thoughts, they are not dispelling anything that is established as wrong.

Furthermore, the Followers of the Middle Way do not use self-approved reasonings to dispel those wrong thoughts about ultimate truth, because it is impossible for self-approved reasonings to ever be approved in the own system of the Followers of the Middle Way. Those who speak in accord with knowable objects use other-approved reasonings to analyze the isolates that appear as subjects in the relative. When we don't find any existence of their entity whatsoever, that nonfinding is what comes to be known as, and what is fancied to be, "ultimate truth" from among the divisions of the two truths. Nevertheless, that ultimate truth is not the actual ultimate truth, because it is an object of hearing, contemplating, and meditating; it is an object of thought and speech.

Such ultimate truth can be analyzed again using similar reasonings and be found to be beyond existence, nonexistence, and other extreme elaborations. Some people think that the conclusion of this latter analysis is the actual ultimate truth, but it is not. It simply becomes a relative subject when it is isolated following the earlier refutations of existence, nonexistence, and so on. Therefore the negation of ultimate truth as ultimate is a relative phenomena—it is a nominal ultimate truth. Subject, predicate, and reason in that case are all relative truth.

Furthermore, that type of ultimate truth is posited in dependence upon the relative truth. It is unsuitable for phenomena posited in dependence upon something else to be the actual ultimate truth, for they are merely conditioned subjects.

How, you may ask, is the actual ultimate truth established in terms of one's own position and in terms of what is approved by others? The actual ultimate does not fall into any extreme bias such as "being established" or "not being established." No matter what reasonings, of oneself or of others, one uses in attempts to affirm or deny its establishment, one will be incapable of any affirmation or denial. For the actual ultimate is beyond thought and speech.

Some people take the following position: "The Proponents of Things, who do not describe knowable objects in accord with interdependence, view the relative truth as real. When the other-approved reasonings of those whose views accord with interdependence are used to analyze and refute the views on the relative of the Proponents of Things, the reasonings used are not own-position reasonings for Followers of the Middle Way. Nor is the analysis employed an analysis on the ultimate level. For the actual ultimate truth is not an object of conventions. Rather, the analysis applied at that time is an analysis of the conventional, relative truth. Therefore, it is a contradiction to say that the Consequentialists do not posit the relative truth after analysis, even conventionally."

There is no such contradiction. The Proponents of Things assert an incorrect relative truth. From the standpoint of those who speak in accord with interdependence, the relative phenomena they propound do not exist even relatively. To reverse such completely erroneous clinging to existence, the Followers of the Middle Way use other-approved reasonings to merely perform the function of refuting the wrong view. They do not posit, even conventionally, any relative phenomena in their own system that would be the reverse or replacement of what they refuted. Therefore there is no opportunity for a contradiction to apply.

For Followers of the Middle Way, the interdependent and dependently designated relative is empty of inherent nature—it is empty of the four extremes of elaboration.[620] At the same time, it is capable of performing a variety of functions. In this way it resembles illusions and dreams. In reference to such phenomena, the Followers of the Middle Way make presentations of saṃsāra and nirvāṇa and so on. They do so as a repetition of those who speak in harmony with interdependence, who do not use reasonings and analyses to posit the relative.

For example, those who speak in harmony with interdependence may say, in an other-approved way and without analysis, that consciousness exists for sentient beings and that wisdom does not exist for buddhas. They may also say things such as "wisdom exists for the buddhas" in order to guide those who do not speak in harmony with interdependence, such as the True Aspectarian Proponents of Mind Only. But when they make those statements, they do so as a repetition of others and to address a specific purpose. The Followers of the Middle Way repeat after others in the same fashion, without analysis.

Nevertheless, when Followers of the Middle Way engage in the analyses of the other-approved reasonings of those who speak in harmony with interdependence, they refute both the assertion that wisdom exists conventionally for buddhas and the assertion that wisdom does not exist conventionally for buddhas. Neither the existence nor the nonexistence of wisdom is truly established.

It is therefore absolutely not the case that Consequentialists posit the relative truth following analysis.[621] There are no divisions of the relative into correct and incorrect based on the adulteration of nonafflictive ignorance. *All* relative phenomena are designated via incorrect conception. They are all erroneous. Although there are, therefore, no such distinctions of correct and incorrect regarding the relative, one can speak of the classifications of "correct" and "seeming" in dependence upon the adulteration of afflictive ignorance. This will be explained as follows.

The relative truth of those who do not speak in harmony with interdependence is adulterated by afflictive ignorance. It comprises the phenomena of confusion and is posited as the seeming relative. Yet when the noble ones, who have relinquished afflictive ignorance, engage conventions without analysis, they do not accept such seeming relative as even belonging to the relative.

When the Followers of the Middle Way arise from their meditative equipoise within true reality and, in their postmeditation, engage the conventions of the relative without analysis, they merely act in accordance with the mindfulness and supreme knowledge that are aware of the illusionlike and dreamlike nature of appearances. They do not posit any relative truth as a product of analysis in that state.

It should be noted, though, that simply being a Follower of the Middle Way does not automatically qualify one as a practitioner who, viewing the relative as an illusion, engages in all avenues of conduct free from analysis. For there are also Followers of the Middle Way of lesser acumen, those who see the relative as being real in and of itself and who engage in conduct on that basis. Their conduct is not fully embraced by an experiential integration[622] of the Middle Way view.

Moreover, the seeming relative that appears in a deceptive way in reliance on the mere relative, which appears due to the adulteration of nonafflictive ignorance,[623] exists merely in dependence upon the confused consciousnesses that apprehend it. It is not the case that it does not exist at all among knowable objects. For, if it were not a knowable object, it would follow that the confused appearances that appear as the seeming relative truth of subjects and objects could not be affirmed as even the mere relative using the tenable, other-approved reasonings of those who speak in harmony with interdependence. Furthermore, when the apprehender and apprehended of the relative truth appear due to ignorance regarding the mere, illusory relative, if objects are not apprehended as what is known by the erroneous mind, it is impossible for the erroneous apprehension of the perceiving subject to be established either.

Thus according to those who speak in harmony with interdependence, on the level of no analysis the phenomena of the relative are capable of performing a variety of functions despite lacking an inherent nature. If these illusionlike phenomena are analyzed with other-approved reasonings, they are not even established as illusionlike phenomena. They transcend speech and thought. That transcendence of speech and thought as well is, for as long as it remains an object of supreme knowledge,[624] relative. When all objects and subjects of consciousness are pacified, that is the actual ultimate truth. It can be realized only by the meditative equipoise of the noble ones in training or beyond training.[625] It is not, however, utterly nonexistent like the horns of a rabbit.

Does that meditative equipoise entail the movement of wisdom, or does it not? The object of the noble ones' equipoise, in which all objects and subjects are pacified, is comprehended only by noble ones. It cannot be demonstrated as existent or nonexistent via speech or thought by other, ordinary beings.

How do the Followers of the Middle Way, who are free from the extremes, describe the dichotomy of themselves versus other persons, namely worldly people who propound other-approved reasonings? Of course, when analyzed neither type of person exists. However, in the nonanalytical context of what is approved by those who speak in harmony with interdependence, they speak of themselves as people who abide in ultimate truth, the middle that is free from the extremes. There are also other, worldly people who abide in the relative truth. They rely on this dichotomy as a nonanalytical repetition of others, voiced for specific purposes such as making presentations of challengers and defenders in a debate.

In such a context, they further describe the Followers of the Middle Way as being of different types. The genuine Followers of the Middle Way are the noble ones, in and beyond training, who dwell in meditative equipoise within the true nature of reality. As for the worldly people other than those genuine Followers of the Middle Way, first there are the worldly

noble beings: the beings on the paths of training who, in the postmeditation phase, speak in harmony with interdependence and perform conduct
in relation to the relative. Secondly, there are ordinary worldly beings who
speak in harmony with interdependence. This second category is in turn
of two types: those who speak of only some knowable objects in harmony
with interdependence and those who speak of all knowable objects in harmony with interdependence.

The first category refers to some persons who have entered the Buddhist
or non-Buddhist philosophical systems. They speak of some things as performing functions in the manner of imputed designation, as opposed to
the manner of substantial establishment. This way of describing the performance of functions accords with interdependence, because phenomena that are designated via dependence are established as interdependent
phenomena.

The second category refers to those who cognize all knowable objects
as interdependent: if any phenomenon were to inherently arise, it would
entail either eternalism or nihilism. Even conventionally the continua of
phenomena would be severed. Therefore, since all phenomena arise in
dependence upon discrete phenomena that are different from each other,
their continua are not severed conventionally. However, members of this
category do not realize interdependence as emptiness.

And, finally, the worldly people who do not describe knowable objects
in harmony with interdependence are just that: worldly people who are
not Followers of the Middle Way.

Are the persons who are Followers of the Middle Way people who
describe knowable objects in accord with interdependence? Or are they
not? One cannot answer these questions categorically. The Followers of
the Middle Way do not express knowable objects in their own system in a
way that harmonizes with interdependence.[626] On the other hand, for the
purpose of taming their students of different types, they describe knowable objects in a variety of ways: sometimes in a way that harmonizes with
interdependence, sometimes in a way that does not—they can use both
approaches.

Then, what of the persons who speak in harmony with interdependence? Are they Followers of the Middle Way? Or are they not? From the
perspective of what is approved by others, we say that those who have realized interdependence as emptiness and who speak of knowable objects as

being interdependent merely from the perspective of what is approved by others are both persons who speak in harmony with interdependence and Followers of the Middle Way. For there is no contradiction in both labels applying to one basis. However, it is held that those who realize interdependence and emptiness but describe knowable objects as interdependent from their own perspective or in their own system cannot suitably be called Followers of the Middle Way.

You may voice the following consequence: "It follows that being either a noble or ordinary worldly person necessitates *not* being a Follower of the Middle Way. For both of those types of person are not noble ones who dwell in the meditative equipoises of those in training and those beyond training." We agree that both noble and ordinary worldly beings are not genuine Followers of the Middle Way. But in terms of being Followers of the Middle Way in a congruent fashion, we would say that the reason of the above consequence is not included in its predicate. Ordinary and noble worldly beings who posit interdependent knowable objects as emptiness merely from the perspective of what is approved by others have a semblance of comprehension, through direct and inferential valid cognition, of the mere freedom from elaborations that is the meditative equipoise of the noble ones in or beyond training. They engage in all their analyses from the perspective of what is approved by others, and refrain from fixating on elaborations such as refutation and affirmation in their own system. They do not take delight in any extreme that could be spoken or conceptualized. Further, they are Followers of the Middle Way in a congruent sense because they do not assert that they accept the other-approved reasonings they employ.

When the Followers of the Middle Way speak of the extreme-free way in which interdependence is equivalent to emptiness, the Proponents of Things attempt to refute them using reasonings that either accord or do not accord with interdependence. How do the Followers of the Middle Way respond?

They respond only by saying, "We do not accept your reasons and predicates, and your inclusions[627] are contradictory to your own tenets." This response is perfect, because it vanquishes the brazenness of the challenger.

How is it that the Proponents of Things' inclusions are not established for even themselves? They use proofs that they consider to be real in themselves to prove objects of affirmation that they also believe to be valid and real. In this way they attempt to prove something nonexistent using a nonexistent as the proof. They [believe that their reasonings] refute a truly existent object of affirmation. No matter what arguments the Proponents of Things set forth to the Followers of the Middle Way, they say nothing other than the above. The responses of the Consequentialists, moreover, cannot be surpassed. The superiority of the answers of the Consequentialists is expressed in quotations such as the following:

> Therefore the learned use the consequence response:
> The four doors of liberation.

Concerning the phenomena of the two truths, what is their ontological status among knowable objects? There is no need to mention the response to that question from the perspective of the own-system of the Followers of the Middle Way when they are engaged in analysis. Even when not analyzing, they do not describe phenomena of the two truths as definitely existing or not existing among knowable objects. However, when the Followers of the Middle Way align themselves with what is renowned to other, worldly beings, they say without analysis that all phenomena of the two truths are suitable as objects to be known by the mind. Even those who speak of the Middle Way that is beyond the world say the same thing. They make such statements as a repetition of others in order to tame their students. Further, they make such statements without analysis and in harmony with other-approved reasonings of worldly people who speak in harmony with interdependence.

The following two types of phenomena correctly exist conventionally as knowable objects: 1) the mere relative, which resembles an illusion and arises due to nonafflictive ignorance and 2) the phenomena of the dependently designated two truths that comprise the relative and that are renowned to noble ones.

The following two types of phenomena do not correctly exist as confusion-free knowable objects: 1) the relative truth adulterated by afflictive ignorance and 2) appearances adulterated by immediate causes of mistakenness, such as a white conch appearing as yellow.

[That is how the Followers of the Middle Way describe, for others, the

different levels of ontological status of the phenomena of the two truths.]
In consideration of this topic, Neyu Zurpa[628] said:

The most final and sublime certainty of unerring realization
that depends upon a relative apprehending mind apprehending
the apparent phenomena that are the illusionlike relative is the
wisdom of postmeditation of the tenth ground. Since its objects
and perceiving subjects are the correct relative, the actual correct relative only exists as a genuinely knowable object in the
postmeditation of the tenth ground. Other relative phenomena do not exist as genuine knowable objects.

And Maja Changchub Tsöndrü said:

Since the appearance of objects increases in extent once one
attains the grounds, mistaken appearances also increase. The
attainment of the wisdom of buddhahood entails the pacification of the engagement of mind in relative phenomena. Therefore, at the stage of buddhahood the continuum of confusion
is severed.

Those who propound the relative truth renowned to ordinary beings,
the relative that arises due to afflictive ignorance, say that the illusionlike
mere relative and the relative adulterated by [immediate] causes for mistakenness, as exemplified by one moon appearing as two, do not exist as
correct knowable objects. However, they say and also think that definienda
such as fire and defining characteristics such as performing the functions
of cooking and burning are things that are real in themselves and exist as
correct knowable objects.

From the perspective of someone perceiving appearances that are
adulterated by immediate causes of mistakenness, both the subjects and
objects of the perceptions exist as knowable objects. This is so because, if
the causes of mistakenness by which the appearances of subject and object
arose did not come together, the confused consciousness apprehending
that appearance as a knowable object would not arise.

The two moons perceived by adulterated perceptions are objects suitable to be known by a mind, but in the worldly perspective (adulterated by the ignorance that is the long-term cause of mistakenness) wherein the existence of only one moon is renowned as the correct relative truth, the perception of two moons is not one of a correct knowable object. This is the way in which things are posited in the world.

Thus, in order to guide their students, the ordinary and noble Followers of the Middle Way describe, without analysis, knowable objects in a manner consistent with those who perceive them: the correct relative truth that is renowned to ordinary beings and the incorrect relative adulterated by the immediate causes of mistakenness. When analyzing, however, they do not assert any phenomena of the two truths as knowable objects. For, if any phenomenon of the two truths were established as a knowable object, real in itself when analyzed, that establishment would contradict the notion that all phenomena are empty of inherent natures.

In sum we can speak of three modes of relative phenomena, all of which are conceptual imputations: 1) the illusionlike incorrect relative, imputed by nonafflictive ignorance, 2) the incorrect relative arisen from afflictive ignorance, consisting of [imaginary] function-performing things that are perceived to be real in themselves [by ordinary beings], and 3) the incorrect relative arisen from the adulteration of immediate causes of confusion, which even ordinary beings hold to be false conventionally.

Nonabiding nirvāṇa, or dharmadhātu—the object of the true, complete awakening with respect to all phenomena in all aspects—and wisdom—that which comprehends such an object—are beyond singularity and multiplicity. They comprise the actual ultimate truth, which is free from conceptual imputations. They are not of the nature of imputed phenomena, the confusion of the relative, and of obscurations. Different from it are all relative phenomena—saṃsāra and nirvāṇa, the two truths, and so on. All those relative phenomena are mere conceptual imputations—their apparent manifestations along with their true natures are both empty of their own entities. They have no nature established as real or as unreal.

As to the mental states that impute such relative phenomena, some are distorted even on the level of imputation. If, for example, one were to impute the existence of cold fire or of the horns of a rabbit, one's imputations could not possibly correlate to anything conventionally, from the perspective of being in harmony with interdependence. Other imputations are in harmony, conventionally, with interdependence. The hotness of fire, the nonexistence of rabbit horns, the result of happiness arising from the cause of virtue—all of these are imputations in accord with interdependence arisen due to beginningless, innate ignorance. Conventionally, they arise as undeceiving interdependence. From that perspective, they afford no opportunity for confusion, because they are designated via dependence.

That is a description of relative phenomena: saṃsāra and nirvāṇa, the two truths, and so on. They are to be realized as being empty of their own entities. If one realizes emptiness, one will also ascertain that karmic cause and effect is undeceiving. It is crucial to exert oneself in methods for realizing emptiness while at the same time not confusing what to adopt or what to reject.

Some[629] who have not understood this point say, "Pillars are real as things that are pillars, but they are not truly existent as things that are objects of refutation by reasons." They claim that through this statement alone they are able to explain how even conventionally the thing that is a pillar is empty of its own entity.

When they speak of "pillars as things that are pillars," they are contradicting the thesis they claim to hold that "the thing that is a pillar is empty even conventionally of its own entity." They are not satisfied with simply determining that all conceptually imputed apparent phenomena are emptiness. Rather, in order to realize emptiness, they seek out the referent object behind the imputation. They say that determining the emptiness of that referent object is the perfectly pure emptiness. They say that the cognition that all interdependent phenomena are empty of their own entities is nihilism; it does not suffice as a genuine realization of emptiness.

This approach is not the intention of the protector Nāgārjuna. The emptiness of any given phenomenon is realized by determining the emptiness of the imputation of the apparent phenomenon. Refraining from determining the emptiness of a quality that does not exist among knowable objects will do not even the slightest harm to those who desire liberation. For there is no basis for conceiving qualities that do not exist among knowable objects to be real.

The phenomena that are to be determined as emptiness are the knowable objects, the imputed phenomena, from form through omniscience. These and these alone are the phenomena that are taught to be empty. Our counterparts, on the other hand, advocate the opposite.

We refute confused, imputed phenomena, such as sprouts, which are undeceiving results, as being real in and of themselves. You may object to this approach, saying, "By refuting the entity of the apparent phenomenon, you remove the potential to employ it as a subject in a logical statement. Anything you try to prove about it, therefore, is in fact unprovable."

Yet for us no knowable objects, such as sprouts, exist in either of the two truths when analyzed. We merely take a confused apparent phenomenon (for example, a sprout) as a subject in a logical statement for the purpose of refuting *your* assertion that it exists as a knowable object. Apart from that, no subjects are posited as knowable objects in the own-system of the Followers of the Middle Way. Since we ourselves do not posit any knowable objects, no logical statements about them apply in *our own system.* Therefore we do not say anything such as, "By our own system of valid cognition, such-and-such object of affirmation is thus proven."

Nevertheless, we are capable of refuting the misconception that a truly existent sprout is produced by a truly existent seed. Our approach to refutation is mirrored by the way in which the Proponents of Things refute the tīrthikas: they do not accept "primal matter" and so on in their own system as a knowable object, but they nonetheless take that other-approved phenomenon as a subject and, in logical statements, refute the misconception that it exists among knowable objects. The same principle applies here.

I have here presented a brief discussion on the essence of the Middle Way, including many good explanations, some penetrating affirmations and refutations connected to the assertions of the great Tsongkapa, and an elucidation on the unsurpassable way of the definitive meaning. The infinite teachings about these topics have been passed down by the perfect Buddha and the glorious protector Nāgārjuna along with his heart disciples. The intention of these teachings has been integrated with heart experience by the masters of the glorious Takpo Kagyü. From among these masters, the peerless lord Mikyö Dorje is like the single eye of the Kagyü teachings. Since I have abbreviated and presented only a fraction of his words in the great *Ṭīkā,* the latter text should be consulted for a more extensive exegesis.

2.3. THE STATEMENT OF THE AUTHOR'S COLOPHON AND THE
TRANSLATOR'S COLOPHON TO THE TREATISE[630]

Thus concludes the *Entrance to the Middle Way*, which clarifies the ways of the profound and the vast. It has been composed by the master Chandrakīrti, whose mind is immersed
in the supreme vehicle, who possesses unassailable wisdom
and compassion, and who reversed clinging to true existence
by milking a painting of a cow.

In the center of the Kashmiri city of Anupatna, in the Ratnagupta Temple, during the reign of the Kashmiri king Shrī
Aryadeva, the Indian abbot Tīlaka and the Tibetan lotsāwa
Bandey Patsap Nyima Drak made this translation in accordance with the Kashmiri edition of the text. Later, at the
Ramoche Temple in Rasa, the Indian abbot Kanakavarma
and the same lotsāwa, through comparisons with the eastern
Aparanta edition of the text, made corrections to and finalized the translation.

Thus concludes the *Entrance to the Middle Way*, which clarifies the ways
of the profound and the vast. It was composed by Chandrakīrti, whose
mind is immersed in the supreme vehicle, who is endowed with unassailable wisdom and compassion, and who reversed clinging to true existence
by milking a painting of a cow.

Thus also concludes the *Feast for the Fortunate*, an explanation of the
Entrance to the Middle Way that abbreviates and easily pulls along the
Chariot of the Takpo Kagyü Siddhas and that preserves the meaning of the
latter commentary's words free from confusion.

In the center of the Kashmiri city of Anupatna, in the Ratnagupta
Temple, during the reign of the Kashmiri king Shrī Aryadeva, the Indian
abbot Tīlaka and the Tibetan lotsāwa Bandey Patsap Nyima Drak made
the translation of the root text [into Tibetan] in accordance with the
Kashmiri edition of the text. Later, at the Ramoche Temple in Rasa,[631]
the Indian abbot of grammar *(da tröpa/brda spros pa)* Kanakavarma and
the same lotsāwa ("lotsāwa" being derived from Sanskrit words that mean
"the one who brings the world together" or "the one who makes the world

aspire" or "the eyes of the world") compared the previous text with the
eastern Aparanta edition, made corrections to the translation's literary
structure, and correctly finalized its meaning.

It may be added:[632]

> Though all phenomena are unobservable from the beginning and
>   free from elaborations, in a single instant of your wisdom,
> Karmapa, you *know* all objects of *the three times*;[633] you are *self-*
>   *arisen*[634] wisdom's great *play*,[635] the *tathāgata*[636]
> *Meaningful to see*,[637] hear, and recall; you are the unconquerable
>   guru, the lake-born vajra, protector of all beings;
> I bow to you who benefit beings by the excellent feast of the
>   millions of dharma wheels of *Sarasvati's*[638] speech.

> All the hosts of old mother beings are to be placed, without bias, in
>   the cool shade of the parasol of your enlightened activity.
> Moved to action by unbearable compassion, we are to join them
>   with the states of stable benefit, joy, and peace.
> To that end, Mipham Chökyi Wangchuk, a bhikṣhu of the Shākya
>   clan, has drawn the elixir of definitive meaning
> From the fine vase of Nāgārjuna's mind and imparted it to those of
>   supreme fortune.

> This lapis lazuli of Nāgārjuna's good way, the treasury of jewels of
>   inconceivable freedom from extremes, has been cast away by
>   some scholars even though it was their very own.
> Swimming in a brew of the poisoned broth of logicians instead,
>   they bind themselves in wrong thinking.
> Since my love for them cannot allow me to let them languish,
>   I offer this jewel, the essence of the glorious Chandrakīrti's
>   thought.
> Though I have written in precise accordance with his textual
>   tradition, if there are mistakes, may they be forgiven by the wise.

> May the new moon of the virtue gathered here adorn the topknot
>   of liberation, the source of happiness,

In the glorious celestial city of the Takpo Kagyü.
By this, may the Karma Kagyü lineage, the essence of the victors'
teachings, be free from decline endlessly into the future.
With the ocean of scripture and realization's nectar ever rising, may
the teachings of the practice lineage eternally blaze.

May I as well please oceans of buddhas with excellent conduct for
the benefit of beings to the reaches of space.
May I ripen oceans of sentient beings into oceans of pure realms;
may I live long, be free of illness, and see the accomplishment of
my wishes.
Not dwelling here, in saṃsāra, or there, in peace, may my profound
methods and wisdom be supreme.
In this supreme support of a body and mind in the higher realms,
may I bring forth the special accomplishments of hearing,
contemplating, and meditating.
Through the excellent activities of explaining, debating,
composing, and so on, may the ocean of my aspirations be
perfectly accomplished.

This book is merely an entryway for beginners into texts such as the
great *Ṭīkā*. From beginning to end, it preserves the *Ṭīkā's* intended meaning while abbreviating its length. It has been composed by the one who
receives his two tutors' foot dust at the crown of his head, the one who
maintains the guise of a Shākya bhikṣhu, Mipham Chökyi Wangchuk.
Begun when I was twenty-three years old and completed when I was
twenty-five, it was written at the glorious Ogmin Tsurpu, the great seat at
which many scholars and meditators gather.

I dedicate all the merit of this effort: may it be a cause for the teachings
of the Buddha to remain for a long time; for all sentient beings to enjoy
the glory of benefit and happiness; and for the great feast of explanation,
debate, and composition to fill the entire world.

This *Feast for the Fortunate*, a commentary on the *Entrance to the Middle
Way* that easily pulls along the *Chariot of the Takpo Kagyü Siddhas*, is excellently accomplished. May virtue and excellence increase! May auspicious-
ness and glory blaze as ornaments to the flourishing of the teachings!

The[639] unequalled teacher is the lord of the Shākyas.
His heart intention is the excellent tradition free of extremes.
The ones who founded that tradition are Nāgārjuna and his son.[640]
They are the eyes of intelligence for all the world.

Their heart intention, intrinsic emptiness *(rangtong/rang stong)*,
Is wishfully taught "clearly" by many.
Yet we have the good fortune, rare as a daytime star,
Of receiving an unmistaken explanation from the Good Sarasvati.[641]

There are many who follow the explanations
Of this new Sarasvati with faith,
But since their view is covered by the clouds of logicians, they do
    not see the meaning.
I wrote this text to help them all.

Led by my supreme tutors,
Several individuals contributed to the editing and finalization:
Intelligent ones such as Choklang *(phyogs glang)* and Longyang
    (klong yangs)
And some other scholars of the hundreds of tripiḍaka texts.

The scribes were Kunga Gyalpo *(kun dga' rgyal po)*,
Karma Tsering *(karma tshe ring)*, and others.
The woodblocks were carved by ten people:
Gyamön Wangpo Tsöndrü[642] *(rgya mon dbang po brtson 'grus)*,
    Tsegyal *(tshe rgyal)*, and so on.

The benefactor who provided all favorable conditions,
Nangso Gopa *(nang so sgo pa)*, along with his retinue,
Is wealthy in both the temporal and the spiritual.
He supported this effort out of a motivation of great faith.

All sentient beings who make a connection with this teaching
In body, speech, or mind; by writing,
Explaining, reading, or listening to it—

May they perfect the realization of the profound freedom from
extremes.

In particular, may they, in one life and one body,
Achieve the supreme state of Karmapa.
Through their ability to host a great feast of explanation, debate,
and composition,
May they become great lords of the teachings.
SHUBHAṂ

Under the direction of The Dzogchen Ponlop Rinpoche, in reliance on the explanations of Acharya Lama Tenpa Gyaltsen and Acharya Tashi Wang-chuk, and by the invaluable assistance of many translators, scholars, and teachers, this translation of the Ninth Karmapa, Wangchuk Dorje's *Feast for the Fortunate* was made under the auspices of Nitartha Institute by Tyler Dewar of the Nitartha Translation Network. May it be virtuous!

⦂ Appendix I

EXCERPT FROM *LUCID WORDS*

The section of Chandrakīrti's *Lucid Words* referred to in the Karma-pa's analysis of the Consequentialist-Autonomist distinction in *Feast for the Fortunate*[643]

Translator's note: This section of Chandrakīrti's Prasannapadā, or Lucid Words (ACIP TD3860, 05B-11B), is part of Chandrakīrti's commentary to Nāgārjuna's Fundamental Wisdom, verse 1.1, which says, "Not from them-selves and not from others, / Not from both nor causelessly— / In things, of whatever type they may be, / Arising never exists." This entire section relates to the meaning of "not from themselves." The commentary examines the issue of how to appropriately refute the Enumerators, a non-Buddhist Indian phil-osophical school that asserts that 1) phenomena arise from themselves, i.e., from their own essential nature, and that 2) that essential nature is pres-ent in an unclear or unmanifest way at the time of phenomena's causes. In particular, Chandrakīrti compares the approaches of Buddhapālita and of Bhāvaviveka regarding how the Enumerators are to be refuted by Followers of the Middle Way. He defends Buddhapālita's approach of highlighting the absurd consequences of the Enumerators' position and refutes Bhāvaviveka's approach of using structured logic statements to affirmatively prove the non-existence of arising from self. Roman numeral section headings have been inserted by the translator and are accompanied by footnotes indicating the section of Feast for the Fortunate to which they correspond. This is challeng-ing material. Readers may wish to read this appendix three times if they do not understand some sections on the first read. Material in square brackets, which appear much more frequently than in the body of Feast for the Fortu-nate due to Chandrakīrti often not explicitly stating the subjects of sentences and his using the passive voice, has been inserted by the translator.

I[644]

The master Buddhapālita said, "Things do not arise from themselves, because their arising would be pointless and because their arising would be endless.[645] Things that already exist by way of their own identity do not need to arise again. If they arose even though they [already] existed, there would never be a time at which they were not arising."

II[646]

Some, [namely Bhāvaviveka], criticized that [statement of consequences] by saying, "That [refutation] is not logical, because it does not employ arguments or examples and because it does not dispel the countercriticisms of others. Since [Buddhapālita's] words are consequential, the opposite meanings of his probandum and of his reason are clearly implied. Thus [Buddhapālita unwittingly] implies that things arise from others, that arising has meaning, and that arising has an end. In this way he contradicts the tenets [of his own position]."

III[647]

However, we see that such criticisms are themselves illogical. Firstly, the claim that [Buddhapālita is at fault] when he "does not employ arguments or examples" is incorrect. [Buddhapālita] is probing his counterpart [in a debate], [in this case] someone who asserts that [things] arise from themselves, by saying, "When you say 'things arise from themselves,' you are saying that an existent, the cause, gives rise to precisely itself. However, one cannot see any need for an existent to arise again. One can, [however], see that [such a process] would be endless. You do not accept that something that has already arisen arises again, nor do you accept that arising is endless. Therefore, your logic is untenable and contradicts your own assertions."

[Buddhapālita] debates in a way that has [the same desired] effect [of forcing the proponent of arising from self to acknowledge his or her own internal contradictions] as using arguments and examples would. [Moreover, his approach is free from the undesirable effect of having to hold to a position of his own in the process of doing so]. Why would [Buddhapālita's] counterparts, [the Enumerators], not accept [that their position is erroneous]?

If a debate method that revealed the internal contradictions of counterparts did not cause the counterparts to relinquish their previously held view, [we can only conclude that] they are shameless [and immune to logical discourse]. Arguments and examples will certainly do no more [to help them] relinquish [their wrong view]. We do not debate with the insane.

Therefore, when the master [Bhāvaviveka] inappropriately uses [autonomous] inferences, he is merely showing his own affection for inferences, nothing more.

IV[648]

It is unacceptable for a Follower of the Middle Way to use autonomous inferences, because [Followers of the Middle Way] do not accept any positions that are alternatives [to the counterparts' position]. As Āryadeva said:

> Against someone who does not hold any position
> Of existence, nonexistence, or both existence and nonexistence,
> One cannot [prevail] in argument,
> Even if [one tries] for a long time.

And, from Nāgārjuna's *Dispelling Objections*:

> If I had a thesis,
> I would have a fault.
> Since I have no thesis,
> I am strictly faultless.

> If direct perception or any other form of valid cognition
> Were to observe some [truly existent] objects,
> It would be possible to engage in affirmation and refutation [on the
>   basis of those].
> Since that is not the case, I cannot be criticized.

V[649]

Since Followers of the Middle Way do not state autonomous inferences, why would they use an autonomous thesis such as "Things do not arise from themselves"? To such a thesis the Enumerators would respond, "What is the meaning of your thesis, '. . . do not arise from themselves'?

Does 'from themselves' mean 'from their own essential nature that is their result,' or does it mean 'from their own essential nature that is their cause'? If it refers to their result, you simply affirm what is already established for us.⁶⁵⁰ If it refers to their cause, your meaning will [merely] contradict [our assertion without proving its illogicality]: for us, everything that arises exists in the essential nature of its cause, and it is [from this essential nature] that [results] arise."

Thus, such an autonomous reasoning would, when spoken to an Enumerator, either affirm [for the Enumerators] what is already established for them or contradict [the Enumerators without doing anything further to refute them]. Therefore, why would we employ an argument such as "because they exist [already]" that would subject us to the efforts of removing such faults? Since [Buddhapālita's consequences] do not entail the faults [described above] that would be adduced as countercriticisms by [the Enumerators], it is not necessary for the master Buddhapālita to respond to such countercriticisms.

VI⁶⁵¹

[After hearing the above defenses of Buddhapālita, Bhāvaviveka might respond by saying], "Suppose I grant that Followers of the Middle Way should refrain from stating autonomous inferences because no position, argument, or example is established for them. [And suppose I grant] that therefore [Followers of the Middle Way] do not prove any thesis that refutes arising from self nor do they dispel the thesis [of arising from self] held by others, [the Enumerators], using an inference that is established for both parties [in the debate].

"It would still be necessary to state the contradictions inherent in the others' thesis using inferences [that are established] for [the persons who hold the thesis] themselves. Therefore one must possess, from one's own perspective, a position, argument, and example that are free of the faults [that could be drawn by the Enumerators].⁶⁵² Since [Buddhapālita] did not state those, and since he did not clear away the countercriticisms [the Enumerators would voice when confronted with the thesis "Things do not arise from themselves,"] [Buddhapālita] is definitely at fault."

That is not the case. On the contrary, [after a Follower of the Middle Way sets forth absurd consequences of "arising from self,"] the onus is on the Enumerators to generate in their counterparts—[us, the Followers of the Middle Way]—a certainty in the [Enumerator] thesis that mirrors the certainty that they themselves have. Whatever methods they use to understand that their position is sensible, they must explain those methods to us. This is the custom in debate: [the Enumerators], as counterparts [to the Followers of the Middle Way, who have presented them with absurd consequences of their thesis], must justify the thesis they hold.

[Yet the Enumerators] do not *have* arguments [that prove their thesis]. Since they have no [valid] arguments or examples, the proofs that they employ to prove their thesis are nothing more than a repetition of the thesis itself. Since they hold to an untenable position, they are not fooling anyone but themselves [when they put forth reasons to prove their position]. [Their reasons] are incapable of generating certainty in others.

It is clear that this very incapacity of [the Enumerators'] affirmations to [prove] their thesis is [the best] means of undermining [the Enumerators' position in a debate]. What sense would there be in trying to do so through stating inferences in order to refute them?

[At this point, Bhāvaviveka might respond], "It is still necessary to state the contradictions [inherent in the Enumerators' system] using inferences [that are accepted by] the Enumerators themselves." [We would respond by saying that] the master Buddhapālita has [already] stated those very [inferences], [as will be explained below].

[Buddhapālita] said, "Things do not arise from themselves, because their arising would be pointless . . ." The term "their" [in his reason] bears [the meaning] "[things] that already exist by way of their own identity." That is so because "Things that already exist by way of their own identity do not need to arise again" is a commentary on the [previous] brief statement ["Things do not arise from themselves, because their arising would be pointless."] The [commentarial] statement also, [implicitly], bears a concordant example—[a clearly manifest vase]— that is accepted by [the Enumerators] and that has the properties of the probandum, [that things do not arise from themselves], and the means of affirmation, [existing by way of identity]. "Already existing by way of their own identity" is connected to the argument or reason. "Because their arising would be pointless" is connected to the meaning of the predicate to be proven.

Consider the following, well-known example of a five-part [probative argument]:

1) Sound is impermanent,

2) because that which is produced is impermanent.

3) That which is produced is seen as impermanent,

4) as in the case, for example, of a vase.

5) Therefore, since it is produced, [sound] is impermanent.

"Being produced" is the argument or reason employed in that example.

Here, too, [Buddhapālita implies a five-part logic statement]:

1) Things do not arise from themselves,

2) because it would be pointless for things that already existed by way of their own identity to arise again.

3) It is seen that that which [already] exists by way of its own identity, such as vases and so on that clearly appear in front of [someone], do not depend on [their own] rearising.

4) In the same way, if [you] think that vases and so on exist by way of their own identity [even] at the stage of [their production when they are] lumps of clay and so on, then,

5) [since they already] exist by way of their own identity even at times such as those, they are devoid of arising.[653]

In that [logic statement], "already existing by way of their own identity" is used as the argument [or reason] and [also] clarifies the application [of the reason]. It is unmistaken with respect to refuting the rearising [of things that already exist by way of their own identity]. It is an inference held by the Enumerators themselves[654] and is used [by Buddhapālita] to highlight contradictions in the Enumerators' own position.

Therefore, how can Bhāvaviveka say that [Buddhapālita's reasoning] "is not logical, because it does not employ arguments or examples"? Not only did [Buddhapālita] not fail to state reasons and examples, he also did not fail to counter the criticisms of others. For the Enumerators do not assert that a vase, clearly manifest before them, becomes clearly manifest again. Thus he correctly chooses [the vase] as his example.

Furthermore, [Buddhapālita] makes a clear distinction regarding what he is refuting with his reasoning: his probandum refutes the arising of things that have the potential to arise but have not yet clearly arisen. Therefore on what grounds does [Bhāvaviveka] accuse [Buddhapālita] of the faults of affirming what is already established [for the Enumerators] and of having a [merely] contradictory argument or reason?

In summary, when Buddhapālita uses the inferences of [the Enumerators] to highlight the contradictions of their system, [the Enumerators] would not respond with the criticisms that Bhāvaviveka says they would. Therefore it is not the case that Buddhapālita did not counter the criticisms of others. Bhāvaviveka's criticisms of Buddhapālita are unfounded.

The phrase "and so on" in the "vases and so on" [of the probative argument above] signifies all things that are asserted [by the Enumerators] to arise. Thus [the example] does not [have the fault of] being unascertainable in the sense of not including woolen cloths, etc.

There is another way to set forth a probative argument [by drawing on the implications of Buddhapālita's original consequence statement], "[Considering] referent objects with the exception of the person[655]—all objects that [you Enumerators] describe as arising from themselves: they do not arise from themselves, because they [already] exist by way of their own identity, just as in the example of the person."

[If the Enumerators respond], "Refuting 'arising' does nothing to invalidate our assertion of 'manifesting,'" they will also be undermined: "arising again" applies [directly] to manifesting, since [manifesting and rearising] are identical terms that refer to the lack of observation previously and the presence of observation subsequently. Thus arising expresses nothing other than manifesting, and the refutation of arising is also a refutation of manifesting.

One may think, "Since Buddhapālita did not state [the above probative arguments directly], how did you arrive at this analysis [and ascribe it to Buddhapālita]?" The words of [Buddhapālita] carry great meaning. In an abbreviated manner, they bear the meaning of all that has been stated above. Explaining [the original brief statements naturally] leads to all of the meanings [that I have explicitly described here]. There is nothing [in what I have said] that is not indicated [in Buddhapālita's original statements].

VII[656]

The reversed meaning of consequences is connected solely to our counterparts, not to us, because we do not have any thesis. Therefore, how would we contradict our own tenets? For it is only in accordance with our wishes when our counterparts' [assertions] are befallen by many [logical] flaws through the reversed meaning of the consequences we state. How could it be the case that the master Buddhapālita, a follower of the unerring way of Nāgārjuna, made statements that afforded opportunities for others [to refute him]?

When someone who speaks of the absence of an inherent nature sets forth [absurd] consequences to someone who speaks of the existence of an inherent nature, how would the reversed meaning of their consequences [fall back on themselves in an undesirable way]?

Words do not disarm their speakers as if they were [bandits] armed with sticks and nooses. Rather, the speaker makes the words—if the words have the potential to do so—follow after his or her intention.

The use of consequences yields no other result than refuting the thesis of the counterpart. The reversed meaning of the consequences does not follow.

VIII[657]

Further, the master Nāgārjuna said *(Fundamental Wisdom)*:

> Before the defining characteristics of space,
> Not even the slightest space existed.
> If [space] existed before its characteristics,
> It would absurdly follow that it had no characteristics. (5.1)

And, in the same vein *(Fundamental Wisdom)*:

> If form existed without its causes,
> It would absurdly follow that form was causeless.
> But no object [of perception] whatsoever
> Is causeless. (4.2)

Also *(Fundamental Wisdom)*:

> Nirvāṇa is not a thing.
> [If it were], it would absurdly follow that it bears the characteristics
>   of aging and death.
> There is no existent thing
> That does not have aging and death.

As indicated above and elsewhere, [the master Nāgārjuna] mostly used consequences as the means to dismantle the positions of others. So, why does [Bhāvaviveka] see the master [Nāgārjuna's] statements, [even though they are only consequences explicitly], as being the cause [for inferring] several probative arguments because of being "endowed with great meaning," while [at the same time] withholding that consideration regarding the [consequence] statements of the master Buddhapālita?

He might reply, "[The difference is that] the extensive statement of probative arguments [by extracting them from brief consequence statements] is the tradition [and responsibility] of the authors of commentaries [to root texts]," but that as well is not [correct]. For even the master Nāgārjuna himself, when authoring the commentary to *Dispelling Objections*, did not use probative arguments.

IX[658]

Furthermore, this logician, wishing merely to show that he is very learned in the treatises of logic, accepts the view of the Followers of the Middle Way, but at the same time states autonomous probative arguments. [His approach] can be seen as a wellspring of many serious faults. To [explain] why, I will first provide his own probative argument: "Ultimately, the inner sense sources can be ascertained to not arise from themselves, because they exist—just as in the case, for example, of an existent consciousness."

X[659]

Why did he apply the distinction "ultimately"? He may reply, "Because, on the worldly, relative level, the assertion of arising should not be refuted. Furthermore, even if one refuted arising [on the level of the relative], the refutation would be invalidated because of one's own acceptance [of relative arising]."

That is illogical. Arising from self is not to be accepted [in any context, including] the relative. The sūtras say:

When a sprout arises from its cause, a seed, it does not create itself; it is not created by others; it is not created by both; it is not created by Ishvara; it is not transformed by time; it does not originate from subtle particles; it does not originate from its "original nature"; it does not arise causelessly.

Similarly *(The Sūtra of Vast Play, Lalitavistarasūtra, Gyacher Rolpey Do/rgya cher rol pa'i mdo):*

If a seed exists, so it is for the sprout.
The sprout is not what the seed is.
It is not the same nor is it other.
Its true reality is beyond permanence and extinction.

And, from this very text *(Fundamental Wisdom)*:

When something arises in dependence upon something else,
The one is not the other,
Nor is it different from the other.
Thus permanence and extinction are transcended. (28.10)

He may claim, "I applied the distinction, ['ultimately'], in dependence upon the systems of others, [the Enumerators]," but that as well is wrong, because [we Followers of the Middle Way] do not accept [the Enumerators'] presentations, even in the relative. It should be seen as advantageous [rather than problematic] when the tīrthikas, who fall from a correct perception of [both of] the two truths, are refuted in regard to both truths. Thus it is unreasonable to apply this distinction in dependence upon the systems of others.

It would be effective [in some instances] to apply this distinction when [communicating with] worldly people, but worldly people do not conceive of arising from self, [which is what is being refuted here]. Worldly people, without analyzing anything such as [arising] "from self" or "from other," simply think, "Results arise from causes." The master [Nāgārjuna] also made his presentations in accordance with [the world]. So, in all respects, this distinction ["ultimately"] should be ascertained as meaningless.

If [Bhāvaviveka] applied this distinction wishing to refute arising on the relative level, he would incur the faults of having a subject that was not established for him and an argument that was not established for him, because he does not accept the eyes and so on, the inner sense sources, as [existing] on the ultimate level. He may reply, "Since the eyes and so on exist [on the relative level], there is no fault," but then what does "ultimately" qualify?

If he applied the distinction as a way to refute the ultimate arising of relative [phenomena] such as eyes, he should have said, "Relative phenomena, such as the eyes, do not ultimately arise . . .," but he did not say that. Even if he did, [his phrasing] would still be illogical, because his counterparts, [the Enumerators], assert [phenomena] such as the eyes to be substantial existents and deny that they are only imputed existents. He would incur the fault of having a subject that was not established for his counterpart.

Still he may retort, "In the case of 'sound is impermanent [because it is produced],'⁶⁶⁰ both the subject and the predicate are construed as generalities. [Their status in terms of relative or ultimate] is not specified, because if it was, there would be no [opportunity] to employ the conventions of inference and what is to be inferred. [For example], if you [specified the subject] by saying, 'sound arisen from the four major elements . . .,' that [subject] would not be established for the counterpart, [a Vaisheṣhika].⁶⁶¹ If you said, '[sound that is] the quality of space,' that would not be established for oneself, a Buddhist.

"Similarly, when the Vaisheṣhikas hold the thesis of sound being impermanent, if they stated [the subject to be] 'produced sound,' that [subject] would not be established for their counterparts, [the Jains].⁶⁶² If they used 'clearly manifest [sound],' [the subject] would not be established for themselves. Continuing in the same vein, if a Buddhist [employed a subject] whose disintegration involved causes [other than that subject's own arising], [the subject] would not be established for the Buddhist. If the subject's disintegration did not depend on any cause [other than that subject's own arising], the subject would not be established for other, [non-Buddhist] parties.

"For the same reasons that apply [to the examples above], in which the subject and predicate are set forth as mere generalities, we may employ the subject [in the probative argument directed at the Enumerators that refutes arising from self] free of specifications [such as relative or ultimate]."

That again is wrong. Here the predicate that [Bhāvaviveka] wishes to affirm is the refutation of arising. Yet [Bhāvaviveka] himself accepts that mere erroneous [consciousnesses] will fail to discover a subject that was a thing that [could serve as] the support for [such a predicate]. Mistakenness and nonmistakenness are different.⁶⁶³ It is just as in the case of a person with an eye disease seeing falling hairs: due to their mistaken [consciousness], they perceive something to exist, even though it does not. But how could even the slightest [truly] existent object be observed? When people whose eyes are healthy [perceive objects], they do not superimpose falsities such as falling hairs. In the same way, when nonmistaken [consciousnesses] do not superimpose falsities, how could they observe even the slightest of objects, [the phenomena of] the relative [truth], which do not exist? Echoing this [logic], the master [Nāgārjuna] himself said *(Dispelling Objections)*:

> If direct perception or any other form of valid cognition
> Were to observe some [truly existent] objects,
> It would be possible to engage in affirmation and refutation
>   [on the basis of those].
> Since that is not the case, I cannot be criticized.

Since mistakenness and nonmistakenness are different, what exists for a mistaken [consciousness] does not exist in the context of nonmistakenness. What need to even mention [Bhāvaviveka's] subject, the relative eyes? Because he fails to avoid the faults of having [both] a subject and a reason the bases of which are not established [for both parties], his response[664] falls short.

There is also no similarity between his example, [the probative argument of sound and impermanence, and your thesis]. In the example, the generality of sound and the generality of impermanence, without any specifications, exist for both parties [of the debate].[665] Here, the generality of the eyes [and so on, the inner sense sources], is not accepted [in the same way] even on the relative level by those who speak of emptiness and those who speak of nonemptiness. Since the same is true with respect to the ultimate [truth], his example is not relevant.

The fault of having a baseless position also applies to his reason ". . . because they exist." It also has a basis that is not established.

XI[666]

As to why this is the case, the logician [Bhāvaviveka] himself accepts [that his logic is erroneous]! This will be explained as follows.

[Consider Bhāvaviveka's treatment of this probative argument] set forth by others. [The hearers say], "The producers, or causes, of the inner sense sources exist, because the Tathāgata said so. Whatever is said to be so by the Tathāgata is just so, such as the statement, 'Nirvāṇa is peace.'"

To that reasoning of [the hearers], Bhāvaviveka responded [in his *Lamp of Knowledge*[667]] with the following:

What do you assert to be the meaning of your reason? Do you mean to say, "because he said so on the relative level," or do you mean, "because he said so on the ultimate level"? If you intended the relative, the reason would not be established for you.[668] If you intended the ultimate, it is as [Nāgārjuna] said *(Fundamental Wisdom)*:

No phenomenon is established as existing,
Not existing, or both existing and not existing. (1.7ab)

This [quotation] dispels [the notion] that conditions could produce any result that was either existent, nonexistent, or both. [Nāgārjuna continues *(Fundamental Wisdom)*]:

Thus how could a "producing cause" [exist]?
It would be illogical. (1.7cd)

The meaning of that [quotation] is that [the phenomena that produce the inner sense sources] are not [actual] producing causes. Therefore, since on the ultimate level that which is produced and the producer are not established, [your reasoning] is either not established [from the ultimate perspective] or contradictory [from the relative perspective].

The above criticisms are the words of [Bhāvaviveka] himself. Since he himself acknowledged that a reason is not established in just the way [he described to the hearers], whatever inferences he sets forth that involve arguments [referring to existent] things will not be established for himself in regard to the reason and so on. Therefore all of his means of affirmation will be lost. The [nonestablishment that Bhāvaviveka identifies for the hearers] applies to [his own refutations as well].

When he says, "Ultimately, the inner sense sources do not arise from conditions that are different from themselves, because they are different [from those conditions], just as in the case of a vase," or, when he says, "It can be ascertained that the producers of the inner sense sources, such as the eyes, which are asserted by others to be ultimate [phenomena], are not conditions, because they are different [from the inner sense sources], just as in the case of cotton and so on," the "difference" [that he speaks of] and the other [components of his reason] are not established for himself!

[Again, examine how he treats this reasoning of the hearers]: "The inner sense sources definitely arise because special conventional terms are used with respect to that which possesses [appearances of] their objects." To this, wishing to show the nonestablishment of the reason, [Bhāvaviveka] replies, "Well then, when a yogin rests in ultimate equipoise, if his or her eyes of supreme knowledge seeing the authentic suchness of things were to affirm the existence of arising, going, and so on, then [your reason would be established. But since the eyes of supreme knowledge of yogins resting in ultimate equipoise do not affirm the existence of arising and so on], your reason—'because special conventional terms are used with respect to that which possesses [appearances of] their objects'—is not established. [Furthermore], 'going' has [already] been refuted by the refutation of arising."⁶⁶⁹

The same faults can be ascribed to his own arguments, such as "Ultimately, there is no motion on the path not yet traversed, because [the latter] is a path, just as in the case of the path already traversed." The reason [in that probative argument] is not established for [Bhāvaviveka] himself. The meaning of this can be drawn from [Bhāvaviveka's own criticisms above]. It is the same with the following: "Ultimately, the eyes along with their supports do not view forms, because they constitute the eye faculty, just as in the case of [an inoperative eye faculty, such as the eye faculty during sleep]." [Bhāvaviveka] also said, "The eyes do not view forms, because they are derived from the elements, just as in the case of forms," and "Earth is not of a hard nature, because it is an element, just as in the case of wind." In the case of all these [probative arguments], the reason and so on are not established for [Bhāvaviveka], thus [Bhāvaviveka's own criticisms above of the hearers] apply [to himself as well].

[Furthermore], [Bhāvaviveka's] counterparts, [the Enumerators], upon hearing his reason, ". . . because they exist," might wonder, "Is it the case that the inner sense sources do *not* arise from themselves, due to the reason of existing, in the same manner as the existence of consciousness?⁶⁷⁰ Or do they *arise* from themselves in the same manner as vases and so forth?" In this way, [his reason] is unascertainable [for them]. He may object, "I affirmed vases and so on [as not arising from themselves] in an equal manner," but [actually] he did not, because he never mentioned vases and so on.

XII[671]

To all of these criticisms, one may reply, "The faults that you ascribe to the inferences of others will equally apply to your own inferences. Do you not also incur the faults of subjects and reasons that are not established? You should not criticize the faulty components of only [Bhāvaviveka's] approach if they equally apply to yours. All of your criticisms [of Bhāvaviveka] are therefore unfounded."

[Not so]. Those who state autonomous inferences will incur the faults [described above], but we do not use autonomous inferences. The inferences [that we use] merely refute the theses of others. Thus when others, [the hearers], think [such thoughts as], "The eyes see [things]," they assert the eye to be a phenomenon that does not view itself. They also accept that [the eyes] do not arise unless there is a phenomenon viewing other [phenomena].

[The hearers can be refuted in the following way]: "Whatever does not observe itself also does not observe others, just as in the example of a vase. Therefore the eyes, existing as something that does not observe itself, also do not observe other [phenomena]. In contradiction with [your claim that eyes] do not observe themselves, they do observe [other objects] such as blue. This contradicts an inference that you yourselves accept." In this way, [the hearers' misconceptions] are cleared away using inferences that are established for them.

Since we state inferences in just this way, in what way could our position incur the same faults that we ascribe to [Bhāvaviveka]?

You may inquire, "Is it [actually] possible to use an inference that is established for [only] one [party in the debate] to invalidate [their position]?" Yes, it is. [In fact, the dispelling of misconceptions] can only take place through [the counterpart's accepting] a reason that is established for him or herself. [They cannot be persuaded] by [arguments that are] accepted only by someone else.

This is, indeed, the way things proceed in the world. In the world, sometimes victory or defeat is determined by the pronouncement of a witness who both parties—[for example], the challenger and the defender—hold in authority. At other times, [defeat is admitted] by one's own words alone. Defeat and victory are, however, never decided merely by the proclamations of someone else. As it is in the world, so it should be in logic, for only the conventions of the world can apply in the treatises of logic.

Some say that inferences accepted by others cannot invalidate the others' positions, because what is desired [in logical debate] is the refutation of precisely what is accepted by others. Still others say that affirmations and refutations can only be accomplished by that which can be stated definitively by both [parties in a debate], and that no [affirmation or refutation] is possible [in situations where the argument] is established for only one [party] or when there is doubt [about the argument in the mind of either party]. But those [people] need to understand the description given here of how inferences must be set forth in dependence upon the presentation of conventions in the world.

In terms [of the possibilities of] refutation via scripture, a refutation does not necessarily depend on a scripture established for both parties. It may also take place by using a scripture that is accepted only by [the person being refuted]. In all instances of inferences for oneself, what is established for oneself is [of course] most conclusive, and never is establishment by two parties [required]. Therefore, [in order to clear away misconceptions of others], it is senseless to state the definitions [relied on by] logicians. The buddhas help ignorant beings to be tamed simply by using whatever makes sense to those beings. Enough of this extensive elaboration!

⋮ Appendix II
ATISHA'S *KEY INSTRUCTIONS OF THE MIDDLE WAY*

In the language of India: *Madhyama-upadesha-nāma*
In the language of Tibet: *Umey Men-ngak Shejawa/dbu ma'i man ngag zhes bya ba*
In the English language: *Key Instructions of the Middle Way*

Homage to the Lord of the World

> The light of your speech
> Opens the lotus in the heart
> Of myself and others, all deluded beings.
> Supreme, genuine being, I bow to you.

These are the key instructions of the Mahāyāna's Middle Way. From the perspective of those who see only the near side,[672] all causes and results and so on are real in just the way they appear, and are presented as such. On the ultimate, or genuine, level, however, when the appearances of relative phenomena themselves have been investigated and disproved by the great reasonings,[673] there is not even one hundredth of a hair's breadth of anything to hold on to. One must comprehend this with certainty.

On a comfortable seat, sit with your legs crossed. There are two types of phenomena to contemplate: physical phenomena and nonphysical phenomena. Physical phenomena are assemblages of subtle particles. When one analyzes these particles by splitting them into their own sections, not even the smallest part is left [that cannot be dismantled]. Not even the tiniest appearance [of a real entity] remains.

The nonphysical refers to mind. The mind of the past has ceased and dissolved. The mind of the future has not arisen or come into being. The mind of the present is extremely difficult to identify: it has no color or shape; it is like space. Therefore it is not established [as a thing]. Furthermore, it is beyond being one or many things, it has never arisen, and it is luminous by nature. We use these and other forms of the sword of reasoning to investigate and analyze phenomena. Through this, we realize that they do not inherently exist.

Since both physical and nonphysical phenomena are not established as any entity and do not exist, the prajñā of discriminating investigation also does not exist. For example, when one rubs two pieces of wood together to create fire, both pieces of wood are burned. In the end, the fire that has done the burning also dissipates on its own. In the same way, once all specifically and generally characterized phenomena have been established as nonexistent, the prajñā [that discovered this reality] no longer appears; it is luminous, not existing in any manner whatsoever.

Therefore, dispel all faults [of meditation] such as dullness and torpor. In the gap [of the experience of the insight described above], do not allow the mind to conceive of or cling to anything. Abandon all recollection and mental engagement. For as long as the enemies, thieves, or bandits of thoughts and attributes do not arise, let your mind rest.

When you wish to rise, slowly release the cross-legged posture. With an outlook of illusion, perform as much virtue as you can in body, speech, and mind. Fortunate ones who practice in this way with dedication and consistency for a long time will see happiness in this very lifetime. Like the center of the sky, they will be free from effort and strain in naturally and spontaneously actualizing all positive qualities.

The postmeditation practice is to understand that all phenomena are like illusions and so on. However, from the time one attains the vajralike samadhi onward, one does not experience post-meditation. For if one did, what difference would there be between buddhas and bodhisattvas? There are further scriptural quotations and reasonings [to prove the difference between buddhas and bodhisattvas regarding equipoise and postmeditation], but I will not state them here.

[When buddhahood is attained], the benefit of others happens in precise accordance with the wishes of the beings to be tamed by oneself, due to one's own aspirations [of the past]. There are a great number of further scriptural quotations and reasonings [that could be explained], but these will not be elaborated on here.

The *Key Instructions of the Middle Way*, composed by the paṇḍita Dip-aṃkara, is now complete.

The translator, bhikṣhu Tsültrim Gyalwa,[674] *translated, edited, and finalized this edition in the Trülnang Temple of Lhasa.*

> *In the great temple of Trulnang in Rasa,*
> *I, a Tibetan monk, Lekpey Sherab,*[675]
> *Supplicated the wise one, Dipaṃkara,*
> *And then translated this text.*

> *The elder Dipaṃkara*
> *Holds the textual tradition of the three types of person.*
> *"Do not wander down mistaken paths!"—*
> *This is what I, Naktso Tsültrim Gyalwa, declare.*

⋮ Appendix III

THE FIVE GREAT REASONINGS OF THE
MIDDLE WAY

1. **The Vajra Slivers** *(dorje zekma/rdo rje gzegs ma)*
The vajra slivers reasoning analyzes causes. It is synonymous with the "refutation of arising from the four extremes" that is the main reasoning used by Chandrakīrti to refute the self of phenomena. When one analyzes to find whether things arise from themselves, from others, from both self and other, or causelessly, one finds no arising whatsoever, and determines that, because they do not arise, phenomena lack an inherent nature.

2. **The Refutation of the Result's Presence and Absence**
(yö me kye gok/yod med skye 'gog)
The refutation of presence and absence analyzes results. Focusing on a given result, such as a sprout "arisen" from a seed, one investigates whether the result was present at the time of its cause, or whether it was absent, both present and absent, or neither present nor absent. When one finds no permutation from among these four in which arising is observable, one concludes that the result does not truly arise from the cause, for true arising would necessarily involve one of these four.

3. **The Refutation of the Four Permutations**
(mu shi kye gok/mu bzhi skye 'gog)
The refutation of the four permutations analyzes both causes and results. If inherent production were to occur, it would necessarily involve at least one of the four following permutations: 1) one cause producing one result, 2) one cause producing many results, 3) many causes producing one result, and 4) many causes producing many results. When one finds no applica-

tion of any of these permutations when analyzing, one concludes that all causes and results lack an inherent nature.

4. Beyond One or Many *(chig du dral/gcig du bral)*

"Beyond one or many" analyzes the entities of phenomena themselves. One investigates to see whether any given phenomenon is one thing or many things. Multiplicity implies a collection of many single units. Therefore, when one searches any phenomenon and finds no single unit that cannot be mentally or physically dismantled into further constituent parts, one concludes that phenomena lack an inherent nature and do not truly exist.

5. Interdependence *(tendrel/rten 'brel)*

The reasoning of interdependence analyzes all phenomena and is known as "the king of reasonings," since, in contrast with the above four, which are capable of refuting only the extreme of clinging to existence, the reasoning of interdependence is capable of refuting both extremes of existence and nonexistence. When one investigates to see if there is any phenomenon that bears its own nature, identity, or character without relying on another phenomenon to arise or be designated, one finds no phenomena that are not dependently arisen or dependently designated. Since true existence implies independent existence, one concludes that no phenomena truly exist. Furthermore, to dispel clinging to nonexistence, one reflects on how the phenomena that are determined to lack an inherent nature are not utterly nonexistent, for they appear in the world and arise in dependence upon other phenomena in a way that is renowned in the world.

⫶ Appendix IV
HOW TO DO ANALYTICAL MEDITATION ON THE
ENTRANCE TO THE MIDDLE WAY: A BRIEF GUIDE

For[676] any formal session of hearing, contemplating, and meditating, one is encouraged to begin by taking refuge in the Buddha, dharma, and saṅgha and giving rise to the excellent motivation of bodhichitta.

The first step is assuming a comfortable posture. The recommended general posture for meditation has seven points:

1. The legs can be comfortably crossed. If you cannot sit cross-legged, sitting in a chair with both legs perpendicular to the ground is fine.

2. The hands can rest, palms down, on top of the knees or thighs. Alternatively, the hands can be placed in the "gesture of equipoise" by laying one hand on top of the other, with both palms facing up and the two thumbs touching each other, around the level of the navel.

3. The back is straight but relaxed enough not to require constant muscular effort. Taking a deep breath while stretching your spine in the beginning will help align the spine in a way that it naturally sits upright.

4. The shoulders are even and relaxed, yet slightly drawn backward to facilitate a straight spine.

5. The chin is slightly tucked in to press down gently on the Adam's apple.

6. The mouth is slightly open, with the tip of the tongue joined with the upper palate above the teeth.

7. The eyes gaze softly downward, naturally open yet with no specific visual focus, toward the space in front of the nose.

One begins in earnest by practicing shamatha, or "calm-abiding," meditation to settle the mind and to support the qualities of relaxation and focus that will be required for the analysis. There are many ways in which one can practice shamatha, but one straightforward method is to focus one's attention on the coming and going of the breath.

Breathing naturally, place your attention on the movement of the breath as it enters and leaves the nostrils. In particular, rest your mind on the out-breath, while allowing the mind to relax spaciously during the inbreath. Allow your mind to simply be with the process of focusing on the out-breath and relaxing with alertness during the inbreath. You do not need to generate any other thoughts, nor do you need to combat or suppress thoughts that arise. If you notice that a thought has distracted you, simply acknowledge that a thought has arisen and return to relating to the breath as just described. It does not matter how many times you return to the breath after becoming distracted, nor does it matter how many thoughts arise in your mind without necessarily distracting you in a coarse way from the breath. Repeating the practice again and again, and cultivating familiarity with resting the mind, with or without thoughts, is foremost.

Depending on how familiar you are with the practice, you may wish to practice shamatha for ten, fifteen, twenty, or thirty minutes, etc., prior to beginning your analysis. In any case, you should have a sense of being both relaxed and focused as a result of resting your mind before you start analyzing. Don't set the bar too high: whatever constitutes a relative state of being relaxed and focused for you will suffice.

To do an analytical meditation on a section of the *Entrance to the Middle Way*, it is best to have not only read the section you will be contemplating many times, but to have received teachings on it from a capable teacher in person, and to have had the opportunity to ask questions or discuss difficult points with fellow students. If this is not possible, simply read the section several times and contemplate its meaning *before* engaging in the formal session of analytical meditation. In this way, you will be practicing *analysis* as an essential prerequisite to *analytical meditation*.

For the main practice of analytical meditation, it is always good to have an authoritative scriptural reference to serve as a basis for the topic of analysis. Many practitioners find it helpful to recite a verse or prose quotation out loud three times as a way to tune their minds in to the topic of investigation. In the case of analytical meditation on the *Entrance* or on sections of *Feast for the Fortunate*, verses or prose quotations from the Buddha or from the authoritative Indian treatises are abundantly available in the main body of this book.

It is also good to have a "game plan" mapped out, on paper or mentally, with regard to the topics of contemplation you would like to cover during the session, along with the stages of analysis you would like to go through. It is advisable not to try to crowd the session with too many topics, but to start off sparsely and build up from there. For example, you might plan to yourself, "From the refutation of the self of persons, I would like to do an analytical meditation on the twenty reverse views of the transitory collection. From among these, I want to investigate how form is not the self." You might start off with just that one topic on your "list" for the session. Later, if you feel that including more topics will help your analysis, you could, for example, add the other three views that relate to the form aggregate. Alternatively, you could use the first view of the transitory collection and apply that to each of the five aggregates: forms are not the self, feelings are not the self, discriminations are not the self, formations are not the self, and consciousnesses are not the self.

After the initial period of shamatha, begin by mentally or verbally reciting the quotation to yourself, one, three, or however many times you feel inclined to recite. For a meditation on the twenty reverse views of the transitory collection, you could recite the root text from the *Entrance*:

> Form is not the self; the self does not possess form;
> The self does not exist in form; form does not exist in the self.
> These four statements should be understood to apply to all the
>   aggregates.
> The reversals of these statements represent the twenty views of
>   the self. (6.144)

Now, bring your planned topic of analysis clearly to mind. Analyze, using the questions and topics of investigation you had set up for yourself earlier. Working with the current example of "Form is not the self," you might begin by asking, "How do I conceive of my body as the self? What part of my body do I consider to be the self? Do I consider my whole body to be the self, or just certain parts of the body?" Shāntideva, in his *Bodhi-charyāvatāra*, outlines wonderful stages of examination of the body as the self in the ninth chapter, on wisdom. You may feel inspired to ask yourself some of the questions that Shāntideva provides at this stage.

When analyzing, permit yourself to make the analysis speak to your own experience. This is not just a theoretical examination of how a body cannot fulfill the characteristics of a self. Rather, the question is, how does *my* body appear as the self to *me*? In what ways do my thoughts take the body as the support for the thought of "I"? When I ask myself whether or not the body is the self, what thoughts does my mind offer in response? Engage in a dialogue in this way with yourself, allowing your map of the session and the words and concepts of the source text to keep you on track.

When you analyze in this way, at any stage of your analysis certainty may arise with regard to the main topic. For instance, you might be engaged in analysis of how you think your head is the self when you have a head-ache, yet when your back aches your thoughts of the self are centered on your back. A clear thought may arise, "The body is not 'me.' My mind simply has habits of identifying with the body in certain situations—other than that, there is no 'self' in the body at all." Alternatively, a mere *feeling* of certainty in selflessness may briefly arise in your experience. You might not have brought your analysis to its full conceptual conclusion, but your experience in the present moment feels markedly different, and this differ-ence is, without doubt, related to your contemplation.

The instruction at this stage is to drop the analysis and rest within this certainty. We do not need to set lofty goals as to what constitutes cer-tainty, thinking, "For as long as I have not directly realized emptiness, I will not rest my mind, but continue analyzing." If we push ourselves in that way, not only will we never receive an opportunity to rest, the qual-ity of our analysis will also probably not improve very much. Therefore, when a mere feeling of certainty arises, or when we have a clear concep-tual insight related to the topic of analysis, we rest within that feeling, that experience of unique certainty, for as long as it lasts. After a few moments, mundane discursive thoughts will start to arise again. When this happens, we resume our analysis and check in with our "game plan" to see what we will analyze next. We analyze once more, using our thoughts in a con-trolled way. When due to our analysis we experience certainty again, we rest again, as before.

This practice of alternating analysis and investigation with resting in

certainty is called *analytical meditation*. By analyzing and resting, analyzing and resting, we deepen our experience of the topic of contemplation.
Selflessness and emptiness shift in our experience from dry understandings to realities that move us in some way. By resting in this conceptually generated certainty again and again, our understanding of emptiness
becomes more and more refined, so that, at some point, we will be primed
to experience the nonconceptual reality of emptiness, without the intermediary of thought or analysis.

Another gauge by which we may choose to alternate analysis with
resting was taught by Jamgön Kongtrul Lodrö Thaye in his *Treasury of
Knowledge*:

> If, due to intense analysis, the ability to rest deteriorates,
> Do more resting meditation and replenish the stillness.
> If due to prolonged resting you no longer want to analyze,
> Do analytical meditation and strengthen the mind's clarity.

Thus, if we become distracted as a result of discursiveness generated by
analyzing, we should temporarily let go of the analysis and practice the
basic technique of shamatha to allow our mind to settle once more. Furthermore, if we find that our resting meditation has led to torpor, we clear
away the torpor by resuming our topic of analysis.

In any case, when we become accustomed to alternating the two activities of analyzing and resting with certainty, there may come a point at
which, in relation to certain topics, we do not need to rely on much analysis at all in order to give rise to certainty. Simply recalling the topic of
analytical meditation will cause us to recall the certainty that is a product of our previous analysis. By recalling the certainty in this way, resting
becomes the main activity of our meditation, and we no longer need to
rely on extensive analysis. For this reason, analytical meditation has been
summarized in three stages:

1. In the beginning, it is important to analyze.
2. In the middle, it is important to join analysis with meditation.
3. In the end, it is important to leap into the space of resting meditation, without relying on analysis.[677]

One can use these basic guidelines to do analytical meditation on any
topic in the *Entrance to the Middle Way* or *Feast for the Fortunate*. At the

end of the analytical meditation session, practice a brief period of shamatha once more to allow the certainty from the session to sink in further and to create a "speed bump," if necessary, between the postmeditation state and any excessive discursive momentum that might have resulted from analysis. Conclude by dedicating the merit of your efforts to the enlightenment of all beings, yourself included, and by making positive and compassionate aspirations that accord with the dharma.

⋮ Appendix V

THE ROOT TEXT OF THE *ENTRANCE TO THE MIDDLE WAY*

In the language of India, *Madhyamakāvatāra-kārikā-nāma*
In the language of Tibet, *Uma la Jukpe Tsikle-ur Jepa She Jawa/dbu ma la 'jug pa'i tshig le'ur byas pa zhes bya ba*
In the English language, the *"Entrance to the Middle Way,"* Set in Verse

Homage to the noble Mañjushrī, the youthful one.

Hearers and middling buddhas arise from the lords of sages,
Buddhas are born from bodhisattvas,
And compassionate mind, nondual intelligence,
And bodhichitta are the causes of the victors' heirs. (1.1)

Since it is asserted that love is the seed of the victorious ones'
    abundant harvest,
Is like the water that causes it to grow,
And is the ripening that allows it to be enjoyed for a long time,
I therefore praise compassion first. (1.2)

First, thinking "I," they cling to a self.
Then, thinking "This is mine," attachment to things develops.
Beings are powerless, like a rambling water mill.
I bow to compassion for these wanderers. (1.3)

Beings are like a moon on rippling water:
They move and are empty of inherent nature.

The victors' heirs see this and, so that these beings may be freed
    completely,
Their minds are overcome by compassion. (1.4)

Fully dedicating their virtue with the *Aspiration of
    Samantabhadra,*
They abide in supreme joy—this is called "the first."
From that time onward, the one who attains that state
Is called by the term "bodhisattva." (1.5)

They are born into the family of the tathāgatas
And relinquish the three entanglements.
These bodhisattvas possess extraordinary joy
And can cause a hundred worlds to quake. (1.6)

Advancing from ground to ground, they excellently move ever
    higher.
At that time, all paths to the lower realms are sealed off.
At that time, all grounds of ordinary beings are exhausted.
They are taught to be like the eighth of the noble ones. (1.7)

Even those who abide on the first level of the view of perfect
    bodhichitta
Surpass those born of the sages' speech and the solitary
    realizers
Through their merit, which continues to perfectly increase.
On the ground *Gone Far Beyond*, their knowledge also becomes
    superior. (1.8)

At that time, the first cause of perfect buddhahood,
Generosity, becomes preeminent.
They give even their flesh respectfully,
Which provides a cause for inferring the unseen. (1.9)

All beings strongly desire happiness,
Yet for humans, there is no happiness without material
    enjoyments.

Knowing that enjoyments, in turn, come about through
   generosity,
The Sage spoke of generosity first. (1.10)

Even for those who are wanting in compassion, ill-tempered,
And focused exclusively on their own concerns,
The enjoyments they desire,
Which thoroughly pacify their suffering, arise from
   generosity. (1.11)

Even they, through an occasion of giving,
Will one day come to meet a noble being.
Perfectly cutting through the continuum of existence,
They will attain the result and proceed to peace. (1.12)

Before long, those committed to benefiting beings
Will achieve joy through giving.
Since it is for both those who are loving and not-so-loving in
   character,
The teaching on generosity is foremost. (1.13)

If the joy the heirs of the victors feel
Upon hearing "Please give to me"
Cannot be matched by the joy of the sages entering peace,
What need to mention their joy of giving everything? (1.14)

The suffering they experience when cutting off and giving their
   flesh
Brings the sufferings of others in the hells and so forth
Directly to the bodhisattvas' minds.
They then swiftly apply themselves to ending that suffering. (1.15)

Generosity that is empty of gift, recipient, and giver
Is known as a transcendent perfection.
Generosity in which attachment to those three arises
Is taught to be a mundane perfection. (1.16)

In this way they excellently abide in the mind of the heirs of the
    victorious ones.
On the genuine support, they discover a beautiful light.
This joy is just like the water crystal jewel:
Completely dispelling the thick darkness, it is victorious. (1.17)

This completes the first bodhichitta generation from the *Entrance to the
Middle Way*.

Since they have the abundant qualities of discipline,
They refrain from faulty discipline even in their dreams.
Because the movements of their body, speech, and mind are pure,
They accumulate the actions of the genuine ones' tenfold path. (2.1)

This virtuous path in its tenfold aspect, though practiced before,
Here becomes supreme and extremely pure.
Like an autumn moon, they are always pure
And beautified by peaceful light. (2.2)

But if they viewed themselves as pure practitioners of discipline,
For that reason their discipline would not be pure at all.
Therefore, these bodhisattvas are always perfectly free
Of the movement of dualistic mind toward the three spheres. (2.3)

Having enjoyments, yet in the lower realms,
Comes about due to the degeneration of the legs of discipline.
When both capital and interest become exhausted,
One will not receive enjoyments again. (2.4)

At the time when one has freedom and favorable conditions,
If one does not protect oneself,
One will later fall into an abyss deprived of freedom.
Who will lift one up from that state then? (2.5)

Therefore, the Victorious One followed his teaching on generosity
With the teaching on discipline.
By growing the seeds of qualities on the field of discipline,
The enjoyment of their fruits will never cease. (2.6)

For ordinary beings, those born of the victors' speech,
Those set on solitary enlightenment,
And heirs of the victors, the cause of definite goodness
And the higher realms is none other than discipline. (2.7)

Just as an ocean and a corpse do not remain together,
And just as something auspicious and inauspicious cannot
    coexist,
The great being who masters discipline
Does not remain together with depraved ethics. (2.8)

If discipline involves observing the three spheres—
The relinquisher, the thing relinquished, and the being toward
    whom the relinquishing is performed—
That discipline is taught as a mundane perfection.
Discipline empty of attachment to those three is transcendent.
    (2.9)

These heirs of the Victor, born of the moon, are not of cyclic
    existence, yet they are the glory of cyclic existence.
They are immaculate; this stainless ground,
Like the light of an autumn moon,
Dispels agony from the minds of beings. (2.10)

This completes the second bodhichitta generation from the *Entrance to
the Middle Way.*

Since the light of the fire that burns
All the kindling of knowable objects arises
On this third ground, it is called *The Luminous.*
At that time, a brilliance like the sun or like copper dawns in the
    heirs of the sugatas. (3.1)

If someone, through unwarranted anger,
Cut the flesh and bones from the body of a bodhisattva
For a long time, ounce by ounce,
The bodhisattva would engender patience, especially for the one
    who is cutting. (3.2)

For bodhisattvas who see selflessness,
All phenomena—what is cut, the cutter, the time of the cutting,
    the method of cutting, and so on—
Are seen to be a like a reflection.
Therefore they have patience. (3.3)

If you get angry at someone who does you harm,
Does your anger reverse what has already been done?
Therefore, anger is definitely pointless in this life
And is contradictory to one's aims in future lives as well. (3.4)

Patience is the very thing that is asserted
To exhaust the results of previously committed nonvirtuous
    actions.
Since harming and being angry toward others causes them
    suffering,
Why lead yourself to the lower realms by planting such a seed? (3.5)

Anger toward heirs of the victorious ones
Destroys, in a single instant, the merit accumulated
Through generosity and discipline during a hundred eons.
Therefore, there is no greater misdeed than impatience. (3.6)

Impatience makes one unattractive and casts one in bad company.
It steals the intelligence that distinguishes between proper and
    improper discipline,
And quickly propels one to the lower realms.
Patience produces the opposite qualities to those just
    explained— (3.7)

Patience makes one beautiful, connects one with genuine beings,
And gives one skill in distinguishing between
What is proper and improper.
Later, one will take birth as a god or human and see the exhaustion
    of misdeeds. (3.8)

Ordinary beings and heirs of the victors,
Recognizing the faults of anger and the benefits of patience,

Should relinquish impatience and always quickly hold to
The patience praised by the noble ones. (3.9)

Even if one's patience is dedicated to the enlightenment of perfect
    buddhahood,
If it entails observation of the three spheres, it is a mundane
    perfection.
If it is free from such observation, the Buddha has taught
Such patience to be a transcendent perfection. (3.10)

On this ground, the bodhisattvas gain the concentrations and
    higher cognitions,
And completely exhaust attachment and aggression.
They also become capable of continually
Conquering worldly attachment toward desirables. (3.11)

The Sugata primarily taught
The three dharmas of generosity and so on to laypeople.
These three accomplish the accumulation of merit
And are the causes for the buddhas' form kāyas. (3.12)

Here the heirs of the victors who dwell in the sun of *The
    Luminous*
First perfectly dispel their own darkness
And then earnestly long to conquer the darkness of beings.
Though on this ground they are very sharp, they do not get
    angry. (3.13)

This completes the third bodhichitta generation from the *Entrance to the
Middle Way.*

All good qualities without exception follow after diligence,
The cause of the accumulations of both merit and knowledge.
The ground on which diligence blazes
Is the fourth, *The Radiant.* (4.1)

On this ground, for the children of the Sugata
There dawns a brilliance surpassing the glow of copper,

Born from especially cultivating the factors of perfect
   enlightenment.
Everything connected with the views of "me" and "mine" is
   completely exhausted. (4.2)

This completes the fourth bodhichitta generation from the *Entrance to the Middle Way*.

The great beings on the ground *Difficult to Overcome*
Cannot be defeated by any of the māras.
Their concentration becomes preeminent, and their excellent
   intelligence
Becomes very skilled at thoroughly examining the nature of the
   truths. (5.1)

This completes the fifth bodhichitta generation from the *Entrance to the Middle Way*.

On *The Approach*, their minds abide in equipoise
And they approach the qualities of perfect buddhahood.
They see the suchness of dependent arising's mere conditionality,
And, through abiding in supreme knowledge, will attain cessation.
   (6.1)

Just as someone with sight can easily lead
An entire group of blind people wherever they wish to go,
Knowledge takes the poor-sighted qualities
And leads them to the state of the victors. (6.2)

Since how bodhisattvas realize sublime, profound suchness
Is taught by scripture and reasoning,
I will explain in a way that precisely accords
With the textual tradition of the noble Nāgārjuna. (6.3)

Even when they are ordinary beings, when they hear about
   emptiness
They experience supreme joy again and again inside,

The tears from this supreme joy moisten their eyes,
And the hairs on their bodies stand on end. (6.4)

Ones like this have the seed of knowledge for perfect buddhahood.
They are a vessel for in-depth teachings on suchness.
They should be taught the ultimate truth.
They will gain the qualities that follow from that. (6.5)

They always take up and abide by perfect discipline,
They give generously and rely on compassion.
They cultivate patience and, so that beings may be freed,
Fully dedicate their virtue to enlightenment. (6.6)

They respect the bodhisattvas who strive for perfect enlightenment.
The one who is learned in the ways of the profound and vast
Will gradually attain the ground of *Supreme Joy*.
Therefore, those who strive to attain that ground should listen to
   teachings about this path. (6.7)

They do not arise from themselves; how could they arise from
   others?
They do not arise from both; how could they arise causelessly?
There is no purpose whatsoever to something arising from itself.
It is illogical for something that has arisen to arise again. (6.8)

If you think that something arisen arises again,
It would be impossible to observe the arising of sprouts,
And seeds would arise in infinitude until the end of existence.
Moreover, how would a sprout ever cause the disintegration of
   its seed? (6.9)

For you, the sprout could have no shape, color, taste, potential, and
   ripening
That were different from those of the seed, its enabling cause.
If a thing loses its earlier attributes and becomes a different entity,
How could the later one be of the same nature as the previous? (6.10)

If as you say seeds are not different from sprouts,
Either a sprout would be imperceptible at the very stage of the
    sprout, just like a seed is,
Or, since the two are the same, a seed would be observable at the
    time of the sprout.
Therefore, we do not accept that seeds and sprouts are the same.
    (6.11)

Since a result is seen only after the cessation of its cause,
Not even worldly people accept that the two are the same.
Therefore, this idea that things arise from themselves
Is illogical, both in suchness and in the world. (6.12)

For someone who asserts arising from self, that which is produced,
    the producer,
The action of producing, and the performer would all be the same.
Since they are not the same, arising from self is not to be accepted,
Because it entails the faulty consequences that have been
    extensively explained. (6.13)

If things arose in dependence upon other things,
Thick darkness would arise from a fire's flames
And everything would arise from everything,
Because all nonproducers would be equal to producers in being
    different. (6.14)

You say, "Since their causes have the distinct ability to produce
    them, results can be identified definitively.
Something that has the ability to produce, though different from
    its product, is still a cause.
Causes and results are in the same continuum, and results arise only
    from specific producers.
Therefore, the consequence that rice sprouts would arise from
    barley seeds and so on does not apply." (6.15)

You do not assert that barley, anthers, shellac, and so on
Are producers of rice sprouts, because they have no capacity to
    produce rice,

Because they are not part of the same continuum, and because they
   are not similar.   ·
In the same way, the rice seed as well is not the rice sprout's
   producer, because it is *different* from the rice sprout. (6.16)

A sprout does not exist simultaneously with its seed.
Since their otherness does not exist, how could a seed be different
   from a sprout?
Therefore, since a sprout cannot be established as arising from its
   seed,
Let go of this position of arising from other. (6.17)

You say, "Just as one arm of a balance moves up
At the same time that the other moves down,
So it is with the arising and ceasing of the produced and producer."
The arms of the balance are simultaneous, but causes and results
   are not; therefore your example does not fit. (6.18)

We assert that something in the process of arising does not yet
   exist;
Something that is in the process of ceasing has not yet ceased.
So how are causes and results congruent to the example of a scale?
This arising that you assert, devoid of a performer, is illogical.
   (6.19)

If the eye consciousness exists separately from its producers that are
   simultaneous with it—
The eye and so on and the discriminations that arise together with
   the eye consciousness—
What purpose is there in an existent arising again?
If you say the eye consciousness does not exist simultaneously
   with its producers, we have already explained the faults of that
   position. (6.20)

If a producer is a cause that gives rise to a different product,
The product must be either existent, nonexistent, both, or neither.
If it exists, what need for a producer? If it does not, what would a
   producer do?

THE KARMAPA'S MIDDLE WAY

And if it is both or neither, of what use would a producer
  be? (6.21)

"Abiding in their natural view, worldly people assert that what they
  see is valid cognition,
So what need is there to propound logic?
Worldly people know that results arise from causes that are
  different—
What need is there for logic to prove that arising from other
  exists?" (6.22)

Since all things can be seen genuinely or falsely,
Every thing bears two natures.
The Buddha taught that the object of genuine seeing is suchness
And that false seeing is the relative truth. (6.23)

False seeing is also said to have two aspects:
That with clear faculties and that with faulty faculties.
In dependence upon consciousnesses endowed with good faculties,
Consciousnesses endowed with faulty faculties are asserted to be
  wrong. (6.24)

What is apprehended by the undamaged six faculties
Is known by the world
And is true for the world.
Everything else is held by the world to be false. (6.25)

The essential nature that is conceived by tīrthikas,
Who are carried away by the sleep of ignorance,
And the conceptions of illusions, mirages, and so on
Do not exist even from the worldly perspective. (6.26)

Just as the perceptions of diseased vision
Do not invalidate the consciousnesses free from diseased vision,
So the mind devoid of stainless wisdom
Does not invalidate the stainless mind. (6.27)

It is called the "relative" because ignorance obscures the true nature.
It contrives things to seem real.
Contrivance was taught by the Sage to be relative truth.
All contrived things are relative. (6.28)

The mistaken entities that are conceived
As hairs and so forth due to diseased vision
Will be seen correctly by someone with clear vision.
It should be understood that the suchness of ultimate truth is the
    same. (6.29)

If worldly perceptions were valid cognition,
Worldly people would perceive suchness.
What need would there be for the other, noble beings, and what
    would the noble path accomplish?
The foolish are not suitable sources of valid cognition. (6.30)

Since in all cases the worldly perspective is not valid cognition,
The worldly perspective does not invalidate analyses of suchness.
If, in conversation with worldly people, a worldly object was denied
    by ultimate reasonings,
The ultimate reasonings would be invalidated by the worldly
    perspective, because the object refuted is renowned in the world.
    (6.31)

Because worldly people will merely plant a seed
And say, "I produced this boy"
Or think, "I planted this tree,"
Arising from other does not even exist for the world. (6.32)

Since sprouts are not different from seeds,
At the time of the sprout the seed does not disintegrate.
Since they are also not the same,
We do not say that the seed exists at the time of the sprout. (6.33)

If things inherently arose due to their own characteristics,
Realizing emptiness would deny and destroy them.

But since it is illogical for emptiness to cause things' destruction,
We conclude there are no truly existent things. (6.34)

When things are analyzed,
Apart from the suchness that is their true nature
No abiding thing can be found.
Therefore, the world's conventional truth should not be analyzed.
     (6.35)

Reasonings prove that arising from self and other
Are illogical in suchness.
Since they also prove that arising is illogical conventionally,
On what basis do you speak of "arising"? (6.36)

Empty things, such as reflections,
Depend on collections of causes and conditions and are accepted in
     the world.
For example, a consciousness can arise
From an empty reflection and bear that reflection's aspect. (6.37)

In the same way, though all things are empty,
They arise vividly from empty things.
Since things have no nature in either of the two truths,
They transcend both eternalism and nihilism. (6.38)

Actions do not inherently cease,
And, although there is no all-base, results have the ability to arise
     from them.
Therefore, even though a long time might transpire after the end of
     the action,
It should be understood that a result correctly arises. (6.39)

Due to seeing certain objects in a dream,
Lust will arise in fools, even after they wake up.
In the same way, results exist even though they arise
From actions that have ceased and have no inherent nature. (6.40)

Although false objects are equal in terms of not existing,
Someone with diseased vision will see images of hairs
But not the images of other false objects.
In the same way know that results, once they ripen, do not ripen
    again. (6.41)

Intelligent ones see that negative results ripen from negative actions
And that positive results ripen from positive actions;
Knowing that both positive and negative actions do not exist, they
    will become liberated.
The Buddha halted speculation about actions and their results.
    (6.42)

"The all-base exists," "The person exists,"
And "Only these aggregates exist"—
These statements were made to those
Who could not grasp the very profound meaning. (6.43)

Even though he was free of the view of the transitory collection,
The Buddha spoke of "I" and "mine."
In the same way, though things have no inherent nature,
The statement "They exist" is a provisional meaning. (6.44)

Without an apprehended object, the apprehender cannot be seen.
Excellently realizing the three realms to be merely consciousness,
The bodhisattvas who abide in supreme knowledge
Realize that suchness is mere consciousness. (6.45)

Just as when the wind blows on a great ocean
Waves arise, in the same way
From the "all-base," the seed of everything,
Mere consciousness originates through the all-base's own
    potential. (6.46)

Therefore the entity of the dependent nature
Is the cause for the imputed existence of things.

It originates without outer apprehended objects,
Exists, and has a nature that is not an object of elaborations. (6.47)

What is your example of a mind without an outer object?
If you say, "It is like a dream," this must be investigated.
For when I am dreaming, my mind does not exist.
Thus your example does not apply. (6.48)

If the recollection of the dream while awake
Establishes the existence of mind, outer objects in dreams would be
    established in the same way.
Just as you recall, "I saw something,"
So the outer objects would exist. (6.49)

You say, "It is impossible for there to be an eye consciousness during
    sleep.
It does not exist; there is only mental consciousness.
Its images are clung to as external objects,
And the waking state is just like this dream example." (6.50)

In the same way you hold that outer objects
Are unarisen in dreams, so the mind of dreams is also unarisen.
The eye, the object of the eye, and the mind generated by those:
All three of these are false. (6.51)

The triad of the ear and the other sensory triads are also unarisen.
Just as they are in dreams, so here in the waking state,
Things are false, and mind does not exist.
There are no objects of experience and also no faculties. (6.52)

Just as the triad of perceptions exists while awake,
So the triad exists in dreams for as long as one is still dreaming.
Just as upon awakening from dreams the dream triad does not exist,
It is the same when waking from the sleep of ignorance. (6.53)

The eye consciousness arisen from a diseased eye faculty
And the hairs seen due to the disease itself

Are both real from the perspective of that consciousness,
But from the perspective of a person that clearly perceives objects,
  both are false. (6.54)

If mind existed without a knowable object,
Someone who looked at the same object as someone with diseased
  vision
Would cognize hairs—even if they had no diseased vision.
Since that is not the case, your position is inadmissible. (6.55)

You say, "If a mind perceiving a given appearance does not arise,
It is because that mind's *potential* to perceive it has not ripened,
Not because there are no objects."
Since such potential does not exist, your rebuttal is not established.
  (6.56)

It is impossible for potential to exist in what has arisen.
The unarisen is also devoid of potential.
A featureless "basis of features" does not exist.
If it did, it would follow that the childless woman's son would
  have potential. (6.57)

You assert potential because consciousnesses will arise in the future.
Yet there is no potential, and there is no consciousness that will
  arise from it.
"Objects that are established through dependence on each other
Are not established at all"—thus teach the genuine ones. (6.58)

If consciousness arose from the ripening of habitual tendencies
  planted by the ceased consciousness of the past,
It would follow that consciousnesses arise from the potential of
  other consciousnesses.
The moments of their continua would be different from each
  other,
And it would follow that anything could arise from anything.
  (6.59)

If you say, "members of a continuum are different,
But they are not of different continua.
Therefore there is no fault," that is beyond your ability to prove.
It is illogical for instances of a continuum not to be different. (6.60)

Phenomena that depend on each other, such as Maitreya and
    Upagupta,
Are not part of the same continuum, precisely because they are
    different from each other.
Phenomena that are separate by virtue of their own characteristics
Cannot be parts of the same continuum. (6.61)

"An eye consciousness perfectly arises
Immediately upon the ripening of its own potential.
The potential that is the support for a given consciousness
Is known in the world as a 'physical eye faculty.'" (6.62)

"Consciousnesses that arise from sense faculties
Depend on their own potential, not on outer apprehended
    objects.
They are themselves the appearances of blue and so on.
Not realizing this, worldly beings think of and accept them as
    outer apprehended objects." (6.63)

"In dreams, mind with the aspect of form arises
From the ripening of its own potential, not from any form as an
    outer object.
It is the same in the waking state:
Mind exists without outer objects," so you say. (6.64)

If in dreams a mental consciousness, without an eye faculty,
Arises as blue appearances and so on,
Why would an eye consciousness not arise in a blind person,
Who does not have an eye faculty, due to the ripening of that
    consciousness' seed? (6.65)

According to you, the sixth consciousness' potential
Ripens in dreams but not in the waking state.

Yet if such potential does not ripen in the waking state,
Why would it not be illogical to say it does not exist in
    dreams? (6.66)

The absence of an eye faculty is not a cause for a blind person to
    perceive visual objects.
Similarly, sleep is not a cause for the ripening of potential during
    dreams.
Therefore you should accept that, even in dreams,
The eye is the false perceiving subject that causes cognition. (6.67)

All the answers they give
Are just repetitions of their thesis.
Seeing that, we close this debate—
Nowhere did the buddhas teach that "things exist." (6.68)

Through meditating on their masters' key instructions,
Yogins may see the entire earth to be filled with skeletons.
But the three components of this perception also do not arise—
This perception was taught to be an incorrect mental engagement.
    (6.69)

If, as you say, the mental objects of repulsiveness meditation
Were the same as the objects of sense consciousnesses,
Everyone who directed their minds to the same place the yogins
    were looking
Would perceive skeletons, and the samādhi would not be false. (6.70)

The perception of a water-river as a pus-river by hungry ghosts
Is equivalent to the perception of a faculty with diseased vision.
In sum, understand the following point:
Just as there is no knowable object, there is also no mind. (6.71)

If there existed an actual dependent consciousness
That were empty of both apprehender and apprehended,
How would you cognize its existence?
If you say, "It exists without being apprehended," that is
    unacceptable. (6.72)

The dependent consciousness does not experience itself.
You may say that memory, arising in subsequent moments, is what
   proves self-awareness.
But memory is nonexistent, and relying on it to prove another
   nonexistent
Does not prove anything. (6.73)

Even if self-awareness did exist,
It is illogical to say it is recalled by memory,
Because it is different from memory, just like the self-awareness
   of someone else.
The same reason will also defeat any further rebuttals. (6.74)

A memory that is different
From a consciousness experiencing an object does not exist
   for us.
There is simply the memory, "I saw it."
This is just how conventions work in the world. (6.75)

Therefore, since self-awareness does not exist,
What consciousness will perceive your dependent nature?
Since agents, actions, and objects are not the same thing,
For a consciousness to apprehend itself is unreasonable. (6.76)

If the dependent nature, whose essential nature
Is unarisen and unknowable, exists as a thing,
Why would the childless woman's son not reasonably exist?
What harm has he caused you? (6.77)

If the dependent nature does not even slightly exist,
What type of dependent nature could be the cause of the relative?
Attachment to the idea of substantial existence
Destroys even the presentations of what is renowned in the world.
   (6.78)

Those who dwell outside the path of the master Nāgārjuna
Have no method for accomplishing peace.

They lapse from the two truths, the relative and suchness,
And, by so lapsing, do not achieve liberation. (6.79)

The conventional truth is the method;
The ultimate truth is what arises from the method.
Those who do not know the distinctions between these two
Will, due to wrong thinking, follow inferior paths. (6.80)

I do not accept relative truth
In the way you assert the dependent nature to be a thing.
For the sake of the result I say, "Things exist," even though they
    do not.
Thus I speak from the perspective of the world. (6.81)

For an arhat who has abandoned the aggregates and entered
    peace,
The relative does not exist.
In the same way, if something does not exist in the world,
I do not say that it exists in the world. (6.82)

If the worldly perspective poses no threat to your views,
Then go ahead—refute it!
Debate with the worldly people about what relative truth is,
And I will side with whoever comes out the strongest. (6.83)

When it is said that the bodhisattvas on the approach of *The
    Manifest*
Realize the three existences to be only consciousness,
The meaning is that their realization refutes a permanent creator
    such as the self.
They realize that the creator is only mind. (6.84)

Therefore, to increase the intelligence of the wise bodhisattvas,
The All-Knowing One, in the *Descent into Laṅka Sūtra*,
Conquered the mountain peaks of tīrthika views with the vajra of
    his speech
In order to clarify his intention. (6.85)

In their own treatises, the tīrthikas
Spoke of the person and so on as creators.
Not seeing them as creators,
The Victorious One taught the creator of the world to be mind
only. (6.86)

"Expansion (gye) into suchness" indicates "buddhahood" (sangye).
In the same way, when the Buddha taught worldly beings about
"mind only" in the sūtras,
The meaning is that mind is foremost.
Negating form is not the intended meaning of those sūtras. (6.87)

If the Buddha knew that the three realms are mind only
And refuted form in the sūtra,
Why would that great being, in the same sūtra,
Say that mind arises from ignorance and karmic actions? (6.88)

Mind itself sets up varieties of sentient beings, worlds,
And worldly environments.
All beings are taught to arise from actions,
And when mind is relinquished there is no karma. (6.89)

Form does indeed exist conventionally,
But it is not a creator like mind is.
Therefore creators other than mind
Are refuted, but form itself is not. (6.90)

For someone abiding in a worldly outlook,
The five aggregates, which are accepted in the world, exist.
For someone in whom the wisdom realizing suchness has
dawned,
For that yogin, the five will not originate. (6.91)

When form is found not to exist, do not cling to the existence
of mind!
When mind is cognized as existent, do not cling to the
nonexistence of form!

In the sūtras on the way of supreme knowledge, the Buddha
   relinquished them equally.
In the abhidharma, he described them equally as existent. (6.92)

Holding your position will destroy the presentation of the two
   truths.
And, since we have refuted it, your "substance" will not be
   established.
Through these stages of explanation, know that all things
   primordially
Do not arise in suchness yet arise for the world. (6.93)

The sūtras that teach that outer appearances do not exist
But that mind appears as all varieties
Were taught for those who are extremely attached to form.
They refuted form only for that purpose, and are provisional
   meaning. (6.94)

This was taught by the Teacher as none other than provisional
   meaning,
And it is also logical that it is provisional meaning.
Scriptures clarify that other similar sūtras
Are provisional meaning. (6.95)

"If there are no knowable objects, consciousness is also refuted—
This is easy to understand," so teach the buddhas.
Since the nonexistence of knowable objects also refutes the
   existence of consciousness,
The Buddha refuted knowable objects first. (6.96)

In this way, know the background of any given scripture.
Understand that sūtras that teach about something other than
   suchness
Are provisional meaning; quote them for appropriate
   students.
Understand that sūtras that teach emptiness are definitive
   meaning. (6.97)

It is also illogical for phenomena to arise from both themselves and
    others,
Because all the faults explained before would apply to that
    assertion.
We do not make this assertion in the world, nor do we make it
    regarding suchness.
Why? Because arising from either of them individually is not
    established. (6.98)

If things arose without any causes at all,
Everything would always arise from everything.
Worldly people would not have to go through hundreds of
    hardships to engage causes,
Such as planting seeds, to make results arise. (6.99)

If beings were empty of causes, then, just like the scent and color
Of utpala flowers in the sky, they would be imperceptible.
Yet the world, in all its intense brilliance, is perceptible.
Therefore, just like your own mind, understand that the world
    arises due to causes. (6.100)

The elements do not have the essential nature
That you think they possess.
Since you are so deeply ignorant of this world,
How could you correctly realize anything about the world
    beyond? (6.101)

When you refute a world beyond,
You should understand that you are incorrectly viewing the nature
    of knowable objects,
Because your view is based on the body.
It is the same when you assert the true existence of the elements'
    essential nature. (6.102)

The nonexistence of the elements has already been explained
In a general way during the sections that refuted
Arising from self, other, both, and no causes.

Although they are not refuted extensively here, the elements do not
exist. (6.103)

Since there is no phenomenon that arises from self, other, both,
Or that does not depend on causes, all things are devoid of inherent
nature.
Worldly people are covered by the thick darkness of ignorance,
like the sky covered by clouds.
For them, things exist; therefore objects appear in an incorrect way.
(6.104)

Due to diseased vision, some people will incorrectly perceive
strands of hair, double moons,
Eyes on peacocks' feathers, and bees.
In the same way, due to the problem of ignorance, the unwise
Perceive the variety of conditioned phenomena by conceptualizing
them. (6.105)

"Actions arise due to bewilderment; without bewilderment,
Actions would not arise—" this is definitely something to be
realized only by the unwise.
The wise ones whose sun of excellent intelligence clears away the
thick darkness of ignorance
Will comprehend emptiness and gain liberation. (6.106)

"If things do not exist in suchness,
They cannot exist conventionally either, like the childless woman's
son.
Yet since phenomena do exist conventionally,
They therefore exist inherently." (6.107)

The objects, such as strands of hair,
Perceived by people with diseased vision are unarisen.
Therefore debate first with people with diseased vision;
Then take the same approach with beings who have the diseased
vision of ignorance. (6.108)

You can perceive what is unarisen, such as dreams, cities of
     gandharvas,
Mirage water, hallucinations, and reflections.
Since these are equal to the childless woman's son in not existing,
Why do you not see the childless woman's son? Your view is
     illogical. (6.109)

In suchness things do not arise.
Yet, unlike the childless woman's son,
They can be perceived by the world.
Therefore your position has no definitiveness. (6.110)

The childless woman's son does not arise by way of its essential
     nature
In suchness, nor does it exist in the world.
In the same way, all things are devoid of arising by way of their
     essence
In the world and in suchness. (6.111)

Therefore the Teacher said that all phenomena
Are primordially peace, free of arising,
And perfect nirvāṇa by nature.
Therefore never is there any arising. (6.112)

Vases and so on do not exist in suchness,
But they exist in terms of what is thoroughly renowned in the
     world.
All other things are the same way,
So the consequence that they are like the childless woman's son
     does not apply. (6.113)

Since things do not arise causelessly,
Nor through the causes of Īshvara and so on,
Nor from self, other, or both,
Therefore they excellently arise *in dependence*. (6.114)

Since all things perfectly arise dependently,
All wrong conceptions are rendered powerless.
Therefore this reasoning of dependent arising
Cuts through the net of all bad views. (6.115)

Conceptions will occur if things are held to exist,
But how things do not exist has been thoroughly analyzed.
When things are seen not to exist, conceptions about their
    existence will not arise,
Just as fire will not burn without fuel. (6.116)

Ordinary beings are bound by conception,
And yogins, free from conception, are liberated.
The wise ones teach that the reversal of conception
Is the result of analysis. (6.117)

Nāgārjuna did not present analysis in his treatise because he was
    fond of debate.
Rather, he taught about suchness so that beings could attain
    liberation.
But if when suchness is explained
The texts of others fall apart, there is no fault in that. (6.118)

Attachment to one's own view and
Aversion to the views of others are nothing more than conception.
Therefore, if you first overcome attachment and aggression
And *then* analyze, you will be liberated. (6.119)

Seeing with their intelligence that all mental afflictions and
    problems
Arise from the view of the transitory collection,
And realizing that the self is the object of that view,
Yogis and yoginīs refute the self. (6.120)

The tīrthikas assert that the self is an enjoyer, is a permanent thing,
Is not a creator, has no qualities, and is inactive.

Based on subtle differences regarding those assertions,
Different tīrthika systems arose. (6.121)

Since, like the childless woman's son, it does not arise,
Such a self does not exist.
It is not the support for the conception of "I,"
And we do not assert its existence even relatively. (6.122)

All of the self's features that were taught
By the tīrthikas in their various treatises
Are invalidated by the reason of nonarising, which the tīrthikas
     themselves accept.
Therefore none of those features exist. (6.123)

Therefore there is no self that is different from the aggregates,
Because, apart from the aggregates, there is no way the self could be
     apprehended.
Nor do we assert such a self to be the support for the worldly
     conception of "I."
For even those who do not perceive it have a view of self. (6.124)

Moreover, those who have spent many eons as animals
Have never seen this unarisen, permanent self,
Yet they are still seen to engage in the conception of "I."
Therefore a self that is different from the aggregates does not exist
     at all. (6.125)

"Because the self is not established as different from the aggregates,
The focal object for the view of the self is strictly the aggregates."
Some say that all five aggregates are the support
Of the view of the self; others assert that such a support is only
     mind. (6.126)

If the aggregates were the self,
There would be several selves, because there are several aggregates.
The self would be substantial, and viewing it would constitute
     engaging in a substance.
The view of a self would therefore not be erroneous. (6.127)

At the time of attaining nirvāṇa, the self would be severed.
In the moments before nirvāṇa, the self would arise and
  disintegrate.
Since there would be no agent, there would be no karmic results,
And one would experience the results of actions accumulated by
  others. (6.128)

If the continuum existed in suchness, such faults would not apply.
But the faults of the continuum have already been explained in
  earlier analyses.
Therefore the aggregates and the mind are untenable as the self,
Since the end of the world and so on do not exist. (6.129)

According to you, when a yogin sees selflessness
Things would definitely become nonexistent.
If you assert that the idea of a permanent self is what is
  relinquished,
Your aggregates or mind could not be the self. (6.130)

When your yogins cognized selflessness,
They would not see the true nature of form and other phenomena.
Attachment and other afflictions would arise in them when they
  engaged forms,
Because they would not have realized the essence of the aggregates.
  (6.131)

You say, "The Teacher said that the aggregates are the self;
Therefore we assert the same."
That statement was made to refute a self that is different from the
  aggregates.
It was taught in other sūtras how form and so on are not the self.
  (6.132)

It was taught in other sūtras that forms and feelings are not the self,
That discriminations are not the self, that formations are not the self,
And that consciousnesses are not the self.
Therefore, the teaching of the above-mentioned sūtra did not assert
  that the aggregates are the self. (6.133)

When you say that the aggregates are the self,
You are referring to the collection of the aggregates, not to the
    entities of the aggregates.
The collection of the aggregates is not a protector, nor is it a tamer
    or witness.
Since the collection does not exist, it cannot be the self. (6.134)

At that time, the parts of a chariot that form a collection
Would become the chariot, and the chariot and the self are
    equivalent.
The sūtras taught that the self is an imputation made on the basis
    of the aggregates.
Therefore the mere assembly of the aggregates is not the self.
    (6.135)

If you say that shape is the self, shape is physical.
For you, physical phenomena could be the self,
But the collection of consciousness and so on could not be
    the self,
Because those aggregates do not have any shape. (6.136)

It is illogical for the appropriator to be the same thing as the
    appropriated.
If they were the same, objects of action would be the same thing as
    their performers.
If you think there are objects of action devoid of performers,
That is not the case, because without performers there are no
    objects of action. (6.137)

The Sage taught the self to be imputed in dependence
Upon the six elements—earth, water, fire, wind, consciousness, and
    space—
And upon the six supports for contact,
The eye and so on. (6.138)

He also definitively taught that the self is imputed
Through apprehending primary minds and mental events.

Therefore the self is not those phenomena, nor is it their mere
collection.
Those phenomena cannot logically be the objects of the conception
of "I." (6.139)

You say that when yogins realize selflessness they relinquish the
view of a permanent self,
But you do not even assert such a self as the support for the
conception of "I."
Your description of how the cognition of selflessness
Uproots the view of a self is marvelous indeed! (6.140)

While looking at a snake's nest in the hole of your house's wall,
To dispel anxiety you say, "There is no elephant there."
This is how you try to pacify the fear of snakes.
Oh dear, how others will laugh! (6.141)

The self does not exist in the aggregates
And the aggregates do not exist in the self.
You may think of them as different,
But they are not different, so any relationship between them of
support and supported is merely a conceptual imputation.
(6.142)

We do not assert that the self possesses form—since the self
does not exist,
No meaning of "possession" is applicable.
Extrinsic possession is as in "Devadatta has a cow"; intrinsic
possession is as in "Devadatta has a body,"
But the self is not the same as or different from form. (6.143)

Form is not the self; the self does not possess form;
The self does not exist in form; form does not exist in the self.
These four statements should be understood to apply to all the
aggregates.
The reversals of these statements represent the twenty views of
the self. (6.144)

When the vajra that is the realization of selflessness
Conquers the mountain of views of the transitory collection,
The twenty high peaks on that massive mountain
Disintegrate, together with the self. (6.145)

Some assert the person as a substantial existent
That cannot be expressed in terms of being the same as or
    different from the aggregates or in terms of being permanent or
    impermanent, and so on.
They assert it to be an object of knowledge of the six
    consciousnesses
And the basis for the conception of "I." (6.146)

Just as mind is not seen as inexpressible in relation to form,
No existent thing is cognized as inexpressible.
If the self is an established thing,
Then, like mind, it could not be inexpressible. (6.147)

According to you, a vase is not established as a thing
And its entity is inexpressible in relation to its form and so on.
Just so, since the self is inexpressible in relations to the aggregates,
It is impossible to cognize its own existence as being established.
    (6.148)

You do not assert that consciousness is different from its own
    entity.
You do assert it as a thing that is different from form and so on.
Things, therefore, must be seen to have those two qualities.
The self does not exist, because it is devoid of these qualities of a
    thing. (6.149)

Therefore the support for the conception of "I" is not a thing,
Is not different from the aggregates, is not the entity of the
    aggregates,
Is not the support of the aggregates, and does not possess the
    aggregates.
It is established merely in dependence upon the aggregates. (6.150)

A chariot is not asserted to be different from its parts.
It is not the same as its parts, nor does it possess them.
It does not depend on its parts, nor do its parts depend on it.
It is not its parts' mere assembly, nor is it their shape. (6.151)

If the mere collection of parts were the chariot,
A chariot would exist in every single one of its parts.
Since there are no parts without something to possess them,
Mere shape as well cannot be the chariot. (6.152)

If for you the shapes of the parts when they form the chariot
Are exactly the same as the shapes before the chariot's assembly,
Then just as there was no chariot in the discrete parts before,
There is also no chariot now. (6.153)

Now, when the chariot has been formed,
If the wheels and so on had shapes that are different from the earlier
    shapes,
The new shapes would be perceptible—but they are not.
Therefore the chariot is not merely shape. (6.154)

Since your "collection" does not even slightly exist,
There can be no shape of a collection of parts.
How could you give the label of "shape"
To nothing at all? (6.155)

It is just how you assert it to be:
If the aspect of a result arises in dependence upon an unreal cause,
That result is also not real.
Know that this is so regarding all things. (6.156)

The chariot example shows that it is illogical for a mental state
    apprehending a vase
To arise in dependence upon particles of form and other such
    phenomena.
Since they are free of arising, form and so on do not exist either.
Therefore they too are untenable as shape. (6.157)

The sevenfold reasoning shows that the chariot
Is not established in suchness or in the world.
Yet, without analysis, here in the world
The chariot is imputed in dependence upon its parts. (6.158)

It is common for beings to refer to a chariot as something that has
  parts and sections,
And to say that it is a performer.
The chariot is also established for people as an appropriator.
Do not destroy the relative that is renowned in the world. (6.159)

"How can the chariot exist, since when it is analyzed in these seven
  ways it is seen not to exist at all?"
Thus the yogis and yoginīs do not find the existence of the chariot.
Through this they also easily engage in suchness,
But, in the relative, the existence of the chariot should be accepted
  in accordance with the world. (6.160)

When the chariot does not exist,
Both the part-possessor and its parts are nonexistent.
Just as in the example of both the chariot and its parts getting
  burnt,
When the fire of intelligence burns the part-possessor, the parts
  are burned as well. (6.161)

Similarly, worldly consensus asserts
That the self is an appropriator in dependence
Upon the aggregates, the six constituents, and the six sources;
That the appropriated are the objects of action; and that the self is
  their performer. (6.162)

Since it is not a thing, the self is not stable or unstable;
It does not arise or disintegrate;
It is not permanent, impermanent, both, or neither,
And is not the same as or different from the aggregates. (6.163)

The conception of "I" is always present in beings.
It arises in connection with
The supports for the imputation of the self.
The self that is its object exists only in the ignorant, nonanalytical
perspective of the world. (6.164)

There are no objects of action without performers.
Therefore there are no entities connected to the self without a self.
Viewing self and entities connected to the self as empty,
Yogis and yoginīs gain complete liberation. (6.165)

Vases, sweaters, canvases, armies, forests, rosaries, trees,
Houses, chariots, hotels, and so on—
All these things should be accepted in the way they are labeled by
beings,
Because the Lord of Sages did not dispute with the world. (6.166)

Parts, qualities, desire, characteristics, firewood, and so on
And part-possessors, quality-possessors, desirous ones, bases of
characteristics, fire, and so on,
If analyzed in seven ways as in the case of the chariot, do not exist.
Apart from that, they exist by way of what is renowned in the
world. (6.167)

Something is a cause only if it produces a result,
And if it does not, there is no reason for it to be called a cause.
Results, as well, arise only if they have causes.
Therefore, state which would arise from which, and which would
be the prior support for which! (6.168)

If, for you, causes produced results by contacting them,
Since the two would have the same potential, there would be
no difference between the producer and its result.
If causes did not contact results, they would be undifferentiable
from noncauses.
There is no third concept that could apply to the relationship. (6.169)

If your causes do not produce results, there is nothing to call a
   "result."
Therefore there is no cause devoid of a result.
Since both causes and results are like illusions,
These faults do not apply to us, and, for the worldly perspective,
   things exist. (6.170)

"Does your refutation refute its intended target through contacting
   it, or does your refutation involve no contact?
The faults you ascribe to us equally apply to your own logic."
"When arguing in that way, you defeat only your own position.
You are incapable of refuting your desired object of refutation."
   (6.171)

"Your words, which contain consequences that equally apply to
   you, express frivolous arguments.
With them, you illogically denigrate all things.
Therefore, noble beings will not accept you,
Because you are just quibblers with no position of your own."
   (6.172)

When you ask, "When your refutation refutes its intended object,
   does it contact it or not,"
The fault that you ascribe to us
Will only apply to those who hold a definite position;
Since we do not hold such a position, it is impossible for this
   consequence to apply to us. (6.173)

When the sun is reflected in a pool of water, its attributes,
Such as eclipses, are clearly seen in the reflection.
Although it is illogical for the sun and its reflection to have contact
   or no contact,
The mere convention of "the reflection" arises in a dependent way.
   (6.174)

Even though it is not real, a reflection can help beautify one's face.
In the same way, in order to clean the face of supreme knowledge,

Arguments are used whose ability to refute or affirm can be
  witnessed.
Although they lack ultimate tenability, understand that these
  arguments can help us realize an object of affirmation. (6.175)

If the arguments that produce the understanding of our objects
  of affirmation were established as things,
And if the objects of affirmation actually existed as something to
  be understood,
The reasonings of contact and so on would be applicable to us.
But since they do not exist, your complaints bring about only your
  own dejection. (6.176)

Our examples are able to easily bring about the realization
That all things are nothings.
Yet you have no method by which you can conveniently cause
  others to understand that things possess an inherent nature.
Why entrust worldly people to the web of your bad logic? (6.177)

Having understood the rest of the refutations taught above,
Employ them in response to the positions of contact and so on.
How it is that we who are not quibblers
Should be understood from our position as it was just explained.
  (6.178)

So that beings may be liberated, the Buddha taught two types of
  selflessness:
The selflessness of phenomena and the selflessness of persons.
The Teacher again taught these two types of selflessness
To students by dividing them into many different types. (6.179)

In elaborate fashion, the Buddha explained the sixteen
  emptinesses.
Abbreviating that explanation,
He again taught four.
These are asserted to belong to the Mahāyāna . (6.180)

Since its nature is emptiness,
The eye is empty of the eye.
In the same way, the ear, nose, tongue,
Body, and mind are explained to be emptiness. (6.181)

They do not stay together
And do not disintegrate.
Therefore, the eyes and the rest of the six faculties
Lack an inherent nature—this lack of inherent nature
Is asserted to be the *emptiness of the inner*. (6.182)

Because its nature is emptiness,
Form is empty of form.
Sound, smell, taste, tangible objects,
And mental objects are the same way. (6.183)

The lack of inherent nature of form and so on
Is asserted to be the *emptiness of the outer*.
The lack of inherent nature of both outer and inner
Is the *emptiness of the outer and inner*. (6.184)

The wise explain the lack of phenomena's inherent existence
To be "emptiness."
This emptiness is also asserted to be empty
Of the entity of emptiness. (6.185)

The emptiness of what is called "emptiness"
Is asserted to be the *emptiness of emptiness*.
It was taught in order to reverse the fixation
Of those who think of emptiness as a thing. (6.186)

Since they pervade without exception
The worlds of sentient beings' environments,
And since the example of the limitless ones shows their
    infinitude,
The directions are "great." (6.187)

The ten directions'
Emptiness of themselves
Is the *emptiness of the great.*
It was taught in order to reverse fixation on greatness. (6.188)

Since it is the supreme objective,
Nirvāṇa is the ultimate.
Its emptiness of itself
Is the *emptiness of the ultimate.* (6.189)

In order to reverse the fixation
Of those who think nirvāṇa is a thing,
The Knower of the Ultimate
Taught the emptiness of the ultimate. (6.190)

Because they arise from conditions, the three realms
Are definitively described as being conditioned.
The three realms' emptiness of themselves
Is taught to be the *emptiness of the conditioned.* (6.191)

Phenomena free from
Arising, abiding, and impermanence are unconditioned.
Their emptiness of their own entity
Is the *emptiness of the unconditioned.* (6.192)

That which does not have an extreme
Is called "beyond the extremes."
Its emptiness of precisely itself
Is explained as the *emptiness of what is beyond extremes.* (6.193)

Since it is free
From a beginning at the start and an end at the finish,
Saṃsāra is described as being beginningless and endless.
Since it is free from coming and going, (6.194)

Cyclic existence, like an illusion, is devoid of its own entity.
This is the *emptiness*

Of the beginningless and endless.
It was definitively explained in the treatises. (6.195)

"To discard" is definitively explained
As "to cast away" or "to abandon."
What should not be discarded
Is that of which one should never let go. (6.196)

What is not to be discarded
Is empty precisely of itself.
Therefore, this emptiness is called
The *emptiness of what is not to be discarded.* (6.197)

The essence of conditioned phenomena and so on
Is not created by the students—the solitary realizers
And bodhisattvas—or by the Buddha himself.
Therefore the essence, emptiness, of conditioned phenomena
　　(6.198)

And so on
Is explained to be their nature.
Its emptiness of itself
Is the *emptiness of nature.* (6.199)

"All phenomena" refers to the eighteen constituents, the six types of
　　contact,
The six feelings that arise from contact,
Physical phenomena, nonphysical phenomena,
And conditioned and unconditioned phenomena. (6.200)

All of these phenomena are void of their own entity.
This emptiness is the *emptiness of all phenomena.*
"Suitable as form" and so on are not things.
This is the *emptiness of defining characteristics.* (6.201)

Form bears the defining characteristic of "suitable as form."
Feeling is of the character of "experience."

Discrimination apprehends characteristics;
Formation refers to "forming." (6.202)

Individually cognizing objects
Is the defining characteristic of consciousness.
The aggregates' defining characteristic is suffering.
The character of the constituents is that of a poisonous snake.
 (6.203)

The Buddha taught that the sources
Are the doors for the arising of suffering.
The defining characteristics of dependent arising
Are assembly and contact. (6.204)

The perfection of generosity is giving;
Discipline is to be without torment;
Patience is to be free from anger;
Exertion is to be without nonvirtue. (6.205)

Concentration is to draw together;
Supreme knowledge is to be free from attachment—
These are held to be the defining characteristics
Of the six perfections. (6.206)

The Perfect Knower taught
That the concentrations,
The limitless ones, and the formless states
Bear the definition "free of disturbance." (6.207)

The thirty-seven factors of enlightenment
Bear the defining characteristic of "that which brings
 deliverance."
The defining characteristic of emptiness is voidness,
Since in emptiness there is no observation of things. (6.208)

The absence of characteristics is peace,
And the definition of the third gate

Is to be free from suffering and ignorance; the eight forms
   of liberation
Bear the defining characteristic of causing liberation. (6.209)

The powers were taught to be of the nature
Of decisive resolution.
The fearlessnesses of the Protector
Are of the essence of utter stability. (6.210)

The correct and discerning awarenesses, confidence and so on,
Bear the defining characteristic of being unceasing.
To thoroughly accomplish the benefit of beings
Is called "great loving-kindness." (6.211)

To fully protect those who are suffering
Is great compassion; joy
Is defined by utter joy, and impartiality
Bears the defining characteristic of being unadulterated. (6.212)

The unshared qualities of the Buddha
Are asserted to number eighteen.
Since the Teacher cannot be deprived of them,
Their defining characteristic is undeprivability. (6.213)

The wisdom of the knowledge of all aspects
Is asserted to have a defining characteristic of directness.
Others, which are only partial knowledges,
Are not asserted to be direct. (6.214)

The defining characteristics of conditioned phenomena
And the defining characteristics of unconditioned phenomena
Are empty precisely of themselves.
This is the *emptiness of defining characteristics*. (6.215)

The present does not abide;
The past and future do not exist.
The state in which these are unobservable
Is called "nonobservation." (6.216)

Nonobservation is void
Of its own entity.
Since it is unchanging and does not cease,
It is the *emptiness of nonobservation*. (6.217)

Since they arise from conditions,
An entity of their assembly does not exist.
The emptiness of that nonexistence
Is the *emptiness of the nonexistence of things*. (6.218)

The term "thing" refers, in brief
To the five aggregates.
The emptiness of those five aggregates of themselves
Is explained to be the *emptiness of things*. (6.219)

In brief, "nonthing"
Refers to unconditioned phenomena.
Nonthings' being empty of themselves
Is the *emptiness of nonthings*. (6.220)

The absence of an essential nature
Is the *emptiness of nature*.
Since it was not created by anyone,
It is called "nature." (6.221)

Whether buddhas arise
Or not, in reality
The emptiness of all things remains.
Therefore it is excellently proclaimed to be an "other entity." (6.222)

This emptiness, which is also called the "perfect limit" and
"suchness,"
Is the *emptiness of other entities*.
These emptinesses were excellently proclaimed
In the teachings of the perfection of supreme knowledge. (6.223)

Thus the light rays of the bodhisattvas' intelligence bring forth the
brilliance of suchness.

Just like a myrobalan fruit in the palm of the hand,
The bodhisattvas realize that the three realms without exception
    have been unborn from the outset.
Through the power of conventional truth, they proceed to
    cessation. (6.224)

Though they always possess the aspects of mind that are
    commensurate with cessation,
They also generate compassion for beings without a protector.
On higher grounds, the bodhisattvas conquer with their
    intelligence
All of those born from the Sugata's speech and also the middling
    buddhas. (6.225)

Spreading the vast immaculate wings of the relative and suchness,
These sovereign swans fly ahead to lead the flock of beings.
Through the powerful winds of virtue,
They proceed to the other shore of the victorious ones' qualities.
    (6.226)

This completes the sixth bodhichitta generation from the *Entrance to the
Middle Way*.

Here on *Gone Far Beyond*, the bodhisattvas
Can enter into cessation in every moment.
They also attain the perfection of methods, which greatly blazes.
    (7.1)

This completes the seventh bodhichitta generation from the *Entrance to
the Middle Way*.

In order to repeatedly attain virtues greater than before,
On this ground the great beings become irreversible
And enter into *The Immovable*. (8.1)

Their aspirations become extremely pure,
And they are roused from cessation by the victorious
    ones. (8.2)

Since the mind that is free from attachment does not coexist with
faults,
On the eighth ground the impurities and their roots are thoroughly
pacified.
Though the mental afflictions are exhausted and they become
unsurpassable in the three realms,
They are not able to attain what buddhas possess in a limitless way,
similar to space. (8.3)

Even though saṃsāra has stopped for them, they attain the ten
masteries, and through these
They display their own essential nature in many different ways to
the beings of cyclic existence. (8.4)

This completes the eighth bodhichitta generation from the *Entrance to
the Middle Way.*

On the ninth, the bodhisattvas' powers, though needless to
mention, become completely pure.
They also attain the completely pure form of the correct and
discerning awarenesses, qualities that have been theirs all along.
(9.1)

This completes the ninth bodhichitta generation from the *Entrance to the
Middle Way.*

On the tenth ground, the bodhisattvas receive the most sublime
empowerments from the buddhas of all directions,
And their wisdom also becomes utterly supreme.
Just as water flows from rain clouds,
From these bodhisattvas a spontaneously present rain of dharma
falls down for the harvest of beings' virtue. (10.1)

This completes the tenth bodhichitta generation from the *Entrance to the
Middle Way.*

At the time of the first ground, the bodhisattvas see a hundred
   buddhas
And realize those buddhas' blessings.
They are able to remain for a hundred eons,
And correctly engage the beginnings and ends of those ages. (11.1)

These intelligent ones are able to enter into and let go of one
   hundred samādhis;
They can cause one hundred worlds to quake, and they can
   illuminate one hundred realms.
Through their miracles, they ripen one hundred sentient beings,
And, in keeping with the number one hundred, can go to that
   many buddha realms. (11.2)

These children of the Lord of Sages open one hundred gates of
   dharma;
They can display one hundred bodhisattvas in their own body,
Each bodhisattva beautified by a retinue and enjoyments,
And each in turn being surrounded by one hundred bodhisattvas.
   (11.3)

By abiding on *Supreme Joy*, the intelligent bodhisattvas attain the
   qualities explained.
In the same manner, those who abide on *The Stainless*
Attain the thousandfold manifestation of those qualities.
On the next five grounds, the bodhisattvas attain those qualities
   (11.4)

In their hundred thousandfold, billionfold,
Ten billionfold, trillionfold,
And sexillionfold
Manifestations, respectively. (11.5)

The bodhisattvas who abide on *The Immovable* are free from
   thoughts.
They attain qualities that are equal in number
To the number of atoms that exist
In one hundred trillion worlds. (11.6)

The bodhisattvas abiding on the ground
Of *Excellent Intelligence* attain the qualities
That were explained before, in a number
That equals that of the atoms in one hundred vigintillion worlds.
(11.7)

Moreover, on the tenth ground, the bodhisattvas' qualities
Go far beyond what can be expressed verbally.
Nevertheless, to summarize them, their qualities become equal in
number
To however many atoms there are in the inexpressible number of
buddha realms. (11.8)

In each pore of their bodies, they can display,
In a single instant, bodhisattvas together with
Countless buddha forms.
They can also display gods, demigods, and humans. (11.9)

To be just like the full moon in a stainless sky, lighting the way for
all,
Once again you apply effort to achieve the ten powers within your
reach.
In Akaniṣṭha you attain that most exalted form of peace,
The unexcelled rank of buddhahood with the fullest extent of
qualities. (12.1)

Differences in containers do not produce differences in the space
they contain.
In the same way, no distinctions of things exist in suchness.
In your mind, you genuinely integrate the equal taste of all
phenomena.
Perfect knower, in an instant you comprehend all knowable objects.
(12.2)

"If the pacification of elaborations is the suchness of all
phenomena, it could not be engaged by mind.
It is definitely illogical for a perceiving subject to arise without
having engaged its knowable object.

How can something unknowable be known? That is a
contradiction.
Since there is no omniscient knower, how do you teach others, 'The
Buddha comprehends reality'?" (12.3)

In the context of nonarising being the suchness of all phenomena,
the mind that perceives that suchness is also free from arising.
In dependence upon the aspect of nonarising, the seeming
realization of suchness is posited.
Just as it is commonly described that a mind fully knows its object
when it takes on the object's aspect,
Here, in dependence upon conventions, wisdom is posited as
knowing the precise nature. (12.4)

By the blessings of the Buddha, the sambhogakāya resulting from
merit,
The nirmāṇakāya, and the sounds of space and other things
Can teach the suchness of phenomena.
Beings in the world can receive these teachings and realize
suchness. (12.5)

A strong craftsperson will first
Apply effort for a long time to get their wheel to spin.
Later, without any further effort needed,
The wheel spins on its own to make vases and so on. (12.6)

Just so, without any current effort to make it arise,
The activity of the buddhas, who engage the dharmakāya, extends
to the reaches of space.
It is a result of the virtue of beings and of aspirations.
The special causes and results of buddhahood are utterly
inconceivable. (12.7)

When the firewood of knowable objects is burned completely,
The peace that emerges is the dharmakāya of the victorious ones.
It has no arising and no ceasing.
When mind ceases, the buddhas make the kāya manifest. (12.8)

The peaceful sambhogakāya is brilliant like a wish-fulfilling tree;
It is free of thoughts like a wish-fulfilling jewel;
It remains permanently, until beings are liberated, so that they may
     attain the endowments of freedom and happiness;
It appears only to those who are free from elaborations. (12.9)

In a single form kāya that is the natural outflow of the other two
And in a single moment, the lords of sages
Can clearly and unerringly display the details of all their previous
     births,
Even though those lifetimes have already ceased. (12.10)

In a single kāya, buddhas can display without exception
The details about the buddha realms they lived in, the sages that
     inhabited them,
The types of powers, forms, and conduct those sages had,
The number of members of the saṅgha of hearers present and their
     qualities, (12.11)

The different forms the bodhisattvas had,
The types of dharma taught there and the types of births
     they took,
The types of trainings they engaged in after hearing the dharma,
And the types of generosity they offered. (12.12)

Similarly, in a complete way they can display in one kāya
The details of previous times when they were practicing
     discipline,
Patience, diligence, concentration, and supreme knowledge—
     all their forms of conduct
They can display clearly in a single pore of their body. (12.13)

A buddha can display the deeds of past and future buddhas
And also the deeds of the buddhas of the present,
Who dwell in the world to relieve beings to the limits of space
     oppressed by suffering
By teaching the dharma in high, melodic tones. (12.14)

From the time of the buddhas' first generating bodhichitta to their
   going to the essence of enlightenment,
A buddha can display all their deeds clearly,
In one moment, in a single pore of his or her body,
Knowing the nature of these deeds to be like a magical illusion.
   (12.15)

Similarly, in one moment they can display in a pore of their body
All of the deeds of the bodhisattvas,
The noble solitary realizers, and the hearers of the three times.
They can also display all deeds performed during the phase of being
   an ordinary being. (12.16)

These pure ones, by simply directing their intention,
Can display worlds to the reaches of space in the area of one atom,
And make an atom pervade the space of limitless worlds,
But without enlarging the atoms or shrinking the worlds. (12.17)

You, who are free from thoughts, can, in each instant
Until the end of existence, display various types of conduct
Whose number is not equaled
By all the atoms in Jambudvīpa. (12.18)

The powers of the knowledge of bases and nonbases;
The awareness of the ripening of actions;
The comprehension of various higher interests;
The knowledge of the various dhātus; (12.19)

The knowledge of supreme and nonsupreme faculties;
The knowledge of the paths and their respective destinations;
The awareness of the concentrations, liberations,
Samādhis, absorptions, and so on; (12.20)

The knowledge that recalls previous states;
The awareness of deaths and births;
And the knowledge of the exhaustion of contaminants—
These are the ten powers. (12.21)

Specific results arise with precision from specific causes.
The buddhas know and teach about the bases of all these arisings.
The absence of such precision is called a nonbasis.
The freedom from obstruction to the knowledge of these is
explained to be the first power. (12.22)

The buddhas' knowledge can individually engage without
impediment
The four types of actions—desirable, undesirable, mixed actions,
and exhausting actions—
Along with their ripening, in all their great variety.
This knowledge, which pervades all objects of the three times, is
asserted to be the second power. (12.23)

Due to desire and so on,
A great variety of wishes for the good arise in lesser, middling, and
superior forms.
These higher interests in turn may become covered by other factors.
The buddhas' knowledge of all of this, pervading all beings of the
three times, is the third power. (12.24)

The perfect buddhas, skilled in the dhātus' divisions,
Teach the nature of the eye and so on to be a dhātu.
Their limitless knowledge that, at all times,
Engages the distinct features of the dhātus is the fourth power. (12.25)

Regarding the faculties of conceptualization and so on, those that
are very sharp are asserted to be supreme,
And the middling and dull are taught to be nonsupreme.
The buddhas possess fully developed knowledge of the eye and so
on and of how the faculties assist each other in producing results.
This unimpeded knowledge is their fifth power. (12.26)

Some paths lead to buddhahood; some lead to the enlightenment
of solitary realizers;
Others lead to the enlightenment of hearers or to the hungry
ghost realm,

The animal realm, the realms of gods, humans, and hell beings, and
other destinations.
The limitless and unimpeded knowledge of these is the sixth power.
(12.27)

Yogis and yoginīs in the limitless worlds experience different
meditative states:
The concentrations, the eight liberations, the states of shamatha,
And the nine distinct absorptions.
The unobstructed knowledge of these is explained to be the seventh
power. (12.28)

Buddhas remember all of the births they took in cyclic existence
due to ignorance;
They also know the births of others—all sentient beings—
And the bases and locations of these births.
Such unobstructed knowledge is explained to be the eighth
power. (12.29)

Buddhas know the deaths and births of each and every sentient
being
In all world realms as limitless as space.
They know these in all of their variety in a single instant,
In an unattached, completely pure, and limitless way—this is
asserted to be the ninth power. (12.30)

Through the power of their omniscient knowledge, the victorious
ones rapidly
Cognize the dissolution of mental afflictions and habitual
tendencies.
They also know how the intelligence of their students causes the
cessation of mental afflictions.
This limitless and unattached knowledge is asserted to be the tenth
power. (12.31)

Birds do not return because the sky is exhausted;
They return because the strength of their wings is drained.

In the same way, the heirs of the buddhas, along with the hearers,
Return, not having expressed the buddhas' skylike, limitless
    qualities. (12.32)

Therefore, what need to speak of my ability to understand
Or describe the buddhas' qualities?
Nevertheless, since they were briefly elucidated by the noble
    Nāgārjuna,
I have left behind qualms and described merely a fraction. (12.33)

The profound is emptiness;
The other qualities are the vast.
By knowing the ways of the profound and vast,
These qualities will be attained. (12.34)

Once again you arrive in the three existences in an unwavering
    kāya.
Through emanations, you display the deeds of descending, birth,
    enlightenment, and turning the dharma wheel of peace.
Compassionately, you lead all worldly, deceptive beings, who are
    bound in the nooses of hope,
To the ground of nirvāṇa. (12.35)

To dispel all impurities, there is no antidote to apply apart from
    knowing the suchness of phenomena.
Suchness does not rely on the divisions of phenomena's
    manifestions,
And the intelligence that perceives suchness is also not multiple.
Therefore, you taught the unequalled and inseparable vehicle to
    sentient beings. (12.36)

Since worldly beings are afflicted by the pollutants that give rise
    to shortcomings,
They do not enter the deep sphere of experience of the buddhas.
Nevertheless, you, the sugatas, do not give up on them,
    for you possess excellent knowledge together with the
    method, compassion,

And because, before, you made the promise, "I will liberate sentient
beings." (12.37)

Just like the skillful guide who emanated a pleasant city
In order to dispel the fatigue of travelers on their way to a jewel
island,
You teach the lower vehicles and have your students apply their
minds to the way of total peace.
Later on, you teach voidness separately to the ones whose minds are
trained. (12.38)

However many subtle atoms there are
In all the pure realms without exception that are the lands of
buddhas,
For that many eons do the sugatas go to supreme, excellent, genuine
enlightenment.
However, they do not share this secret with everyone. (12.39)

The victorious ones remain for as long as all worldly beings have
not gone to supreme, excellent peace.
For as long as space has not disintegrated,
You, borne by the mother of supreme knowledge and nurtured by
the nanny of loving compassion, remain.
Thus how could you depart to peace? (12.40)

You regard worldly beings, who consume poisonous food due to
the fault of ignorance,
As members of your own family.
The love you feel for them is not even rivaled by that of a mother
whose only child has eaten poison.
Therefore, protector, you do not pass into supreme, excellent peace.
(12.41)

Unskillful beings cling to existence and nonexistence,
By which they fall prey to the sufferings of birth, death, losing
the pleasant, meeting with the unpleasant,

And negative actions—every being in all the worlds there are is an
object of your loving compassion.
Therefore, transcendent conquerors, you feel no fondness for peace
and instead choose not to pass into nirvāṇa. (12.42)

This system has been expressed by the bhikṣhu Chandrakīrti
By drawing on the *Treatise on the Middle Way*
And in precise accordance with scripture
And key instructions. (13.1)

Just as there are no treatises that teach the dharma of emptiness
In the way the *Treatise on the Middle Way* does,
Learned ones should ascertain that there is no other treatise among
Nāgārjuna's followers
That teaches his system like this one. (13.2)

Frightened by the vast, dark ocean of Nāgārjuna's mind,
Some have cast his excellent tradition far away.
Now, his verses, like flower pistils waiting to open, have fully
bloomed
Due to the water of Chandrakīrti, who thus perfectly fulfills the
hopes of disciples. (13.3)

The suchness explained above, profound and frightening, will
be realized
Through beings' previous habituation—it will not be
comprehended by those who merely have done extensive
hearing.
Therefore, just as the conceptually fabricated systems that
propound a self should be relinquished,
So should all fondness be forsaken for the systems outside the way
of Nāgārjuna. (13.4)

May the merit I have gained through explaining the good system
of master Nāgārjuna pervade space in all directions.
With the blue hue of the mental afflictions becoming a brilliant
autumn star in mind's sky,

And with the jewel hood-ornament beautifying the snake of the
  mind,
May the beings in all worlds realize suchness and swiftly proceed to
  the ground of the sugatas. (13.5)

Thus concludes the *Entrance to the Middle Way*, which clarifies the
ways of the profound and the vast. It has been composed by the master
Chandrakīrti, whose mind is immersed in the supreme vehicle, who possesses unassailable wisdom and compassion, and who reversed clinging to
true existence by milking a painting of a cow.

In the center of the Kashmiri city of Anupatna, in the Ratnagupta Temple, during the reign of the Kashmiri king Shrī Aryadeva, the Indian
abbot Tīlaka and the Tibetan lotsāwa Bandey Patsap Nyima Drak made
this translation in accordance with the Kashmiri edition of the text. Later,
at the Ramoche Temple in Rasa, the Indian abbot Kanakavarma and the
same lotsāwa, through comparisons with the eastern Aparanta edition of
the text, made corrections to and finalized the translation.

Under the direction of The Dzogchen Ponlop Rinpoche, in reliance on
the explanations of Acharya Lama Tenpa Gyaltsen and Acharya Tashi
Wangchuk, and by the invaluable assistance of many translators, scholars, and teachers, this translation was made under the auspices of Nitartha Institute by Tyler Dewar of the Nitartha Translation Network. May
it be virtuous!

⦂ Appendix VI

THE KARMAPA'S OUTLINE FOR *FEAST FOR THE FORTUNATE*

2.2.2.1.1.6.2.3.1.1.1.2.1.1.2.2.1.2.3.3.1. THE MAIN TEACHING 228

2.2.2.1.1.6.2.3.1.1.1.2.1.1.2.2.1.2.3.3.1.1. Though causes and results have
no nature their connection is tenable......................................228

2.2.2.1.1.6.2.3.1.1.1.2.1.1.2.2.1.2.3.3.1.2. Establishing that meaning
by way of example..233

2.2.2.1.1.6.2.3.1.1.1.2.1.1.2.2.1.2.3.3.1.3. Eliminating the absurd
consequence of endlessness..234

2.2.2.1.1.6.2.3.1.1.1.2.1.1.2.2.1.2.3.3.1.1. THOUGH CAUSES AND
RESULTS HAVE NO NATURE THEIR CONNECTION IS TENABLE........228

2.2.2.1.1.6.2.3.1.1.1.2.1.1.2.2.1.2.3.3.1.1.1. Teaching our own system...........228

2.2.2.1.1.6.2.3.1.1.1.2.1.1.2.2.1.2.3.3.1.1.2. Refuting the systems of others 232

2.2.2.1.1.6.2.3.1.1.1.2.1.1.2.2.1.2.3.3.1.1.1. TEACHING OUR OWN SYSTEM 228

[2.2.2.1.1.6.2.3.1.1.1.2.1.1.2.2.1.2.3.3.1.1.2. REFUTING THE SYSTEMS
OF OTHERS]..232

2.2.2.1.1.6.2.3.1.1.1.2.1.1.2.2.1.2.3.3.1.2. ESTABLISHING THAT
MEANING BY WAY OF EXAMPLE..233

2.2.2.1.1.6.2.3.1.1.1.2.1.1.2.2.1.2.3.3.1.3. ELIMINATING THE
ABSURD CONSEQUENCE OF ENDLESSNESS............................234

2.2.2.1.1.6.2.3.1.1.1.2.1.1.2.2.1.2.3.3.1.3.1. The actual teaching
on eliminating the absurd consequence of endlessness......................234

2.2.2.1.1.6.2.3.1.1.1.2.1.1.2.2.1.2.3.3.1.3.2. Even though they are
empty, causes and results can be individually ascertained and
are inconceivable..235

2.2.2.1.1.6.2.3.1.1.1.2.1.1.2.2.1.2.3.3.1.3.1. THE ACTUAL TEACHING ON
ELIMINATING THE ABSURD CONSEQUENCE OF ENDLESSNESS........234

2.2.2.1.1.6.2.3.1.1.1.2.1.1.2.2.1.2.3.3.1.3.2. EVEN THOUGH THEY
ARE EMPTY, CAUSES AND RESULTS CAN BE INDIVIDUALLY
ASCERTAINED AND ARE INCONCEIVABLE..............................235

2.2.2.1.1.6.2.3.1.1.1.2.1.1.2.2.1.2.3.3.2. THE ANCILLARY EXPLANATION
THAT THE BUDDHA'S TEACHING ON THE SUPPORT FOR
ACTIONS AND RESULTS IS PROVISIONAL MEANING....................236

2.2.2.1.1.6.2.3.1.1.1.2.1.1.2.2.1.2.3.3.2.1. The teachings on the all-base
and so on are provisional meaning..236

2.2.2.1.1.6.2.3.1.1.1.2.1.1.2.2.1.2.3.3.2.2. Everything that the Tathāgata
taught as existent is provisional meaning...................................238

2.2.2.1.1.6.2.3.1.1.1.2.1.1.2.2.1.2.3.3.2.1. THE TEACHINGS ON THE
ALL-BASE AND SO ON ARE PROVISIONAL MEANING....................241

2.2.2.1.1.6.2.3.1.1.1.2.1.1.2.2.1.2.3.3.2.2. EVERYTHING THAT THE
TATHĀGATA TAUGHT AS EXISTENT IS PROVISIONAL MEANING......238

2.2.2.1.1.6.2.3.1.1.1.2.1.1.2.2.2. THE ANCILLARY REFUTATION
OF THE SYSTEM OF THE PROPONENTS OF CONSCIOUSNESS
(NAMRIK MAWA/RNAM RIG SMRA BA)................................241

Bibliography

ABBREVIATIONS

ACIP   Asian Classics Input Project (see Reference Materials)
ALTG   Acharya Lama Tenpa Gyaltsen, oral teachings
ATW   Acharya Tashi Wangchuk, oral teachings
GTCD   *The Great Tibetan-Chinese Dictionary* (see Reference Materials)
TBRC   The Tibetan Buddhist Resource Center (see Reference Materials)

TIBETAN SOURCES

Āryadeva *('phags pa lha)*. *The Four Hundred Verses (bstan bcos bzhi brgya pa)*. ACIP TD3846

Atisha *(a ti sha)*. *Key Instructions of the Middle Way (dbu ma'i man ngag)*. Electronic file from the Nitartha International Document Input Center (www.nitartha.org).

Bhāvaviveka *(legs ldan 'byed)*. *The Lamp of Wisdom: A Commentary on* Fundamental Wisdom of the Middle Way *(dbu ma rtsa ba'i 'grel pa shes rab sgron ma)*. ACIP TD3853.

Buddhapālita *(sangs rgyas bskyangs)*. *Buddhapalita: A Commentary on* Fundamental Wisdom of the Middle Way *(dbu ma rtsa ba'i 'grel pa sangs rgyas bskyangs)*. ACIP TD3842.

Chandrakīrti *(zla ba grags pa)*. *An Explanation of the* Entrance to the Middle Way *(dbu ma la 'jug pa'i bshad pa)*. ACIP TD3862.

―――. *Lucid Words: A Commentary on* Fundamental Wisdom of the Middle Way *(dbu ma rta ba'i 'grel pa tshig gsal ba)*. ACIP TD3860.

Gendün Chöpel *(dge 'dun chos 'phel)*. 1990. *An Ornament to Nāgārjuna's Thought (klu sgrub dgongs rgyan)*. In *The Compositions of Gendün Chöpel (dge 'dun chos 'phel gyi gsung rtsom)*, vol. 2, pp. 271-376. Lhasa: Bod ljongs bod yig dpe rnying dpe skrun khang.

Gö Lotsawa Shönu Pal *('gos lo ts'a ba gzhon nu dpal)*. 2002. *The Blue Annals (deb ther sngon po)*. 2 vols. Varanasi: Vajra Vidya Library.

Gorampa Sönam Senge *(go rams pa bsod nams seng ge)*. 1975. *Dispelling Bad Views: A Sectional Outline of the* Entrance to the Middle Way *and an Analysis of Each of the Text's Difficult Points (dbu ma 'jug pa'i dkyus kyi sa bcad pa dang gzhung so so'i dka ba'i gnas la dpyad pa lta ba ngan sel)*. In vol. 5 of *The Collected Works of Go Rams Pa Bsod Nams Seng Ge*. Dehra-Dun: Sakya College.

Mikyö Dorje *(mi bskyod rdo rje)*. 1996. *The* Chariot of the Takpo Kagyü Siddhas: The Oral Transmission of the Glorious Düsum Khyenpa—A Detailed Explanation of the Entrance to the Middle Way *(dbu ma la 'jug pa'i rnam bshad dpal ldan dus gsum mkhyan pa'i zhal lung dvags brgyud grub pa'i shing rta)*. Seattle: Nitartha *international* Publications.

_____. 2003. *In Relief of the Noble Ones: The Karmapa's Commentary to the* Ornament for Clear Realization *(mngon rtogs rgyan gyi kar t'ik rje btsun ngal gso)*. 2 vols. Seattle: Nitartha *international* Publications.

Nāgārjuna *(klu sgrub)*. *Countering Objections (rtsod pa bzlog pa'i tshig le'ur byas pa)*. ACIP TD3828.

_____. *Fundamental Wisdom of the Middle Way (dbu ma'i rtsa ba tshig le'ur byas pa shes rab)*. ACIP TD3824.

_____. *Sixty Stanzas on Reasoning (rigs pa drug cu pa'i tshig le'ur byas pa)*. ACIP TD3825.

Pawo Tsuklak Trengwa *(dpa' bo gtsug lag phreng ba)*. 2003. *Banquet for the Wise: A Dharma History (chos 'byung mkhas pa'i dga' ston)*. 2 vols. Varanasi: Vajra Vidya Library.

Rendawa Shönu Lodrö *(red mda' ba gzhon nu blo gros)*. 1983. *The Lamp That Clarifies Suchness: An Explanation of the* Entrance to the Middle Way *(dbu ma la 'jug pa'i rnam bshad de kho na nyid gsal ba'i sgron ma)*. Varanasi: Sakya Students' Union.

Rongtön Sheja Kunrik *(rong stong shes bya kun rig)*. 1999. *The Lamp of the Vital Points: An Explanation of the* Ornament of Sūtras *That Clarifies the Mahāyāna (mdo sde rgyan gyi rnam bshad theg chen gsal bar byed pa'i gnad kyi sgron ma)*. Gangtok: Pema Thinley Sikkim National Press.

Shāntideva *(zhi ba lha)*. *Entrance to the Bodhisattva's Conduct (byang chub sems dpa'i spyod pa la 'jug pa)*. ACIP TD3871.

Tsongkapa Lobsang Drakpa *(tsong kha pa blo bzang grags pa)*. *Illumining the Intention: An Explanation of the* Entrance to the Middle Way *(dbu ma la 'jug pa'i bshad pa dgong pa rab gsal)*. ACIP S5408.

Vasubandhu *(dbyig gnyen)*. *Treasury of Abhidharma (chos mngon pa mdzod kyi tshig le'ur byas pa)*. ACIP TD4089.

_____. *Explanation of the* Treasury of Abhidharma *(chos mngon pa mdzod kyi bshad pa)*. ACIP TD4090.

Wangchuk Dorje *(dbang phyug rdo rje)*. 2004. *Feast for the Fortunate: A Commentary on the* Entrance to the Middle Way *That Easily Pulls Along the* Chariot of the Takpo Kagyü Siddhas *('jug t'ik dvags brgyud grub pa'i shing rta bde bar 'dren byed skal bzang dga' ston)*. Seattle: Nitartha *international* Publications.

———. 2005. *A Brief Summary of the Middle Way and An Abridgement Called "The Lion's Roar" (dbu ma'i bsdu don bsdus pa dang/ zur khol seng ge'i nga ro)*. Kathmandu: Thrangu Dharma Kara Publications.

ENGLISH SOURCES

Acharya Lama Tenpa Gyaltsen. 2002. *Commentary on the Presentation of Madhyamaka in the* Treasury of Knowledge *by Jamgön Kongtrul Lodrö Thaye.* (Root text translation by Karl Brunnhölzl; oral translation by Karl Brunnhölzl). Nitartha Institute.

Ames, William L. 2003. "Bhāvaviveka's Own View of His Differences with Buddhapālita." In Dreyfus and McClintock 2003.

Brunnhölzl, Karl. 2004. *The Center of the Sunlit Sky: Madhyamaka in the Kagyü Tradition.* (Contains a translation of Pawo Tsuklak Trengwa's commentary on the ninth chapter of *Bodhicharyāvatāra*). Ithaca: Snow Lion Publications.

Chandrakīrti. 1994. *Supplement to the "Middle Way" (Madhyamakavatara) and Explanation of the "Supplement to the 'Middle Way'" (Madhyamakavatara-bhashyam)*. Translated and edited by George Churinoff [Gelong Thubten Tsultrim]. Pomaia: Istituto Lama Tzong Khapa.

Chandrakīrti and Jamgön Mipham. 2002. *Introduction to the Middle Way: Chandrakirti's* Madhyamakavatara *with Commentary by Jamgön Mipham.* Translated by the Padmakara Translation Group. Boston: Shambhala.

Chandrakīrti and Mikyö Dorje. 2005. *The Moon of Wisdom: Chapter Six of Chandrakirti's* Entering the Middle Way: *with Commentary from the Eighth Karmapa, Mikyö Dorje's* Chariot of the Dakpo Kagyü Siddhas. Translated under the guidance of Khenpo Tsültrim Gyamtso Rinpoche by Ari Goldfield, Jules Levinson, Jim Scott, and Birgit Scott. Ithaca: Snow Lion Publications.

Chizuko Yoshimizu. 2003. "Tsong kha pa's Reevaluation of Candrakīrti's Criticism of Autonomous Inference." In Dreyfus and McClintock 2003.

Dreyfus, Georges B. J., and Sara McClintock, eds. 2003. *The Svātantrika-Prāsaṅgika Distinction: What Difference Does a Difference Make?* Boston: Wisdom Publications.

Dzogchen Ponlop Rinpoche. 1997. *Commentary on* The Chariot of the Takpo Kagyü Siddhas. (Root text translation and translation of commentary from *The* Chariot of the Takpo Kagyü Siddhas by Mark S. Seibold; revised by Elizabeth M. Callahan, Tingdzin Ötrö, Scott Wellenbach, and Cryssoula Zerbini). Nitartha Institute.

————. 1998. *Commentary on* The Chariot of the Dakpo Kagyü Siddhas: *The Sixth Mind Generation: the Manifest.* (Translation of root verses and commentary from *The* Chariot of the Takpo Kagyü Siddhas by Elizabeth M. Callahan). Nitartha Institute.

————. 1999. *Commentary on* The Chariot of the Dakpo Kagyü Siddhas: *The Sixth Chapter.* (Translation of root verses and commentary from *The* Chariot of the Takpo Kagyü Siddhas by Elizabeth M. Callahan in talks 1-22 and by Mark S. Seibold in talks 23-25). Nitartha Institute.

————. 2000. *Commentary on the* Madhyamakavatara: *Chandrakirti's* Entrance to the Middle Way: *Chapters Seven to Eleven.* (Oral translation by Karl Brunnhölzl; root verse translation by Ari Goldfield). Nitartha Institute.

————. 2004. *Commentary on* Feast for the Fortunate: *Grounds One-Five and Part I of Ground Six.* (Oral translation by Tyler Dewar; root text translation by Tyler Dewar). Nitartha Institute.

————. 2006. *The Lives of the Karmapas.* (English and Chinese edition). Dharamsala: Altruism Press.

Dzongsar Khyentse Rinpoche. 2003. *Introduction to the Middle Way: Chandrakirti's* Madhyamakavatara *with Commentary by Dzongsar Jamyang Khyentse Rinpoche.* Edited by Alex Trisoglio. Electronic file. Khyentse Foundation.

Hookham, S. K. 1991. *The Buddha Within: Tathagatagarbha Doctrine According to the Shentong Interpretation of the Ratnagotravibhaga.* Albany: State University of New York Press.

Hopkins, Jeffrey. 1983. *Meditation on Emptiness.* London: Wisdom Publications.

————. 2007. *Nāgārjuna's Precious Garland: Buddhist Advice for Living and Liberation.* Ithaca: Snow Lion Publications.

Huntington, C. W., Jr. and Geshé Namgyal Wangchen. 1989. *The Emptiness of Emptiness: An Introduction to Early Indian Mādhyamika.* Honolulu: University of Hawaii Press.

————. 2003. "Was Candrakīrti a Prāsaṅgika?" In Dreyfus and McClintock 2003.

Jamgön Kongtrul Lodrö Thaye. 2002. *The Presentation of Madhyamaka in the* Treasury of Knowledge. Translated, edited, and annotated by Karl Brunnhölzl. Sackville, New Brunswick, Canada: Nitartha Institute.

Jamgön Mipham Rinpoche. 2000. *Gateway to Knowledge,* vol 2. Translated under the direction of Chökyi Nyima Rinpoche by Erik Pema Kunsang. Boudhanath: Rangjung Yeshe Publications.

Karma Thinley. 1980. *The History of the Sixteen Karmapas of Tibet.* Boulder: Prajñā Press.

Khenchen Thrangu Rinpoche. 2002. *Essential Practice: Lectures on Kamalashila's Stages of Meditation in the Middle Way School.* Translated by Jules B. Levinson. Ithaca: Snow Lion Publications.

Khenpo Tsültrim Gyamtso Rinpoche. 1986. *Progressive Stages of Meditation on Emptiness.* Translated and arranged by Shenpen Hookham. Oxford: Longchen Foundation.

———. 2003. *The Sun of Wisdom: Teachings on the Noble Nagarjuna's* Fundamental Wisdom of the Middle Way. Translated and edited by Ari Goldfield. Boston: Shambhala.

Klein, Anne Carolyn. 1994. *Path to the Middle: The Spoken Scholarship of Kensur Yeshey Tupden.* (Contains Anne Klein's translation of Tsongkapa's commentary, in *Illumining the Intention*, on verses 6.1-6.7 of the Entrance to the Middle Way). Albany: State University of New York Press.

Lopez, Donald S., Jr. 1987. *A Study of Svātantrika.* Ithaca: Snow Lion Publications.

———. 2006. *The Madman's Middle Way: Reflections on Reality of the Tibetan Monk Gendun Chopel.* Chicago: University of Chicago Press.

Maitreya, Jamgön Kongtrul Lodrö Thaye, and Khenpo Tsültrim Gyamtso Rinpoche. 2000. *Buddha Nature:* The Mahayana Uttaratantra Shastra *with Commentary.* Translated by Rosemarie Fuchs. Ithaca: Snow Lion Publications.

Maitreyanātha/Āryāsaṅga and Vasubandhu. 2004. *The Universal Vehicle Discourse Literature (Mahāyāna sūtrālaṃkāra): Together with its Commentary (Bhāṣya) by Vasubandhu.* Translated from the Sanskrit, Tibetan, and Chinese by L. Jamspal, R. Clark, J. Wilson, L. Zwilling, M. Sweet, and R. Thurman; Editor-in-Chief, Robert A.F. Thurman. New York: American Institute of Buddhist Studies.

Maitreya and Mipham. 2004. *Maitreya's Distinguishing Phenomena and Pure Being: with Commentary by Mipham.* Translated by Jim Scott under the guidance of Khenpo Tsültrim Gyamtso Rinpoche. Ithaca: Snow Lion Publications.

Nāgārjuna. 1995. *The* Fundamental Wisdom of the Middle Way: *Nāgārjuna's Mūlamadhyamakakārikā.* Translation and commentary by Jay L. Garfield. New York: Oxford University Press.

Pettit, John Whitney. 1999. *Mipham's Beacon of Certainty: Illuminating the View of Dzogchen, the Great Perfection.* Boston: Wisdom Publicatons.

Ruegg, David Seyfort. 1981. *The Literature of the Madhyamaka School of Philosophy in India.* Wiesbaden: Otto Harrassowitz.

Shāntideva. 1997. *The Way of the Bodhisattva: A Translation of the Bodhicharyāvatāra.* Translated by the Padmakara Translation Group. Boston: Shambhala.

Stearns, Cyrus. 1999. *The Buddha from Dolpo: A Study of the Life and Thought of the Tibetan Master Dolpopa Sherab Gyaltsen.* (Contains a translation of Dolpopa's *The Fourth Council*). Albany: State University of New York Press.

Thupten Jinpa. 2002. *Self, Reality and Reason in Tibetan Philosophy: Tsongkhapa's Quest for the Middle Way.* New York: RoutledgeCurzon.

THE KARMAPA'S MIDDLE WAY

Tillemans, Tom J. F. 2003. "Metaphysics for Mādhyamikas." In Dreyfus and McClintock 2003.

Tsongkapa. 2000. *The Great Treatise on the Stages of the Path to Enlightenment: Lam Rim Chen Mo.* 3 vols. Translated by the Lamrim Chenmo Translation Committee, Joshua W.C. Cutler, Editor-in-Chief, Guy Newland, Editor. Ithaca: Snow Lion Publications.

————. n.d. *Illumination of the Thought (dgongs pa rab gsal): by Lama Tsongkhapa: Chapter Six, verse 8 onward.* Translated from the Tibetan by Joan Nicell; checked and corrected by Thubten Sherab Sherpa. An FPMT Masters Program Translation.

Vasubandhu. 2005. *Selected Sections from the Abhidharmakośa and Bhāṣya of Vasubandhu.* Translated by Gelong Lodrö Sangpo from La Vallée Poussin's French rendition which was based mainly on Hsüan Tsang's Chinese translation but also on Paramārtha's Chinese translation and Yaomitra's commentary, *Sphutārthā Abhidharmakośavyākhyā.* Produced solely for use of Nitartha Institute. Edited by Gelongma Migme Chödrön. Nitartha Institute.

Wangchuk Dorje. 2004. *Feast for the Fortunate: Which Easily Pulls Along the Chariot of the Takpo Kagyü Siddhas, Commentary to the Entrance to the Middle Way.* (Draft translation by Tyler Dewar). Nitartha Institute.

REFERENCE MATERIALS

Asian Classics Input Project, http://asianclassics.org

Digital Library and Museum of Buddhist Studies, http://buddhism.lib.ntu.edu. tw/BDLM/front.htm

An Encyclopaedic Tibetan-English Dictionary (bod dbyin tshig mdzod chen mo). (Tibetan and English). Vol 1. Translated by Gyurme Dorje and Tudeng Nima. Editor of the Tibetan Text, Tudeng Nima. Executive Editor, Tadeusz Skorupski. Beijing/London: The Nationalities Publishing House/The School of Oriental and African Studies, 2001.

The Great Tibetan-Chinese Dictionary (bod rgya tshig mdzod chen mo). (Tibetan and Chinese). 2 vols. Beijing: Mi rigs dpe skrun khang, 1996.

The Home Page of Borislav Manolov (for research on large numbers), http://www.uni-bonn.de/~manfear/

Kagyu Office: the Official Website of His Holiness Karmapa, http://www.kagyuoffice.org

The Online Dharma Dictionary v. 4, http://rywiki.tsadra.org

Peking Tripitaka Online Search, The Shin Buddhist Comprehensive Research Institute, Otani University, http://web.otani.ac.jp/cri/twrp/tibdate/Peking_online_search.html

The Tibetan Buddhist Resource Center, http://tbrc.org

Notes

1 For more remarks on Nāgārjuna's possible dates, see Ruegg 1981, p. 4, note 11.

2 From the perspective of our ordinary thoughts and ways of relating to the world, the significance of the realities revealed at this stage is anything but "slight." Consequently, this stage can, at first, seem misnamed. Yet as the instructions for the level of thorough analysis, explained below, demonstrate, this stage is not the final culmination of investigating appearing phenomena.

3 See Appendix III.

4 Dreyfus and McClintock 2003, p. 7.

5 The chapter of *Feast for the Fortunate* that examines the differences between the Consequentialists and Autonomists, as well as the debate between Bhāvaviveka and Chandrakīrti, begins on page 159. See also Appendix I (p. 579), which contains the full relevant excerpt from Chandrakīrti's defense of Buddhapālita and refutation of Bhāvaviveka in *Lucid Words*.

6 Nāgārjuna's tradition is generally thought to emphasize the profound aspect of the Mahāyāna teaching, while the tradition of Asaṅga (ca. 300) is said to emphasize the teachings on the Mahāyāna's vast, or extensive, aspect. Also highly noteworthy for its combination of the Mahāyāna's vast and profound elements in one text is the *Entrance to the Conduct of Bodhisattvas (Bodhicharyāvatāra, Chanchub Sempe Chöpa la Jukpa/ byang chub sems dpa'i spyod pa la 'jug pa)* by the great Indian master Shāntideva, who is generally classified as a Consequentialist.

7 Ruegg 1981, p. 113.

8 *Naktso Lotsawa Tsültrim Gyalwa/nag 'tsho lo ts'a ba tshul khrims rgyal ba.*

9 Ruegg 1981, p. 113.

10 In his *Blue Annals (Debter Ngönpo/deb ther sngon po)*, Gö Lotsawa Shönu Pal *('gos lo ts'a ba gzhon nu dpal*, 1392-1481) lists the fours sons of Patsap as Tsangpa Sarbö *(gtsang pa sar sbos)*, Maja Changchub Yeshe *(rma bya byang chub ye shes)*, Dar Yönten Drak *(dar yon tan grags)*, and Shangtang Sakpa *(zhang thang sag pa)*.

11 See the Padmakara Translation Group's Translators' Introduction in Chandrakīrti and Jamgön Mipham 2002 for a discussion of qualifications to this rule within the Nyingma tradition.

12 Brunnhölzl 2004, p. 59.

13 Dzogchen Ponlop Rinpoche 2006, p. 182.

14 For the Karma Kagyü monastic universities, the root text for Vinaya studies is the *Summary of the Vinaya (Vinayasūtra, Dulwa Do/'dul ba mdo)* by Gunaprābha; Mikyö Dorje's commentary is entitled *Orb of the Sun (Nyimey Kyilkhor/nyi ma'i dkyil 'khor)*.

The root text for the Abhidharma is the *Treasury of Abhidharma (Abhidharmakosha, Chö Ngönpa Dzö/chos mngon pa mdzod)* by Vasubandhu; Mikyö Dorje's commentary is entitled *Extracting the Delight of Accomplishment and Bliss (Drup De Chi Jo/grub bde dpyid 'jo)*. The root text for the Perfection of Supreme Knowledge is the *Ornament for Clear Realization (Abhisamayālaṃkāra, Ngöntok Gyen/mngon rtogs rgyan)* by Maitreya and Asaṅga; Mikyö Dorje's commentary is entitled *In Relief of the Noble Ones (Jetsün Ngalso/rje btsun ngal gso)*. The root text for the Middle Way is, of course, Chandrakīrti's *Entrance to the Middle Way*; title information for Mikyö Dorje's commentary is provided below. The main text for the study of Valid Cognition is the Seventh Karmapa's *Ocean of Texts on Reasoning (Rik Shung Gyamtso/rigs gzhung rgya mtsho)*, an exposition on multiple works by Dignāga and Dharmakīrti.

15 Mikyö Dorje 1996, p. xxxx.

16 Mikyö Dorje gives his age at this time as thirty-nine, but the Tibetan system of counting one's age often results in a total that is one year greater than in the Western custom.

17 Mikyö Dorje's colophon only mentions the age at which he began the composition, the place at which he began it, and the place, but not the age, at which he finished it.

18 Fully titled *The Chariot of the Takpo Kagyu Siddhas: The Oral Transmission of the Glorious Düsum Khyenpa—A Detailed Explanation of the Entrance to the Middle Way (Uma la Jukpe Namshe Palden Düsum Khyenpe Shal-lung Tak-gyü Drubpe Shingta/ dbu ma la 'jug pa'i rnam bshad dpal ldan dus gsum mkhyan pa'i zhal lung dvags brgyud grub pa'i shing rta)*.

19 Published by Nitartha *international* in 1996.

20 Mikyö Dorje 1996, pp. xxxx-xxxxi.

21 *Ṭīkā* is a Sanskrit word meaning "commentary" and often indicating the extensive variety.

22 The contents of this sentence in particular were drawn from public oral teachings on the Middle Way by the Very Venerable Khenchen Tsültrim Gyamtso Rinpoche in Seattle, Washington.

23 Mikyö Dorje was certainly not alone among non-Gelukpa commentators who disagreed with Tsongkapa on some key issues, such as the status of the self and other phenomena on the level of relative truth and the object or target of refutation by Middle Way reasonings. However, it is perhaps easy to overlook the fact that, as a careful reading of this book will reveal, Mikyö Dorje and Tsongkapa also agreed on a number of important issues, such as whether or not the hearers and solitary realizers cognize the selflessness of phenomena (both masters hold that they do) and whether or not all instances of clinging to true existence are necessarily afflictive, as opposed to cognitive, obscurations (both masters hold that clinging to true existence *is* necessarily an afflictive obscuration).

24 Mikyö Dorje did compose treatises from the perspective of the other-emptiness doctrine in his earlier years, but it is believed he only did so to appease a tutor. (Dzogchen Ponlop Rinpoche 2006, p. 182)

25 For a translation of Shāntideva's ninth chapter and Pawo Rinpoche's commentary on it, as well as an excellent, thorough discussion of the Middle Way in the Kagyü tradition, see Karl Brunnhölzl's *Center of the Sunlit Sky: Madhyamaka in the Kagyü Tradition* (Ithaca: Snow Lion Publications, 2004).

26 Brunnhölzl 2004, p. 21.

27 For an example of his treatment of the Middle Way in *Treasury of Knowledge*, see *Frameworks of Buddhist Philosophy*, translated by Elizabeth Callahan (Ithaca: Snow Lion Publications, 2007).

28 Dzogchen Ponlop Rinpoche 2006, p. 185.

29 Fully titled *Feast for the Fortunate: A Commentary on the* Entrance to the Middle Way *That Easily Pulls Along the* Chariot of the Takpo Kagyü Siddhas (*Juktik Tak-gyü Drubpe Shingta Dewar Drenje Kalzang Gatön/'jug T'ik dvags brgyud grub pa'i shing rta bde bar 'dren byed skal bzang dga' ston*).

30 These two have been published in a single volume by Thrangu Dharma Kara Publications (Kathmandu, 2005). Brunnhölzl reports that Wangchuk Dorje wrote "both brief and extensive commentaries" on the five sūtra topics, but only the two mentioned here have, to our current knowledge, survived to the present day. (Brunnhölzl 2004, pp. 18-19)

31 The Nitartha *international* Tibetan edition of Mikyö Dorje's text is 733 pages long in a Western-style book format.

32 This verse is quoted by the Karmapa in his commentary to verse 6.119 on page 332.

33 Dzogchen Ponlop Rinpoche explains, however, that, in the lead-up to direct realization, fear of emptiness, born of intellectual understandings of emptiness that have begun to undermine some of the ego's defense mechanisms, can be a positive sign that one is actually approaching realization.

34 Chandrakīrti's tradition differs from that of Shāntideva on this point. In Shāntideva's tradition, one may be genuinely named a bodhisattva on the basis of having given rise to relative bodhichitta, the desire, born of compassion, to attain enlightenment for the benefit of all sentient beings. However, for Chandrakīrti, the authentic application of the bodhisattva label must entail ultimate bodhichitta, an enlightened outlook informed by the realization of the true nature of reality. For this reason, Chandrakīrti calls his chapters on the bodhisattva grounds "bodhichitta generations," or levels of the development of ultimate bodhichitta.

35 ALTG.

36 See, for example, Chandrakīrti and Jamgön Mipham 2002, pp. 310-314. Although Mipham allows for some level of realization of phenomenal selflessness on the part of the hearers and solitary realizers, he does not agree that the arhats *fully* realize phenomenal selflessness. In contrast, the Karmapa holds that the arhats' realization of phenomenal selflessness is complete, but they do not cultivate their familiarity with this realization in a wide variety of contexts. The semantic styles of the two masters' usage of "realization" *(tokpa/rtogs pa)* and "familiarization/meditation" *(gompa/goms pa* or *bsgom pa)* could well be worth further investigation.

37 See note 163.

38 See Dreyfus and McClintock 2002 for a thorough exploration of issues surrounding the history and application of these two terms.

39 As stated previously, buddhas dwell continually in meditative equipoise and have no postmeditation.

40 Also translated as "freedom from projections," "freedom from conceptual fabrications," "freedom from reference points," "freedom from discursiveness," and "simplicity."

41 Genuine reality is not just a negation that indicates nonexistence *(me-gak/med dgag)*.

42 Dzogchen Ponlop Rinpoche 2004, p. 307. The following explanation of the three consequences also follows Dzogchen Ponlop Rinpoche's explanations, from the same source, pp. 307-319.

43 If there are Autonomist masters who do not accept that conventionally the phenomena of relative truth are established by virtue of their own characteristics, these masters would not be a target of Chandrakīrti's refutation. Moreover, an examination of the Karmapa's views on the Consequentialist-Autonomist distinction seems to reveal that the Karmapa disagrees with the notion that the Autonomists assert the valid establishment of phenomena's characteristics on the conventional level. In fact, one of the Karmapa's biggest objections to the explanations by the tradition of Tsongkapa is the one he makes regarding that tradition's depiction of the Autonomists as having a different ontological view than the Consequentialists, particularly with regard to conventional phenomena being established by their own characteristics.

44 The Geluk School.

45 Gendün Chöpel 1990, pp. 291-292.

46 The Tibetan term translated as "postdisintegration" is simply the past-tense form *(shikpa/zhig pa)* of the intransitive verb "disintegrate" *(jikpa/'jig pa)*, constructed as what in English would be called a noun. Consequently, some translate this term as "disintegratedness."

47 In his *Treasury of Knowledge*, Jamgön Kongtrul Lodrö Thaye lists Tsongkapa's eight great difficult points as four negating claims—1) there is no establishment of things by way of their own characteristics even conventionally, 2) autonomous arguments are not accepted even conventionally, 3) self-awareness is not accepted even conventionally, and 4) the all-base consciousness is not accepted even conventionally—and four affirmative claims—5) outer referents are accepted, 6) clinging to true existence is necessarily an afflictive obscuration, 7) postdisintegration is a function-performing thing, and 8) the hearers and solitary realizers realize phenomenal selflessness (Jamgön Kongtrul Lodrö Thaye 2002, p. 47). In his *Entrance* commentary the Karmapa agrees with points 3, 6, and 8 explicitly and certainly seems to favor point 4. If read as applying to the context of analysis, point 1 also seems to fit well with the Karmapa's approach. Since Tsongkapa and the Karmapa had different understandings of what the term "autonomous arguments" means, point 2 would require more research. See Brunnhölzl 2004, pp. 557-560, for alternate listings of the eight points as well as a discussion of what points the Karmapa and other masters accept or refute.

48 Available in English as *Ocean of Reasoning: A Great Commentary on Nagarjuna's Mūlamadhyamakakārikā*, translated by Ngawang Samten and Jay L. Garfield (New York: Oxford University Press, 2006).

49 Tsongkapa (n.d.), p. 53.

50 There has been much discussion about the relationships of the terms "Proponents of Mind Only" *(Sem Tsampa/sems tsam pa)*, "Practitioners of Yogic Conduct" *(Yogāchāra, Naljor Chöpa/rnal 'byor spyod pa)*, and "Proponents of Consciousness" *(Vijñāptivādin, Namrik Mawa/rnam rig smra ba)* and about whether these three terms refer to the same Indian school of thought or to different schools. This issue will not be explored here. However, Chandrakīrti seems mostly to have used the term Proponents of Consciousness in his root text and autocommentary. The Karmapa, in his commentary, sometimes uses the Tibetan-originated term Proponents of Mind

Only, but without explicitly alluding to the possibility of a different school. Yet at the end of the section on the refutation of a nondual dependent nature, the Karmapa makes a curious statement: "There are many subschools, such as the Practitioners of Yogic Conduct and the Proponents of Consciousness, who hold different views about which of the three natures are substantially established and so on. One can elaborate."

51 Acharya Lama Tenpa Gyaltsen, in his teachings at Nitartha Institute, has explored the question of whether or not the "dependent nature consciousness" refuted by Chandrakīrti is synonymous with the all-base consciousness within the Proponents of Consciousness' eightfold collection of consciousnesses. Chandrakīrti does not seem to provide a clear answer to this question, as he never directly equates "dependent nature consciousness" with "all-base consciousness."

52 ALTG.

53 Oral teachings by Dzogchen Ponlop Rinpoche.

54 These two correlate with the two types of ignorance mentioned earlier in this introduction, in the summary of the "Introduction to the Teachings on Emptiness."

55 "Imputed" in this context is used interchangeably with "imaginary."

56 These two schools are definite anomalies within the Buddhist tradition because of their assertions of the existence of the self of persons.

57 "Tīrthikas" most commonly is used by Indian and Tibetan Buddhist philosophers as a term to refer to the Hindu schools of ancient India. However, and especially in the Middle Way context, it can also refer to any philosophical school, including Buddhist schools, that mistakenly posits truly existent phenomena.

58 Oral teachings by Khenpo Tsültrim Gyamtso Rinpoche.

59 The next two lines of the quotation are: "The emptiness endowed with the supreme of all aspects/ Is not like the former emptiness."

60 *Arya-mahābherīhārakaparivarta-nāma-Mahāyāna-sūtra, Pakpa Ngawoche Chenpö Le-u Shejawa Tegpa Chenpö Do/'phags pa rnga bo che chen po'i le'u zhes bya ba theg pa chen po'i mdo.*

61 *Arya-mahāmegha, Pakpa Trin Chenpo/'phags pa sprin chen po.*

62 *Laṅkāvatārasūtra, Langkar Shekpe Do/langkar gshegs pa'i mdo.*

63 *Mañjushrīmūlakalpa, Jampal Tsawe Gyü/'jam dpal rtsa ba'i rgyud.*

64 "Moon" *(Chandra, Dawa/zla ba)* is a poetic reference to Chandrakīrti *(Dawa Drakpa/zla ba grags pa).*

65 "Lotus in hand" is a reference to Avalokiteshvara, from whom the Karmapas are viewed as inseparable.

66 A play on the name of the Eighth Karmapa, whose name, Mikyö, is also the name of the buddha Akṣhobhya.

67 *Dewar shekpa/bde bar gshegs pa:* literally, "blissfully gone ones" or "those who have gone to bliss" or "those who go blissfully," an epithet for buddhas.

68 The *Entrance to the Middle Way* of Chandrakīrti.

69 Here, as to the distinction drawn between dharma wheels and dharma discourses, "dharma wheels" seems to refer to groupings of teachings given by the Buddha for which there were definite and predictable topics, audiences, and locations of the teachings. "Dharma discourses," however, is a grouping of the teachings that does not involve such definitiveness of audience and so forth, but rather is a grouping of spontaneously spoken teachings. "Dharma gates," on the other hand, is a categoriza-

tion that includes all of the teachings of the Buddha, both dharma wheels and dharma discourses. (ALTG)

70 1) The dharma wheel of the four noble truths *(denpa shi/bden pa bzhi)*, 2) the dharma wheel of noncharacteristics *(tsen-nyi mepa/mtshan nyid med pa)*, and 3) the dharma wheel of excellent distinction *(legpar nampar chewa/legs par rnam par phye ba)*.

71 The twelve branches of scripture *(sung-rab yenlak chunyi/gsung rab yan lag bcu gnyis)* are: 1) the Sūtra Collection *(Do-De/mdo sde)*, 2) Melodic Proclamations *(Yang kyi Nyepe De/dbyangs kyis bsnyad pa'i sde)*, 3) Prophecies *(Lungdu Tenpe De/lung du bstan pa'i sde)*, 4) Verses *(Tsiksu Chepe De/tshigs su bcad pa'i sde)*, 5) Directed Statements *(Chedu Jöpe De/ched du brjod pa'i sde)*, 6) Declarations *(Lengshī De/gleng gzhi'i sde)*, 7) Narratives *(Tokpa Jöpe De/rtogs pa brjod pa'i sde)*, 8) Parables *(Detabu Jungwe De/de lta bu byung ba'i sde)*, 9) Previous Births *(Kyerabpe De/skye rabs pa'i sde)*, 10) Extensive Sayings *(Shintu Gyepe De/shin tu rgyas pa'i sde)*, 11) Marvels *(Medu Jungwe De/rmad du byung ba'i sde)*, and 12) Determinations *(Tenla Pabpe De/gtan la phab pa'i sde)*.

72 Lines one, two, and three of this quotation correspond, respectively, to the three levels of analysis: the level of no analysis, the level of slight analysis, and the level of thorough analysis. See Introduction, pp. 3–5.

73 This is an epithet of Maitreya.

74 I.e., to impermanence, suffering, selflessness, and peace as being truly existent things.

75 This quotation also follows the three stages of analysis.

76 The pleasant existences within saṃsāra.

77 The attainment of 1) mere freedom from saṃsāra or 2) the complete omniscience of buddhahood.

78 Also known as Ashvagoṣha *(Tayang/rta dbyangs)*.

79 As to the inclusion of Shāntideva in the list of the Proponents of the Model Texts, this seems to be done here not due to chronology but rather because all major masters of the Buddhism of India and Tibet accepted Shāntideva as a Follower of the Middle Way. However, Shāntideva is usually considered a Consequentialist as opposed to being part of the group of masters whose teachings existed before the Consequentialist-Autonomist split developed.

80 Literally, "[Authors of] the Model Texts of the Middle Way."

81 *Madhyamakālaṃkāra, Uma Gyen/dbu ma rgyan,* composed by Shāntarakṣhita *(Shiwa Tso/zhi ba 'tsho)*.

82 *Madhyamakāloka, Uma Nangwa/dbu ma snang ba,* composed by Kamalashīla.

83 *Satyadvayavibhaṅga, Den-nyi Namje/bden gnyis rnam 'byed,* composed by Jñānagharba *(Yeshe Nyingpo/ye shes snying po)*.

84 Brunnhölzl (2004, p.462) explains that certain streams of explanation in the tradition of Maitreya/Asaṅga came to be known as False Aspectarian Middle Way. This statement by the Karmapa, therefore, seems to be a refutation of that system as a genuine expression of the Middle Way teachings.

85 *Mutekpa/mu stegs pa* or *mutekje/mu stegs byed,* "those who hold up the edges": this term, most often used to describe non-Buddhist philosophical systems, is here used to describe any philosophical system, Buddhist or non-Buddhist, that holds to an extreme view of reality, i.e., of existence, nonexistence, and so on.

86 Another name for Atisha (ca. 980-1052)

87 The three types of supreme knowledge *(sherab sum/shes rab gsum)* are the supreme knowledge arising from hearing *(töpa/thos pa)*, the supreme knowledge arising from contemplation *(sampa/bsam pa)*, and the supreme knowledge arising from meditation *(gompa/sgom pa)*.

88 *bKa' gdams pa* is a lineage founded in Tibet by the Indian master Atisha.

89 Once again *moon (Chandra)* is used as a reference to Chandrakīrti. His name in full means "Famous Moon."

90 Who himself was a direct student of Nāgārjuna.

91 The "lords of the three families" refers to Avalokiteshvara, Mañjushrī, and Vajrapaṇi. (ATW)

92 The second Shamar *(zhva dmar)* incarnation.

93 The first Gyaltsab *(rgyal tshab)* incarnation.

94 The first Sangye Nyenpa *(sangs rgyas mnyan pa)* incarnation. TBRC provides two sets of dates different from those given here: 1455/1457-1510/1525. Kagyü Office gives his dates as 1457-1525.

95 The fifth Shamar incarnation.

96 The greater Saraha is Saraha himself; the lesser Saraha is Shavaripa.

97 This lineage is also called "Kagyü" *(bka' brgyud)* in Tibetan, but it has been translated into English here to provide distinction from the section heading entitled "The lineage of the precious Kagyü itself."

98 Otherwise known as Dromtönpa *('brom ston pa)*.

99 I.e., there are two alternative lineages being described here; one passing through Gampopa to Düsum Khyenpa, the other being received by Düsum Khyenpa directly from the Kadampa masters.

100 *me-gak/med dgag*. This type of negation, in contrast to its counterpart, the implicative negation *(mayin gak/ma yin dgag)*, is a total refutation of its target subject that does not leave any implication of the presence of something else in its wake. For example, the statement, "All phenomena are devoid of true existence" is a nonimplicative negation. Similarly, "The eye lacks true existence" is also a nonimplicative negation, because even though the subject of the statement (the eye) is not inclusive of other phenomena, still the eye's lack of true existence leaves no implication that other phenomena indeed truly exist. By contrast, the statement, "These flowers were not picked during the night" would be an implicative negation: it refutes the possibility of the flowers being picked at night, but implies in its wake that they were picked during the day.

101 Patsab Lotsawa Nyima Drak (Tib. *pa tshab lo tsa ba nyi ma grags)*, b. 1055.

102 Könchok Yenlak and Namgyal Drakpa, as above.

103 As will be obvious, the following two paragraphs are highly cryptic and condensed references to special views and practices in the Vajrayāna. This section of the *Ṭīkā* contains a very long and detailed discussion of this topic, including analyses of several Tibetan masters' views. As in many other sections of this book, the author is assuming that the reader has sufficient background knowledge to appreciate what is being said. Yet since the sūtrayāna, and not the mantrayāna, approach to the Middle Way is the main topic of this book, an attempt will not be made in the footnotes to unpack the mysteries of this brief foray into the mantrayāna. For a helpful discussion about this topic, see Brunnhölzl 2004, pp. 61-68.

104 The first Sangye Nyenpa incarnation.

105 Another name for Shākya Chokden *(shā kāya mchog ldan, 1428-1507)*.

106 Podong Chokle Namgyal (*bo dong phyogs las rnam rgyal,* 1376-1451).

107 Tsongkapa Lobzang Drakpa (*tsong kha pa blo bzang grags pa,* 1357-1419).

108 मध्यमकावतारकारिकानाम

109 དབུ་མ་ལ་འཇུག་པའི་ཚིག་ལེའུར་བྱས་པ་ཞེས་བྱ་བ།

110 In his commentary to Atisha's *Lamp for the Path to Enlightenment,* Jamgön Kongtrul Lodrö Thaye teaches that the titles of Indian treatises are stated in their original language in order to show the authenticity of the text, help students develop appreciation for the efforts of the paṇḍitas and translators, and plant a seed of familiarity with the Sanskrit language. (Jamgön Kongtrul Lodrö Thaye 2005, p. 6)

111 The "three obscurations" are: 1) the afflictive obscurations (*nyönmong kyi dribpa/nyon mongs kyi sgrib pa*), 2) the cognitive obscurations (*sheje dribpa/shes bya'i sgrib pa*), and 3) obscurations of absorption (*nyomjuk gi dribpa/snyo 'jug gi sgrib pa*). (ATW)

112 Here the term "elaboration" (*tröpa/spros pa*), which in Middle Way teachings usually refers in a negative way to conceptual fabrications, is used to indicate the variety and complexity of the enlightened activity of the buddhas. (ATW)

113 Mikyö Dorje says that "someone who accepts the view" of the Middle Way is someone who, through following the venerable Nāgārjuna, has developed a full understanding of the texts that speak of the lack of inherent nature of all phenomena. "Someone who has developed realization," in the tradition of the *Entrance to the Middle Way,* refers to noble beings of any of the three vehicles who rest in the meditative equipoise of the true nature of phenomena. The four permutations of these two types of persons are 1) someone who accepts the view yet has no realization, 2) someone who has realization but does not accept the view, 3) someone who both accepts the view and has realization, and 4) someone who neither accepts the view nor possesses realization. The first, third, and fourth permutations are straightforward. The second (having realization but not accepting the view) is explained as follows: there are some noble beings of the Mahāyāna who have realized, but do not, at least outwardly, accept, the view of the Middle Way. They do so as a skillful means of communicating with certain types of students, namely those who practice the lower vehicles. Also, there are certain types of hearers and solitary realizers—those with dull faculties or those who gain liberation due to supreme knowledge alone (i.e., without compassion)—who have gained realization of the Middle Way but do not have the intellectual capacity to familiarize themselves with the methods and so forth that are presented in the Middle Way tradition. Consequently, these types of beings would not be capable of teaching the view of the Middle Way to others, even though they had gained realization of it in a personal way. Finally, in some cases, due to the power of the methods of the secret Vajrayāna, it is possible for even ordinary beings to gain the realization of the Middle Way in their mindstreams and yet still be incapable of perfectly explaining the view of the Middle Way to others. With respect to the third permutation, someone who has both gained realization of the Middle Way and accepts the view, Mikyö Dorje says that any instance of their accepting the view is only a display for the sake of others, as is explained in the following paragraph.

114 Mañjushrī's name in Tibetan is *Jampalyang/'jam dpal dbyangs. Jam* means "gentle," *pal* means "glorious," and *yang* means "melodious."

115 In Mikyö Dorje's commentary, these two benefits are listed as 1) temporary benefit (*nekab/gnas skabs*) and 2) ultimate benefit (*tartug/mthar thug*).

116 This section explains what is commonly known in the Indo-Tibetan commentarial

tradition as the "four properties, the purpose and so on" (*gö sog chö shi/dgos sogs chos bzhi*). They are: 1) the object of expression (*jöja/brjod bya*), 2) the purpose (*göpa/dgos pa*), 3) the essential purpose (*nying-gö/nying dgos*) or purpose-of-the-purpose (*göpe göpa/dgos pa'i dgos pa*), and 4) the connections (*drelwa/'brel ba*). The "connections" describes the relationships between the first three, and these four are most commonly presented in the order in which they are listed here.

117 As will be explained in the chapter on the Consequentialist-Autonomist distinction (p. 159), the Consequentialists follow Nāgārjuna's declaration that it is self-defeating to hold any thesis about anything from one's own point of view. For the Consequentialists, therefore, all theses and positions are only repetitions of others' views that are voiced from the perspective of others. The Autonomists, on the other hand, contend that in some cases one must hold and express a position of one's own in order to prove the validity of emptiness to others or in order to correct others' wrong thoughts.

118 The five paths are the path of accumulation (*tsok lam/tshogs lam*), the path of juncture (*jor lam/sbyor lam*), the path of seeing (*tong lam/mthong lam*) (which corresponds to the first bodhisattva ground), the path of meditation (*gom lam/bsgom lam*) (which corresponds to bodhisattva grounds two through ten), and the path beyond training (*mi lobpe lam/mi slob pa'i lam*) (which corresponds to the ground of buddhahood).

119 The eleven grounds are the ten bodhisattva grounds and the ground of buddhahood.

120 An epithet for solitary realizers.

121 An epithet for buddhas.

122 Tathāgata is an epithet for the Buddha meaning "thus-gone one."

123 Here the two syllables of the term *nyentö/nyan thos* are used to describe two activities: 1) hearing teachings from the buddhas and 2) causing others to hear them, I.e., propagating or proclaiming them to others.

124 "Inexhaustible" is a quality of the fruition of arhathood attained by hearers, also called the result of separation (*draldre/bral 'bras*). It refers to a state of irreversibility, the state that, once attained, will not be exhausted. (ALTG)

125 "Proponents of Things" primarily refers to the two lower Buddhist philosophical systems of the Sūtra Followers (*Sautrāntika, Do Depa/mdo sde pa*) and the Particularists (*Vaibhāṣhika, Jedrak Mawa/bye brag smra ba*), because these two schools propound truly existent things in the material world (in the form of partless particles) as well as in the realm of consciousness (in the form of indivisible moments of consciousness).

126 The first seven bodhisattva grounds are called "impure grounds" because on them some mental afflictions have not been relinquished.

127 Grounds eight through ten are called pure grounds because on them all mental afflictions have been relinquished.

128 I.e., buddhas.

129 Rendawa Shönu Lodrö (*red mda' ba gzhon nu blo gros*, 1349-1412), the early Tibetan master of the Sakya lineage, in his commentary on the *Entrance to the Middle Way* called *The Torch That Clarifies Suchness (Dekonanyi Salwe Drönme/de kho na nyid gsal ba'i sgron me*) lists six ways in which the example of a water mill is congruent with the suffering of sentient beings in saṃsāra: 1) a water mill is bound by a rope, whereas sentient beings are bound tightly by the rope of karma and mental afflictions created by their fixation on self and entities connected to the self, 2) a water mill is subject to

the power of its operator, whereas sentient beings are subject to the power of dualistic consciousness, 3) the water in a water mill spins about at random in the well, whereas sentient beings spin about in the great well of cyclic existence, 4) the water in a water mill naturally flows downward and is only drawn up with a great deal of effort, whereas sentient beings tend to migrate toward the lower realms of saṃsāra, and can only be released from this downward migration and drawn up to the human and god realms by applying a great deal of effort, 5) the first, middle, and final stages of the cycle of a water mill cannot be readily ascertained, whereas the stages of the sequence of the mental afflictions, karma, and birth of sentient beings are also difficult to ascertain, and 6) a water mill is progressively worn down with use every day, whereas sentient beings are battered daily by the three kinds of suffering. (Rendawa Shönu Lodrö 1983, pp. 46-47) Mikyö Dorje explains the example in a similar way in the *Ṭīkā*.

130 Here in his commentary Mikyö Dorje says "adults" *(genpa/rgan pa)* instead of "genuine beings" *(dampa/dam pa)*.

131 These are explained in detail in the chapter on the qualities of the bodhisattva grounds (p. 505).

132 Dzogchen Ponlop Rinpoche explains that "power" mainly refers to the bodhisattvas' power to purify their own obscurations and their power to help others purify obscurations. (Dzogchen Ponlop Rinpoche 2004, p. 58)

133 The "increase of karmic maturation" *(nampar minpa pelwa/rnam par smin pa 'phel ba)* refers to the stage of a bodhisattva's progress in which the results of the bodhisattva's earlier engagement in generosity and so forth are beginning to bear fruit. (ATW)

134 This verse was translated by Elizabeth Callahan (Nalandabodhi website). The quotation is truncated in Wangchuk Dorje's text and appears here as it appears in the *Ṭīkā*.

135 One hundred vigintillion equals ten to the sixty-fifth power. This number was phrased in the original text as "one hundred thousand times countless *(drangme/grangs med)* (ten to the fifty-ninth power) times ten." In all instances of such complex naming of numbers throughout the text, the English (U.S.) name for the resultant figure was chosen as a substitute for a literal translation of the words in the root verses and commentary.

136 *Möchö kyi sempa/mos spyod kyi sems dpa'.* This term refers primarily to aspirants on the path of juncture, but it can also apply to those on the path of accumulation. Those engaging in the conduct of devoted interest have given rise to relative bodhichitta— the wish to attain perfect enlightenment for the benefit of others—but have not engendered the ultimate bodhichitta, which is born on the path of seeing, or first bodhisattva ground.

137 "Definite separation" is the first stage of fruition of the hearers, the state of "stream enterer." This is the hearers' equivalent of the bodhisattvas' path of seeing. The bodhisattva engaging in the conduct of devoted interest, in not yet having attained the path of seeing of bodhisattvas, is similar to someone possessing the disposition of a hearer who has not attained the definite separation sought after by hearers. (ALTG)

138 *Bhagavatī, Chomden Dema/bcom ldan 'das ma,* used here as an epithet for the *Prajñāpāramitā,* or *Perfection of Supreme Knowledge,* sūtras.

139 The "three spheres" *(kor sum/'khor gsum)* are conceptions of true existence directed

toward three axes or constituents of any given action: the performer of the action, the object to which the action is directed, and the action itself—in short, the agent, object, and action.

140 This refers to the time of taking bodhisattva vows. (ATW)

141 See more on the qualities they attain in the chapter entitled "Qualities of the Bodhisattva Grounds."

142 For example, the sixteen aspects of the four noble truths: impermanence and so on.

143 *Nyentö gangzak zung shi ya gye/nyan thos gang zag zung bzhi ya brgyad*: the hearers' results have four stages, and each of these stages has two subdivisions. The results are therefore traditionally called "the four pairs of results and the eight single results." The four stages are 1) the arhat *(drachom/dgra bcom)*, 2) the nonreturner *(chir midogpa/ phyir mi ldog pa)*, 3) the once-returner *(chir dogpa/phyir ldog pa)*, and 4) the stream-enterer *(gyun shug pa/rgyun zhugs pa)*. Each of these four stages has two subdivisions: 1) those who are entering into the given stage and 2) those who have attained the final result of the given stage. In a manner opposite to the enumeration of the bodhisattva grounds, the results of the hearers are numbered from the most advanced to the most rudimentary. (The arhat is the highest result for hearers; the stream-enterer is the starting point of the resultant stages. Just as the eighth stage of the hearers' fruition is the starting point for hearers, the first bodhisattva ground is the starting point for the bodhisattvas' attainment of the fruition.)

144 Both the pre-stream-enterer and the stream-enterer who has attained the result are examples of an individual who has attained the hearers' path of seeing.

145 A scholar from the Indian Vikramalashīla Monastery who lived around the beginning of the twelfth century. (Ruegg 1981, p. 114)

146 A twelfth century Kashmiri master who authored the only extant Indian commentary to *The Entrance to the Middle Way*. (Ruegg 1981, p. 113)

147 All of these reasonings are directed at someone who asserts that hearers and solitary realizers *do not* realize the selflessness of phenomena. The reasonings show the faulty consequences of such a view. As such, they demonstrate the standard logical approach of the Consequentialists: they set forth a predicate that is either absurd or that the opponents would not want to accept; and, to prove such a predicate, they state a reason that is part of the opponents' belief system, i.e., something they accept. In the case of each reasoning, the Karmapa is *not* trying to prove the predicate. He is trying to show that the reason, which the opponents accept (not the Karmapa) is illogical because of its proving an absurd predicate. These three reasonings, along with the footnotes, will be best understood by being read several times.

148 It would be undesirable for a follower of Chandrakīrti's tradition to accept this proposition, because Chandrakīrti clearly states in verse 1.8 and its commentary that bodhisattvas do not outshine the hearers in terms of their knowledge, or realization, until the seventh ground.

149 For the opponents this is true: the hearers and solitary realizers do not realize the selflessness of phenomena, therefore they have not fully understood how all phenomena lack inherent nature.

150 The part of the sentence from "just as" onward contains the traditional element called the concordant example *(tun pe/mthun dpe)*. The concordant example is used to prove how the reason necessitates or entails the predicate. "Worldly freedom from attachment" refers to the fourth, or highest, meditative concentration of the form

realm, which is experienced within saṃsāra. It proves that the reason entails the predicate, because people who have gained freedom from worldly attachment have not fully understood that things lack inherent nature, and for that reason they are inferior to bodhisattvas in terms of realization. (ALTG/ATW)

151 This is an undesirable proposition for the opponents, because it is universally accepted that arhats completely relinquish all mental afflictions.

152 This refers to the highest level of the formless realm, called "the peak of existence." This is the level, according to the Buddhist presentation, attained by deities such as Īshvara. The peak of existence entails the mental afflictions of saṃsāra since it is not beyond the three realms and individuals who have achieved the peak of existence do not realize the true nature of phenomena. (ALTG)

153 Those who assert that the hearers, etc. do not realize phenomenal selflessness say that the arhats realize that the aggregates, sources, and constituents are devoid of a self of persons, but they do not realize the emptiness of the aggregates themselves. They apprehend them as being impermanent, selfless, of the nature of suffering, and so on.

154 The translations of the *Precious Garland* quotations were greatly assisted and informed by Hopkins 2007.

155 Clinging to the aggregates, clinging to an "I," and the creation of karma.

156 From the *Precious Garland*.

157 Being distinct from each other or being merged.

158 An epithet of the Buddha.

159 From the *Precious Garland*.

160 In the approach to liberation of the lower vehicles, the Buddha taught karma and mental afflictions as things of which one's mindstream must be "emptied" or "exhausted," without placing much emphasis on the fact that the karma and mental afflictions are, from the very outset, "empty" or "exhausted" of their own inherent existence. Therefore this quotation is teaching that, though the approaches of these two vehicles are different, the exhaustion sought after by aspirants of the lower vehicle is indeed of the same quality as the emptiness that is taught in the Mahāyāna as the nonarising nature of all phenomena. The difference in approach is that in the Mahāyāna exhaustion is viewed as the nature of such phenomena as karma and mental afflictions from the very outset, as opposed to a reality that only becomes true at the time of attaining the result of individual liberation.

161 From *Fundamental Wisdom*.

162 From Nāgārjuna's *Praise to the Transcendent*.

163 In this section of his *Ṭīkā*, Mikyö Dorje examines two views held by "some Tibetan masters." The first view holds that there is a difference of extensiveness regarding what is to be proven—the selflessness of phenomena. The second view holds that this distinction applies to the means of proof—the logical reasonings that prove phenomenal selflessness. He says that the first of these views is untenable because the selflessness of phenomena is not established from its own side; therefore no distinction of brevity or extensiveness could apply to it. Furthermore, all three types of noble beings (hearers, solitary realizers, and bodhisattvas) realize the exact same phenomenal selflessness, which is nothing other than the nonexistence of phenomena's true characteristics, which all ordinary beings mistakenly perceive as being real. Secondly, Mikyö Dorje notes that a difference in the extensiveness of reasonings cannot be the

difference between the vehicle of the hearers and the Mahāyāna : if hearers realized phenomenal selflessness on the basis of a brief presentation of reasonings, followers of Mahāyāna would have no need for more extensive reasonings. The extensive proofs of selflessness in the Mahāyāna would merely be redundant. The actual difference in extensiveness between the views of the lower vehicles and the Mahāyāna lies in the extent to which the relationship between appearing phenomena *(chöchen/chos can)* and the true nature of phenomena *(chönyi/chos nyid)* is realized. Hearers and solitary realizers realize phenomenal selfless in relation to the aggregates, sources, and constituents of their own personal continua and in relation to the uncontaminated truth of the path. Bodhisattvas, on the other hand, realize the selflessness of phenomena in relation to countless appearing phenomena of the relative truth—buddha nature, infinite buddhas in infinite atoms, and more. Buddhas, moreover, cognize phenomenal selflessness in relation to all relative phenomena, including the kāyas and buddha wisdoms.

164 I.e., great compassion and the realization of emptiness.

165 The Tibetan term for "perfection" *(parol tu chinpa/pha rol tu phyin pa, Skt. pāramitā)* literally means "gone to the other side" or "gone to the other shore."

166 There are seven nonvirtuous actions of body and speech: three for body (taking life, stealing, and sexual misconduct) and four for speech (harsh speech, inciting discord, lying, and idle chatter). The three virtuous actions of mind are relinquishing the three nonvirtuous mental actions (covetousness, malicious intent, and wrong view).

167 The ten virtuous actions are to refrain from the ten nonvirtuous actions or, alternatively, to practice the opposite of the ten nonvirtuous actions.

168 A corpse will float on the surface of the ocean and then be tossed to the shore.

169 *Narsem kyi ngöpo gu/mnar sems kyi dngos po dgu*: The following nine thoughts: 1) my enemy has harmed me, 2) my enemy is harming me, 3) my enemy will harm me, 4) my enemy has harmed my friend, 5) my enemy is harming my friend, 6) my enemy will harm my friend, 7) my enemy has assisted my other enemy, 8) my enemy is assisting my other enemy, and 9) my enemy will assist my other enemy. (GTCD)

170 Literally, "It binds one in relationships with nongenuine beings."

171 These are four levels of concentration in the form realm. They are simply called the first concentration, the second concentration, the third concentration, and the fourth concentration.

172 The four formless absorptions are four absorption states of the formless realm: 1) limitless space, 2) limitless consciousness, 3) utter nonexistence, and 4) not existence, not nonexistence.

173 Loving-kindness *(jampa/byams pa)*, compassion *(nyingje/snying rje)*, joy *(gawa/dga' ba)*, and impartiality *(tang-nyom/btang snyoms)*.

174 The five higher cognitions are 1) the miraculous higher cognition, 2) the divine eye, 3) the divine ear, 4) recollection of previous states, and 5) knowing the minds of others.

175 Realizing "unmoving interdependence" *(tendrel powa mepa/rten 'brel pho ba med pa)* refers to realizing the emptiness for the bases of the twelve links of interdependent arising and therefore being free from the forward progression *(lugjung/lugs 'byung)* of the twelve links. Realizing the "nondisintegration of interdependence" refers to the same insight producing the result of being free from the reverse progression *(lukdog/lugs ldog)* of the twelve links. (ALTG/ATW)

THE KARMAPA'S MIDDLE WAY

176 Generosity, discipline, and patience.

177 "Marked by one hundred merits" means that the forms of the buddhas, which display attributes such as the major and minor marks of enlightenment, bear the signs of having accumulated a limitless amount of merit.

178 I.e., wisdom.

179 During the explanation of verse 3.1.

180 See p. 760, note 549.

181 The devaputra māras are said to be children of the desire realm gods who, due to their jealousy, interfere with other beings' virtuous actions.

182 Mikyö Dorje cites the example of the teaching on "the eleven truths" in *The Sūtra on the Five Grounds of Bodhisattvas (Sempa Sa Ngape Do/sems dpa' sa lnga pa'i mdo)* and states that those eleven can also be placed into the categories of the two truths.

183 I.e., Nāgārjuna.

184 "Glorious" *(Shrī, Pal/dpal)* is a name that Nāgārjuna received upon his monastic ordination. (Dzogchen Ponlop Rinpoche 2004, p. 15)

185 Another way of referring to the *Fundamental Wisdom of the Middle Way (Mūlamadhyamakakārikā, Uma Tsawa Sherab/dbu ma rtsa ba shes rab).*

186 The Buddhist philosophical systems of the Particularists, Sutra-Followers, and Proponents of Consciousness.

187 Rendawa Shönu Lodrö *(Red mda' ba gzhon nu blo gros,* 1349-1412) was an early Tibetan master who composed a commentary to the *Entrance to the Middle Way* entitled *A Lamp to Illuminate Suchness: An Explanation of the* Entrance to the Middle Way *(dbu ma la 'jug pa'i rnam bshad de kho na nyid gsal ba'i sgron ma).* This commentary is widely regarded as authoritative in the Tibetan lineages of the Middle Way.

188 The four extremes are as expressed in the above theses refuting arising from the four extremes. Alternatively, the four extremes can be listed as existence, nonexistence, both, and neither. The eight extremes are those listed by Nāgārjuna in his *Fundamental Wisdom's* opening praise: cessation *(gakpa/'gag pa)*, arising *(kyewa/skye ba)*, nihilism *(chepa/chad pa)*, eternalism *(takpa/rtag pa)*, coming *(ongwa/'ong ba)*, going *(drowa/'gro ba)*, singularity *(chik/gcig)*, and multiplicity *(tade/tha dad).*

189 I.e., the only perspective from which they say they are Consequentialists is the perspective of others, not their own perspective.

190 The four fearlessnesses of buddhas are listed and explained in the commentary to verse 6.210cd, pp. 480–481.

191 Lochen Kyapchok Palzang composed a commentary to the *Entrance to the Middle Way* entitled *A Thorough Clarification of Suchness as Elucidated in the Ocean of Scriptures: An Extensive Explanation of the* Entrance to the Middle Way *(dbu ma la 'jug pa'i rgya cher bshad pa gsung rab rgya mtsho'i de kho na nyid rab tu gsal ba).*

192 This is challenging material. Readers may wish to read this entire section three or more times if they have difficulty understanding some sections on the first read.

193 A reference to Tsongkapa and his commentators in the Geluk tradition.

194 The valid cognition of the power of things *(ngöpo topshuk kyi tsema/dngos po stob zhugs kyi tshad ma)* is a system of valid cognition in which things, at least conventionally, are regarded as holding their own qualities objectively. For someone who accepts this valid cognition, fire really is hot and burning. Those properties exist in fire and nowhere else; they are testament to the objective "power" of fire. (ATW) Mikyö Dorje describes the "power of things" as the notion that things perform a function

by virtue of their own, real nature, not by depending on other things. The function as well is viewed as being real. (*Ṭīkā*, p. 137)

195 An example of this category is the statement, "Sound, the subject, is impermanent, because it is produced," directed at a Vedantin. The reason (or "inference"), that sound is produced, is accepted by or renowned to the Vedantins themselves.

196 An example of this category is Chandrakīrti's use of consequences in his refutation of arising from other: if things arose from inherently different things, it would follow that darkness could arise from candle flames, because darkness is different from the candle flames. The reason is logically included in the predicate, but the predicate itself is undesirable for someone who accepts arising from other. This absurd consequence highlights the self-contradictions inherent in the view of arising from other. This reasoning is similar to *reductio ad absurdum* in Western philosophy.

197 Neutrality through equivalence means that the opponents' reason is neutral, or powerless, because it equally proves the position opposite to their own. For example, someone might try to logically prove that there are no past or future lives because they cannot be perceived at present. However, their reasoning can equally be used to support the opposite position: the nonexistence of past and future lives cannot be established, because it cannot be seen at present.

198 The reason given is only a reiteration of the predicate and does nothing more to prove it. Chandrakīrti and the Karmapa highlight this fault as it applies to the Proponents of Consciousness at verse 6.68abc, p. 264.

199 This refers to the Consequentialists' own lack of a thesis.

200 In the *Ṭīkā*, Karmapa Mikyö Dorje says that, firstly, the assertion that the Autonomists accept the perceptions and inferences of ordinary beings as valid cognitions is misleading. Even though they do use such presentations *to communicate with* ordinary beings, they do not hold such presentations as being authentic valid cognition from their own side as Followers of the Middle Way. Mikyö Dorje then uses quotations from Bhāvaviveka and Kamalashīla (both Autonomist masters) to corroborate this. He also discusses in detail how the Autonomists do not use logic in the same manner as Dignāga and Dharmakīrti. See Brunnhölzl 2004, pp. 341-360, for an extensive discussion of this topic based on several passages from Mikyö Dorje.

201 The main progenitor of what came to be known in Tibet as the Autonomist school.

202 The quotation is truncated in Wangchuk Dorje's text and appears here as it appears in the *Ṭīkā*.

203 The quotation is truncated in Wangchuk Dorje's text and appears here as it appears in the *Ṭīkā*.

204 Reading *rang sde* for *rang cag* in the Tibetan.

205 This refers to the Consequentialists' approach of using their counterparts' own reasoning in order to show the latter their own mistakes.

206 The *Fundamental Wisdom of the Middle Way*.

207 The contention that either Buddhapālita or Bhāvaviveka was a direct disciple of Nāgārjuna seems to be at odds with most modern Western scholarship. It also does not seem to be held by many contemporary Tibetan masters.

208 Who follow the approach to logic of Bhāvaviveka.

209 Who follow the approach to logic of Buddhapālita.

210 The Consequentialist Follower of the Middle Way.

211 For the purpose of engaging with their counterparts, the Consequentialists temporarily assume that the subject and so on are established by valid cognition.

212 That subjects, predicates, and reasons are neither established by reasoning consciousnesses analyzing the ultimate truth nor are they established by the noble ones' wisdom of meditative equipoise.

213 That "conventional valid cognition" is itself not even valid cognition.

214 This verse is found in the refutation of the Proponents of Consciousness on p. 282.

215 Presumably a reference to Chandrakīrti's autocommentary to the *Entrance to the Middle Way*.

216 See Appendix I for the corresponding section of Chandrakīrti's *Lucid Words*.

217 This corresponds to section I (p. 580) of the *Lucid Words* Appendix.

218 Chandrakīrti's commentary to the *Fundamental Wisdom of the Middle Way*.

219 Here Chandrakīrti, in *Lucid Words*, is quoting Buddhapālita from the latter's commentary to *Fundamental Wisdom*, conveniently entitled *Buddhapālita*.

220 See the corresponding footnote in Appendix I for an explanation of why "endless" appears here instead of "absurd."

221 I.e., that being established at the time of their cause would not entail or necessitate the pointlessness of their arising.

222 They must arise again or, in other words, transform from the state of being unmanifest to the state of being manifest.

223 This corresponds to section II (p. 580) of the *Lucid Words* Appendix.

224 Here Chandrakīrti, in *Lucid Words*, is quoting Bhāvaviveka from the latter's commentary to *Fundamental Wisdom*, entitled *Lamp of Wisdom (Prajñāpradīpa, Sherab Drönma/shes rab sgron ma)*.

225 I.e., probative arguments the properties of which are established for both the defender and the challenger.

226 The "inclusion" is the capacity of the reason to prove the predicate. In this case, however, the Karmapa uses "inclusion" mainly to point to the faults that Bhāvaviveka perceives in the predicate itself, as formulated by Buddhapālita. In the following paragraph the Karmapa will paraphrase Bhāvaviveka's criticism of the "subject-quality," which essentially means the validity of the reason itself. In short, Bhāvaviveka says that Buddhapālita has an inclusion that is contradictory and a subject-quality that is not established.

227 The Enumerators hold that clearly manifest results—not results that exist in an unclear way at the time of their causes—arise from themselves, i.e., from their own essential nature, which exists in causes. Therefore if Buddhapālita's statement holds the implication that Bhāvaviveka claims it does, it does nothing to disprove the Enumerators' position. Thus it contradicts the thesis that things do not arise from themselves. According to Bhāvaviveka, Buddhapālita should have established this thesis through an autonomous reasoning—a formal statement of logic whose subject-quality, inclusion, and example are accepted by both parties of the debate—rather than through consequences alone.

228 This refers to Buddhapālita's statement that, "Things that already exist by way of their own identity do not need to arise again." If this is construed by the Enumerators as Bhāvaviveka suggests it would be, it is problematic, since, for the Enumerators, clearly manifest results *do not* arise again, once they are manifest. For the Enumerators, the notion of "arising from self" is the arising or "manifesting" of a result from a cause that bears the result's "own identity" or "essential nature."

229 See note 228.

230 The "branches of affirmation" are the subject-quality, the inclusion, and an example that upholds the inclusion.

231 And, as we saw in the quotation from *Lucid Words* that began this section, Bhāvaviveka also claims that Buddhapālita's consequence implies that things arise from others. This is explained in the next paragraph.

232 This corresponds to section III (p. 580) of the *Lucid Words* Appendix.

233 In the case of "... because it does not employ arguments or examples," the full reasoning would be "That [refutation] is illogical, because it does not employ arguments or examples."

234 This corresponds to section IV (p. 581) of the *Lucid Words* Appendix.

235 Accepting and maintaining a position of the "nonexistence" of arising from self would, in the context of analysis of the actual state of things, be a conceptual elaboration.

236 Here the Karmapa makes a commentary on the two Nāgārjuna verses that Chandrakīrti includes in this section of *Lucid Words*. He ties the meaning of the verses specifically to Bhāvaviveka's critique of Buddhapālita, with Buddhapālita, rather than Nāgārjuna, speaking in the voice of the first person.

237 This corresponds to section V (p. 581) of the *Lucid Words* Appendix.

238 This corresponds to section VI (p. 582) of the *Lucid Words* Appendix.

239 This follows Chandrakīrti's assertion that Buddhapālita's original consequence statement, "Things do not arise from themselves, because their arising would be pointless and their arising would be endless," *implied* a five-part probative argument, as Chandrakīrti presented in *Lucid Words* and as the Karmapa sets forth below.

240 See footnote 653 (pp. 583–584 in the *Lucid Words* Appendix) for an explanation of how the traditional Indian five-membered probative argument, along with an example from traditional Indian Buddhist logic, is used here. Observe also how the Karmapa simplifies the words in comparison with Chandrakīrti's original phrasing.

241 I.e., number two, "because they already exist by way of their own identity."

242 The Enumerators would not criticize an argument that they themselves accept.

243 The example accepted by others is the "clearly manifest vase." This is something that the Enumerators accept as not needing to arise again. It is the example that Buddhapālita uses to uphold the inclusion of his reason, "because they [already] exist by way of their own identity," which in turn affirms his thesis, that *all* things do not arise from themselves. Just as a clearly appearing vase, since it already exists by way of its own identity, does not need to arise again, so all things—including unmanifest results such as vases when they are lumps of clay—because of existing (according to the Enumerators) by way of their own identity even at the time of their causes, do not need to arise again. Buddhapālita thus uses an argument or reason and an example that are accepted by the Enumerators to force them to accept a thesis that they had not previously accepted.

244 This corresponds to section VII (p. 585) of the *Lucid Words* Appendix.

245 Arising from self, arising from other, arising from both, and causeless arising.

246 Bhāvaviveka is asking about Buddhapālita's consequence statement, "Things, the subject, do not arise from themselves, because their arising would be pointless and because their arising would be endless." The "predicate" of the consequence refers to things "not arising from themselves." According to Bhāvaviveka's thinking, the standard rules of inferential valid cognition that apply to probative arguments (guide-

lines that come mainly from the tradition of Dignāga and Dharmakīrti) dictate that the opposite of the predicate must be true in relation to the opposite of the reason. Consider the classic Buddhist probative argument, "Sound, the subject, is impermanent, because it is produced." In that example, that which is not produced is necessarily not impermanent. Bhāvaviveka attempts to extend this general logic principle of probative arguments to the predicate of Buddhapālita's consequence statement. To Bhāvaviveka, a statement of not arising from self because of being produced pointlessly and endlessly would necessitate accepting arising from other because of being produced sensibly and in a limited way.

247 According to Bhāvaviveka, Buddhapālita implies an acceptance of arising from other. Arising from other is one of the four extreme types of arising, whereas Followers of the Middle Way wish to be free from all four extremes.

248 The reverse inclusion of Buddhapālita's consequence would be: that which arises from itself necessarily is something whose arising is not endless. This inclusion is accepted by the Enumerators. Bhāvaviveka, in what seems a fanciful interpretation, suggests that the reversal of the predicate "not arising from self" is arising from other.

249 In other words, one does not need to prove that "things do not arise from themselves." One need only demonstrate the absurdity of the wrong thought that "things arise from themselves."

250 This corresponds to section VIII (p. 586) of the *Lucid Words* Appendix.

251 The example given by Chandrakīrti in a different section of *Lucid Words* (which is used by Karmapa Mikyö Dorje in the *Ṭīkā*) is a quotation from Nāgārjuna's *Fundamental Wisdom*, 13.1, from which the probative argument, "Conditioned phenomena, the subject, are delusive, because they are deceptive," may be extracted. There, Nāgārjuna is addressing a counterpart who accepts the inclusion that whatever is deceptive is necessarily delusive and who accepts that conditioned phenomena are deceptive. Instead of relying on an absurd consequence, Nāgārjuna uses a probative argument to make the final link between conditioned phenomena and what is delusive. This approach means the same thing as a consequence that demonstrates the absurdity of a view that conditioned phenomena are free from delusion.

252 According to Mikyö Dorje, Shākya Chokden holds the view that, on the level of conduct, Consequentialists follow the Proponents of Things by stating autonomous arguments to avoid the extreme of nonexistence. However, Mikyö Dorje explains that although the Consequentialists avoid the extreme of nonexistence by using reasonings that seem similar to those of the Proponents of Things, this does not mean that they accept those reasonings from their own perspective. To think that the use of identical reasonings must entail the same assertions from one's own perspective is, according to Mikyö Dorje, a view lacking in subtlety.

253 The example means that the sky is beyond being washed or not washed, so it is incorrect to say that there are times when it is or is not being washed, regardless of whether rain falls or not. In the same way, the Consequentialists are always free from any assertions whatsoever in terms of their own perspective, so it is incorrect to say that there are times when they have their own assertions and times when they do not, regardless of the fact that they sometimes use reasoning in a manner similar to the Proponents of Things.

254 This corresponds to section IX (p. 587 of the *Lucid Words* Appendix.

255 This corresponds to section X (p. 587) of the *Lucid Words* Appendix.

256 The Karmapa seems to abbreviate the quotation slightly here, as it appears with the following additional phrases in *Lucid Words*: "it is not transformed by time; it does not originate from subtle particles; it does not originate from its 'original nature.'"

257 In this section of the *Ṭīkā* Karmapa Mikyö Dorje alludes to the explanations of conventional valid cognition in the tradition of Tsongkapa (a master of the "later" period), who, according to Mikyö Dorje, misreads the system of Chandrakīrti by insisting that, for Consequentialists, appearing subjects such as sprouts—the bases for Middle Way reasonings such as "beyond one and many"—are established on the relative level by conventional valid cognition.

258 "Authoritative" translates *tsema/tshad ma*, usually rendered as "valid cognition." Thus the Karmapa is describing the different types of valid cognition through which Bhāvaviveka's approach to logic is undermined.

259 This corresponds to section XI (p. 590) of the *Lucid Words* Appendix.

260 "Name and form" is the fourth in the twelve links of dependent arising. "The inner sense sources" is the fifth link.

261 Bhāvaviveka would say that the "relative" distinction would be contradictory for the hearers, because the hearers assert that the Buddha taught the inner sense sources and their causes as ultimate truths.

262 As was explained above, in Bhāvaviveka's probative argument, "Ultimately, the inner sense sources do not arise from themselves, because they exist," the existence of the sense sources is unascertainable, because, when asked to explain whether he means to say that they exist ultimately or relatively, if he says they exist ultimately, then he contradicts himself; if he says they exist relatively, his subject and reason are not established for his counterparts, the Enumerators. This criticism of Bhāvaviveka's reasoning precisely mirrors the criticisms that he leveled against the hearers.

263 This corresponds to section XII (p. 593) of the *Lucid Words* Appendix.

264 The following verses seem to have been composed by Wangchuk Dorje himself, as they do not appear in the *Ṭīkā*.

265 A reference to Chandrakīrti ("Chandra" being the Sanskrit for "moon").

266 A reference to the Eighth Karmapa, Mikyö Dorje.

267 Reading *btsan dug* for *btsun dud* in the fourth line of the Tibetan.

268 The example of a clearly appearing vase is used because it is a phenomenon that the Enumerators accept exists by way of its own identity and does not need to arise again. The example forces the Enumerators to accept that manifest results do not arise from "themselves"—nonmanifest results—since they accept that those nonmanifest results already exist by way of their own identity and, as such, are in no further need of arising. The reasoning used to defeat the Enumerators in this context was explained extensively beginning with the section entitled "Setting forth the system of Buddhapālita" (p. 169).

269 In other words, if you say, "We do assert that results arise from their own essential nature that exists in their cause, but that does not necessitate the consequence that you draw, which is that already-arisen seeds arise from already-arisen seeds."

270 In other words, contrary to simply seeds producing sprouts, it would absurdly follow that seeds would produce seeds, which would produce seeds, etc.

271 This is an example of something that the Enumerators accept as not canceling itself out or causing its own disintegration.

272 This is an example of a type of seed and a type of sprout that the Enumerators accept

as being of different substance due to having different attributes such as taste, color, and so forth. The implication is that plantain tree sprouts are different from plantain tree seeds, and therefore have different attributes.

273 An "excluding qualifier" is a distinction drawn for the purpose of excluding qualities or phenomena, as opposed to emphasizing what qualities the distinction might include. Its opposite is the "including qualifier" *(yongchö/yongs gcod)*. As the section on the Consequentialist-Autonomist distinction explains, Bhāvaviveka wishes to *exclude* the possibility of refuting conventional arising or arising from the worldly perspective.

274 As the Karmapa has previously explained, worldly people do not analyze such notions of things "arising from themselves" or "arising from others." Worldly people simply think, "results arise from causes," which is different from entertaining a philosophical speculation, even conventionally, of "arising from other."

275 Throughout the commentary, "other" *(shen/gzhan)* is sometimes replaced by "different" for the sake of variety. No difference in meaning is implied.

276 The six causes are 1) enabling causes *(je-gyu/byed rgyu)*, 2) simultaneously arising causes *(lhenchik jungwe gyu/lhan cig 'byung ba'i rgyu)*, 3) causes of a similar outcome *(kalnyam gyi gyu/skal mnyam gyi rgyu)*, 4) congruent causes *(tsungden gyi gyu/mtshungs ldan gyi rgyu)*, 5) omnipresent causes *(kundrö gyu/kun 'gro'i rgyu)*, and 6) completely ripening causes *(nam-min gyi gyu/rnam smin gyi rgyu)*.

277 The "last type of arhat" refers to the "arhat without remainder," who passes into nirvāṇa without the five aggregates.

278 I.e., nowhere is it seen that bright flames are produced by thick darkness.

279 In this case the hearers' probandum (what they are trying to prove) is that causes produce results and that causes and results are different from each other. The reason given to prove the probandum is "because the definitiveness is perceptible." Here Chandrakīrti and the Karmapa charge that the reason, definitiveness being perceptible, is just a reiteration of the probandum, that causes and results are other. The hearers' argument amounts to saying, "We are certain that causes truly produce results, because we are certain." Mikyö Dorje's commentary in the *Ṭīkā* on this point is helpful: "If you say, '[The definitiveness] is established, because it seen directly by the eyes,' it is true that the eyes see rice seeds and rice sprouts. Yet they do not see a difference in substance between the seed and sprout, nor do they see [the latter] arising from [the former]."

280 These are outlined in the *Ṭīkā*, where in particular the view the early Tibetan master Chapa Chökyi Senge *(phyva pa chos kyi seng ge, 1109-1169)*, who claimed that the Middle Way refutation of the hearers did not speak to the essential points of the hearers' assertions, is examined. Also refuted is the notion that arising from other is to be accepted conventionally, whereas only the other three possibilities of arising are to be refuted in both truths.

281 In other words, the logicians of this school are suggesting that the "otherness" of causes and results is established in a context of earlier and later moments, not in a context of simultaneity.

282 The example of Maitreya and Upagupta illustrates the relationship between any two given persons: two people can be established as being different from each other in mutual dependence, but two people who exist simultaneously cannot be in a cause-result relationship.

283 Here it is being proposed that the eye consciousness is the cause, and the mind and mental events, such as feelings, that go along with it are its results.

284 The usage of the phrase "and so on" here indicates the proposed applicability of this reasoning to all other engaging consciousnesses in relation to their own specific faculties (i.e., ear, nose, tongue, etc.), observed objects, and resultant mental events.

285 Literally, "The Naked Ones."

286 In the *Ṭīkā*, Mikyö Dorje explains that the Enumerators, Particularists, and some Tibetans assert that an existent result arises; that the Differentiators, the Followers of Sūtra, and the Performers of Yogic Conduct assert that a nonexistent result arises; and that the Jains assert that a result that is both existent and nonexistent arises.

287 A reference to the Gelukpa lineage and, in particular, to the views of Tsongkapa and his interpreters.

288 "Diseased vision" is a rough translation of *rab-rib*, an ailment of the eyes that is difficult to correlate with the terminology of modern medicine. Symptoms of *rab-rib* include seeing false apparitions of falling hairs.

289 For example, the horns of a rabbit may be thought of, but since they do not appear in the common worldly perspective, there is no label "horns of a rabbit" used conventionally for the purpose of adopting or rejecting.

290 This statement appears to refer to verses 6.24 through 6.26 and their autocommentary by Chandrakīrti.

291 The reason, horses and oxen created by magicians' spells being established by the consciousness that apprehends them, does not affirm the predicate: that the Autonomists establish the relative truth as a genuine object from their own perspective.

292 In other words, not only would their reasoning not prove what they were trying to prove, it would prove the opposite. Here an anonymous interlocutor is suggesting that, because of the Autonomists' saying that an illusion-horse exists for the consciousness perceiving it (whose faculties have been adulterated by the spells of a magician), the Autonomists affirm the existence of relative phenomena using relative valid cognition. According to the Consequentialists, however, that same reason (an illusion-horse existing for the adulterated consciousness that perceives it) would prove the opposite: it would prove that the Autonomists affirm the fact that the relative truth is incorrect or confused, because the example is one of a confused consciousness apprehending a nonexistent object. So the original reasoning proves that even the Autonomists hold that the phenomena of the relative truth are not perceptible by any valid cognition.

293 The appearance of strands of hair to someone with diseased vision is an example of the incorrect relative. Though the hairs appear real and valid to the people perceiving them, there is no benefit in according them any status of valid existence, even conventionally.

294 Mikyö Dorje's comments at this section of the *Ṭīkā* are helpful: "[The same appearances] deceive naïve beings, but for noble beings they are the mere relative—illusion-like, dependent arisings."

295 In other words, the notion that clinging to true existence necessarily constitutes an afflictive, as opposed to a cognitive, obscuration.

296 The example is illustrating the tendency to criticize that which is free of fault, spending efforts that just end up spoiling what was originally unproblematic. In the section of the *Ṭīkā* that corresponds to this one, Mikyö Dorje also includes Gorampa

Sönam Senge with Zilungpa. Remarkably, Mikyö Dorje implicitly indicates that he and Tsongkapa agree on this issue and explicitly faults Zilungpa and Gorampa for attacking Tsongkapa. This section of the *Ṭīkā* thus constitutes a rare instance of Mikyö Dorje defending Tsongkapa from the criticisms of others.

297 I.e., hearers, solitary realizers, and bodhisattvas.

298 "Tanakpa" is used here as an alternative name for Gorampa Sönam Senge (*go rams pa bsod nams seng ge*, 1429-1489), the great Middle Way master of the Sakya lineage. Gorampa and Mikyö Dorje agree on many points in their commentaries on the *Entrance to the Middle Way*, such as whether the two truths are the same or different in entity (both masters say that the two truths are beyond being the same or different due to the reason of mutually depending on each other for their own designations) and whether there is a difference between Consequentialists and Autonomists with regard to the correct and incorrect relative (both masters say that the Consequentialists and Autonomists posit these categories in the same fashion). The issue at hand here—whether there is a difference with regard to the ontological status of the relative truth and the conventional truth—brings to light a key point on which the two masters differ. The passage of Gorampa referenced here is found in his commentary to the *Entrance to the Middle Way* entitled *Dispelling Bad Views: A Sectional Outline of the Entrance to the Middle Way and an Analysis of Each of the Text's Difficult Points (Uma Jugpe Kyü kyi Sabchepa dang Shung Sosö Kawe Ne la Chepa Tawa Ngensel/dbu ma 'jug pa'i dkyus kyi sa bcad pa dang\ gzhung so so'i dka ba'i gnas la dpyad pa lta ba ngan sel)* (Gorampa Sönam Senge 1979, p. 608). Whereas Gorampa distinguishes between what is "conventional" and what is "relative," Mikyö Dorje and Wanghcuk Dorje seem to treat the two terms as synonyms. Another point on which Mikyö Dorje and Gorampa differ is explained above in a footnote to the discussion regarding Zilungpa's position on whether afflictive obscurations pervade clinging to true existence.

299 Gorampa seems to be classifying relative *truth* into the two categories of correct relative *truth* and false relative *truth*, with the latter category being composed of phenomena that would not qualify as *existents*. The Karmapa, however, and as explained in the text, holds the false relative as not belonging to the relative *truth* at all.

300 For Chandrakīrti, "valid" means "without any error," which would refer to a consciousness free from ignorance of any kind whatever.

301 The implication is, "If the perceiving subjects of worldly people do not realize the true nature or actual status of a given object—emptiness of inherent nature—then those perceiving subjects cannot be said to be valid cognizers, because they are unaware of the object's true nature."

302 The anonymous interlocutor here is meant to portray Tsongkapa and his commentators in the Geluk lineage.

303 The second half of the sentences here would contain the meaning of the last three lines of verse 6.30.

304 Persons and trees are phenomena that *are* different from each other, but they do not, and cannot, depend on each other for production. In the same way, if boys and trees and their seeds were inherently different, it would be impossible for them to depend on their seeds for their own production.

305 This heading first appeared on p. 192.

306 The quotation is truncated in Wangchuk Dorje's text and appears here as it is found in this section of the *Ṭīkā*. Wangchuk Dorje's text concludes the truncated quota-

tion by saying, "Thus, [the Buddha] taught up through wishlessness" (the first three focuses of the quotation being the components of the "three doors of liberation").

307 Tsongkapa and his commentators in the Geluk lineage.

308 "That which has a bulbous belly, is thin at its bottom, and performs the function of carrying water" is the traditional definition for "vase" used in Tibetan debate courts. "Vase" is one of the most common examples used by the Indo-Tibetan logical tradition for a function-performing thing.

309 This heading first appeared on p. 192.

310 "Mirrors and faces" is a reference to the causes and conditions for a reflection to appear; "wood, pebbles, and spells" is a reference to the causes and conditions for an illusion to appear. Indian and Tibetan texts speak of magicians applying spells to a stone or a piece of wood in order to project the appearances of horses, oxen, etc.

311 "Emanations" *(trulpa/sprul pa)* here conveys a lack of solidity: "something ethereal arising from something ethereal."

312 George Churinoff's translation of Chandrakīrti's autocommentary explains that Druma *(Jönpa/ljon pa)* is a king of a class of spirits called "kinnaras" *(mi-am chi/ mi'am ci)* and appears frequently in the sūtras in conversations with the Buddha. (Chandrakīrti 1994, p. 108, note 95)

313 A reference to the positions of Tsongkapa that a thing called postdisintegration *(shigpa/zhig pa)* serves as the connection between actions and their results. "Postdisintegration" is used here as an experimental translation of *zhig pa* because of the emphasis placed on *zhig pa* as the past-tense form of *jigpa/'jig pa,* "to disintegrate."

314 6.37 and 6.38ab and the commentary to those verses.

315 Minds or consciousnesses that are not tainted by faulty sense faculties.

316 Maja is considered an "Early Follower of the Middle Way" *(dbu ma snga ma)* and was a student of the famed early Tibetan logician, Chaba Chökyi Senge *(phyva pa chos kyi seng ge,* 1109-1169).

317 This is most likely a reference to Maja's commentary on the *Entrance to the Middle Way,* entitled *Brief Notes on the* Entrance to the Middle Way *(Uma la Jugpe Chenbu/ dbu ma la 'jug pa'i mchan bu).*

318 In brief, a nonimplicative negation refutes a given phenomenon without providing an opportunity for the positing of another phenomenon. The statement that "There is no eye," as is found in the *Heart Sutra,* is an example of a nonimplicative negation. An implicative negation is a negation that allows for the possibility of positing something else. A traditional example of an implicative negation is "Fat Devadatta does not eat during the day." Since he is fat it is implied that he eats. Since he does not eat during the day, the original negation implies the positive statement "Devadatta eats at night." Maja Changchub Tsöndrü and the Karmapa use these two types of negation here by saying that, in the relative truth, the arising of mere results from mere causes is implied by the negation of the notion that causes cease or disintegrate; whereas, in the ultimate truth, the negation of the cessation of causes also negates the existence of any cause or result.

319 Though this heading represents the second subsection of the heading "Though causes and results have no nature their connection is tenable," it does not appear in the Tibetan text of either Mikyö Dorje or Wangchuk Dorje's commentaries beyond its initial listing. Its insertion in this location follows the choice of the editors of the 1996 Nitartha *international* Tibetan edition of Mikyö Dorje's commentary. Mikyö Dorje's

commentary continues beyond these two paragraphs with an extensive analysis of the idea of "postdisintegration" as a function-performing thing.

320 6.39.

321 *Gongshi* (lit. "basis of intention") is an important term in discussions of what constitutes a provisional meaning teaching. When asking what the *gongshi* of a particular provisional meaning teaching is, one is essentially asking, "What did [the Buddha] *really* have in mind when he taught about such-and-such phenomenon, which does not exist but which the Buddha provisionally stated did?" Three elements must be established for a teaching to be considered provisional meaning: purpose (as in the explanation of the previous paragraph about relating to students of certain dispositions), basis of intention, and the teaching's vulnerability to refutation if taken literally *(ngö la nöje/dngos la gnod byed)*.

322 "Intention" translates the same *gongpa/dgongs pa* that is found in *gongshi/dgongs gzhi*. "Special intention" here means "an intention that reflects something other than the literal meaning of the statements themselves."

323 This is possibly a reference to one of the eighteen subsects of the hearers.

324 I.e., buddhas.

325 The next four-line verse in the Tibetan was not translated due to its unclear meaning.

326 The Tibetan for this heading, *chok ngama/phyogs snga ma*, could be literally rendered as "the preceding position."

327 It is important to note here that this root verse, along with verses 6.46 and 6.47, expresses the view of the Proponents of Consciousness. It is not the position of Chandrakīrti or the *Entrance to the Middle Way*.

328 Also translated as "false imagination."

329 Here the implicit three-part reasoning given by the Proponents of Consciousness is as follows: "The mistaken consciousness at the time of dreams, the subject, exists, because it is recalled after having awoken." In saying that the reason is not included in the predicate, Chandrakīrti and the Karmapa are saying that the dream consciousness is recalled after having awoken, but this does not mean that the dream consciousness existed.

330 Here the three-part reasoning, implicitly set forth by the Followers of the Middle Way, is: "Outer objects, the subject, would also exist, because they are also recalled, just like consciousness is recalled." If the Proponents of Consciousness say that the reason is not included in the predicate—that the reason of recollection cannot prove existence—they have undercut their own argument that consciousnesses in dreams should be considered existent phenomena.

331 Karmapa Mikyö Dorje discusses how Chandrakīrti's refutation of the Proponents of Consciousness differs from that of Bhāvaviveka and also criticizes Tsongkapa's views on this topic pertaining to what may be accepted as "existent" in the relative truth.

332 The Tibetan at this line literally reads, "For as long as one has not awoken."

333 Karmapa Mikyö Dorje continues to dissect the positions of Tsongkapa.

334 This is a reference to the sixth grammatical case in Tibetan grammar, the connecting particle *(dreldra/'brel sgra)*.

335 The possibility that "potential" is connected to a consciousness of the past or future.

336 A classic example of something that does not exist among knowable objects.

337 The commands are harbingers and causes of results to come.

338 As we saw earlier (pp. 195–197), during the general refutation of arising from other, phenomena must exist at the same time to be considered *other* or *different*. If phenomena exist at different times, such as earlier and later moments of a continuum, it is impossible for them to be other.

339 The phenomena connected to the truth of suffering and the truth of the origin of suffering.

340 The phenomena connected to the truth of cessation and the truth of the path.

341 The phrase "repetition of the thesis" here means that the Proponents of Consciousness, when making these assertions, are simply making claims that embellish or are added to their original thesis, but these claims do nothing to actually prove the original thesis—that consciousness can exist without outer objects.

342 The skeletons one is instructed to visualize do not actually exist.

343 There is no truly existent "river" there in the first place. Therefore it is unnecessary to speak of whether the river is "water" or "pus."

344 One consciousness would have to be experienced by another consciousness, which would have to be experienced by another consciousness, and so on.

345 This sentence may be an acknowledgment of the popular position, held by other masters, that self-awareness exists conventionally and that the *Entrance to the Middle Way* should be understood only to refute the *ultimate* existence of self-awareness.

346 The text literally reads "any *special* [rebuttals]."

347 This example is illustrating the same principle as the "Maitreya and Upagupta" explanation above.

348 Verse 6.32 and commentary, p. 220.

349 The quotations below appear as in the *Ṭīkā*. These translations follow those of Thurman 2004, pp. 122-123 and p. 182.

350 It is possible to read the Tibetan of the root verse as, "If the dependent nature did not exist in the slightest,/ What would be the cause of the relative?" With his statement here, however, the Karmapa refutes that reading: this verse is to be understood as a *refutation* of the Proponents of Consciousness, not as a rebuttal by them.

351 A Hindu philosophical system.

352 The quotation is truncated in Wangchuk Dorje's Tibetan, and is only mentioned, but not quoted, in the *Ṭīkā*. It appears here as it is found in Chandrakīrti's autocommentary.

353 A key doctrine of the Particularist school. The "five bases" are 1) forms, 2) primary minds, 3) mental events, 4) nonassociated formations (formations that are neither form nor mind), and 5) unconditioned phenomena.

354 A text by Bhāvaviveka for which he also composed an autocommentary

355 The quotation is truncated in Wangchuk Dorje's text and appears in full here.

356 Attainment *(tobpa/thob pa)* and nonwastage *(chü mi zawa/chud me za ba)* are doctrines of the lower philosophical systems; the all-base is a doctrine of the Proponents of Consciousness.

357 *Blaze of Reasoning* is Bhāvaviveka's autocommentary to *The Essence of the Middle Way*.

358 The term tīrthika literally means "those who support the extremes."

359 "This dharma tradition" would presumably refer to the Buddhadharma in general.

360 These verses refer to one of the Buddha's fourteen "unanswerable questions": questions that were put to the Buddha which the Buddha refused to answer because of the

basic confusion of the questioner with regard to the phenomena that were the subjects of the question. One of these questions was, "Does the Tathāgata exist after passing into parinirvāṇa or not?" Therefore the implicit statement made by Nāgārjuna in
these verses seems to be, "The buddhas do not hold any position of the Tathāgata's
existing or not existing after parinirvāṇa, because they are free from all views of the
Tathāgata's existence or nonexistence in the first place. If you wish to have an answer
to your question, you should ask a philosopher who holds positions of existence or
nonexistence. They might be able to be creative enough to offer you an answer based
on their own confused concepts."

361 *Sang-gye (sangs rgyas)* is the Tibetan word for Buddha and/or buddhahood. Its first
syllable, *sang*, literally means "to purify" or "to be cleansed of," and its second syllable,
gye, literally means "to expand," "to blossom," or "to develop."

362 The reasons why mind is foremost are explained in the section entitled "The reasons
why mind only is foremost" beginning on p. 293.

363 To simplify this, when the Buddha said mind alone is the creator of the world, he did
not intend his sayings about "mind only" to imply that form and other phenomena do
not *exist*. He simply meant to refute the notion that form and other phenomena *function* as creators in the way mind does. The distinction between mind and form is not
one of ontological status. It is one of importance with respect to karmic function.

364 This quotation is also truncated in the *Ṭīkā*.

365 This ancillary section refutes Tsongkapa's contention that deadness, *(shiwa/shi ba)*
as opposed to dying *(chiwa/'chi ba)*, is what causes the birth of the subsequent life.
Mikyö Dorje relates this assertion to Tsongkapa's more commonly repeated position,
that postdisintegration, as opposed to disintegration itself, serves as a cause for the
arising of things.

366 A pure realm in Buddhist cosmology depicted as being at the summit of the universe.

367 Therefore (to explicitly conclude the sentiment of the commentary), mind is important and to be considered foremost in comparison with other phenomena in terms of
its function.

368 This quotation is also truncated in the *Ṭīkā*.

369 "All five aggregates" is another way of saying "form and mind," because "form" refers
to the first aggregate, form, and "mind" refers to the other four aggregates: feeling,
discrimination, formation, and consciousness.

370 In order for a statement of the Buddha to be considered provisional meaning, it must
be shown to have three criteria: an *ulterior intention (gongshi/dgongs gzhi)*, something
else that the Buddha wished the beings to come to realize through the provisional
meaning; a *purpose (göpa/dgos pa)*, a positive result that will come about by describing something as existent even though it does not really exist; and a *refutation of the
literal statements (ngö la nöje/dngos la gnod byed)*, the susceptibility of the statement
to logical refutation if it is taken literally.

371 The verb for "to quote" in Tibetan is *drang/drangs*. It can also mean "to lead" and is
the same verb found in the first syllable of *drangdön/drang don*, the Tibetan term for
"provisional meaning." Thus the deeper etymology of provisional meaning, or *drang-
dön*, is that such statements by the Buddha are to be used to *lead* students to a deeper
understanding of ultimate truth. They lead students to the ultimate truth, but are not
themselves descriptions of ultimate truth.

372 "Interpreted" once again translates *drang*.

373 This quotation is truncated in Wangchuk Dorje's text and appears here as it appears in the *Ṭīkā*.

374 This is a reference to the imaginary, or imputed, nature.

375 This seems to refer to "consciousness in the way it is described by the Proponents of Consciousness."

376 Literally from the Tibetan, "The Naked Ones."

377 The "nine principles of word and meaning" of the Jains, or Naked Ones, are 1) the life force, 2) the lifeless, 3) dharma, 4) nondharma, 5) the mental afflictions, 6) vows of ethics, 7) happiness, 8) suffering, and 9) karmic formations.

378 "Maitreya" is being used as a random example of a person; there is no special correlation with Buddhism's future buddha known as Maitreya.

379 Dharma and nondharma here carry the sense of virtue and nonvirtue, i.e., what is in accordance with the genuine dharma and what is not.

380 This verse is truncated in Wangchuk Dorje's text.

381 The text uses "Proponents of Entity" here as an epithet for the Indian Chārvāka school. The Chārvākas' view is different from the assertion of arising from self, because those who assert arising from self assert that the cause and result are of the same substance. Here, however, a cause is not asserted at all: phenomena arise because of their very own entity, with no need for relation to a cause whatsoever, regardless of whether that cause is of the same or different substance as the result.

382 George Churinoff, in his translation of Chandrakīrti's autocommentary, describes "panasa" as referring to "the breadfruit or Jaka tree, *Artocarpus integrifolia*." (Chandrakīrti 1994, p. 103, note 78)

383 An example of something utterly nonexistent.

384 Another reference to the Chārvākas.

385 A meaning translation was chosen over a literal translation here because of the awkwardness of this line in Tibetan, which literally reads, "Because you possess the body, an equivalent support of that view." The commentary to this line is also rendered in a meaning translation rather than a literal translation.

386 The body is a phenomenon that, upon investigation, demonstrates the incorrectness of the Chārvākas' view.

387 This section heading first figured into the sectional outline on p. 150.

388 This section heading first figured into the sectional outline on p. 150.

389 "Unmoving" *(mi yowa/mi gyo ba)* karma is karma generated from the practice of meditation that propels one to birth in the form and formless realms.

390 I.e., beyond clinging to notions of the existence, or presence, of bewilderment (which leads to the existence, or presence, of actions or karma) and the nonexistence, or absence, of bewilderment (which leads to the nonexistence, or absence, of actions or karma).

391 An example of something utterly nonexistent

392 The quotation is truncated in Wangchuk Dorje's text and appears here as it appears in the autocommentary, as it is not adduced in the *Ṭīkā*.

393 This section heading first figured into the sectional outline on p. 150.

394 They do not find any interdependent phenomena to exist *in the first place* that could be qualified by emptiness.

395 Though not specifically referenced here, this sentence seems to refer to a quotation from the sūtras that appeared earlier in *Feast for the Fortunate*, on pp. 328–329.

396 This is the second of the "four reliances" taught by the Buddha. The first, third, and

fourth are "do not rely on the person—rely on his or her teachings," "do not rely on provisional meaning—rely on definitive meaning," and "do not rely on deluded consciousness—rely on enlightened wisdom."

397 This quotation, only one line of which appears in Wangchuk Dorje's text, is not adduced in either the *Ṭīkā* or the autocommentary. The translation follows an as yet unpublished translation by Karl Brunnhölzl.

398 The following three quotations are truncated in Wangchuk Dorje's text and appear here as they appear in the *Ṭīkā*.

399 Tsongkapa and his followers.

400 "Self" and "entities connected to the self" also correspond to the English words "me" and "mine."

401 Attachment, aggression, and ignorance.

402 A Buddhist school of the hearers.

403 A Buddhist school of the hearers.

404 Tsongkapa and his followers.

405 Some Saṃmitīyas assert a self that is the mere collection of the aggregates, while other Saṃmitīyas assert that the self is the mind.

406 The Tibetan text occasionally alternates between *kuntak/kun brtags* and its homonym, *kuntak/kun btags*, "imaginary" and "imputed," respectively. I have rendered *kun btags* as "imaginary or imputed" in this instance to alert the reader to the interchangeability of these two terms.

407 The "three methods of analysis" are analyses of three different views of imputed self: 1) the permanent, singular, and independent self imputed by the non-Buddhists, 2) the self asserted by the Saṃmitīyas to be either mind or the collection of the aggregates, and 3) the self asserted as inexpressible by the Vātsīputrīyas.

408 These "twenty peaks" are twenty views of the self and are explained in verse 6.144, p. 377.

409 See note 377 on p. 751 for a list of the nine principles. These principles are an assertion of the Chārvākas.

410 Asserted by the Particularists and the Sūtra Followers.

411 Asserted by the Sūtra Followers.

412 Asserted by the Proponents of Consciousness.

413 Asserted by the Proponents of Consciousness and some proponents of *shentong* (*gzhan stong*), or "emptiness of other."

414 Asserted by some proponents of *shentong*.

415 Asserted by Tsongkapa and his followers.

416 Asserted by Tsongkapa and his followers.

417 The following critique is aimed at Tsongkapa and his followers.

418 "Four permutations" (*mu shi/mu bzhi*) is a description, renowned in Tibetan logic, of a relationship between two categories of phenomena. If two categories of phenomena are described to have four permutations, there are some phenomena that are members of the first category but not the second, some that are members of the second but not the first, some that are members of both categories, and some that are members of neither. In this case, therefore, Tsongkapa is described by the Karmapa as holding the assertion that 1) there are instances of the view of the transitory collection that are not the view of a self, 2) there are instances of the view of a self that are not the view of the transitory collection, 3) there are phenomena that are both the view of a self

and the view of the transitory collection, and 4) there are phenomena that are neither the view of a self nor the view of the transitory collection. "Four permutations" is one of four descriptions used in Tibetan logic to identify the possible scope of relationship between any two categories. The other three are "mutually inclusive" *(dön chik/don gcig)*, wherein both categories are equivalent to each other (as in "thing" and "impermanent phenomenon"), "mutually exclusive" *(galwa/'gal ba)*, wherein the two categories share no common members (as in "impermanent phenomenon" and "permanent phenomenon"), and "three permutations" *(mu sum/mu gsum)*, wherein a larger category shares some, but not all, of its members with a smaller category, the members of which are all included in the larger category (as in "color" as a larger category and "the color red" as a smaller category).

419 Although somewhat disconcerting in English, the practice of switching between the third and second persons in the Tibetan text has been mirrored in the translation of this section in order to maintain the flow of the author's style.

420 "It would follow that it is also not a factor to be relinquished" is the thesis joined to the reasons that follow.

421 This sentence comprises "the first reason" referenced two paragraphs below in the Karmapa's commentary.

422 In other words, Tsongkapa and his followers try to make a distinction between the self that is the support for actions and their results and the self that is to be refuted by logic; but nowhere in the scriptures, says the Karmapa, can explanations about the latter self—explanations that would highlight a distinction between two different notions of self and thus grounds for Tsongkapa's claim—be found.

423 This sentence comprises "the second reason" referenced below.

424 The main consequence, as stated above, is that the view of the self, asserted by Tsongkapa, etc. to be a support for actions and results is not a factor to be relinquished.

425 The Karmapa here seems to be using two examples of food categories to illustrate what he views as an excessive fondness for categorization on the part of Tsongkapa and his followers. In the example, all the names refer to types of food, which is analogous to the view of a self and the view of a transitory collection, which the Karmapa holds to be synonyms. Splitting these categories into specific instances with the hope of drawing a substantial distinction between them, he says, is pointless.

426 "Disintegrating" refers to the present moment of things, whereas "postdisintegration" refers to the state in which things have already disintegrated. "Disintegrating thing" is, in Buddhism, a synonym for "thing," which is in general held necessarily to exist in the present moment.

427 That all things are persons that support the connection between actions and results.

428 The action would already have taken on two parts, or components, in the two types of support.

429 I.e., a consciousness apprehending the "self."

430 If you say that the object of refutation by reasons does not exist in a substantial or imputed way, but it does not necessarily follow that that it cannot be taken as an object of mind, . . .

431 If you say that that which can be taken as an object of mind does not necessarily exist among knowable objects, you lose the position of knowable objects being equivalent with that which can be taken as an object of mind. This equivalency is a traditional and basic tenet of Buddhist logic.

432 That the object of refutation by reasons exists among knowable objects.

433 Literally, "from their own side."

434 As in "Sound, the subject, is impermanent, because it is produced."

435 In the Karmapa's reading of the system of Tsongkapa, phenomena are empty of true existence, which is the object, or target, of refutation by reasons. Once this true existence is identified, the Karmapa says, its emptiness as well must be verified. In other words, "true existence," in Tsongkapa's system, would need to be verifiably shown as empty of true existence. The true existence of which it is empty would also need to be verified in a similar way. The process of verifying the emptiness of true existence of the object of refutation would thus be endless.

436 If you accept that the object of refutation must be established as emptiness in an infinite process but say that this does not mean that the object of refutation by reasons itself is not an object of refutation by reasons, . . .

437 Note explanations and translations related to the Enumerators' classification schemes in this section were greatly assisted by, and often closely follow, Hopkins 1983, pp. 321-326.

438 See two paragraphs below in the Karmapa's commentary.

439 The "sixteen" consists of five sense objects (forms, sounds, smells, tastes, and tangible objects), five "mental faculties" (the eye, ear, nose, tongue, and skin), five physical faculties (speech, arms, legs, anus, and genitalia), and the intellectual faculty *(yi/yid)*, the nature of which is both mental and physical.

440 Readers may note that "person" here translates *kyebu/skye bu* or *puruṣha*, whereas at other points in this book "person" also translates *gangzak/gang zag* or *pudgala*. The two different origin-language terms are considered in general to be synonyms.

441 In the Enumerators' system the person exists "alongside" the nature, with the nature creating everything that the person experiences.

442 See note 439.

443 Forms through tangible objects.

444 Earth, water, fire, wind, and space.

445 The five sense faculties and the five physical faculties outlined above.

446 Literally, "blessed."

447 The archaic example of "another man's wife" is drawn from old Indian culture. It refers to the shyness a married woman was said to typically feel when men who were not her husband looked at her.

448 A synonym for nature, or prakṛiti.

449 In other words, the primal matter is left with "nothing to do," since the manifestations "do not want to" arise anymore.

450 The person becomes isolated because it no longer has any objects to enjoy.

451 These three are all qualities, or different manifestations, of the I-principle.

452 Happiness corresponds with lightness, suffering corresponds with motility, and ignorance corresponds with darkness.

453 Reading *sdug bsngal gyi cha ldan rdul can dang* for *sdug bsngal gyi cha ldan rnam 'gyur can dang.*

454 Reading *skyes bu'i dbang po sogs bdag gi ba rnams* for *skyes bu'i dbang sogs bdag gi ba rnams.*

455 Literally, "Apprehension of/fixation toward 'I/me'" or "I-fixation." The phenomenon referred to by this term is the everyday thought of "I" or "me" that arises in ordinary sentient beings.

456 For the Enumerators, the person is neither a nature (i.e., a cause) nor a manifestation (i.e., a result). Therefore it is not produced and does not produce anything. Thus the reasoning of nonarising is accepted by the Enumerators.

457 The view of the transitory collection apprehends the aggregates as the self, and holding the view that the self is the aggregates entails both eternalism and nihilism. Regarding the time before nirvāṇa, one clings to eternalism by believing that the aggregates are a truly existent self. Regarding the time after nirvāṇa, one clings to nihilism by believing that the self, previously truly existent, becomes nothing at all.

458 I.e., not yield a result.

459 The verse is truncated in the Tibetan and appears in full here.

460 The fourteen things left unspoken by the Buddha, listed in condensed form in the verse below, are 1) whether the world is permanent, 2) impermanent, 3) both, or 4) neither; 5) whether the world has an end, 6) does not have an end, 7) both, or 8) neither; 9) whether the Buddha exists after passing into nirvāṇa, 10) does not exist, 11) both, or 12) neither; and 13) whether the body and life force are identical or 14) different.

461 The four noble truths are traditionally taught to have sixteen aspects, four corresponding to each truth. Selflessness is the first of the four aspects related to the truth of suffering.

462 The Saṃmitīyas and the Vātsīputrīyas.

463 That "the schools from the Particularists through the Autonomists assert that the aggregates are the basis of imputation of the self and that the self is an imputed existent."

464 That "the Consequentialists say that the aggregates are the cause of the imputation of the self, but they do not assert them to be either the basis of imputation of the self or the basis of illustration of the self."

465 The Tibetan language has an advantage in these quotations because dak/bdag, the Tibetan word for "self," can also be used as the first person pronoun.

466 The quotation is truncated in Wangchuk Dorje's text and appears here as it appears in the Ṭīkā.

467 The text literally reads "mind" (sem/sems), but it is clear that this refers to the fifth aggregate, consciousness, because of the added phrase "... and so on, the four mental aggregates."

468 Literally, "the four aggregates of name" (ming shiy pungpo/ming bzhi'i phung po).

469 I.e., the assembly of the aggregates.

470 Chandrakīrti's autocommentary adds: "However, it is not to be understood that it refutes the branch of conventional truth, that which is imputed dependently."

471 Chandrakīrti's autocommentary is very clear at this section: "The six elements are earth, water, fire, wind, space, and consciousness. In dependence upon them, one imputes the existence of the self. The six supports for contact are the contact of the eye meeting with the other constituents up through the contact of the mind meeting with other constituents. In dependence upon these, one imputes the existence of the self. The eighteen movements of mind are the six movements of happy mind (the happy movements of mind that depend on forms, sounds, smells, tastes, tangible objects, and mental phenomena), the six movements of the unhappy mind, and the six movements of the neutral mind. In dependence upon these, one imputes the existence of the self. Also, through apprehending the phenomena of primary mind and mental events, one imputes the existence of the self. Since the Buddha taught that one

imputes the existence of the self *in dependence upon* these phenomena—the elements and so on—the self cannot be these phenomena. Nor is it logical for the self to be the mere collection of those phenomena. Since none of those phenomena are suitable as the self, it is illogical to engender a conception of 'I' in relation to those phenomena. In the same way the aggregates cannot be the object for the conception of 'I.' Nor can such an object be different from the aggregates. Therefore, since the object for the conception of 'I' does not exist, yogins fully understand that the self is unobservable. They fully understand also that entities connected to the self have no essence. These yogins clear away all conditioned phenomena and, free from the appropriated aggregates, they pass into nirvāṇa. This analysis, therefore, is very beautiful."

472 In other words, the Saṃmitīyas, beyond simply saying that the process of refuting the two assertions is similar, take a further step and say that if you successfully refute the imputed self, you will have refuted—put a stop to completely—the notion of the connate self. If this were true, however, the mere understanding of how a permanent, singular, independent self does not exist would cause all sentient beings to gain liberation with very little effort. (ALTG)

473 In traditional Mahāyāna Buddhist cosmology, the ground of the universe is considered to be made of gold. The metaphor illustrates the formidable capability of ignorance to endure for a long time.

474 In other words, the twenty views of the transitory collection are innate views as opposed to imaginary or imputed views.

475 The appearance of "the Vātsīputrīyas" in this sentence follows the text of the *Ṭīkā*. Although Wangchuk Dorje's text mentions the Saṃmitīyas at the outset of this paragraph, that mention has been removed, following Mikyö Dorje, in order to make the text more internally consistent for the reader. At his commentary to verse 6.120, for example, Wangchuk Dorje clearly identifies the Vātsīputrīyas as holding the view of a self that is inexpressible in terms of being the same as or different from the aggregates. "The Vātsīputrīyas," therefore, appears as the subject of all sentences in the English translation of this section whose subject is implicitly the Vātsīputrīyas in the Tibetan text.

476 Vātsīputrīyas.

477 Literally, "It is not something not different from its parts."

478 I.e., the last two components of the sevenfold analysis: 1) the mere assembly and 2) shape.

479 The first five steps of the sevenfold reasoning, which were refuted in the previous sections of the refutation of the self of persons. Specifically, these five positions are 1) a self different from the aggregates, 2) a self identical to the aggregates, 3) a self that possesses the aggregates, 4) a self that depends on the aggregates, and 5) a self on which the aggregates depend.

480 Some versions of the Tibetan text here say ". . . at the time when the chariot is cognized . . ."

481 "Formations and sprouts" are, respectively, the results of "ignorance and seeds," ignorance being the first of the twelve links of interdependence and formations being the second.

482 The word "chariot" does not appear in the root verse, but is inserted here based on the Karmapa's commentary and on the appearance of "chariot" in verse 6.159.

483 This triad resembles the three determinants of a provisional meaning teaching (see

note 321), except it has "basis of imputation" as its first component instead of "basis of intention."

484 This sectional outline appears in a unique way (with letters, roman numerals, and italicized text) because, strictly speaking, it is not part of the main sectional outline of *Feast for the Fortunate*; it is, rather, an ancillary discussion that takes place in the section entitled "The way of explaining the conventions of objects of action and performers."

485 These are: 1) the absorption of cessation, 2) the state of nondiscrimination, 3) the absorption of nondiscrimination, 4) deep sleep, and 5) fainting.

486 This quotation, which is truncated in Wangchuk Dorje's text and appears here as it appears in the *Ṭīkā*, is actually an excerpt from a commentary on the text mentioned, not the root text. The commentary quoted here is that of Rongtön Sheja Kunzik (*rong ston shes bya kun gzigs*, 1367-1449) entitled *The Great Drum of the Gods: A Well-Condensed Explanation of* Distinguishing Phenomena from True Reality *(chos dang chos nyid rnam par 'byed pa'i rnam bshad legs par 'doms pa lha yi rnga bo che)*.

487 Also called the Drikung Gongchik (*'bri gung dgongs gcig*), this Middle Way text of the Drikung Kagyü lineage is highly revered by scholars in many other Kagyü schools, including the Karma Kagyü. The Eighth Karmapa, Mikyö Dorje, authored a commentary to this text.

488 The other two properties are both permanence and impermanence and neither permanence nor impermanence.

489 These quotations are truncated in Wangchuk Dorje's text and appear here as they appear in the autocommentary and the *Ṭīkā*.

490 This quotation proves that the self is not something stable.

491 This quotation proves that the self is not something unstable.

492 This quotation proves that the self does not arise or disintegrate.

493 This quotation proves that the self is not permanent, impermanent, both, or neither.

494 This quotation proves that the self is not the same as or different from the aggregates.

495 Literally, "Dialectic opponents who make incorrect refutations."

496 The quotation is truncated in Wangchuk Dorje's text and appears here as it appears in the *Ṭīkā* and in the autocommentary.

497 Due to highly challenging syntax in Mikyö Dorje's Tibetan poetry, the lines excerpted by Wangchuk Dorje, eleven of ninety-one Tibetan lines, are the only ones that appear here. Mikyö Dorje's main criticism in his verses centers on his reading of Tsongkapa's presentation of the object of refutation by reasonings. Similar analyses of Tsongkapa's object of refutation by reasonings have been preserved in *Feast for the Fortunate* by Wangchuk Dorje. They can be found, for example, in the commentary to verse 6.120 in the section from p. 340, line 8 to p. 348, line 26.

498 The *Vajra Ḍākinī* itself is a tantra of the Buddha.

499 Bhavabhaḍa goes on to refute the possibility of reflections being autonomous, function-performing things in their own right.

500 In other words, Bhāvaviveka attempts to counter the Proponents of Things' initial complaint about Middle Way hypocrisy by giving refutations a status different from other causes, such as barley seeds that produce barley sprouts. The Proponents of Things, however, will not buy into this delineation, because for them—and, indeed,

for Chandrakīrti as well—refutations function as causes every bit as much as seeds function as causes (one produces an intellectual understanding of the opposite of what was believed before, the other produces a physical sprout perceived by the eyes and other sense faculties). Chandrakīrti successfully counters his opponents' criticisms by teaching them how although all causes—seeds and refutations alike—are devoid of their own inherent natures, they are still capable of producing results: a seed can produce a sprout. A reflection in the mirror can help one to wash one's face. And a refutation can remove a wrong idea. The wrong idea removed here is that things *inherently*, or, in other words, *when analyzed,* arise.

501 This heading first figured into the sectional outline after the explanation of verse 6.7 on pp. 148–149.

502 This heading first figured into the sectional outline after the explanation of verse 6.7 on pp. 148–149.

503 Both quotations below are truncated in Wangchuk Dorje's text and appear here as they appear in the *Ṭīkā.*

504 The Tibetan text here is phrased in a way that each of the following sixteen headings should be understood to implicitly begin with "The extensive explanation of . . ."

505 The translation of *ter zuk tu nepa mepa/ther zug tu gnas pa med pa* here follows the Karmapa's breakdown of its Sanskrit etymology in the commentary below.

506 The quotation is truncated in Wangchuk Dorje's text and appears here as it appears in the *Ṭīkā.*

507 *Brahmachārya, tsangpar chöpa/tshangs par spyod pa*, the vows of celibacy.

508 The words between brackets are from the autocommentary.

509 I.e., for bodhisattvas on the path or for buddhas.

510 This refers to the stage of analysis that corresponds to the second line of Āryadeva's famous quotation: "In the beginning one reverses nonvirtue./ In the middle one reverses the view of a self./ In the end one reverses all views./ Those who know this way are wise."

511 Referring to line three of Āryadeva's quotation.

512 Despite Wangchuk Dorje's use of the phrase "root text and commentary" below in connection with this quotation, the quotation's source text was not readily identifiable. The quotation was not found in the editions of Chandrakīrti's autocommentary or Chandrakīrti's *Clear Words* that were available.

513 Only the first line is quoted in both Wangchuk Dorje's text and the *Ṭīkā.* Three more lines were translated and appear here to give the reader context.

514 Dolpopa Sherab Gyaltsen *(dol po pa shes rab rgyal mtshen,* 1292-1361) was the earliest exponent of the other-emptiness, or shentong *(gzhan stong),* system in Tibet. Although his views were assailed from all corners in Tibet, he is also considered to be a great scholar of the Kālachakra Tantra and treatises related to it. (See Stearns 1999)

515 The next two lines of the quotation are: "The emptiness endowed with the supreme of all aspects/ Is not like the former emptiness."

516 This refers to a very specific type of time period in Buddhist cosmology and is equivalent to the age of degeneration *(kaliyuga, nyik dü/snyigs dus).* (ATW)

517 Shambhala is a pure realm associated with the Kālachakra Tantra. Dolpopa was one of the great masters of the Kālachakra's teachings. Rigdens are said to be the kings of Shambhala.

518 This trilogy, which consists of commentaries on the *Kālachakra Tantra*, the *Hevajra Tantra*, and the *Chakrasaṃvara Tantra*, was among the sources Dolpopa most frequently used to support his views. (See Stearns 1999, pp.3-4 and p. 178, note 11)

519 The translation of these verses, which are truncated in Wangchuk Dorje's text and appear here as they appear in the *Ṭīkā*, follows that of Cyrus Stearns. (Stearns 1999, pp. 127-128)

520 In other words, after three lesser ages, which last 5,400 years each.

521 The Karmapa seems to be stringing out a reason, for dramatic effect, that he knows would not be accepted by Dolpopa.

522 I.e., because the undeceiving quality of conventional karmic causes and results is *not* true in the way that it appears to the minds of ordinary beings.

523 If you say that the undeceiving quality of karmic causes and results *not* being true in the way that it appears to the minds of ordinary beings does not make it unnecessary for beings to correctly engage adopting and rejecting in relation to conventional karmic cause and effect . . .

524 The undeceiving quality of actions and results and the rabbit-horn ladder.

525 Again, the Karmapa seems to be laying out a reason he expects the hypothetical Dolpopa not to accept.

526 By not accepting the earlier reason, "he" accepted that single and multiple are not real in the way they appear to worldly beings' minds.

527 The Tibetan words here are *yöpa/yod pa* for "existence" and *yinpa/yin pa* for "being" (in the equative sense).

528 Being refuted in the frame of reference of knowable objects *does* necessitate existing among knowable objects . . .

529 The natural implication of the two negatives is to say, for example, that a refutation of nonexistence must imply an affirmation of existence, and a refutation of existence must imply an affirmation of nonexistence.

530 You may say that the need to identify true existence as a hypothetical possibility does not necessitate the hypothetical status of its opposite, the lack of true existence . . . but it does.

531 This is a meaning translation of the Tibetan text, which refers to the eight grammatical particles of Tibetan grammar and how the attempted rebuttal would be beyond the scope of those eight.

532 Contradiction and connection form a classic pair of opposites in Buddhist logic.

533 The two main traditional classifications of types of connection.

534 These quotations appear as they are found in the *Ṭīkā*.

535 "Brahmin" in this quotation could refer to one practicing the discipline of celibacy.

536 I.e., a prophecy of Tsongkapa's views.

537 *Pak Seng/'phags seng*: "The tradition of Haribhadra" refers to the lineage of explanation associated with Maitreya's *Ornament for Clear Realization*.

538 The following quotation is translated as it appears in the *Ṭīkā*.

539 The following quotation is translated as it appears in the *Ṭīkā*.

540 Another name for followers of the Geluk tradition.

541 This is a reference to the Particularists' views as described in the *Treasury of Abhidharma* (verse 6 is quoted at this section of the *Ṭīkā*) and its autocommentary by Vasubandhu. The Particularists' description of nirvāṇa is connected to their assertion of the truth of cessation and, in particular, to their concept of "cessation through anal-

ysis" *(so sor tak gok/so sor brtags 'gog)*. Cessation through analysis, they say, consists not of just one, but of multiple, instances that are considered to be substantial entities. Each of these substances is attained in a manner equal in number to the instances of attaining freedom or separation from the impure mental events. These instances of freedom or separation are also considered to be substantial entities. Therefore, they say, the instances of the attainment of this cessation are equal in number to the instances of separation from the impure mental events. (Vasubandhu 2005, pp. 6-7)

542 The accumulation of merit (the generosity example that follows falls in this category) and the accumulation of wisdom.

543 "Defining characteristics" *(tsen-nyi/mtshan nyid)* can, in cases such as this, be understood to be very close in meaning to "definition."

544 The suffering of suffering, the suffering of change, and the all-pervasive suffering of formations.

545 The poisonous snakes example seems to illustrate that, just as grasping on to a poisonous snake will bring harm to oneself, in the same way grasping on to the constituents causes one to suffer in saṃsāra.

546 These are the four graduated levels of concentration in the form realm. They are simply called the first concentration, the second concentration, the third concentration, and the fourth concentration.

547 Loving-kindness, compassion, joy, and impartiality.

548 These are the four graduated levels of concentration, or samādhi, in the formless realm. They are limitless space *(namka taye/nam mkha' mtha' yas)*, limitless consciousness *(namshe taye/rnam shes mtha' yas)*, utter nonexistence *(chi yang mepa/ci yang med pa)*, and not existence, not nonexistence *(yö min me min/yod min med min)*.

549 The thirty-seven factors of enlightenment are (1-4) the four close placements of mindfulness *(drenpa nyer shak shi/dren pa nyer bzhag bzhi)*: the mindfulnesses of body *(lü/lus)*, feelings *(tsorwa/tshor ba)*, mind *(sem/sems)*, and phenomena *(chö/chos)*; (5-8) the four correct relinquishments *(yangdak pongwa shi/yang dag spong ba bzhi)*: the relinquishment of nonvirtue that has arisen *(mi gewa kyepe pongwa/mi dge ba skyes pa'i spong ba)*, the nonproduction of nonvirtue that has not arisen *(mi gewa ma kyepa mi kyepa/mi dge ba ma skyes pa mi bskyed pa)*, the production of virtue that has not arisen *(gewa ma kyepa kyepa/dge ba ma skyes pa bskyed pa)*, and the further propagation of virtue that has arisen *(gewa kyepa pelwa/dge ba skyes pa spel ba)*; (9-12) the four miraculous legs *(dzuntrul gyi kangpa shi/rdzu 'phrul gyi rkang pa bzhi)*: aspiration *(dünpa/'dun pa/)*, exertion *(tsöndrü/brtson 'grus)*, concentration *(sempa/sems pa)*, and analysis *(chöpa/dpyod pa)*; (13-17) the five pure faculties *(namjang wangpo nga/rnam byang dbang po lnga)*: faith *(depa/dad pa)*, exertion *(tsöndrü/brtson 'grus)*, mindfulness *(drenpa/dran pa)*, samādhi *(ting nge dzin/ting nge 'dzin)*, and supreme knowledge *(sherab/shes rab)*; (18-22) the five pure powers *(namjang top nga/rnam byang stobs lnga)*: (same five as listed in "the five pure faculties"); (23-29) the seven branches of enlightenment *(changchub yenlak dün/byang chub yan lag bdun)*: correct mindfulness *(drenpa yangdak/dran pa yang dag)*, excellent differentiation of phenomena *(chö rab tu nam je/chos rab tu rnam 'byed)*, correct exertion *(tsöndrü yangdak/brtson 'grus yang dag)*, correct joy *(gawa yangdak/dga' ba yang dag)*, correct pliancy *(shinjang yangdak/ shin sbyangs yang dag)*, correct equanimity *(tang-nyom yangdak/btang snyoms yang dag)*, and correct samādhi *(ting-nge dzin yangdak/ting nge 'dzin yang dag)*; and (30-37) the noble eightfold path *(paklam yenlak gye/'phags lam yan lag brgyad)*: correct

view *(yangdakpe tawa/yang dag pa'i lta ba)*, correct examination *(yangdakpe tokpa/ yang dag pa'i rtogs pa)*, correct speech *(yangdakpe ngak/yang dag pa'i ngag)*, correct limits of action *(yangdakpe le kyi ta/yang dag pa'i las kyi mtha')*, correct livelihood *(yangdakpe tsowa/yang dag pa'i 'tsho ba)*, correct effort *(yangdakpe tsolwa/yang dag pa'i rtsol ba)*, correct mindfulness *(yangdakpe drenpa/yang dag pa'i dran pa)*, and correct samādhi *(yangdakpe ting-nge dzin/yang dag pa'i ting nge 'dzin)*.

550 The three gates of liberation *(nampar tarpe go sum/rnam par thar pa'i sgo gsum)*—emptiness, the absence of characteristics, and wishlessness—are taught to correlate to the stages of ground, path, and result, respectively. They are also described by the *Great Tibetan-Chinese Dictionary* as "three samādhis that bring about the attainment of liberation." (GTCD, p. 1569)

551 The full Tibetan here reads, "the perceptual state *(kye che/skye mched)* of limitless space."

552 In the section on the qualities of buddhahood.

553 These are the correct and distinct awarenesses *(soso yangdakpe rikpa/so so yang dag pa'i rig pa)* of phenomena *(chö/chos)*, meaning *(dön/don)*, contextual etymology *(ngepe tsik/nges pa'i tshig)*, and confidence *(pobpa/spobs pa)*.

554 In the chapter on the ninth bodhisattva ground.

555 This fourfold grouping is also called "the four limitless ones" *(tse me shi/tshad med bzhi)*.

556 As a note of interest, Chandrakīrti's autocommentary at this point delves into a very extensive commentary on the eighteen unmixed qualities.

557 This heading first appeared in the sectional outline on p. 143.

558 The medicinal fruit of a tree, the embellic myrobalan *(āmalakī, kyurura/skyu ru ra)* or *Phyllantus embellic*. When fresh, this fruit is highly transparent, and has thus been used in Indo-Tibetan literature as an example of being able to see everything very clearly. (GTCD, p. 190 and Chandrakīrti and Jamgön Mipham 1992, pp. 323 and p. 382 note 236)

559 This quotation, which does not appear in the *Ṭīkā* (Mikyö Dorje describes its contents and says that it is to be found in the autocommentary), is truncated in Wangchuk Dorje' text and appears here as it appears in the autocommentary.

560 The quotation is truncated in Wangchuk Dorje's text and appears here as it appears in the *Ṭīkā*.

561 Dzogchen Ponlop Rinpoche explains that "imputed" is an operative word here because it differentiates Asaṅga's explanation of the absorption of cessation from that of the Particularists, who assert the absorption to be substantially existent. (Dzogchen Ponlop Rinpoche 2000, p. 14)

562 This term would perhaps be better rendered by "the perfect end" in this context.

563 This sentence was extracted from the *Ṭīkā* in order to give this paragraph more clarity.

564 I.e., the last four perfections in the enumeration of ten, which correspond to the last four bodhisattva grounds.

565 Chandrakīrti's autocommentary provides more information: "When supreme knowledge takes on special appearances, it becomes methods, aspirations, powers, and wisdom. Supreme knowledge is only known strictly as 'the perfection of supreme knowledge' in a very specific presentation. This specificity does not apply in other cases."

566 The quotation is truncated in Wangchuk Dorje's text, is paraphrased in the *Ṭīkā*, and appears here as it appears in Chandrakīrti's autocommentary.

567 "Ten sexdecillion" equals ten to the fifty-second power. The Tibetan text here literally says, "ten countless [figures]," employing the classic Indo-Tibetan numeral system in which "countless" refers to ten to the fifty-first power.

568 This quotation does not appear in the *Ṭīkā*. It does appear in the autocommentary, yet in an incomplete form. Wangchuk Dorje's truncations are all that are rendered here. In terms of points conveyed, the quotation seems to be, for the most part, a more prolix rendition in prose of the verse-form quotation above.

569 The quotation is truncated in Wangchuk Dorje's text and appears here as it appears in the *Ṭīkā*.

570 The word *lama/bla ma*, rendered contextually by "unsurpassable" here, may also be rendered as "guru"—"they become guru to the [beings in] the three realms."

571 At this point in the *Ṭīkā*, Mikyö Dorje adds an interesting comment: "About the mental body, some Tibetans claim that Chandrakīrti asserts it to be a nonmaterial body that is composed of consciousness and is small and attractive. In effect these people are thinking that Chandrakīrti has chosen to follow the Proponents of Consciousness in asserting the body, faculties, and so forth to be consciousness. Yet if Chandrakīrti refutes as untenable the approach of the Proponents of Consciousness even on the nonanalytical, conventional level, think about it: does your ascription of that view to Chandrakīrti have any vision? Does it have any life?"

572 This mastery specifically relates to the bodhisattvas' ability to take birth at any desired time. (ATW)

573 This mastery is specifically related to the location or type of birth. (ATW)

574 This refers to the ultimate teachings. (ATW)

575 This quotation appears in the *Ṭīkā*, as it does in the autocommentary, in an incomplete form. Wangchuk Dorje's truncations are all that is rendered here.

576 "One octodecillion" equals ten to the fifty-seventh power. The Tibetan literally reads, "Countless (ten to the fifty-first power) times one hundred thousand times ten."

577 This heading first appeared in the sectional outline on p. 99.

578 This epithet is a positive way of referring to our own human world, which in traditional Buddhist cosmology is called Jambudvīpa, the southern continent. In this world, one need not feel afraid or fearful with regard to practicing the dharma.

579 To summarize, the twelve sets of qualities enable bodhisattvas of the varying grounds to: 1) see a certain number of buddhas, 2) realize the blessings of those buddhas, 3) remain for a certain number of eons, 4) correctly engage in the beginnings and ends of those eons, 5) enter into and arise from a certain number of samādhis, 6) cause a certain number of worlds to quake, 7) illuminate a certain number of realms, 8) ripen a certain number of sentient beings, 9) go to a certain number of buddha realms, 10) open a certain number of gates of dharma, 11) display a certain number of bodhisattvas in their body, and 12) have those bodhisattvas in turn be surrounded by a retinue of the same number of bodhisattvas.

580 One sexillion equals ten to the twenty-first power.

581 The Tibetan text here has a long-winded way of multiplying numbers to arrive at a resultant figure. This complexity was abandoned in the translation and, instead, only the resultant numbers of the multiplications appear. The same approach is followed for the verses and commentaries that contain large numbers below.

582 One hundred vigintillion equals ten to the sixty-fifth power.

583 The Tibetan phrase here, *jö du mepe yang jö du mepa/brjod du med pa'i yang brjod du med pa*, could also potentially refer to the number called "inexpressible" (one hundred octodecillion or ten to the fifty-ninth power) multiplied by itself, which would yield a result of ten octotrigintillion (ten to the one hundred eighteenth power) buddha realms.

584 In this enumeration of five realms of saṃsāra, the jealous gods are taken out. Half of the jealous gods are categorized with the gods, and the other half of the jealous gods is categorized with the animals. (ATW)

585 This heading first appeared in the sectional outline on p. 99.

586 These are "five pure places only inhabited by noble ones" *(pakpa shatak gi ne tsangma nga/'phags pa sha stag gi gnas gtsang ma lnga)*: 1) Not as Great *(mi chewa/mi che ba)*, 2) The Untormented *(mi dungwa/mi gdung ba)*, 3) Extensive Vision *(shin tu tongwa/ shin tu mthong ba)*, 4) The Appearance of Excellence *(gyanom nangwa/gya nom snang ba)*, and 5) Akaniṣṭha *(ogmin/'og min)*. These five places exist on the fourth level of concentration in the form realm (Jamgön Mipham Rinpoche 2000, p. 94). As the Karmapa will describe beginning with the next sentence, there seems to be a paradoxical issue at hand here as to whether or not the Akaniṣṭha in which buddhas attain enlightenment is the same Akaniṣṭha that is a member of the fivefold list of form-realm pure lands. Both Wangchuk Dorje and Mikyö Dorje seem to refrain from offering in an explicit way a final answer as to what type of Akaniṣṭha is being referenced by Chandrakīrti.

587 See note 191 on p. 738.

588 Alternatively, "meditates."

589 "Suchness" and "variety" are known as the two wisdoms of the buddhas: the wisdom of suchness knows the ultimate nature of phenomena and the wisdom of variety knows phenomena individually in all their multiplicity, vastness, and extent.

590 "Purification" and "expansion" are the literal meanings of the two syllables of the Tibetan word for buddha or buddhahood, *sang-gye/sangs rgyas*.

591 This sentence could also be rendered as follows: "It is illogical for a perceiving subject to arise with definitiveness without having engaged its knowable object."

592 The Tibetan *ta bur/lta bur* here is challenging to translate in a noncolloquial way in English. A colloquial rendering that perhaps better captures the meaning here is as follows: "In dependence upon the aspect of nonarising, wisdom is posited as realizing suchness—it's kind of like that."

593 "Continuum's end" *(gyun ta/rgyun mtha')* refers to the end of the tenth bodhisattva ground.

594 It seems important to use the terms "existence" and "nonexistence" in this discussion because of the parallels with all the other Middle Way reasonings; however in this context of the wisdom of the buddhas, phrases such as this one could also be rendered by "If the buddhas did not *have* wisdom . . ."

595 This is identified as "the condensed version" *(düpa/sdud pa)* in Wangchuk Dorje's text. This name could refer to any of several "condensed" *Perfection of Supreme Knowledge* sūtras. The quotation is identified in Nitartha *international's* edition of the Tibetan as being found in volume Ka of the Derge Kangyur, *shes rab sna tshogs*, p. 5b.3.

596 This quotation is truncated in Wangchuk Dorje's text and appears here as it appears in the *Ṭīkā*.

597 The quotations are truncated by Wangchuk Dorje and are presented in a different

order in the *Ṭīkā*. The quotations appear here in the order selected by Wangchuk Dorje but with the content that appears in the *Ṭīkā*.

598 Those who have attained one of the four types of results for hearers (stream enterer, once-returner, nonreturner, and arhat) or those who have attained one of the eight categories created when the four main results are divided into the entrance into that result and the abiding stage of the result.

599 The *Great Tibetan-Chinese Dictionary* identifies these twenty as the five stream enterers, the three once-returners, the ten nonreturners, the enterers into arhathood, and the rhinoceroslike solitary realizers. (GTCD, p. 449)

600 Karl Brunnhölzl's translation of this term as "natural outflow" has been followed here in preference to the literal "causally concordant." These kāyas, explained later in the Karmapa's commentary, are the natural outflow of the dharmakāya and form kāyas.

601 *"Kyenpe top/mkhyen pa'i stobs"* ("The power of knowledge of . . ."), the phrase closing out (or beginning, in English) the names of all the powers, will be deleted from the remaining Tibetan phoneticizations and transliterations for brevity.

602 The translation of this paragraph is tentative.

603 Up to now in this book, "dhātu" *(kam/khams)* has been rendered differently in different contexts. Sometimes dhātu refers to the eighteen sensory "constituents" (visible form and the other objects, the eye and the other faculties, and the eye consciousness and the other consciousnesses); sometimes it refers to the three "realms" (the form realm, the formless realm, and the desire realm); sometimes it refers to "elements" such as earth, space, and so on. Chandrakīrti's autocommentary at this section, however, indicates that "dhātu" in the context of the fourth power refers to *all* of the above-mentioned usages and then some. Since no translation convention has been employed in this book by which one word could apply to all of these senses of "dhātu," it has been left in its Sanskrit form for this section of the text.

604 The autocommentary here reads: "'Nature,' 'essence,' and 'emptiness' are synonyms."

605 Reading *mig sogs dag gi rang bzhin* for *mig sogs ngag gi rang bzhin*.

606 These are presented by the *Great Tibetan-Chinese Dictionary* and the online *Dharma Dictionary v.4* as the seven faculties that are supports (the eye, ear, nose, tongue, body, mind, and life force), the two faculties that are supported (the male faculty and the female faculty), the five faculties of feeling (happiness, suffering, mental comfort, mental discomfort, and neutrality), the five pure faculties (faith, diligence, mindfulness, samādhi, and supreme knowledge), and the three uncontaminated faculties (the creation of complete knowledge, complete knowledge itself, and the attainment of complete knowledge). (GTCD, p. 1933)

607 Or "vehicles to buddhahood."

608 Also translated as "five degenerations," "five residues," and "five dregs."

609 In his autocommentary, Chandrakīrti cites the following example as originating from a tale in the sūtra called *The White Lotus of Genuine Dharma (Saddharmapundarika, Damchö Pema Karpo/dam chos padma dkar po)*.

610 In the *Ṭīkā* the following misconception is attributed to "some Vajrayāna practitioners of the Nyingma tradition."

611 Literally, "the four activities including request." These are four phases of the ritual of the ceremony for full ordination: the request to be ordained is recited once by the ordainee, and the actual verses of taking the vows are recited three times, totaling "four rituals."

612 The text literally says, "the first verse," but the comments here seem to apply to verse 13.1 and the first two lines of verse 13.2.

613 The text literally says, "the later verse[s]," which appears to refer to the last two lines of verse 13.2.

614 The Consequentialists.

615 This appears to refer to the Autonomists as the example of Followers of the Middle Way who make presentations of the relative in accordance with the Particularists.

616 Vasubandhu.

617 The translation of this paragraph has been slightly loosened in an attempt to accommodate a poetic relationship between the root verse and its commentary.

618 It may be noteworthy here to observe that the root verse and the commentary are constructed slightly differently from each other in terms of what it is that causes the closed pistils of Nāgārjuna's verses to open. In the root verse it is the water, but in the commentary it is clearly "the cooling light rays of Chandrakīrti's intelligence." The implied connection between Chandrakīrti's name, "famous *moon*," and the night-blooming flowers, Nāgārjuna's writings, which bloom due to *cool light rays* of intelligence, makes quite a beautiful image.

619 Cool, delicious, light, soft, clear, free from impurities, not harmful to the stomach, and not harmful to the throat.

620 Existence, nonexistence, both, and neither.

621 Although not reflected in the translation due to the structural difficulty which would be required, this sentence is a logical thesis, the reasons corresponding to which are the contents of this and the next two paragraphs. In other words, this paragraph and the next two prove why the Followers of the Middle Way never posit the relative truth in a context of analysis.

622 *Nyam-len/nyams len* is usually rendered as "practice," but something closer to its literal meaning, "to bring into experience," has been followed here.

623 Reading *nyon mongs pa can ma yin pa'i ma rig pas* for *nyon mongs pa can gyi ma rig pas.*

624 I.e., conceptual discrimination.

625 "In training" refers to the hearers, solitary realizers, and bodhisattvas, and "beyond training" refers to buddhas.

626 In their own system—from their own perspective—knowable objects of the relative are not observed in any way that could be expressible, including by way of interdependence. So the notion of "describing knowable objects in accord with interdependence" would not apply.

627 I.e., the inclusions of the reasons in the predicates.

628 Neyu Zurpa Yeshe Bar (*sne'u zur pa ye shes 'bar,* 1042-1118).

629 The *Ṭīkā* directs the following critique explicitly at Tsongkapa.

630 This heading first appeared in the section outline on p. 89.

631 Lhasa, Tibet.

632 These verses appear to be the composition of Wangchuk Dorje himself, with some verses strongly resembling the closing verses of Mikyö Dorje.

633 A reference to the First Karmapa, Düsum Khyenpa, "Knower of the Three Times."

634 A reference to the Third Karmapa, Rangjung Dorje, "Self-Arisen Vajra."

635 A reference to the Fourth Karmapa, Rolpe Dorje, "Playful Vajra."

636 A reference to the Fifth Karmapa, Deshin Shekpa, "Tathāgata."

637 A reference to the Sixth Karmapa, Tongwa Dönden, "Meaningful to See."

638 A reference to the Eighth Karmapa, Mikyö Dorje, who was also known as Yangchen Gawa *(dbyangs can dga' ba)*, "Adored by Sarasvati."

639 Some of the following verses are translated loosely.

640 Āryadeva.

641 Mikyö Dorje.

642 It is possible that "Gyamön," "Wangpo," and "Tsöndrü" are names of three different people.

643 Corresponding to the section "The way in which Consequentialists and Autonomists related to each other through affirmations and refutations," p. 168.

644 This section corresponds to the section in *Feast for the Fortunate* entitled "Setting forth the system of Buddhapālita," p. 169.

645 At this point the Tibetan in both Wangchuk Dorje's text and ACIP actually says *shin tu thal bar 'gyur ba'i phyir*, "and because [their arising] would be absurd," but that phrase has been replaced with *skye ba thug pa med pa nyid du 'gyur ba'i phyir*, "and because their arising would be endless." This replacement was chosen for the sake of consistency and ease of understanding, because in the Tibetan text of *Feast for the Fortunate* and *Lucid Words* the commentary that follows Buddhapālita's original quotation is written as if "endless," not "absurd," was the originally stated consequence. Discussion of "absurd" does not happen anywhere beyond the original quotation.

646 This section corresponds to the section in *Feast for the Fortunate* entitled "Stating the refutation of Bhāvaviveka," p. 169.

647 This section corresponds to the section in *Feast for the Fortunate* entitled "Because we do not use autonomous reasonings that are established by any valid cognition of our own, there is no fault in our not stating examples or reasons," p. 172.

648 This section corresponds to the section in *Feast for the Fortunate* entitled "Because we do not set forth consequences that contain autonomous implications of their opposite meaning, we do not contradict ourselves," p. 173.

649 This section corresponds to the section in *Feast for the Fortunate* entitled "Because we do not state arguments and so on that are established by any valid cognition of our own, there is no need to clear away the faults involved in the theses and arguments we state to the defender," p. 173.

650 The Enumerators believe that resultant things exist in an unmanifest way in their own causes, and that these causes are the essential nature of the result. So to say that things do not arise from their own essential nature that is the result is simply to restate the position of the Enumerators themselves.

651 This section corresponds to the section in *Feast for the Fortunate* entitled "Although we do not have assertions of our own, we do use arguments, examples, and so on for the purpose of refuting others," p. 175.

652 A position and so on the individual components of which the Enumerators themselves would accept according to their own system

653 This follows the traditional Indian five-membered format for a probative argument. The five steps are 1) the thesis, 2) the reason, 3) the example (which upholds the reason's inclusion in, or entailment of, the predicate of the thesis), 4) the application (which explicitly ties the subject to the reason), and 5) the summary (which restates the thesis as affirmed by the reason). The phrasing of the argument that Chandrakīrti voices on behalf of Buddhapālita is slightly more complicated than the traditional

example of "sound is impermanent" cited first. In particular, at the fourth stage (i.e., of the application) Chandrakīrti departs from the general subject of "things" with which he began and introduces the more specific subject of unmanifest vases that exist by way of their own identity at the time of their causes. This strikes the heart of the Enumerators' position, because the Enumerators wish to reserve a special place for unmanifest results by saying that the latter "arise" or "manifest" into a manifest result. The reason of "already existing by way of their own identity," however, forces the Enumerators to accept the absurdity of their position, since something that already exists would not have any further need of arising.

654 The Enumerators accept that results already exist by way of their own identity at the time of their causes.

655 The Enumerators assert that the person is a phenomenon that does not arise—it is primordially existent.

656 This section corresponds to the section in *Feast for the Fortunate* entitled "The reversed meaning of consequences is connected to others, the Enumerators and so on, not to our position," p. 176.

657 This section corresponds to the section in *Feast for the Fortunate* entitled "Nāgārjuna himself, when refuting others, defeated them primarily by way of consequences," p. 177.

658 This section corresponds to the section in *Feast for the Fortunate* entitled "Stating the system of Bhāvaviveka," p. 178.

659 This section corresponds to the section in *Feast for the Fortunate* entitled "Stating that system's many faults," p. 179.

660 The classical Buddhist probative argument cited as an example of traditional Buddhist logic defeating the assertions of certain Hindu schools.

661 The Vaisheṣhikas assert that sound, as opposed to being a derivative of the four major elements, is a quality of space. (Hopkins 1983, p. 506)

662 The Jains assert that sound "manifests" due to conditions, but that it exists previous to its manifestation and is therefore not a product. (Hopkins 1983, p. 507)

663 Bhāvaviveka wishes to assert the absence of arising, which is perceived by the non-mistaken consciousnesses of noble beings. But as the subject to support that assertion, he posits the inner sense sources such as the eyes, which are relative phenomena, perceived by the mistaken consciousnesses of the relative truth. It would thus require two different types of beings to perceive these two different elements of his probative argument.

664 Which suggests employing subjects that are mere generalities.

665 In the case of the reasoning proving the impermanence of sound, the Buddhist who advances the reasoning to the Hindu is a Proponent of Things, a follower of a lower vehicle philosophical system.

666 This section corresponds to the section in *Feast for the Fortunate* entitled "Bhāvaviveka has [in other contexts] acknowledged the faulty nature [of the approach he uses here]," p. 181.

667 Bhāvaviveka's commentary to *Fundamental Wisdom*.

668 For the hearers, the inner sense sources exist ultimately.

669 These comments by Bhāvaviveka are made in the context of his commentary on the second chapter, the examination of coming and going, of Nāgārjuna's *Fundamental Wisdom*. The refutation of arising takes place in the first chapter.

670 The Enumerators hold that consciousness is not produced; thus saying it does not arise from itself would be no problem for them.

671 This section corresponds to the section in *Feast for the Fortunate* entitled "Showing how Chandrakīrti is free from the fault of contradiction," p. 182.

672 Ordinary beings, those who see only the "near side" of appearances that seem to truly exist, as opposed to the "far side" of the true nature of appearances, emptiness.

673 The five great reasonings of the Middle Way.

674 Naktso Lotsawa.

675 This line is a tentative translation of *bod kyi rdog btsun legs pa'i shes rab kyis.*

676 The following very brief description of the basic technique of analytical meditation is based on oral teachings by Dzogchen Ponlop Rinpoche and Acharya Lama Tenpa Gyaltsen at Nitartha Institute.

677 Dzogchen Ponlop Rinpoche taught these three stages at the 2007 Nitartha Summer Institute when giving oral teachings on analytical meditation based on several texts, including Jamgön Mipham's *Beacon of Certainty (Ngeshe Drönme/nges shes sgron me).*

⋮ Index

cognition(s)
five higher, 135, 737n174
of selflessness, 373
cognitive obscuration(s), 35, 112, 214,
430, 545
*Commentary on Bodhichitta (byang chub
sems kyi 'grel pa)*, 463
*Commentary on the Entrance to the Mid-
dle Way*, 536
*Commentary to the Two Truths (bden
gnyis 'grel pa)*, 437
Commentary to the Vajra Ḍākinī
(Bhavabhaḍa) *(rdo rje mkha' 'gro'i 'grel
pa)*, 420
compassion, 15, 17, 727n34
analyses of Middle Way as expression
of, 53–54
of bodhisattvas, 489
buddhahood and, 148
Chandrakīrti's praise of, 95-98
mindstreams moistened by, 136–37
nirmāṇakāya and, 72
nirvāṇa and, 551
nonreferential, 96–97
patience and, 130
pure intention and, 105
three types of, 96-97
concentration *(bsam gtan)*, 22, 141. *See
also* four concentrations
Concentration of the Space Treasury, 117
conception of "I." *See also* worldly conception of "I"
as aggregates, 373
as always present in beings, 406
basis of, 379
selflessness and, 375
support for, not a thing, 382
conditionality. *See also* mere conditionality *(rkyen 'di pa tsam)*
dependent arising of mere, 389
Precious Garland on, 324
Treatise on the Middle Way on, 324
conditioned phenomena *('dus byas)*, 276,
316, 470-74, 483-87, 555, 742n251
connate view of self, 55–56, 59, 336-43
consciousness. *See also* all-base consciousness; dependent nature consciousness;
eye consciousness; Proponents of
Consciousness; sense consciousness
absurd consequence and, 254, 266

arising of, 252
continuum of, 258
dependent, 245, 270
diseased vision and, 211, 250
in dreams, 245, 249
false seeing and, 208
of future, 254
habitual tendencies and, 257
inherent nature and, 296, 317
mental, 248, 263–64
mere, through all-base, 242
mistaken, in dreams, 246
nondual, 269, 401
perceiving, 251
potential and, 255
potential originating, 260
qualities of a thing and, 381
rising of, 259
sixth, 262
suchness and, 241
triad of, 248
consequence(s). *See also* absurd consequence; root consequence
affirmation and, 170
aggregates/selflessness and, 362
arising from other and, 194
with autonomous implications, 173
Buddhapālita employing, 177
contradictions highlighted by, 160,
739n196
of endless arising, 186
of extinction, 359
Followers of Middle Way and, 183
knowable objects and root, 347
mental afflictions and, 363
Nāgārjuna, 177
of not relinquishing mental afflictions,
363
as probandum, 178
reversed meaning of, 176, 586
of seed/sprout not appearing, 188
of several selves, 357
valid cognition and root, 344
of view of self not relinquished, 373
Consequentialist-Autonomist distinction, 28-30, 159-84
in *Fundamental Wisdom*, 152
Karmapa and, 29, 728n43
Khedrub Je on, 166
Lucid Words on, 30

relinquishment of, 298
transitory collection and, 336
mental body, 762n571
Middle Way, 1. *See also* Followers of the
Middle Way
analyses of, 53–54
Autonomist branch of, 7, 725n5
as beyond the extremes, 469
Chandrakīrti in tradition of, 81
Consequentialist branch of, 6–7, 725n5
debates of, 14–15
dharma system of, 340, 417
Dolpopa on, 445
Early Followers of, 9
entrance into, 7–8
experience of, 5
in India, 2–8
Karma Kagyü lineages of, 9
Karmapa system of, 73
key instructions for, 595
Mind Only system distinct from, 276
Nāgārjuna on, 81, 328
scholars, 11
suchness and, 74
Takpo Kagyü and, 333
in Tibet, 8–14
ultimate truth and, 269
union of two truths in, 90
uniqueness of, 557
Zilungpa on, 304
Middle Way Progenitors, 3, 4
Mikyö Dorje, 9–14, 20, 74, 716nn14–17,
726nn23-24
on Consequentialists, 742n252
on definitiveness, 744n279
on dharmadhātu, 142
on inferences of ordinary beings,
739n200
on mental body, 761n571
on realization, 732n113
on Sangye Nyenpa, 154–55
Milarepa, 85
mind. *See also* consciousness
afflicted, 214
assertions of self as, 358
bodhisattvas and, 123–24
calming, 22
eighteen movements of, 372
form and, 294, 296
with form arising from dreams, 261

knowable object and, 268
Proponents of Consciousness analysis of, 245
rational, 216
untenability of aggregates as, 361
"mind only," 49, 287-92
clarification of, 750n363
provisional meaning of, 297-301, 304
Mind Only school. *See* Proponents of Mind Only; Proponents of Consciousness
Mipham Chökyi Wangchuk, 575
Mipham, Jamgön, 19, 727n36

Nāgārjuna, 1–6, 77, 725n6
on aggregates, 214, 378
Chandrakīrti and, 67, 73, 144-45, 448, 554
compassion and, 53-54, 331
consequences and, 177-78
Consequentialist-Autonomist distinction and, 733n117
on dependent arising, 151-53, 207, 256, 328, 455
Descent into Laṅkā on, 145
on emptiness, 19, 26-27, 153-54, 156, 434, 442, 463
Middle Way tradition of, 81, 84, 87-88, 91, 557-58, 732n113
on two truths, 34, 180, 190, 433
worldly perspective and, 164, 433
Naiyāyikas, 352
Naktso Lotsawa, 27
Namgyal Drakpa, 78
Nāropa, 84
nature
contrived, 435
as creator, 351
emptiness of, 470, 485–86
label given to ultimate lack of, 435
meaning of, 350
in mode of abiding, 438
Nāgārjuna on, 442
of phenomena, 64
phenomena as devoid of, 221
neutrality through equivalence, 160, 739n197
Neyu Zurpa, 569
nihilism
dependent arising and, 220